AF878336

CARTE BLANCHE PHOTOGRAPHY.1

CARTE B

LANCHE

PHOTOGRAPHY.1

THE MAGENTA FOUNDATION

CONTENTS

PHOTOGRAPHY IN CANADA

I'm 43 years old. That means I've been around for 31 per cent of Canada's nationhood. Canada, at 139, is one of the youngest countries on earth. What a wonderful thing! Our lack of modern history leaves us with little choice but to go forward. There's no time for being overly hampered by reflection when there's not much history to do the hampering.

Given our proportionally small modern history, it seems to me that Canadians tend to focus on two overall themes—our landscape and our future.

First, our landscape. Everything about Canada forces us to think about size and distance in new ways. The Canadian Shield is billions of years old. The Ice Ages carved out all those lakes we visit in summer. Everywhere you look in Canada, geological time, with its almost incomprehensible lengths, manifests itself in a landscape that remains wild, untamed and harsh.

Another aspect of Canada's landscape is that it's also, well, big. When doing business or dealing with family issues in Canada, the contemplation of distance cannot be avoided. It should come as no surprise that the telephone was invented here—all of those poor recent immigrants marooned in a quasi-barbaric landscape, desperate to reach out and touch someone and unable, out in the middle of nowhere, to even order in a pizza. These days? A long-distance phone call from Newfoundland to B.C. that once cost a fortune now costs only a few cents. In our heads, we've become championship shrinkers of time and space.

Not only do we tend to overly contemplate our landscape, our future is a minor obsession as well. It remains as undefined as the physical country itself. Unlike most other countries, Canada is still in the process of becoming whatever it could ultimately be. And with this sense of heightened expectation for tomorrow comes a great sense of hope, generosity and optimism.

So how is all of this reflected in the work of Canadian photographers? How many nations' histories neatly overlap the rise of photography? Other countries have millennia of painting, sculpture and architecture to document their pasts. We do have important painting in Canada, too, but photography has emerged as the dominant mode used by Canadian artists to help navigate our path to the future.

Photography is unsentimental. Photography is smart. Photography allows us to focus on the collision points between man and nature, between human and non-human. It allows us to knit together threads that are physically distant. It allows us to focus on a place where our assumptions collide with reality and where our inner worlds mesh with the outer world to create something startling and fresh.

Canadian photographers tend to be methodical in their working habits, and their work tends to be conceptual rather than poetic. Few gooey kisses, cute animals, throbbing sunsets or kissing nudes. And there seems to be less ego in Canadian photography; it's hard to imagine a Canadian photographer having a hissy fit or screaming at an assistant (though I'm sure it does happen).

The work of Canadian photographers also tends to be inclusive—it presupposes a smart audience to receive the work. It seems there's no need to dumb things down or tart them up.

Outsiders are fascinated with Canadians. It's a weirdly sexy country from the outside. It is also assumed that Canadian work is going to be inventive and come from a charitable place. Just as being Canadian often propels a novel in manuscript form to the front of the line in a New York editorial office, curators and collectors are eager to view new works of art from here.

Oddly, there seems to be little sense of a community among Canada's photographers, and from this comes a sense of inferiority and isolation. If your work is so great, why isn't Manhattan or London knocking on your door? The irony is that Manhattan and London are knocking on the door—but the lack of community has muted the sound of those knocks.

In the past decade, as American and Canadian societies have forked into two distinct directions, a sense of confidence has begun to emerge among Canadian artists. They are discovering that their work is not a shadow of something larger but, rather, wholly unique, increasingly risky and technically complex. If The Magenta Foundation can make inroads with this discovery, I support it wholeheartedly.

Canada is one of the few places on earth that has yet to realize its potential. What a thrill to make history every day simply by doing what you love!

DOUGLAS COUPLAND

LA PHOTOGRAPHIE AU CANADA

J'ai 43 ans, ce qui veut dire que j'ai vécu 31 % des années que le Canada soit une nation indépendante. Notre pays n'est pas âgé. En fait, le Canada, agé de seulement 138 ans, est un des pays le plus jeune du monde. Quelle merveille ! En face à ce manque d'histoire moderne, notre seul choix est de l'écrire nous même. Aussi, la lacune historique nous donne la liberté de vivre dans le présent sans être encombré par le passé.

En considérant notre histoire moderne proportionellement petite, il me semble que les Canadiens concentrent leur attention sur deux grands thèmes : notre paysage et notre futur. Les deux sont chargés avec des attentes considérables.

Réfléchisons à notre paysage immense et ancient. Son ampleur nous force à reconsidérer la façon par laquelle nous traitons la taille et la distance. Le Bouclier Canadien date des billions d'années. La période glaciaire a taillé de la terre tous les lacs que nous visitons l'été. Lorsque les pionniers qui traversaient le pays ont vue les chaines de montagnes ils ont certainement été désespérés par leur stature excessive. Partout au Canada, un paysage toujours sauvage et sévère est le produit du temps géologique et sa durée incompréhensiblement longue. Je note aussi que les Américains le croit bizarre quand le sujet du Bouclier Canadien survient dans une conversation avec un Canadien. Nous devenons presque tendres en discutant les filons de nickel, la glaciation, et la protection contre les mouches noires.

Un autre aspect du paysage canadien demeure sa taille immense. La contemplation de la distance ne peut pas être ignoré quand on s'occupe des affaires commerciales ou familiale au Canada. Ce n'est nul surprise que le téléphone est une invention canadienne. Nous devons avoir pitié pour ces pauvres immigrants qui ont été abandonnés en pleine cambrousse dans une région presque barbare. Ils manquaient un moyen de communication, une façon de tendre les bras vers la civilization, la facilité de commander une pizza. De nos jours, un appel de téléphone interurbain de la Terre-Neuve jusqu'à la Colombie Britannique coûte seulement quelques sous. Auparavant, ça coûtait une petite fortune. Par toute apparence, nous avons gagné la guerre contre le temps et l'espace.

Comme j'ai mentionné si-dessus, les Canadiens ont aussi la tendence à surcomtempler leur futur. L'avenir de notre pays demeure aussi vaste et étendu que son domaine physique. Contraire aux autres pays, le Canada n'a pas encore completé sa differenciation en entité définitive. En 500 ans la France sera probablement encore la France et la Chine sera encore la Chine, mais le Canada ? Dieu le sait ! Cette impression élevée du lendemain inspire aussi un sens de générosite, d'optimisme et d'espoire.

Ce n'est pas surprenant d'apprendre que notre société canadienne est parmi ceux les plus paisibles et tolérants du monde. Ce que j'ai toujours noté durant mes voyages européens est la façon que les jeunes canadiens ressortent de leur milieu. La raison pour leur singularité n'est pas seulement à cause de leur costume mais plutôt leur visage ouvert et souriant. Même les Australiens ont l'air plus prudent que Jeanette venant de Montréal ou Paul originaire d'Ottawa.

Alors, comment est-ce que la photograhie canadienne est-elle une réflection de la société canadienne ? Bien sure que la photographie existe aussi dans tous les autres pays, mais leur passé ne chevauchent pas complètement le développement de la photographie. Des milliers d'années ont produit des cultures riches en tableaux, en sculptures et en architecture qui peuvent être consulté pour documenter le passé de tous ces pays. Au Canada nous avons aussi quelques œuvres historiques, mais la majorité de notre documentation a été faite à travers des photos. Ce n'est guerre surprenant que les artistes canadiens le préfère contre toutes autre moyens d'expression artistique.

La photographie n'est pas sentimentale. La photographie est intelligente. La photographie nous donne la capacité d'observer les relations entre l'homme et la nature, entre l'humain et le non-humain. Elle nous permet de tisser ensemble les fils du monde. La photographie nous montre la vision de nos assomptions en collision avec la réalité. C'est là ou quelque chose de nouveau est créée de la réunion de l'univers dans notre cerveau au monde corporel.

Les photographes canadiens on la tendance de travailler méthodiquement. Leurs travaux ont plus souvent un air conceptuel plutôt que poétique. Absent sont les baisers mielleuses et les animaux mignons, les coucher d'un soleil vibrant ou les nues qui s'embrassent. Les photographes canadiens sont aussi moins égoïstes. C'est difficile d'imaginer un photographe canadien qui pique une crise de colère ou qui tempête contre son assistant.

La photographie canadienne est aussi inclusive. L'artiste présuppose qu'il y aura des spectateurs intelligents et alors il n'y a aucune raison de baisser l'intelligence de son œuvre ou de le retaper. Le public voit seulement la vérité.

Il est curieux qu'il n'existe pas vraiment l'impression d'une communauté photographique au Canada. Peut-être ceci est le produit d'une sensation d'infériorité et d'isolation que peut engendrer le Nord. « Si mes travaux sont si bons, pourquoi n'ai-je pas le reconnaissance de Londres ou de Manhattan ? » La réalité est que Londres et Manhattan veulent te reconnaître, mais l'absence d'une communauté photographique au Canada les prévients de te découvrir. Esperons que cela changera.

Les étrangers sont captivés pas les Canadiens. Ils considèrent notre pays bizarrement séduisant. Les populations halogènes ont l'idée que les arts canadiens vont être inventifs et viennent d'une place charitable. De la même façon qu'un manuscript pour un roman composé par un canadien sera bien reçu par n'importe quelle maison de publication de New York, les conservateurs et collectionneurs ont toujours hâte de voir les nouveaux chef d'œuvres que nous allons produire. Durant la dernière décenie, les sociétés américaines et canadiennes ont clairement branché dans deux directions différentes. Pour les Canadiens, de cette route indépendante a émergé une nouvelle confiance et une réalisation que ce que nous produisons n'est pas une imitation d'autres travaux. Plutôt, c'est original, sui generis, et de plus en plus risqué et complexe.

Le Canada est un pays qui n'a pas encore déterminé son identité finale. Si La Fondation Magenta peut contribuer à ce processus je les applaudis. Quel plaisir de faire parti de notre histoire seulement en faisant ce qu'on aime.

DOUGLAS COUPLAND

MADE IN CANADA

I returned to Canada in the spring of 2004 after a 10-year stint in New York City. All that summer, I was asked countless times what my line of work was, and my stock answer quickly became: "I publish books and arrange exhibitions." More often than not, the response I got was: "Have you noticed there is no publishing house here in Canada for the arts?" After hearing that one too many times I decided to create The Magenta Foundation and our first book, *Carte Blanche*.

What exactly inspired me? Many things: the methodical work Canadians put into their projects, the concern for their environment, the sense of pride they show in their work. The biggest trigger was the ability I would have to showcase some really good work and watch careers change because of it. Ultimately, publishers are looking for those rare gems, and Canada has quite a few. While getting better acquainted with Canadian photography these past two years, I realized that finding work to look at is easy; there is no shortage of it. Being inspired by good work is a completely different story. I guess, in a way, by creating Magenta, I am spurring other Canadians in the arts to pay closer attention to what's going on right under their own noses.

I was fortunate enough to have my first body of work published while I was in my 20s, allowing me to experience first-hand what it's like to have your photography seen on an international level. Starting a publishing house for the arts to propel the careers of others was an inevitable career move for me, and I feel honoured to have had such enormous support and encouragement to start this foundation. It's great knowing that as a unified artistic community working together toward the same goal, we are *all* responsible for *Carte Blanche*. Board members Doug Wallace and Clare Vander Meersch are instrumental to Magenta's makeup and success. They are relentless, dedicated, proactive and truly a winning team.

Carte Blanche is unique—both a reference and a piece of art!—and, as the title suggests, it's all about starting fresh and working with full creative freedom. A simple call for submissions plus the recruiting efforts of our 17 jurors brought together Canada's best and brightest photographers.

I have always said that it's an exciting time to be Canadian, because the best is yet to be. On that note, here's a little piece of history. Absorb it. There's so much more to come.

MARYANN CAMILLERI

FABRIQUÉ AU CANADA

J'ai fait mon retour au Canada le printemps de l'an 2004 après avoir habité la ville de New York pour 10 ans. Durant l'été, on m'a souvent demandé mon emploi. Rapidement j'ai trouve ma réponse clichée : « Je publie des livres et organise des expositions d'art. » Souvent la réponse a cette déclaration était une autre question : « Avez-vous remarqué que le Canada est sans une maison de publication pour les arts ? » Après avoir entendu cette remarque une dizaine de fois, j'ai décidé de créer La Fondation Magenta et voilà notre premier livre, *Carte Blanche*.

Alors, où ai-je trouvé mon inspiration ? Des autres canadiens bien sure ! Parmi mes inspirations les plus importantes sont les travaux méthodiques des canadiens, leur préoccupation avec l'environnement et la fierté canadienne que démontrent leurs œuvres. Ma plus grande inspiration était surement l'habileté que j'aurai de partager des bonnes œuvres d'art et peut-être aussi influencer d'une façon positive les carrières d'autres artistes. Le but ultime des éditeurs est de trouver ces pierres précieuses dont le Canada en a en masse. En étudiant la photographie canadienne durant ces deux dernières années, j'ai réalisé quelque chose très importante : bien qu'il n'y a pas un manque de travaux à considérer, être inspiré par un ouvrage exceptionnel est une histoire complètement différente. Je suppose qu'en créant Magenta je force une multitute de canadiens à faire attention à ce qui ce passe directement sous leur nez.

Quand j'etais encore dans mes vingtaines, j'étais assez heureuse d'avoir la chance d'être publié pour la première fois. Je sais personellement ce qui arrive quand un photographe est exposé à un niveau international. Pour moi, la création d'une maison de publication pour les arts qui pourrait aider les carrières d'autres artistes canadiens était une étape inévitable de ma vie. Je suis très honorée d'avoir reçu tant de support et d'encouragement quand j'ai entrepris de créer cette fondation. C'est fantastique de savoir qu'en travaillant ensemble comme une communauté artistique unifiée envers le même but nous sommes *tous* responsable pour la creation de *Carte Blanche*. L'organisation et le succès de Magenta est aussi merci au membres du conseil d'administration, Doug Wallace et Clare Vander Meersch. Ils sont implacables, devoués, et proactives, vraiment un duo fantastique !

Carte Blanche est unique. Simultanément, c'est un livre de référence et un chef d'œuvre. Comme suggère le titre, ce texte traite tout au sujet de repartir de zéro et de travailler avec une liberté créative complète. Avec l'aide de nos 17 jurés et après un simple appel au photographes de nous rendres leurs œuvres photographiques, nous avons rassemblé le meilleur qu'à a offrir le Canada.

Je maintiens que c'est un temps excitant d'être canadien car nous n'avons pas encore atteint notre zénith culturel. Pour nous aider à completer ce voyage, je vous offre un petit bout d'histoire. Savourez-le. Ce n'est pas encore la fin.

MARYANN CAMILLERI

FINE

Raymonde April, Michel Archambault, Barbara Astman, Nicolas Baier, Dean Baldwin, Iain Baxter, Marco Bohr, Diane Borsato, Dianne Bos, Robert Bourdeau, Jim Breukelman, Karin Bubas, Robert Burley, Edward Burtynsky, Olga Chagaoutdinova, Serge Clément, Scott Conarroe, Susan Coolen, Stephanie Cormier, Douglas Coupland, Jackie Cytrynbaum, Andrew Danson Danushevsky, Susan Dobson, Katyuska Doleatto, Jakub Dolejš, David Donald, Evergon, Janieta Eyre, Michael Flomen, Debra Friedman, Eldon Garnet, Chad Gerth, Barbara Gilbert, Rita Godlevskis, Rafael Goldchain, Nathalie Gosselin, Angela Grauerholz, Colwyn Griffith, Frank Grisdale, Sunil Gupta, Toni Hafkenscheid, Rawi Hage, Adad Hannah, Arni Haraldsson, Isabelle Hayeur, Dave Heath, Martha Henrickson, April Hickox, Bettina Hoffmann, Thaddeus Holownia, Vid Ingelevics, Geoffrey James, Louis Joncas, Lisa Klapstock, Eric Klemm, Thomas Kneubühler, Katherine Knight, Victor Korchenko, Suzy Lake, Laura Letinsky, Nina Levitt, Jennifer Long, Arnaud Maggs, Amanda Marchand, Carol Marino, John Massey, Scott McFarland, David Miller, Lori Newdick, Lindsay Page, Alain Paiement, Steve Payne, Nicholas & Sheila Pye, Elise Rasmussen, Mark Ruwedel, Chuck Samuels, Carlos & Jason Sanchez, Michael Schreier, Volker Seding, Sandra Semchuk, Derek Shapton, Cheryl Sourkes, Lisa Stinner, F. Leslie Thompson, Eve K. Tremblay, Tobaron Waxman, Carl Zimmerman

ART

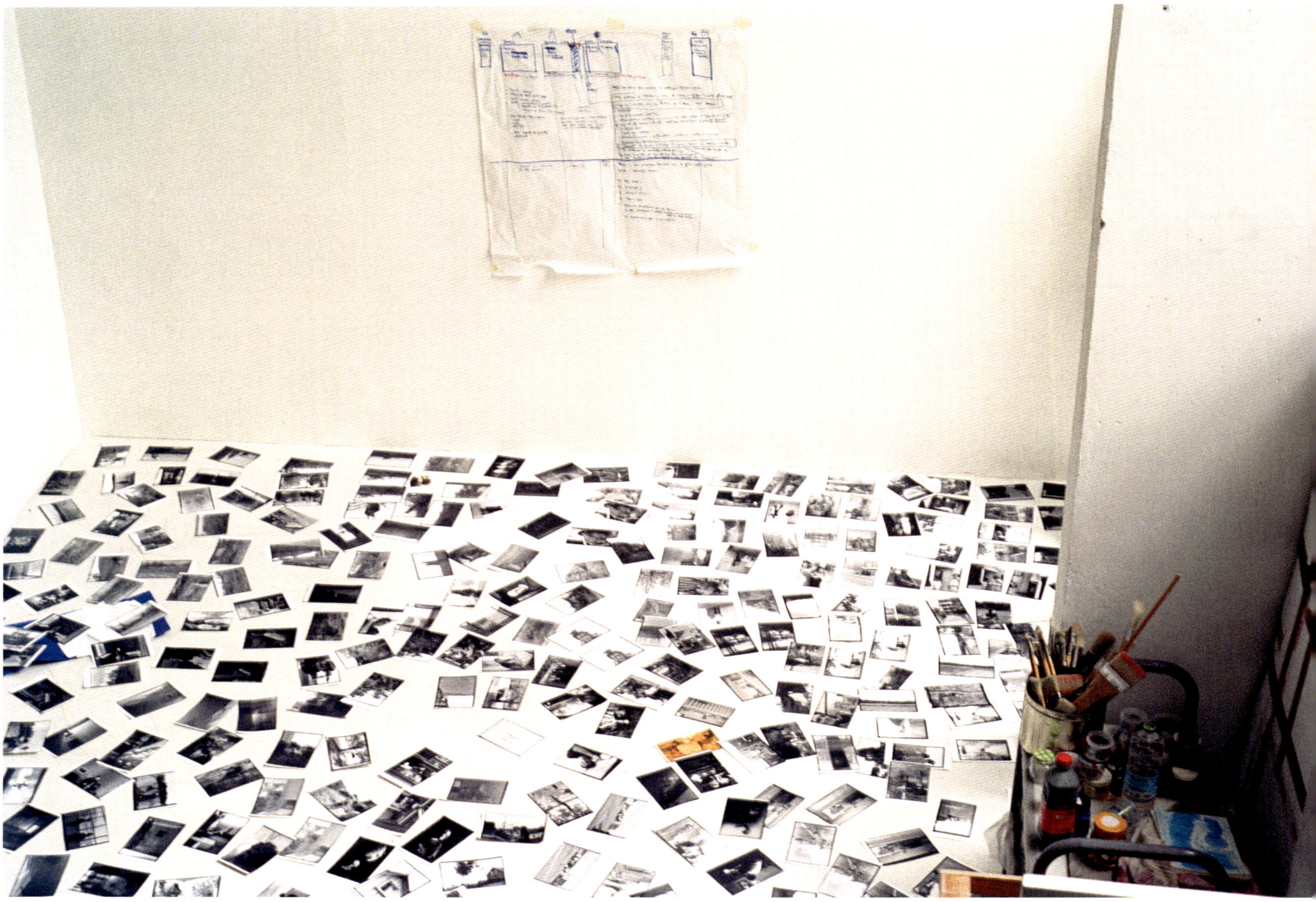

Raymonde April Mosaique (Mosaic)

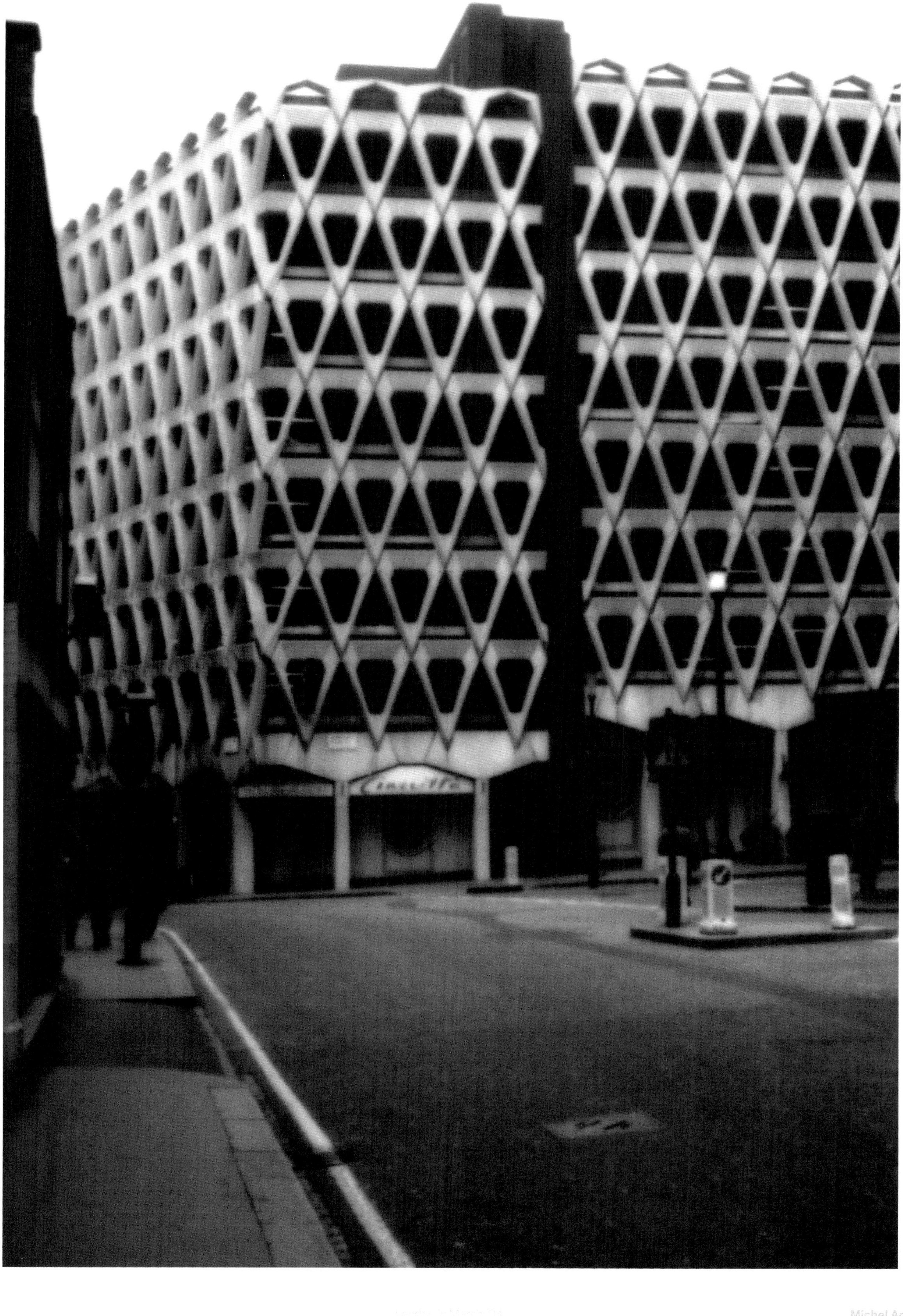

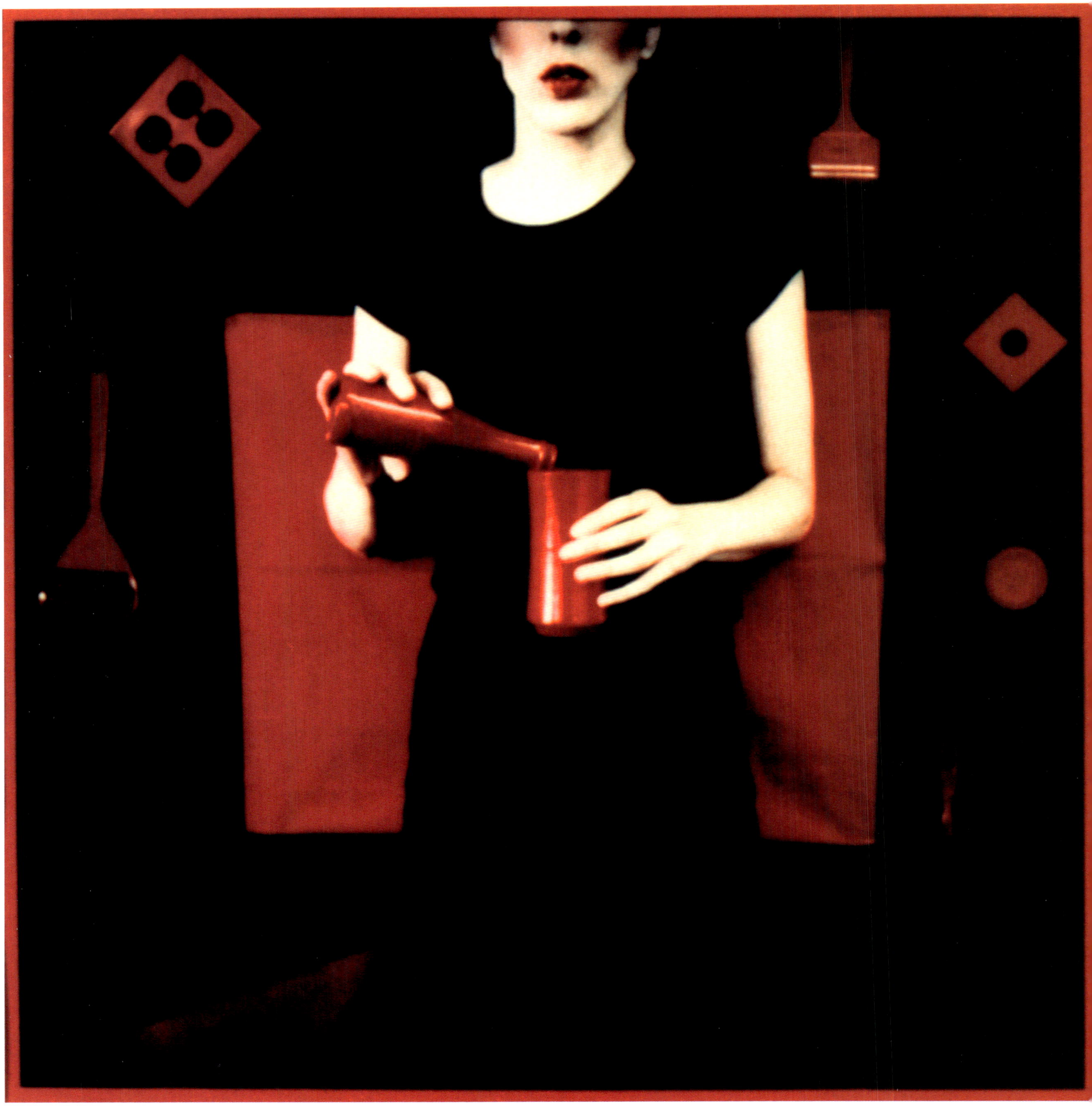

Barbara Astman

Red 3 (from "The Red Series")

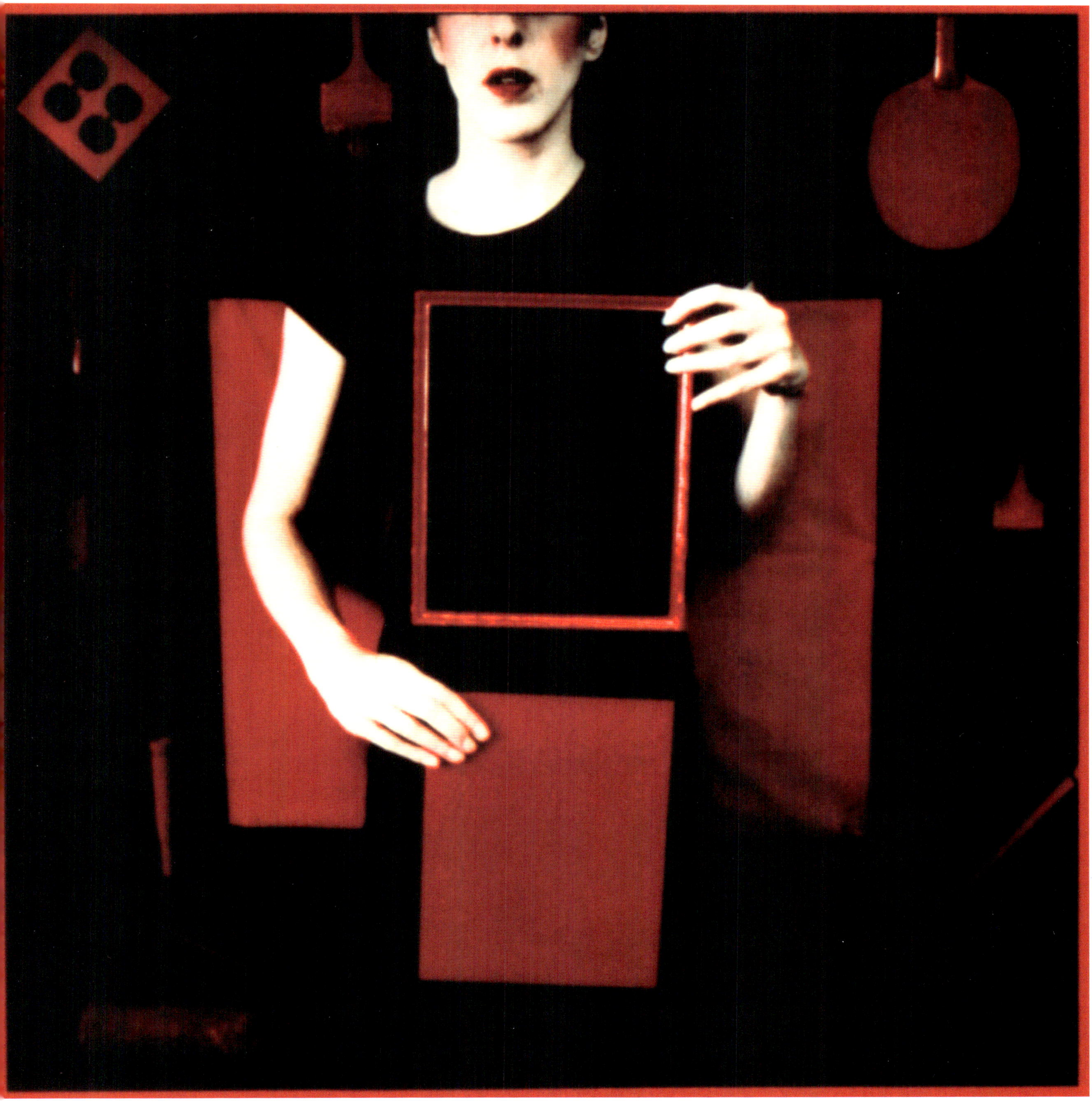

Red 4 (from "The Red Series")

Barbara Astman

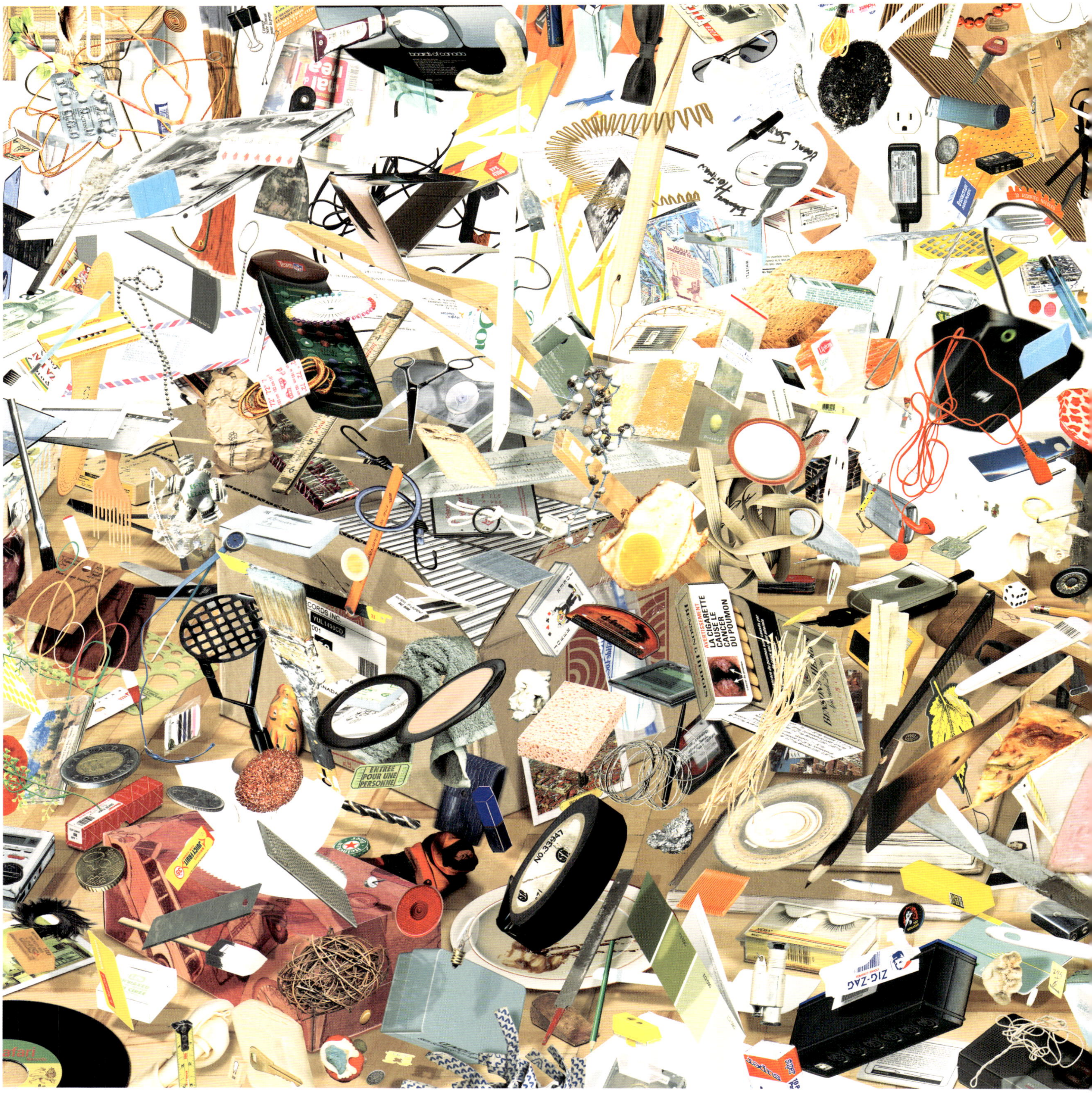

Nicolas Baier

Petits riens

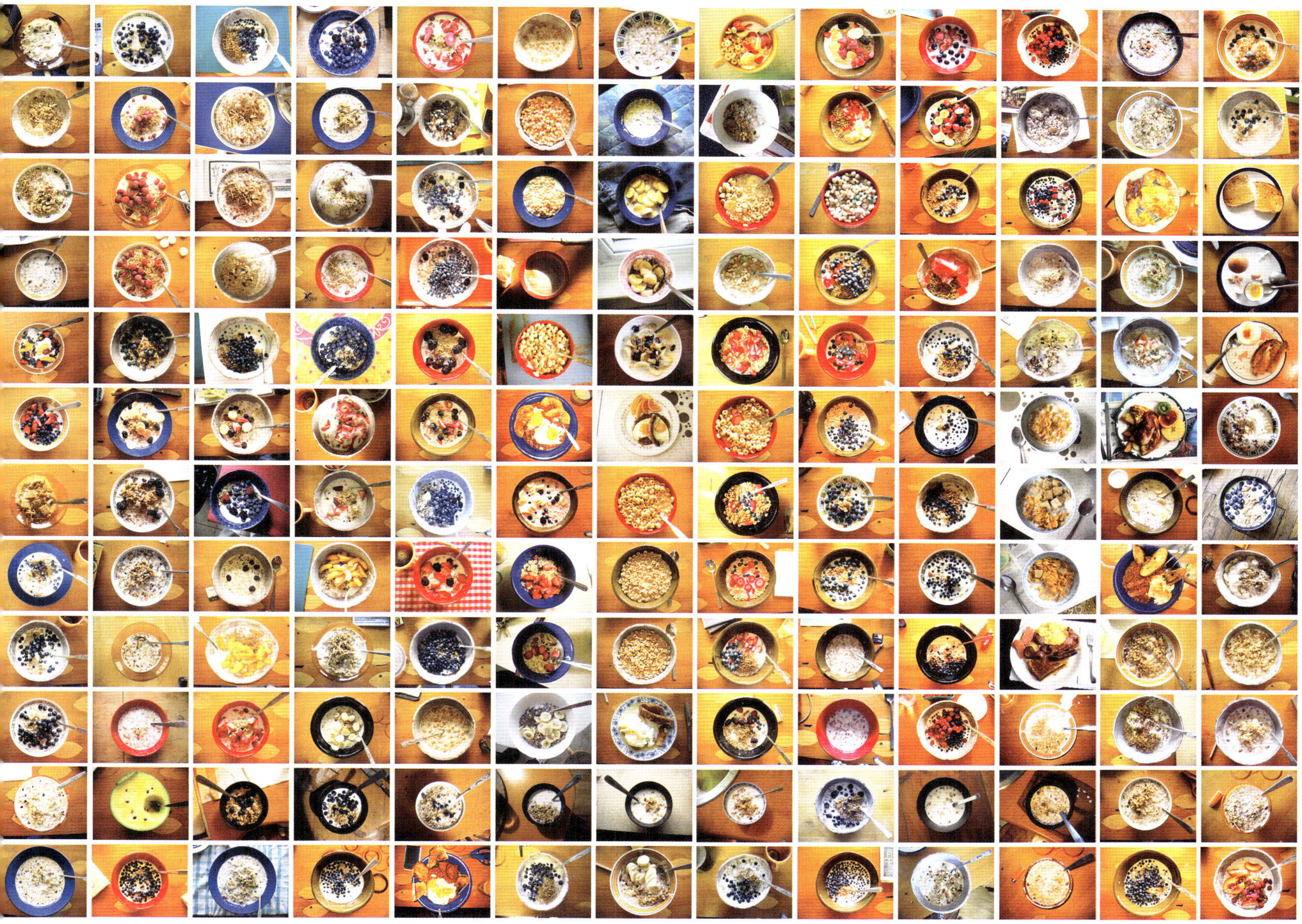

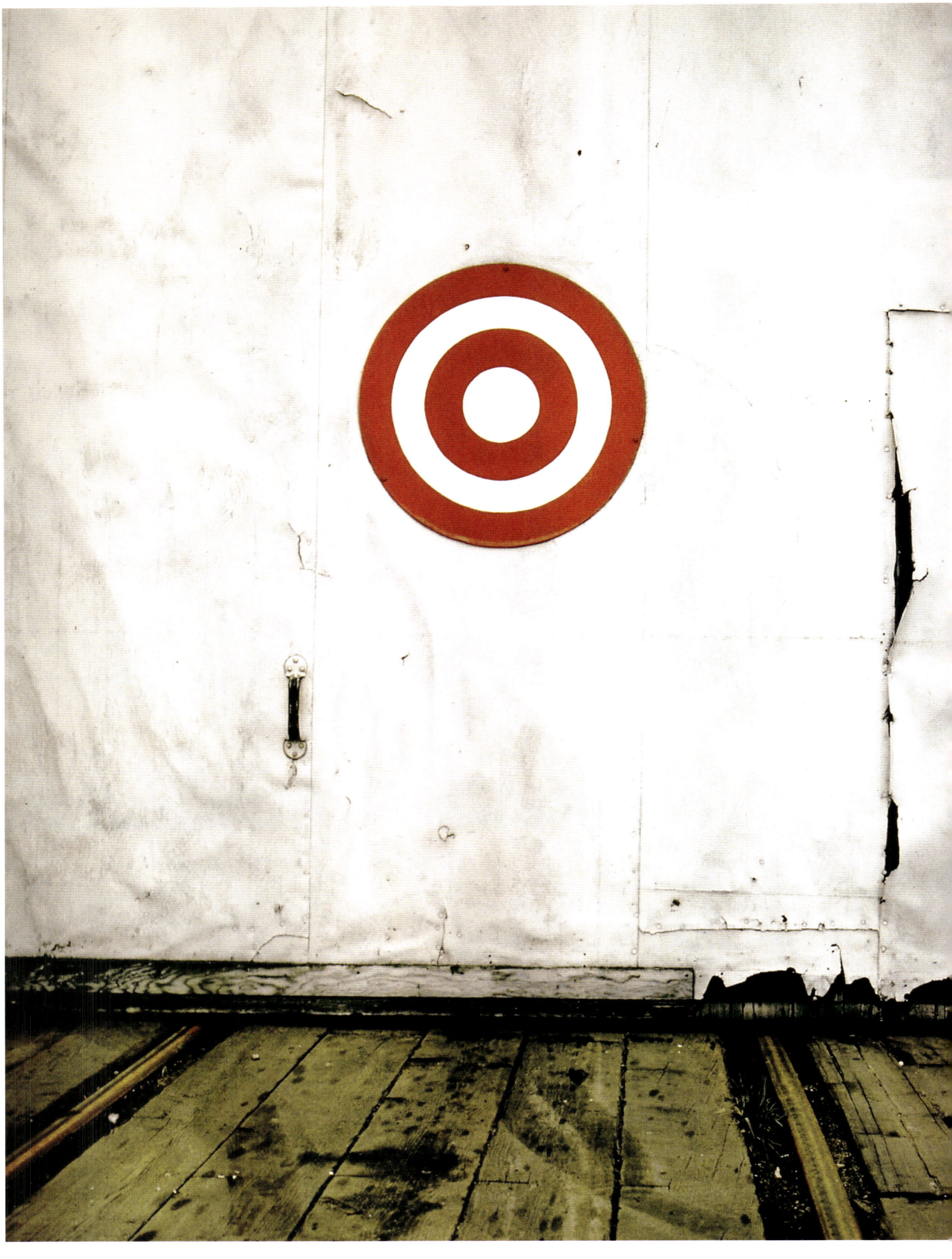

Iain Baxter

Door, Ballantyne Wharf, Vancouver, B.C.

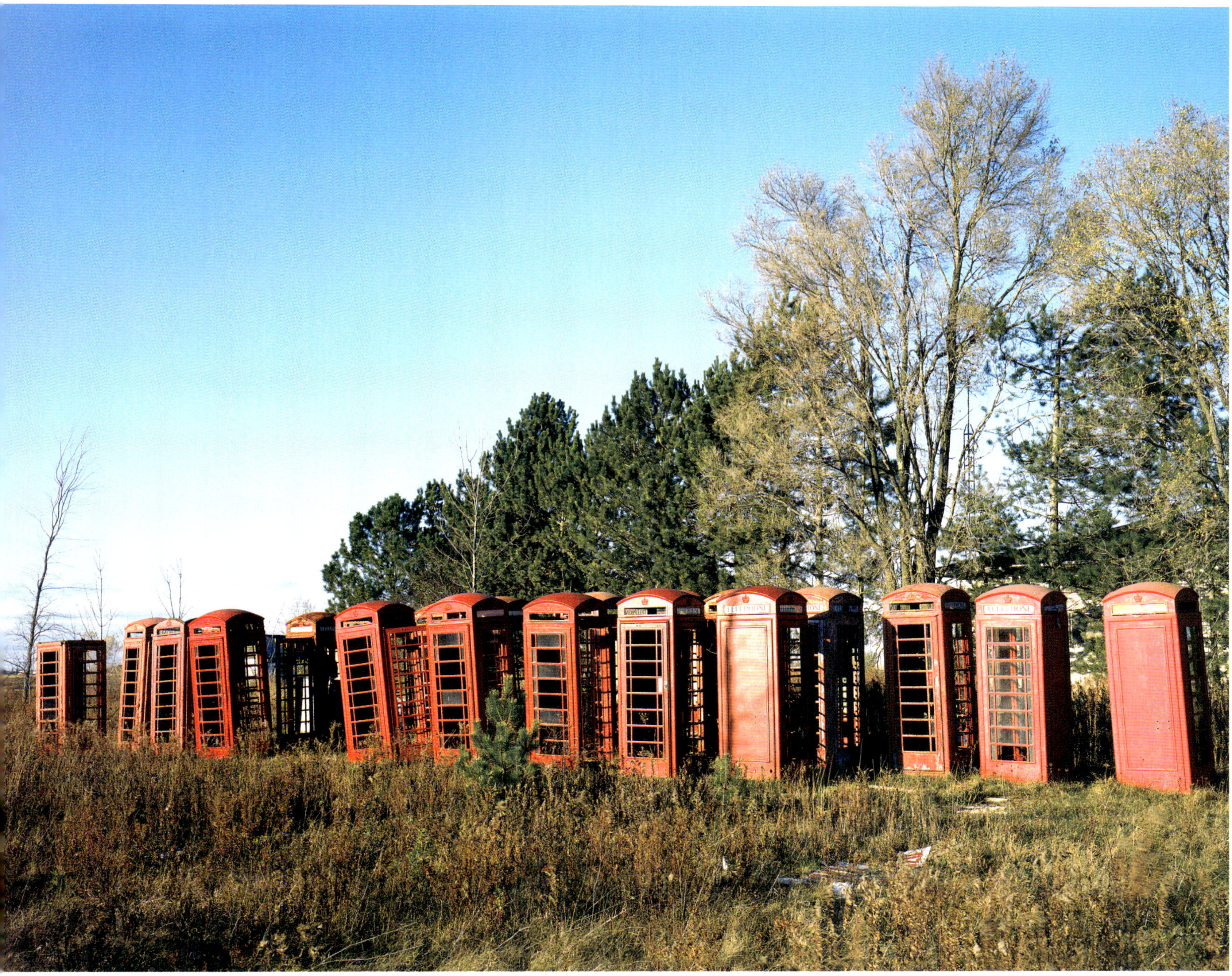

Telephone Booths (from the series “Invisible Cities”)

Marco Bohr

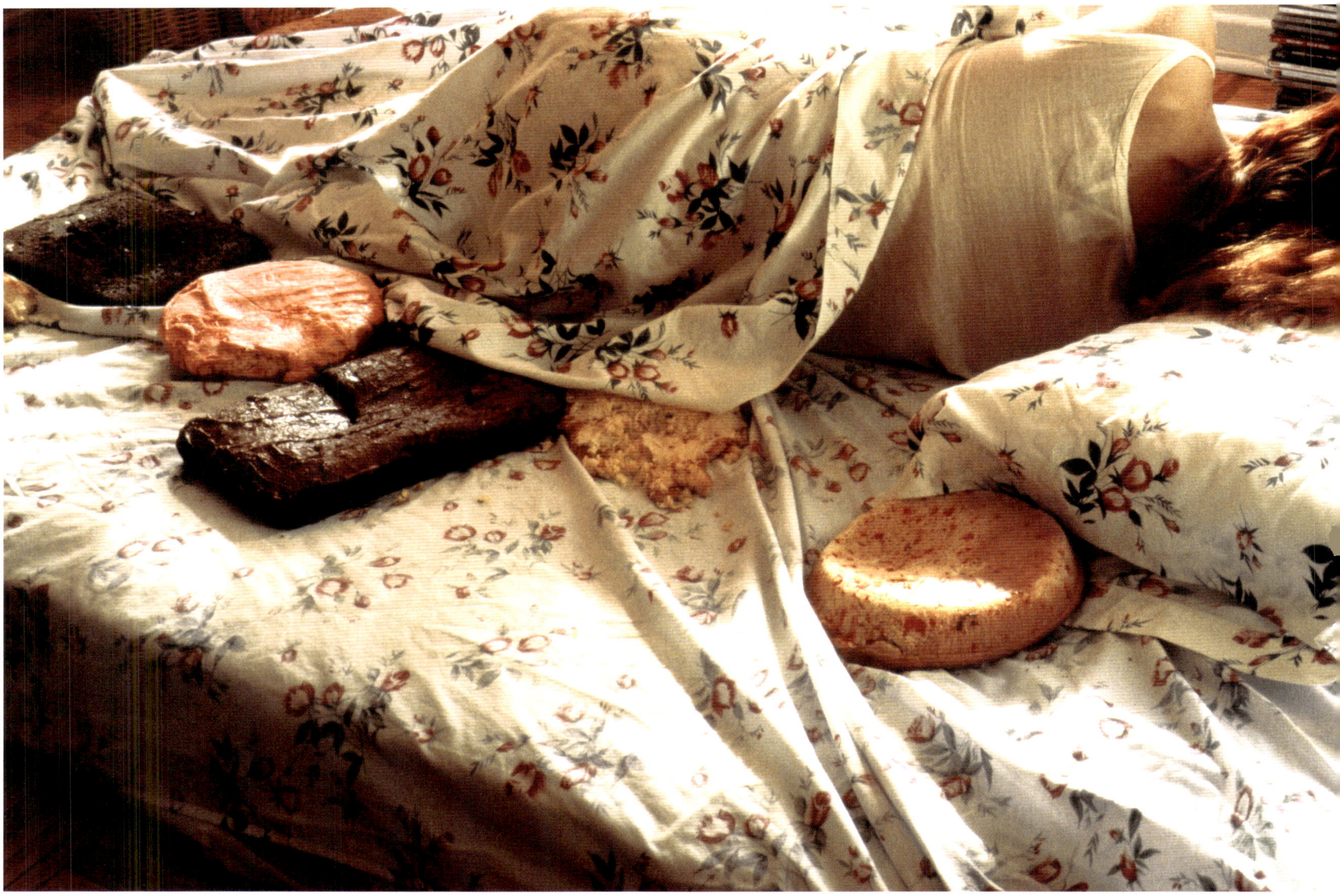

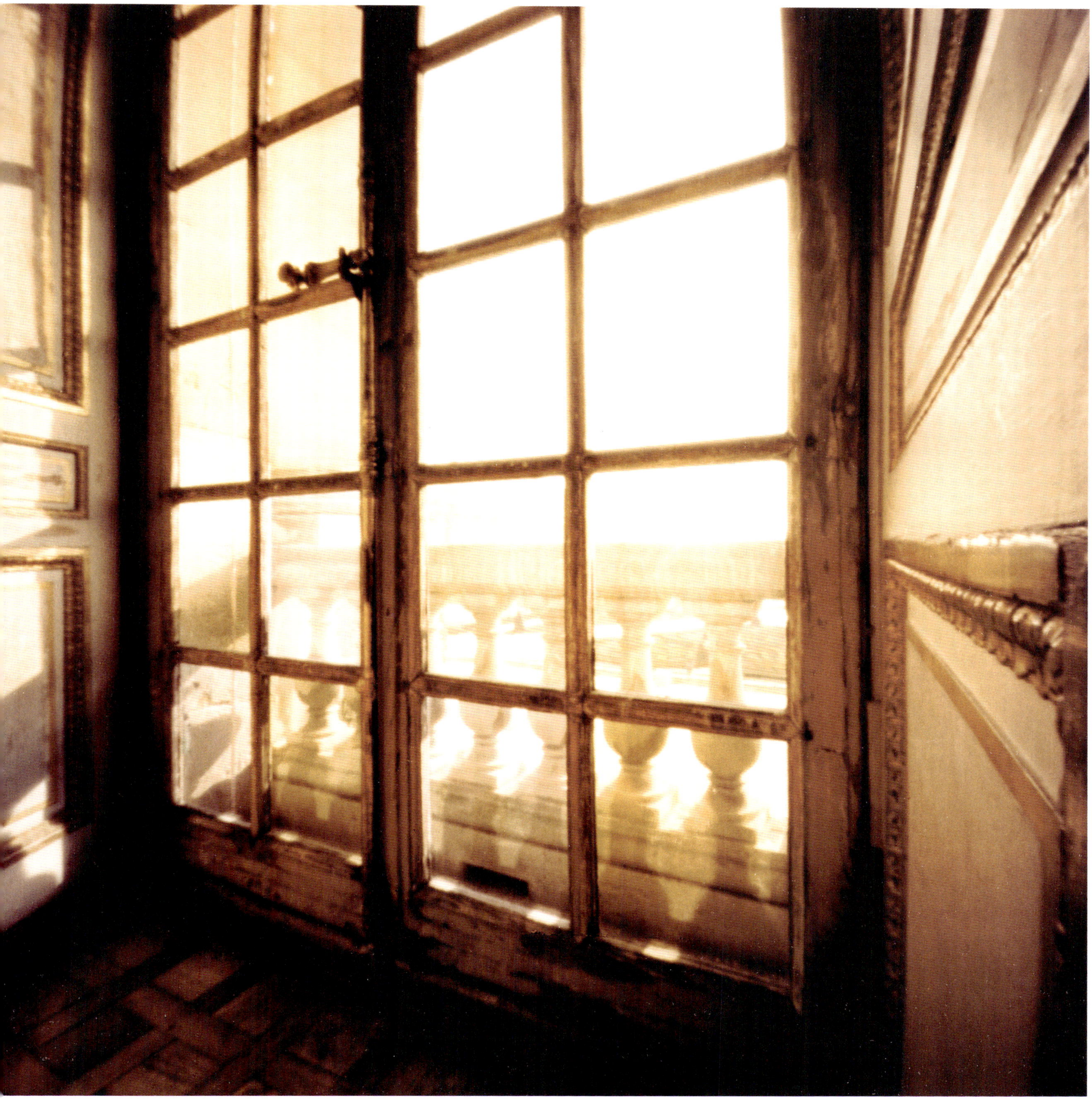

Window, Versailles, 2003

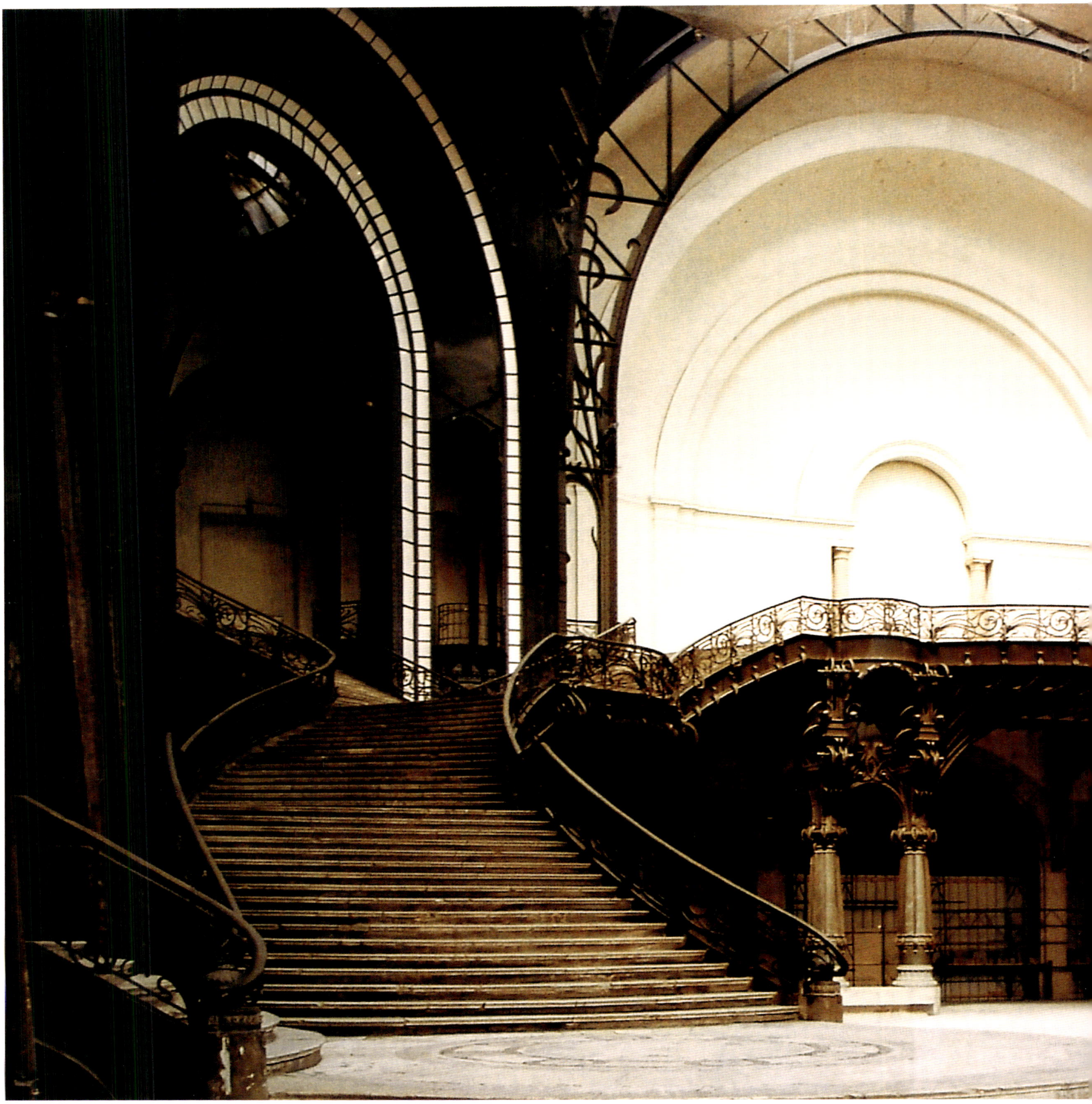

Robert Bourdeau

Le Grand Palais, Paris, France, 2001

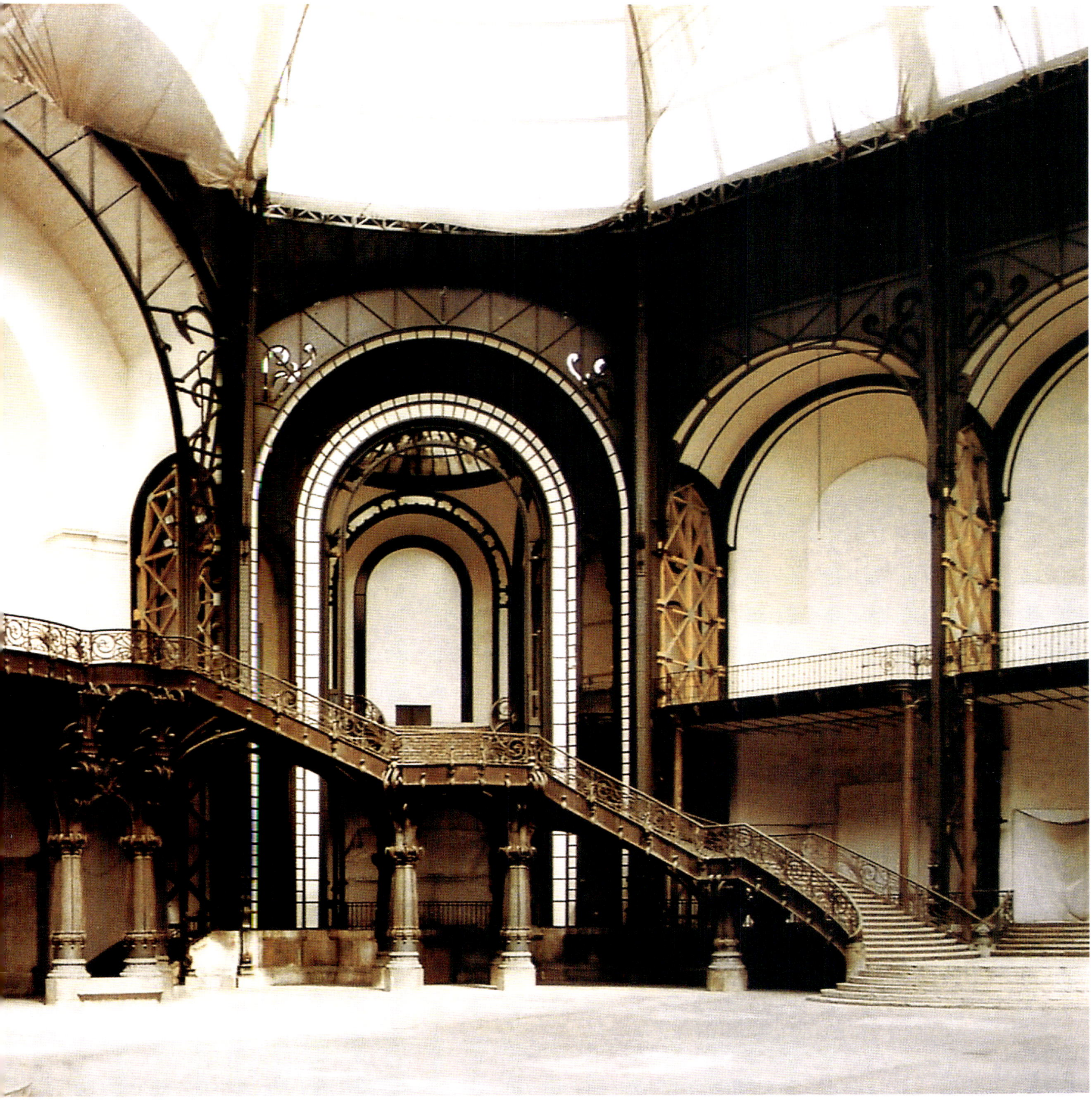

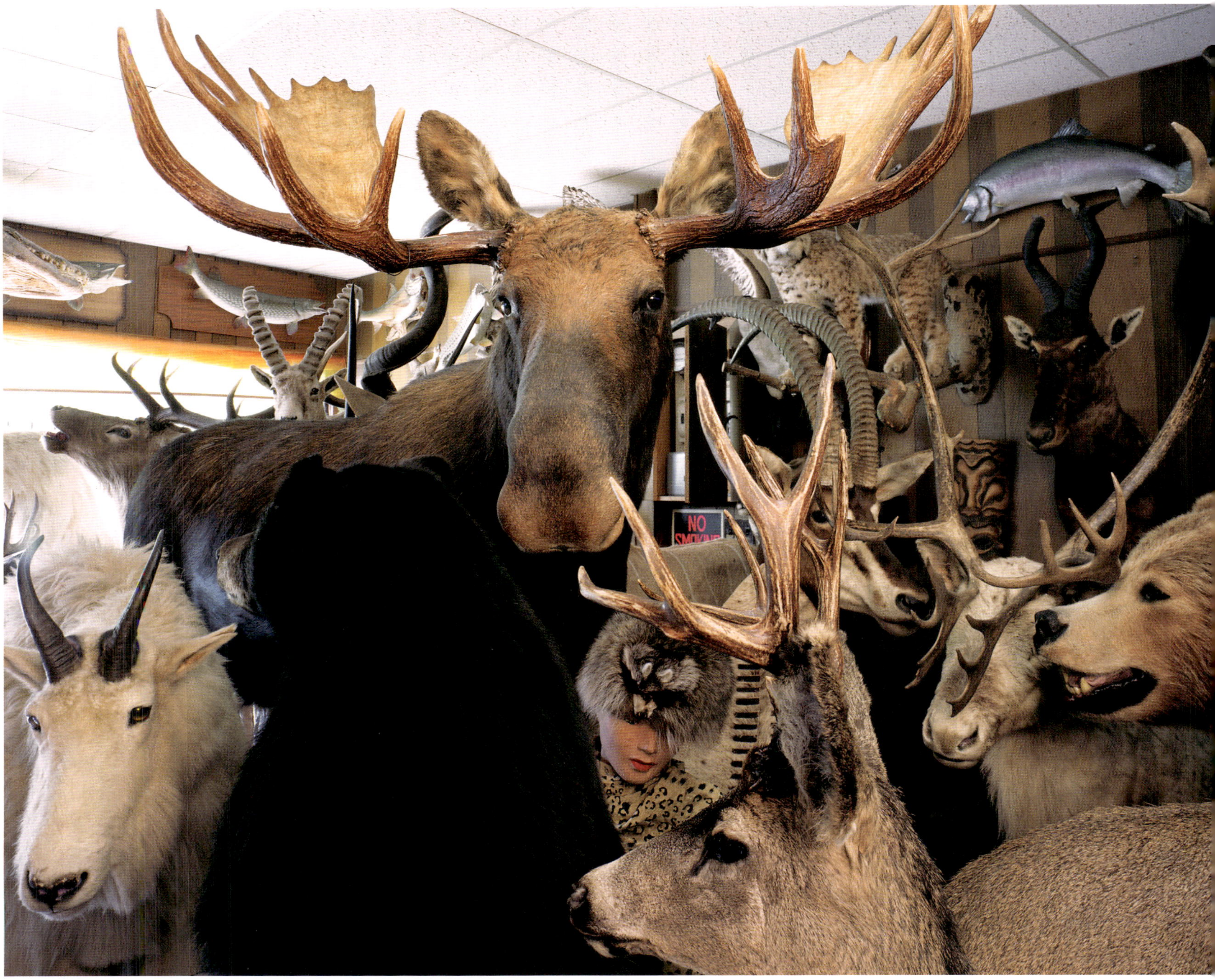
NO

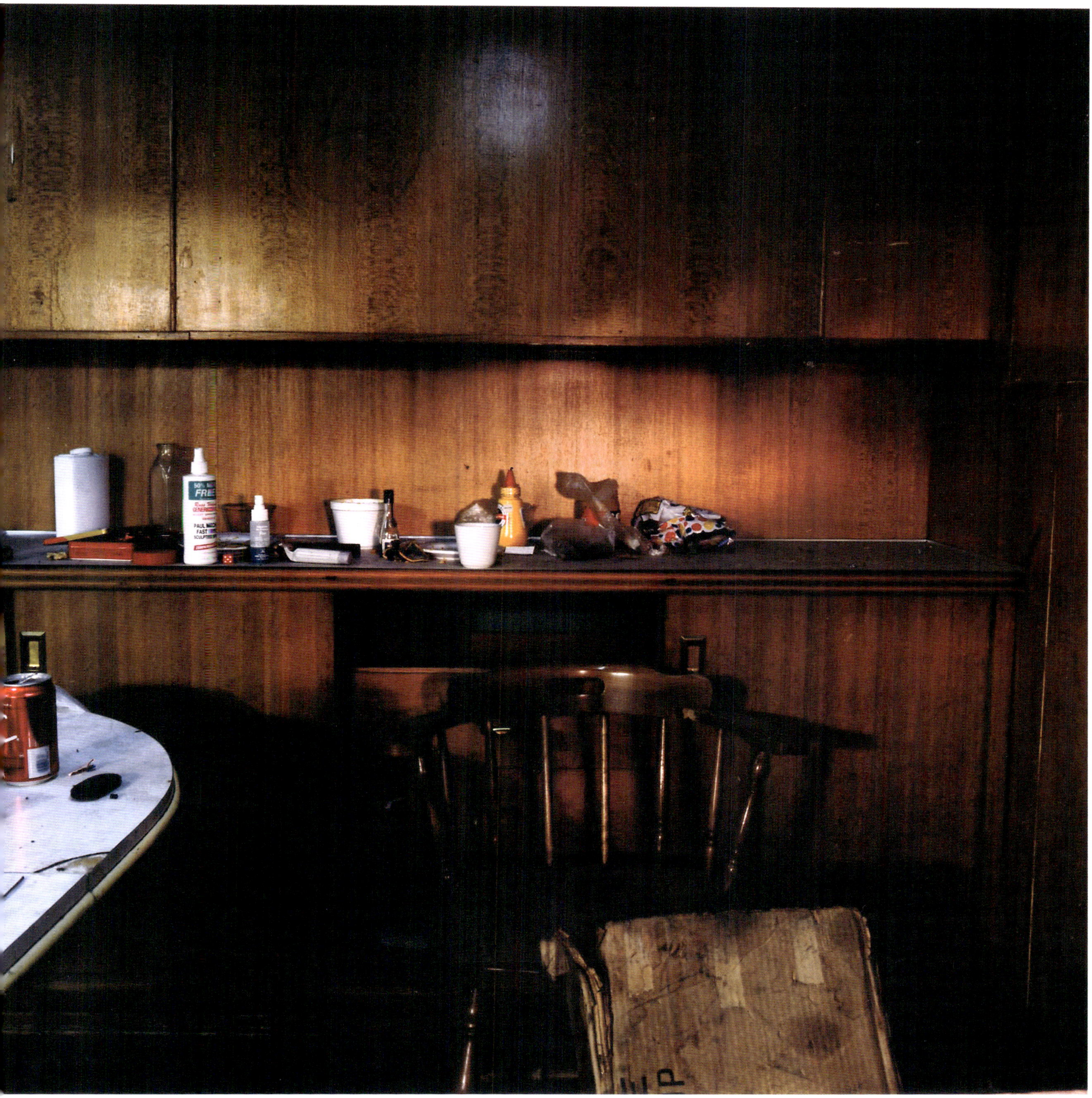

Kitchen 1 (from the series "Leon's Palace")

Karin Bubas

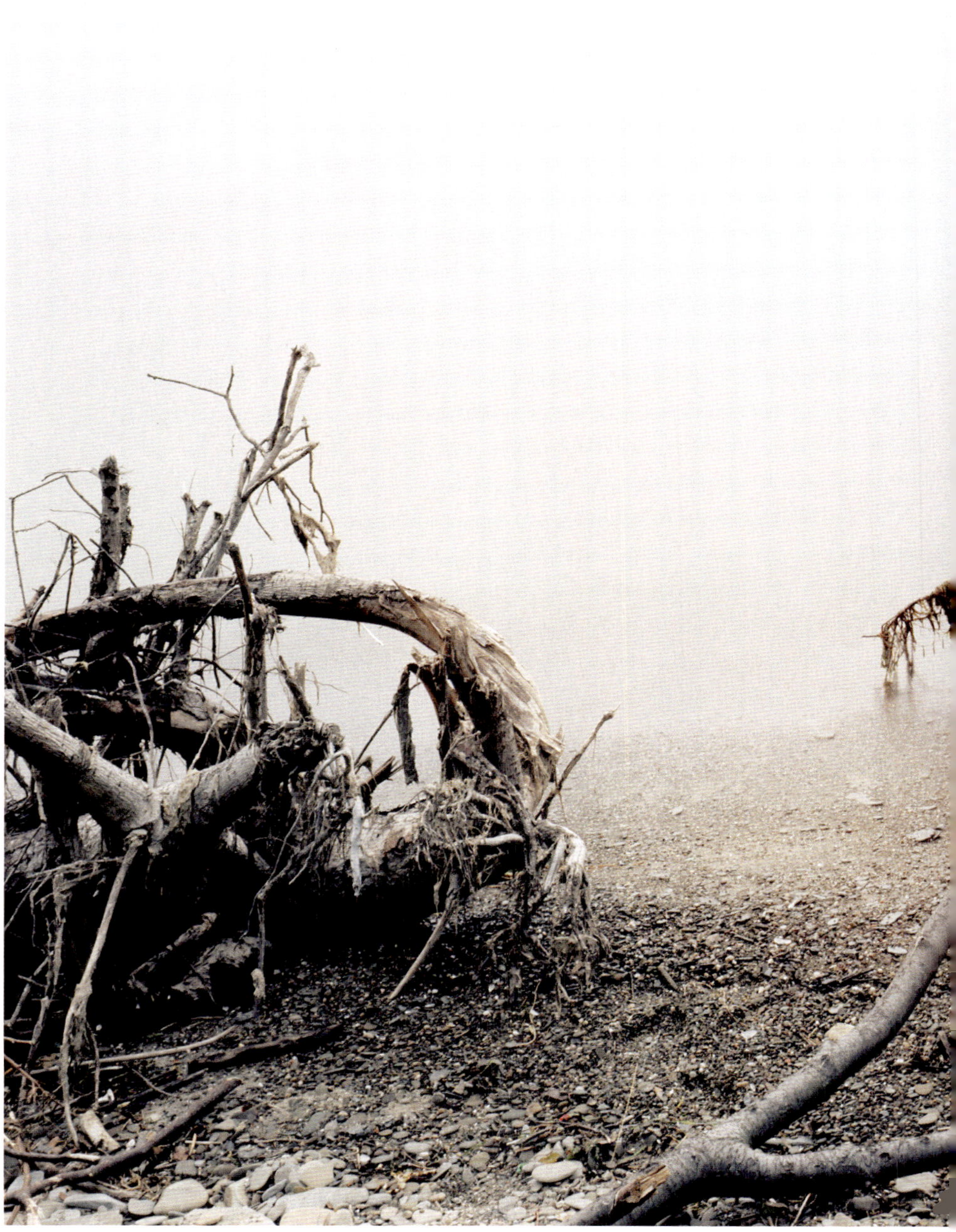

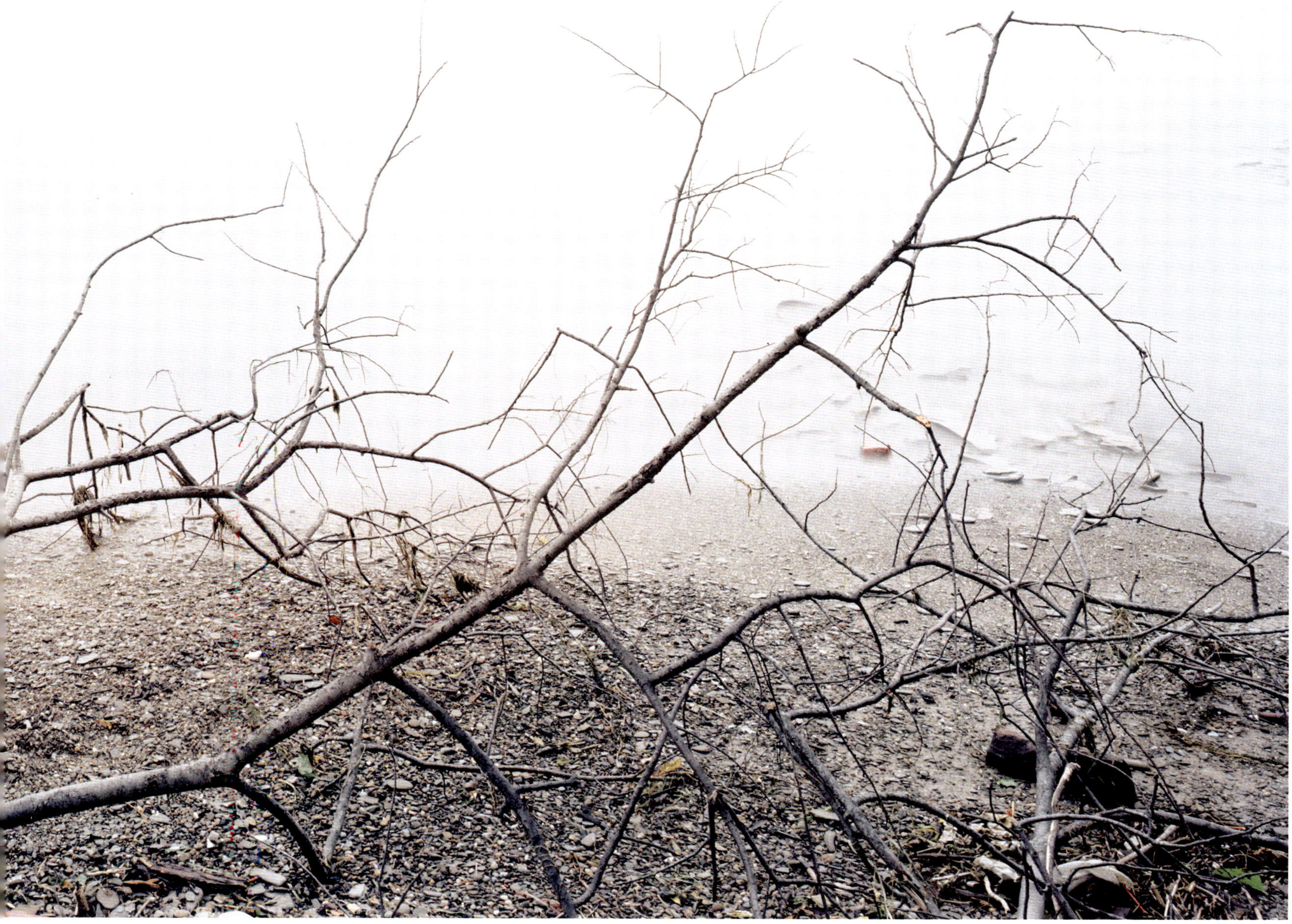

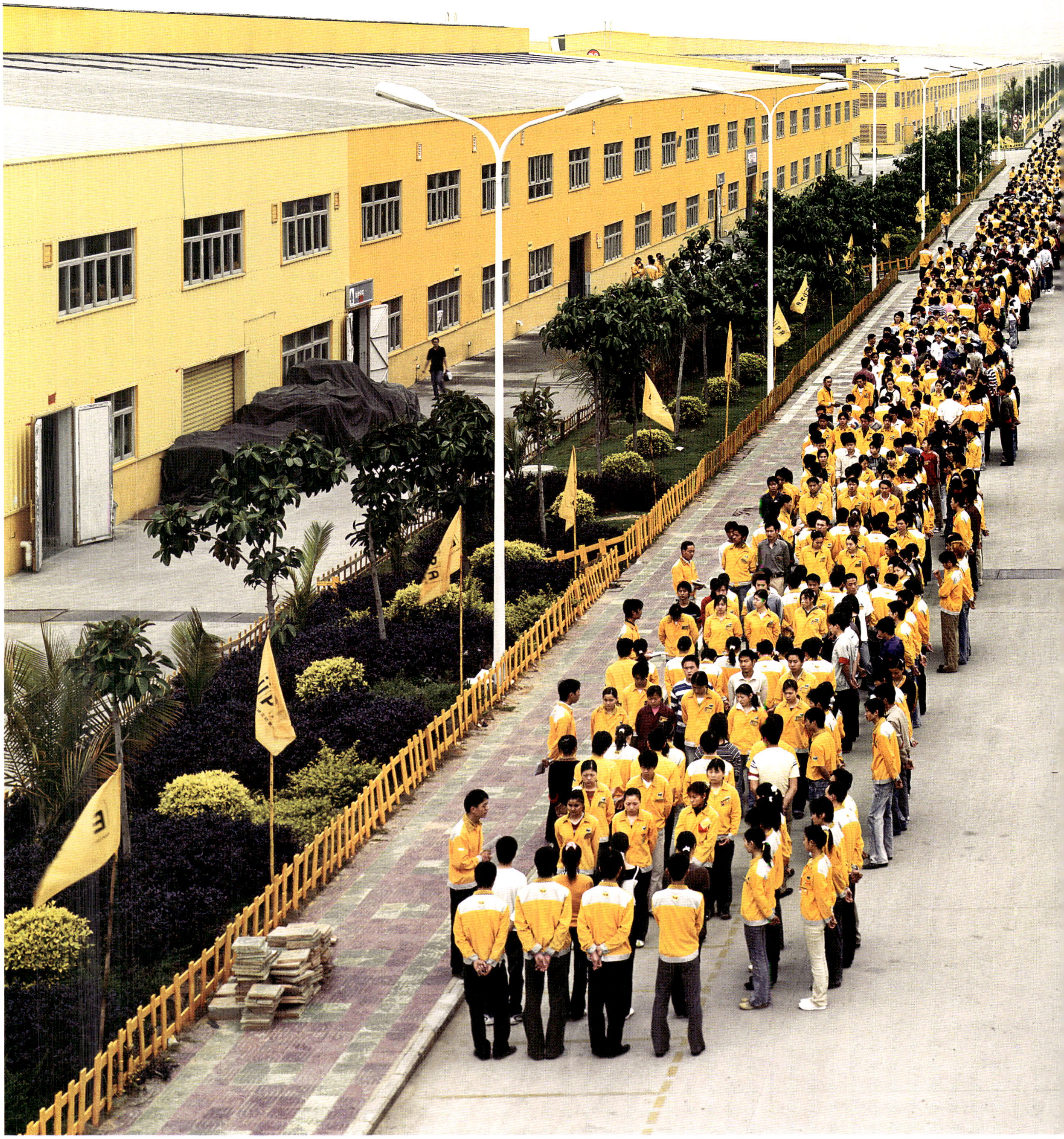

Edward Burtynsky Manufacturing #18, Cankun Factory, Zhangzhou, Fujian Province, China 2005

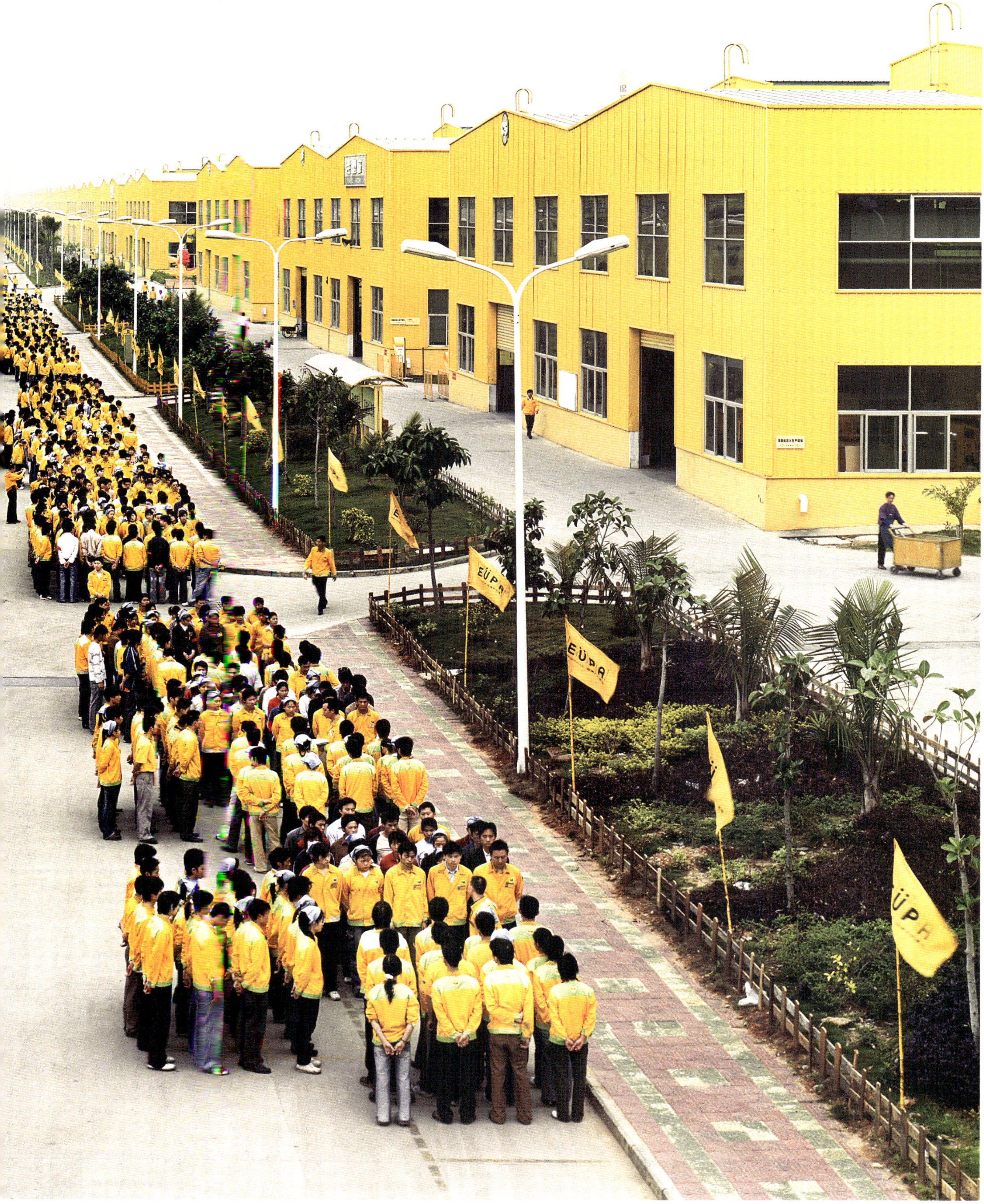
EÜPA
EÜPA

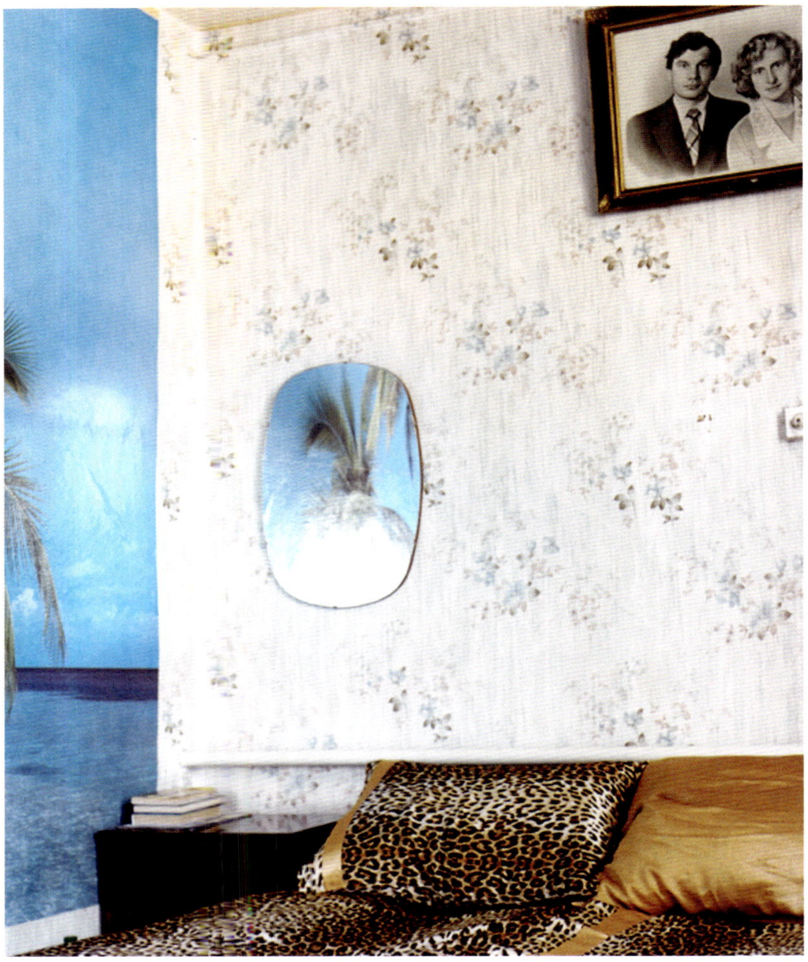

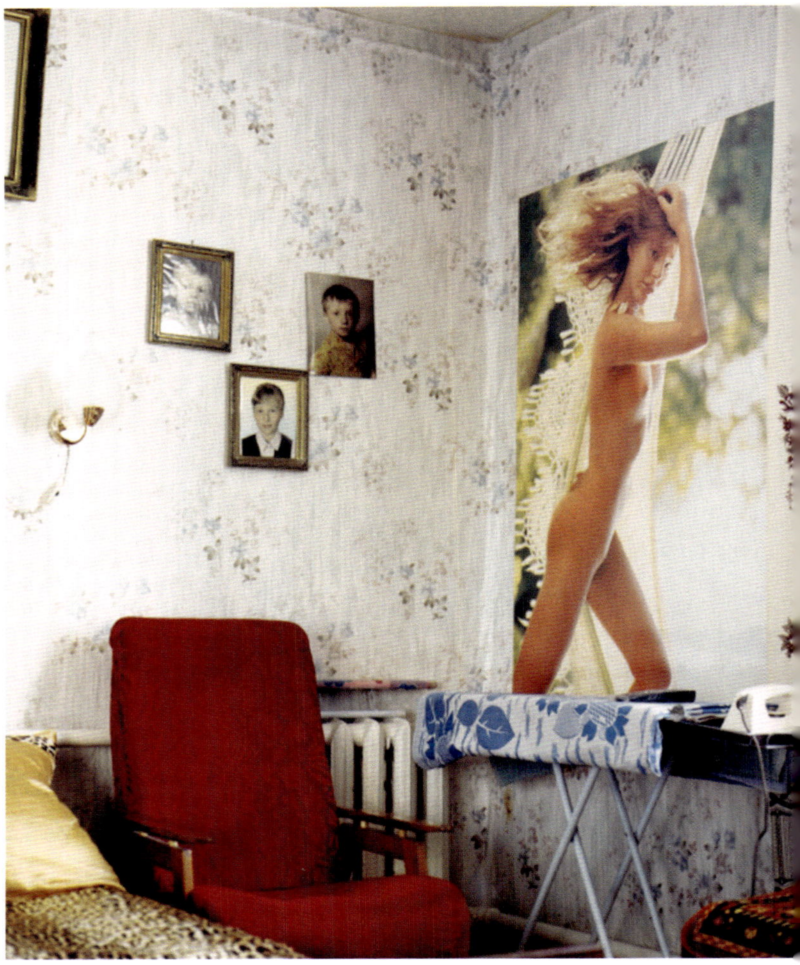

Olga Chagaoutdinova

Bedroom in Siberia (Diptych)

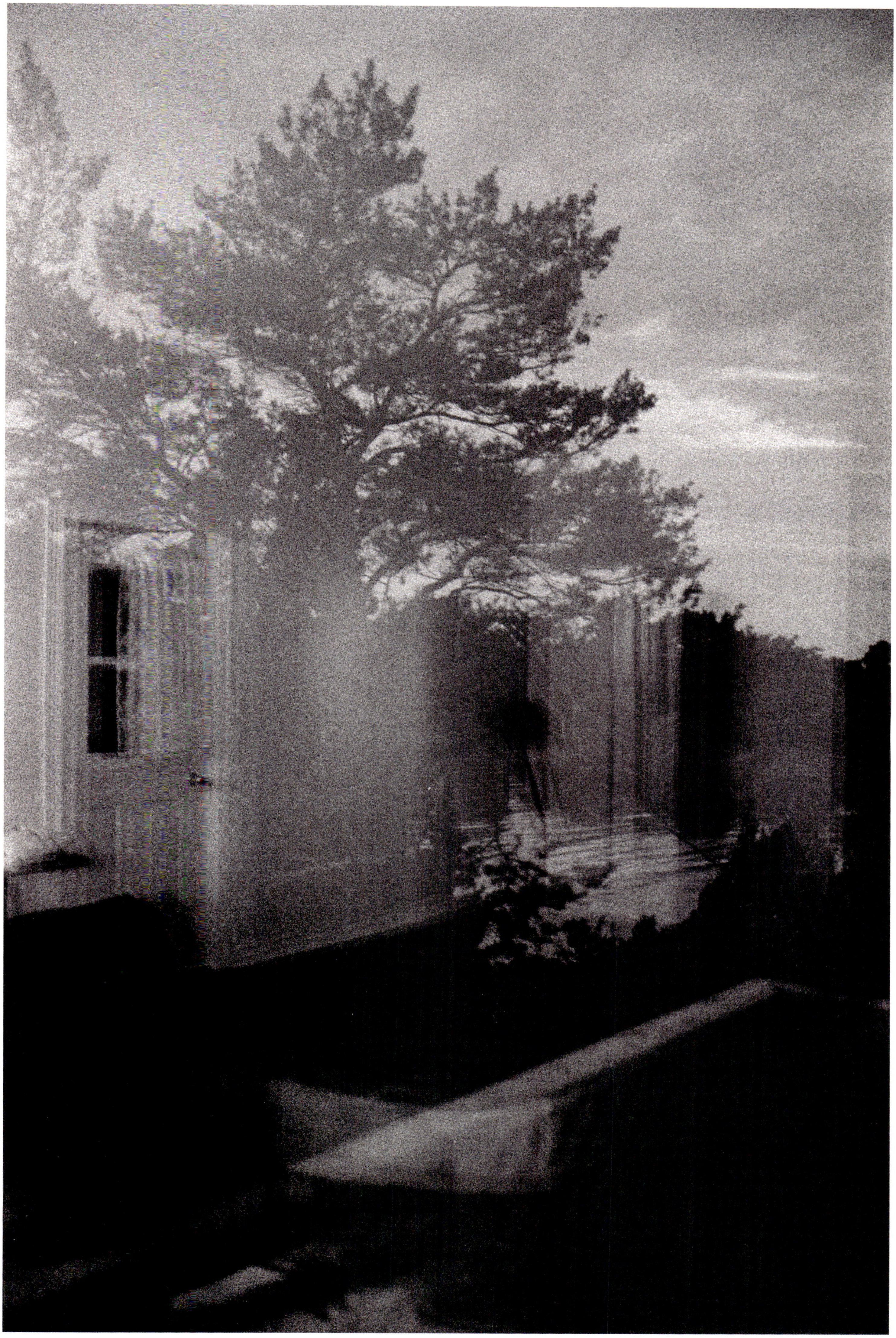

Porte/Rive, Saint-Jean-Port-Joli, Quebec

Serge Clément

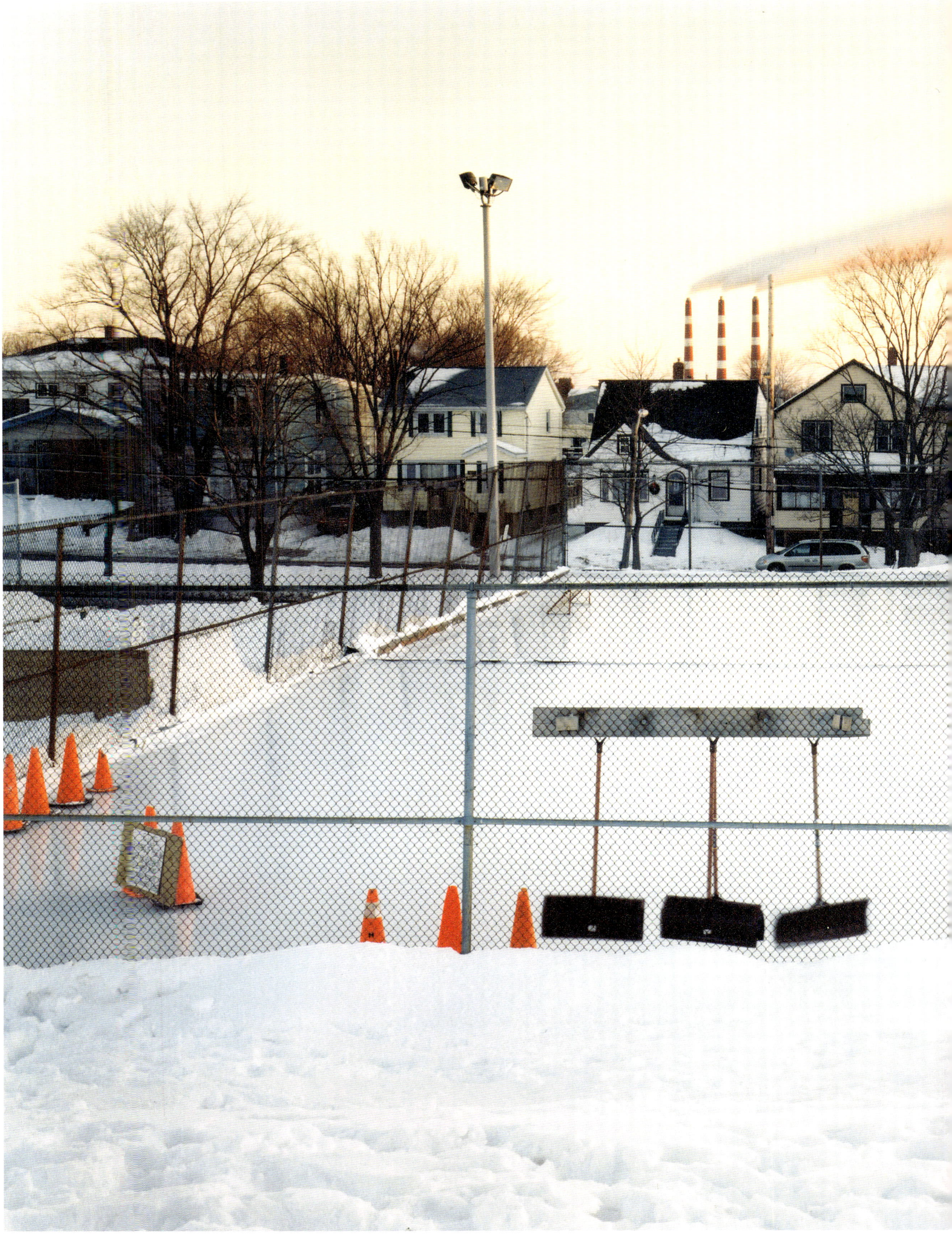

Shinny Rink

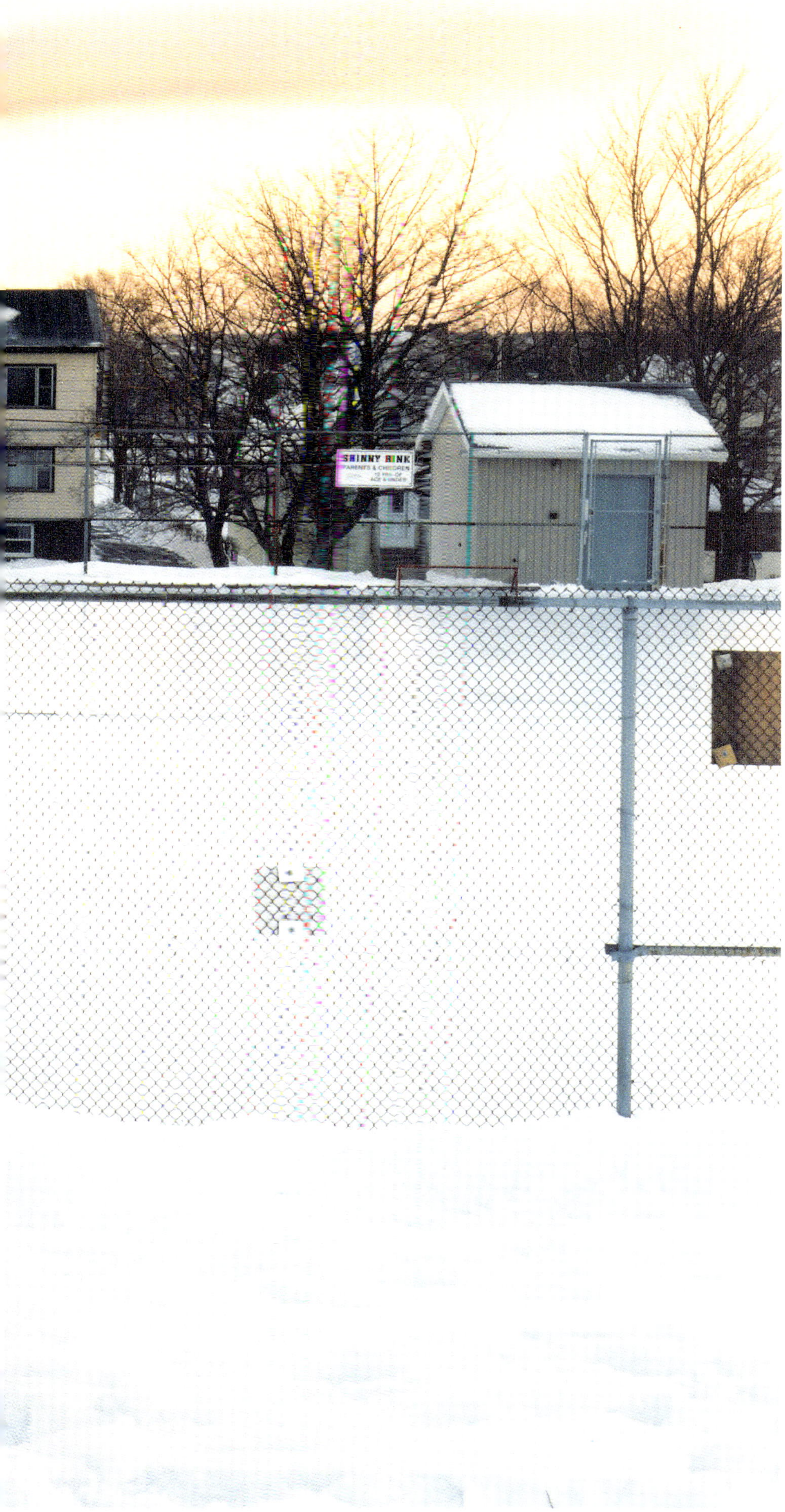
SHINNY RINK

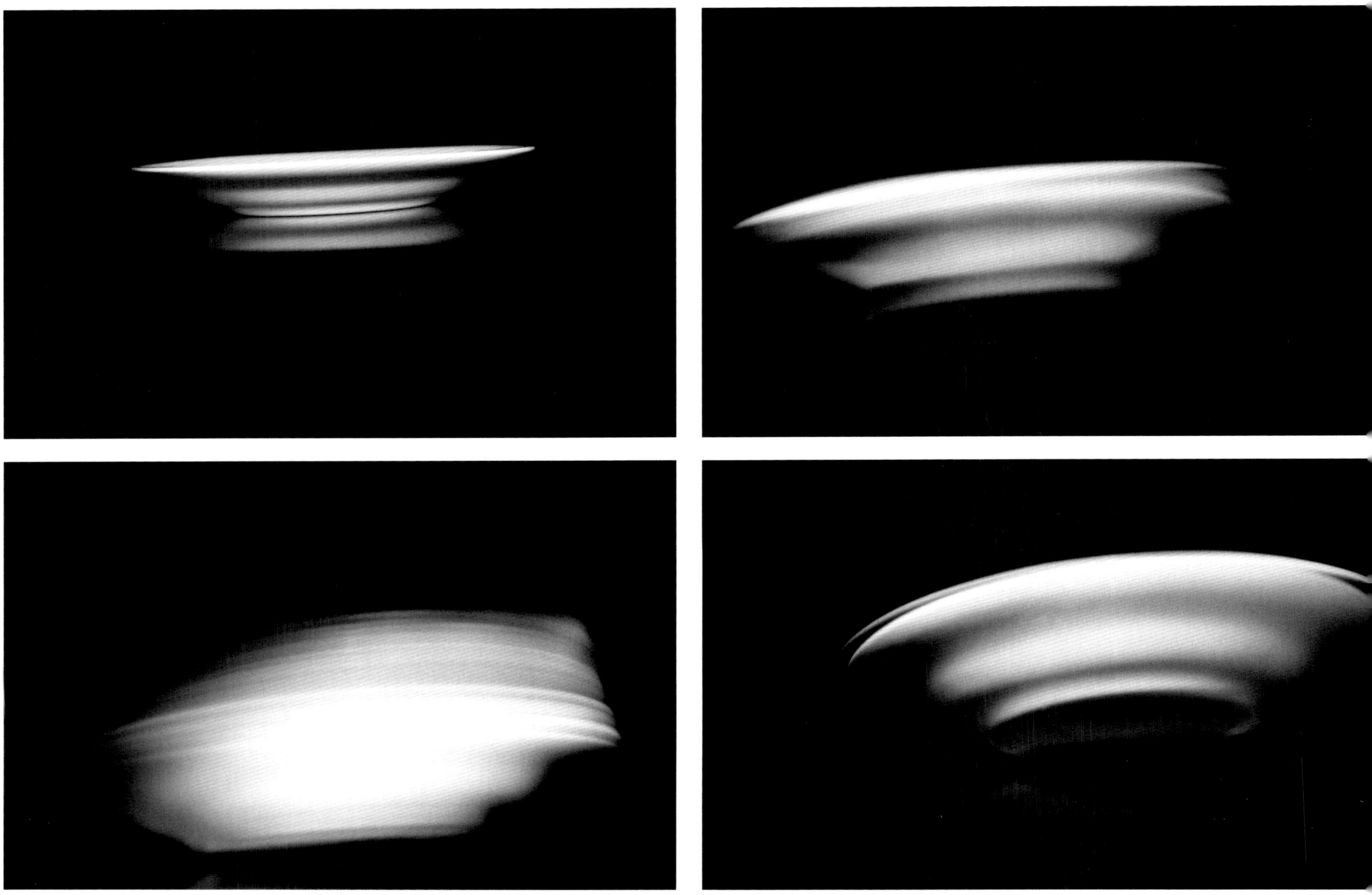

Susan Coolen Sighting (from the series "Astral Projections")

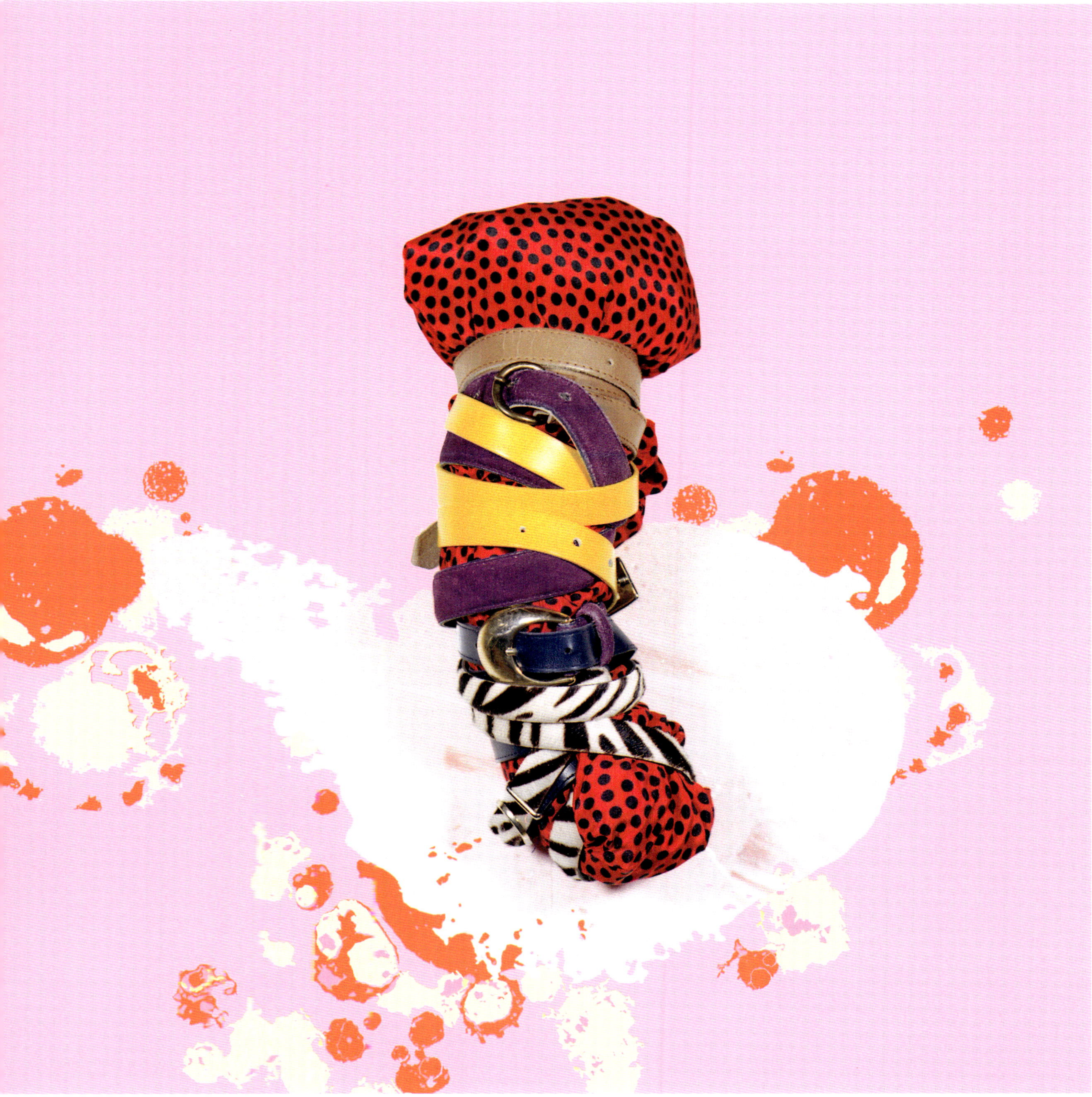

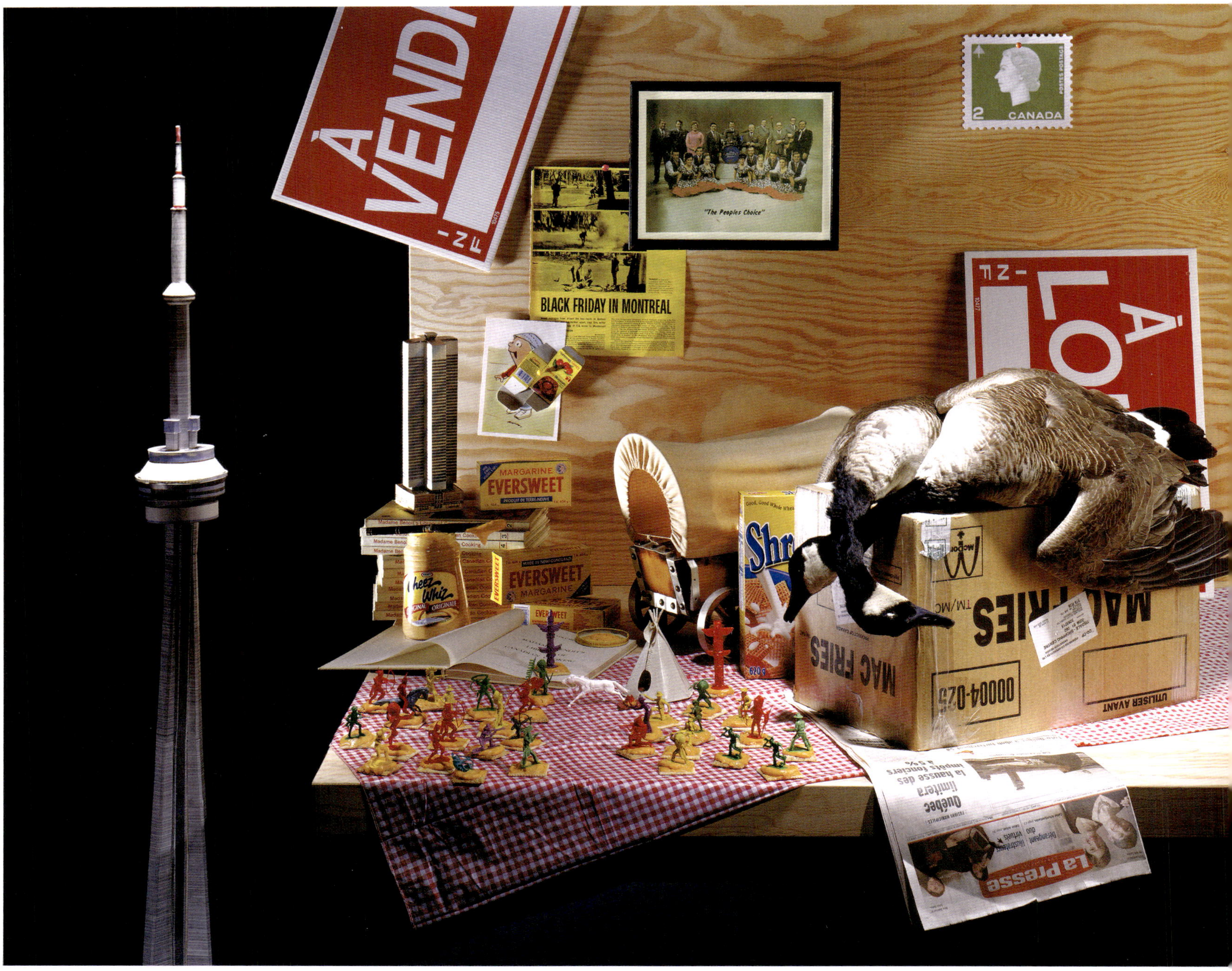

Douglas Coupland

Canada Picture No 2

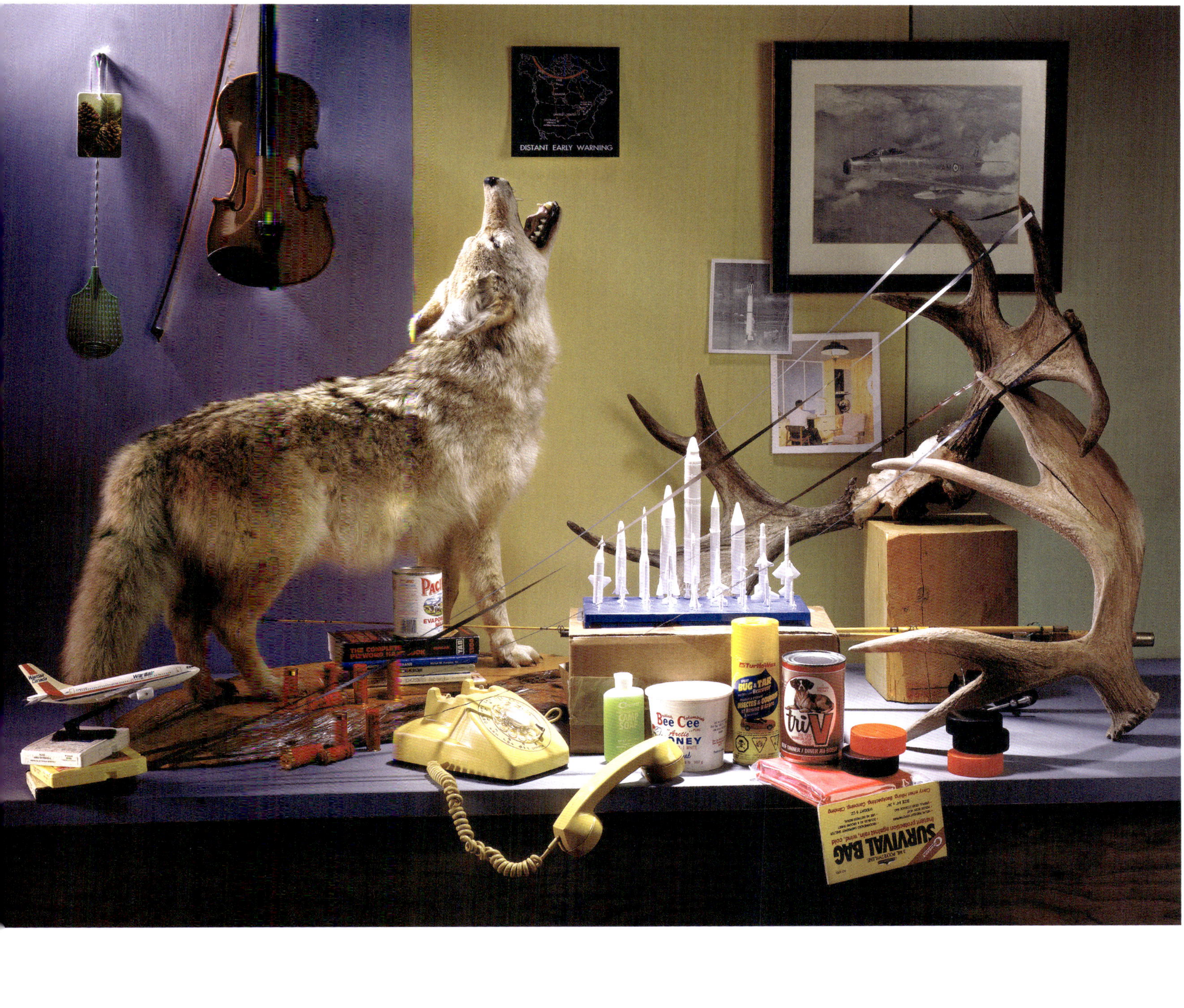

Canada Picture No. 3

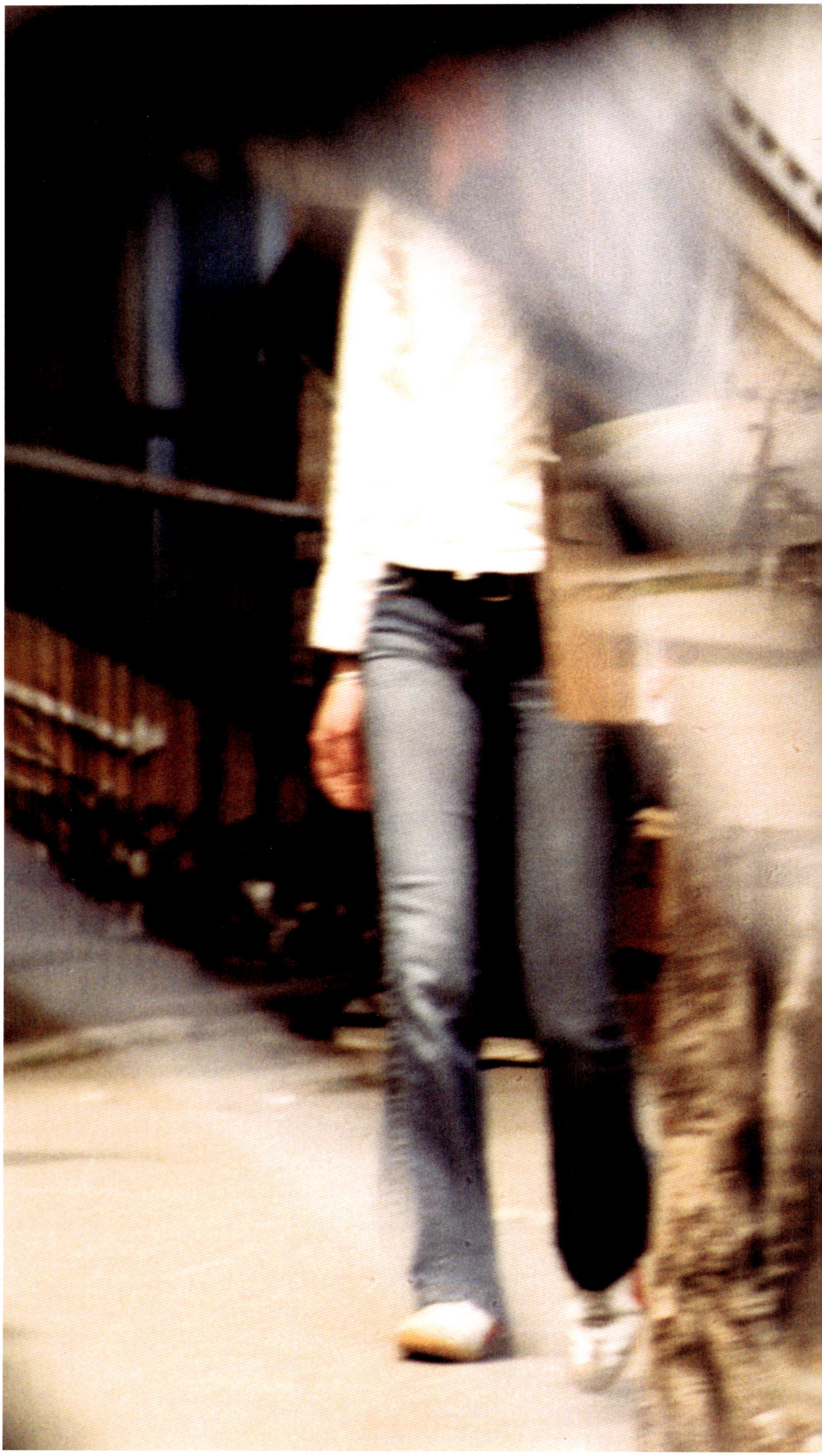

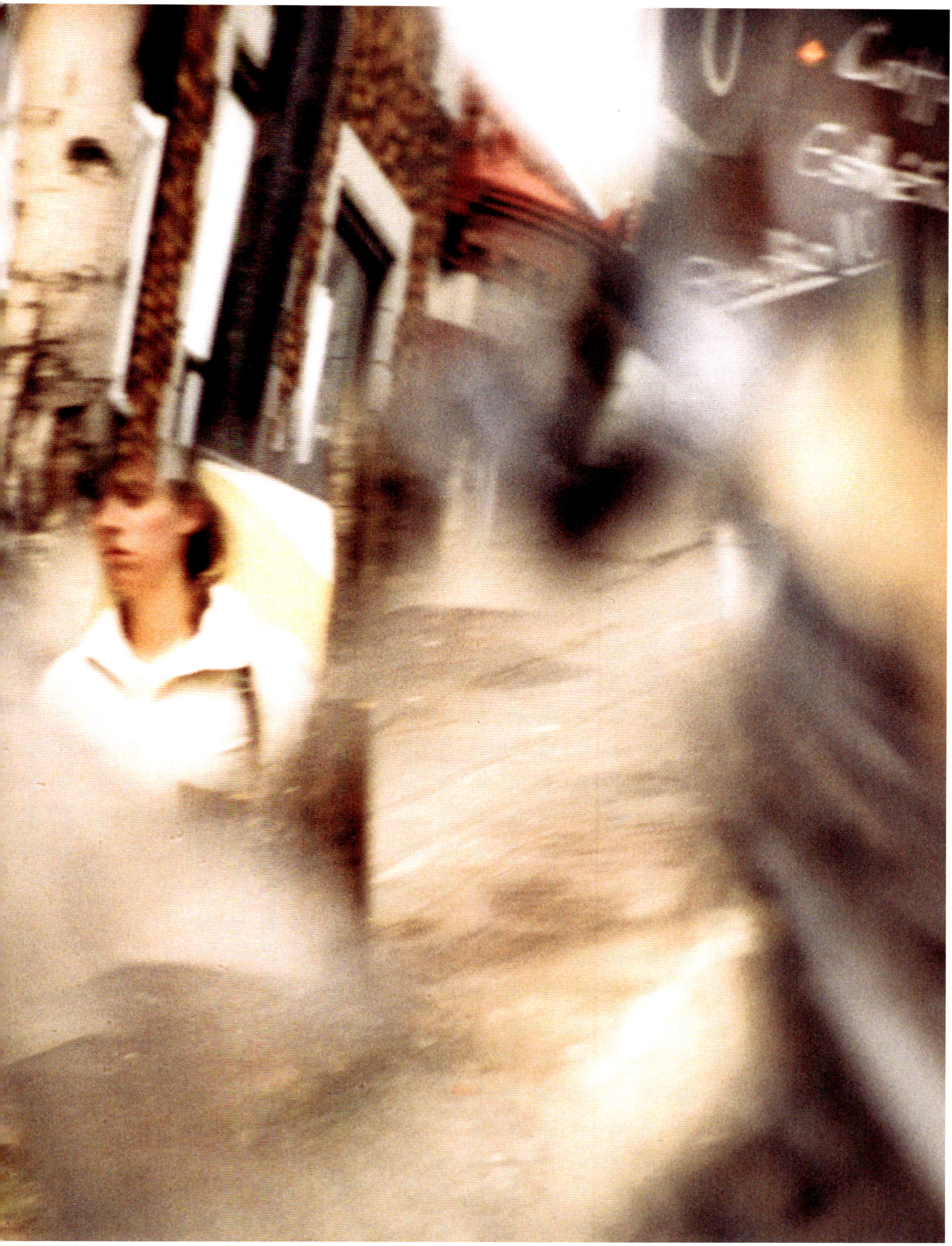

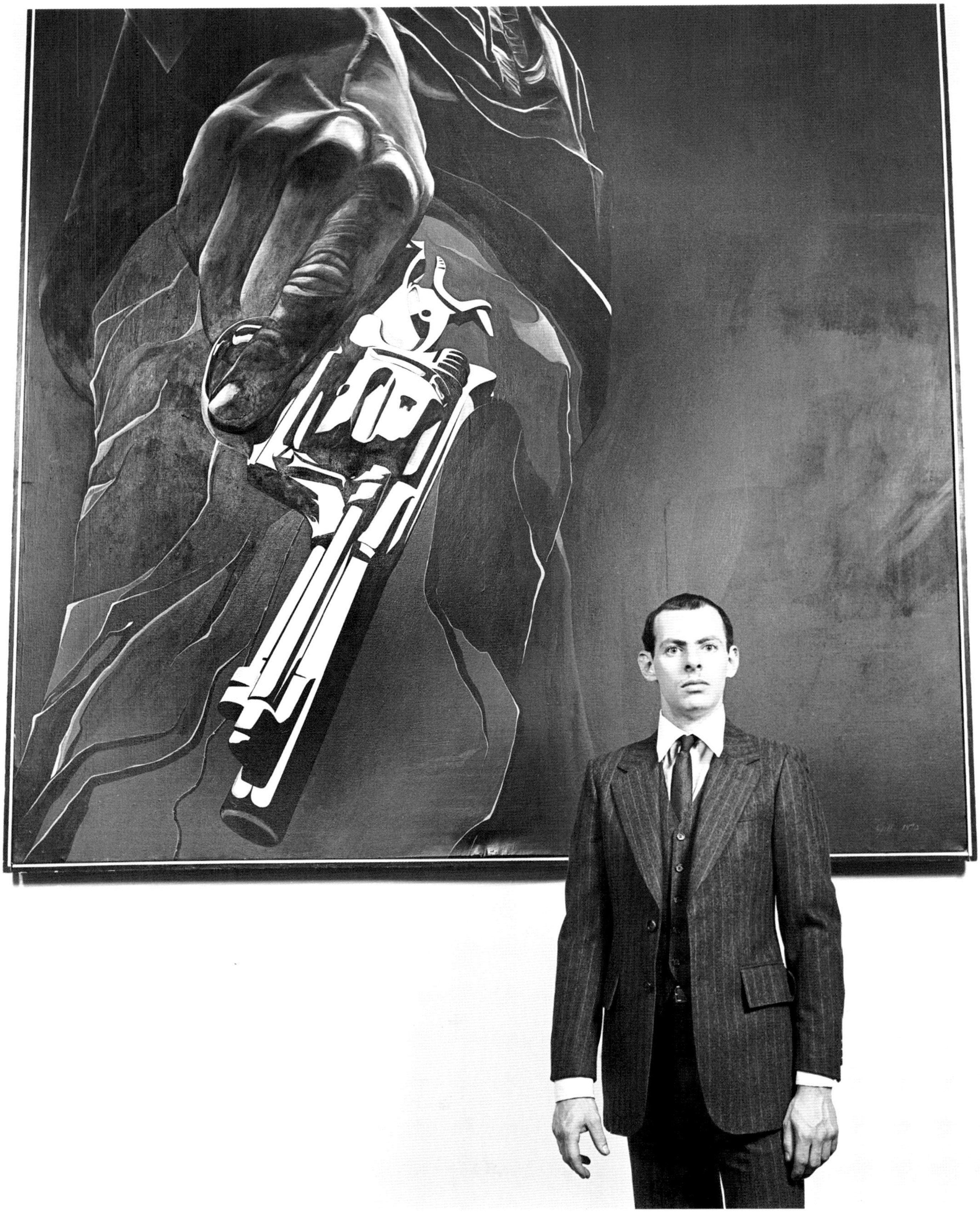

Andrew Danson Danushevsky

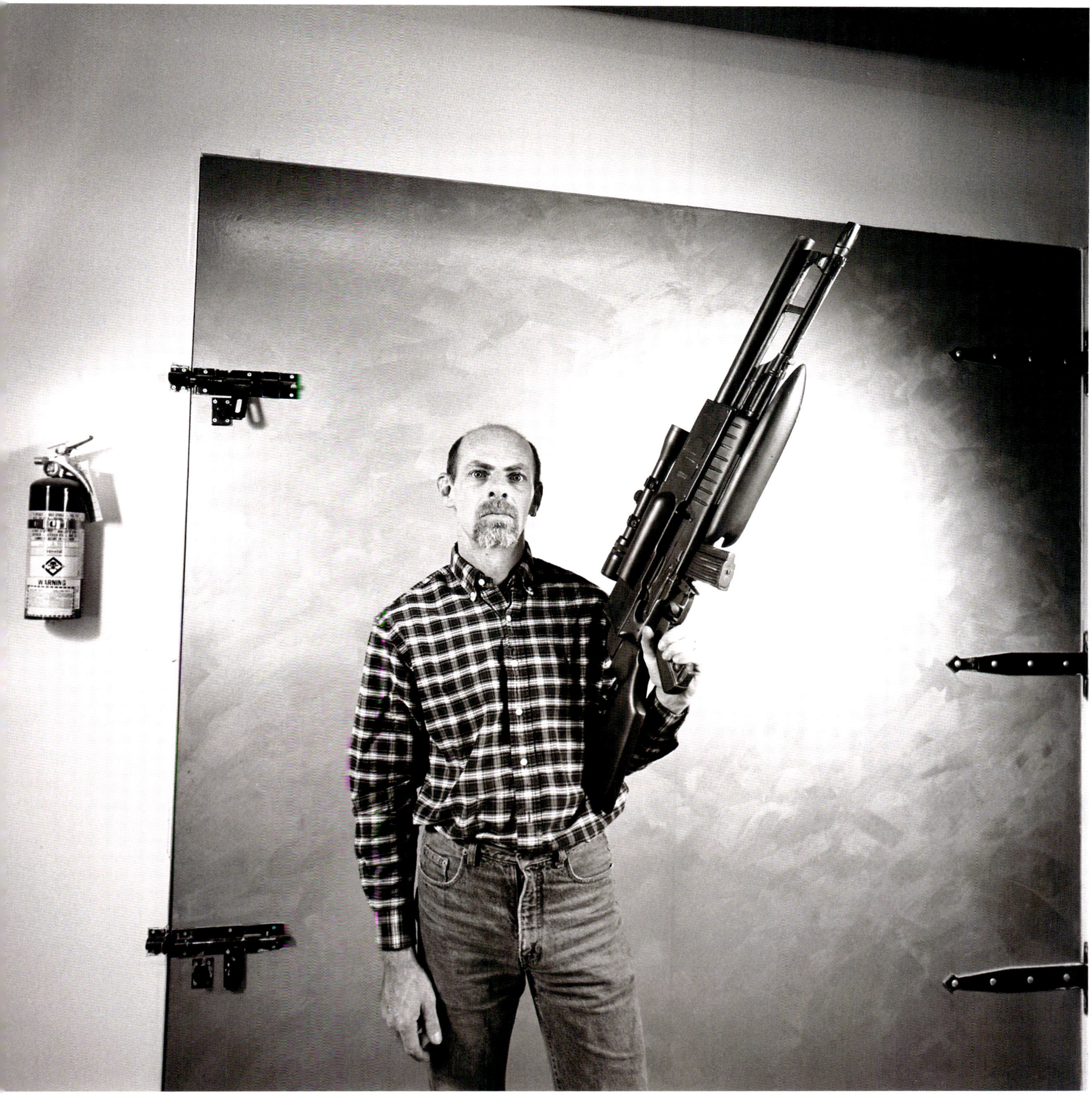

John Jackson 1996

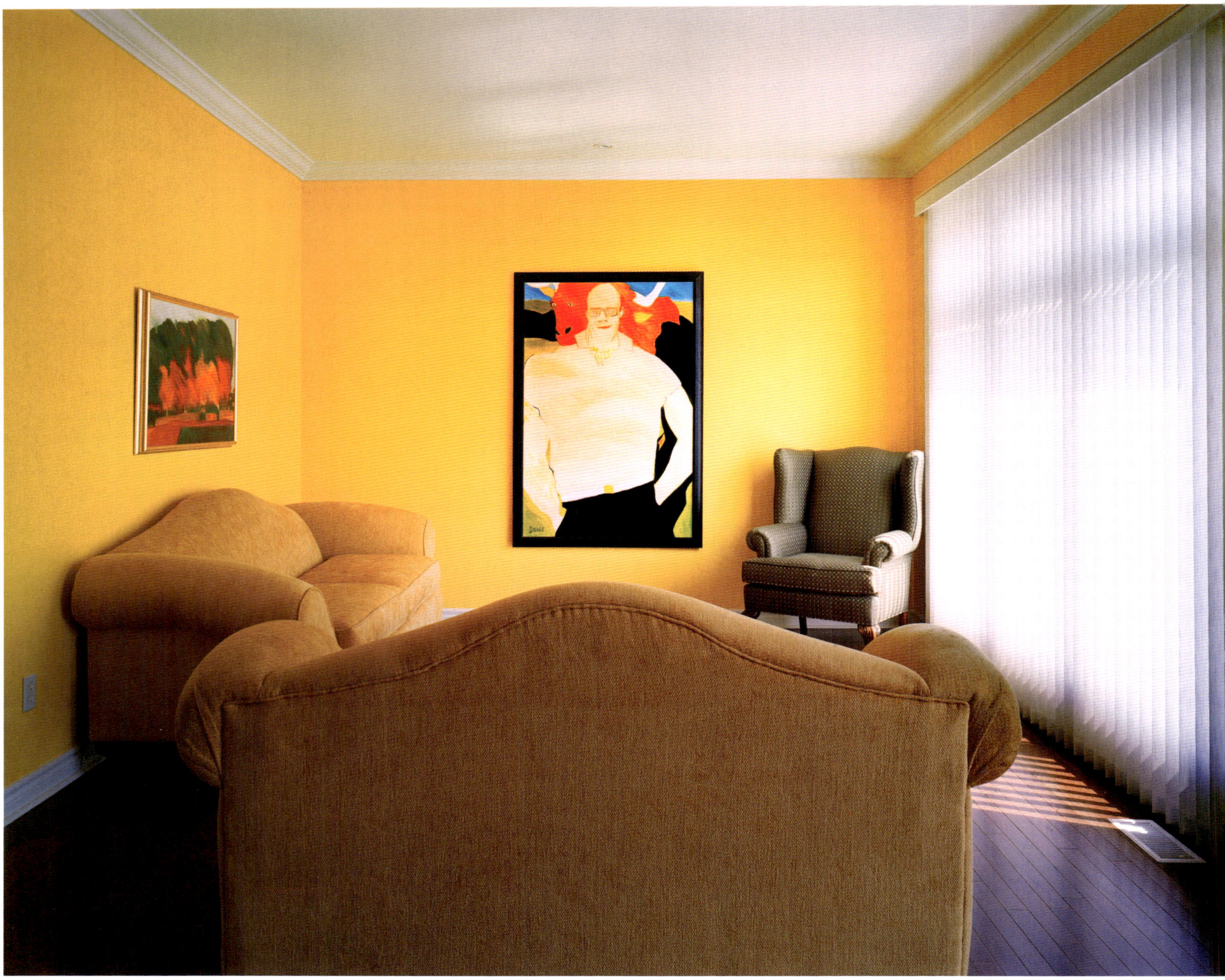

Susan Dobson

Untitled (from the series "Open House")

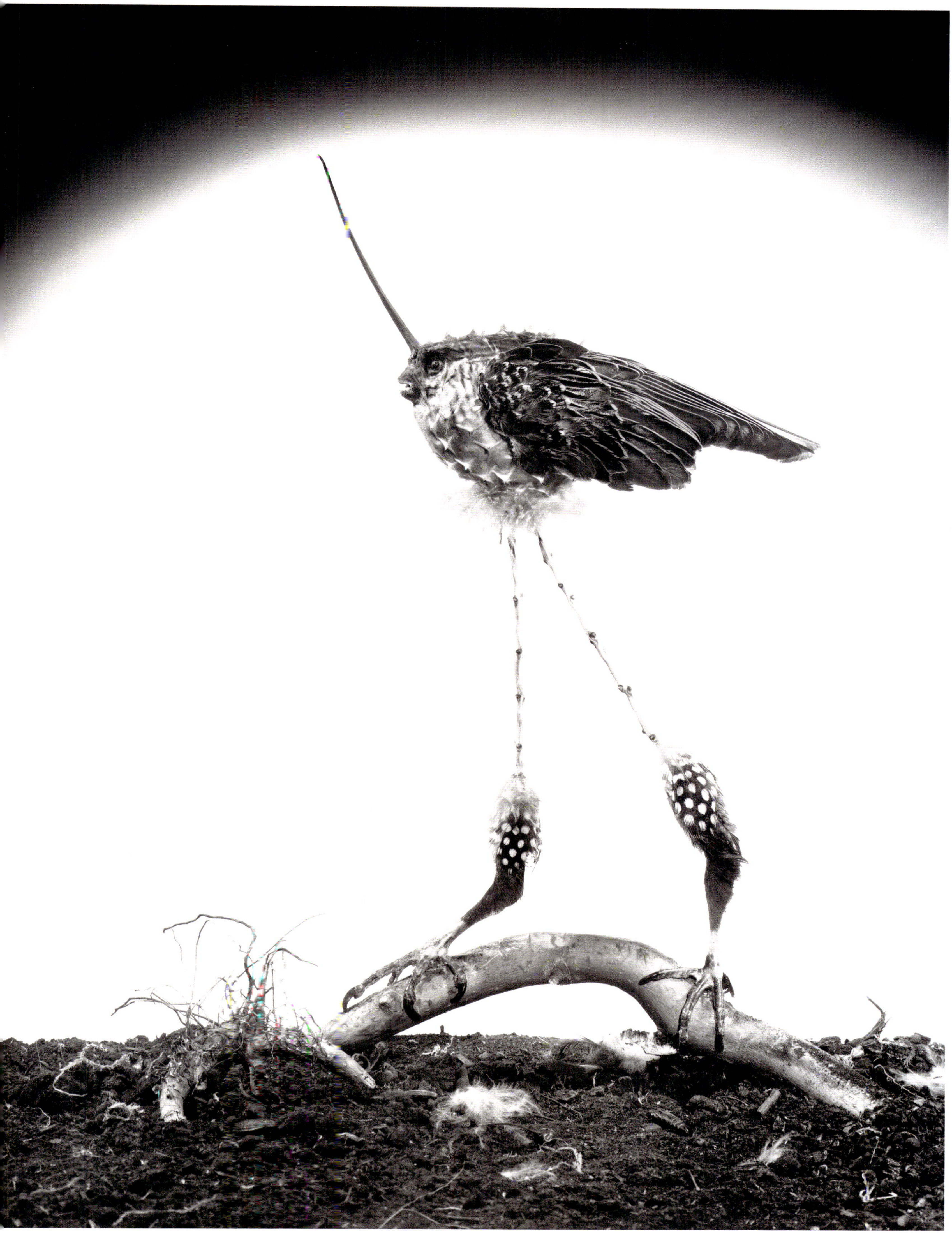

Untitled (from the series "Rebirth")

Katyuska Doleatto

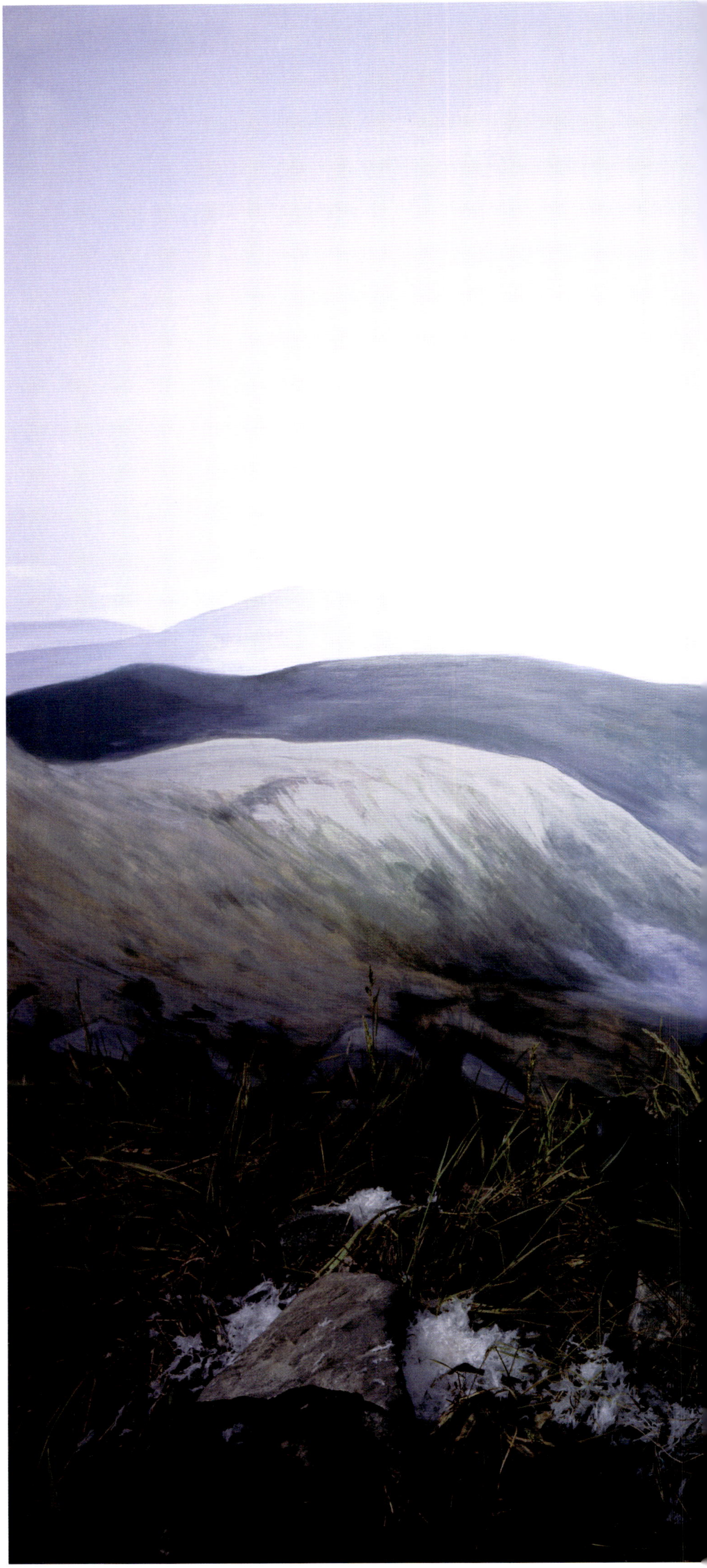

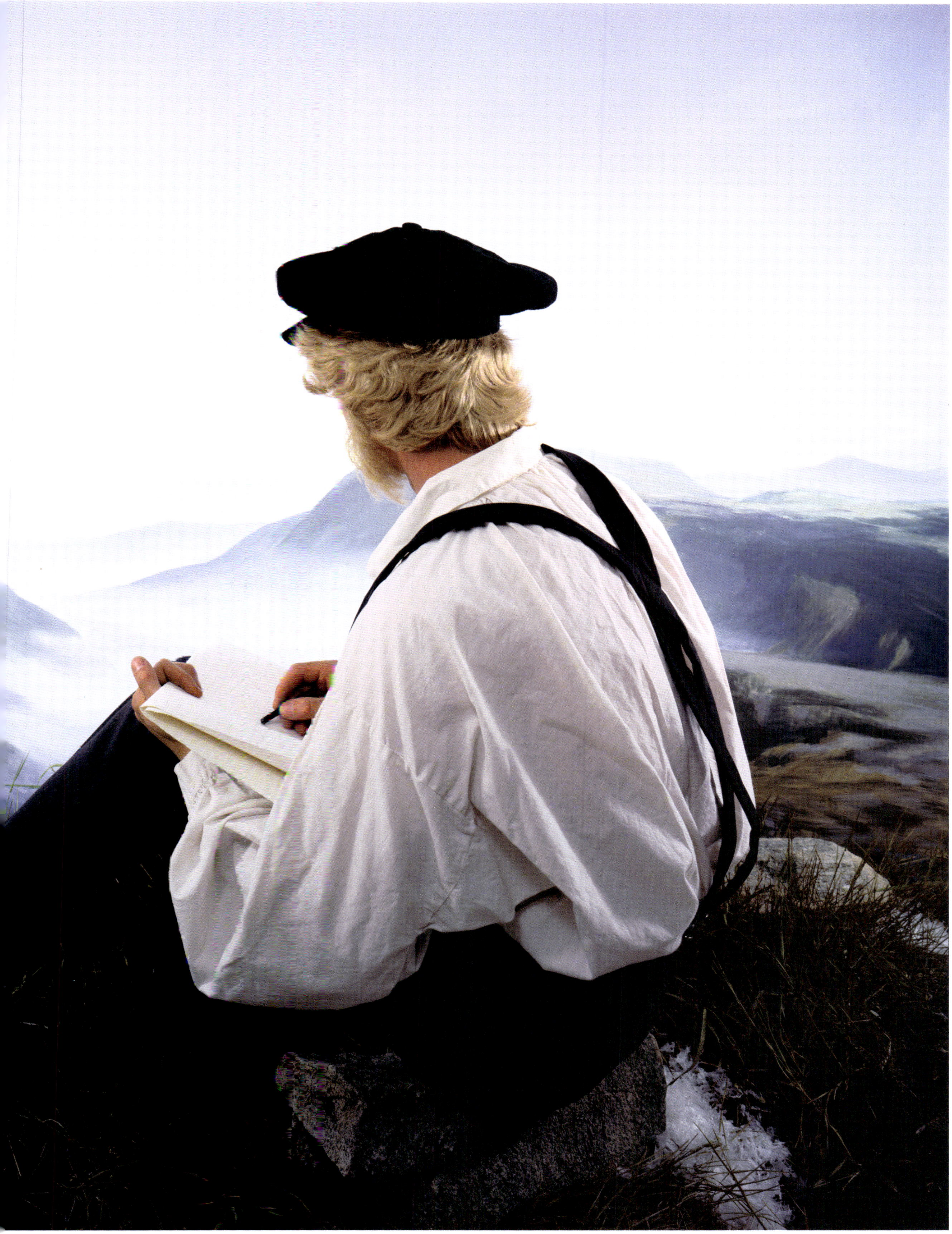

Caspar David Friedrich Sketching My Homeland, 1810

Jakub Dolejš

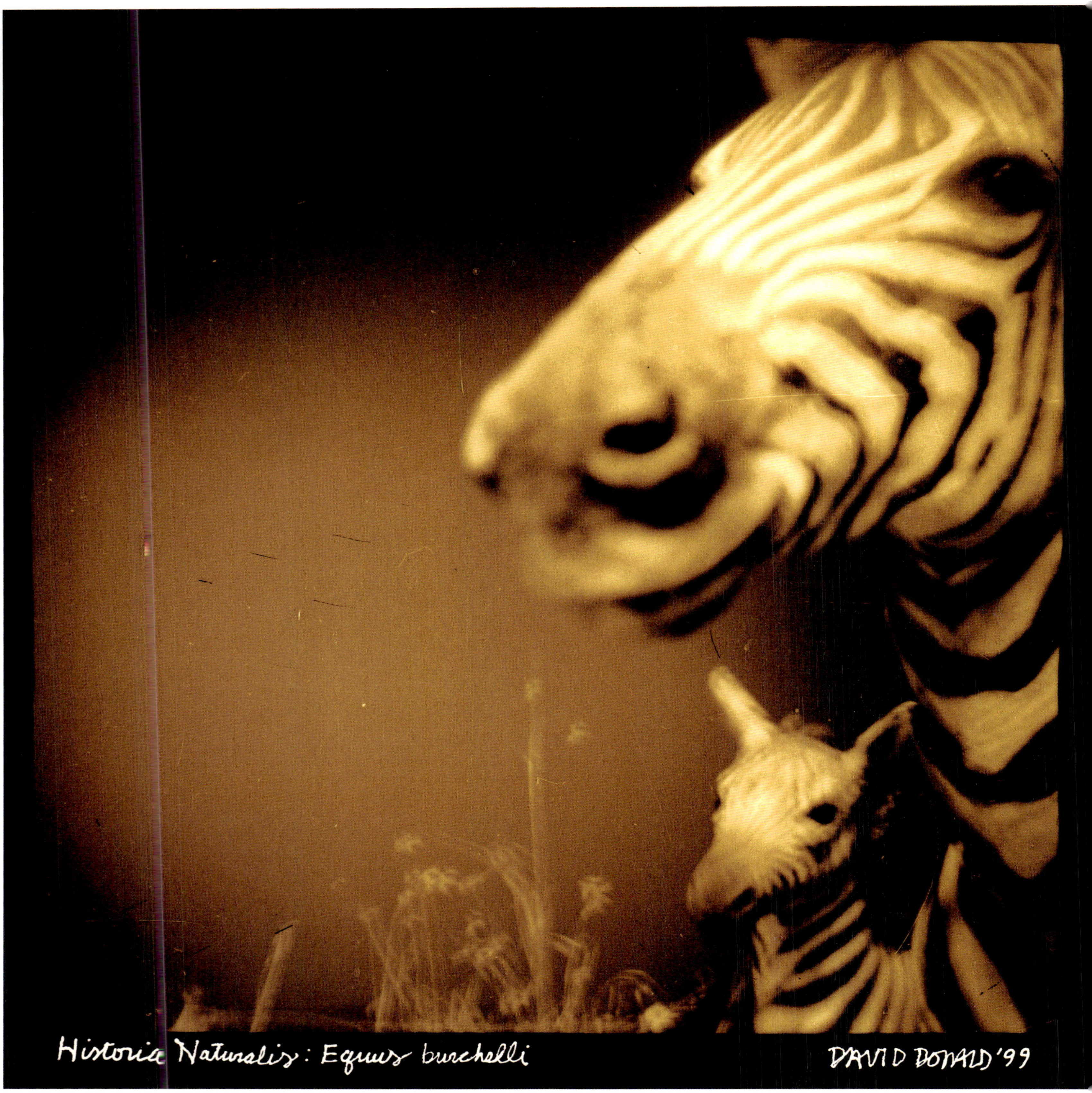

Historia Naturalis: Zoologiae—Equus burchelli

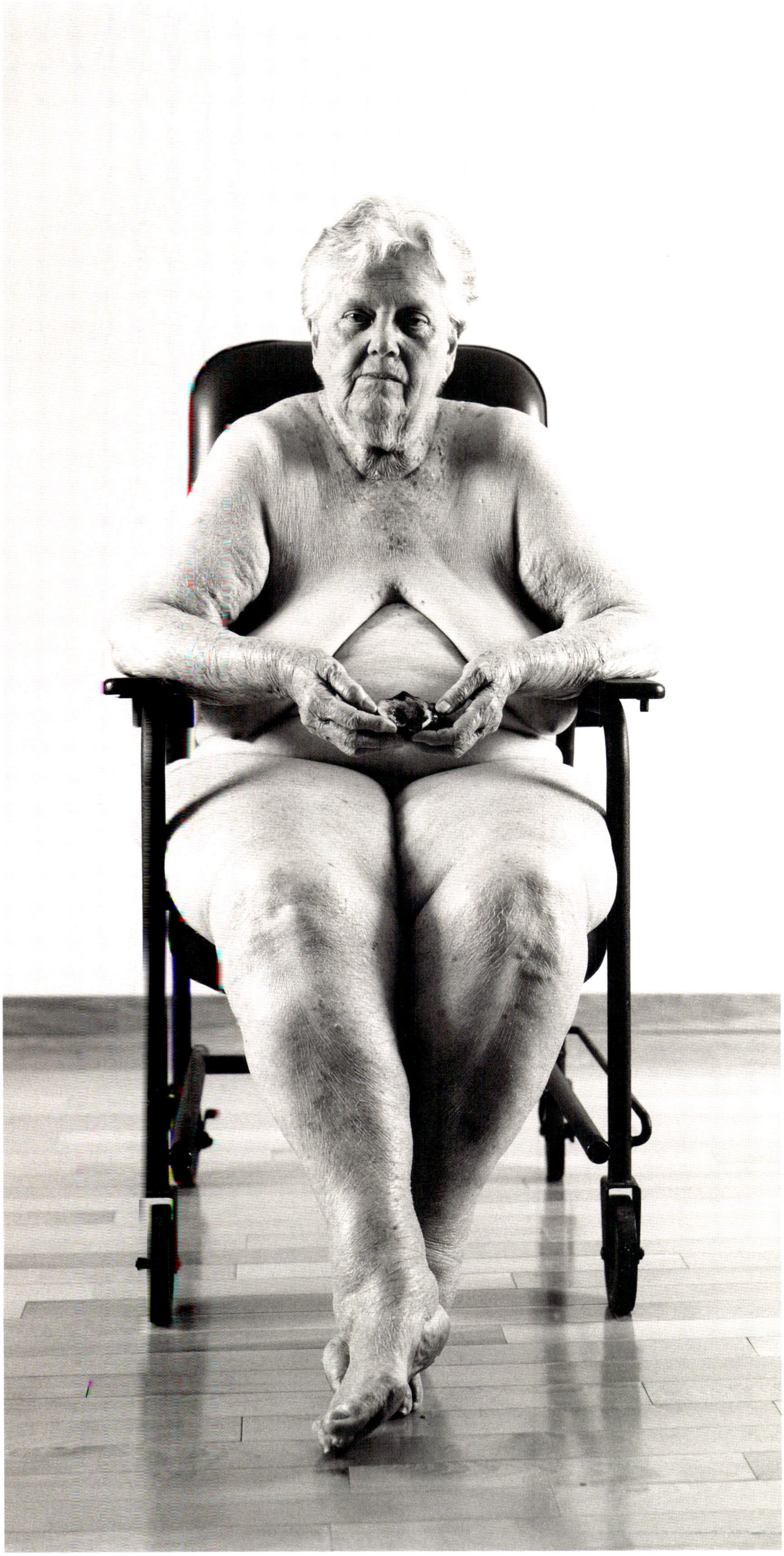

Margaret With Fig

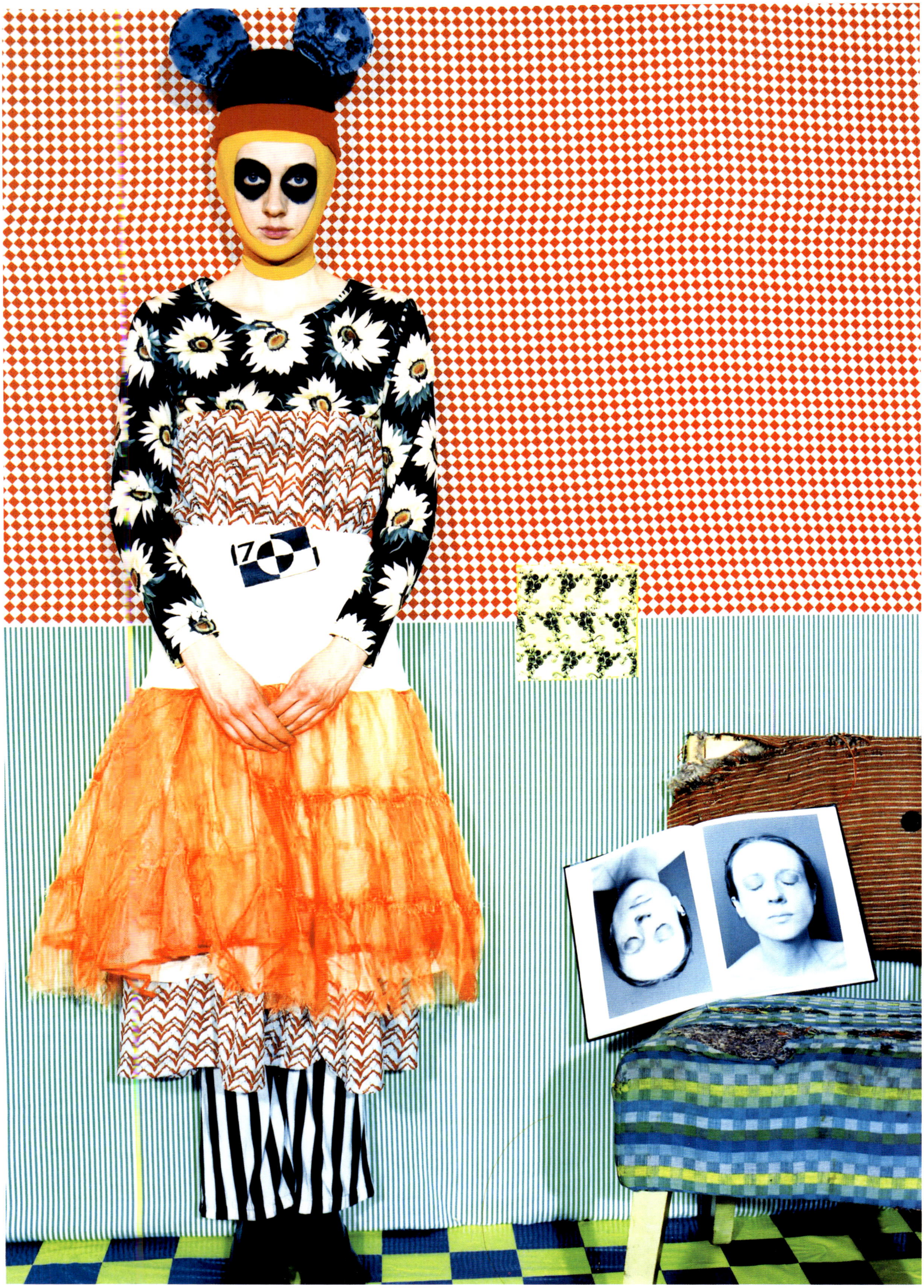

Janieta Eyre

Androgyne, Two Pages From My Diary

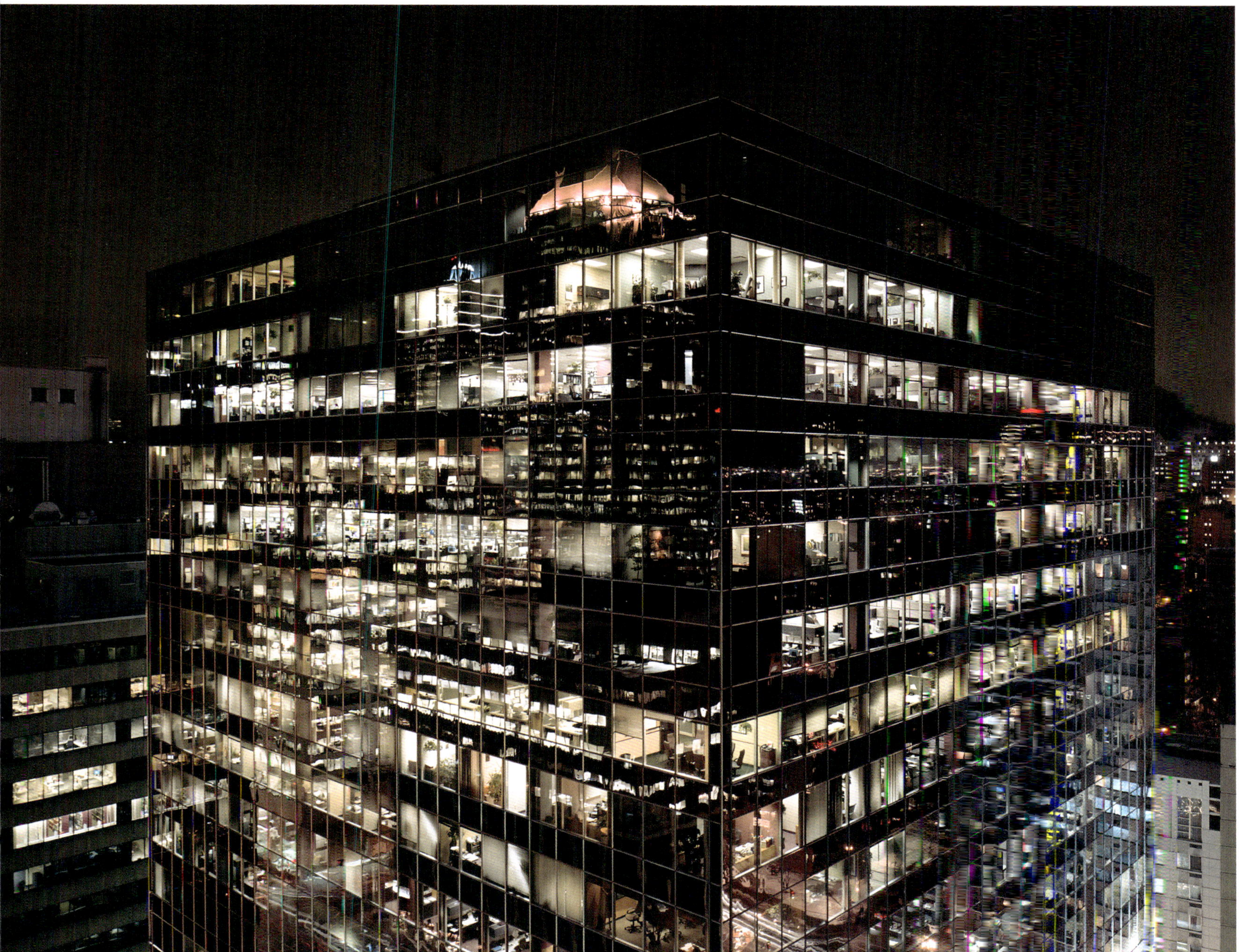

Untitled (from the series "Office 2000")

Thomas Kneubühler

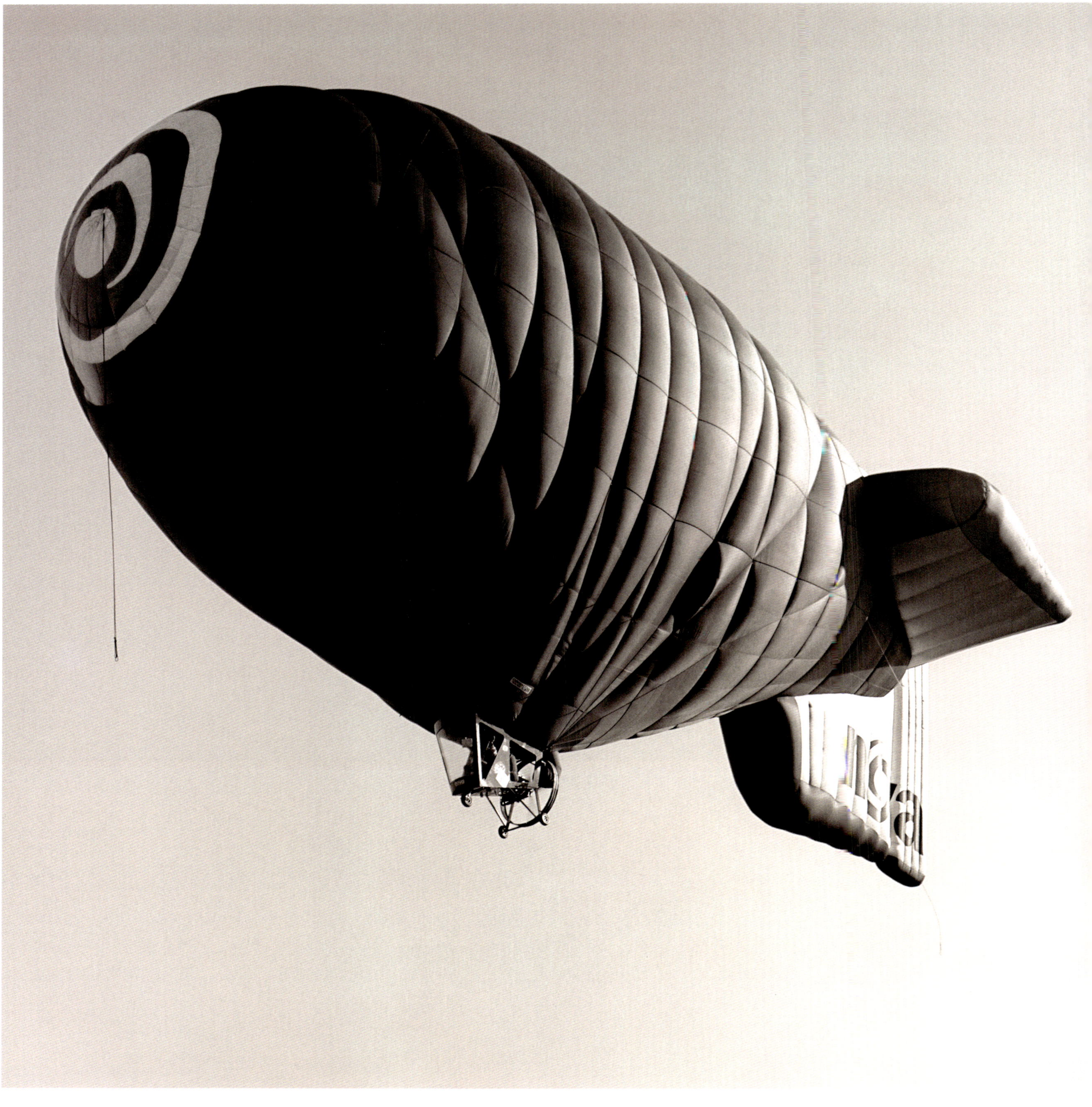

Katherine Knight

Airship

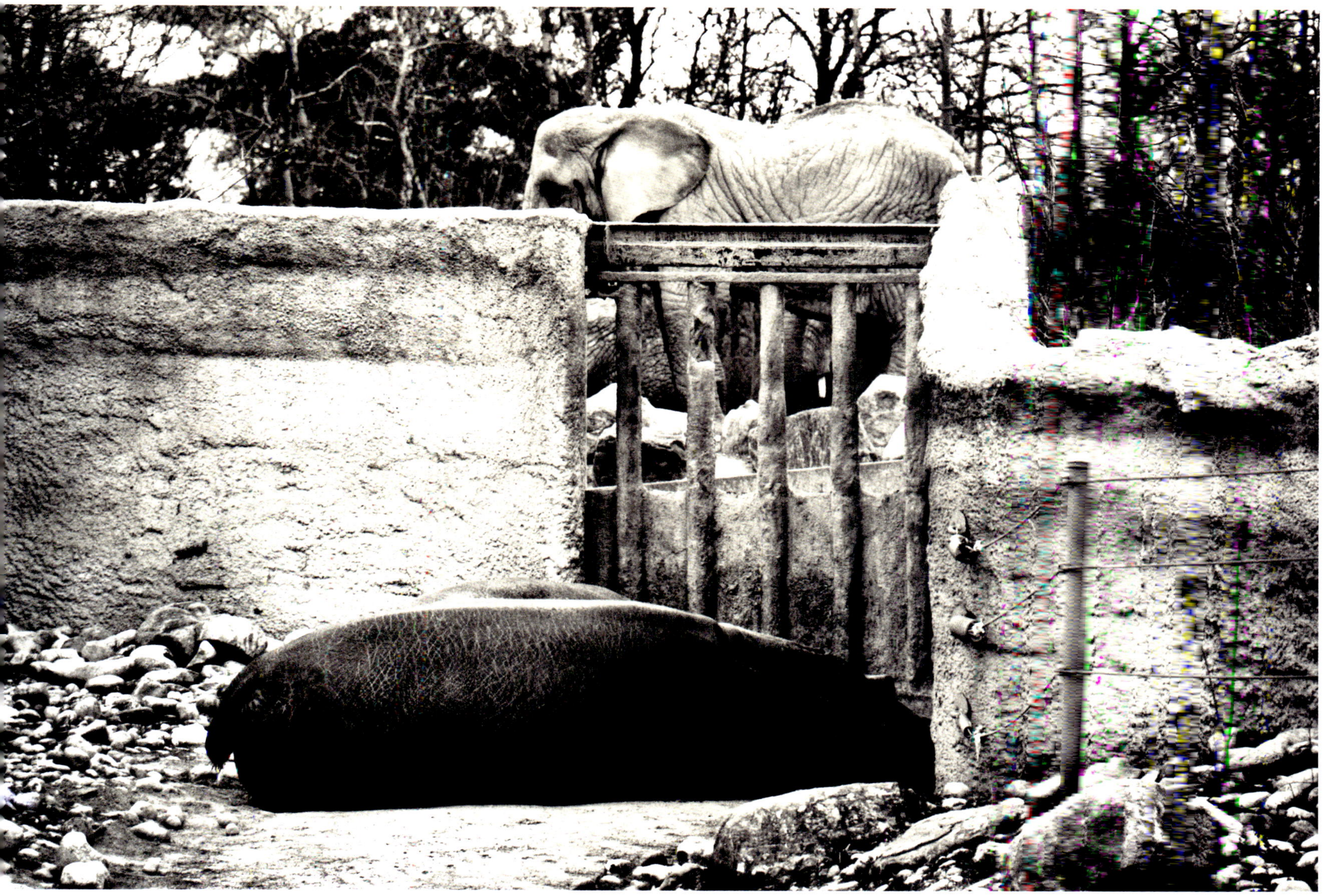

Hippopotamus & Elephant

Victor Korchenko

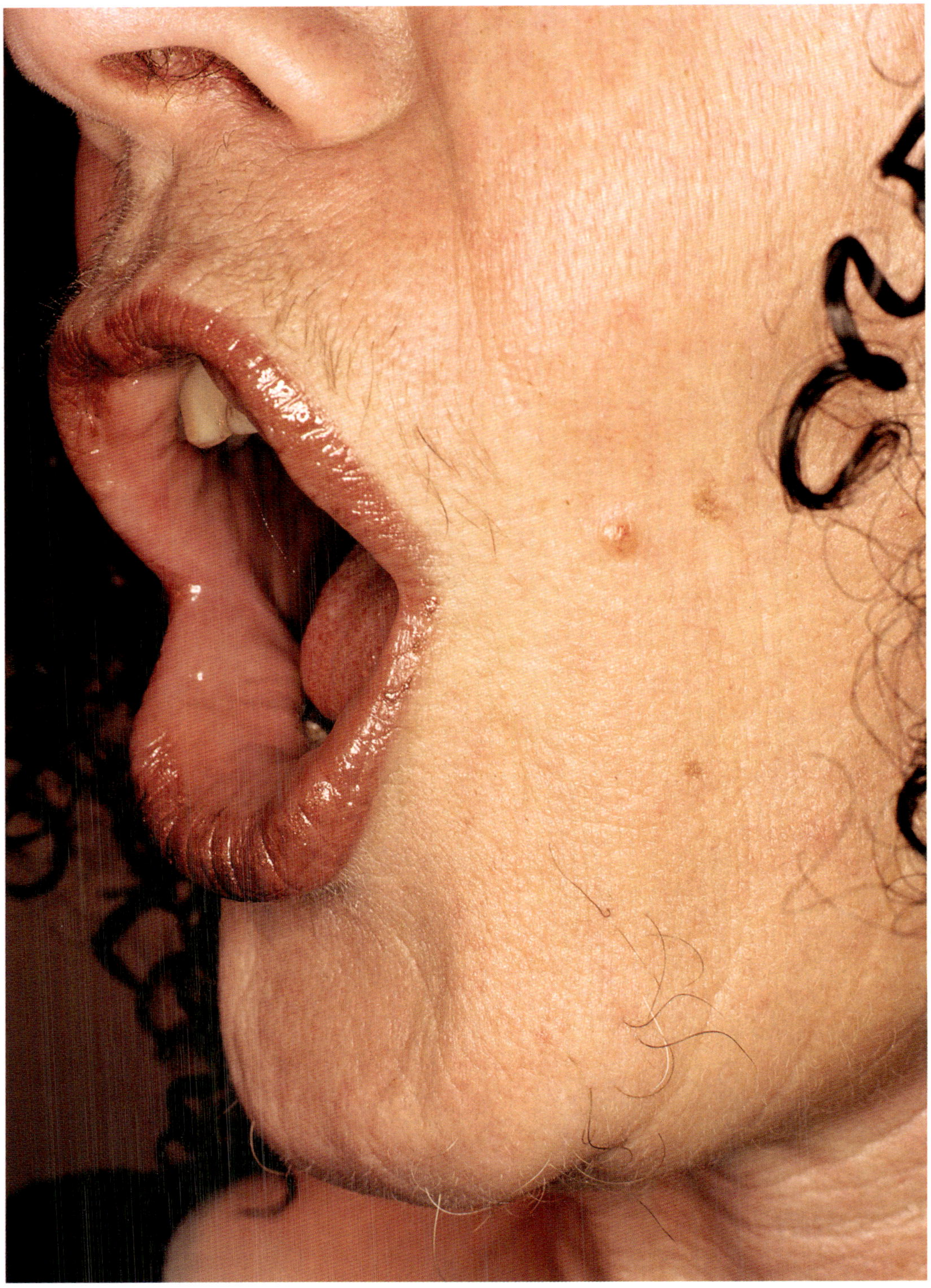

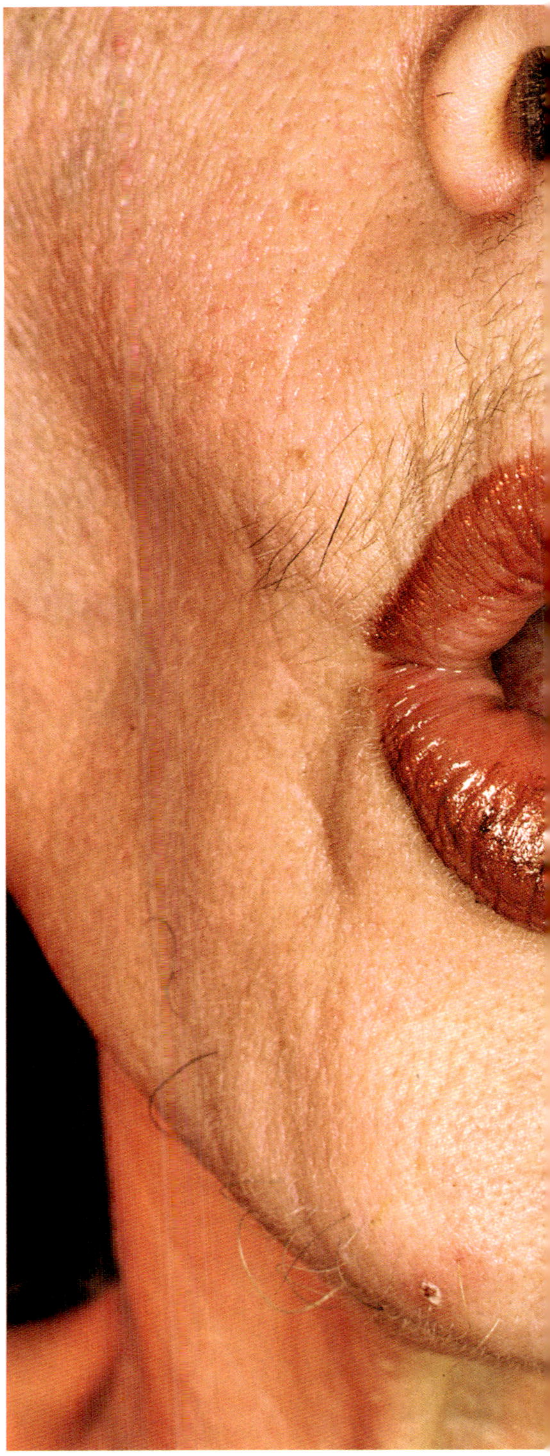

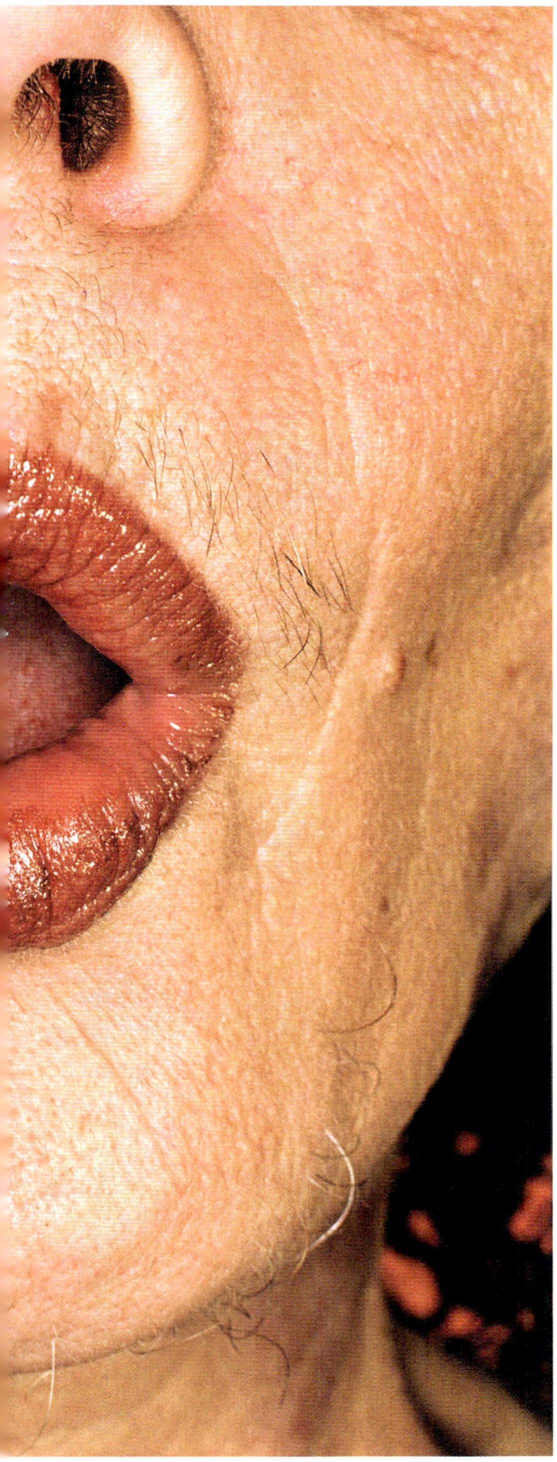

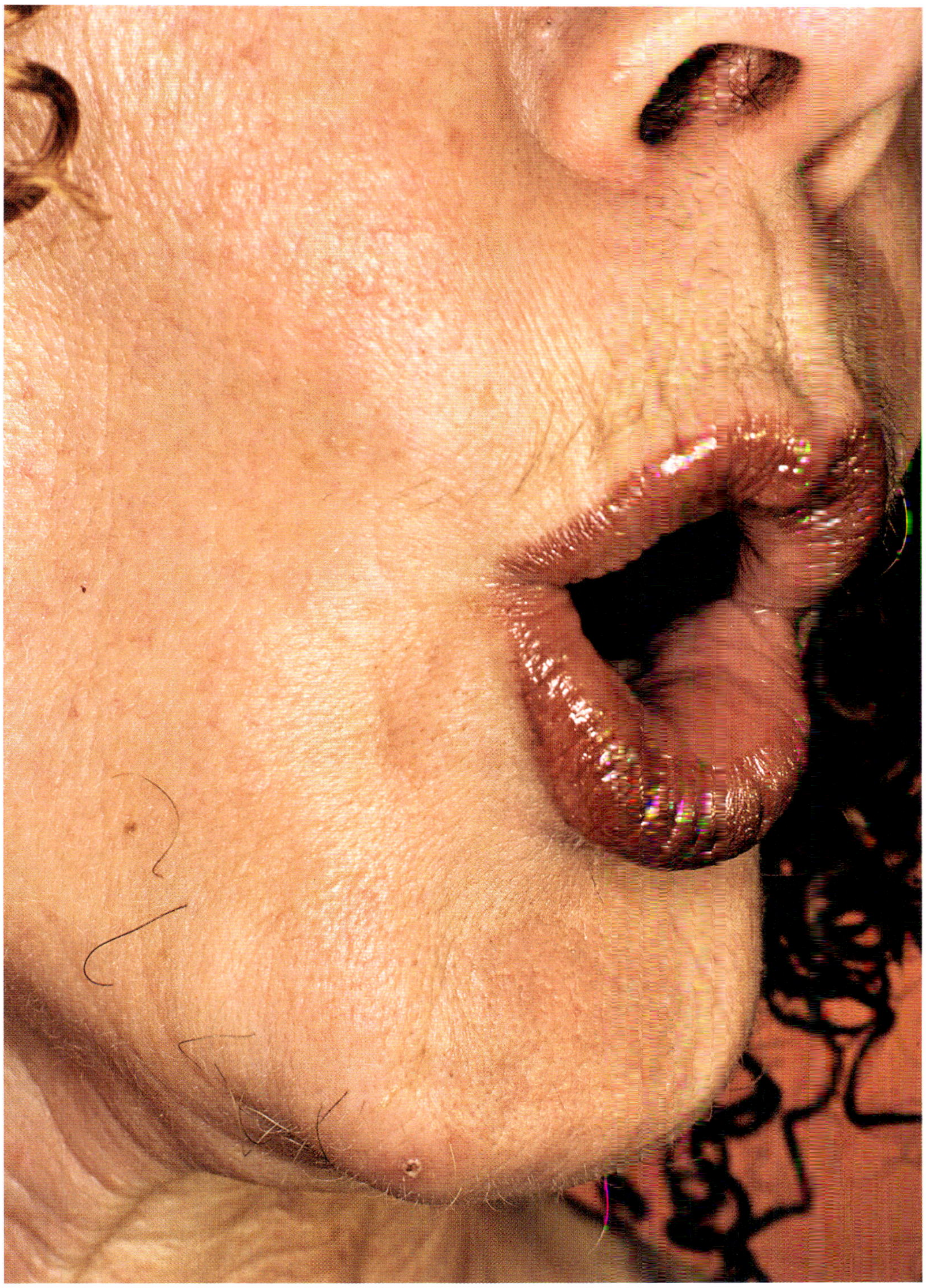

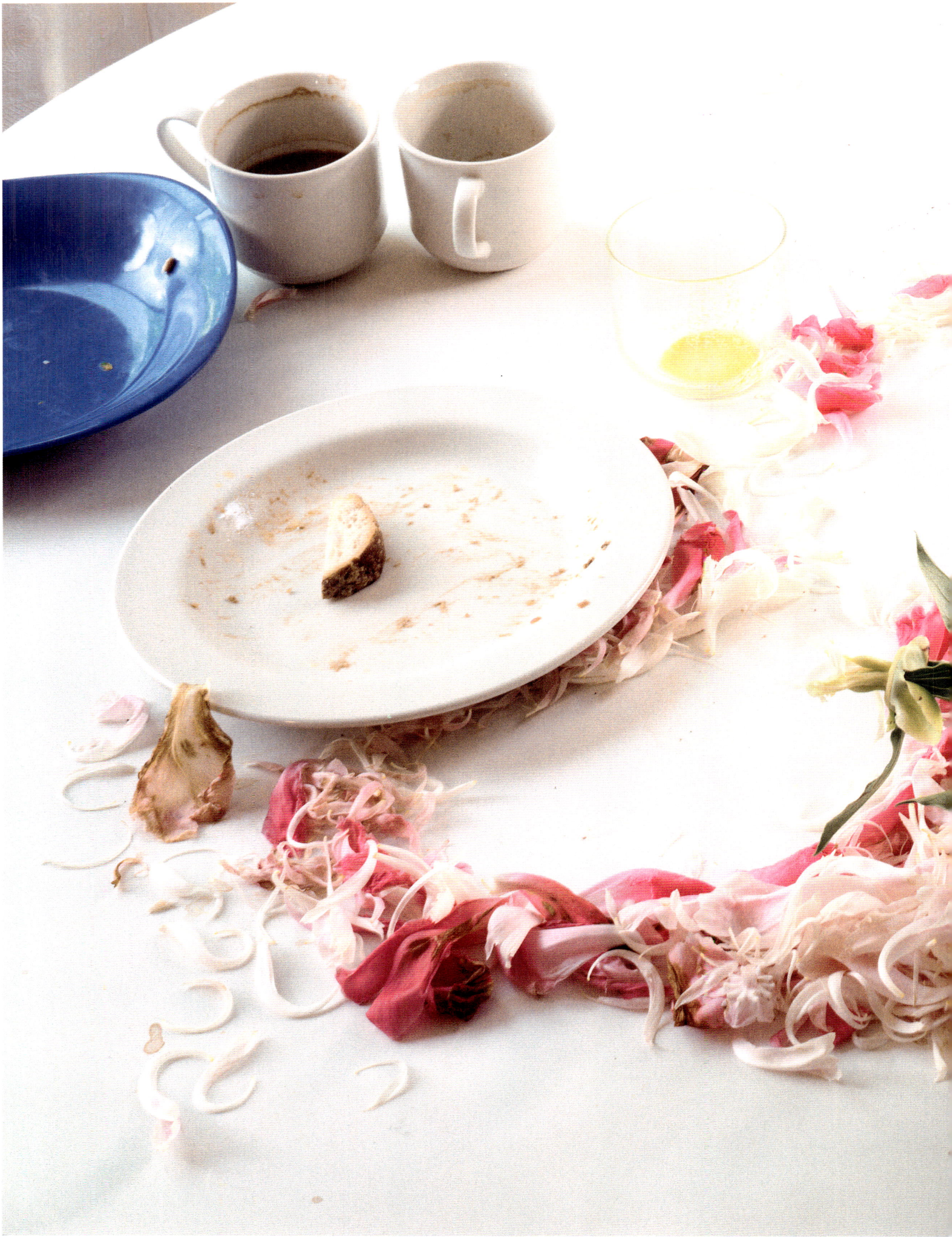

Laura Letinsky

Untitled #22 (from the series "Morning & Melancholia")

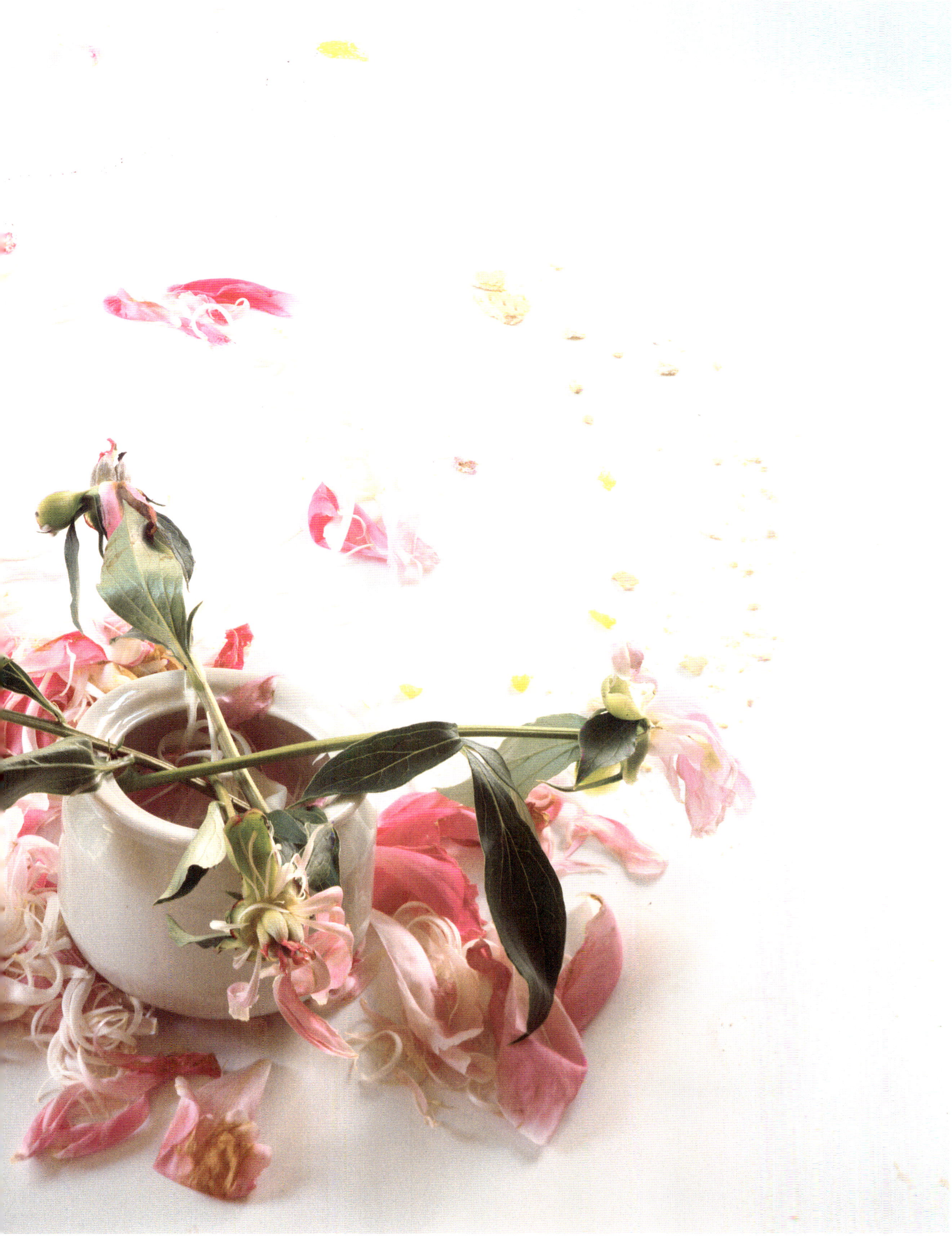

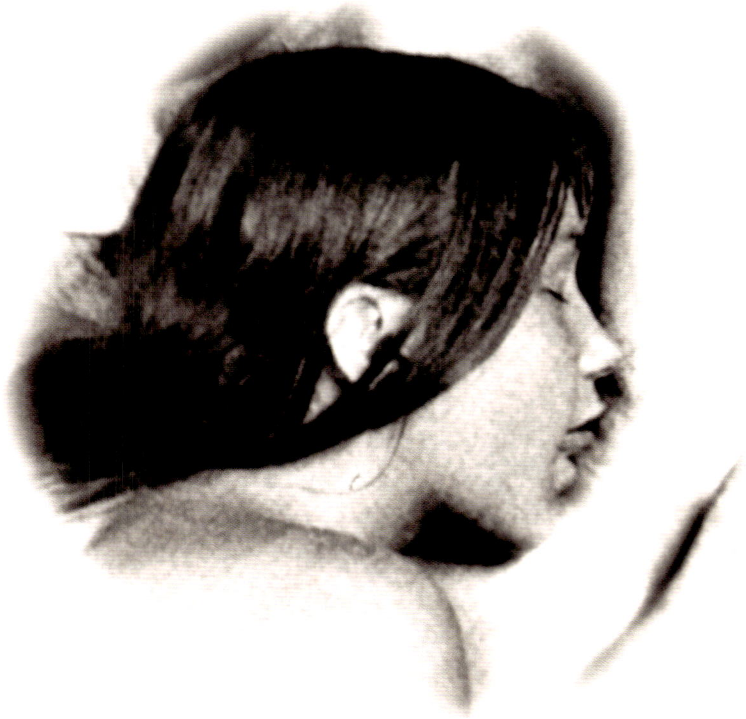

Nina Levitt Untitled (from the series "Lickers & Suckers (1)")

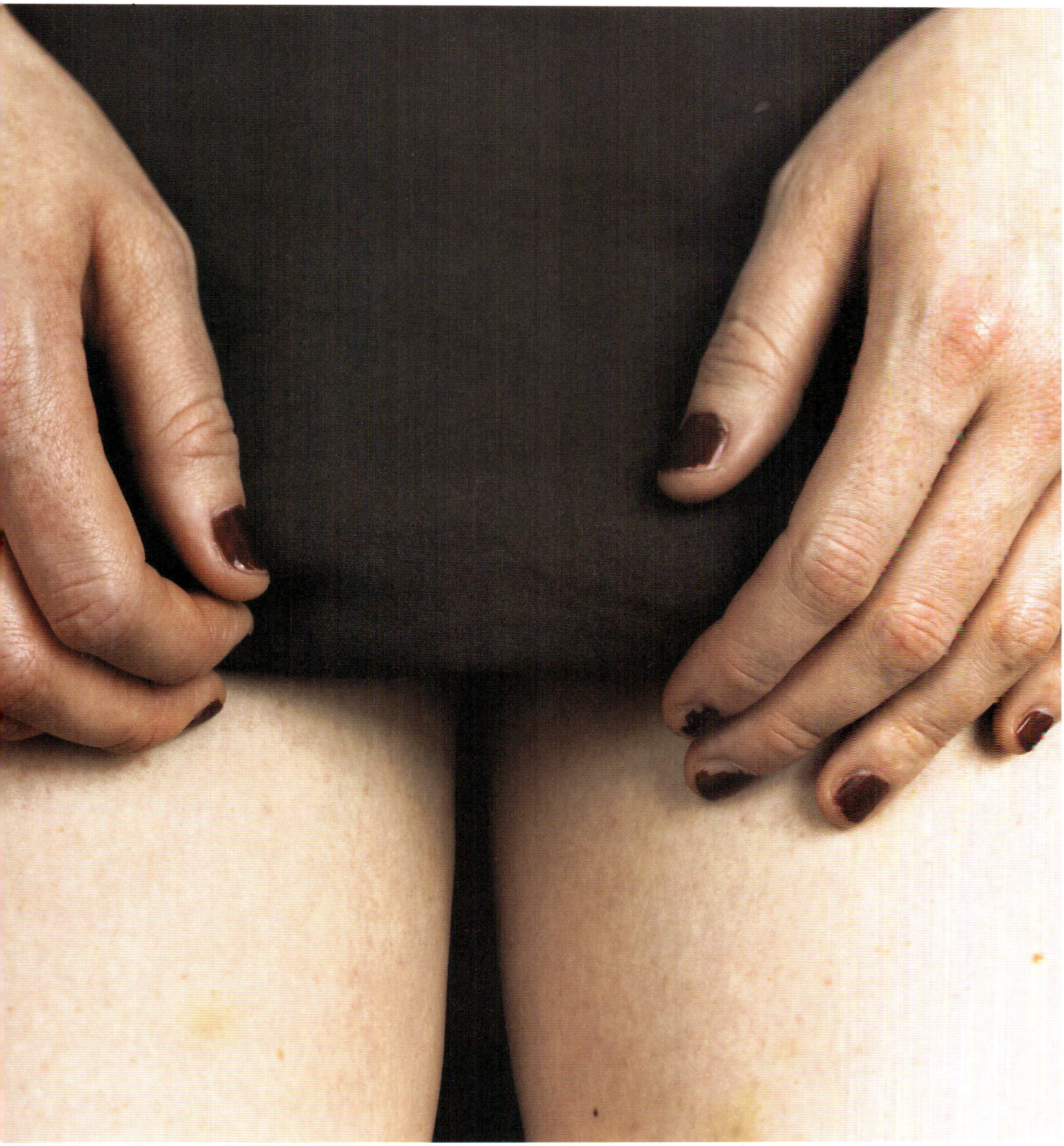

Chipped (from the series "Shifting")

Jennifer Long

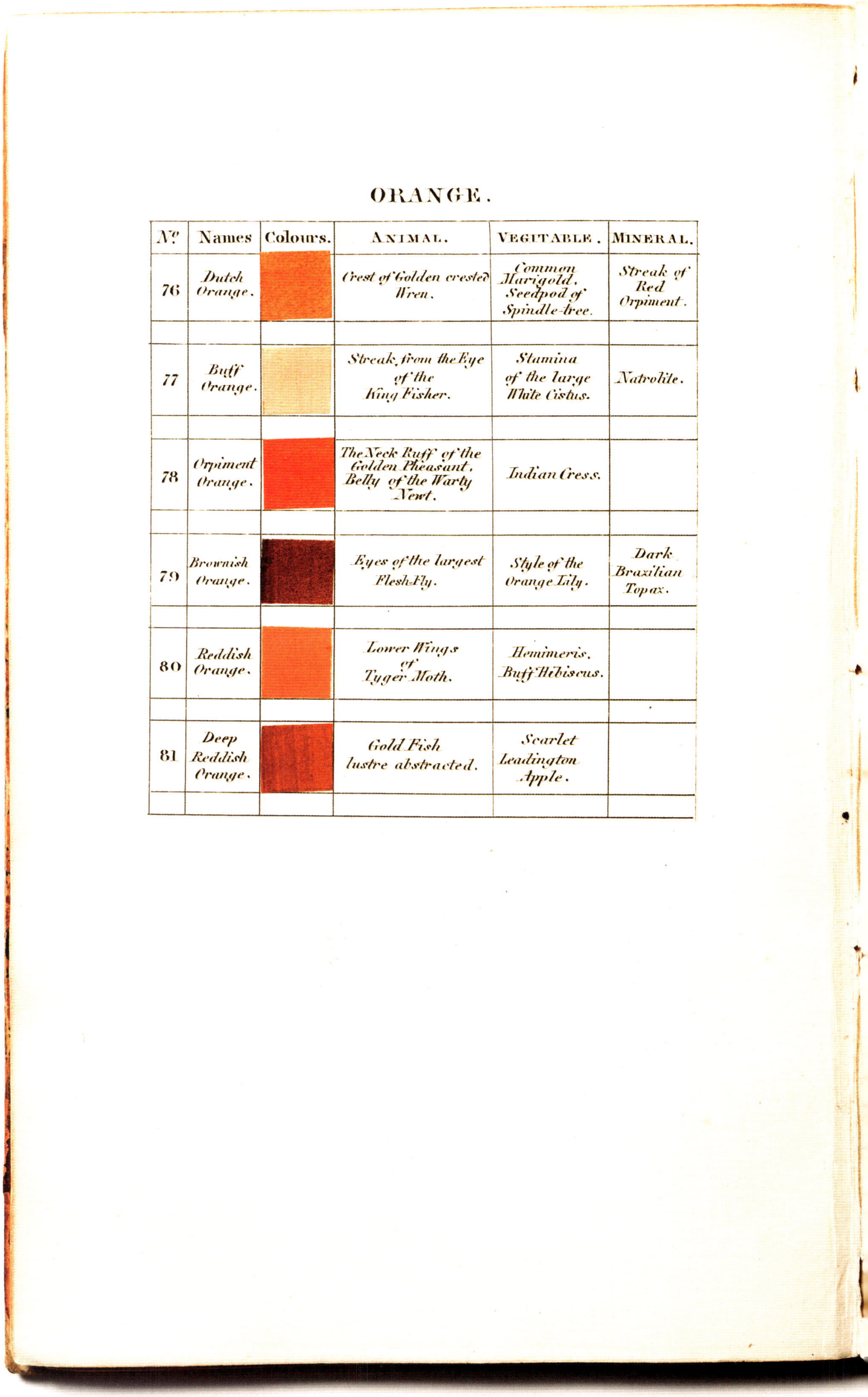

ORANGE.

Nº	Names	Colours.	ANIMAL.	VEGITABLE.	MINERAL.
76	Dutch Orange.		Crest of Golden crested Wren.	Common Marigold. Seedpod of Spindle tree.	Streak of Red Orpiment.
77	Buff Orange.		Streak from the Eye of the King Fisher.	Stamina of the large White Cistus.	Natrolite.
78	Orpiment Orange.		The Neck Ruff of the Golden Pheasant. Belly of the Warty Newt.	Indian Cress.	
79	Brownish Orange.		Eyes of the largest Flesh Fly.	Style of the Orange Lily.	Dark Brazilian Topaz.
80	Reddish Orange.		Lower Wings of Tyger Moth.	Hemimeris. Buff Hibiscus.	
81	Deep Reddish Orange.		Gold Fish lustre abstracted.	Scarlet Leadington Apple.	

RED.

Nº	Names.	Colours.	Animal.	Vegetable.	Mineral.
82	*Tile Red.*		*Breast of the Cock Bullfinch.*	*Shrubby Pimpernel.*	*Porcelain Jasper.*
83	*Hyacinth Red.*		*Red Spots of the Lygæus Apterus Fly.*	*Red on the golden Rennette Apple.*	*Hyacinth.*
84	*Scarlet Red.*		*Scarlet Ibis or Curlew. Mark on Head of Red Grouse.*	*Large red Oriental Poppy. Red Parts of red and black Indian Peas.*	*Light red Cinnaber.*
85	*Vermillion Red.*		*Red Coral.*	*Love Apple.*	*Cinnaber.*
86	*Aurora Red.*		*Vent coverts of Pied Wood-Pecker.*	*Red on the Naked Apple.*	*Red Orpiment.*
87	*Arterial Blood Red.*		*Head of the Cock Gold-finch.*	*Corn Poppy. Cherry.*	
88	*Flesh Red.*		*Human Skin.*	*Larkspur.*	*Heavy Spar. Limestone.*
89	*Rose Red.*			*Common Garden Rose.*	*Figure Stone.*
90	*Peach Blossom Red.*			*Peach Blossom.*	*Red Cobalt Ore.*

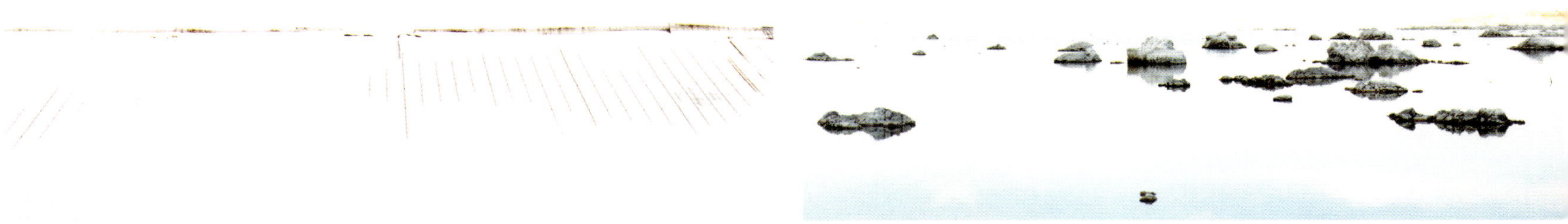

Amanda Marchand

Untitled (from the series "415/514")

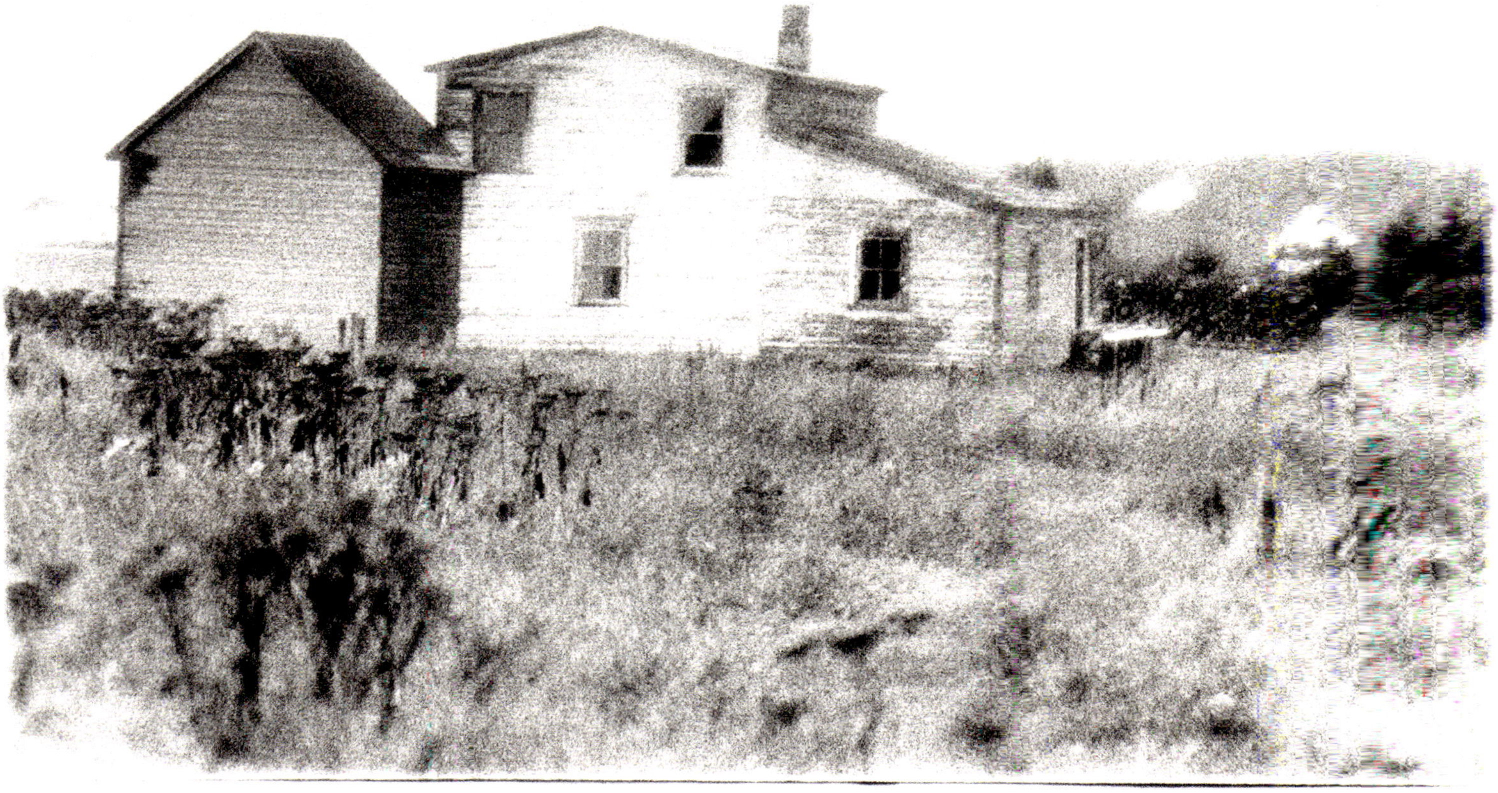

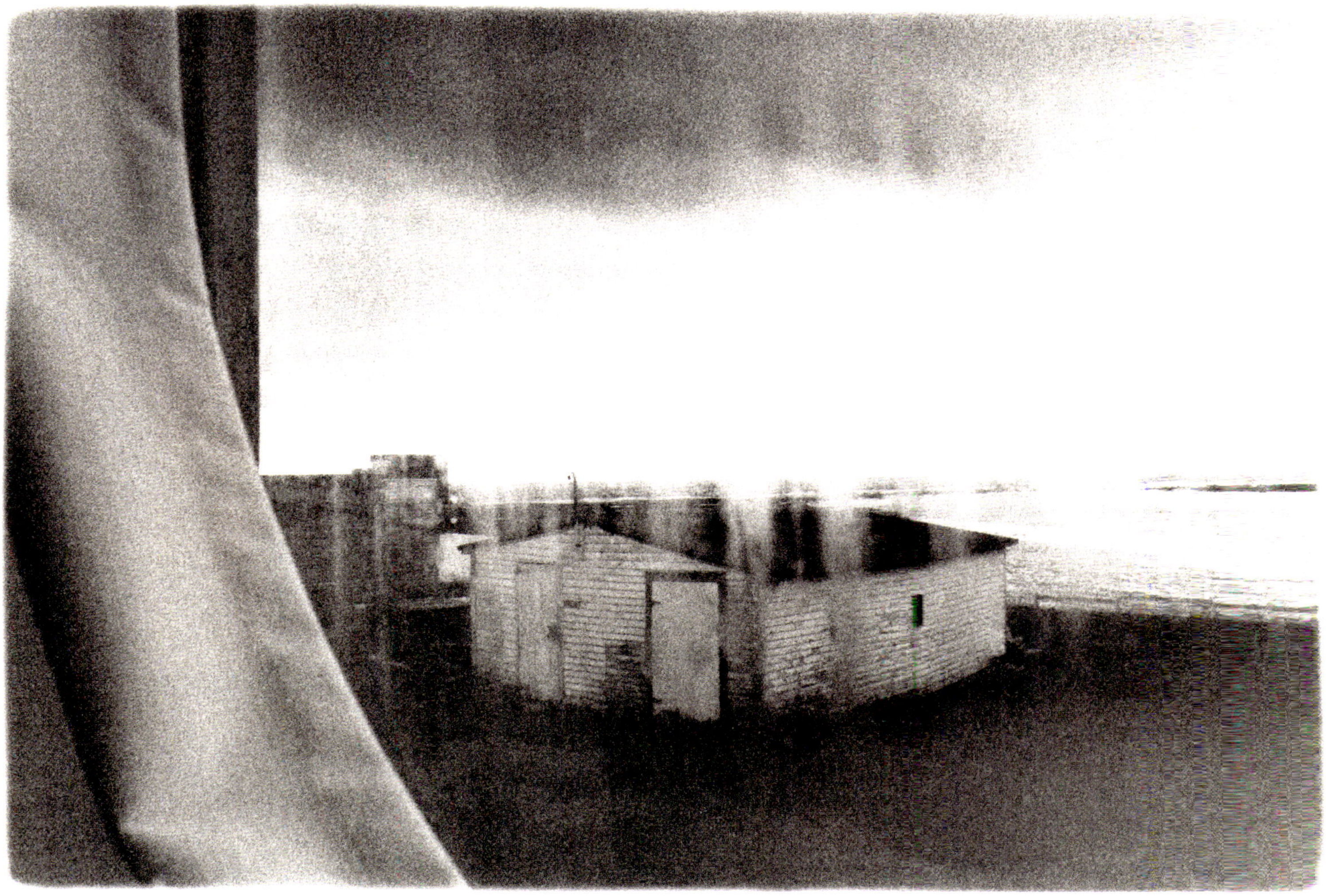

Original
Rainy Dawn

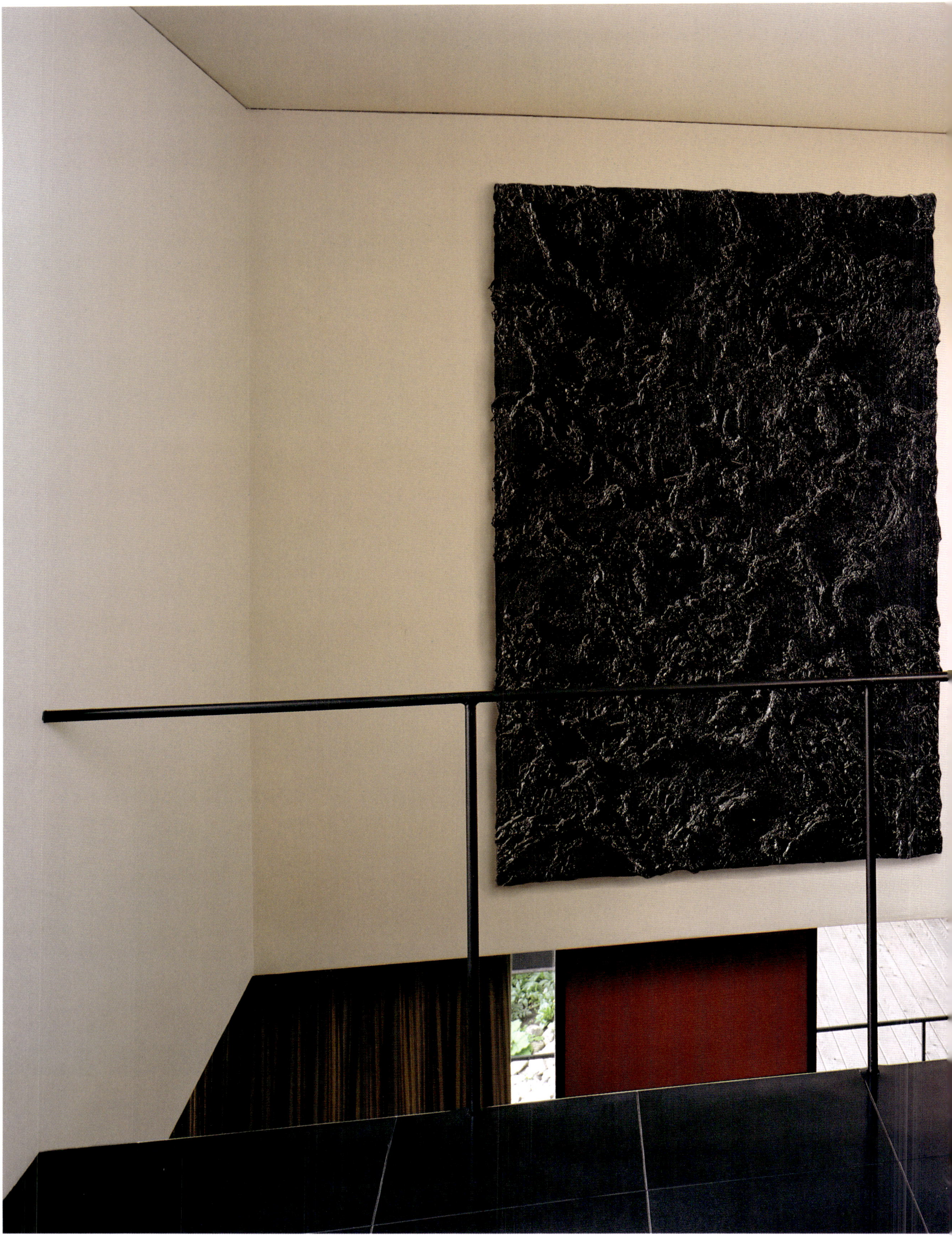

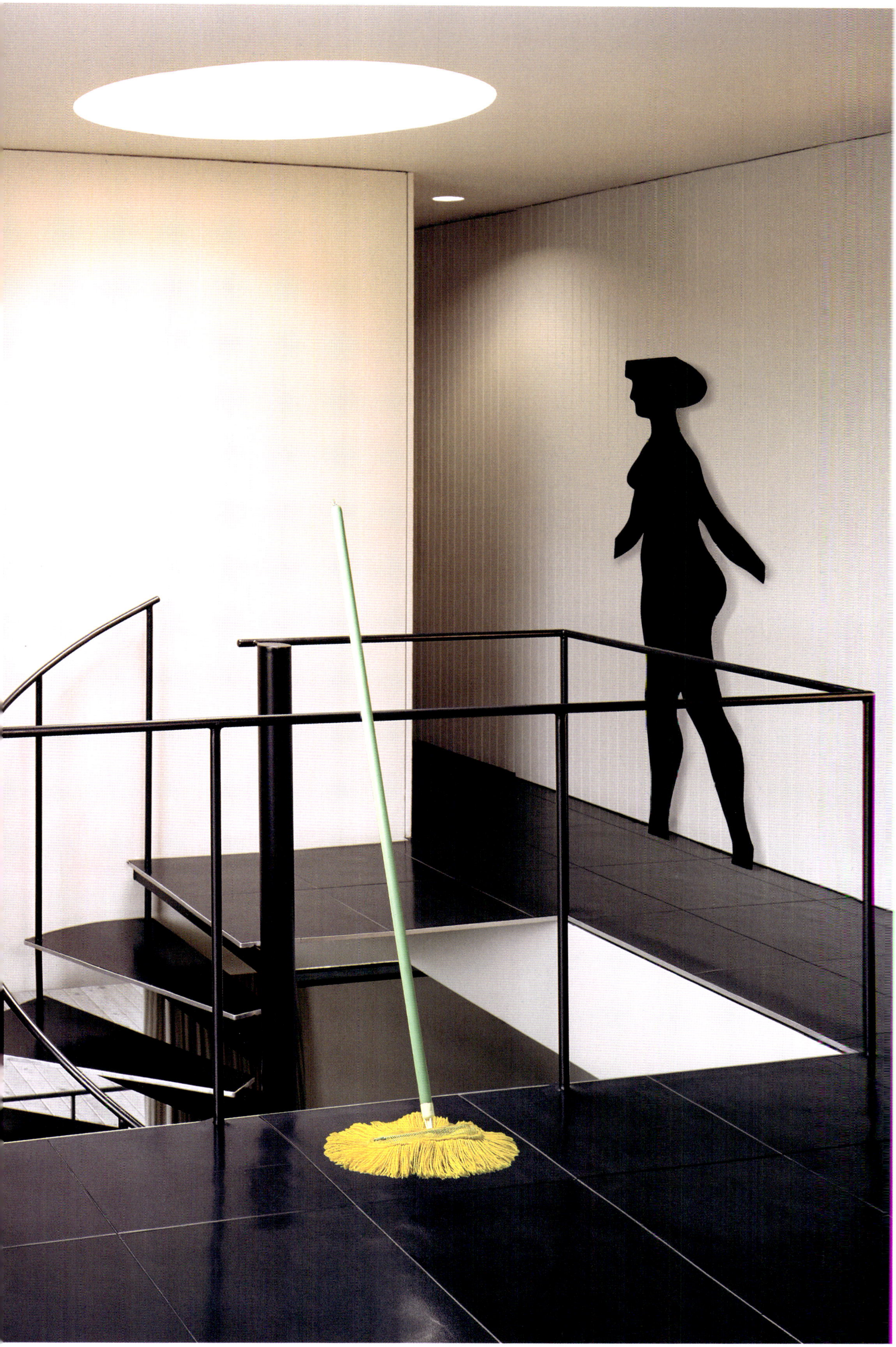

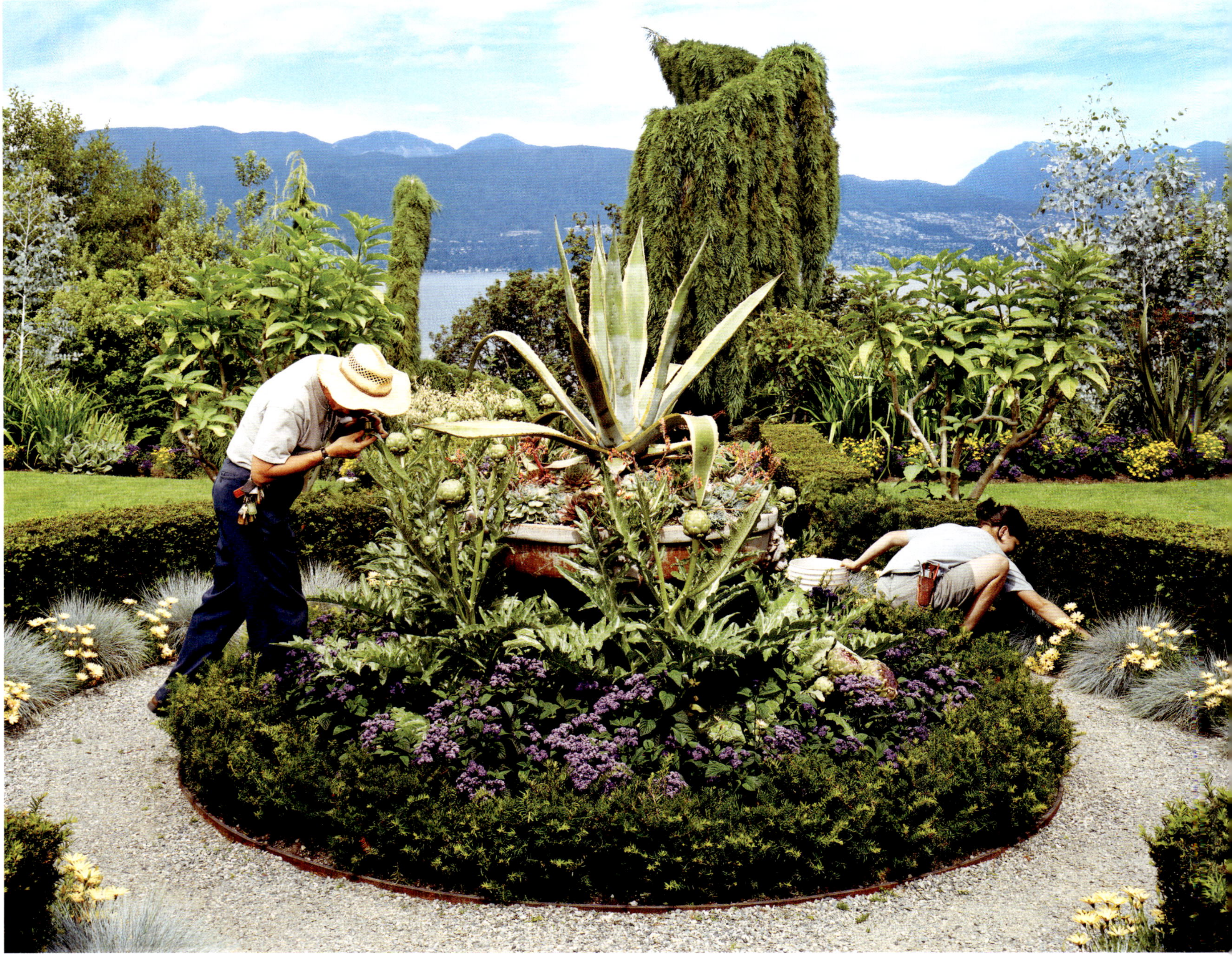

Scott McFarland

Inspecting, Allen O'Connor Searches for *Botrytis cinerea*

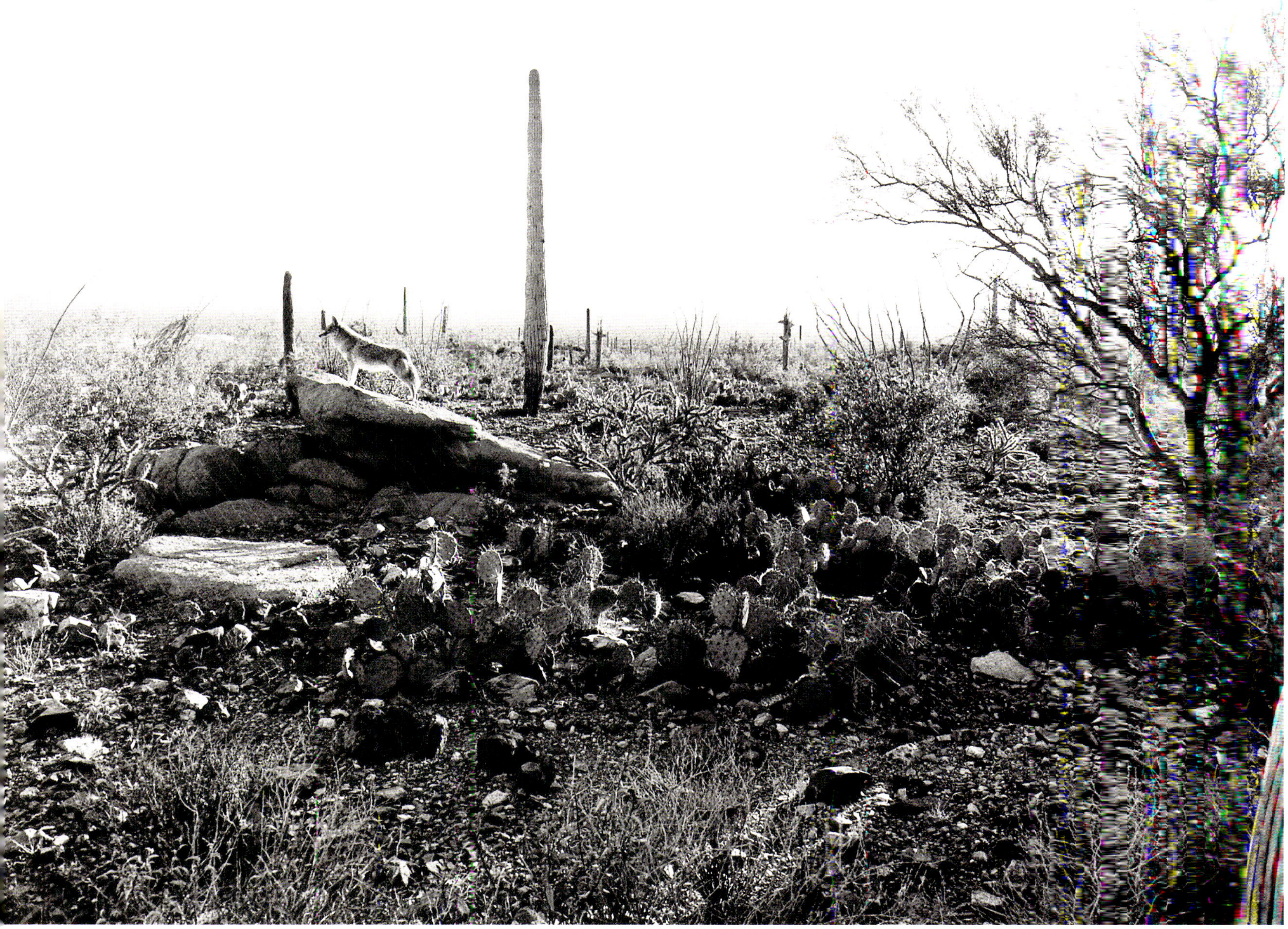

Desert Museum (Tucson, Arizona)

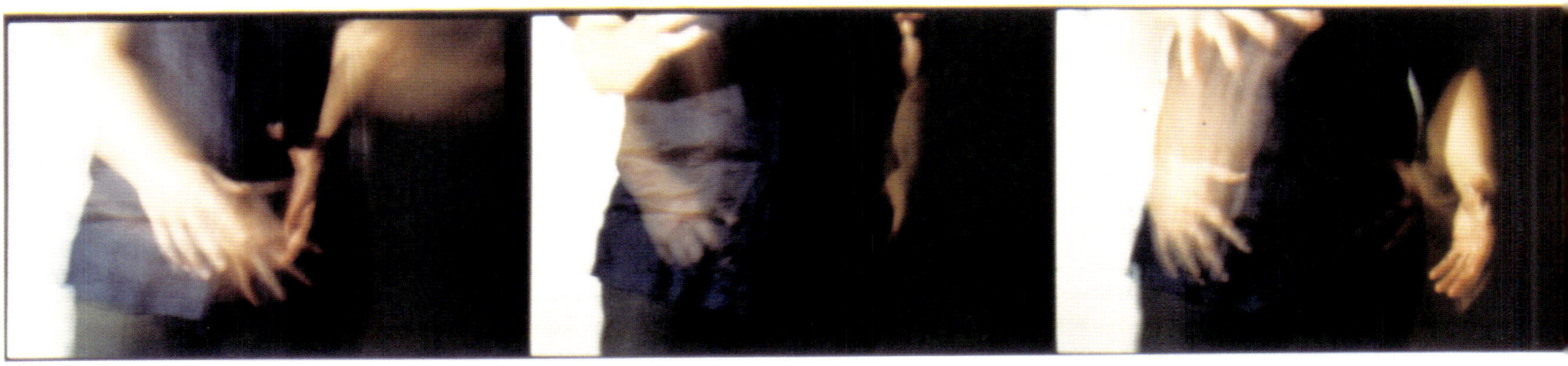

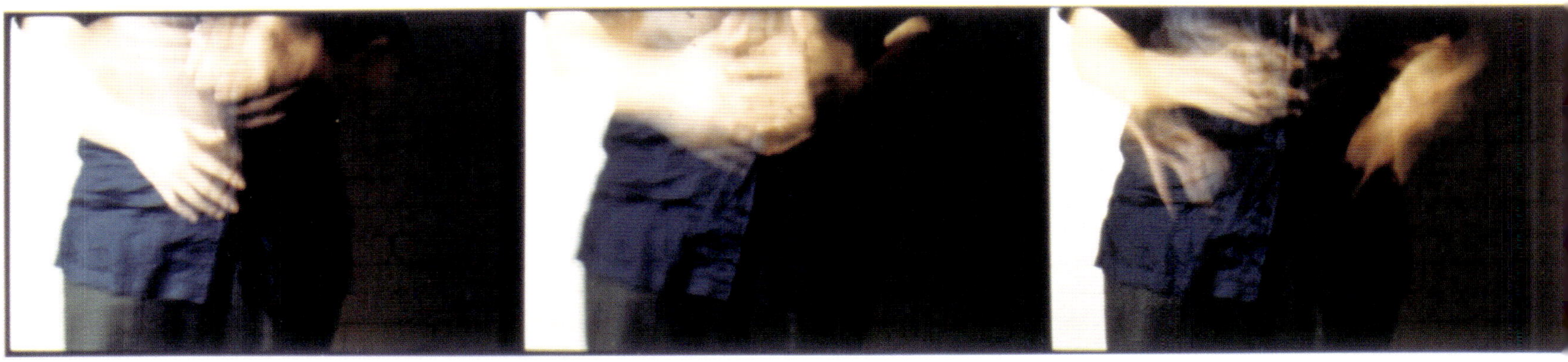

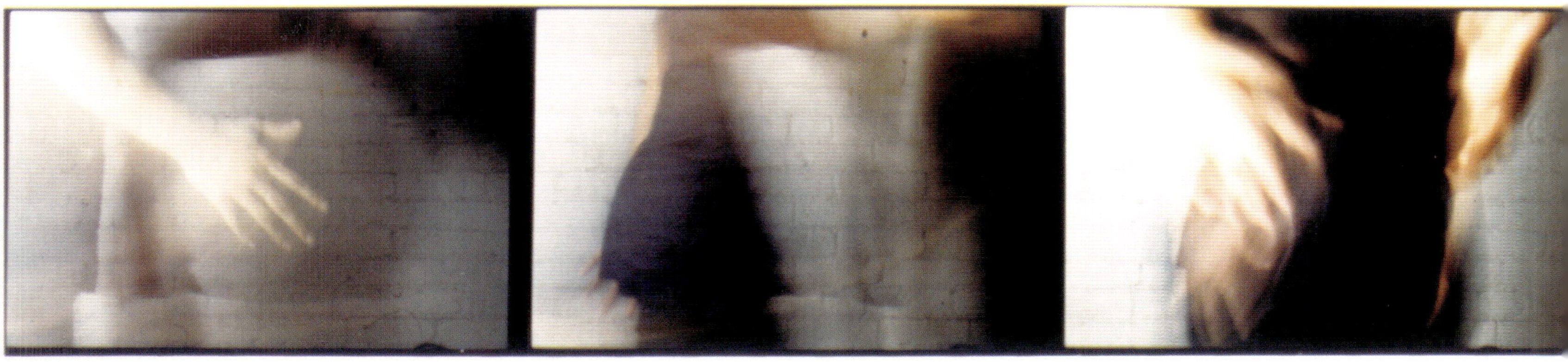

Felonious #1
Felonious #2
Felonious #3

Lori Newdick

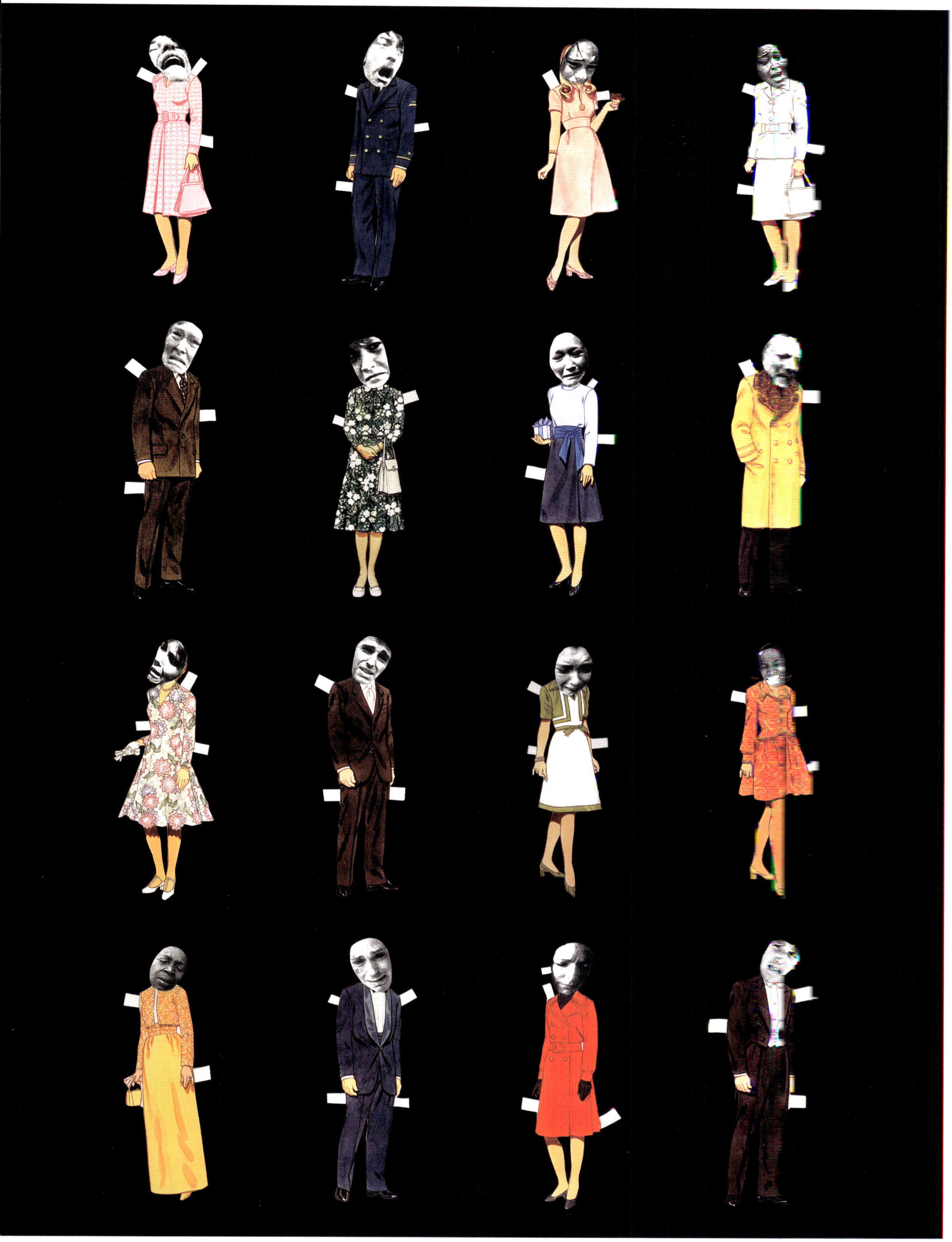

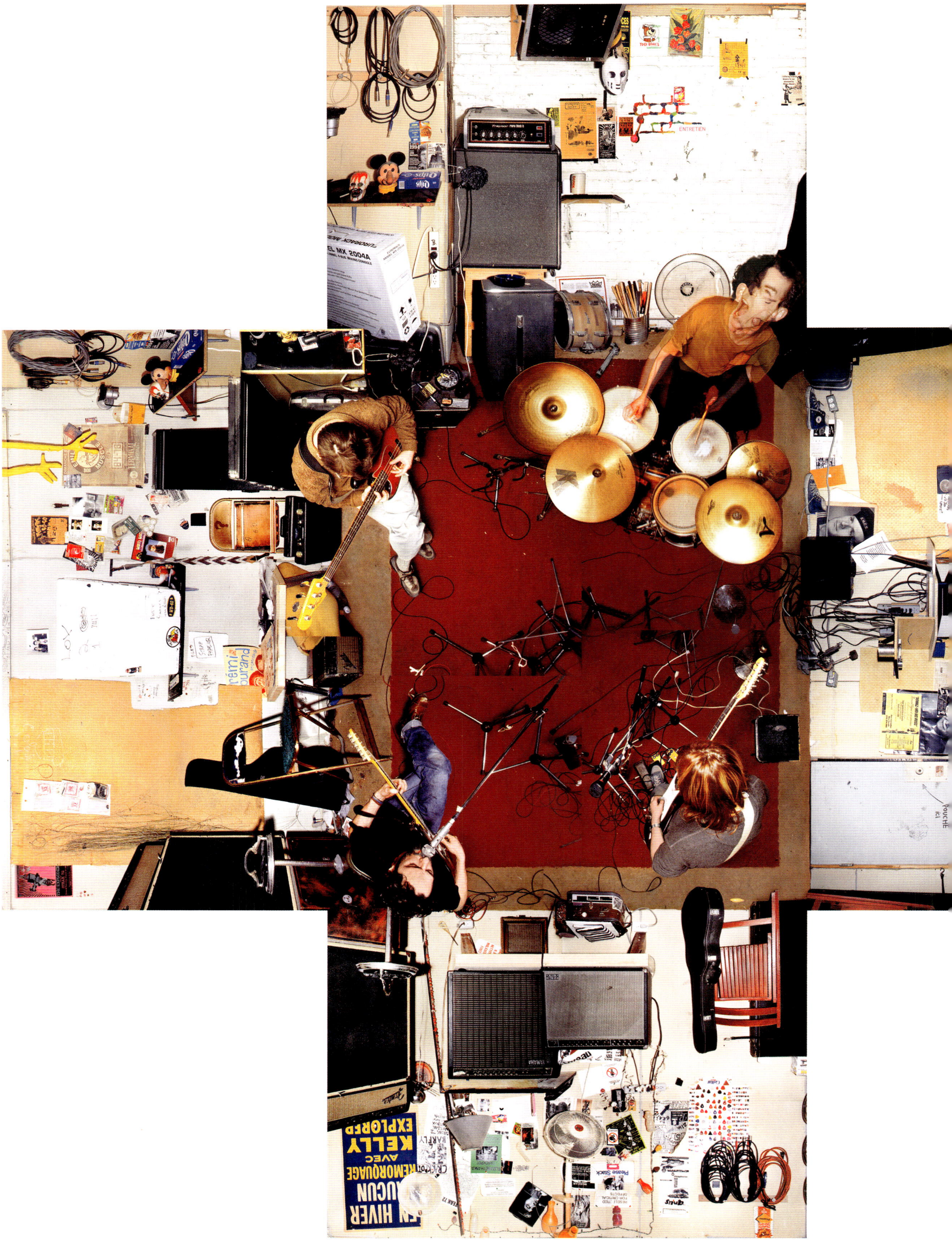
ENTRETIEN

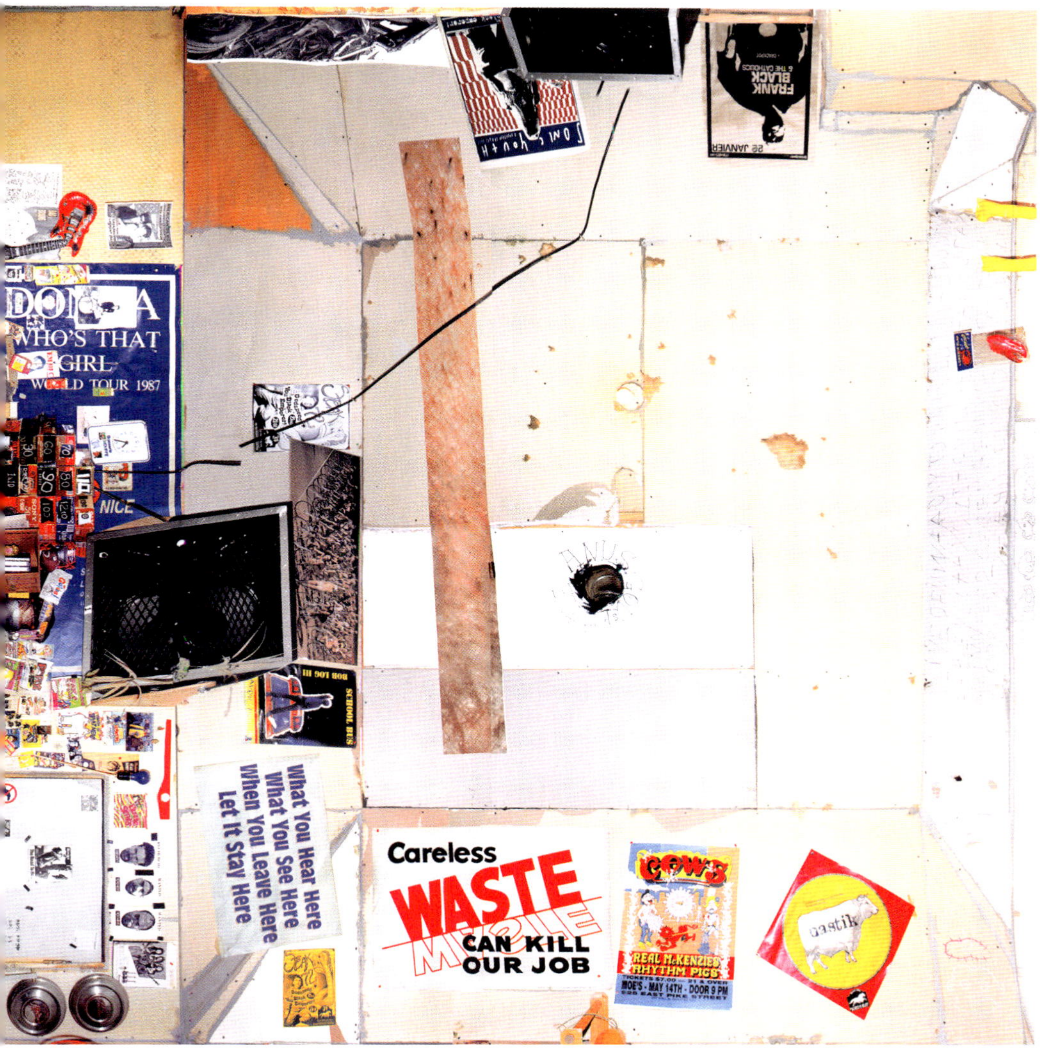
Careless
WASTE
CAN KILL
OUR JOB
What You Hear Here
What You See Here
When You Leave Here
Let It Stay Here
WHO'S THAT
GIRL
COWS
REAL McKENZIES
RHYTHM PIGS

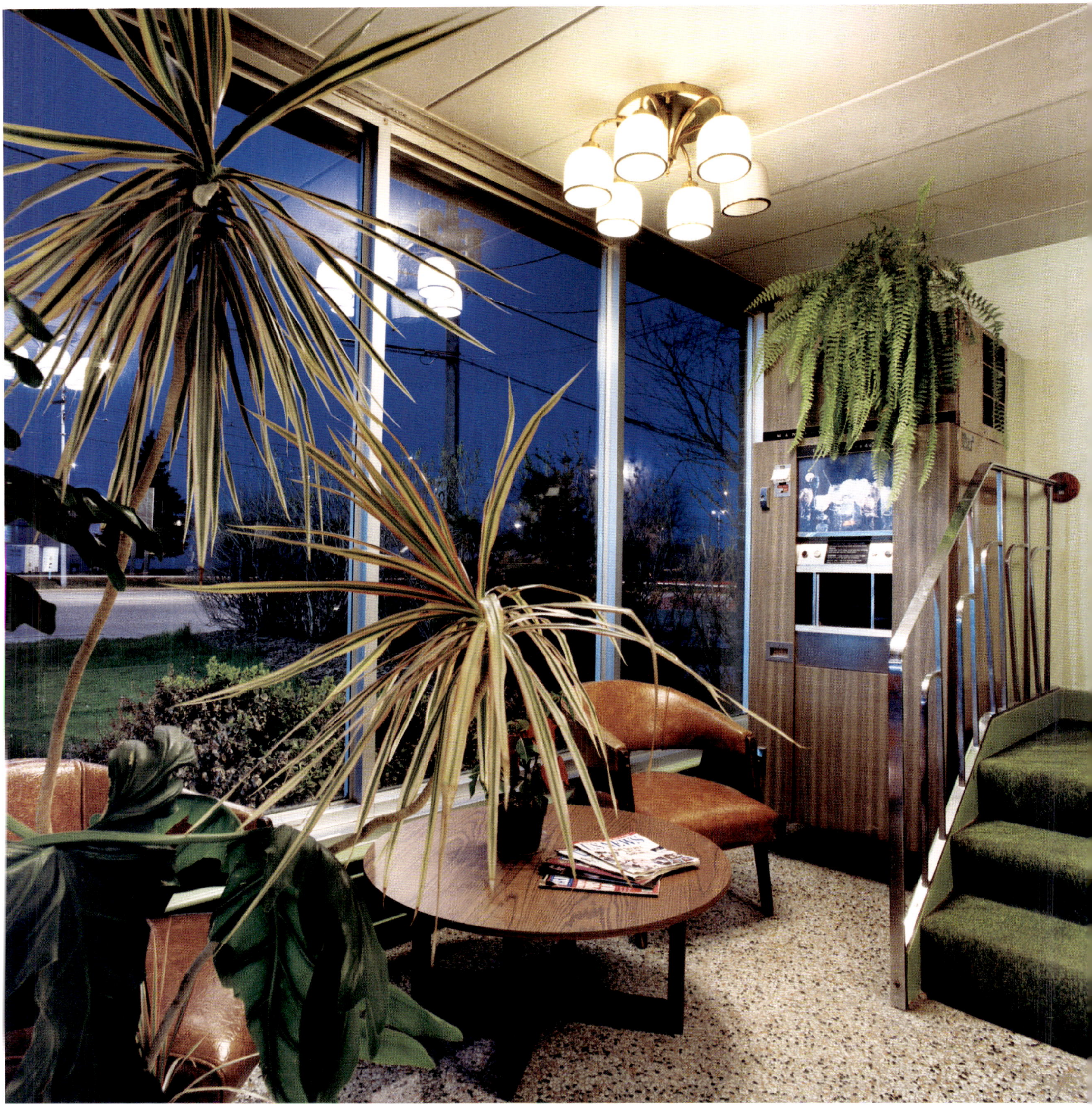

Steve Payne

Hillcrest Lobby (from the series "Motel")

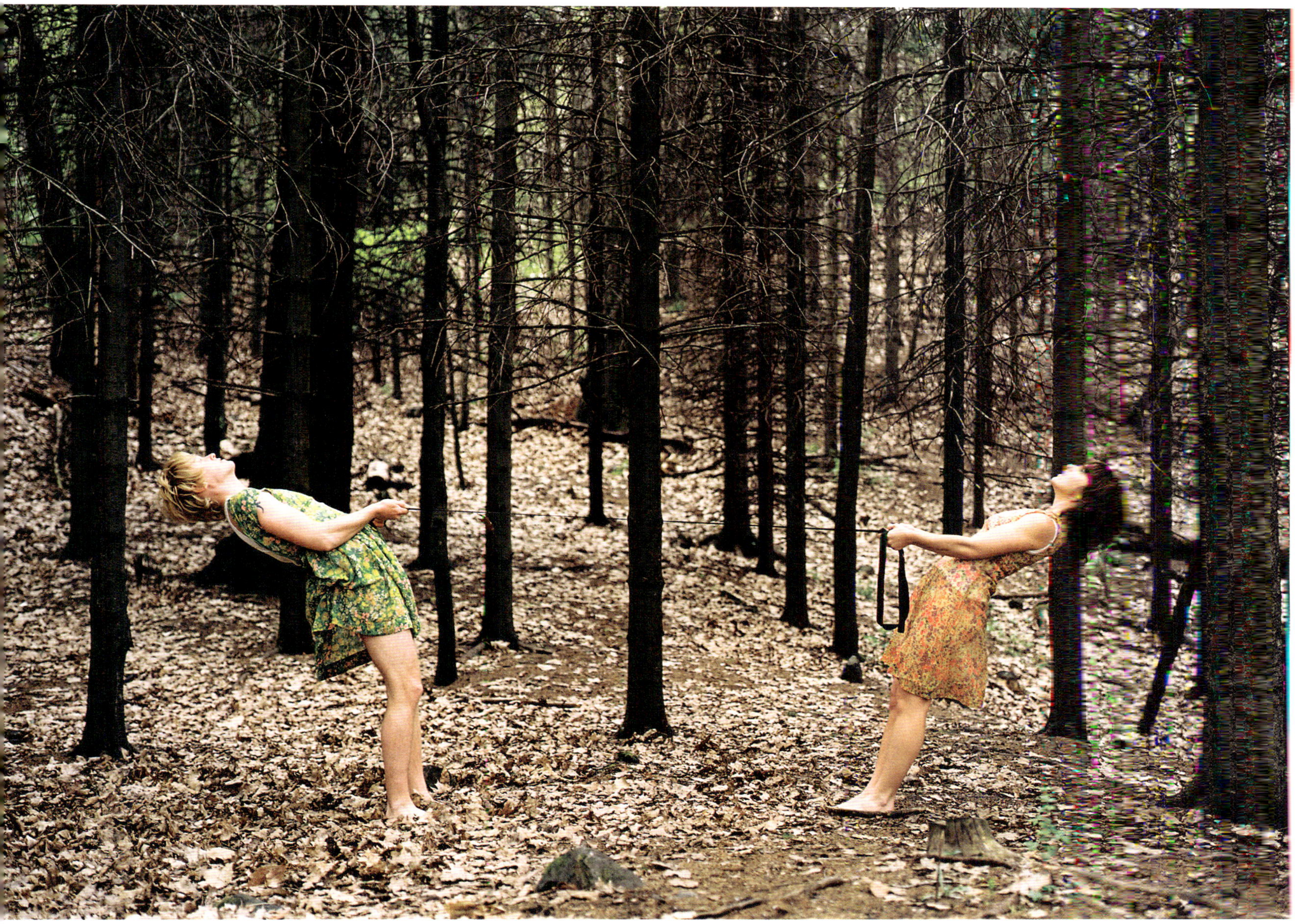

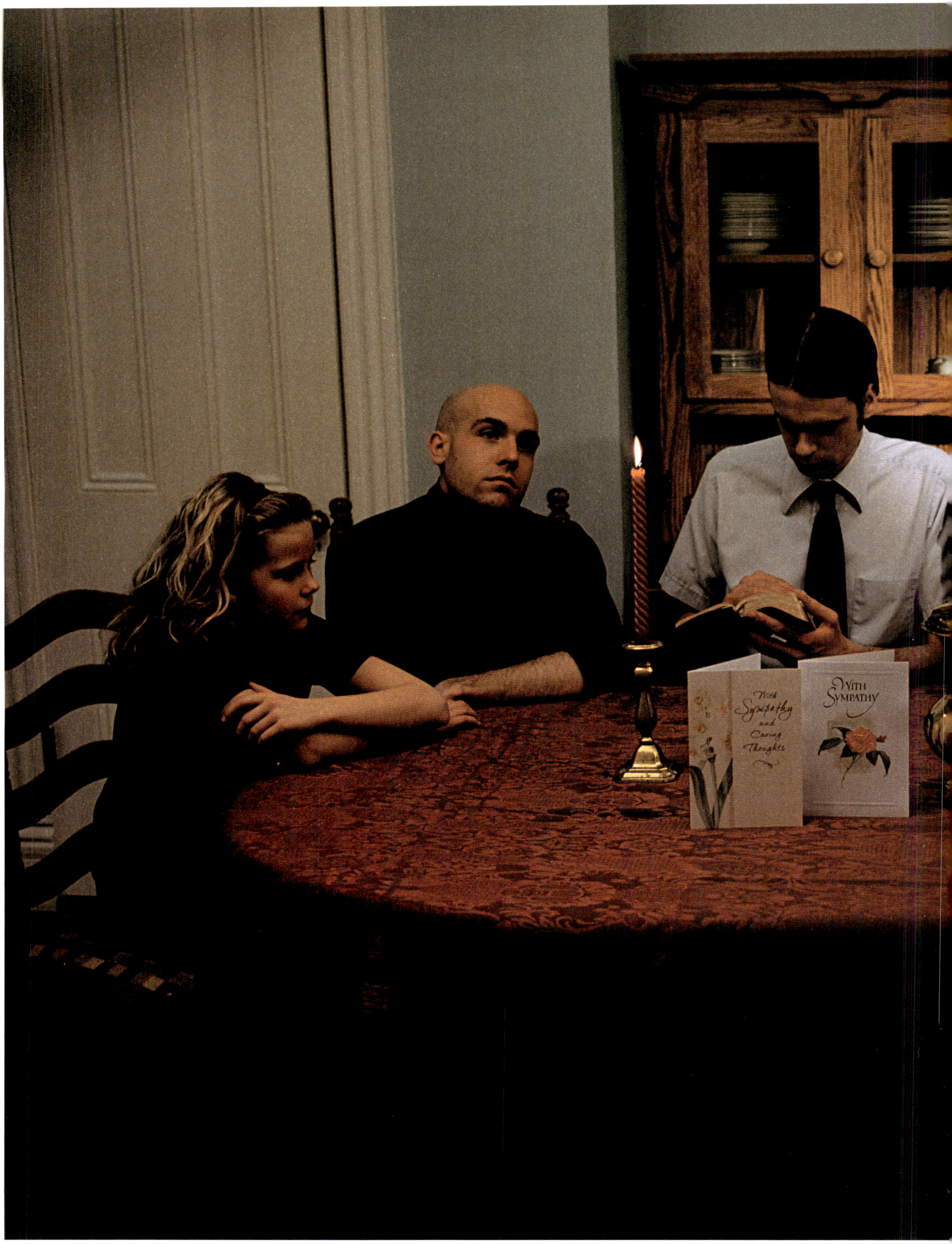

Elise Rasmussen

Untitled #1 (from the series "The Passing of Life")

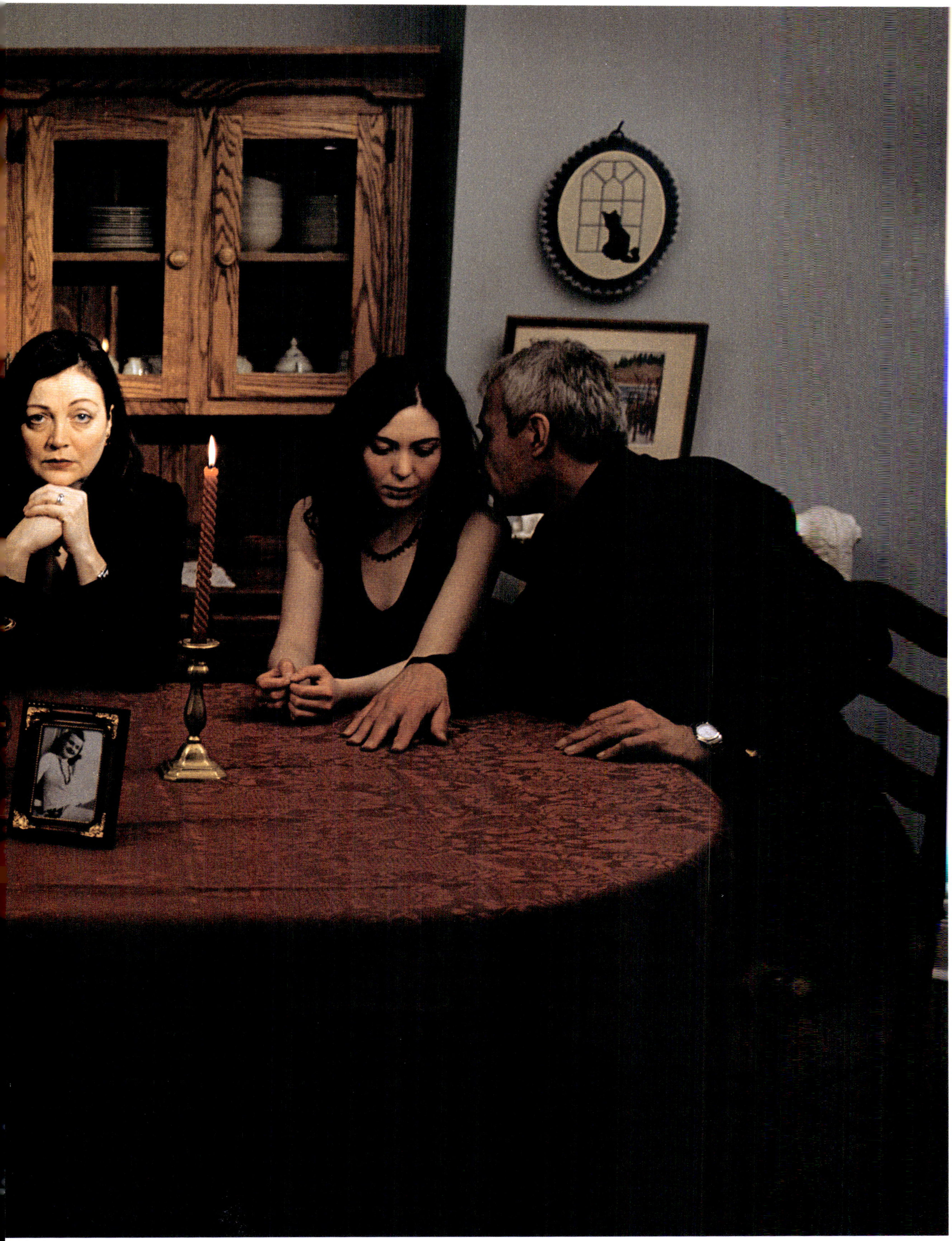

Elle Rasmussen

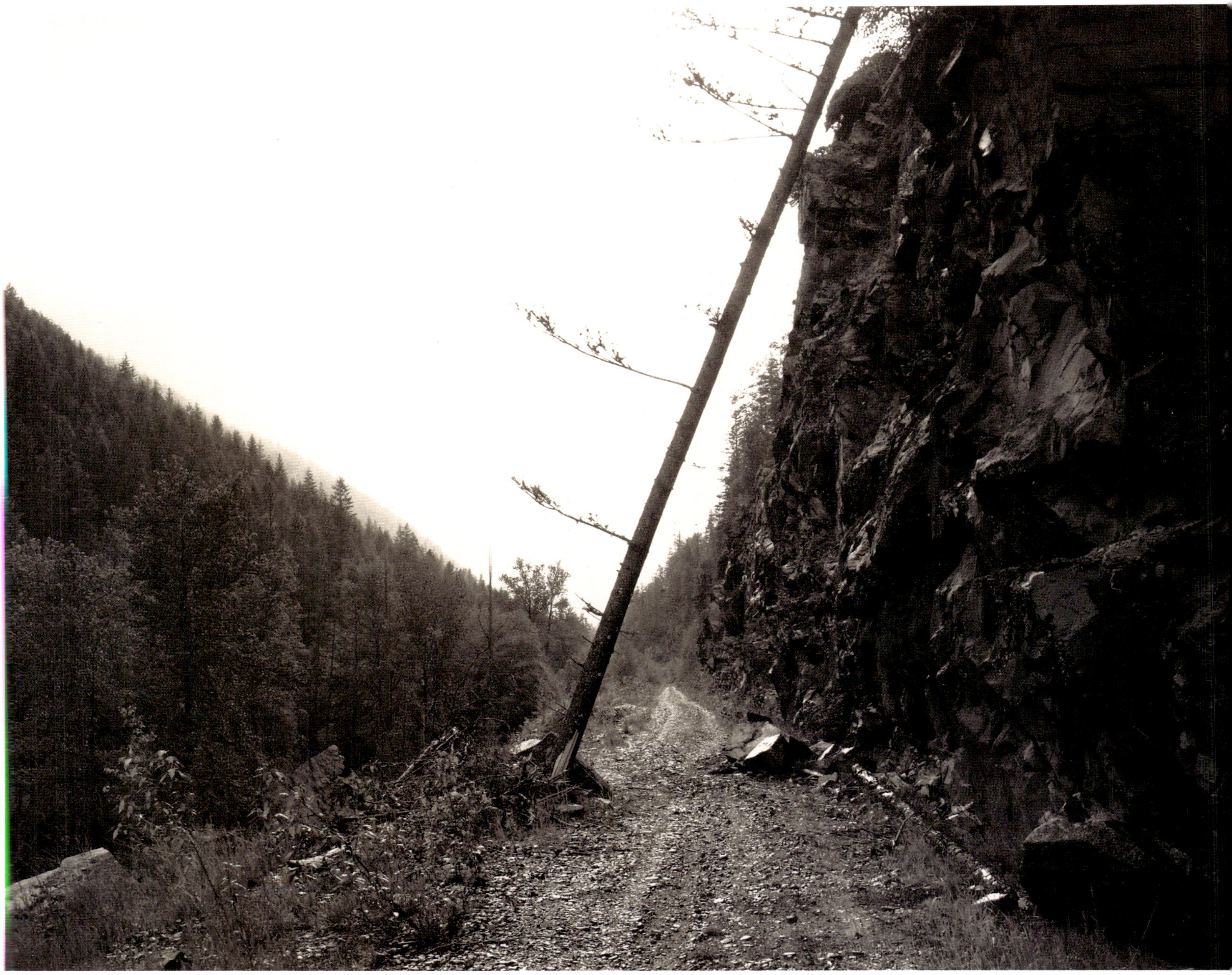

Columbia and Western #3

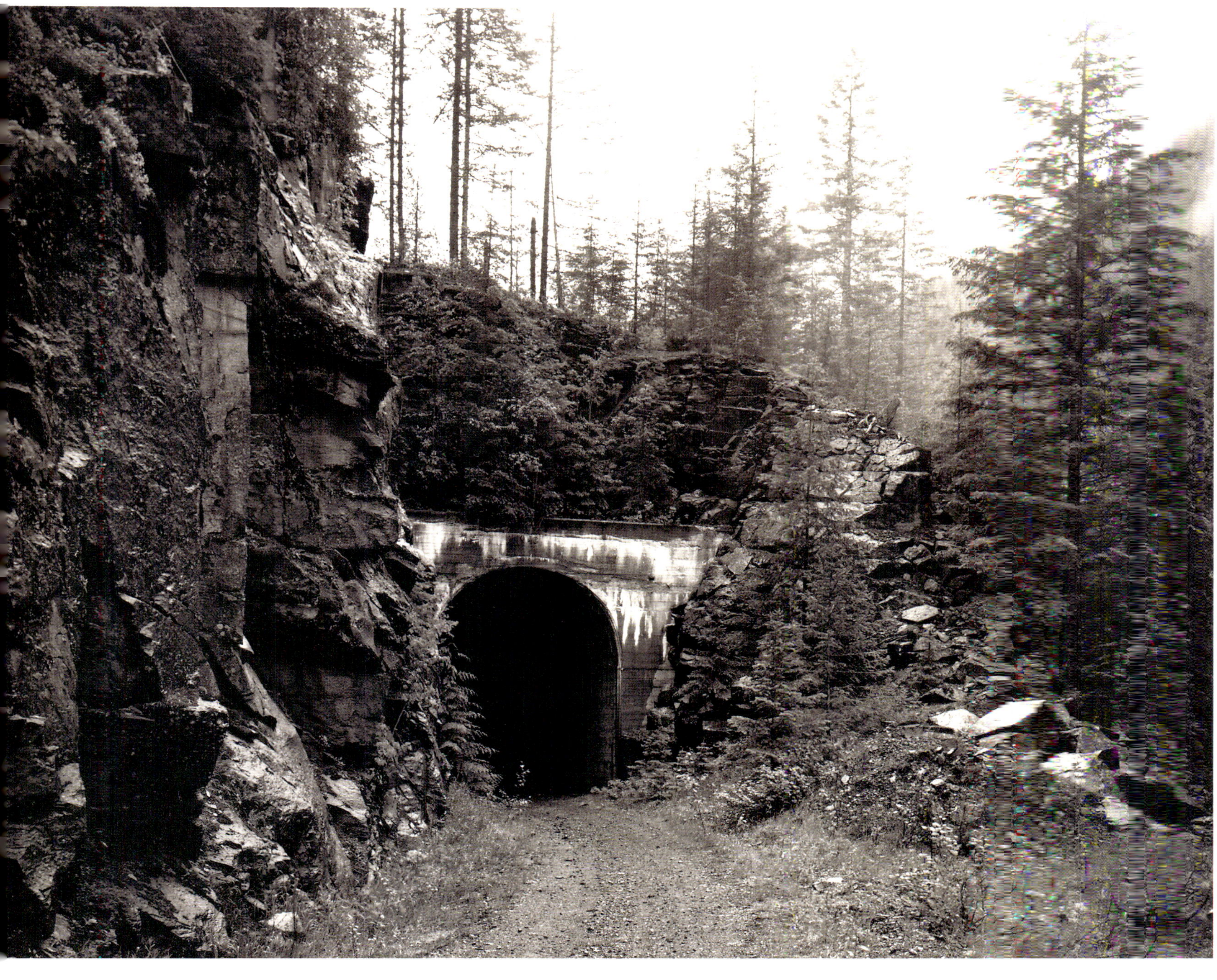

Columbia and Western #8

Mark Ruwedel

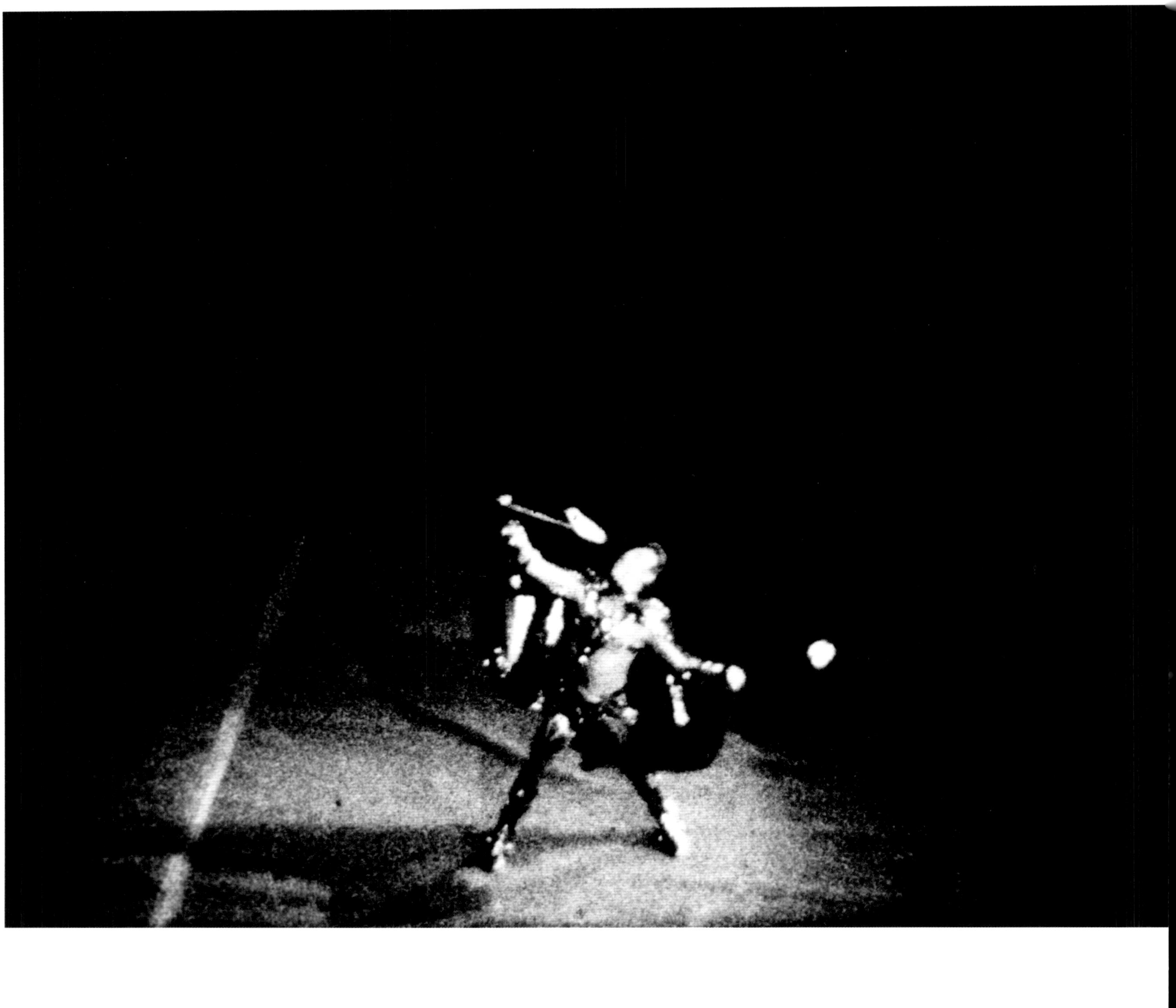

Chuck Samuels

Untitled #26 (from the series "Memory Believes")

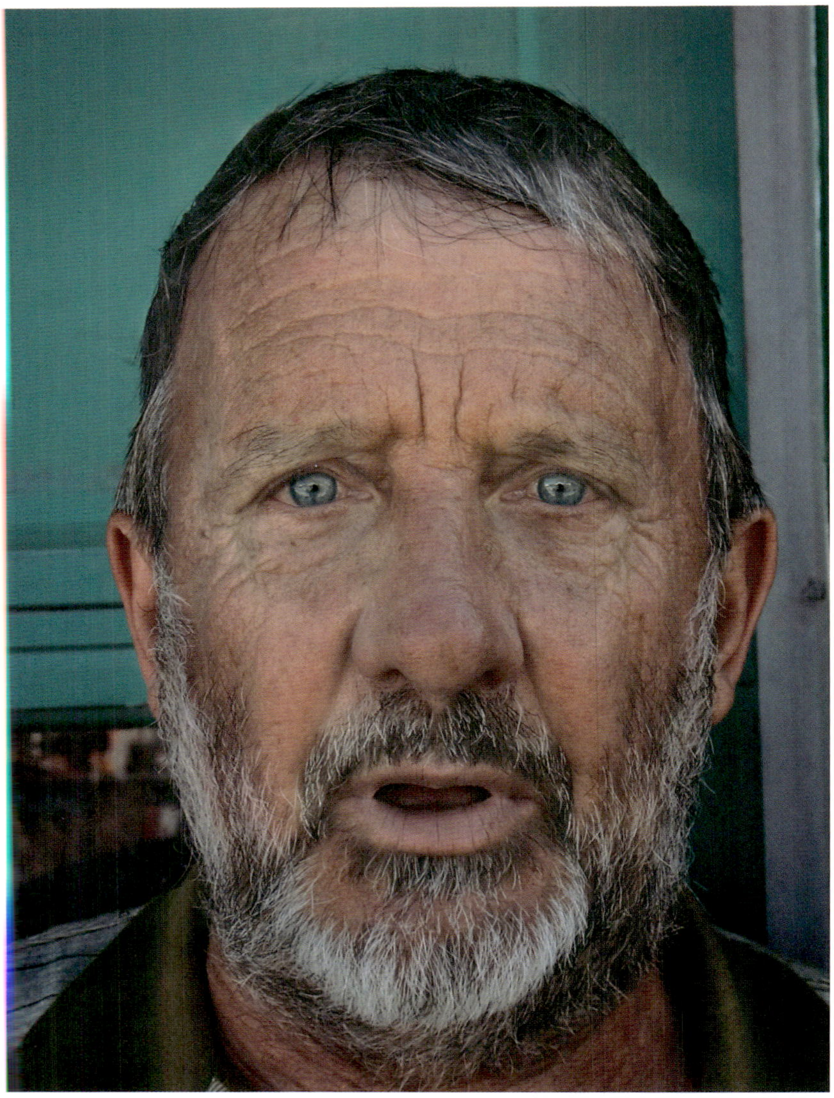

25..07..04, 15..25..48

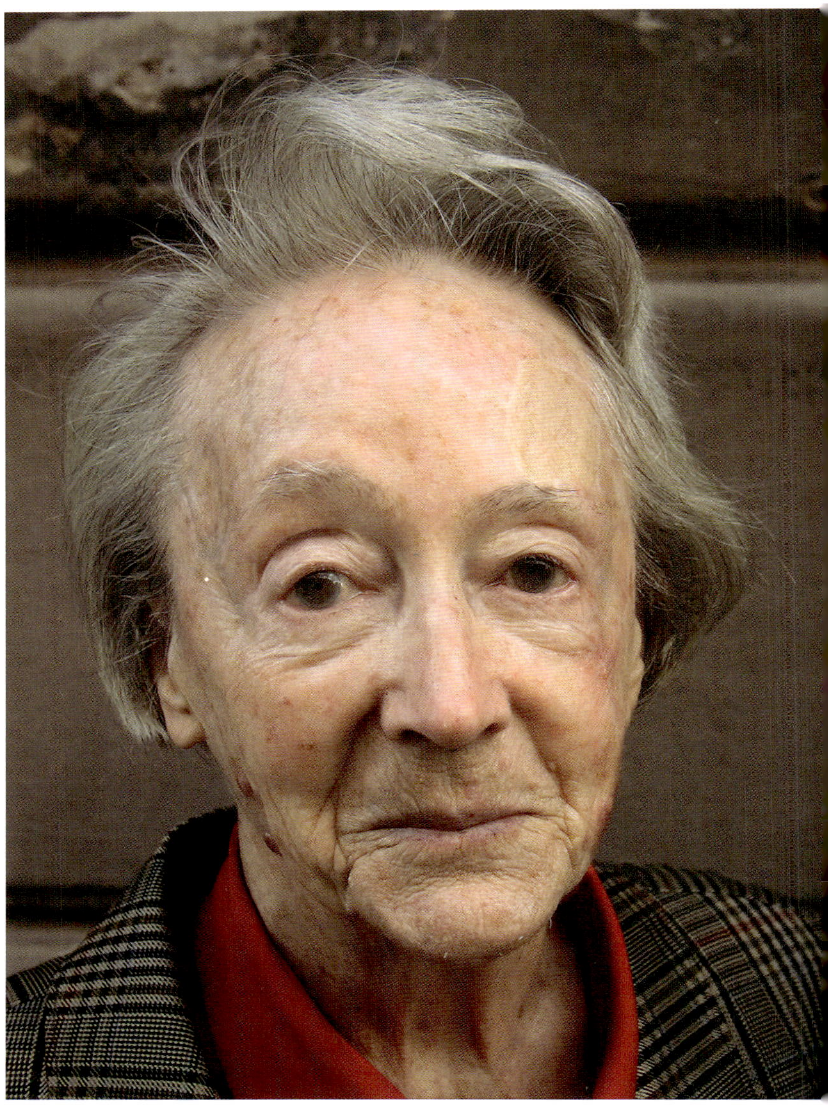

03..10..04, 16..08..09

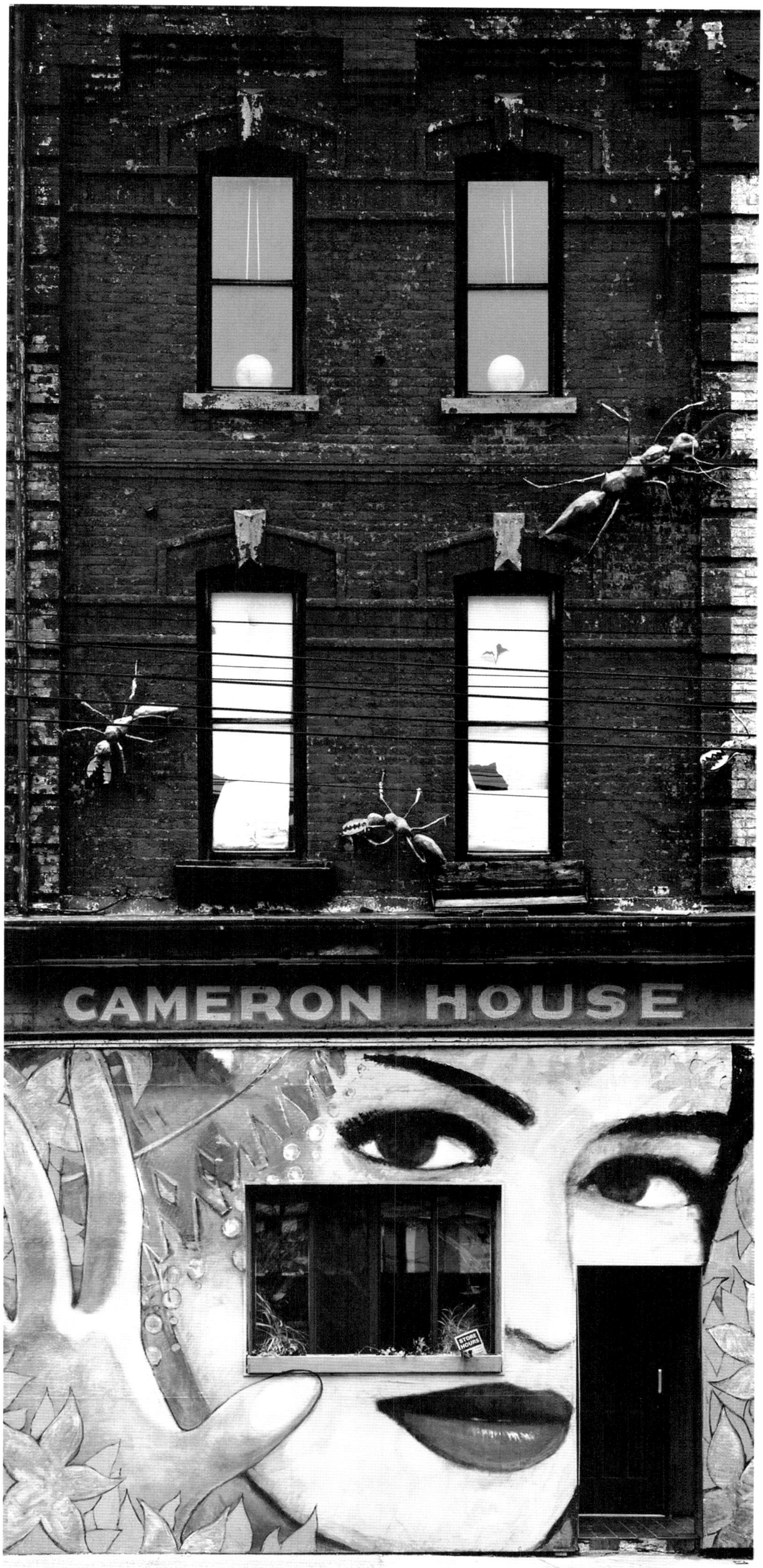

Cameron House, Toronto

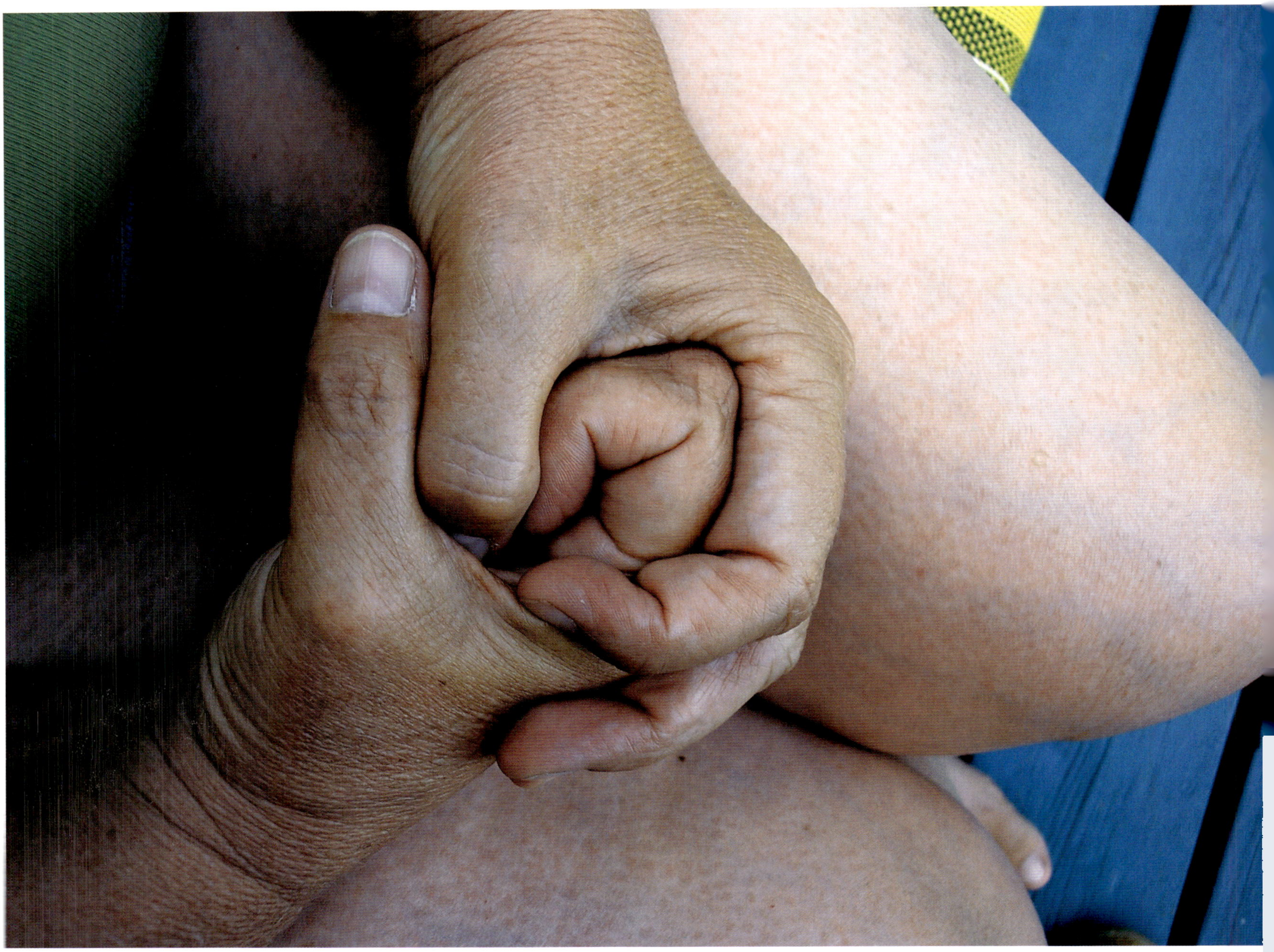

Sandra Semchuk

The Comfort of Fingers (with the co-operation of James Nicholas)

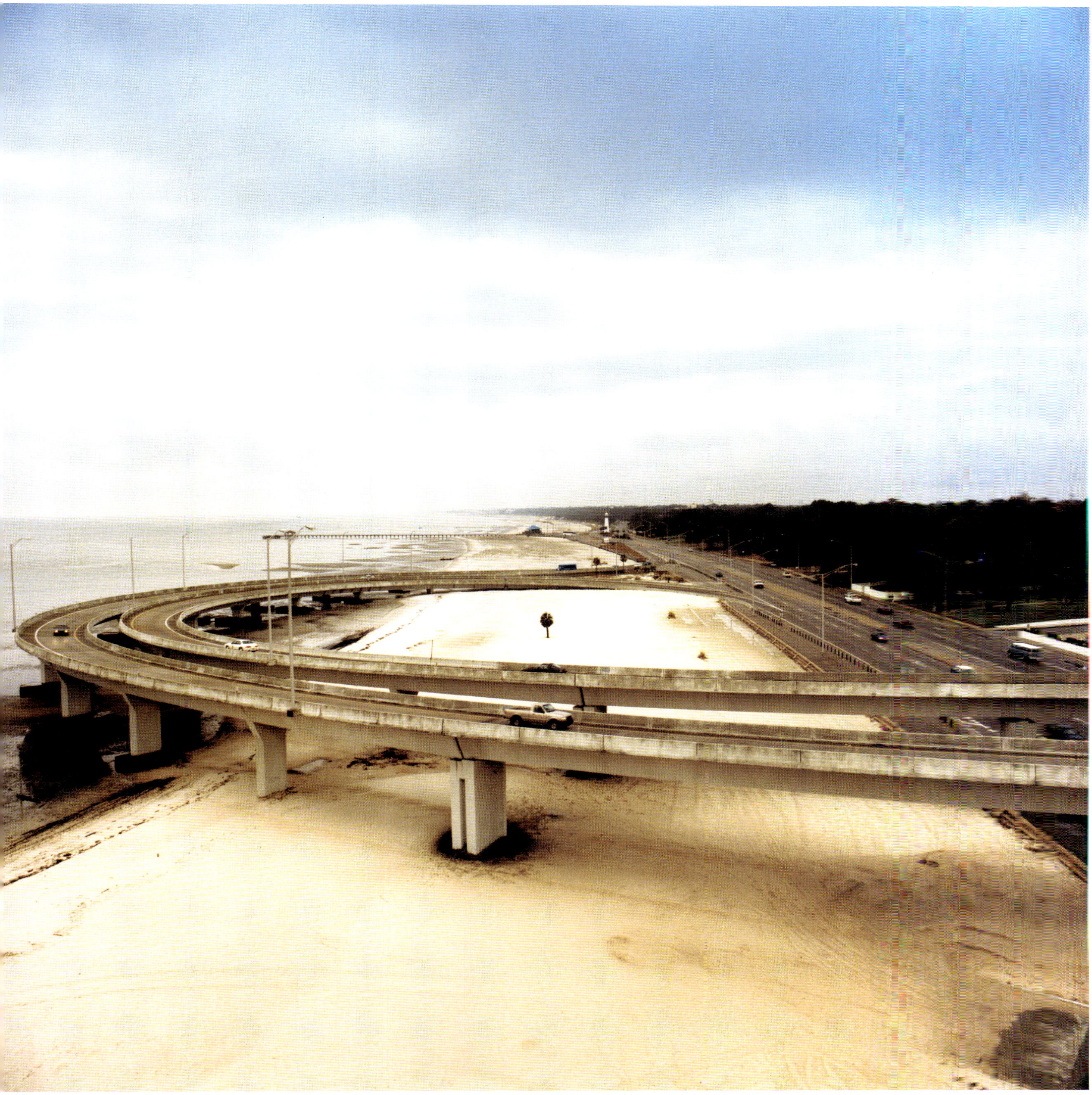

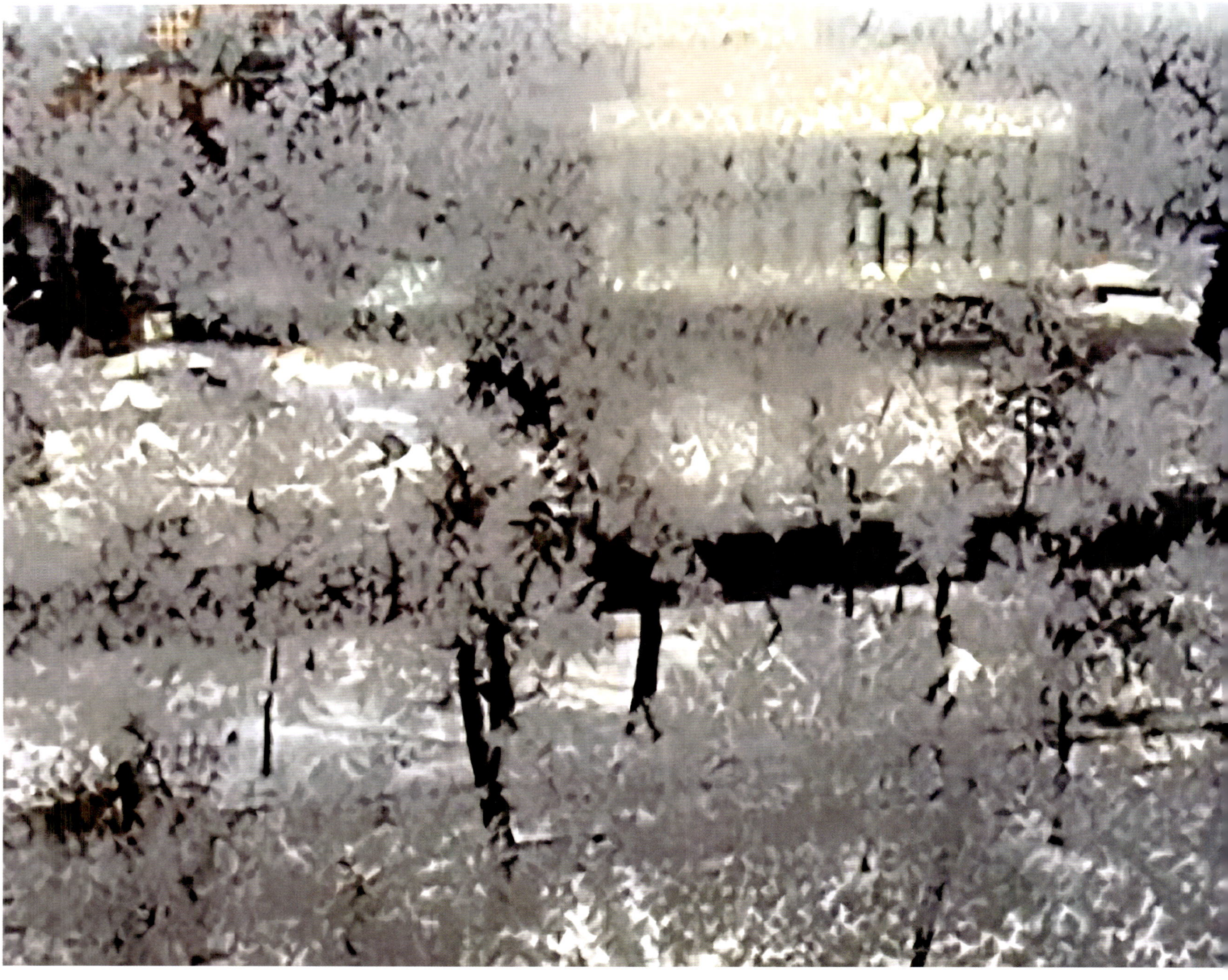

Cheryl Sourkes

Dnipropetrovsk, Ukraine

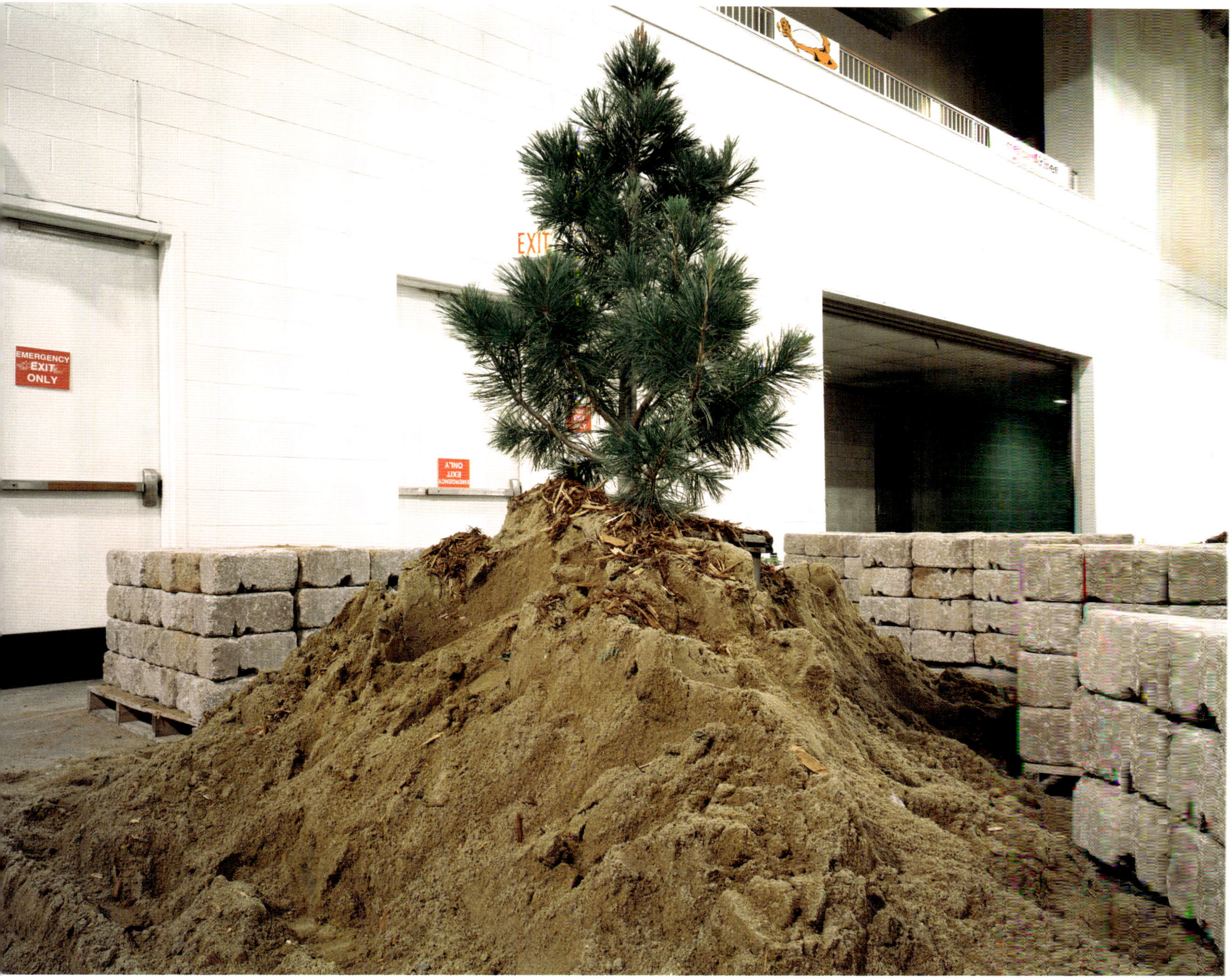

Navy Pier

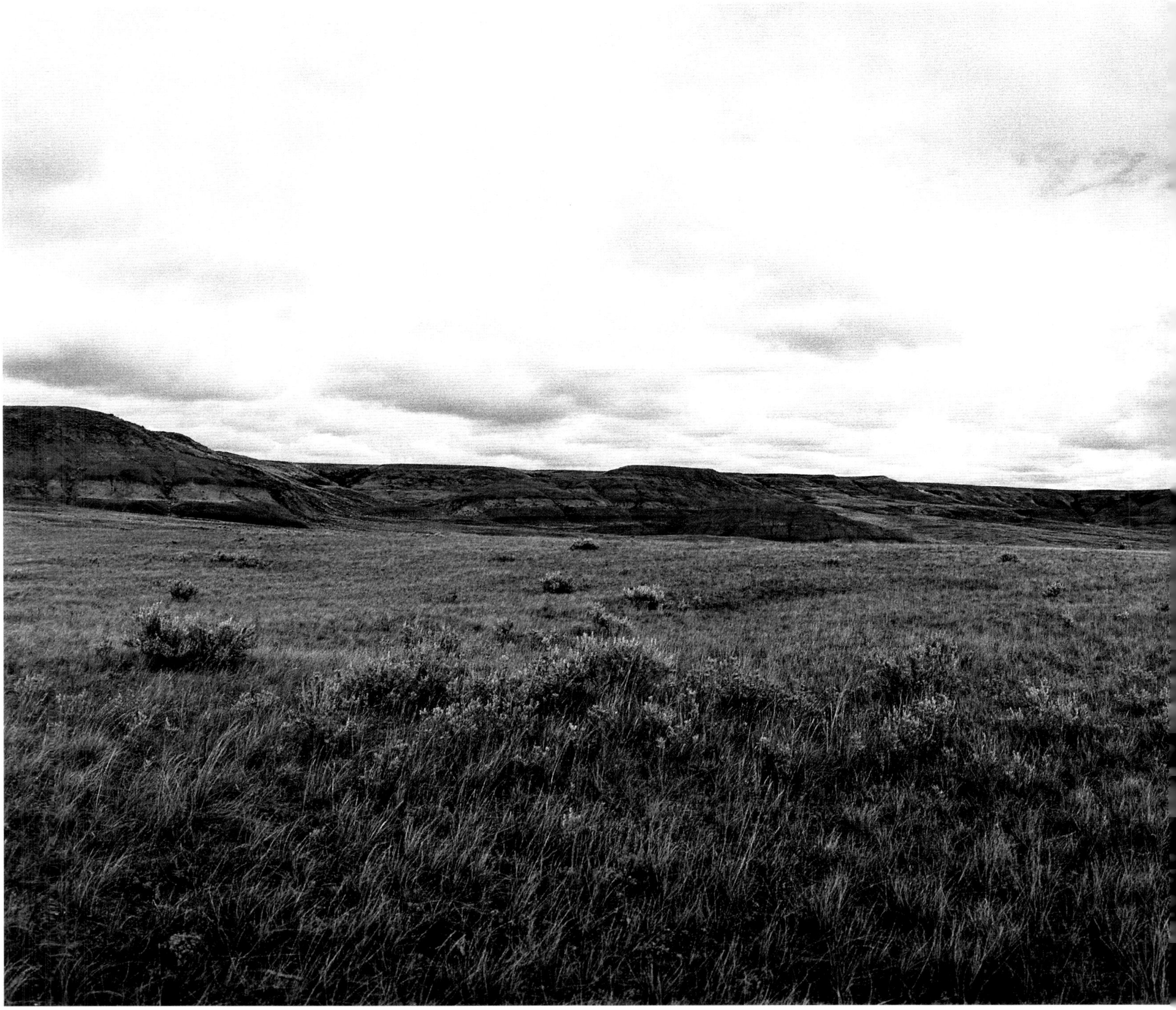

F. Leslie Thompson

Untitled 1 (from the series "Erase Me")

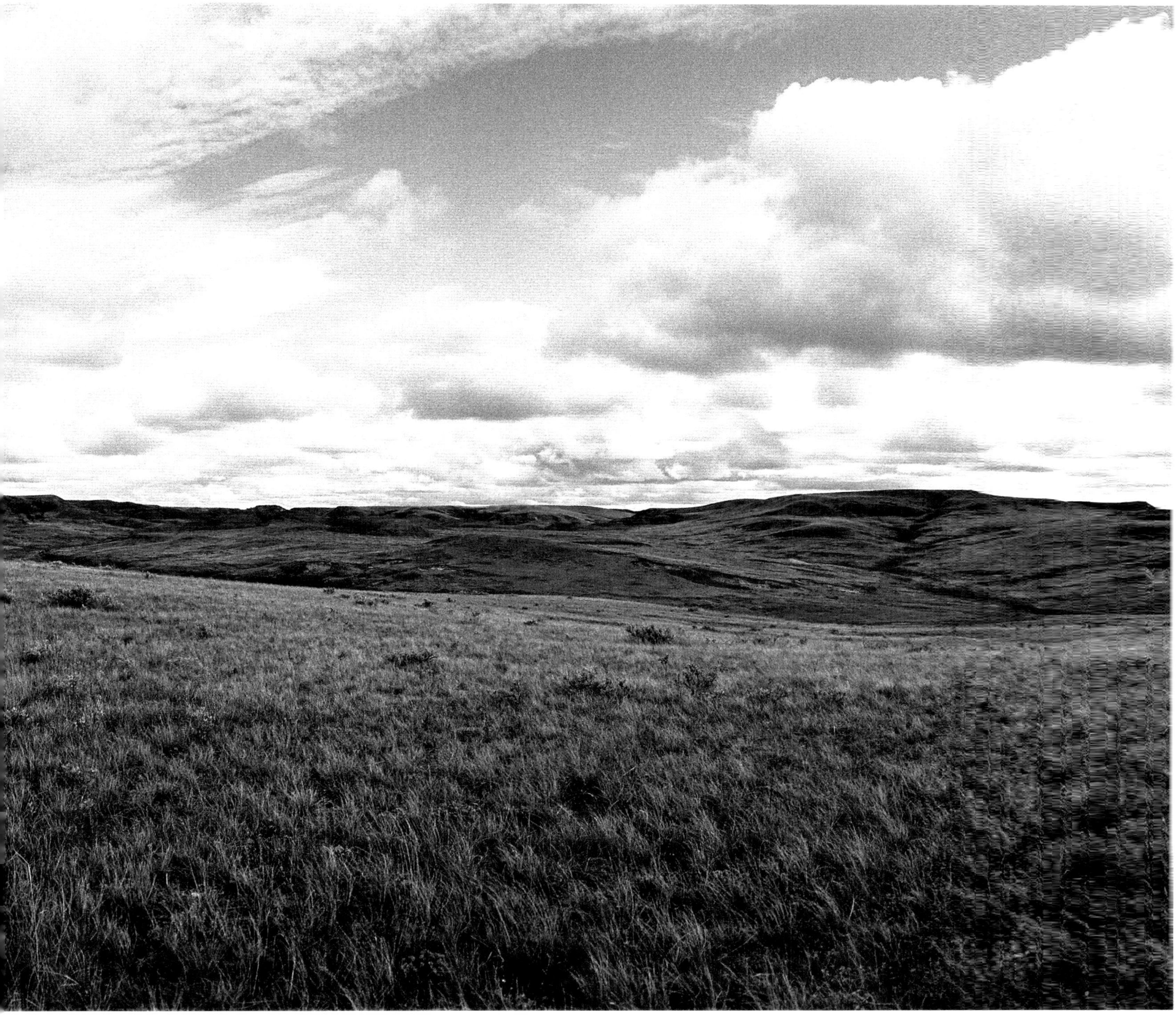

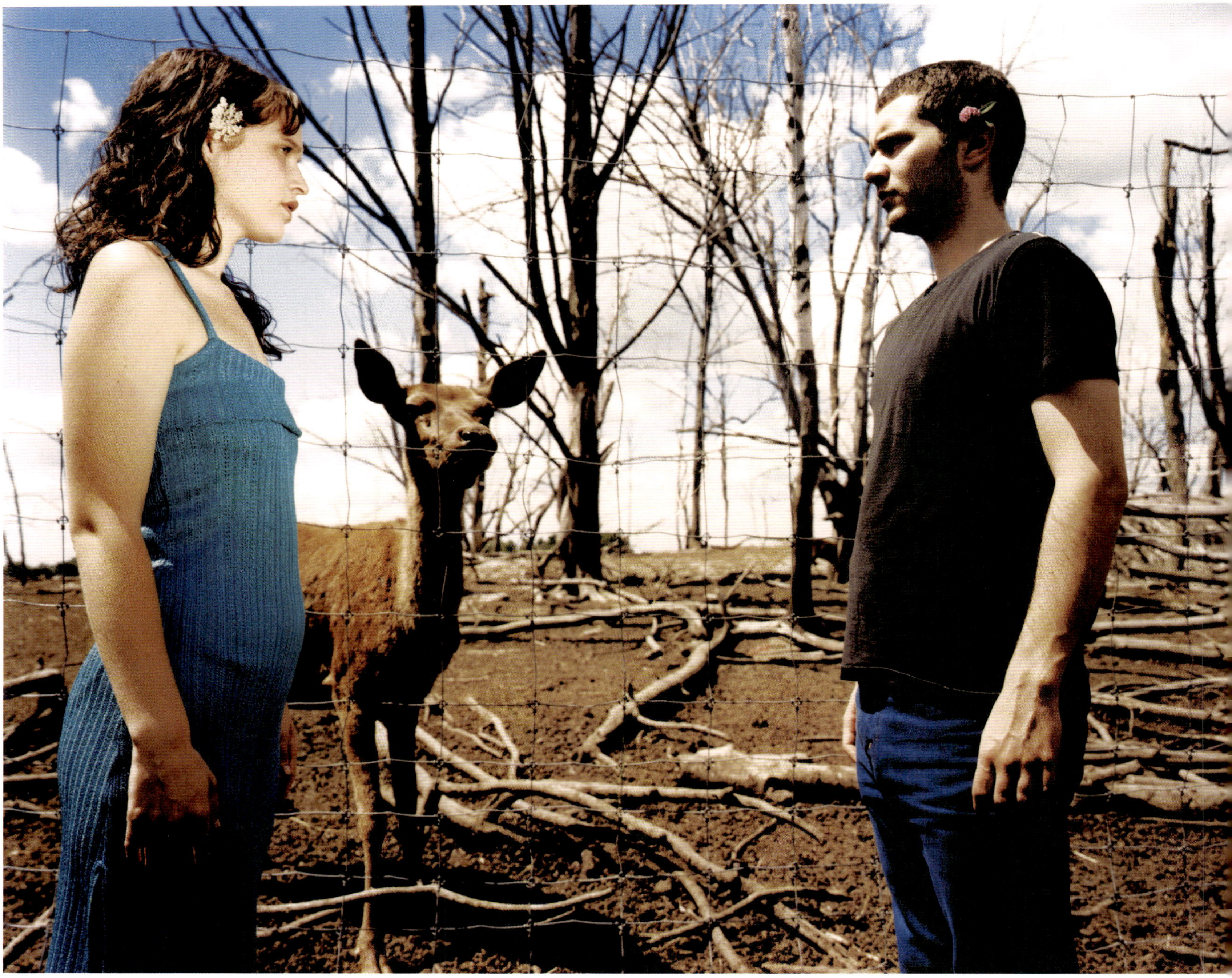

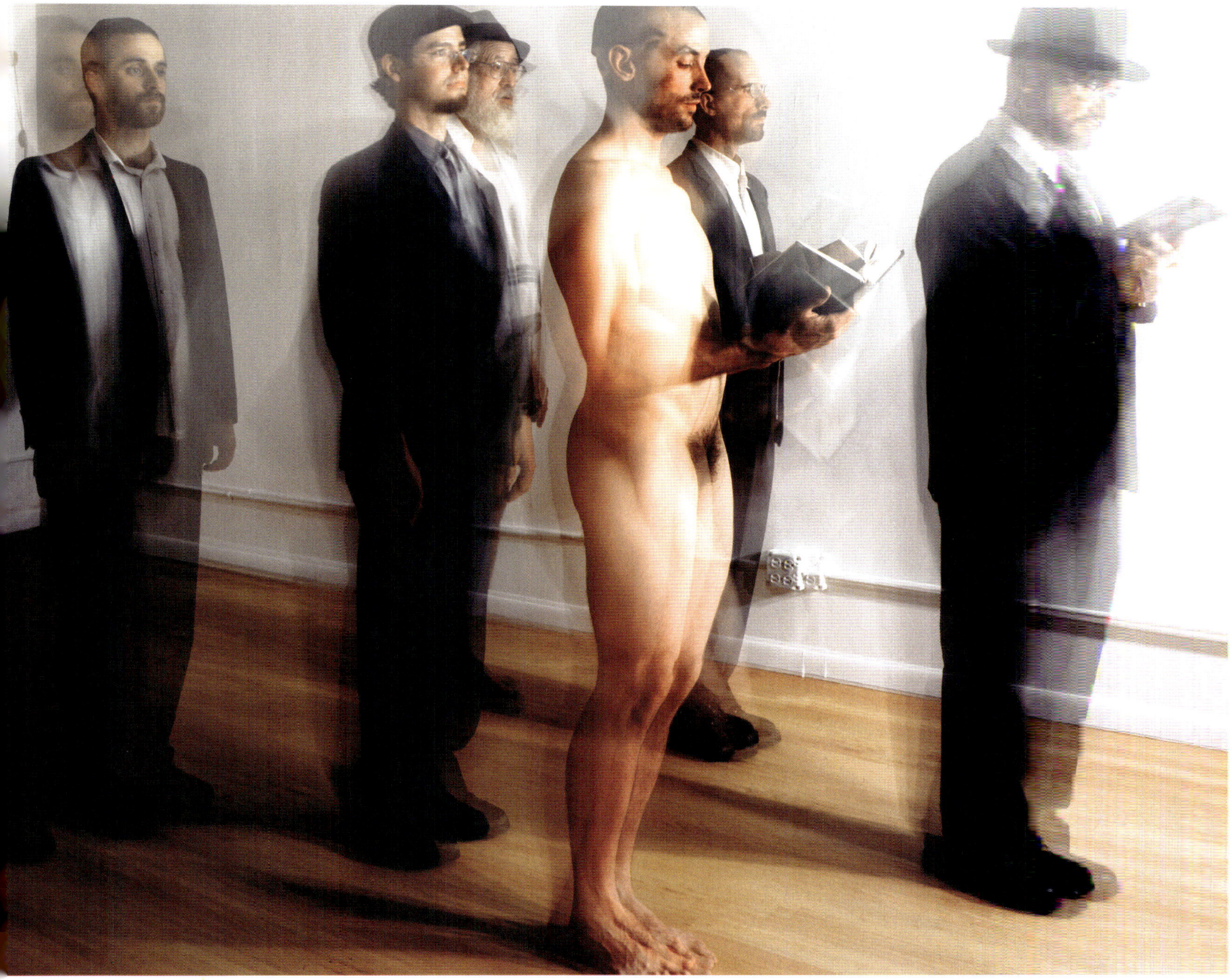

Amidah

Tobaron Waxman

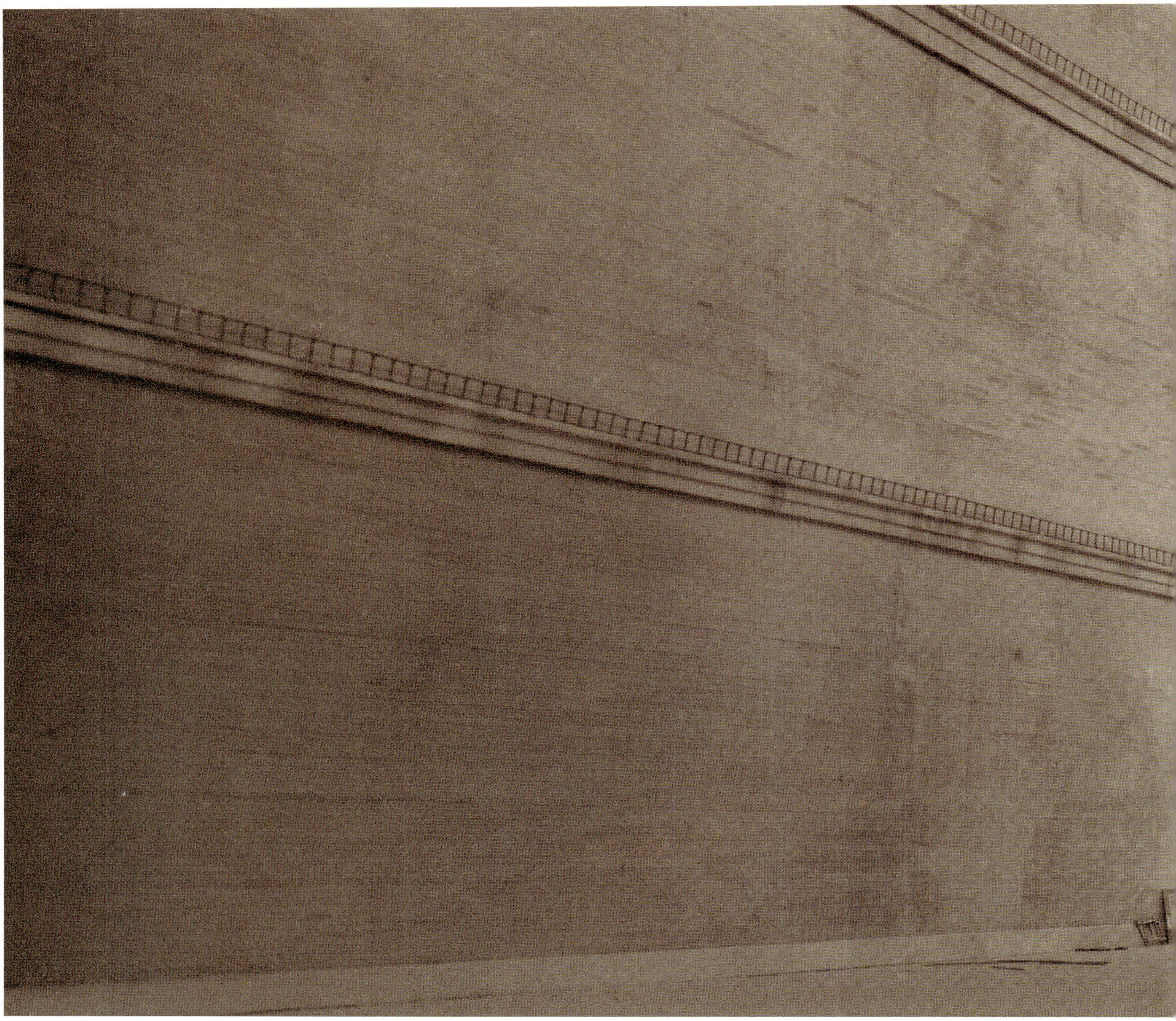

Carl Zimmerman

Mausoleum (Birmingham, England)

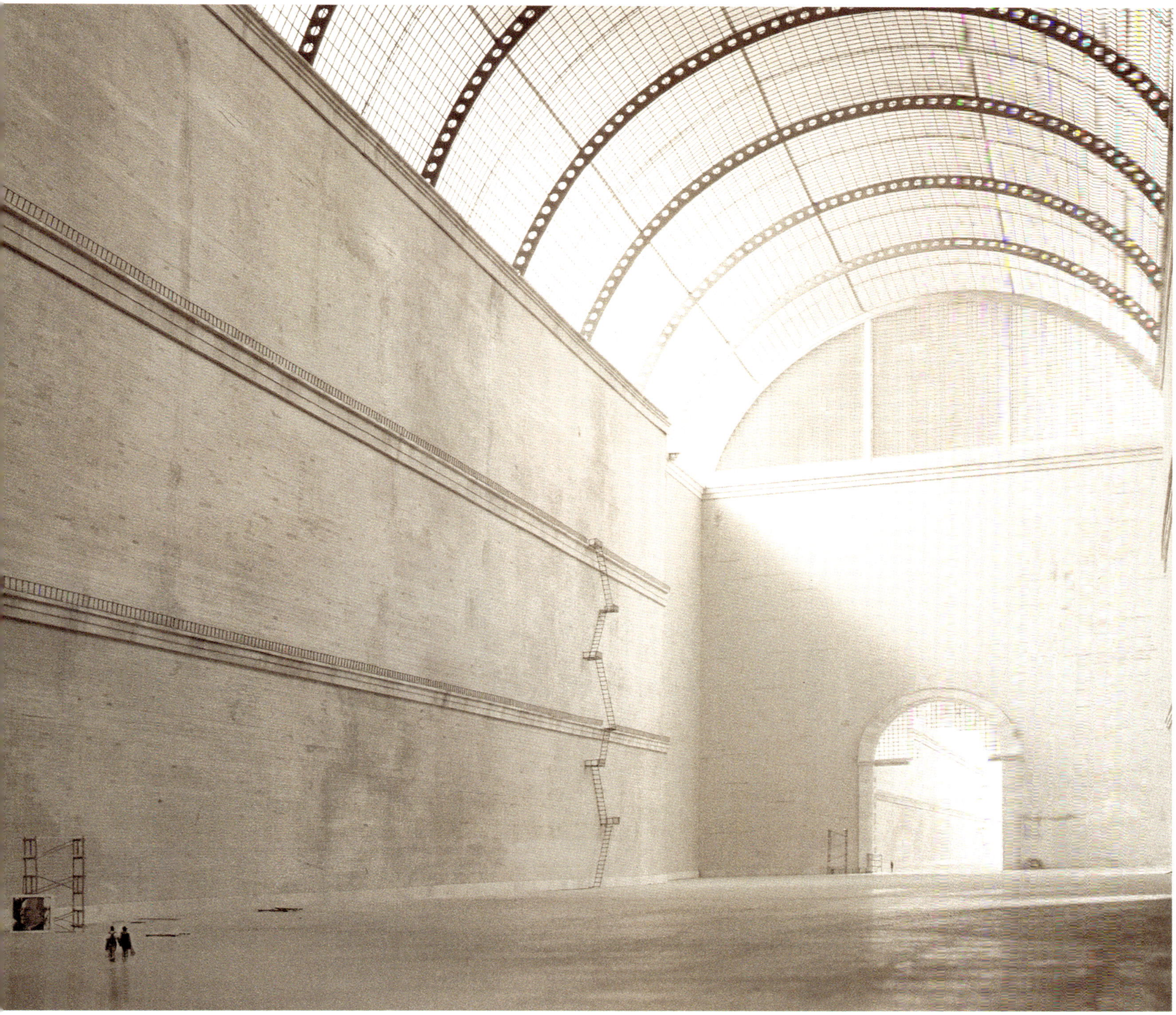

DOCUMEN
PHOTOJO

Patrick Alleyn, Benoit Aquin, Tobi Asmoucha, Brian Atkinson, David Barbour, Phil Bergerson, Normand Blouin, Olivier Boëls, Elaine Brière, Adrian Brown, David Campion, William Ciccocioppo, John Cullen, William DeKay, J. Kevin Dunn, Ethan Eisenberg, Pamela Gawn, Greg Girard, Patti Gower, Christopher Grabowski, Patrice Halley, Naomi Harris, Brian Howell, Ruth Kaplan, Raina Kirn, Todd Korol, Wolf Kutnahorsky, Rita Leistner, Roger Lemoyne, Fred Lum, Ian MacEachern, Bryan McBurney, Fernando Morales, Christinne Muschi, Sandy Nicholson, Farah Nosh, Lucas Oleniuk, Louie Palu, Vincenzo Pietropaolo, Peter Power, Duane Prentice, Pedro Ruiz, Steve Russell, Andrea Ryder, Robert Semeniuk, Peter Sibbald, David Leonard Sidaway, Steve Simon, Lana Slezic, Lyle Stafford, Andrew Stawicki, Deddeda Stemler, Gabor Szilasi, Amanda Tetrault, David Trattles, Kevin Van Paassen, Christopher Wahl, George Webber, Donald Weber, Bernard Weil, George S. Zimbel

TARY +
JRNALISM

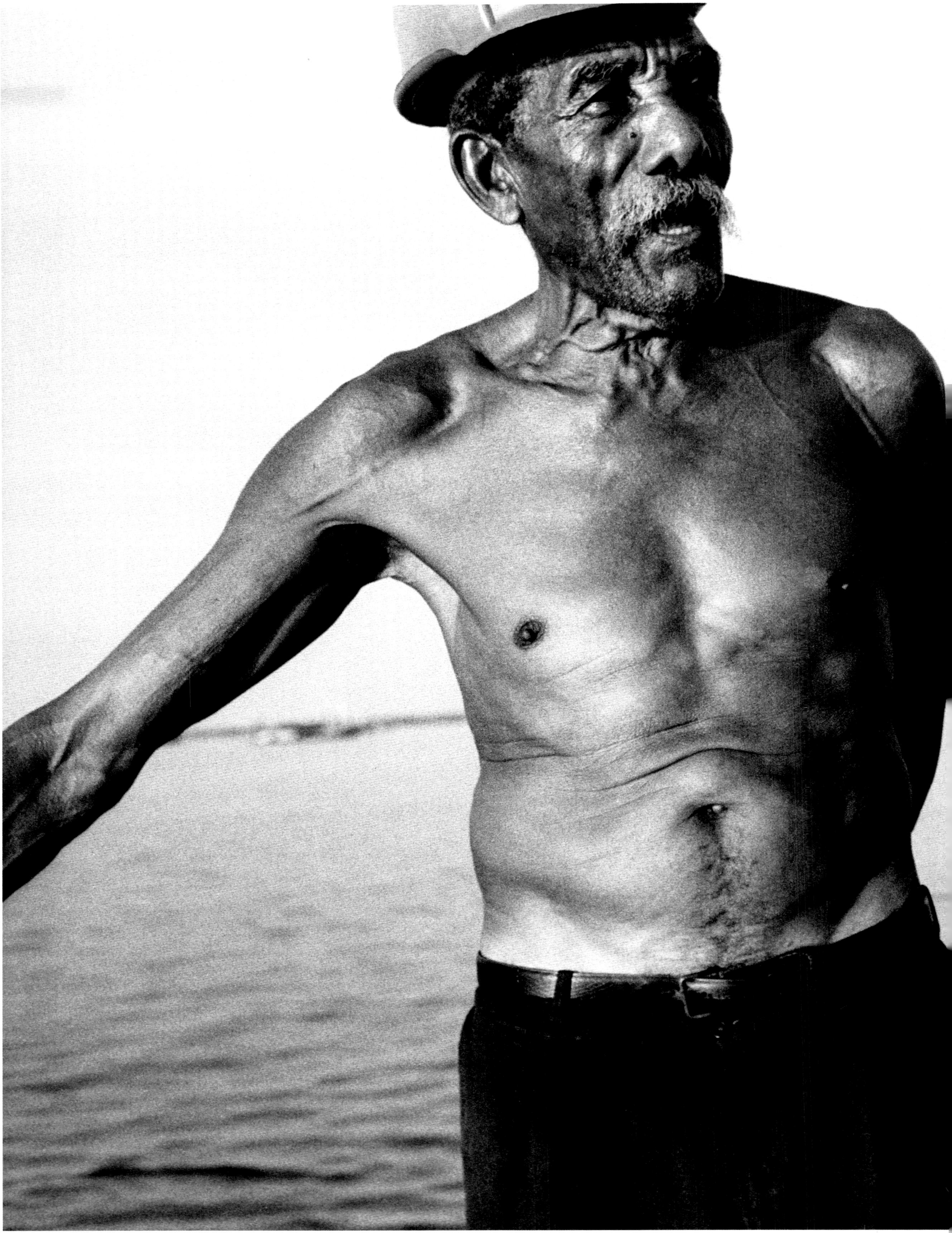

Patrick Alleyn

Puerto Esperanza, Cuba, 2003

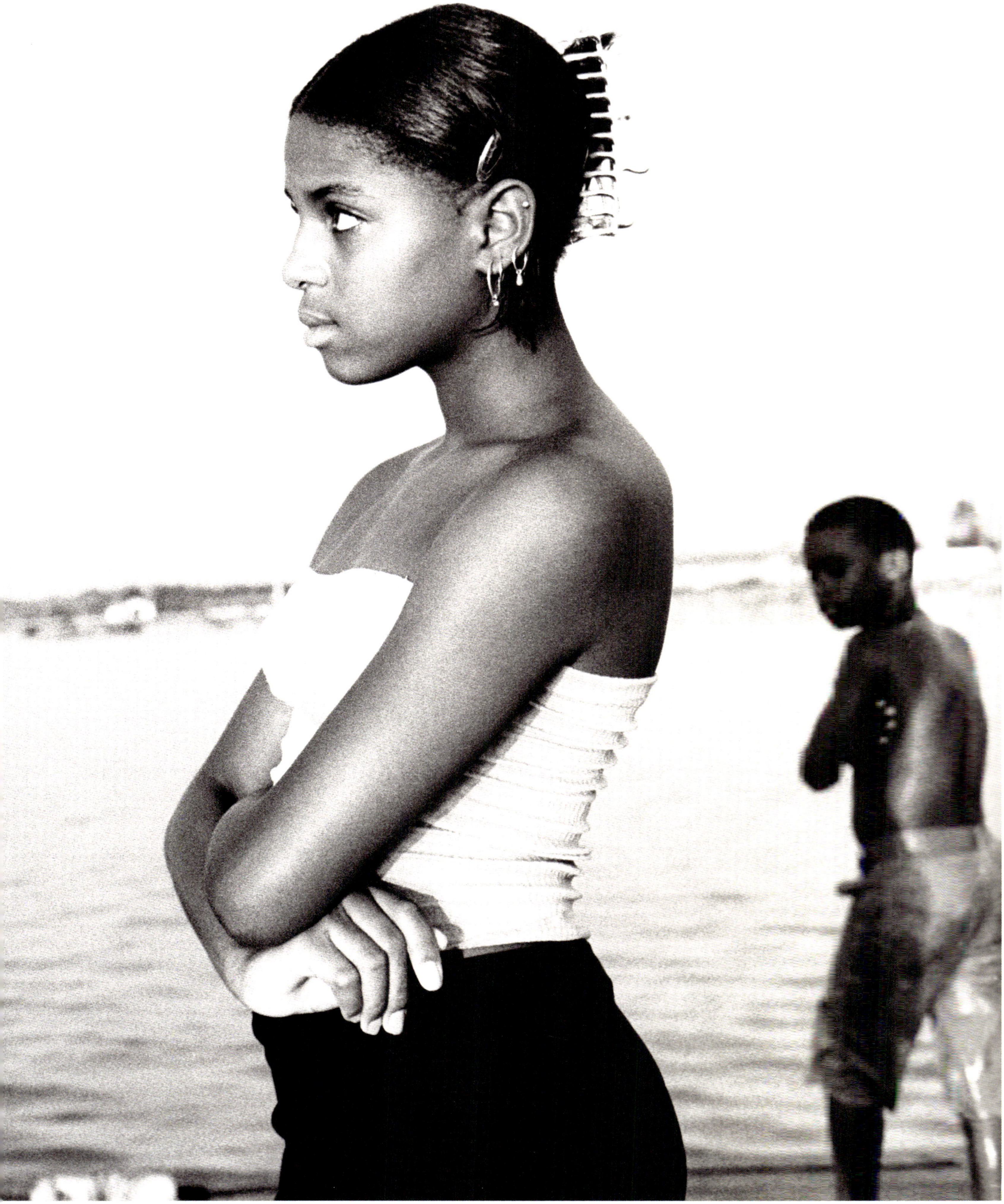

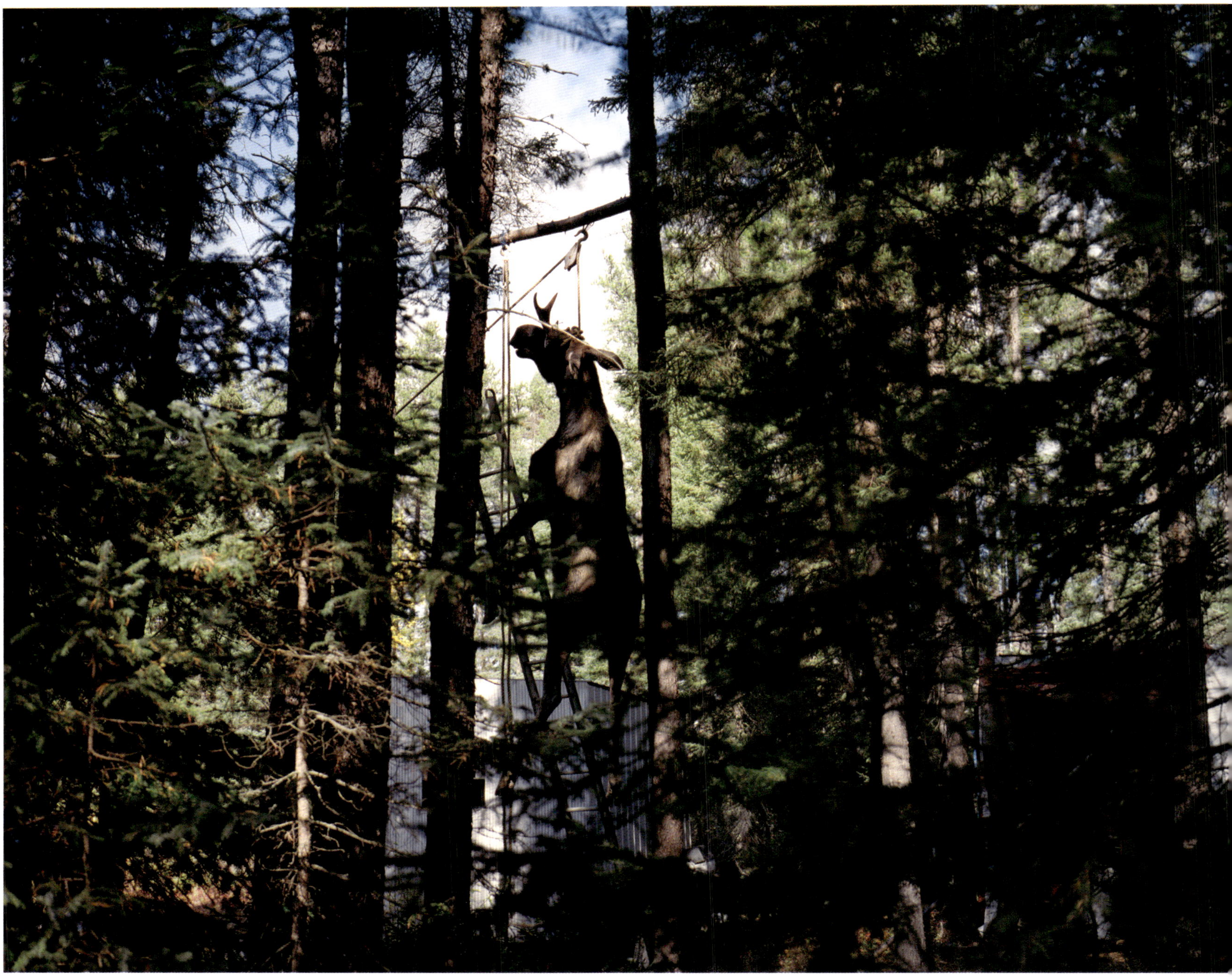

Moose Hunting

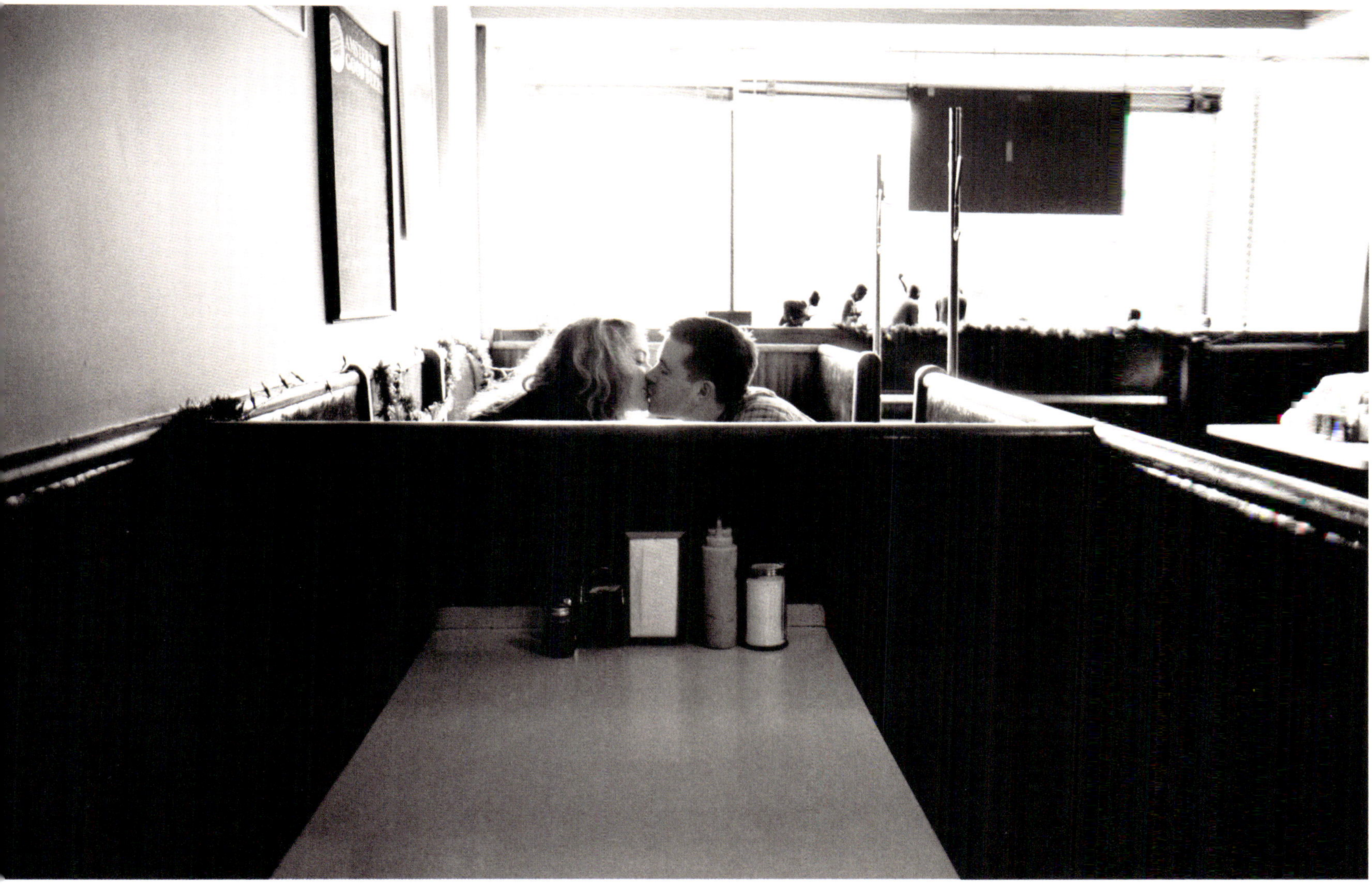

Lakeview Kiss

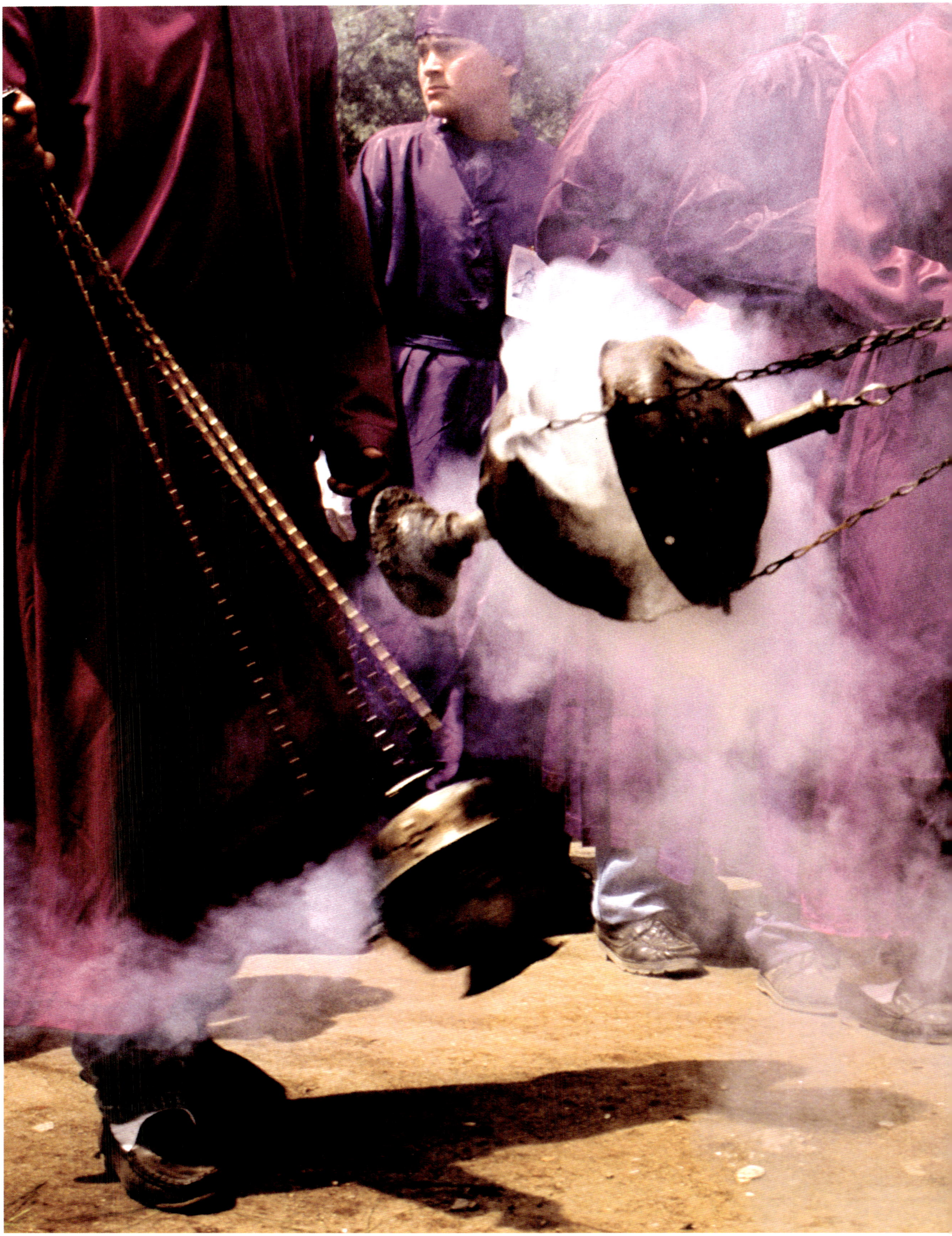

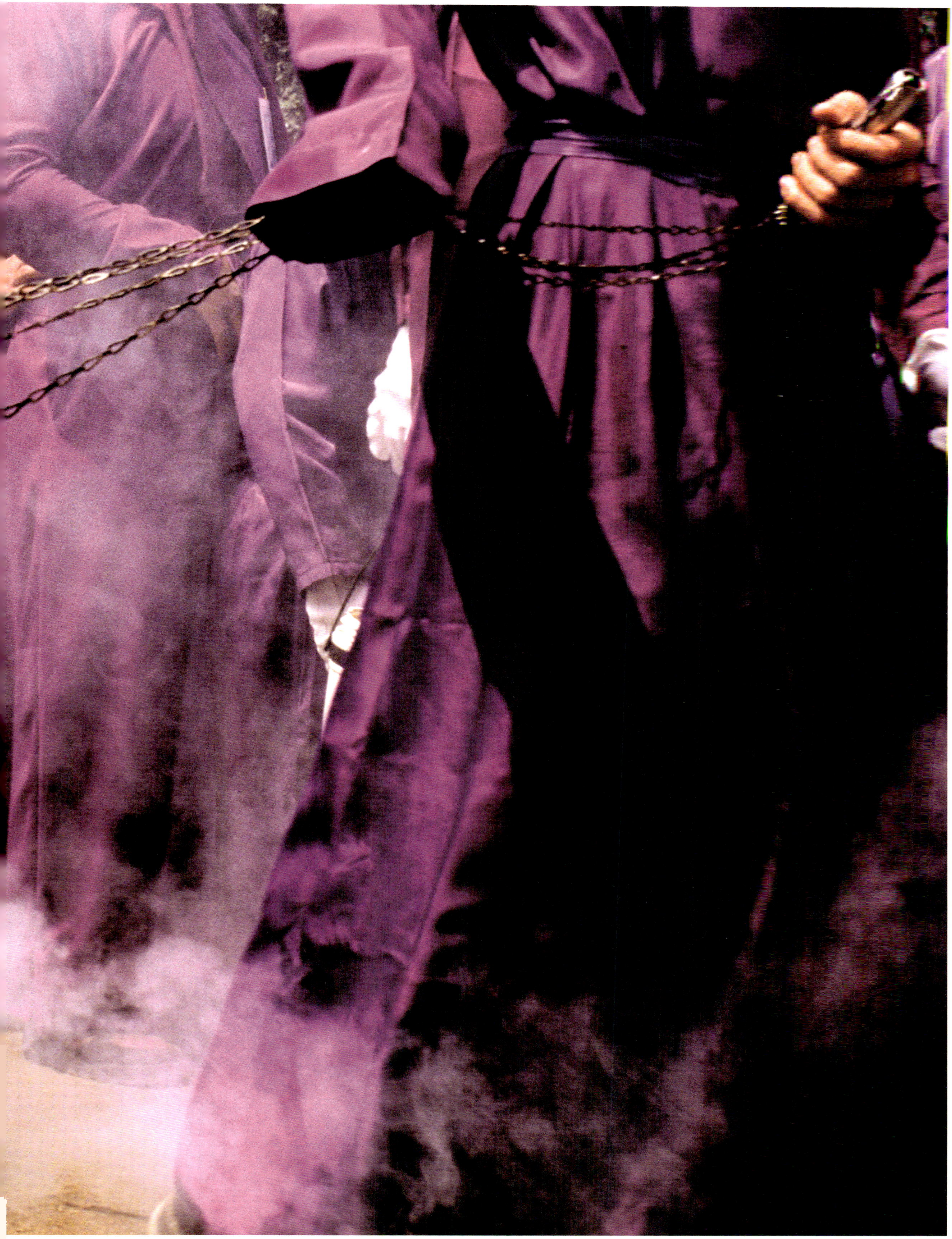

Brian Atkinson

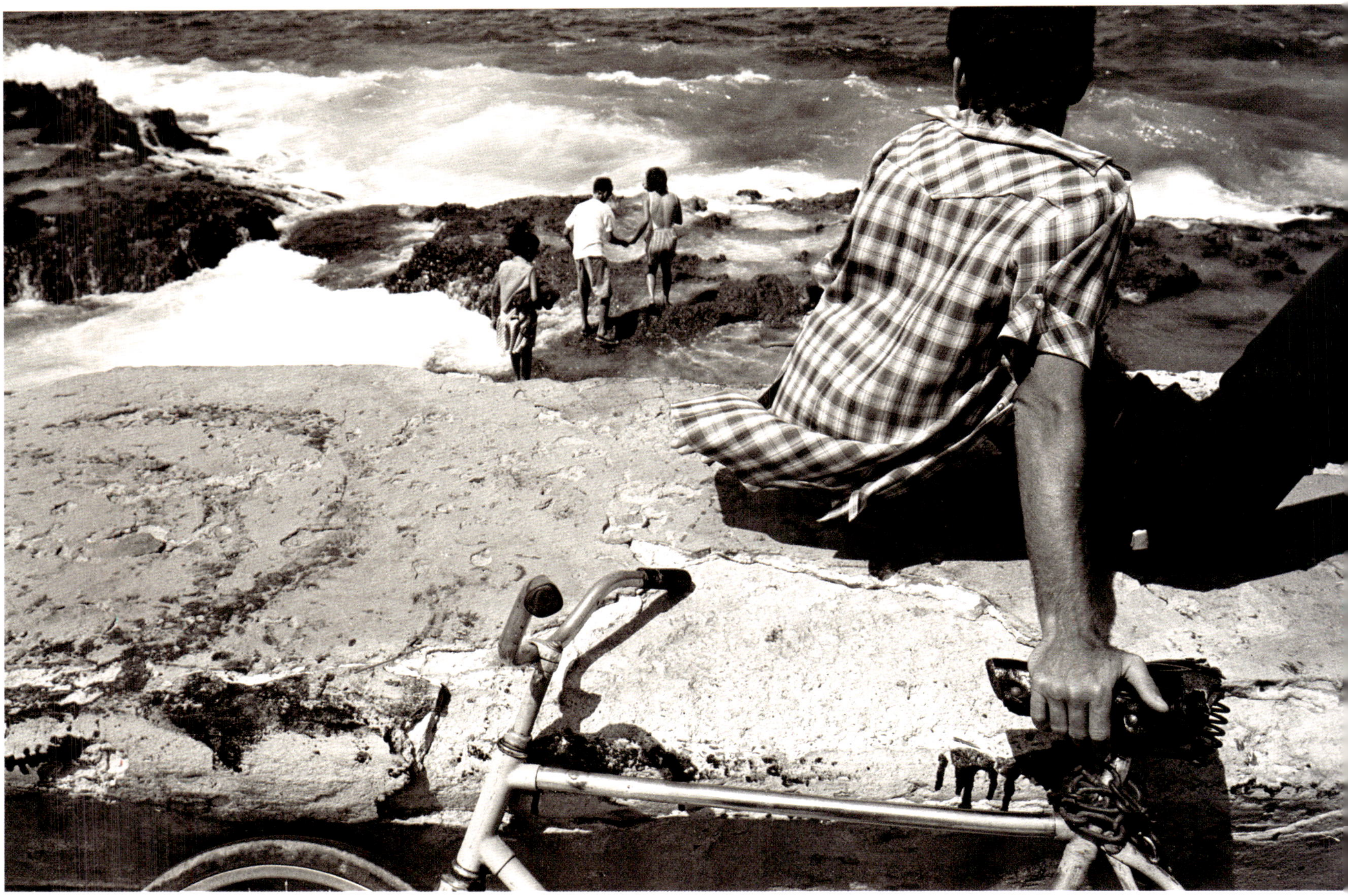

Havana

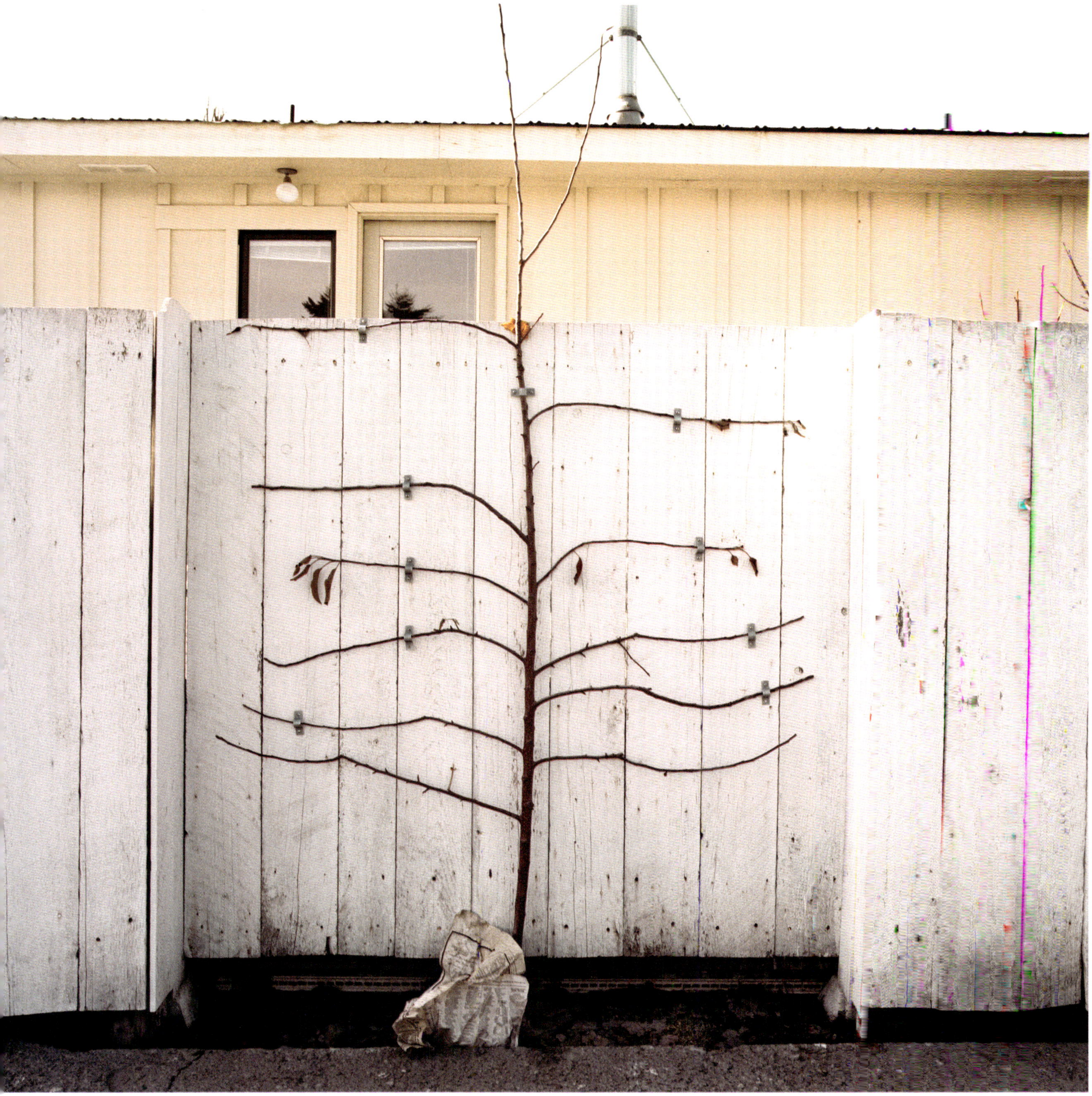

Untitled (Cle Elum, Washington, 1993)

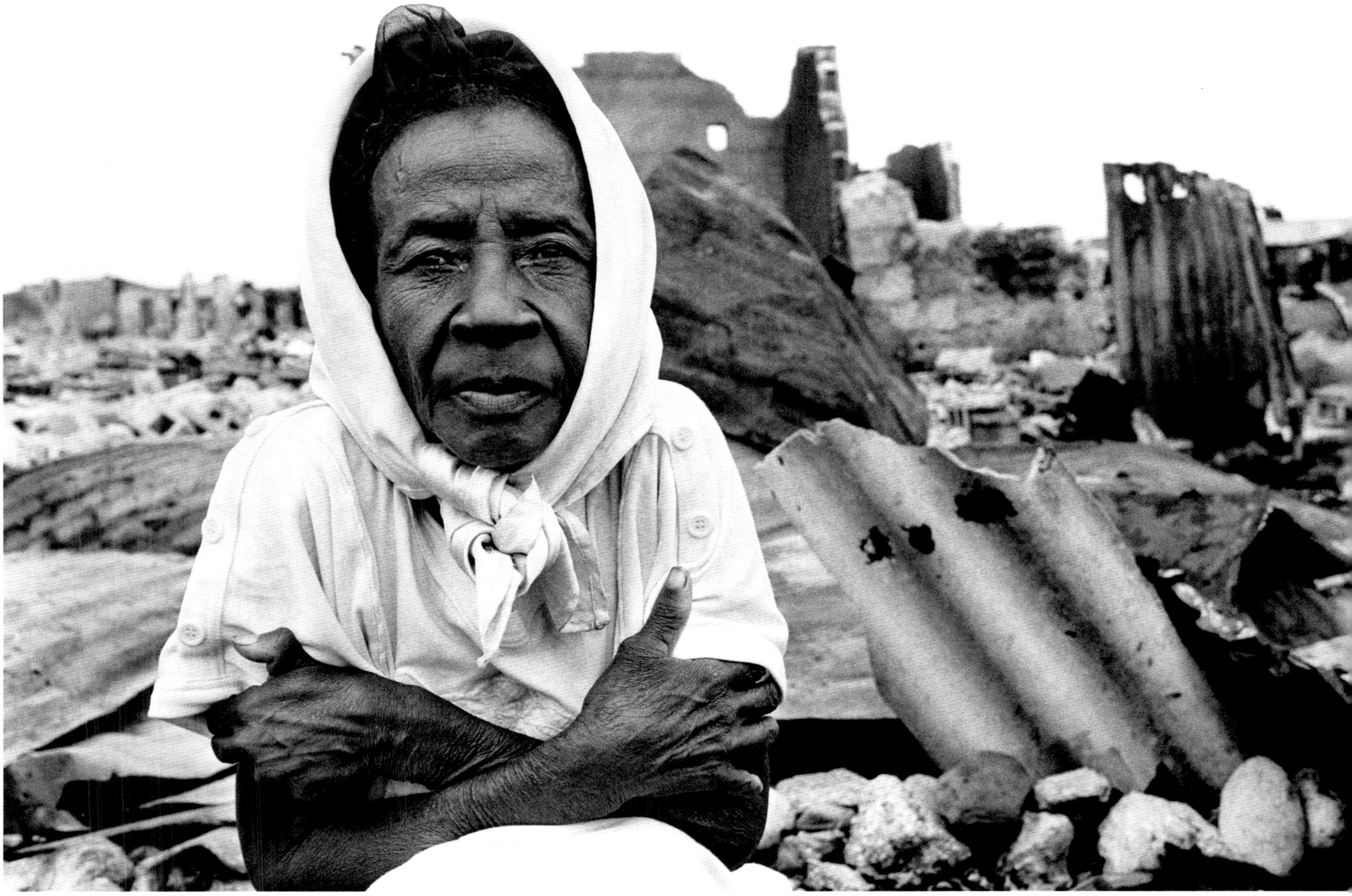

Normand Blouin

La dame en blanc

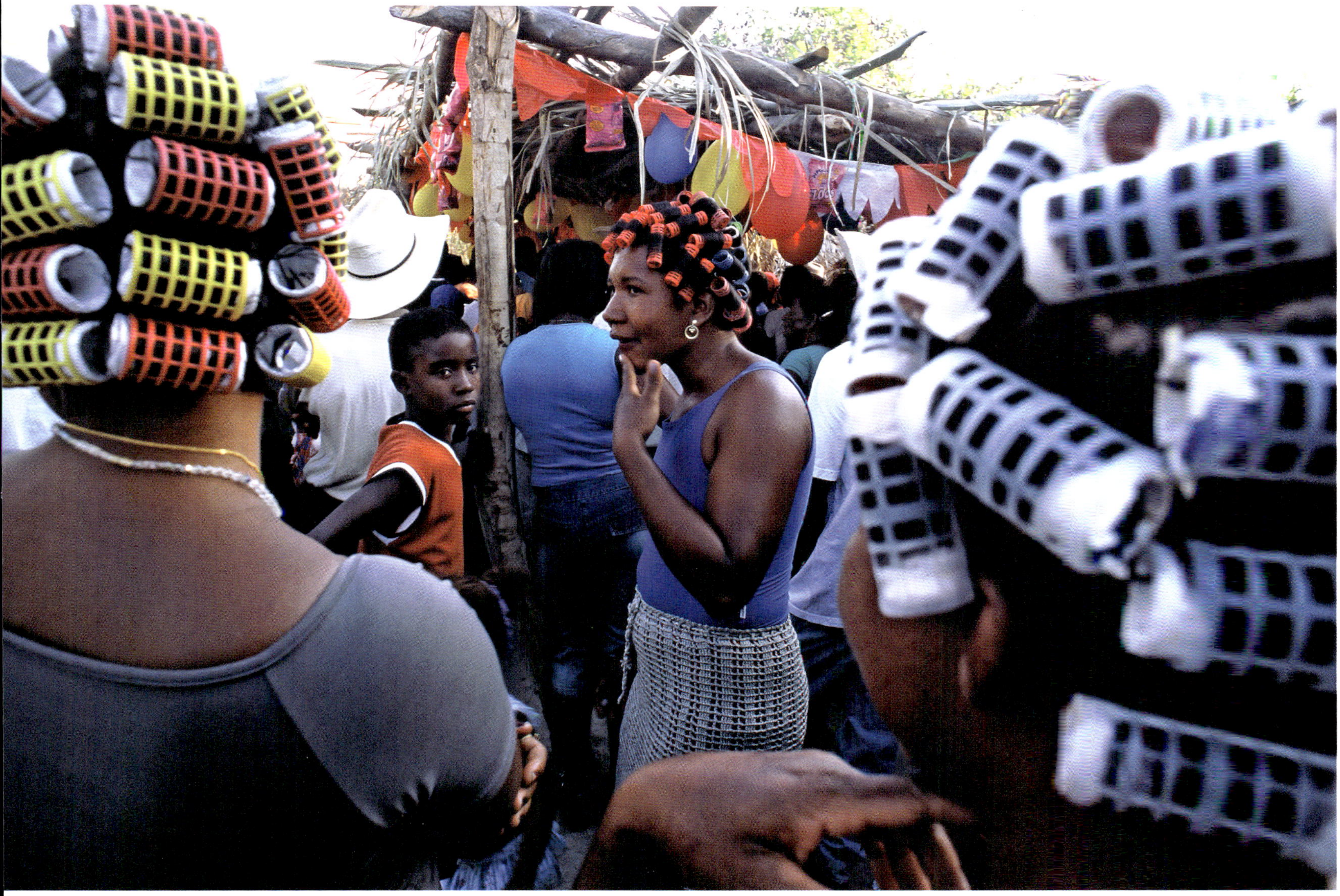

Kalunga Women Getting Ready for Nighttime Dances

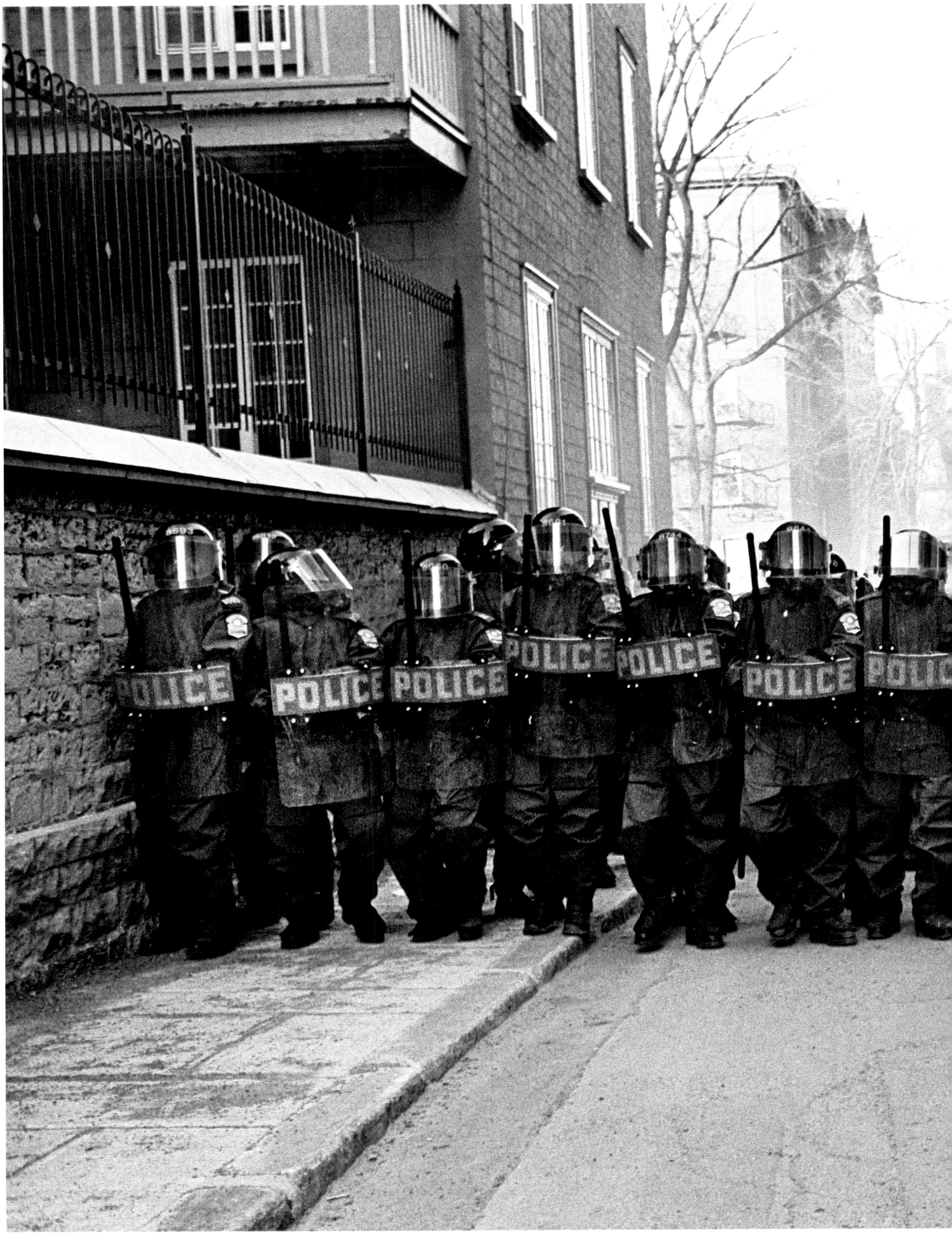

Elaine Brière

Summit of the Americas, Quebec, 2001

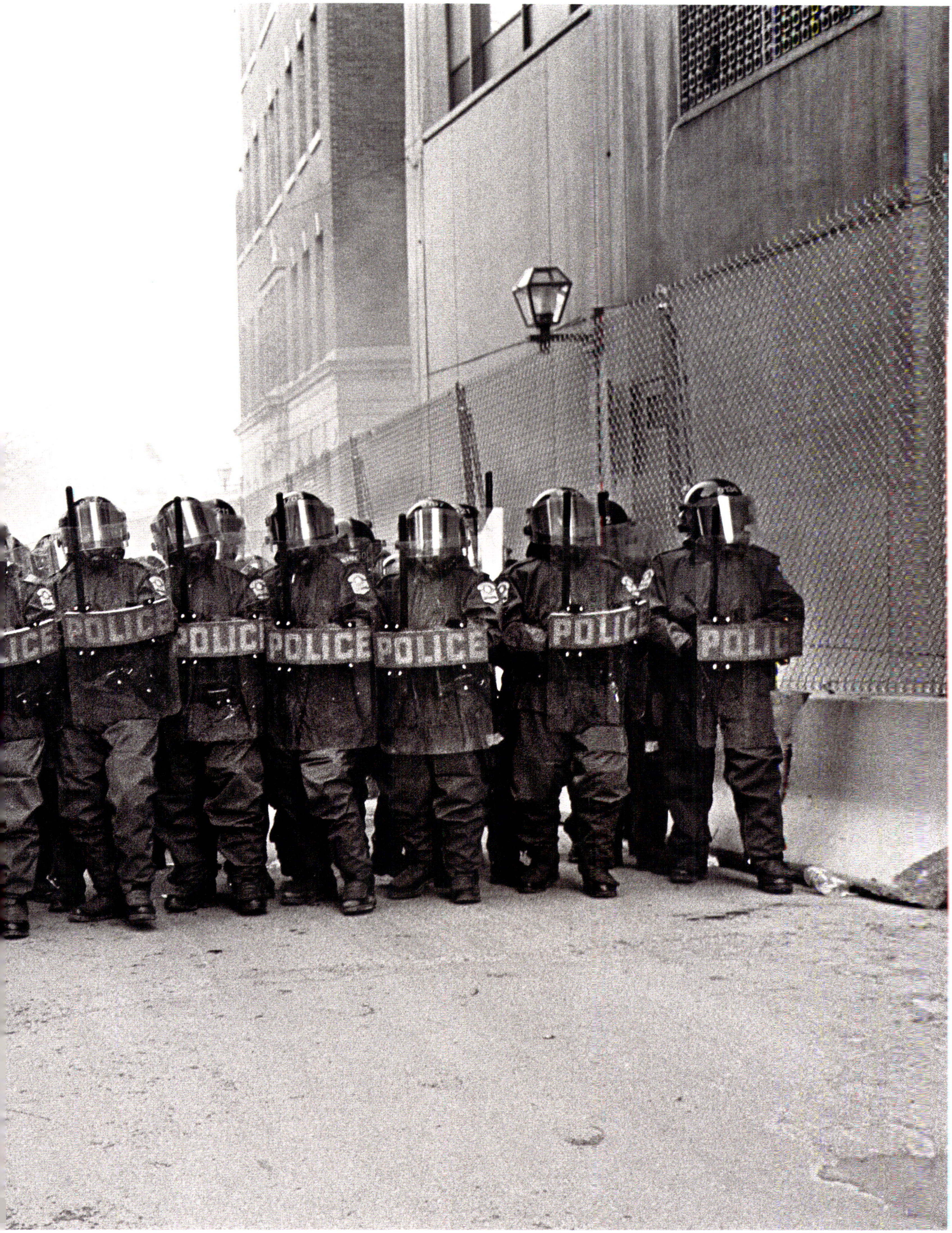
POLICE
POLICE

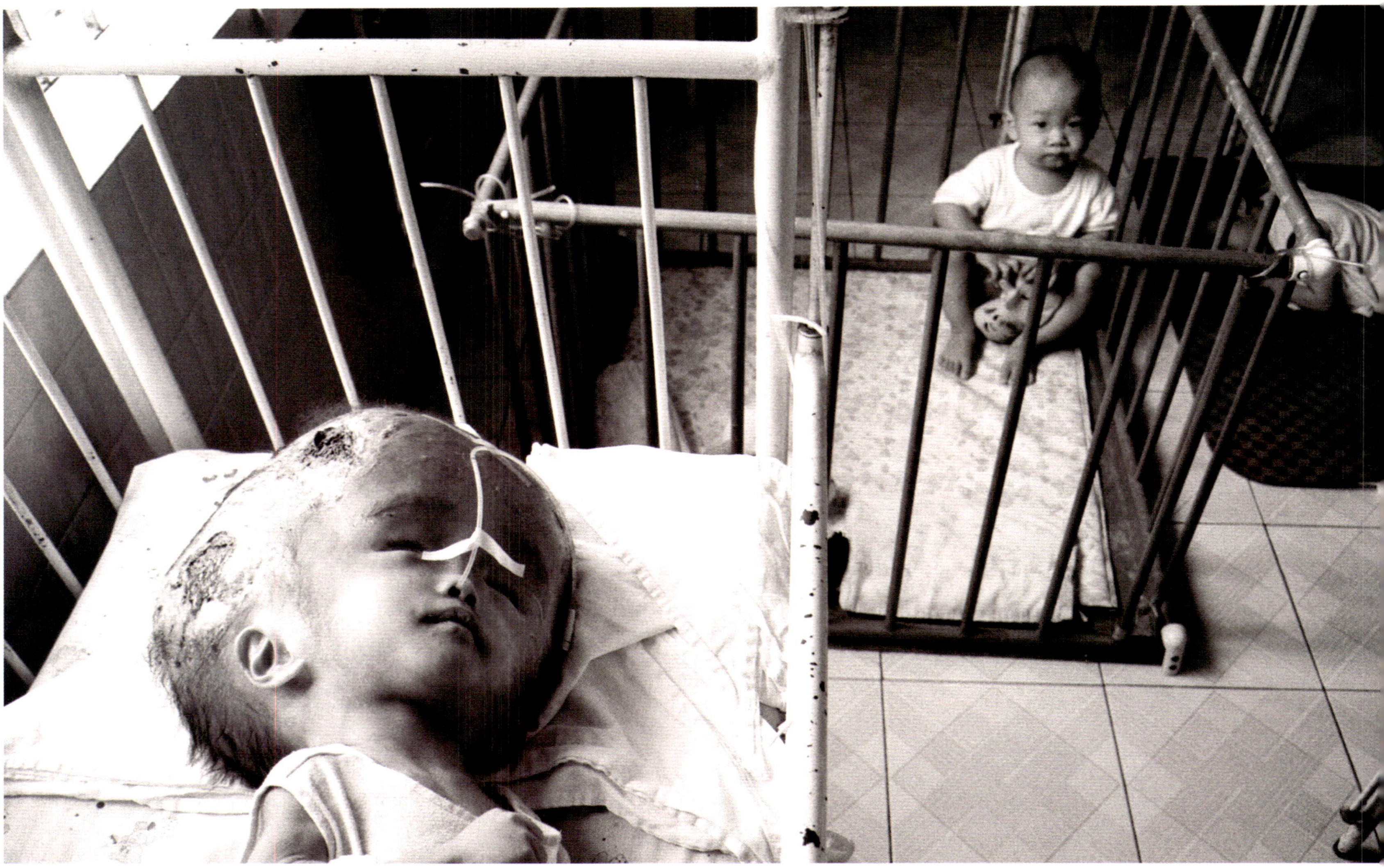

Tu Du Hospital, Ho Chi Minh City

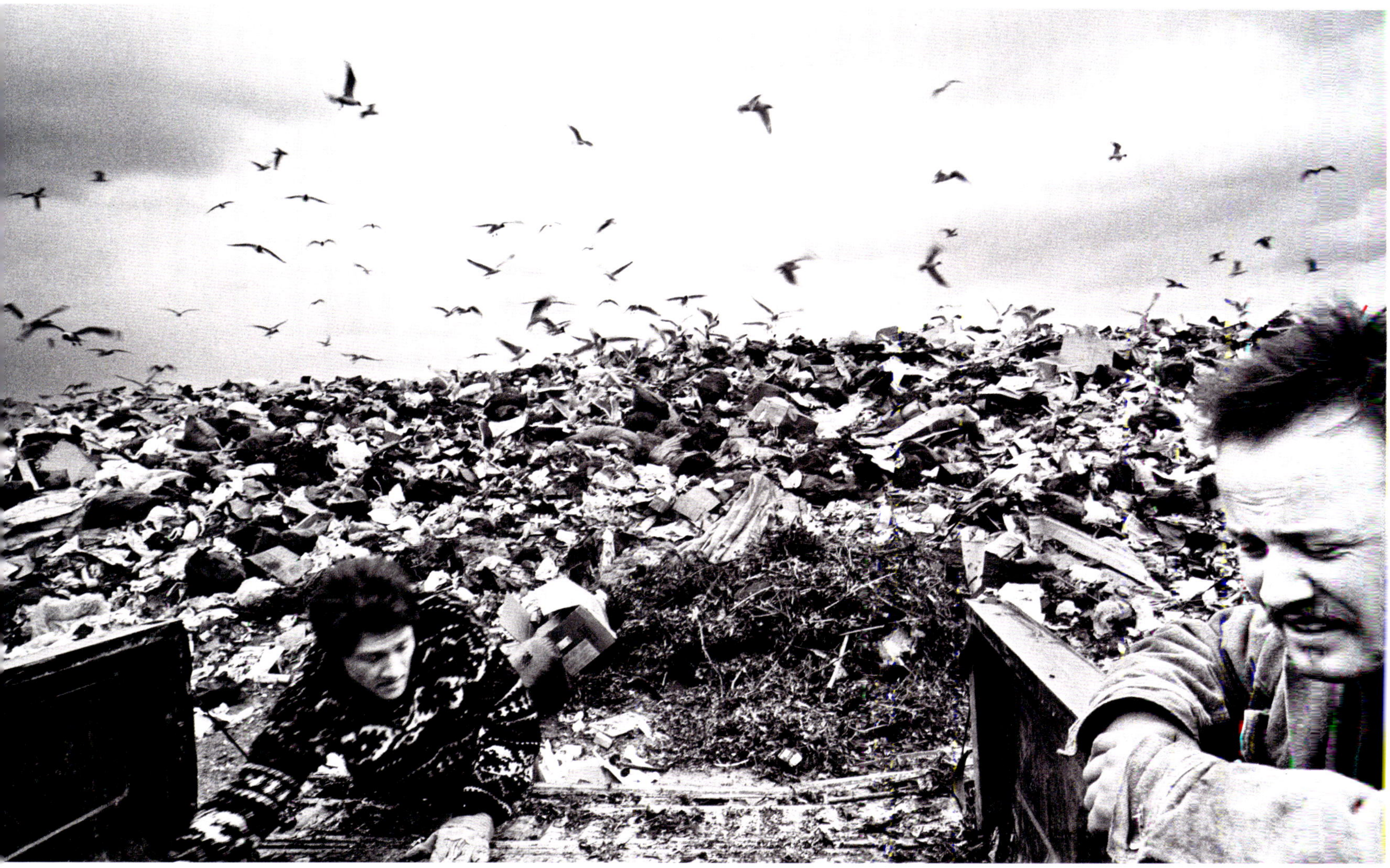

Calgary, 1997 (Garbage Site)

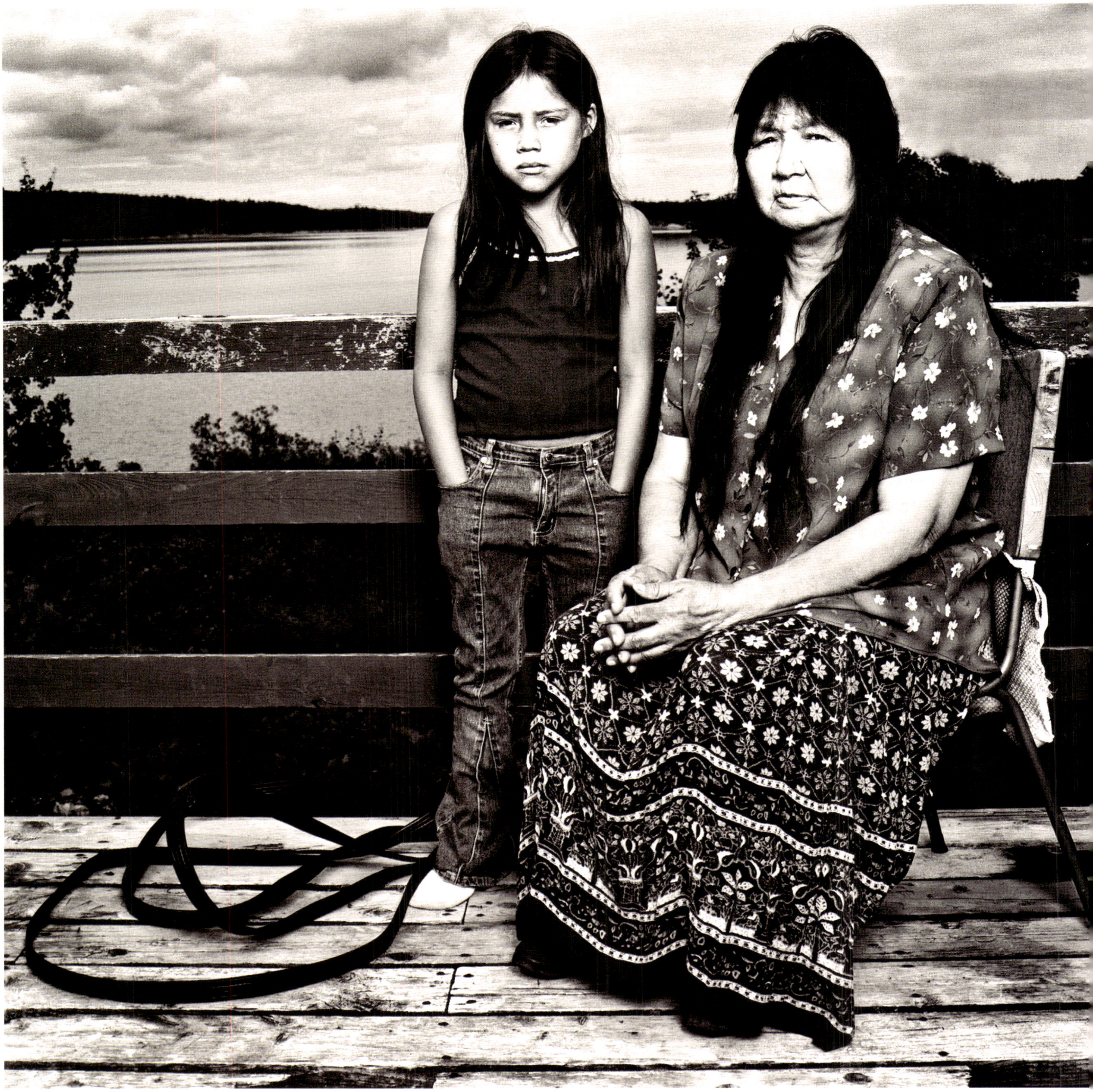

The Pahpasays

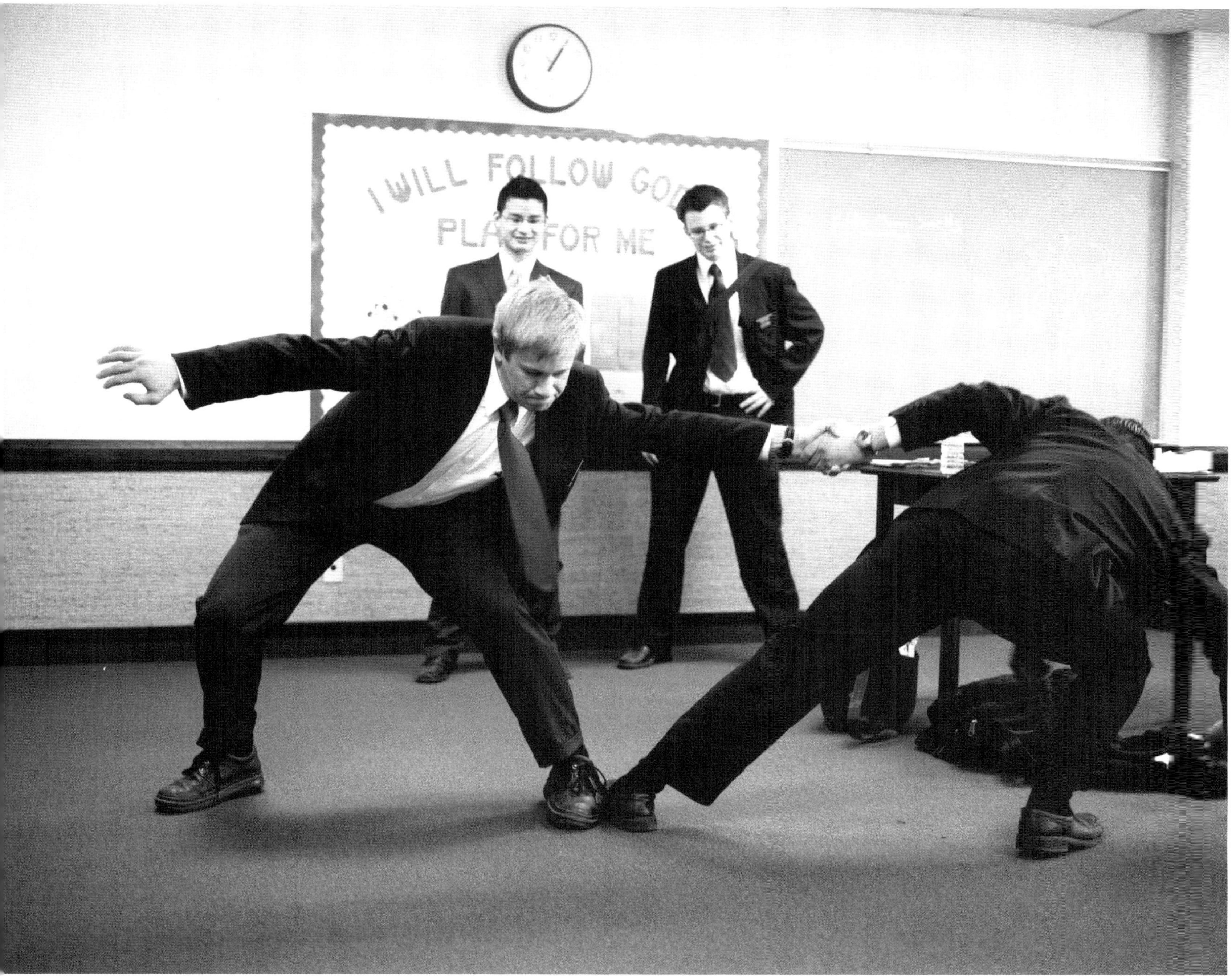
I WILL FOLLOW GOD
PLA FOR ME

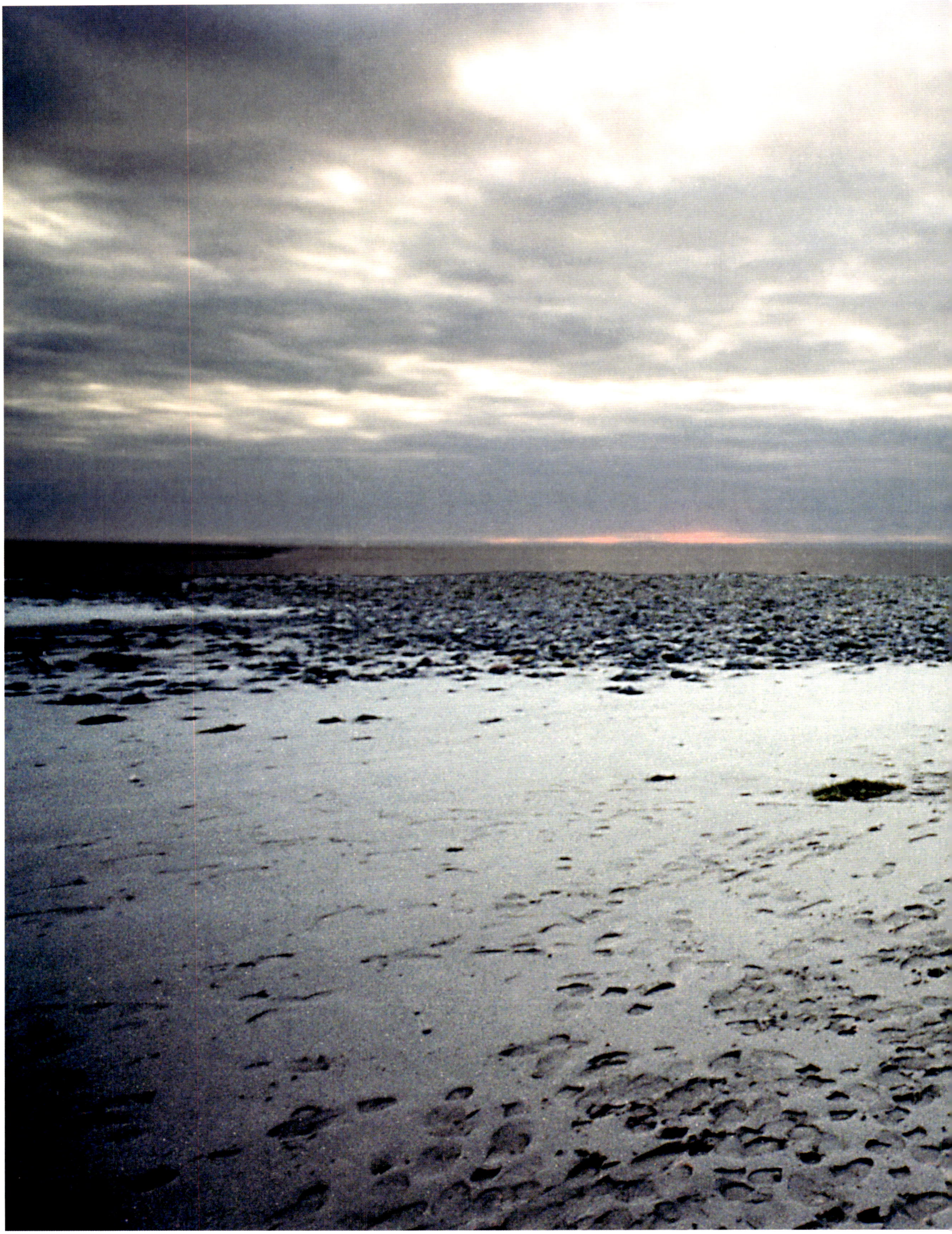

William DeKay

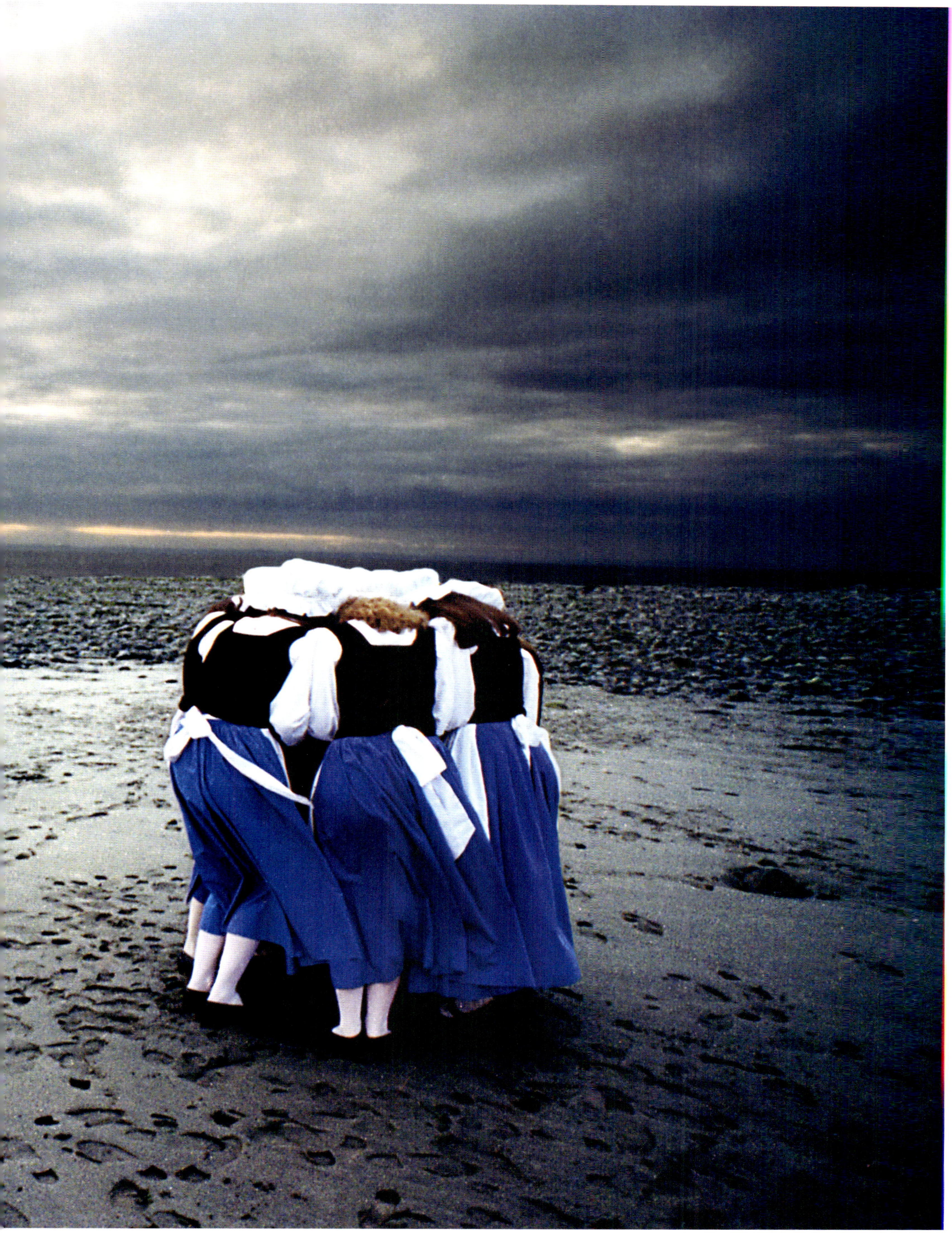

Acadian Dancers

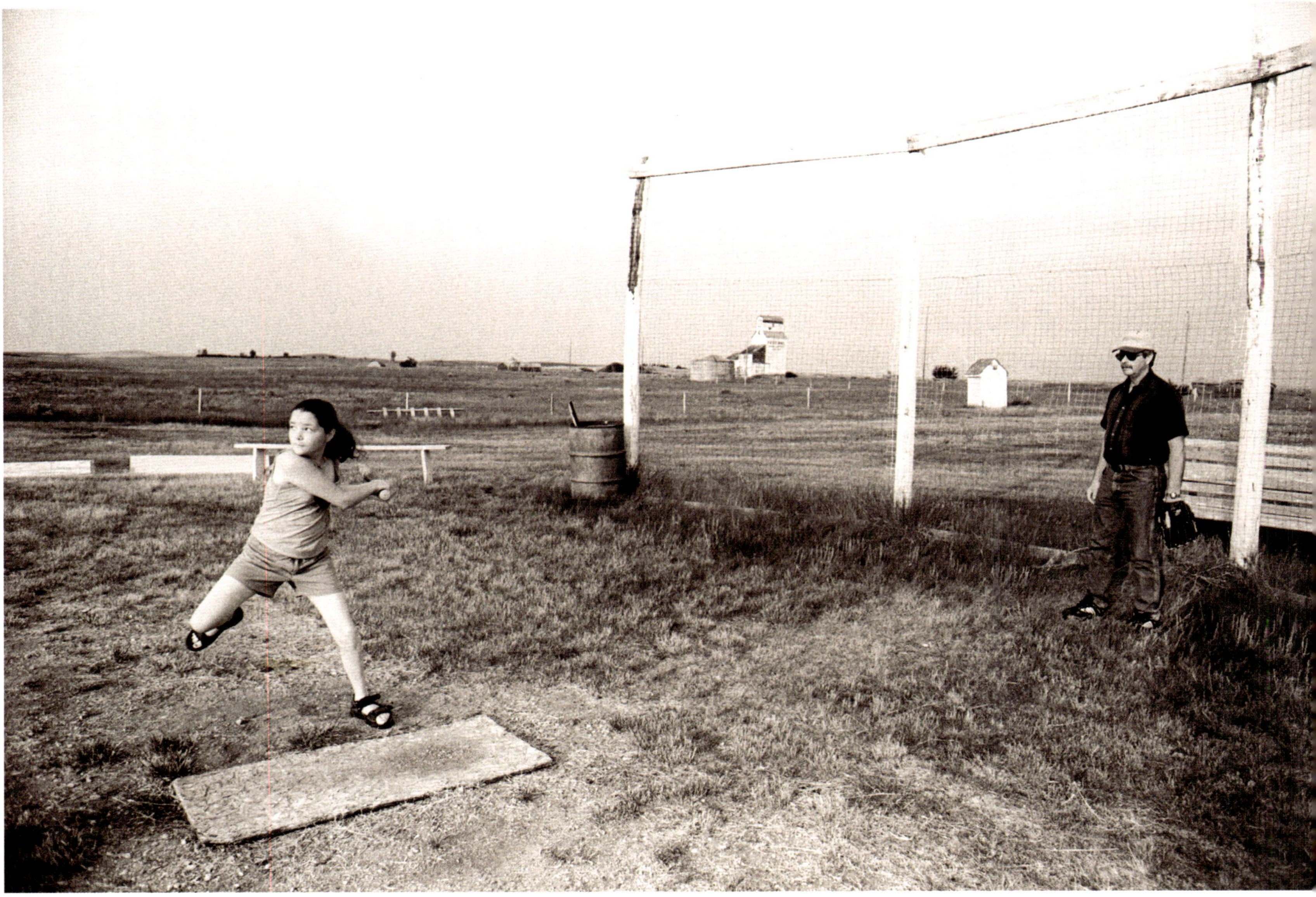

J. Kevin Dunn

Baseball Horizon

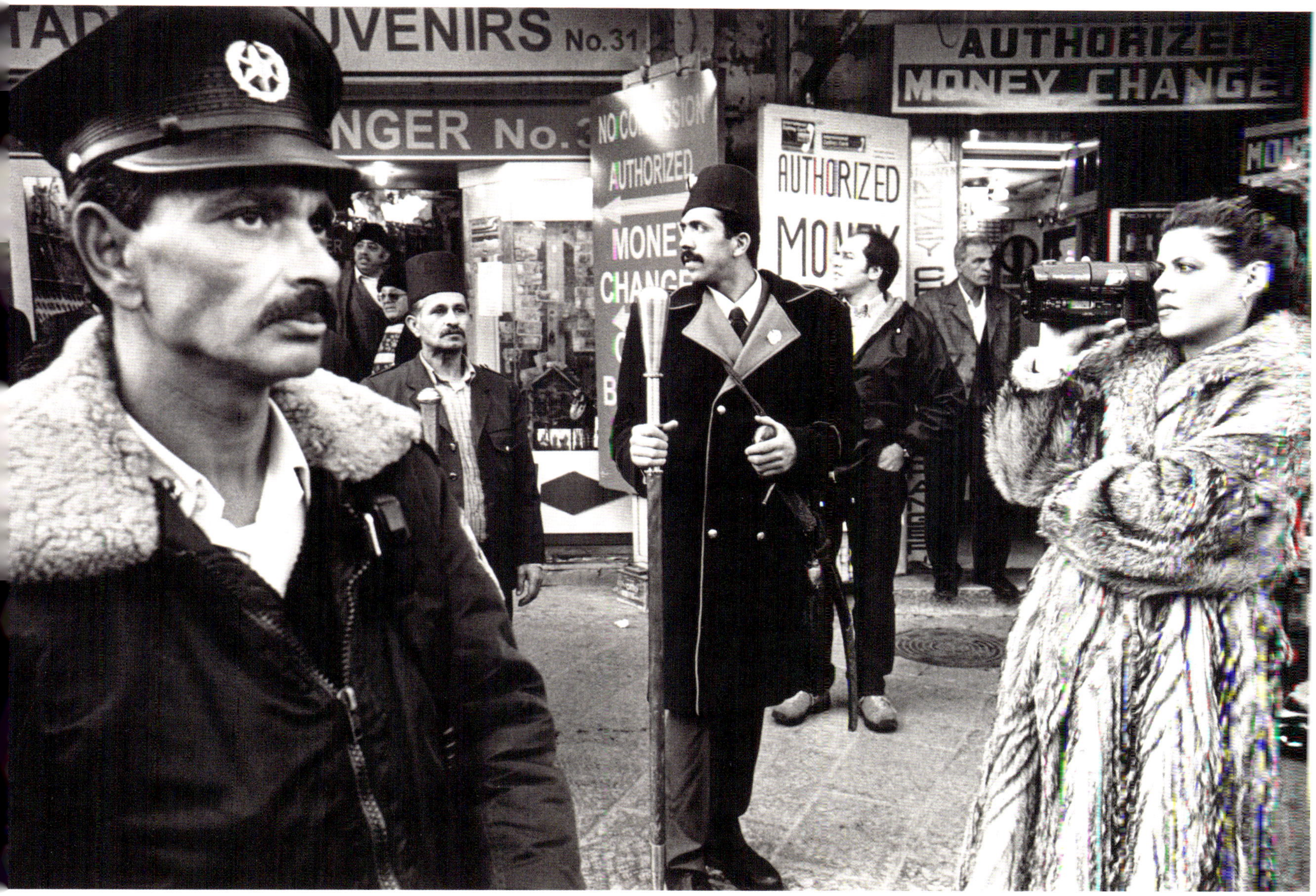

Jerusalem, 2000

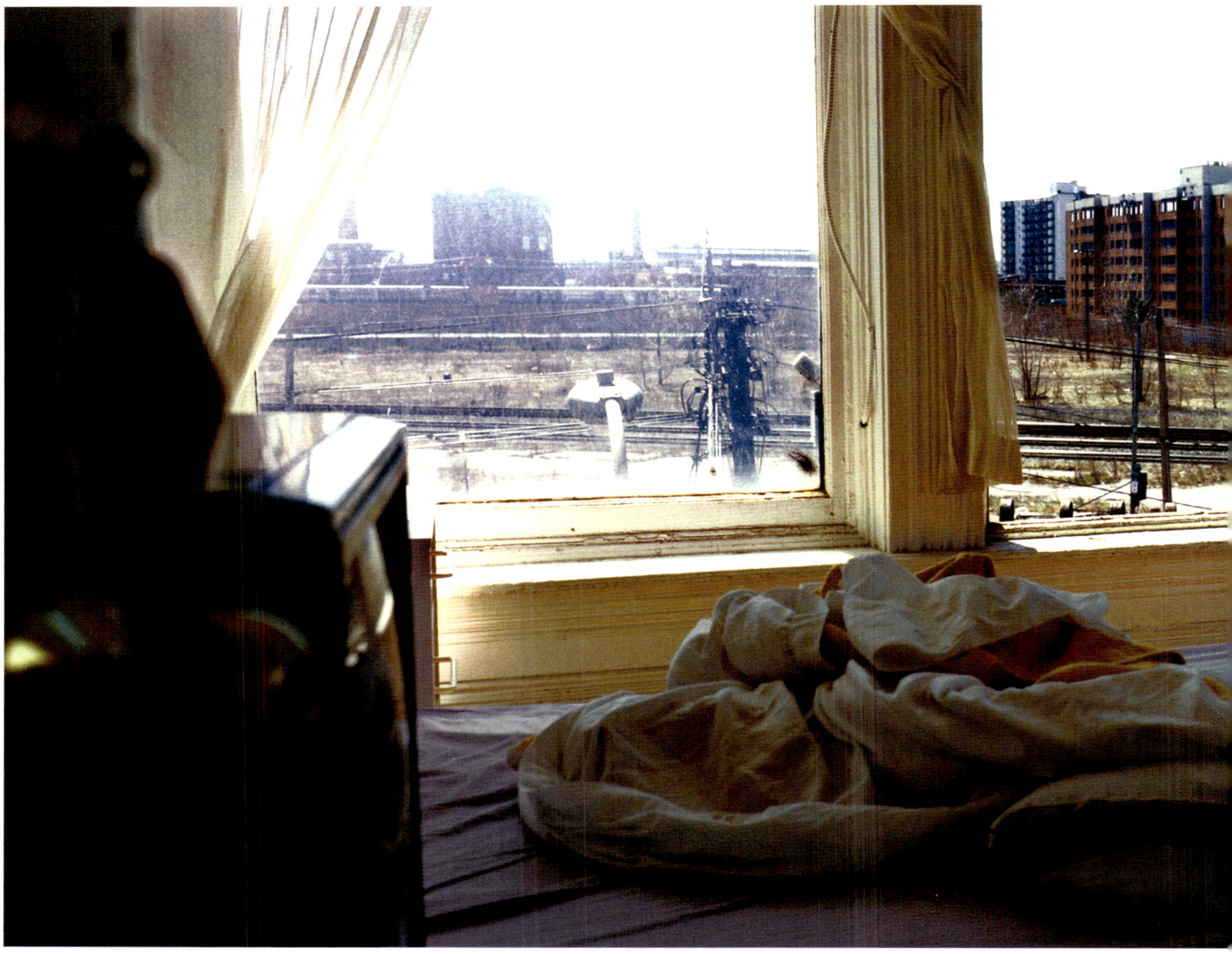

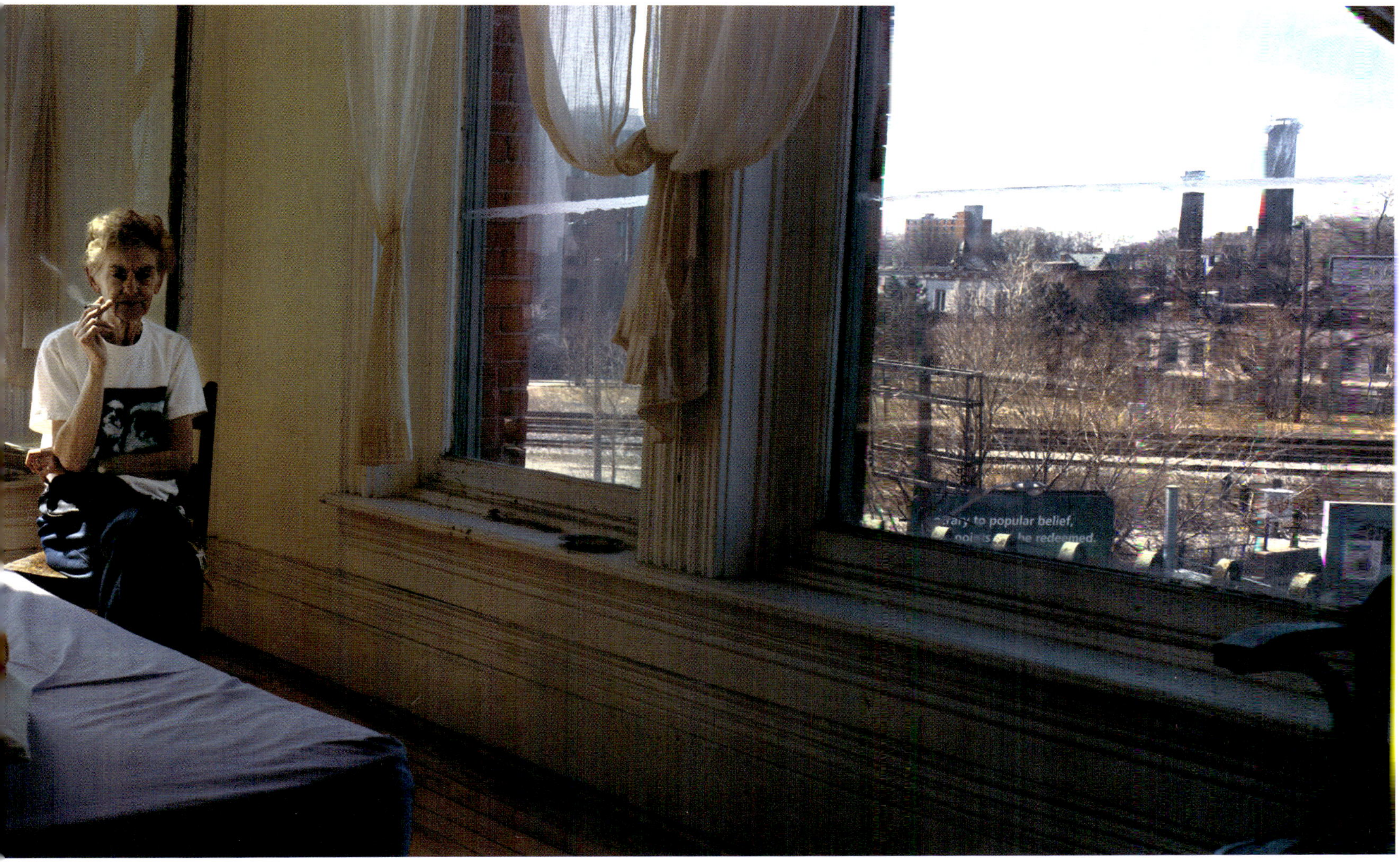

Shirley Lacy

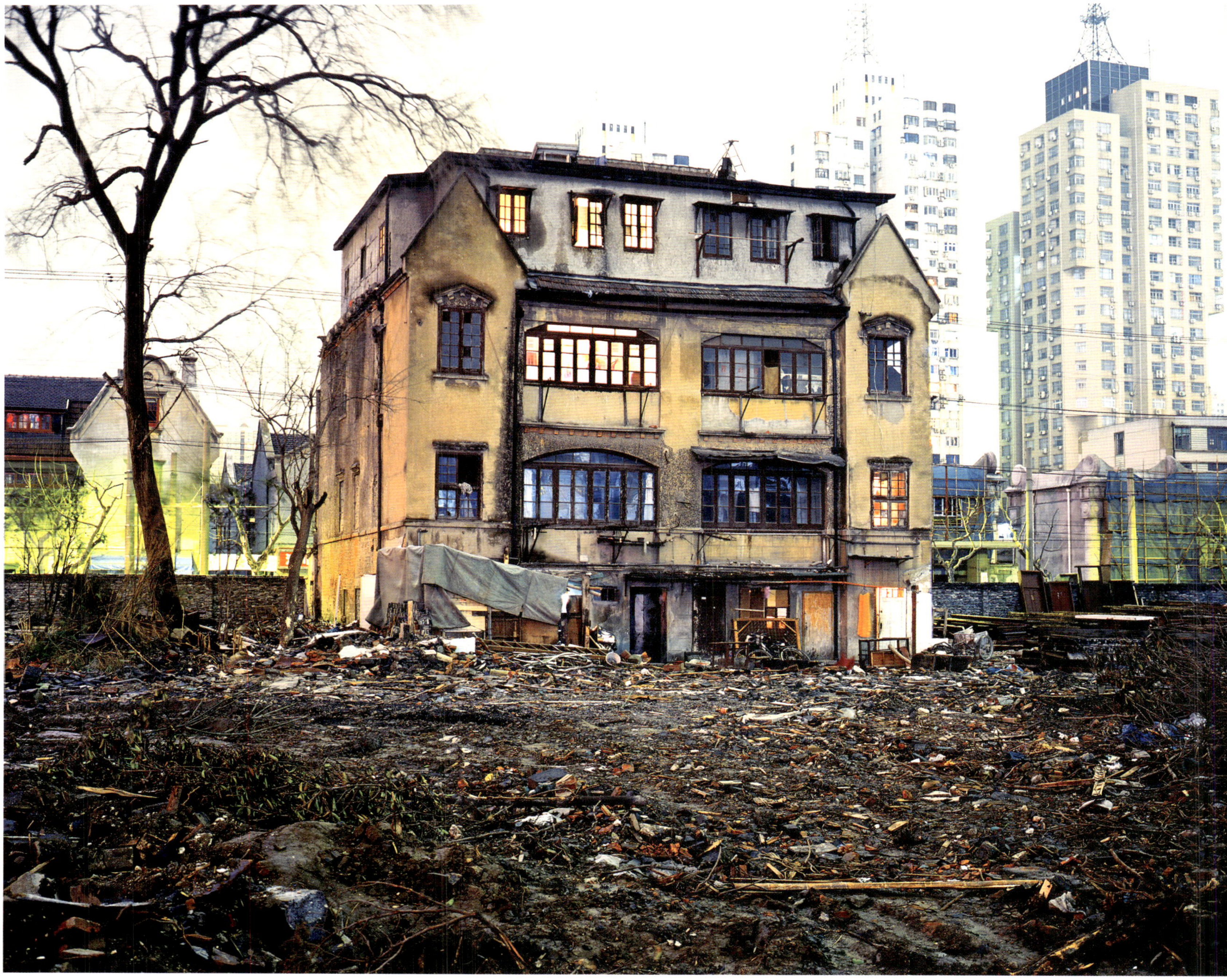

House on Yuyuan Lu, 2001

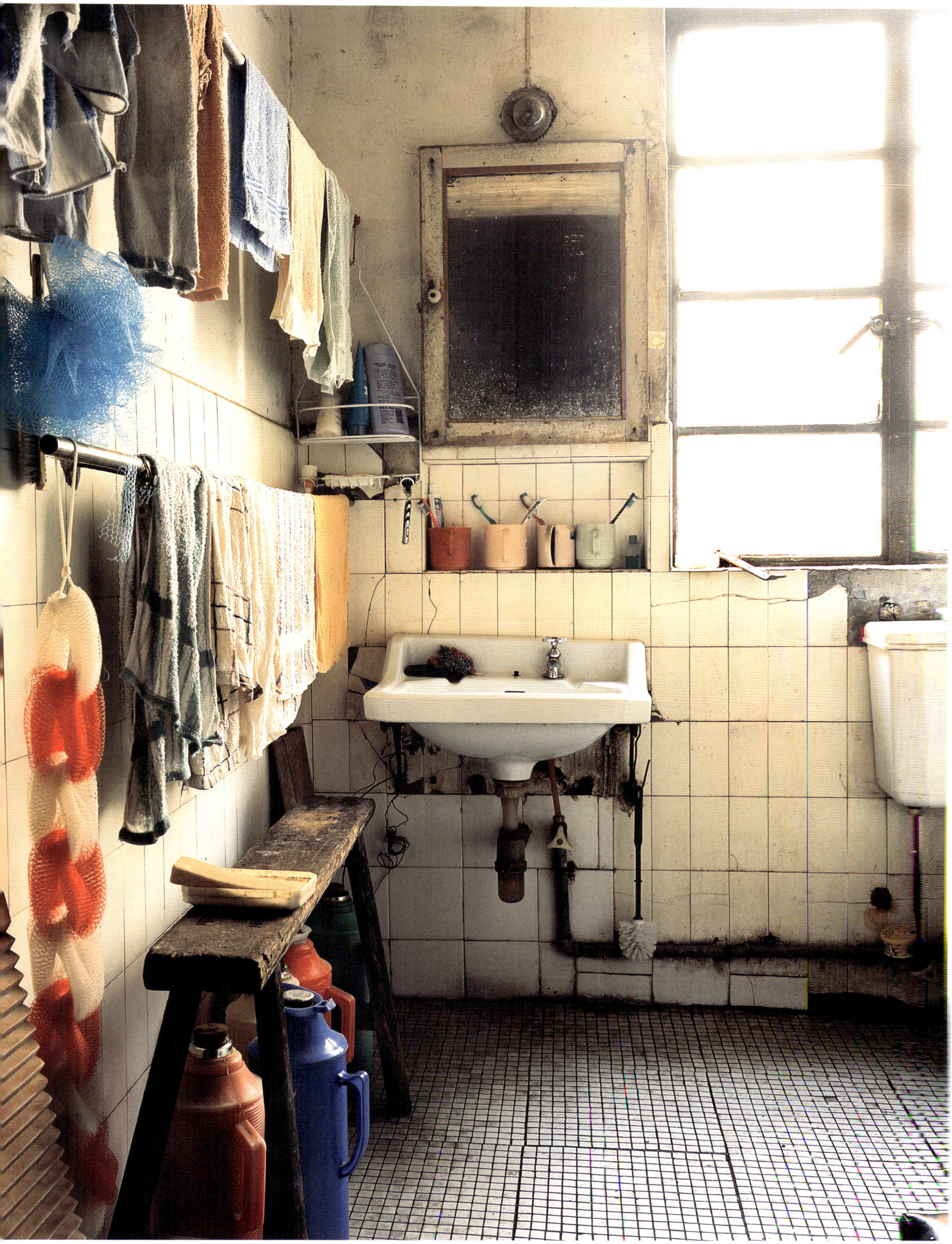

Shared Bathroom, Shanghai, 2003

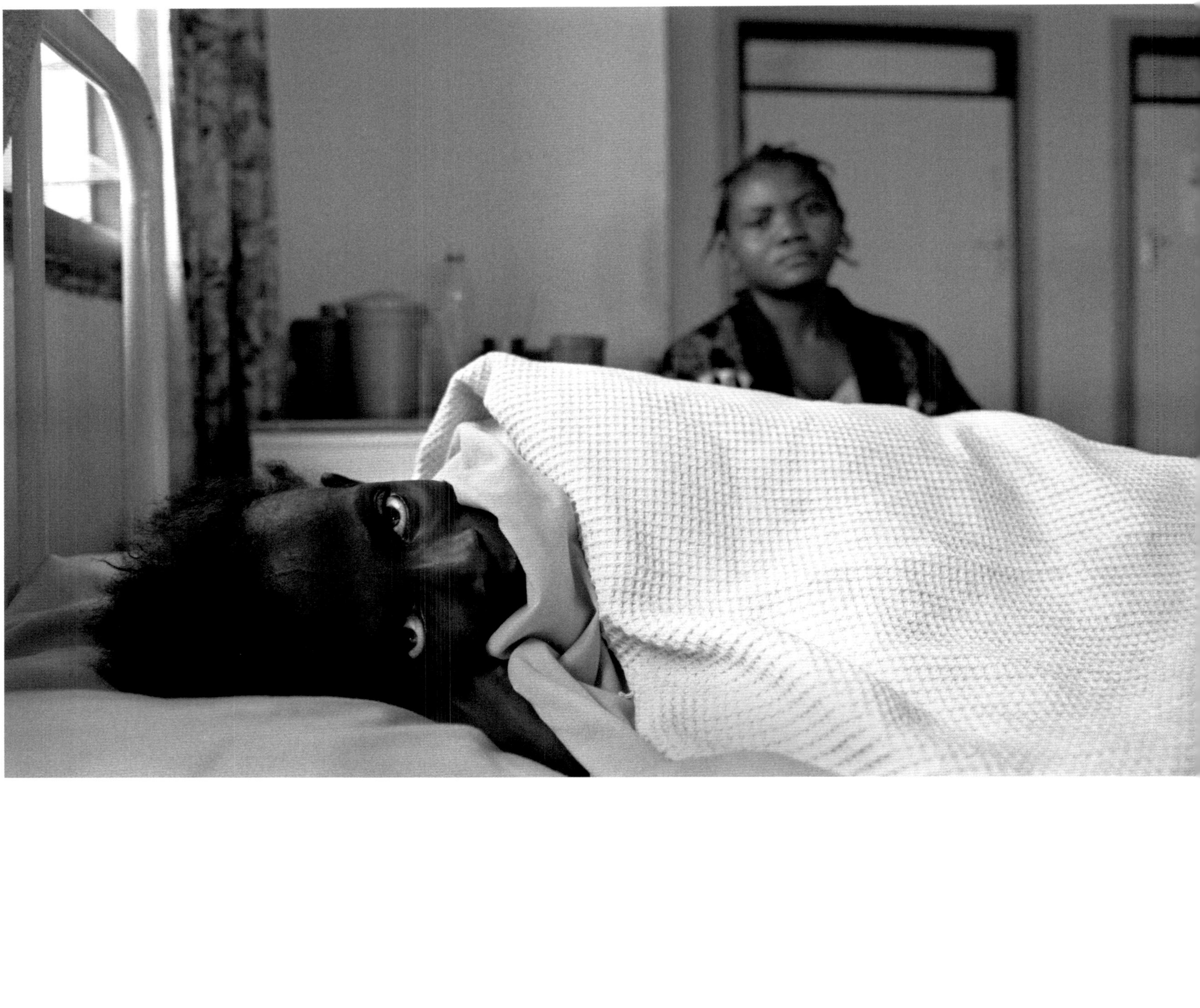

Patti Gower

Lucy Bwanali, AIDS Victim (Lusaka, Zambia)

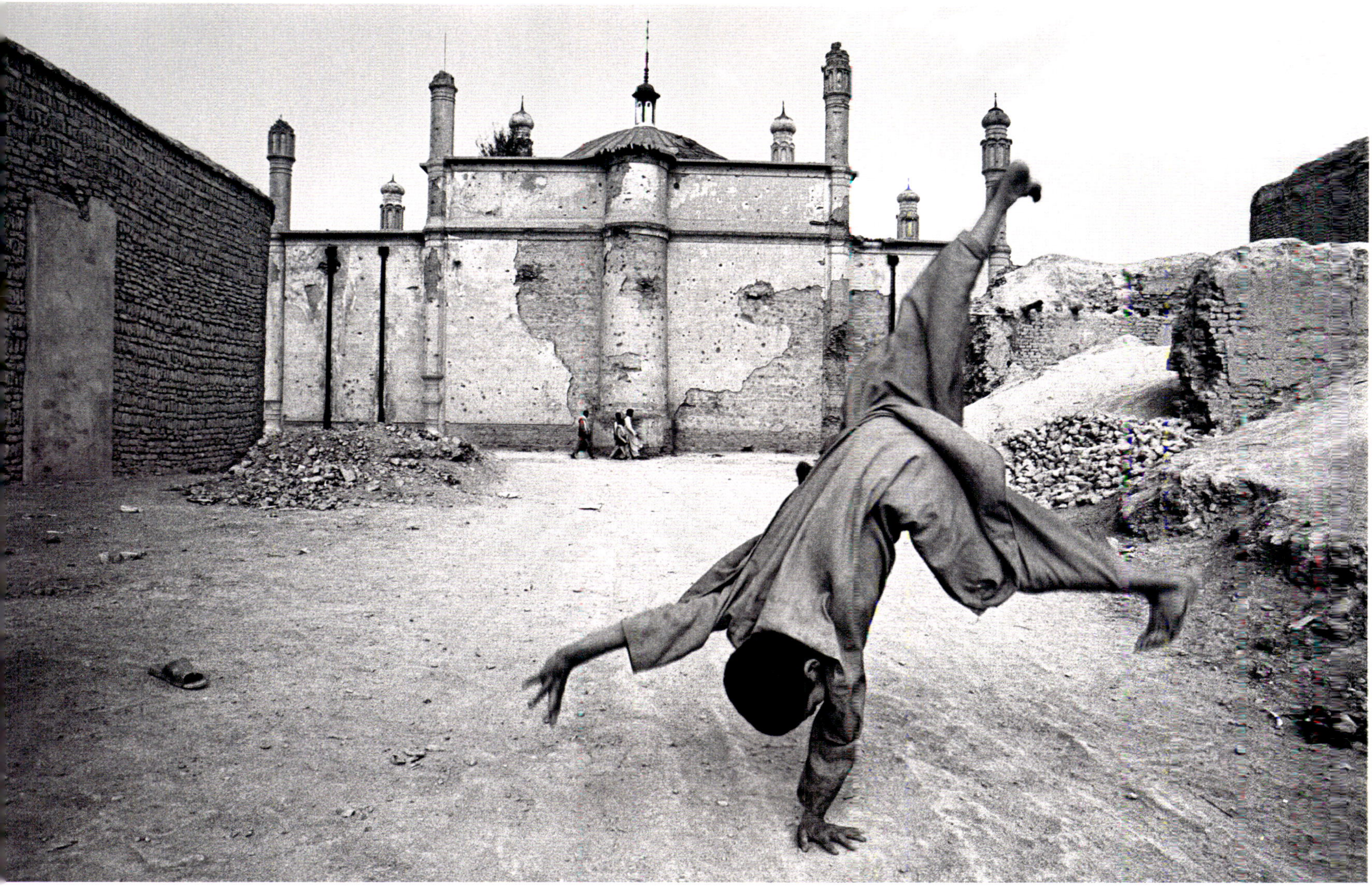

Kabul, September 2003

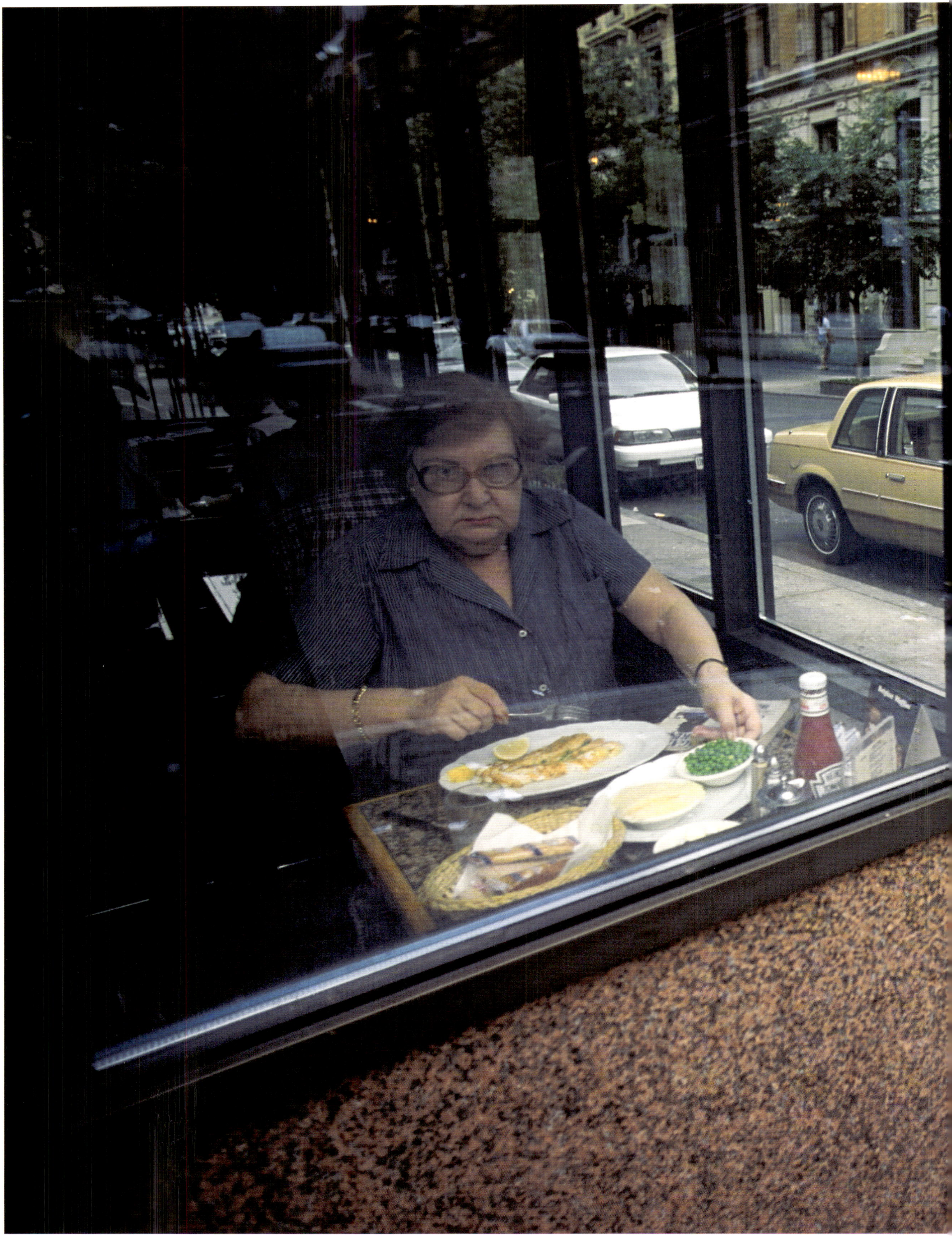

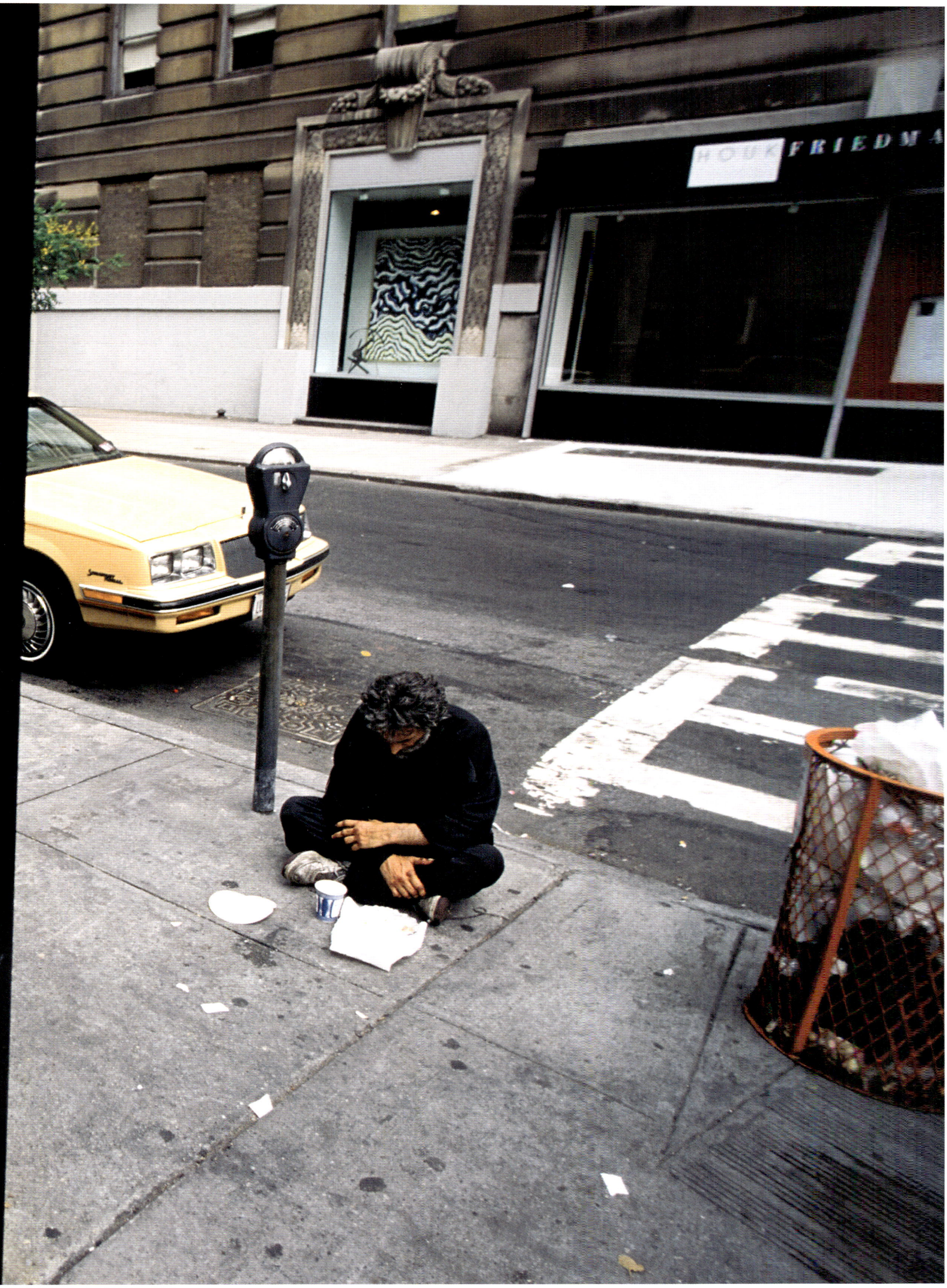

Patrice Halley

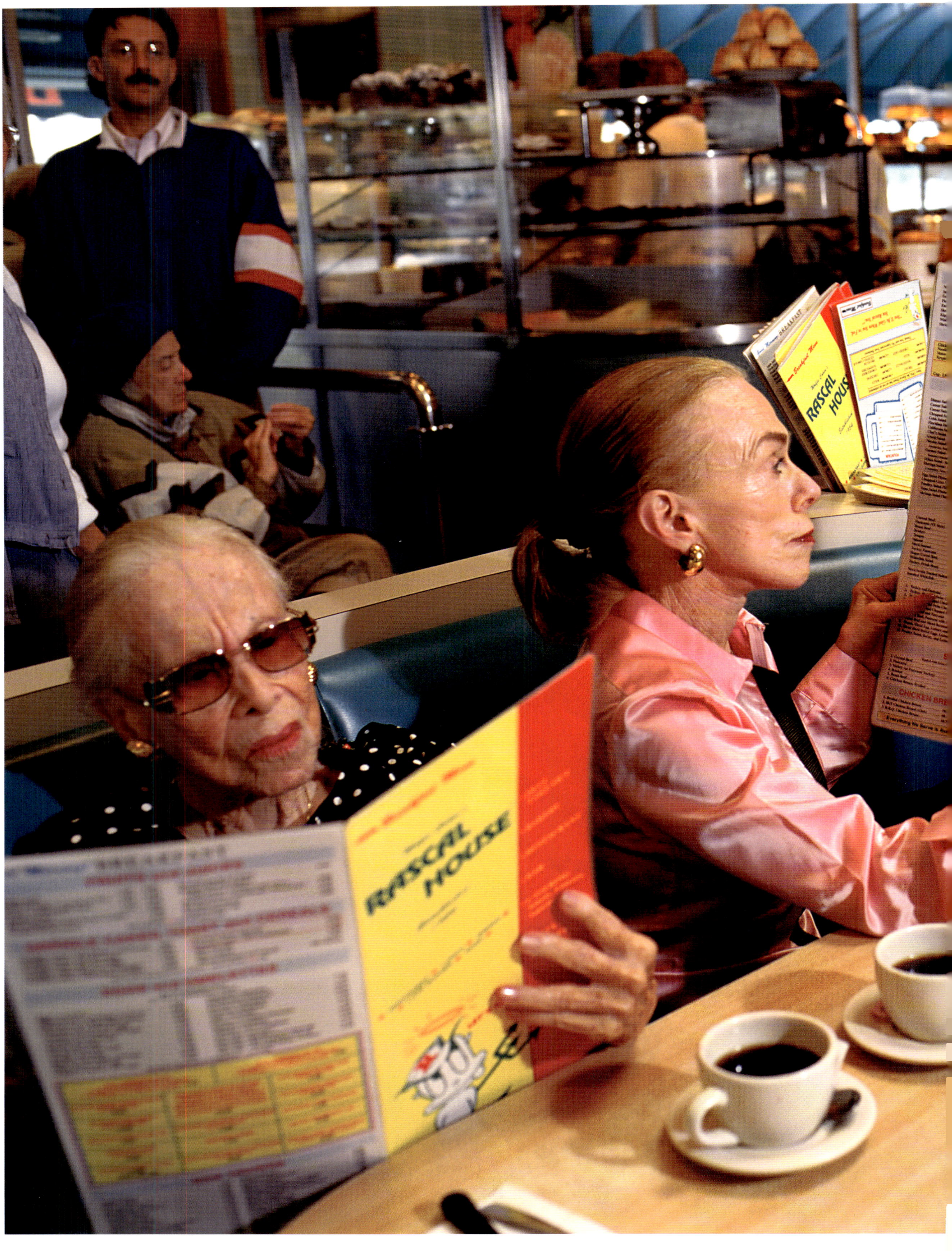
RASCAL HOUSE
RASCAL HOUSE
CHICKEN BRE

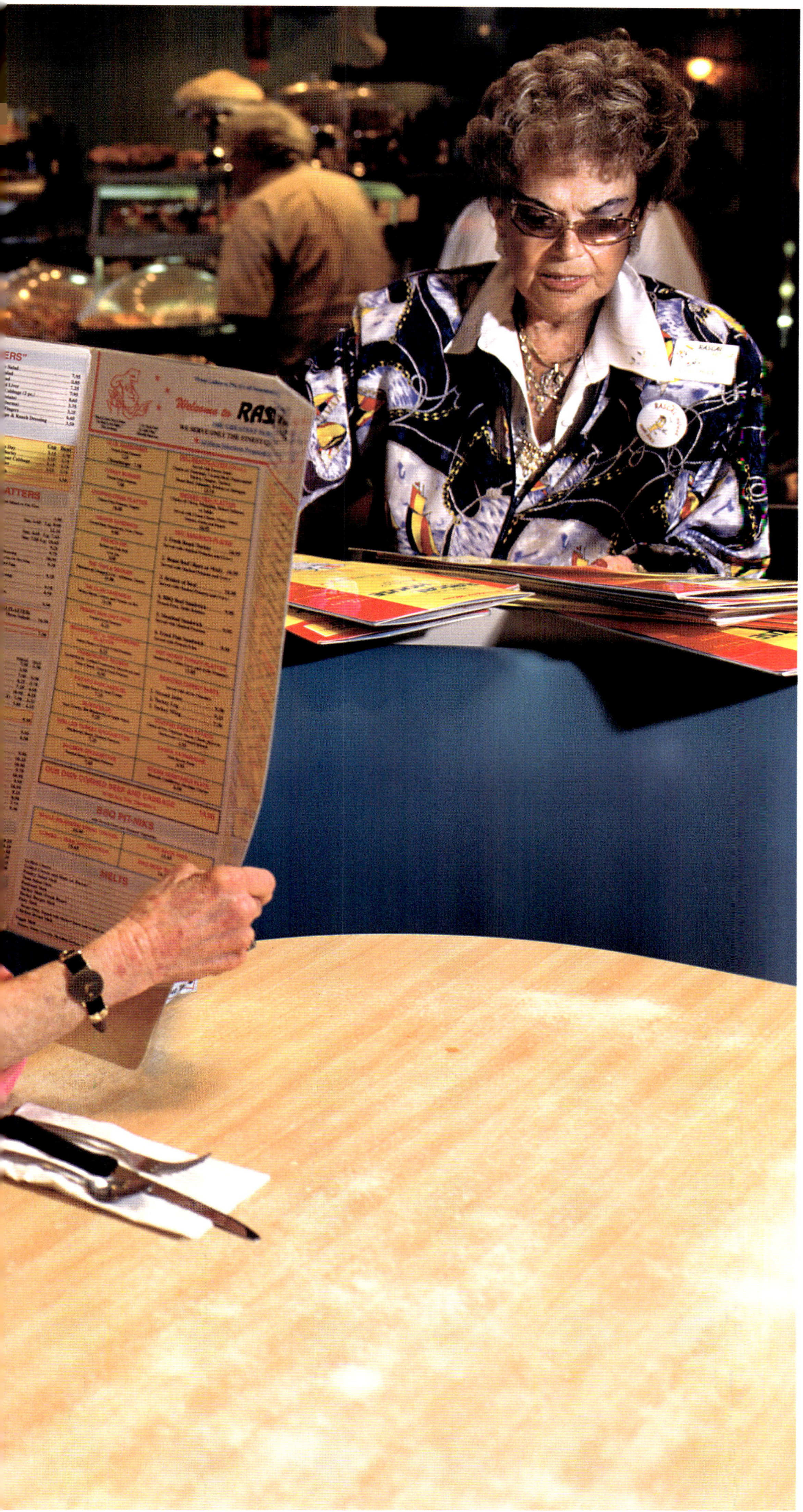

Naomi Harris

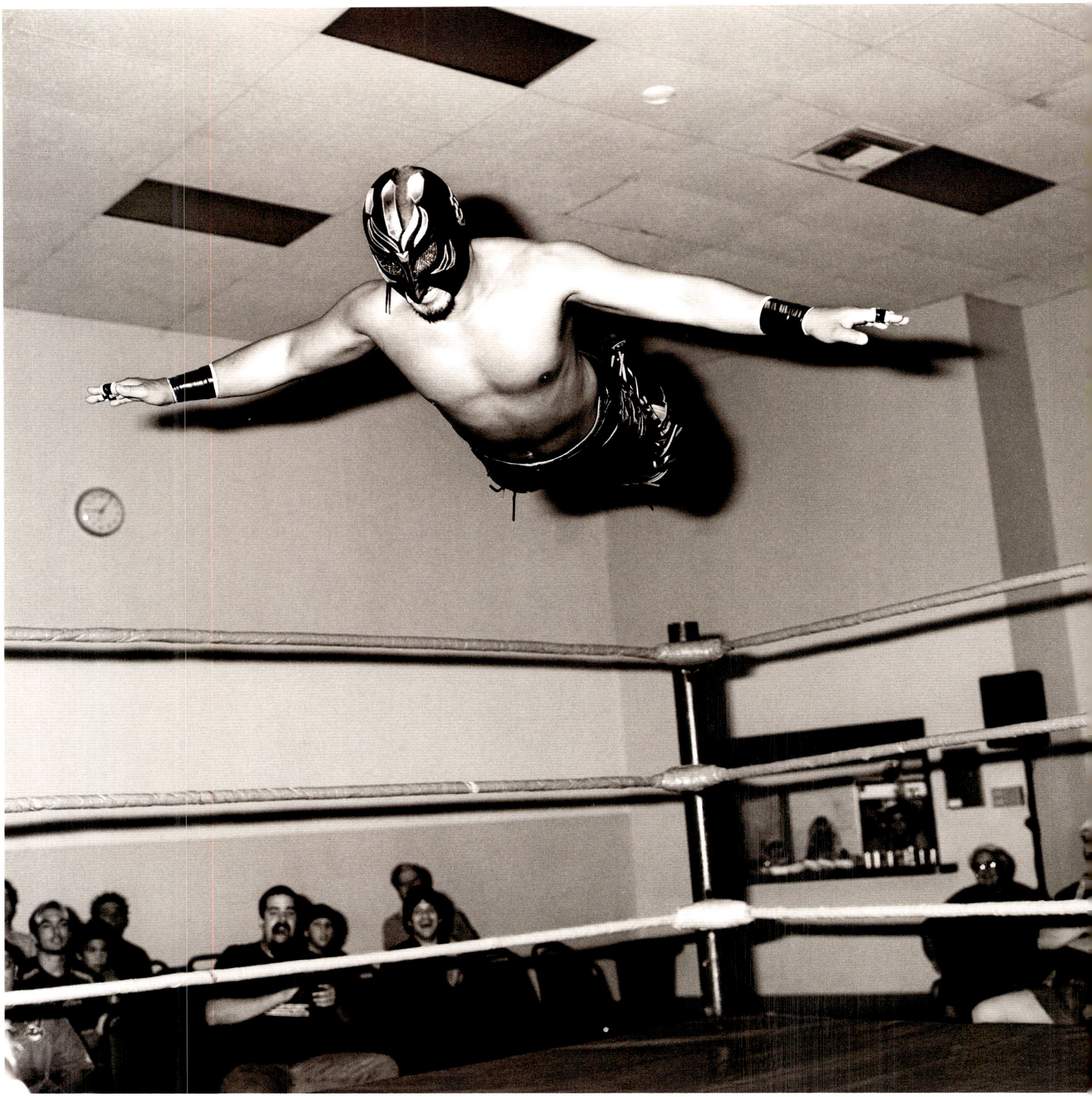

Asian Cougar

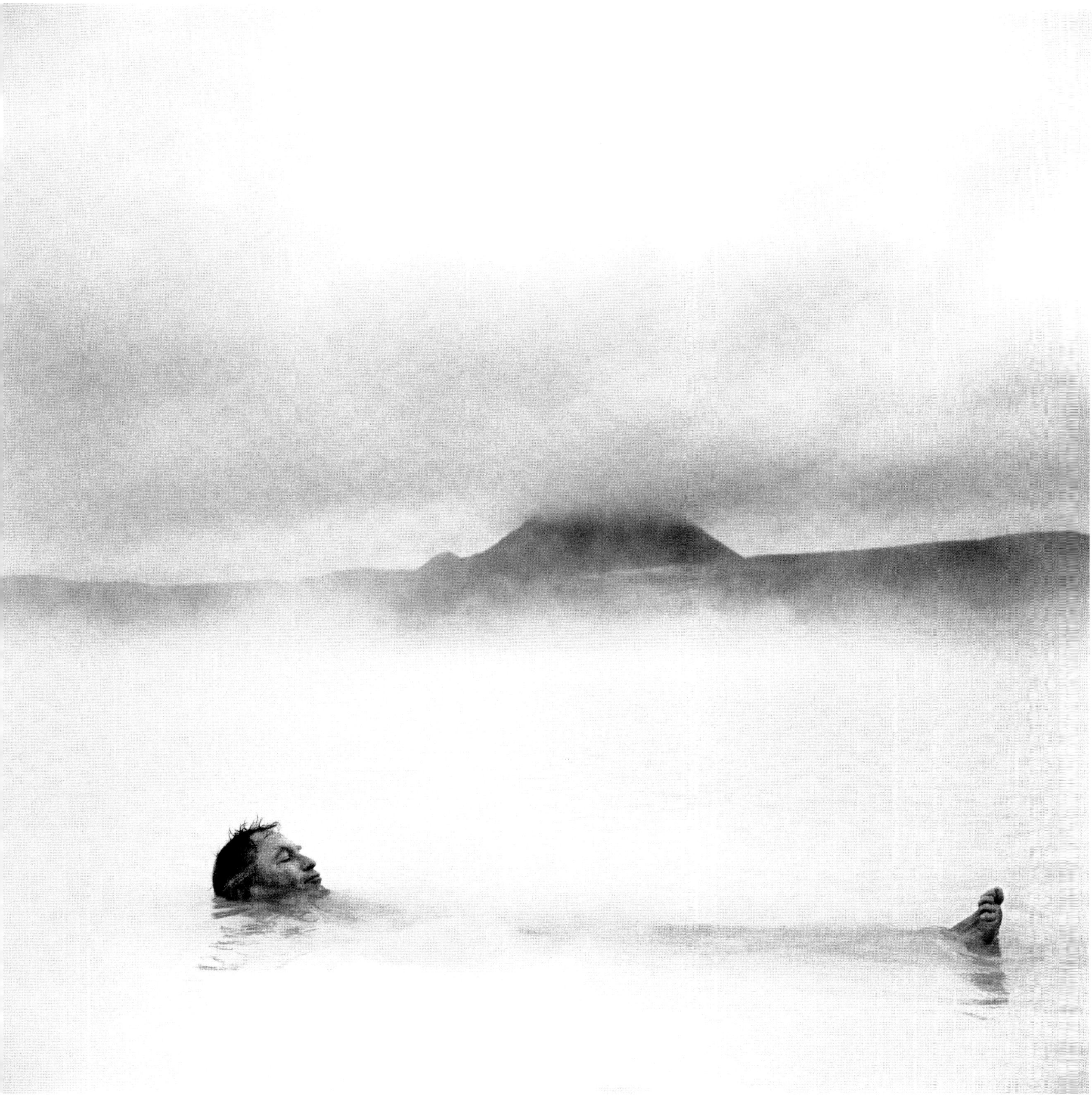

Hot Spring (Myvatn, Iceland, 2002)

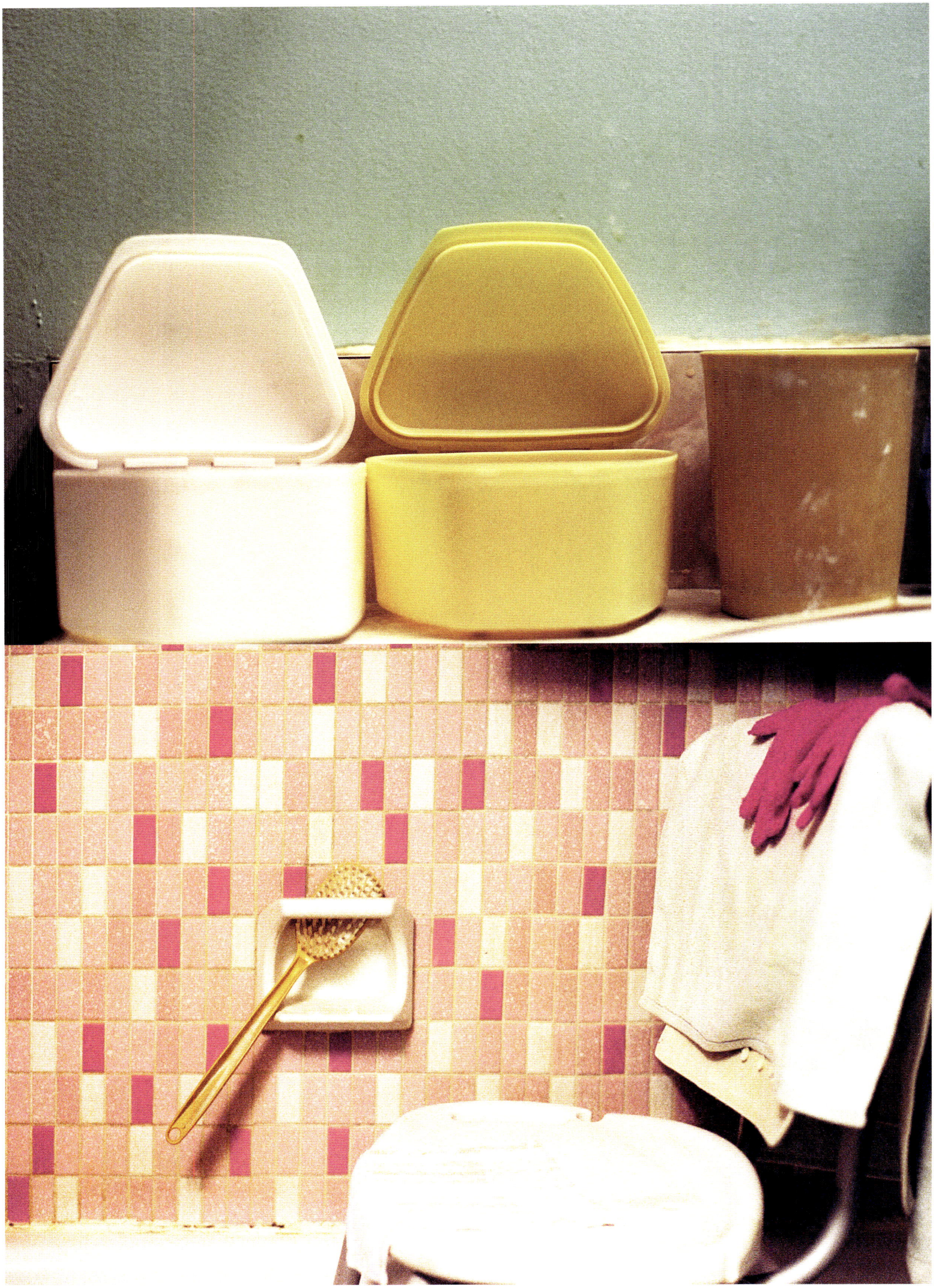

Raina Kirn

Bathroom

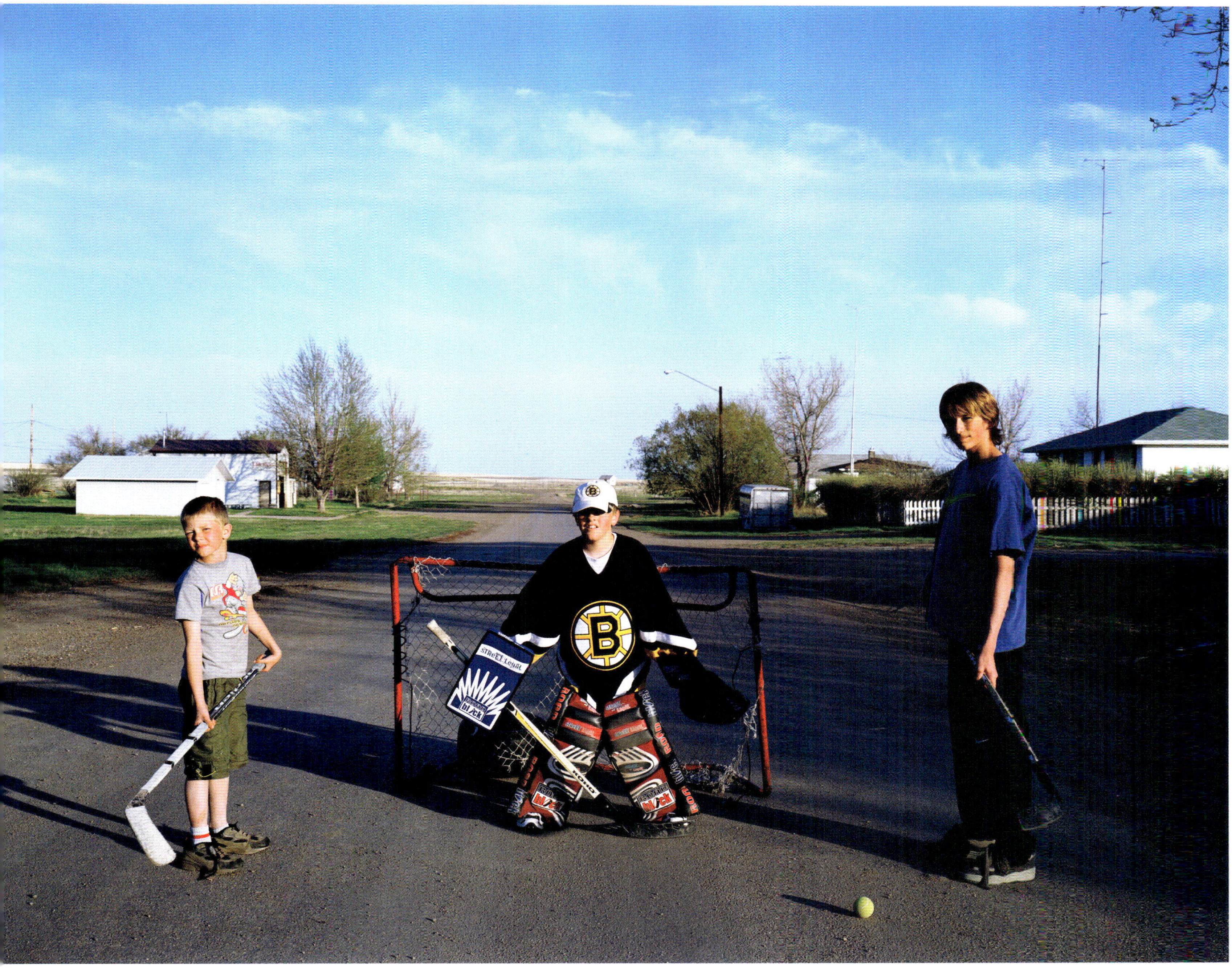

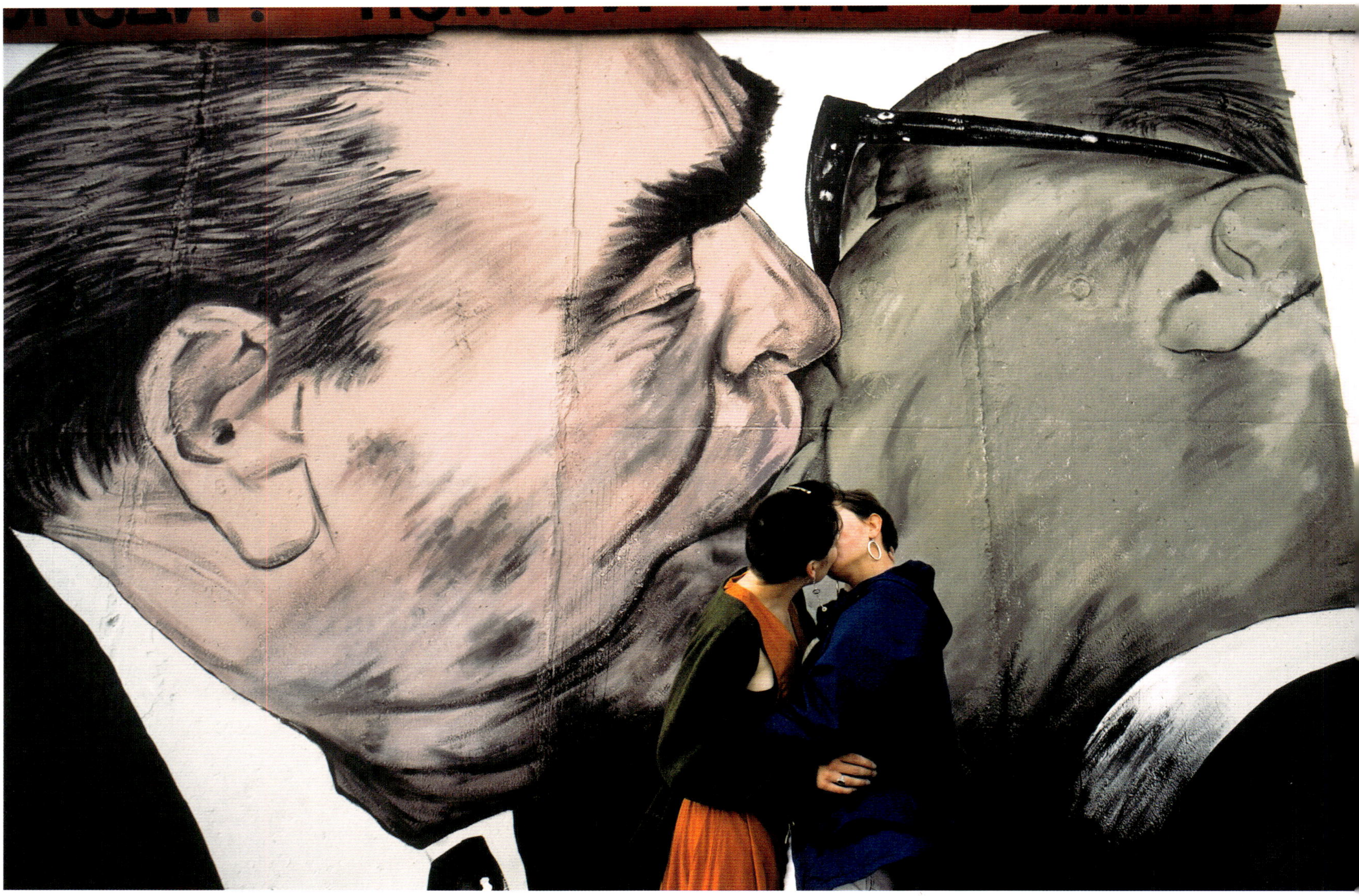

Wolf Kutnahorsky

The Kiss (Prague Prison)

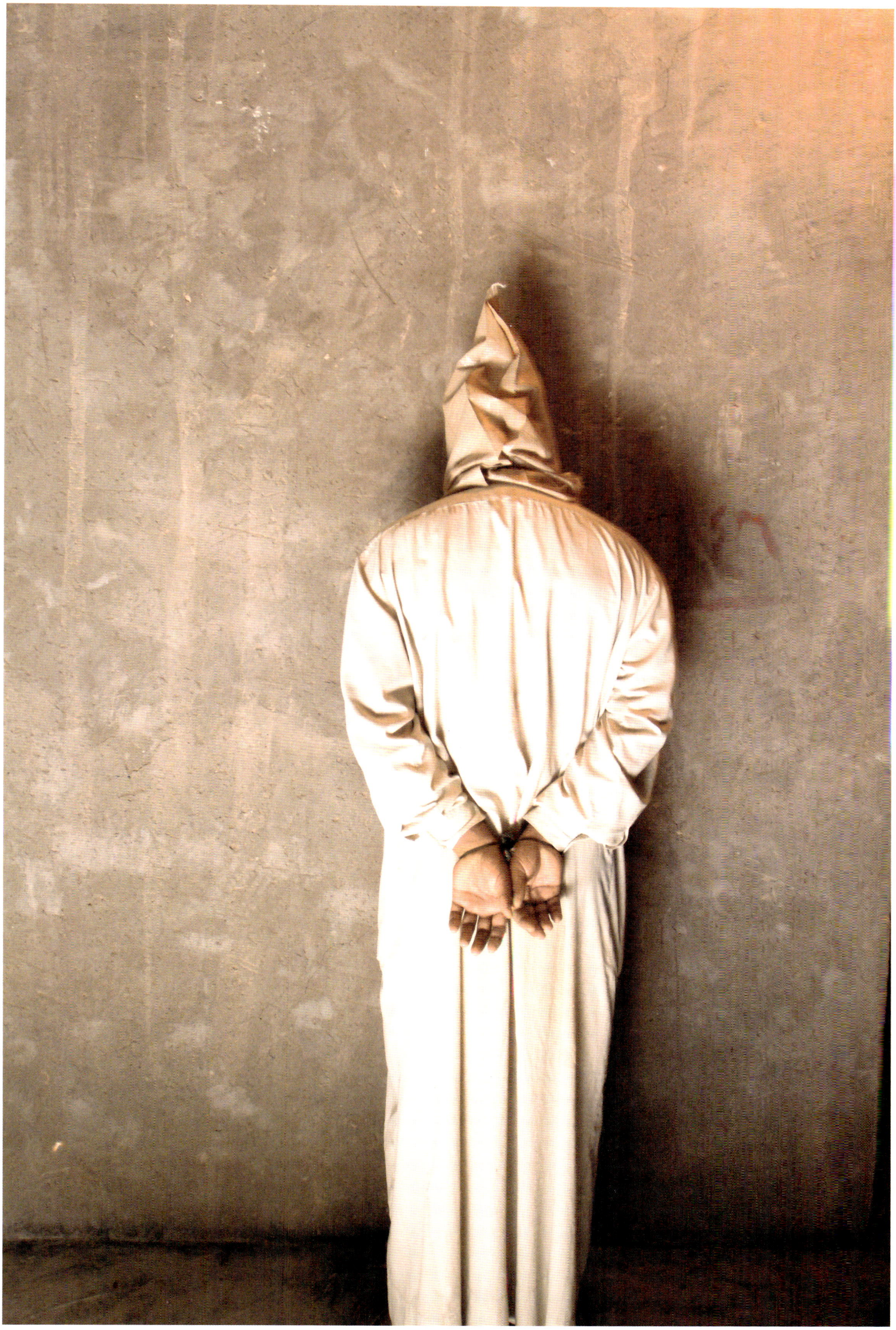

Hooded Iraqi Prisoner

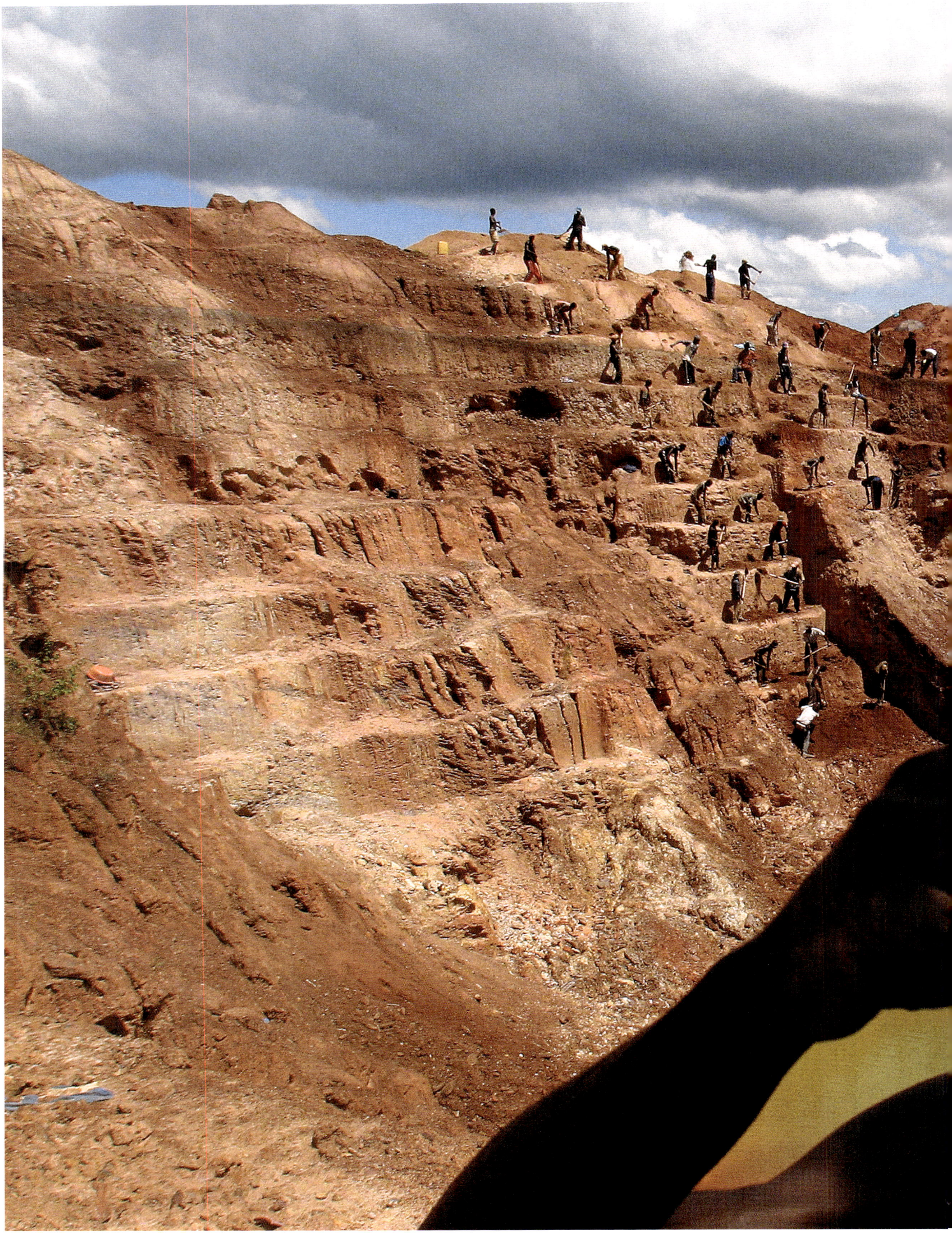

Roger Lemoyne

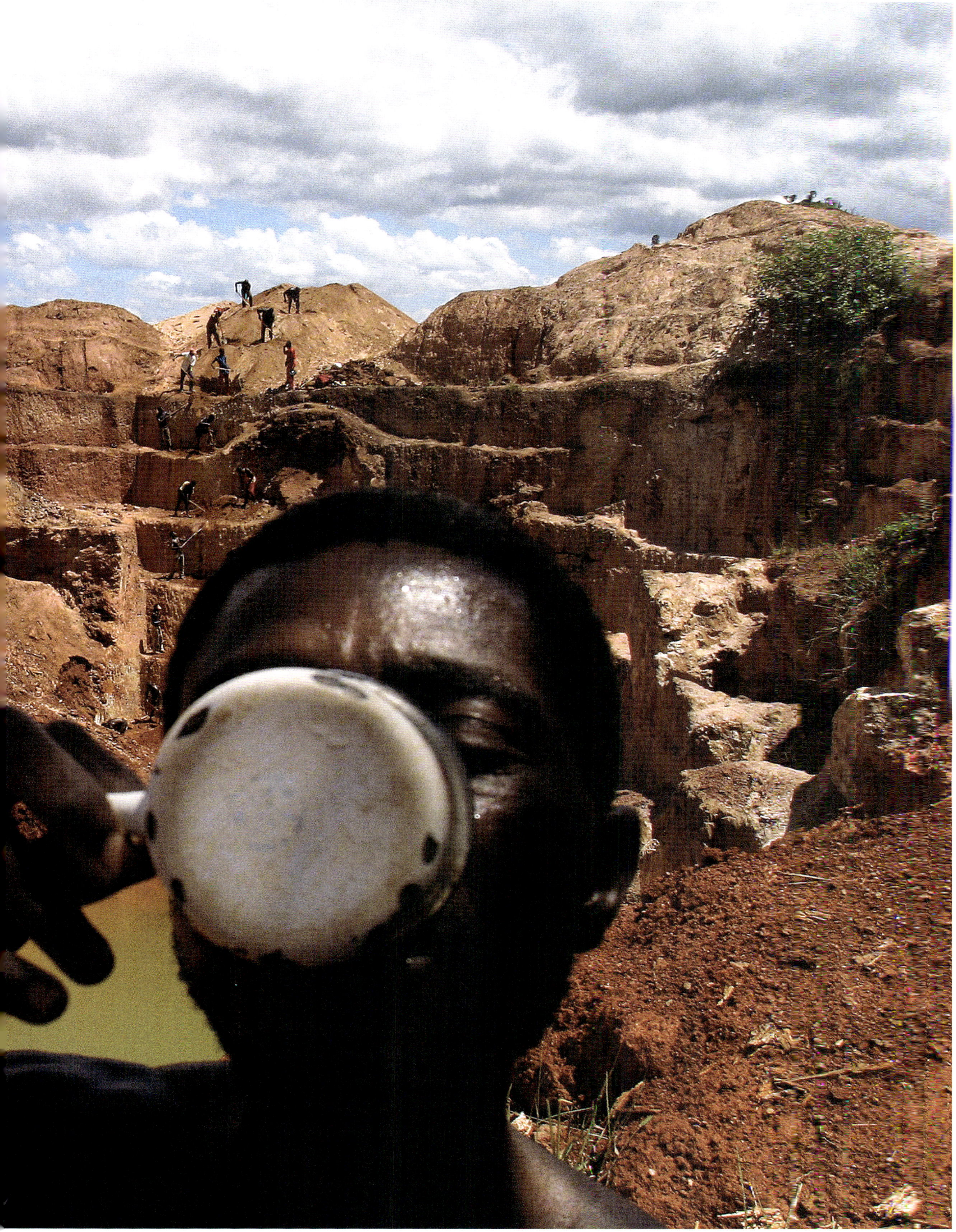

Congolese Men Prospect for Gold (Durba, Democratic Republic of Congo)

Roger Lemoyne

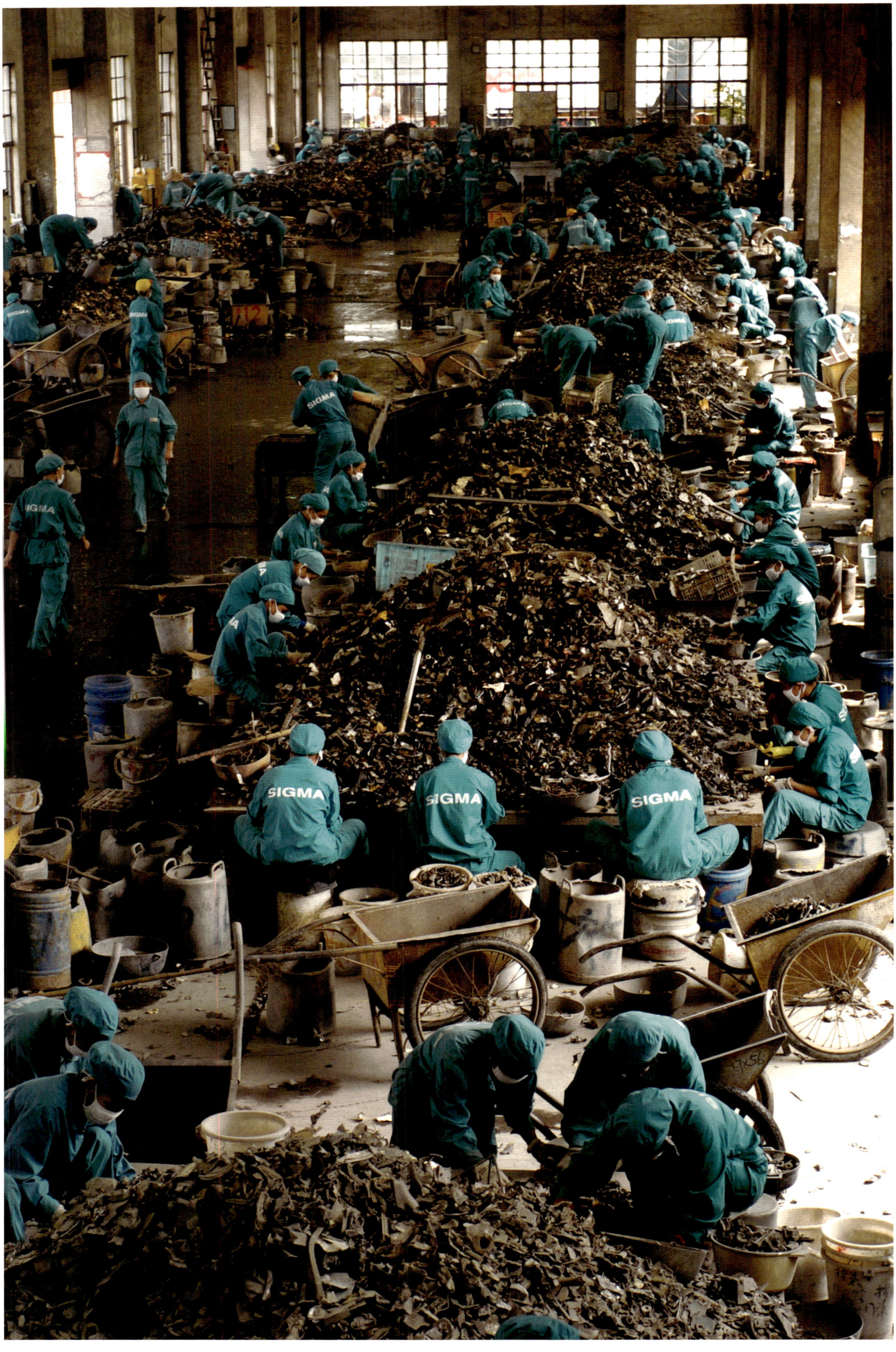

Fred Lum

Factory Workers

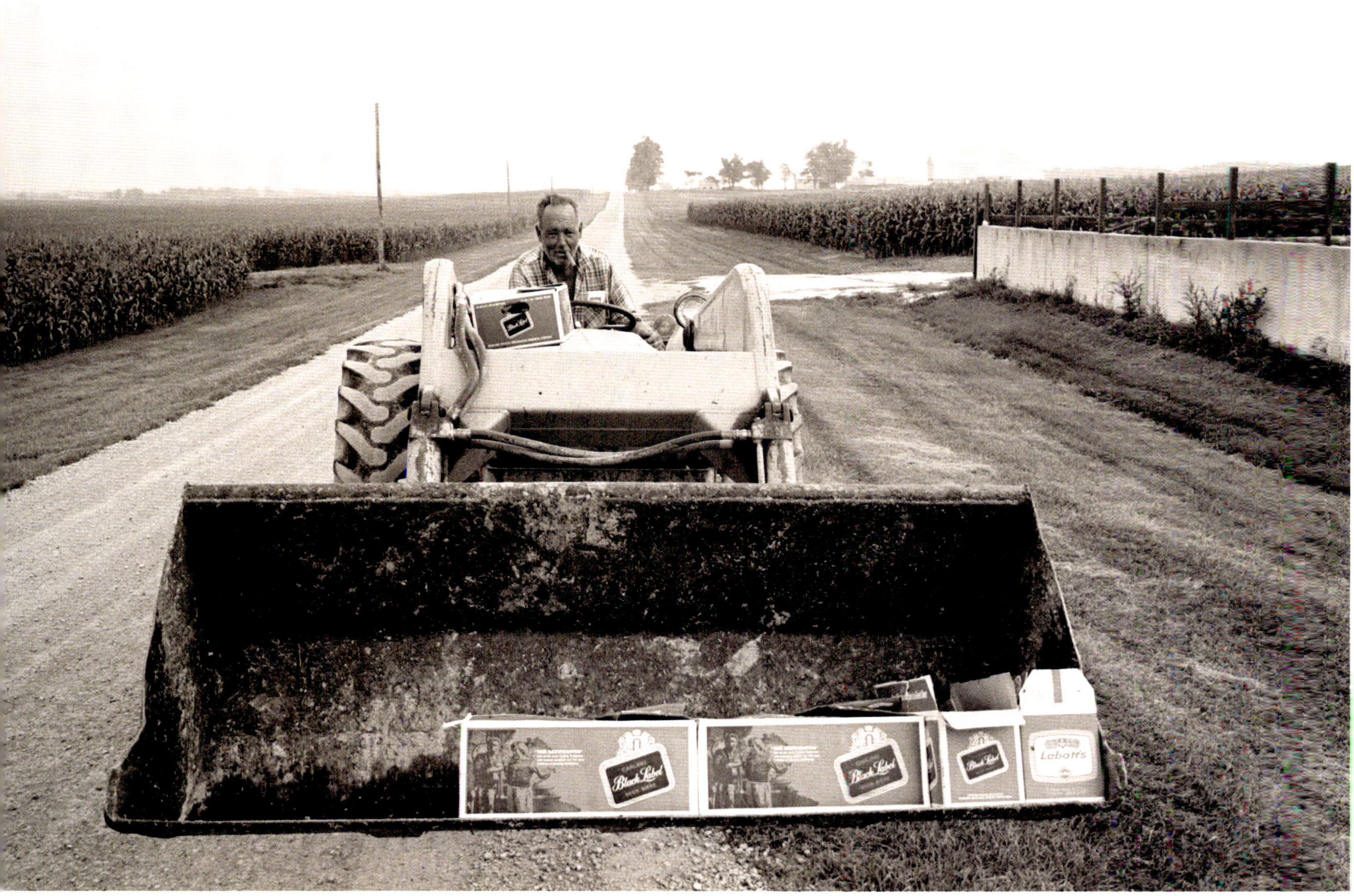

Going for Beer (Exeter, Ontario)

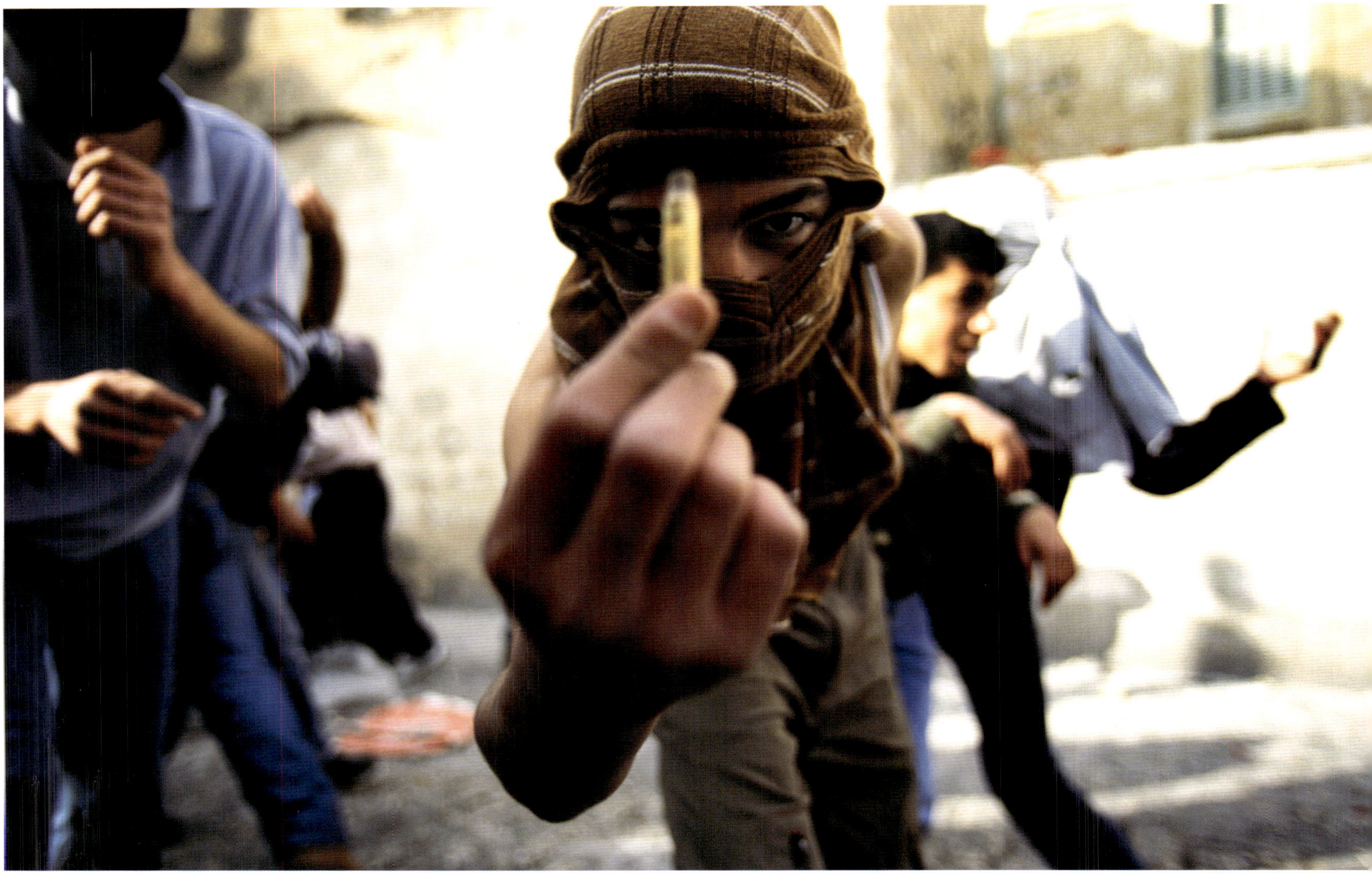

Bryan McBurney

Boy With Bullet

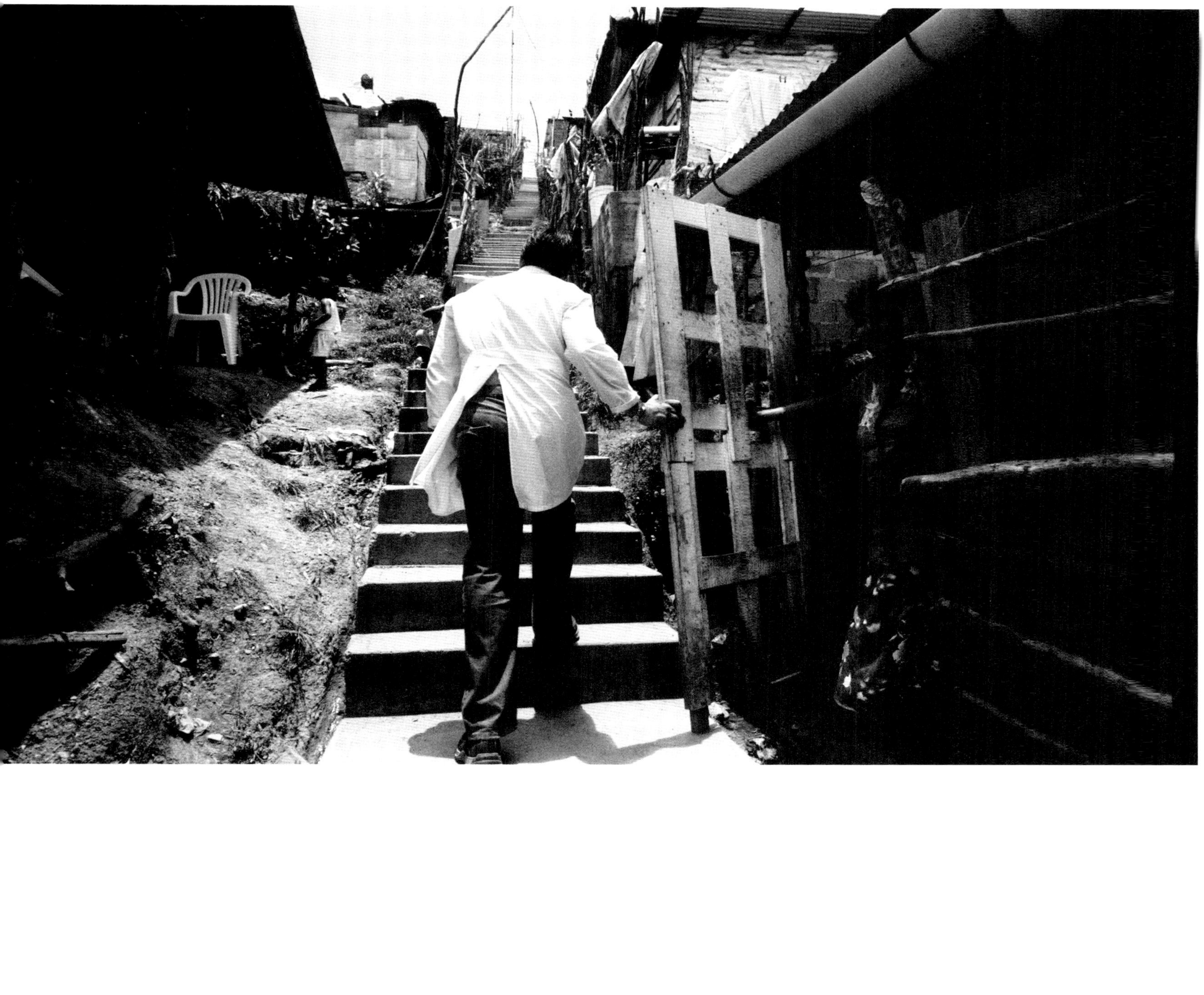

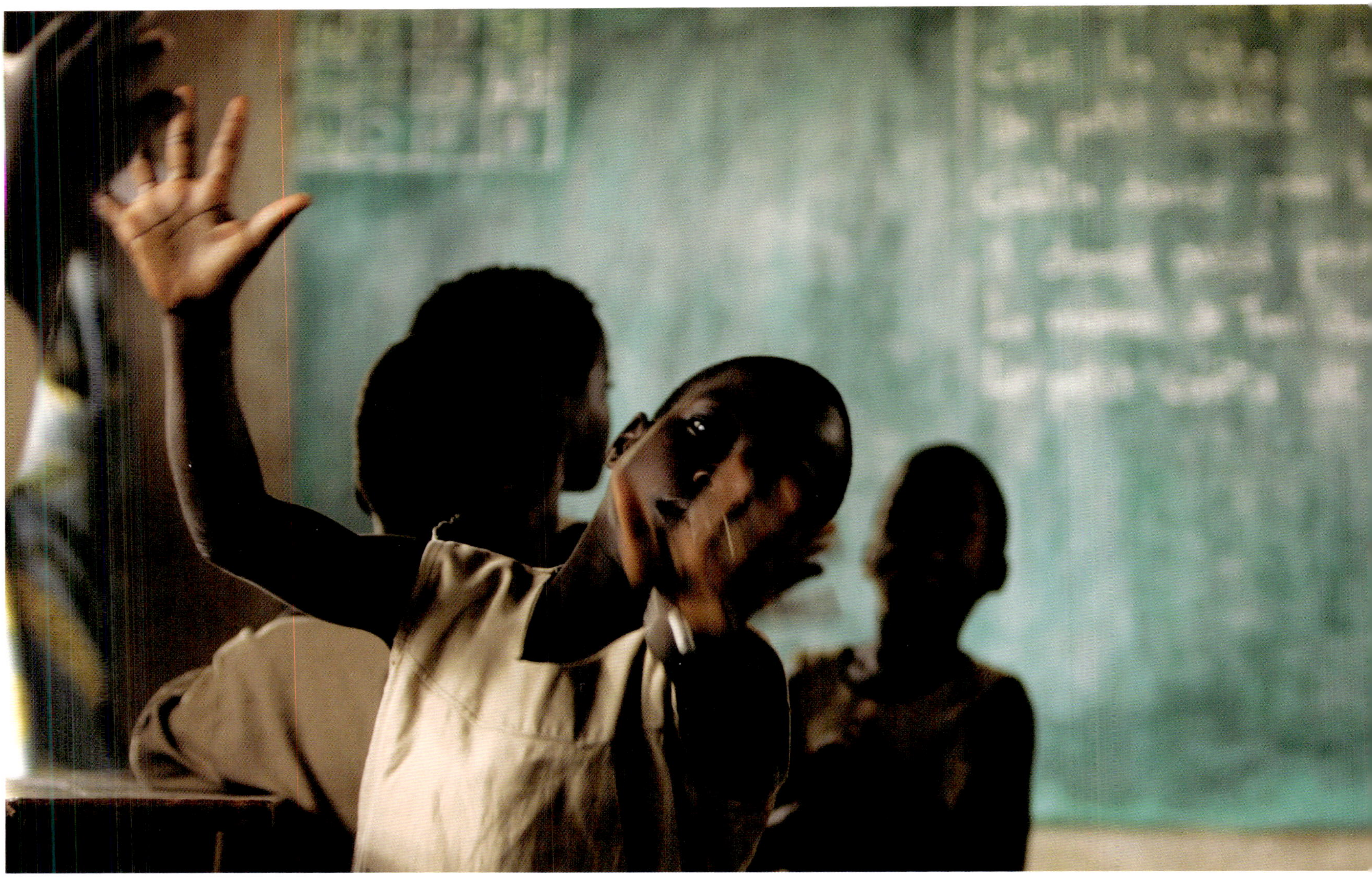

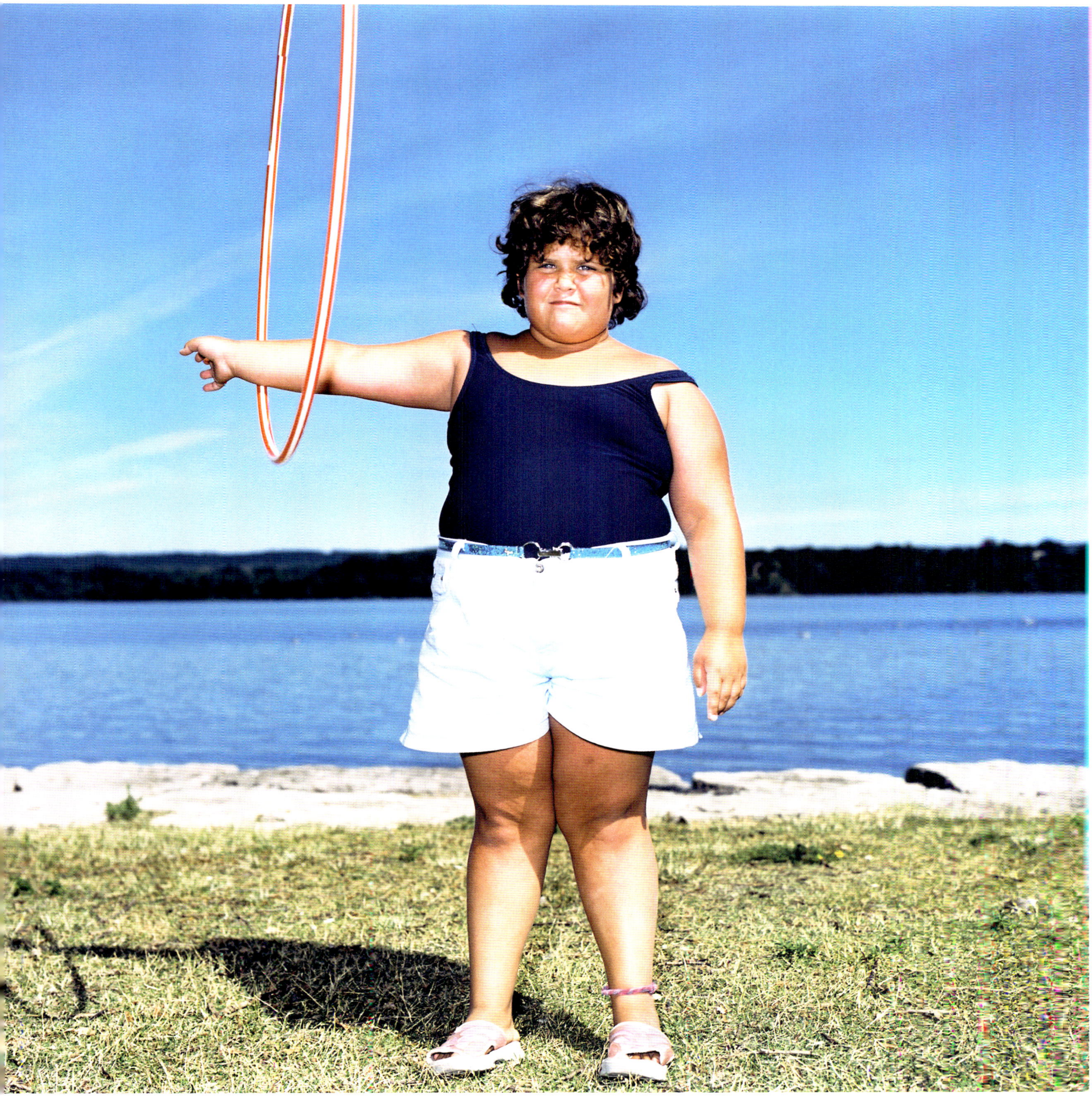

Hula Girl

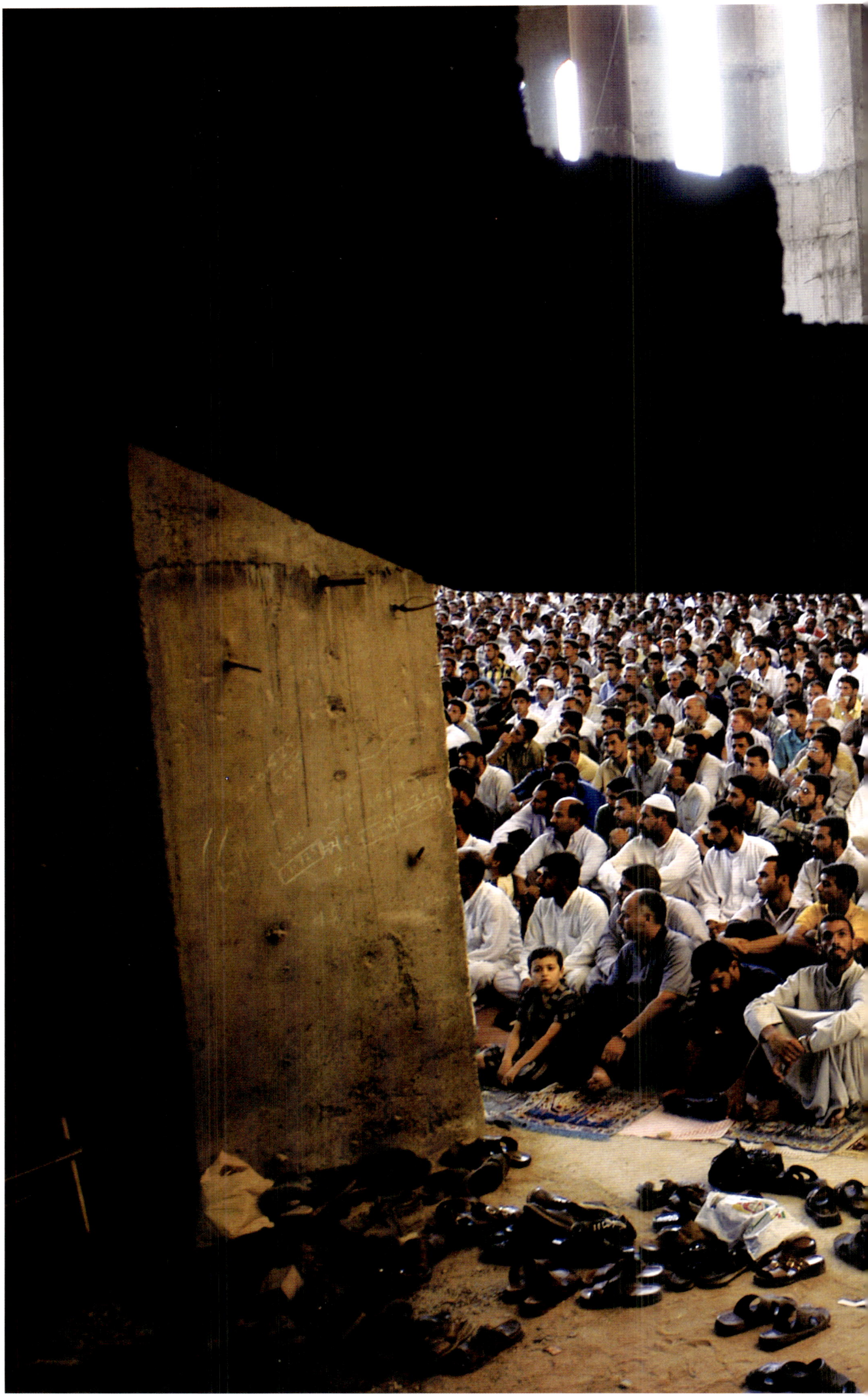

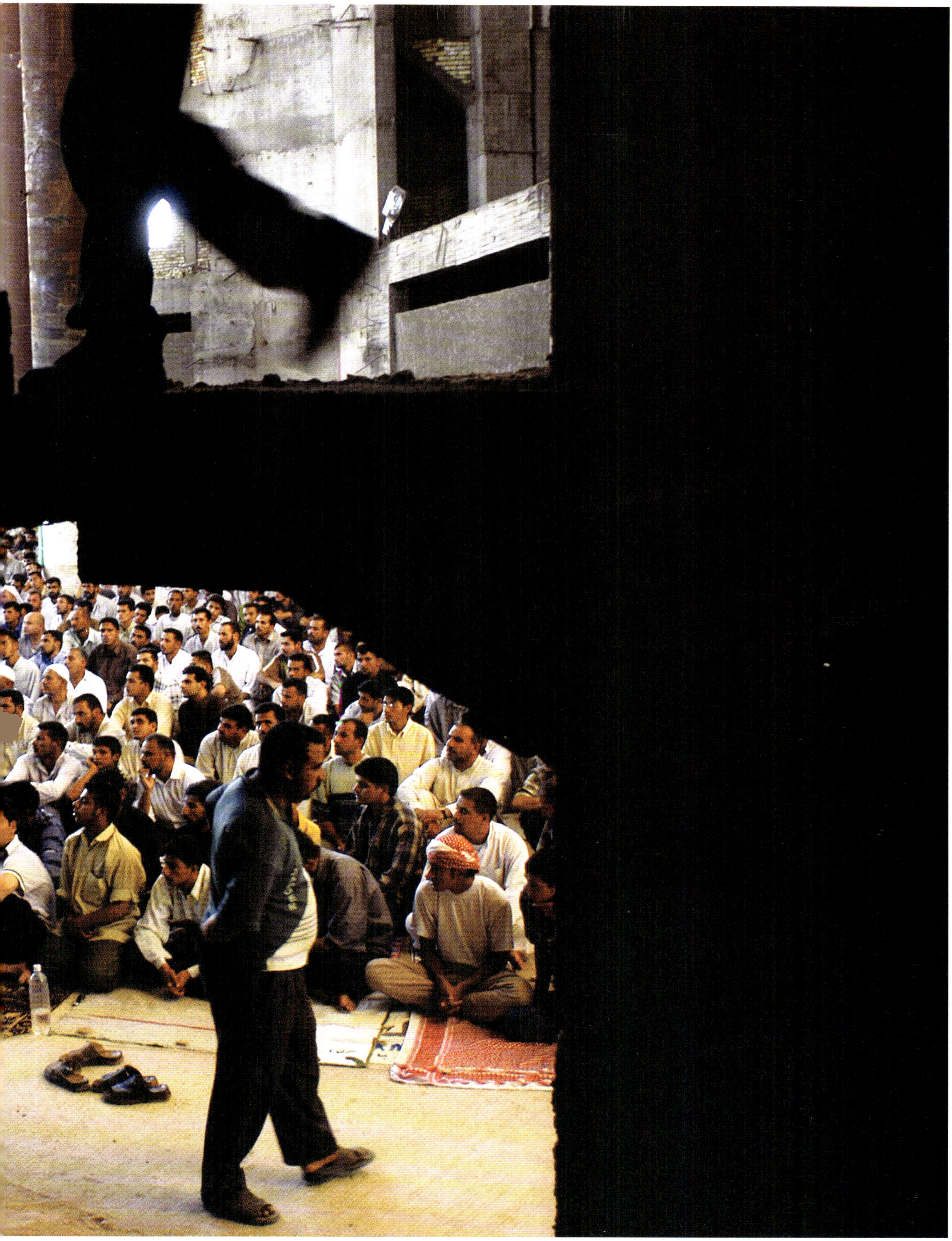

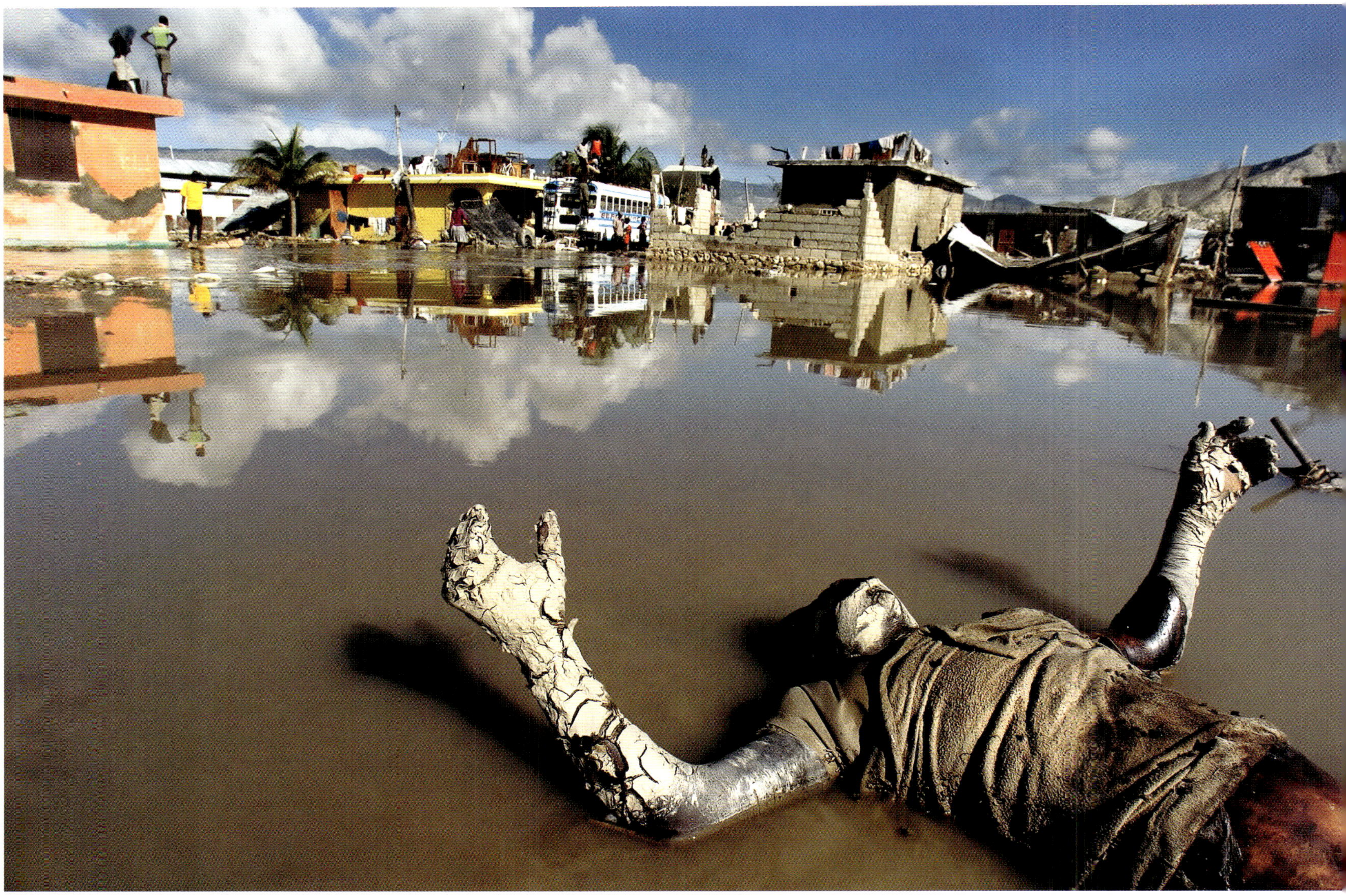

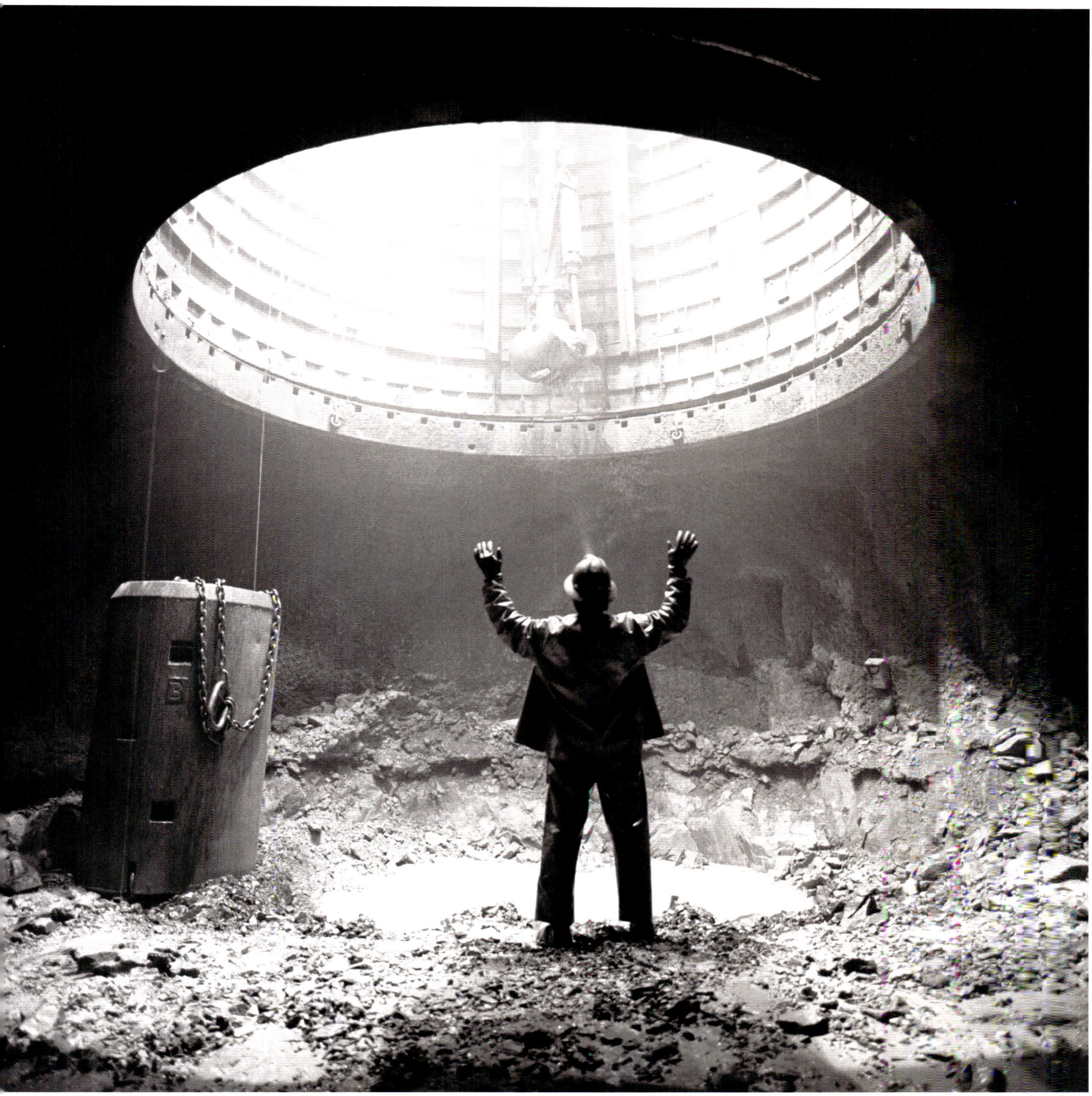

Shaft Miner, Louvicourt Mine No.1 Shaft, 2,500 Foot Level (Val d'Or, Quebec)

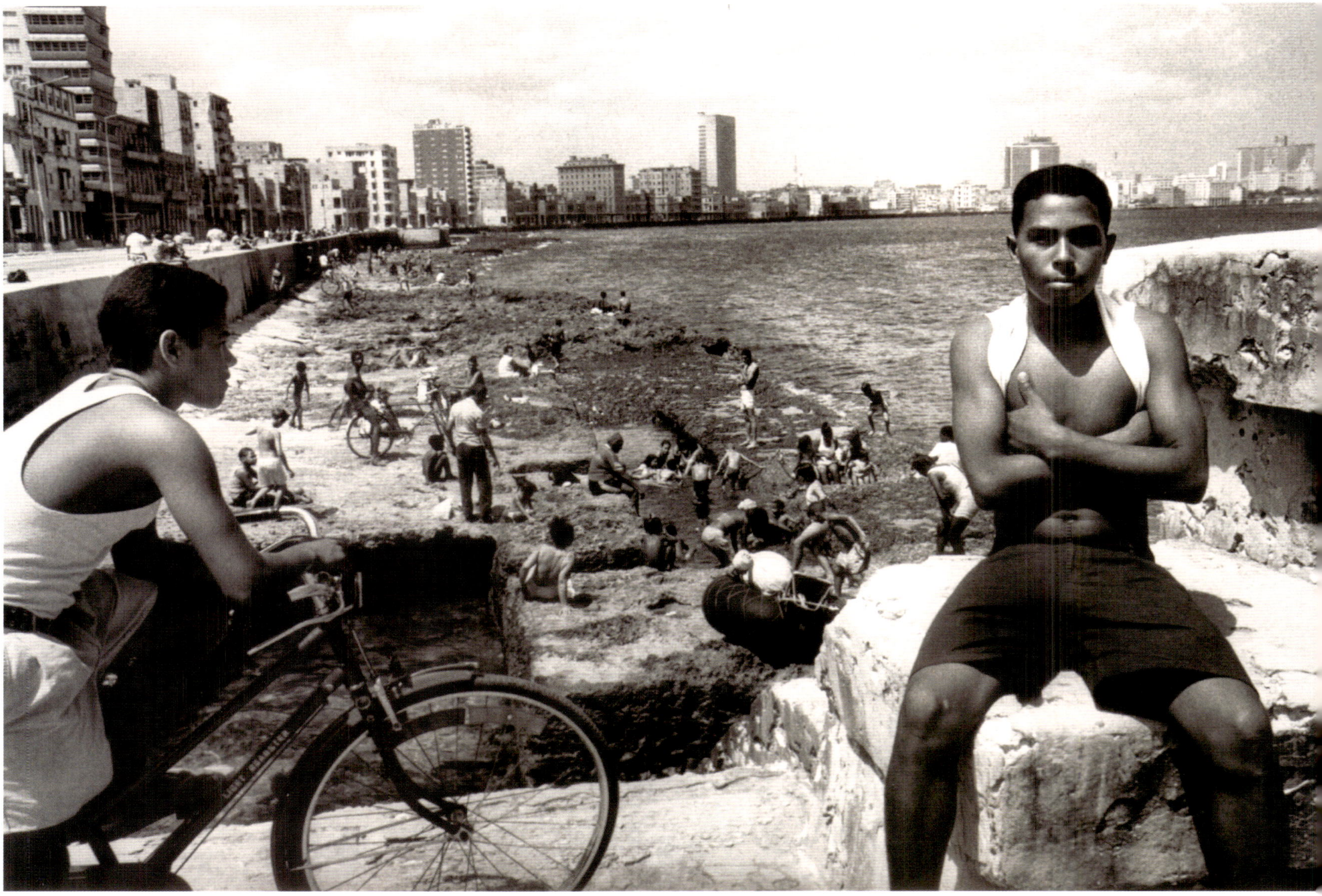

Havana Waterfront

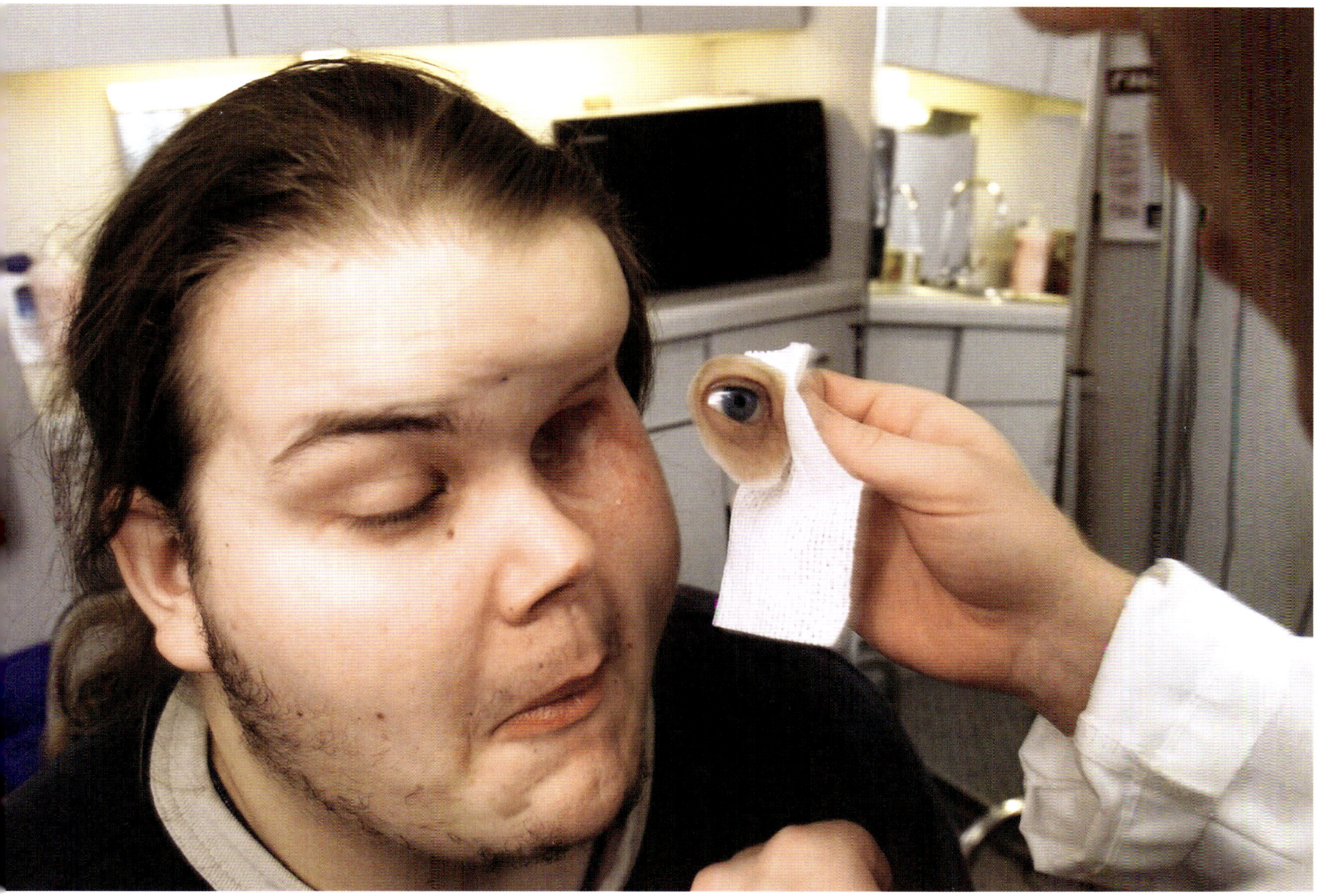

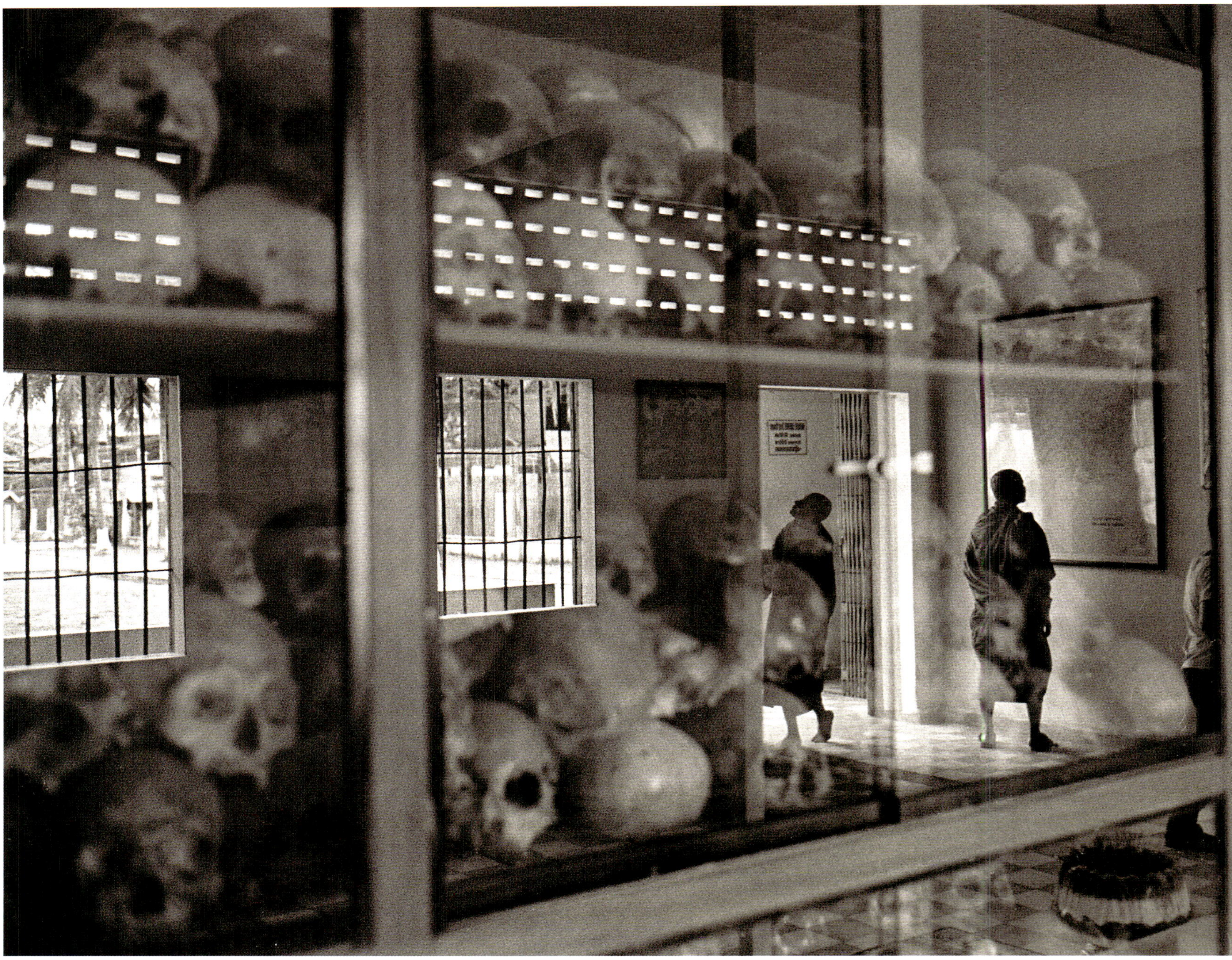

Duane Prentice

Tuol Seng Monks and Skulls

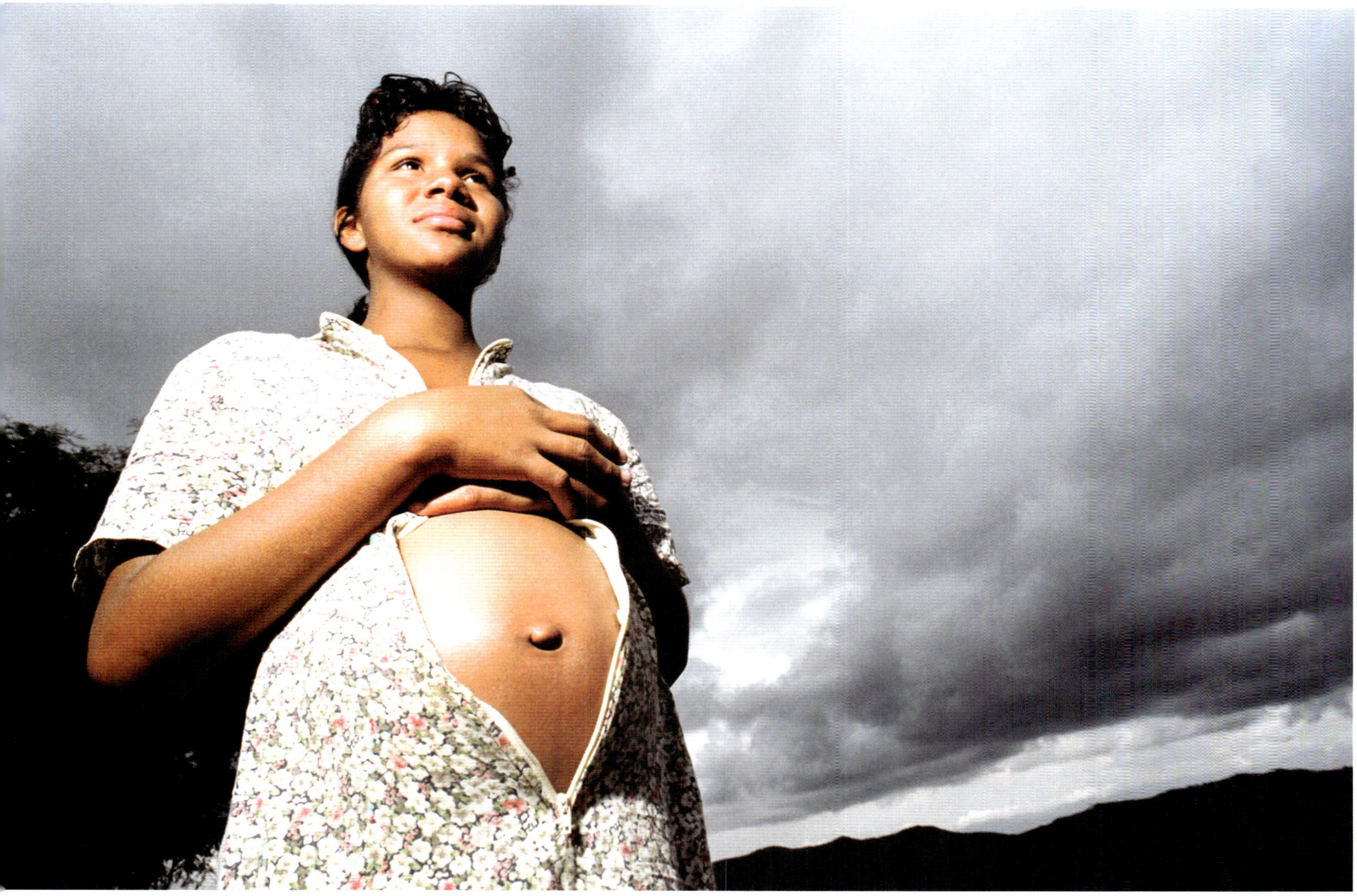

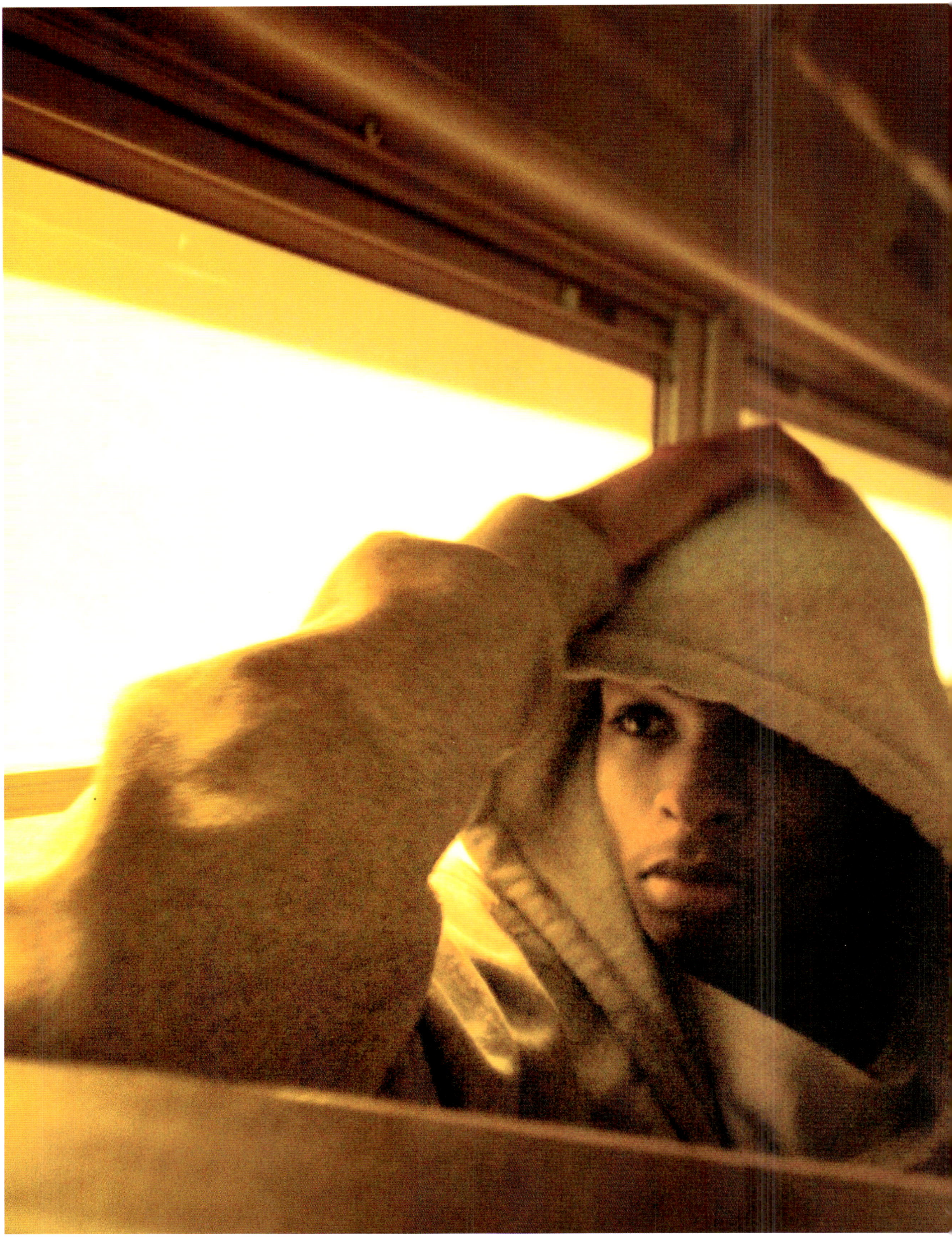

Steve Russell

Basketball

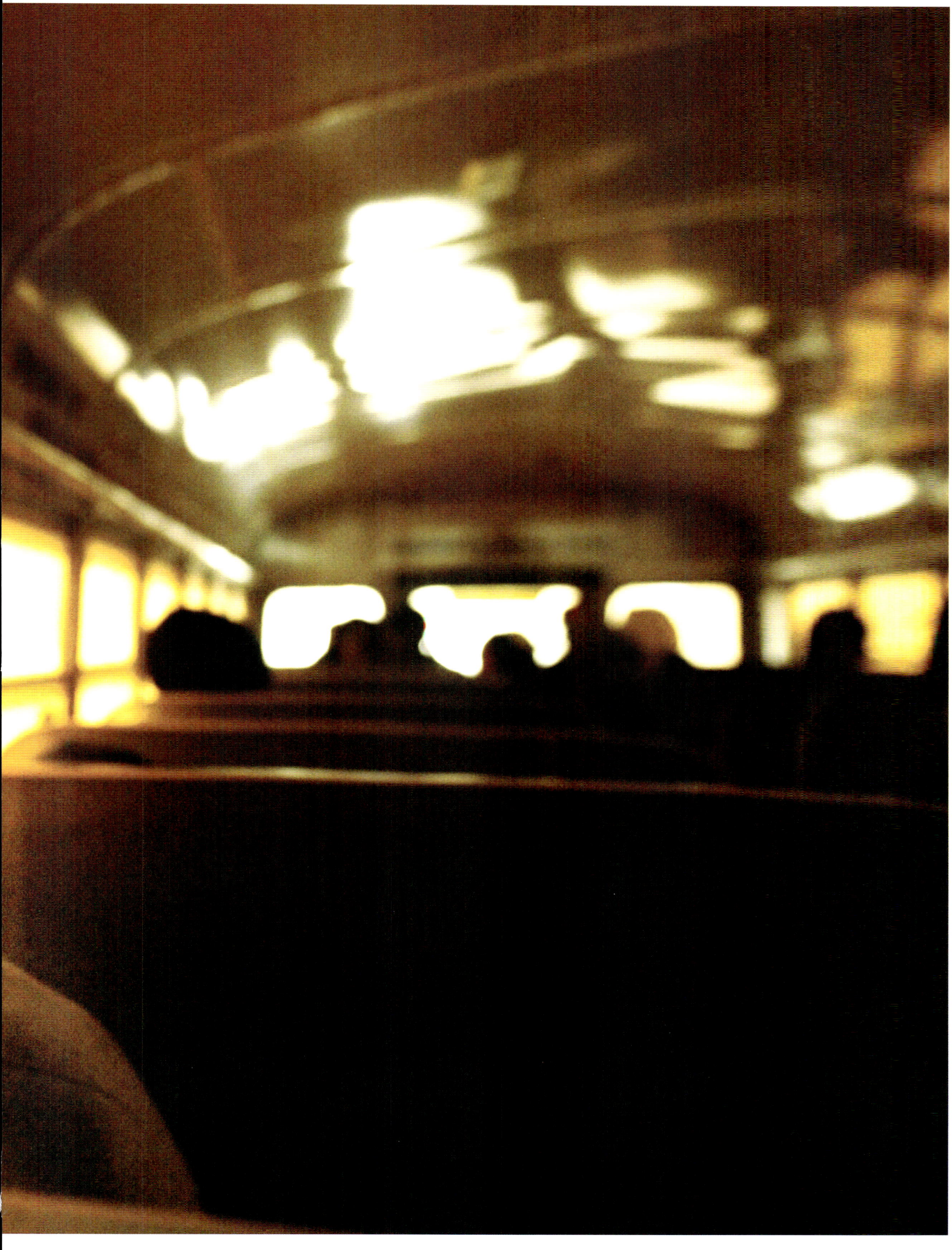

Steve Russell

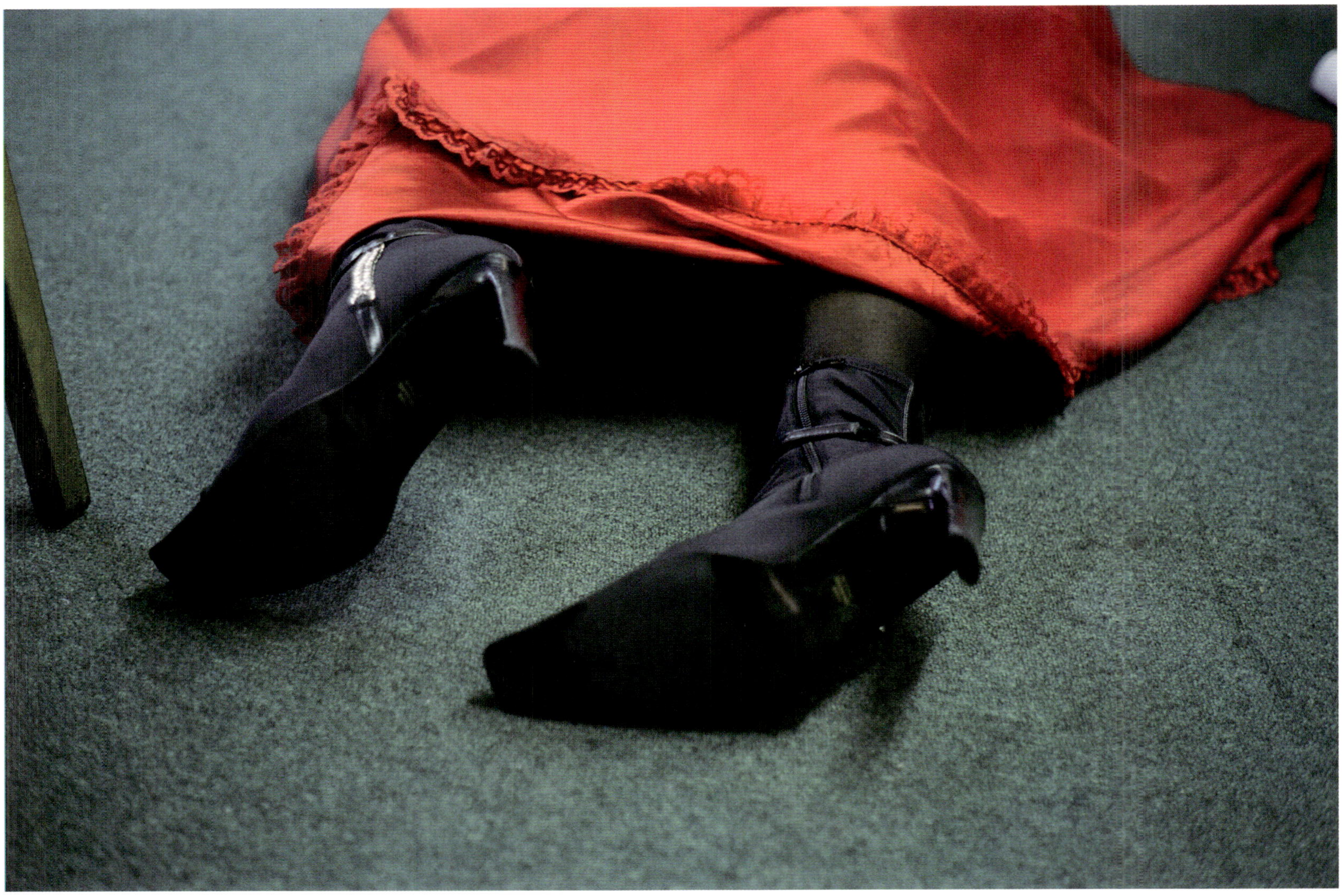

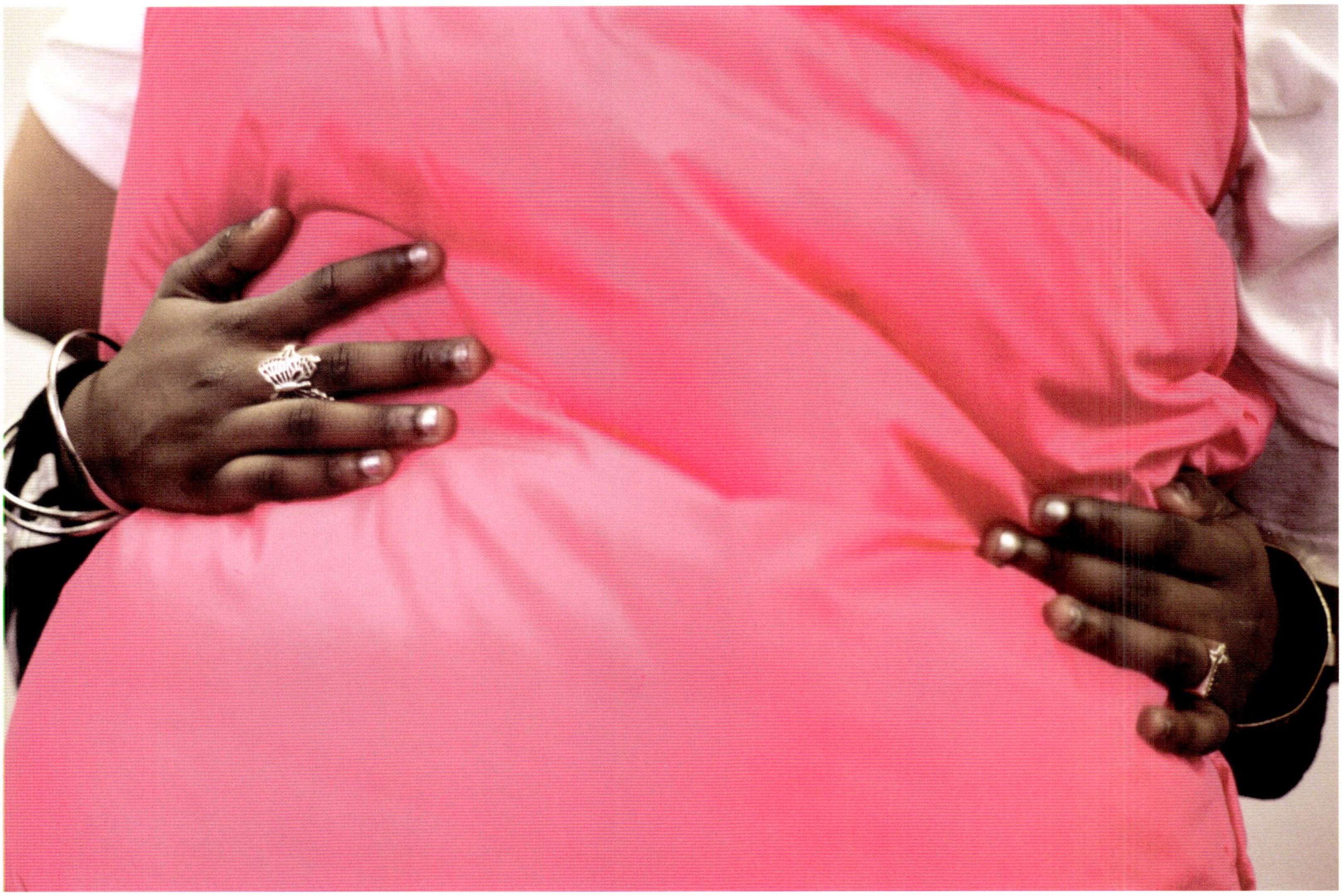

Andrea Ryder

From the Hebrew Pentecostal Series (Brooklyn, New York, 2003)

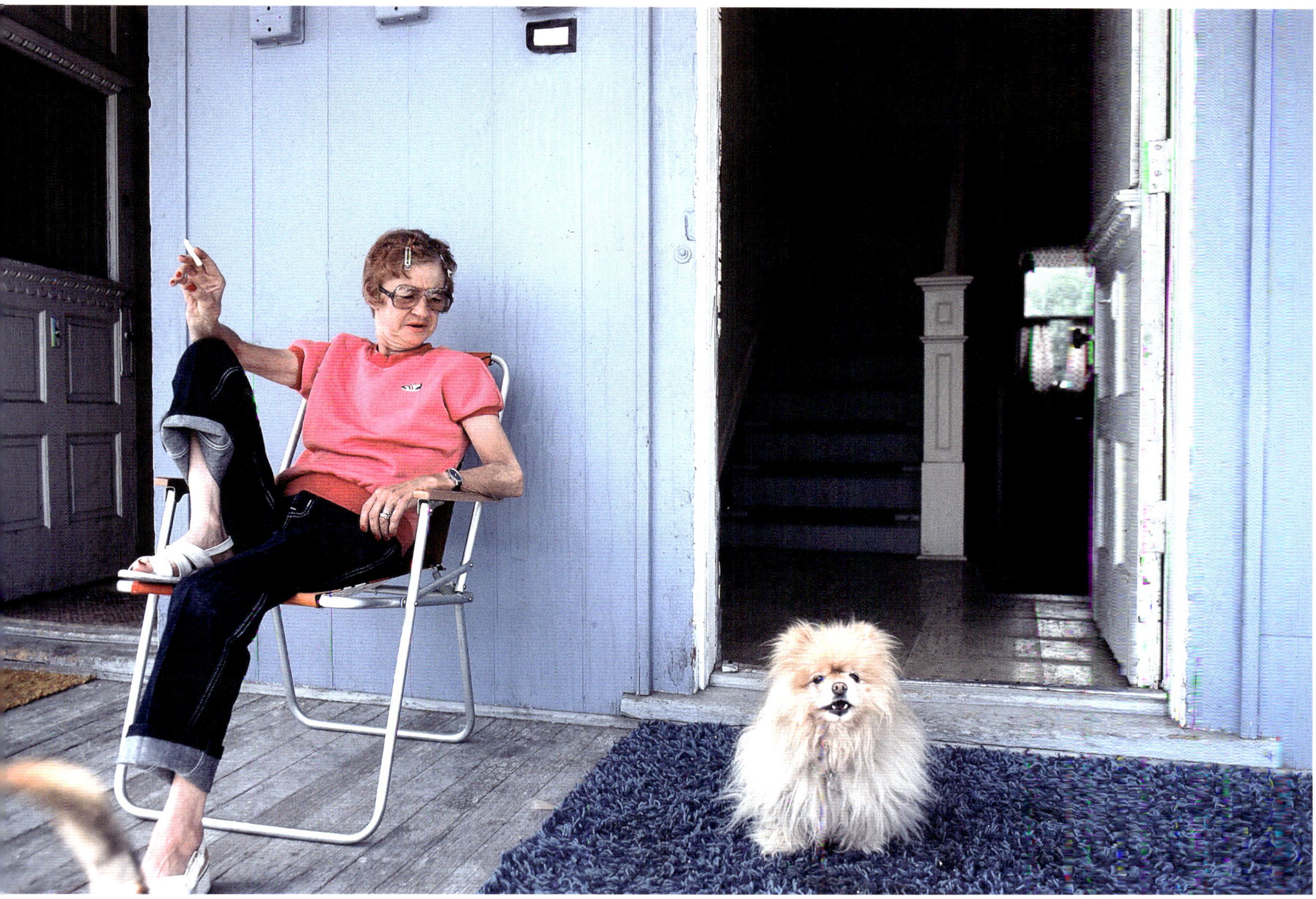

Woman & Dog, Calgary

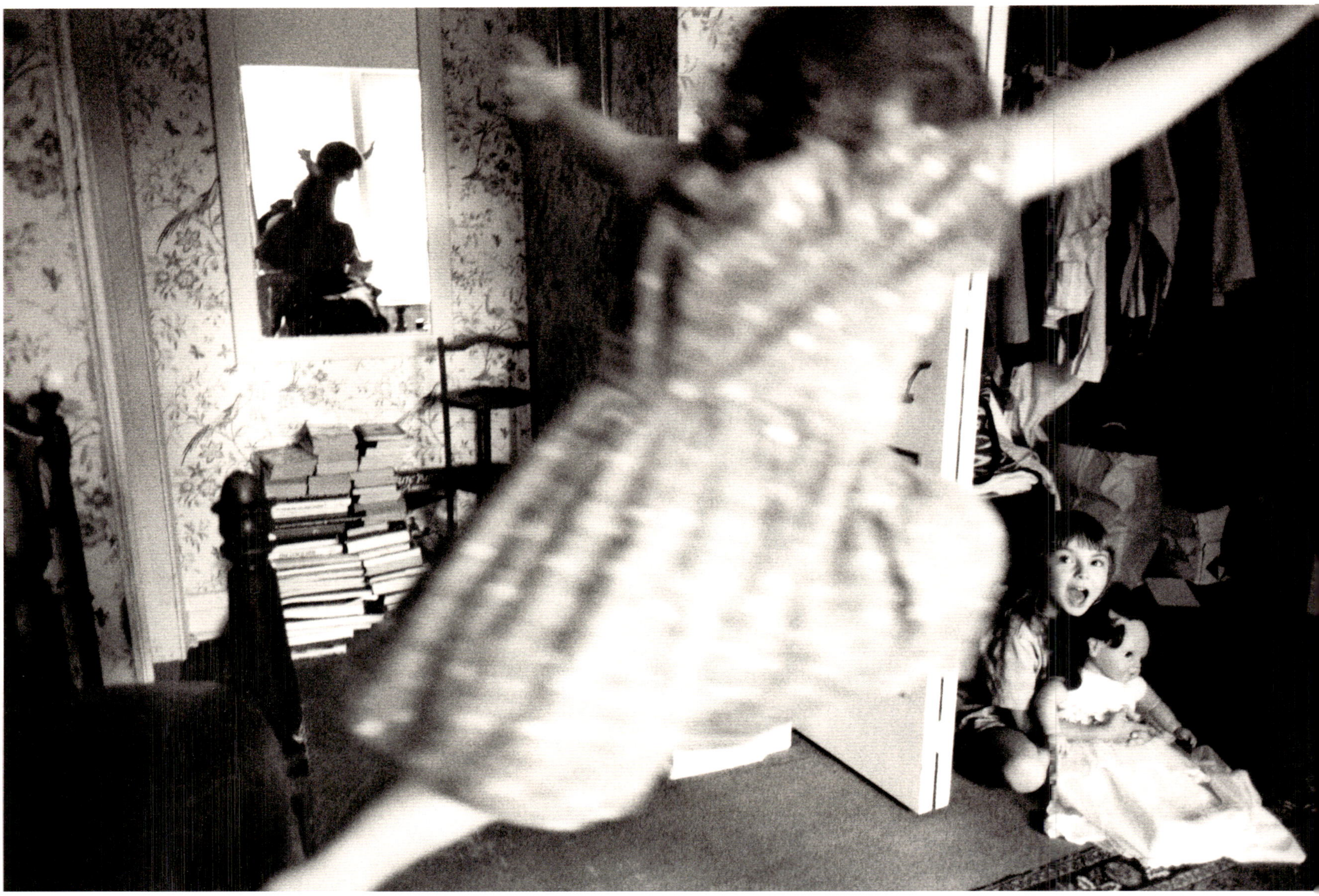

Flying Off Grannie's Bed

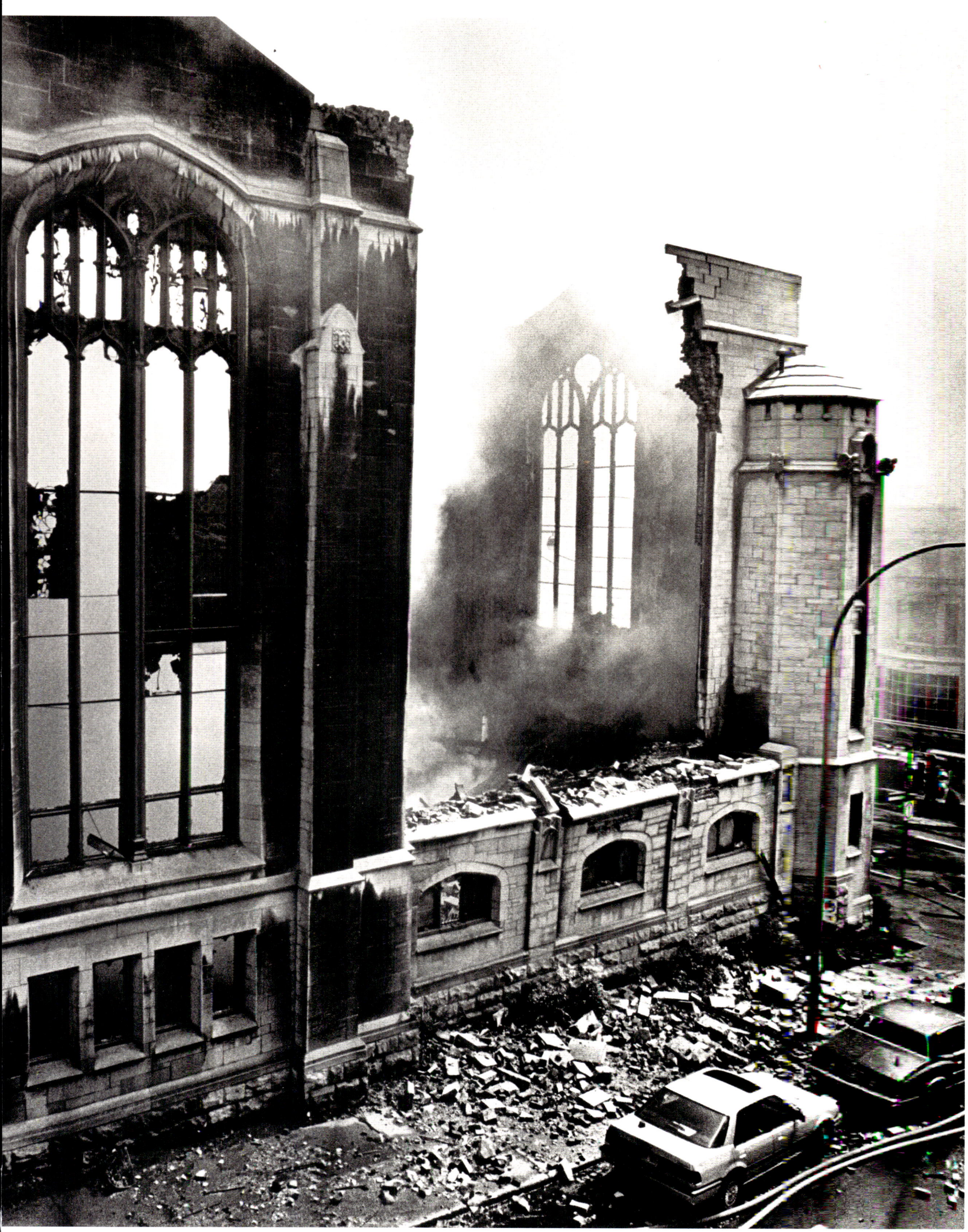

Unitarian Church Fire

David Leonard Sidaway

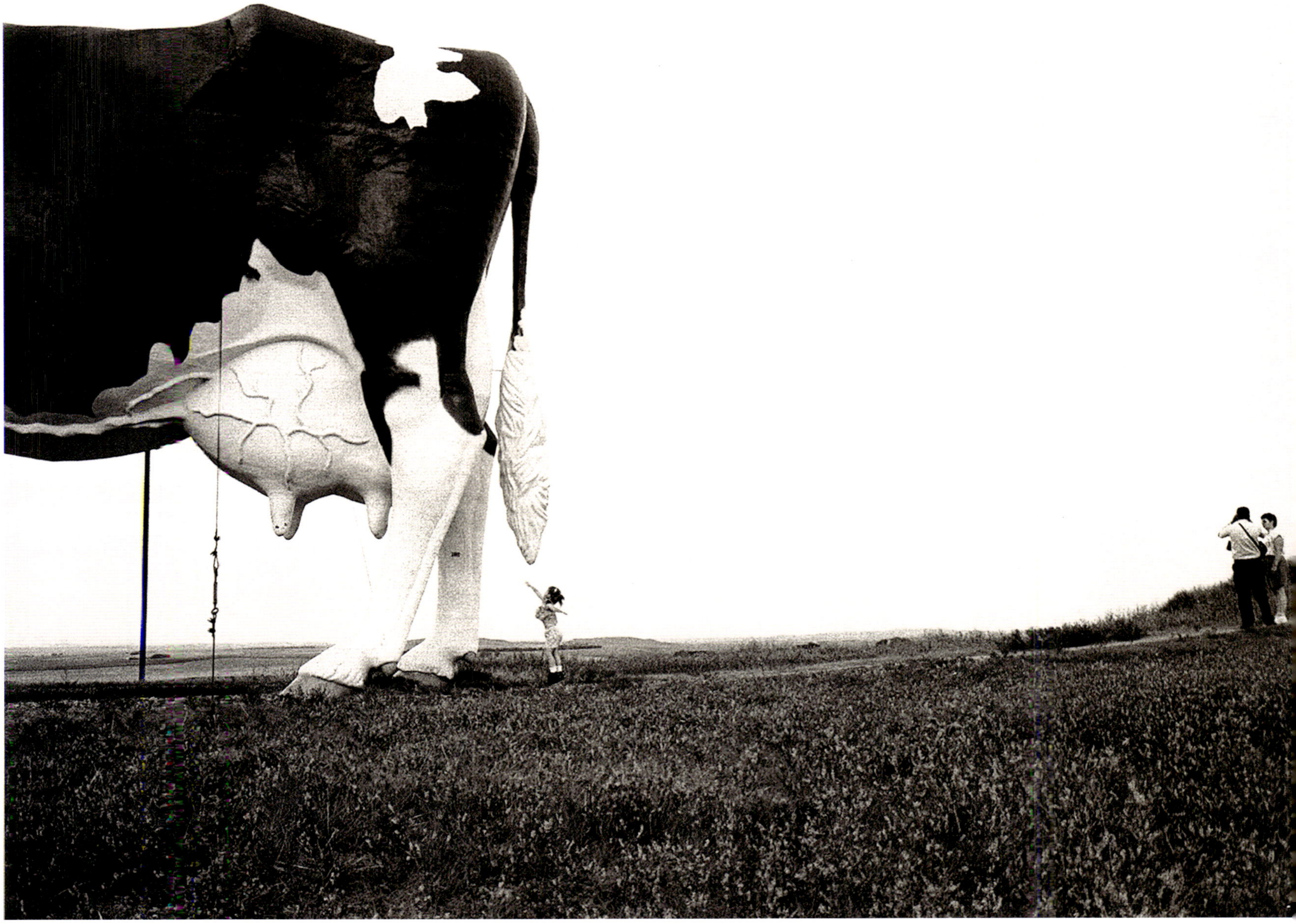

Big Cow

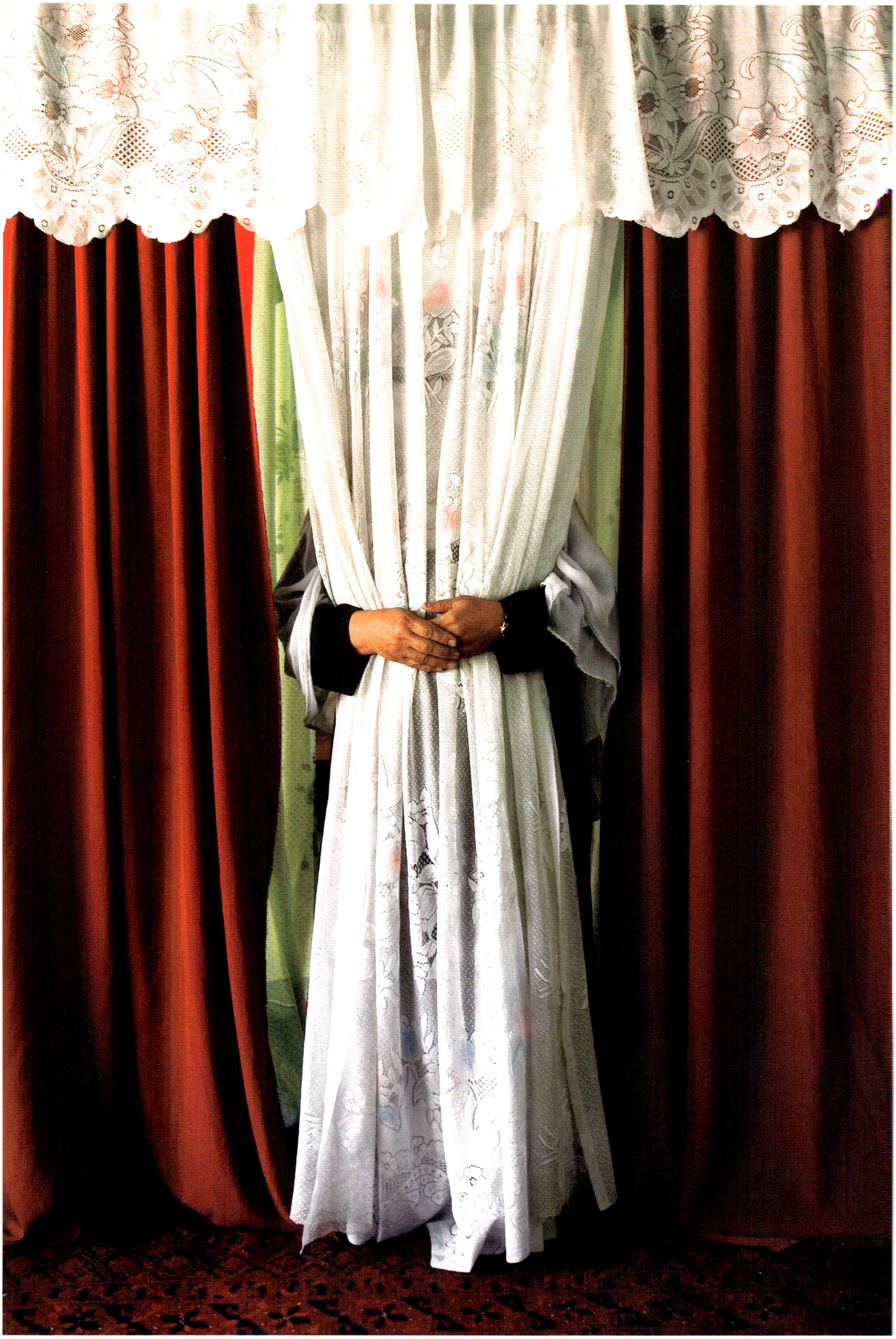

Prostitute

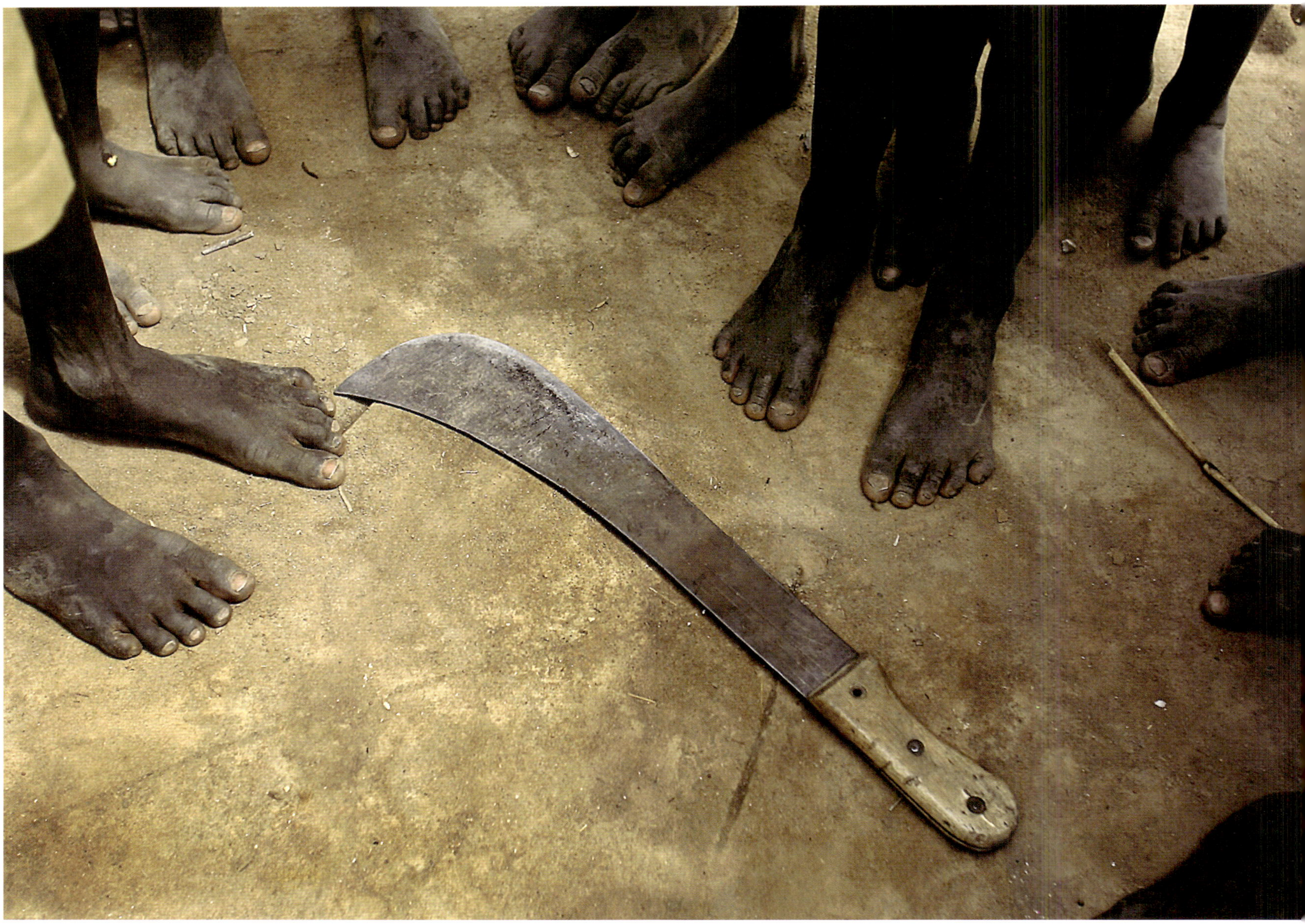

Lyle Stafford

Untitled

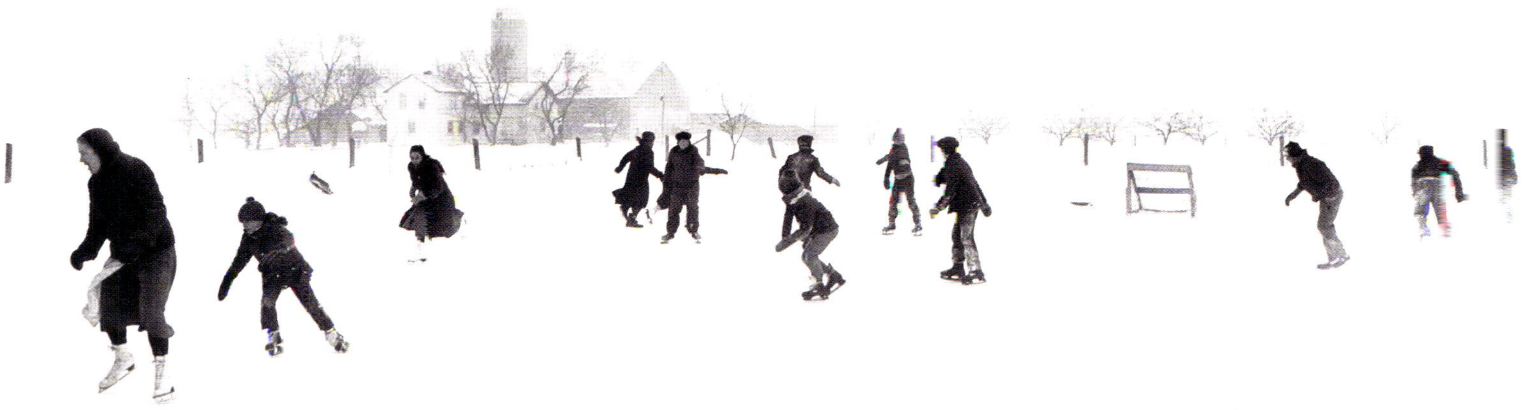

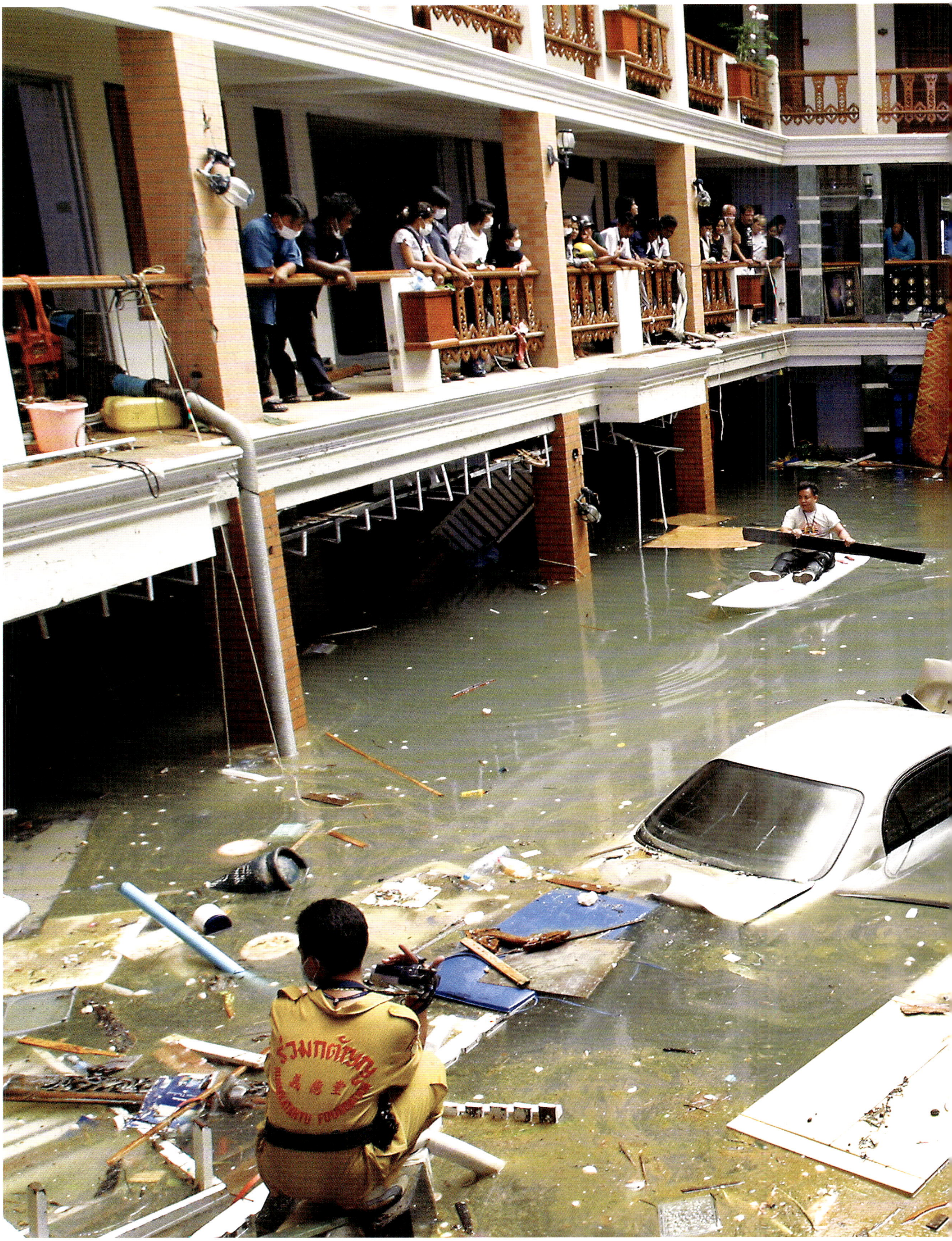

Deddeda Stemler

Flooded Hotel Lobby: Tsunami Aftermath

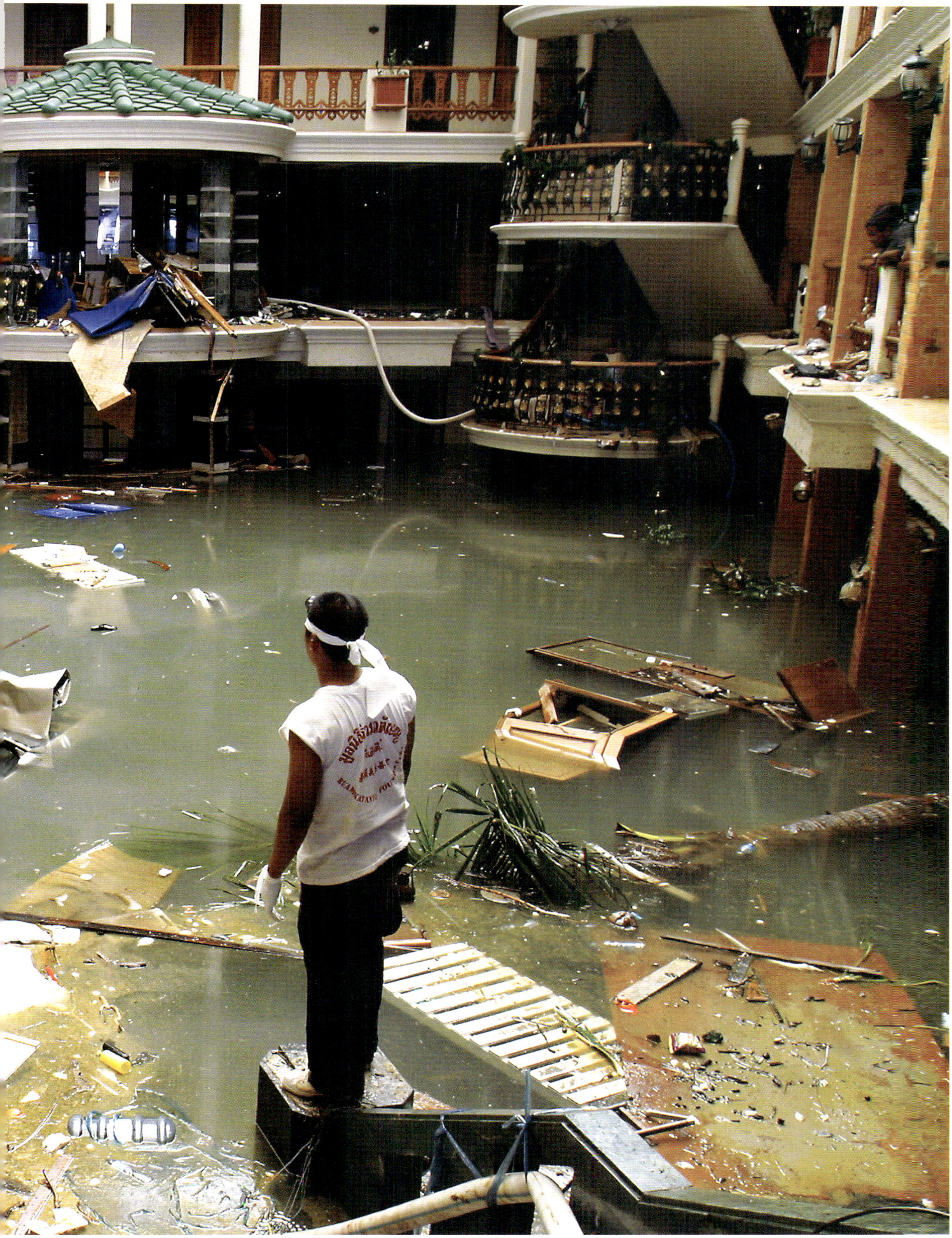

Deborah Schindler

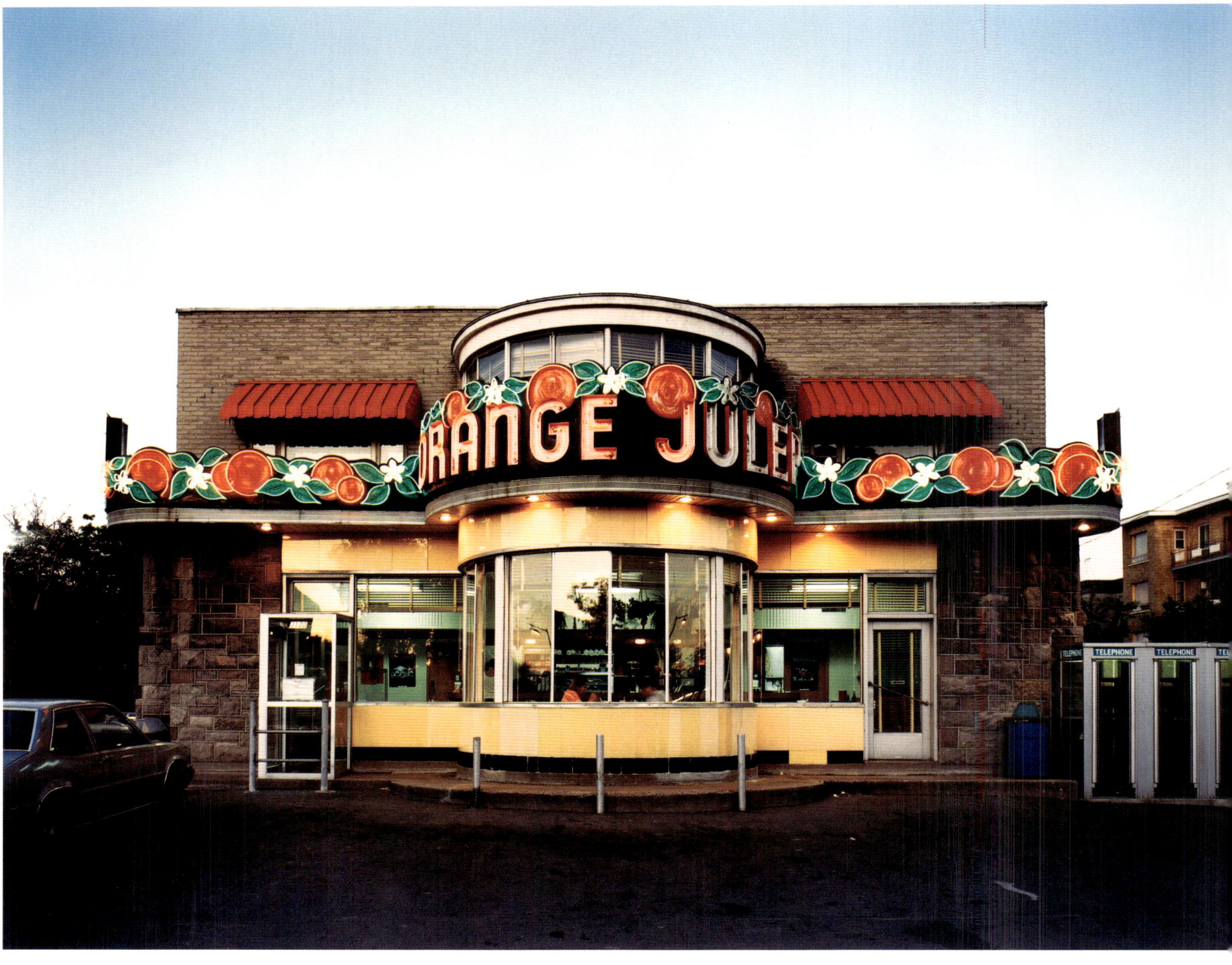

Gabor Szilasi

Orange Julep

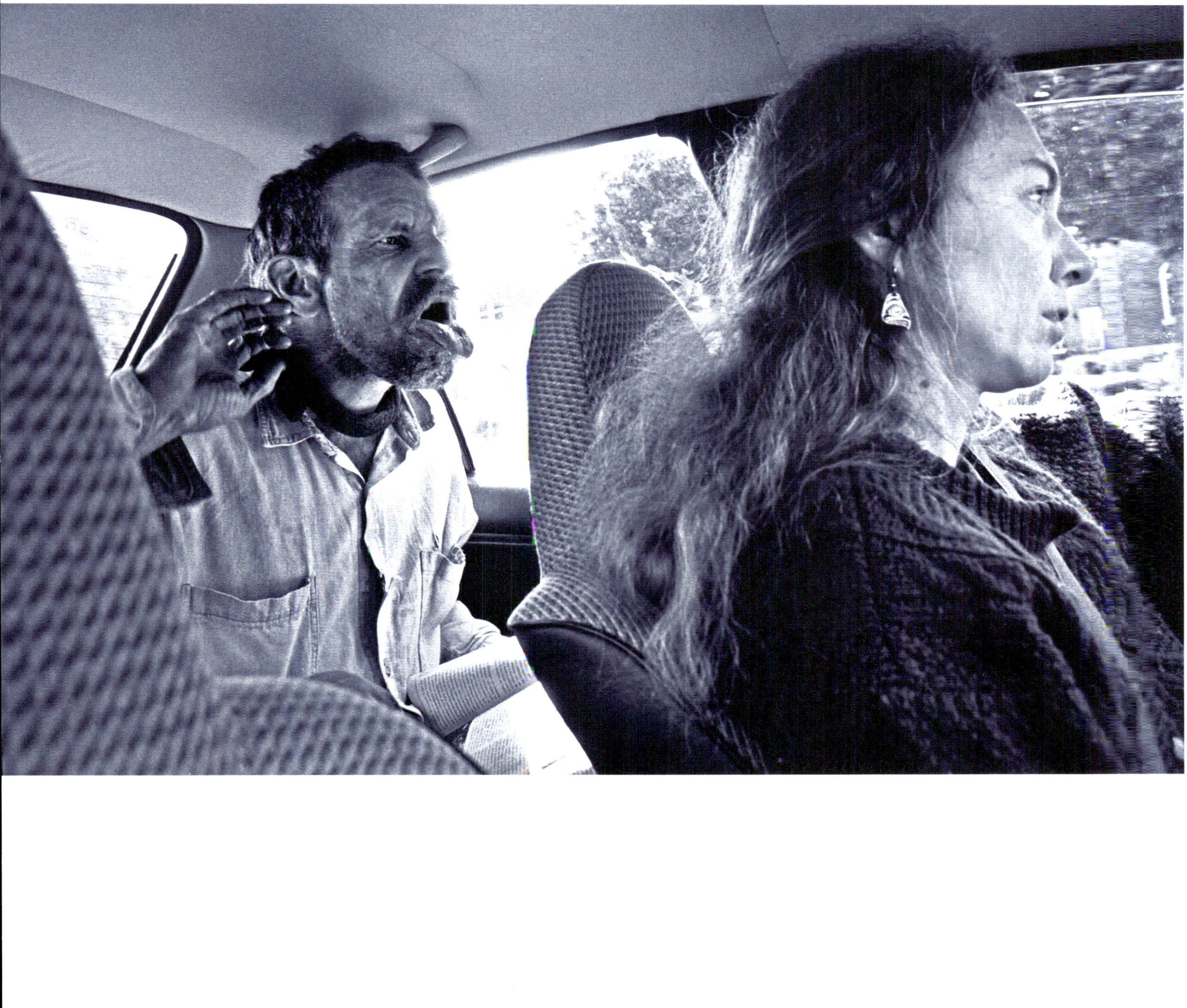

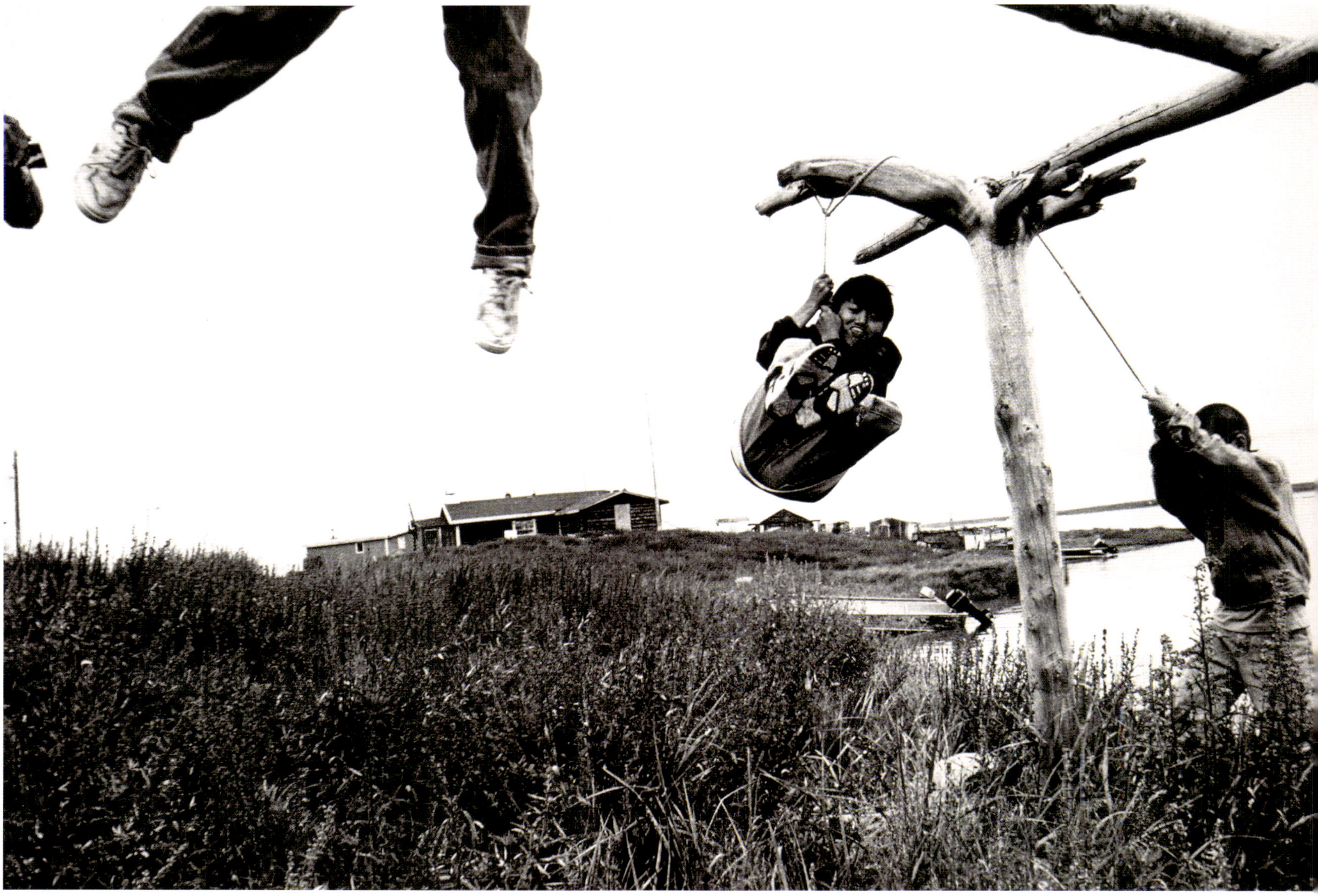

Tuktoyaktuk, N.W.T.

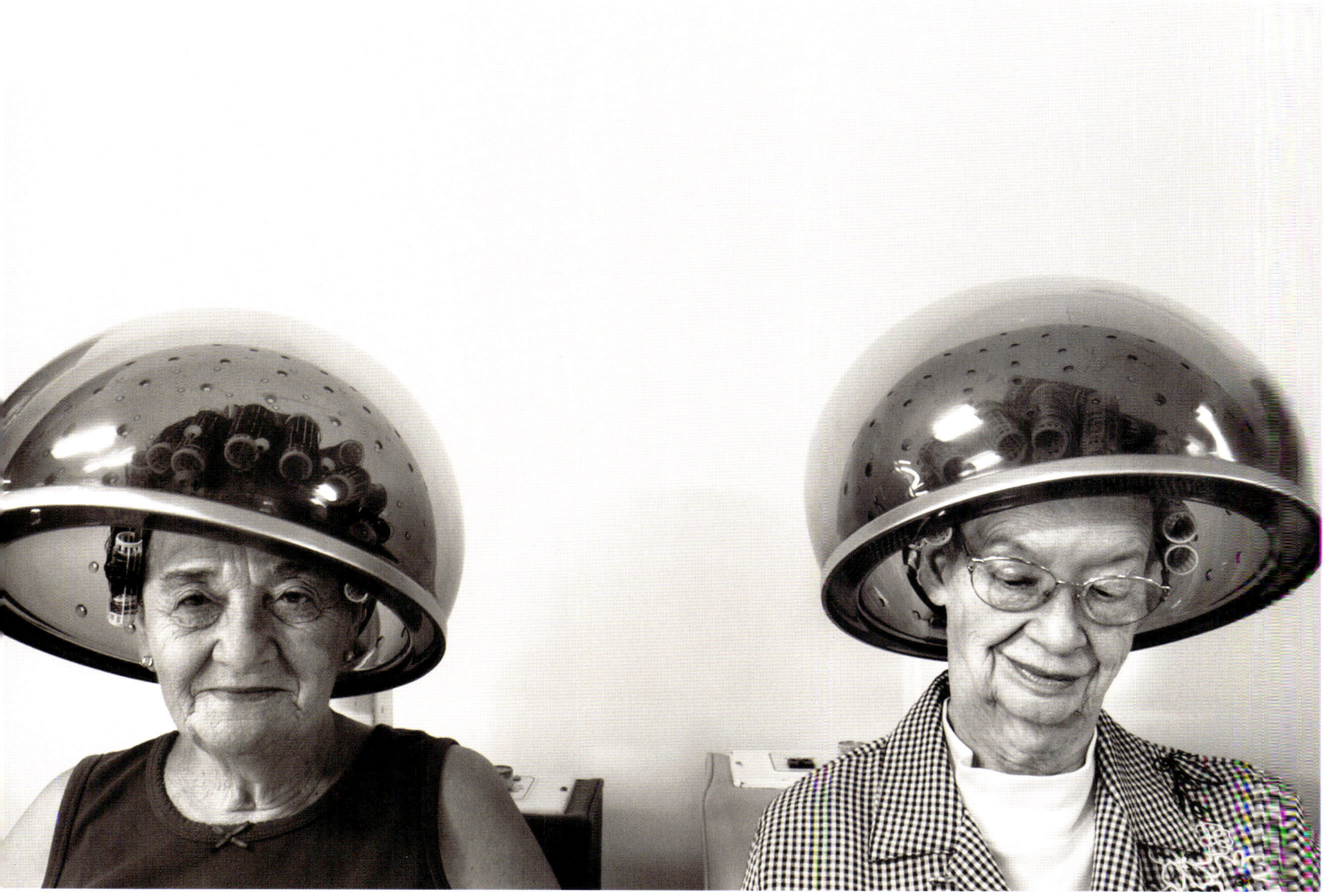

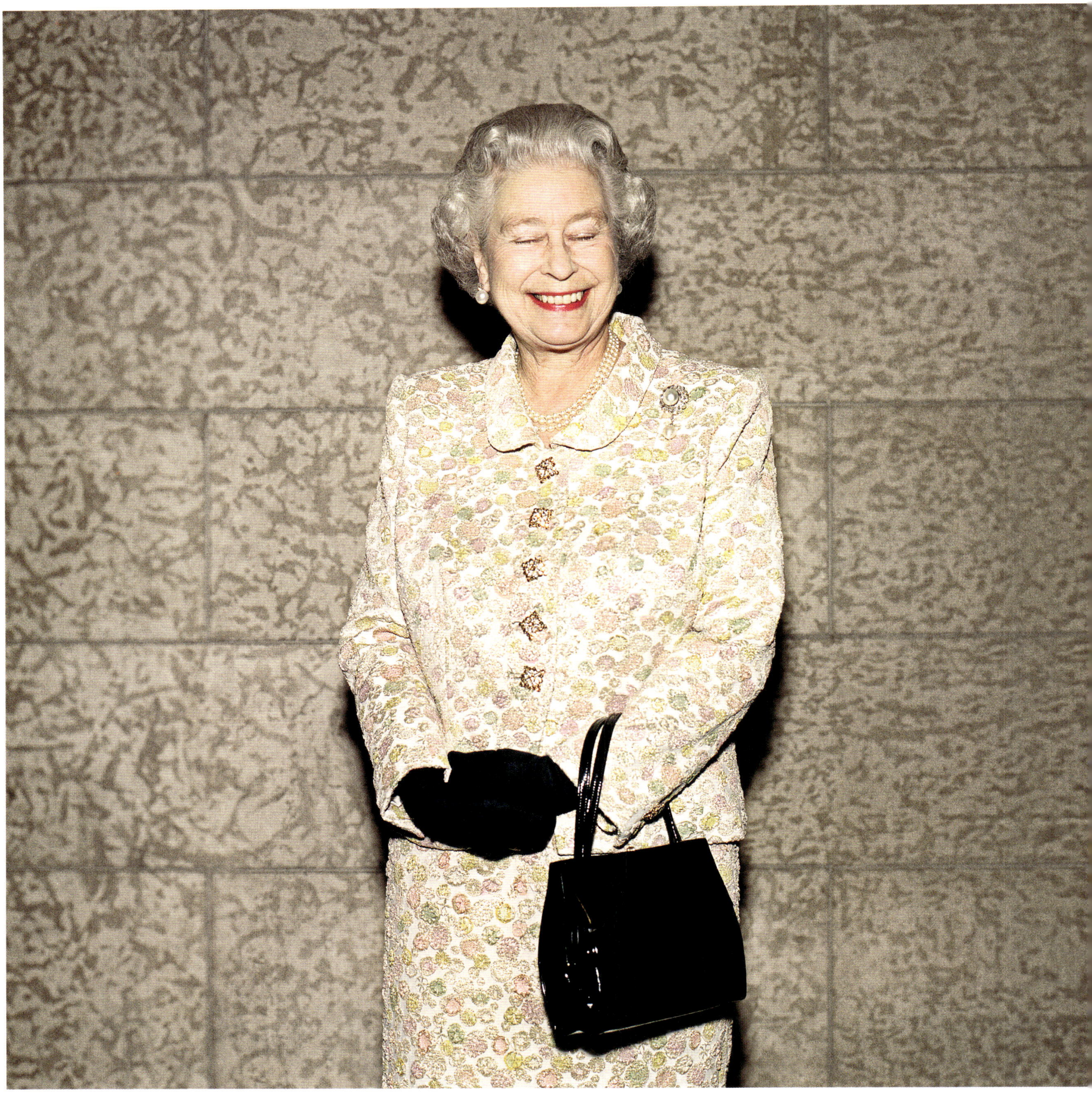

Christopher Wahl Queen (No Eyes)

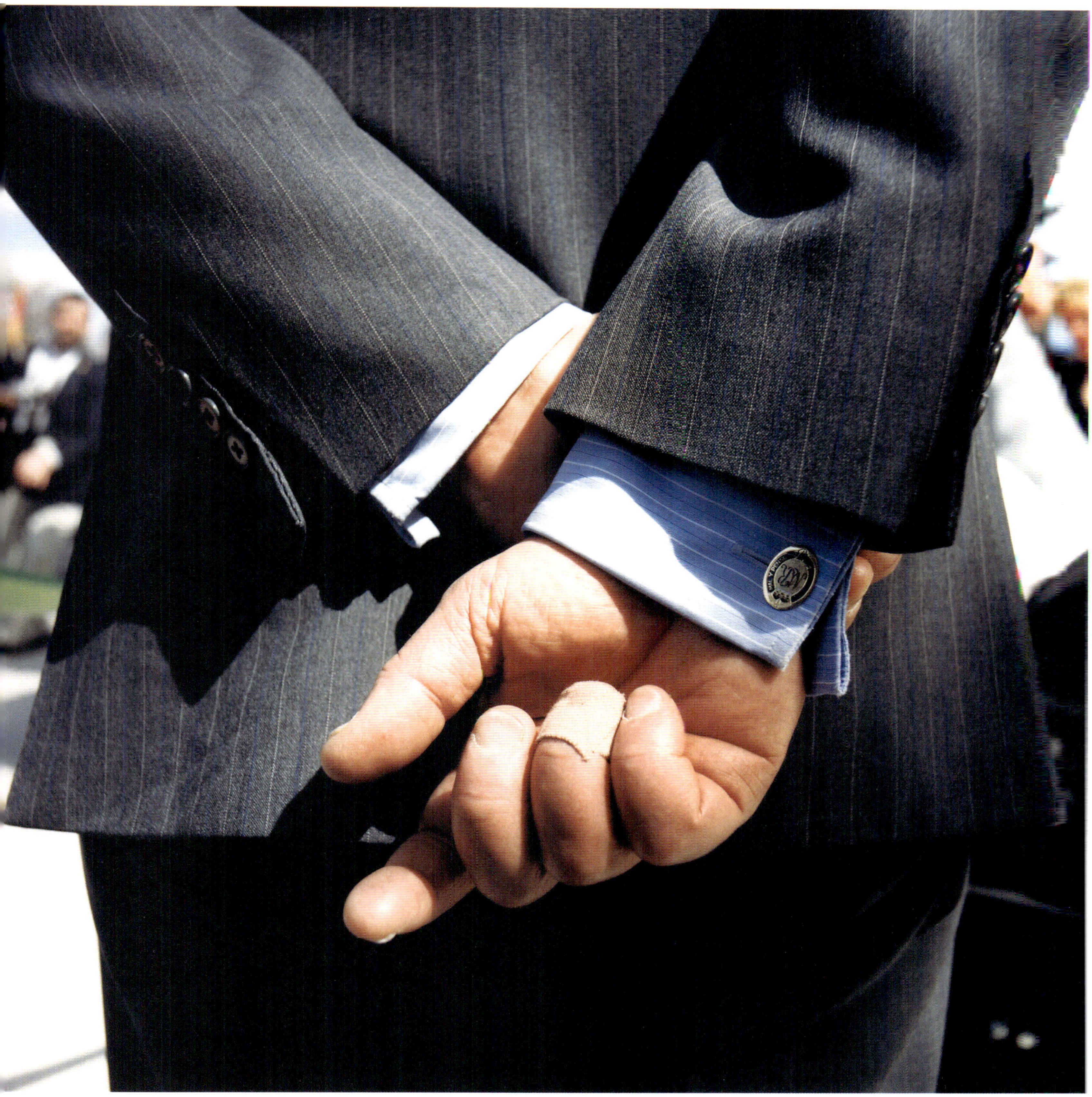

Prince (Hands)

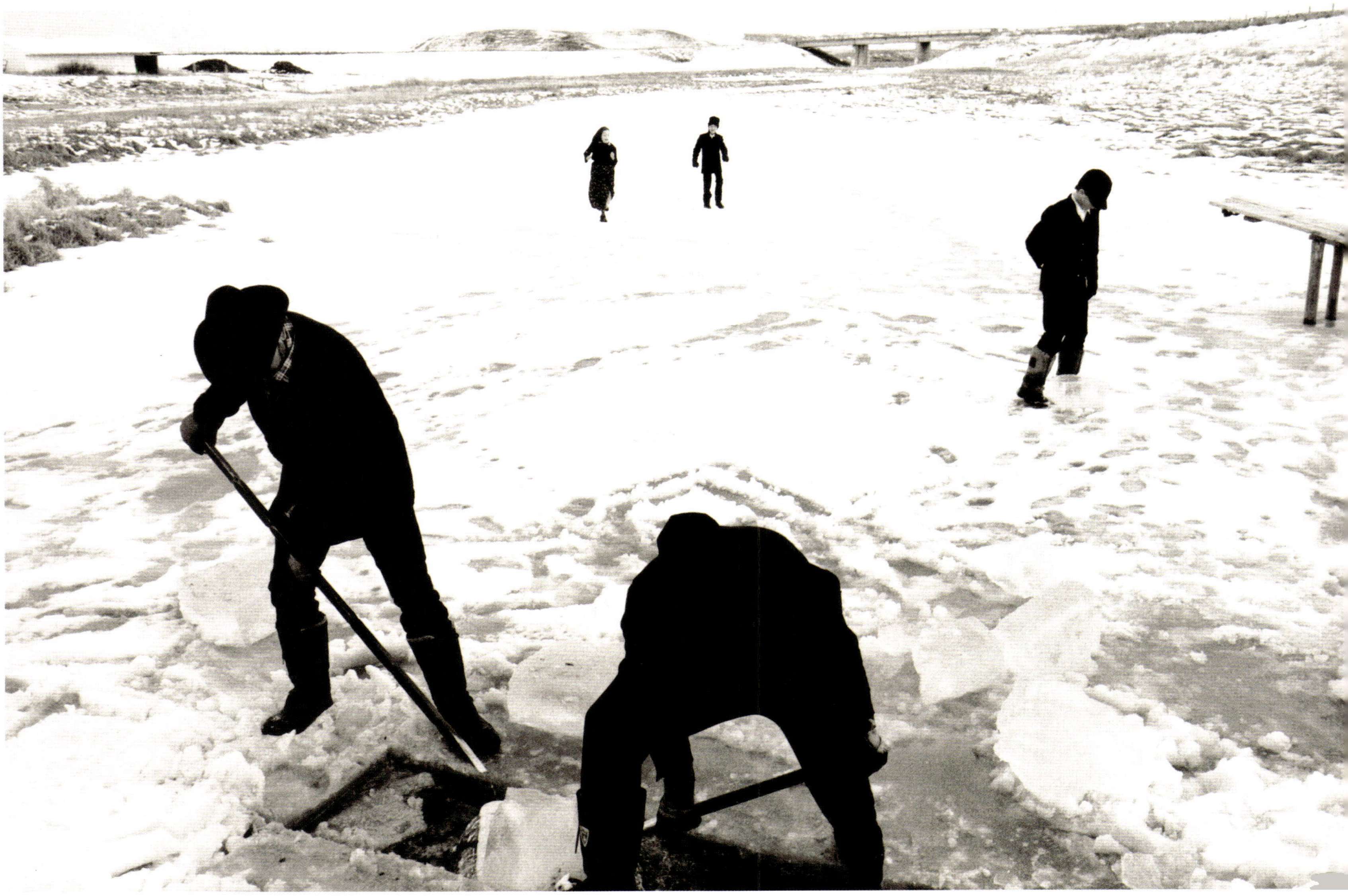

Clearing Ice

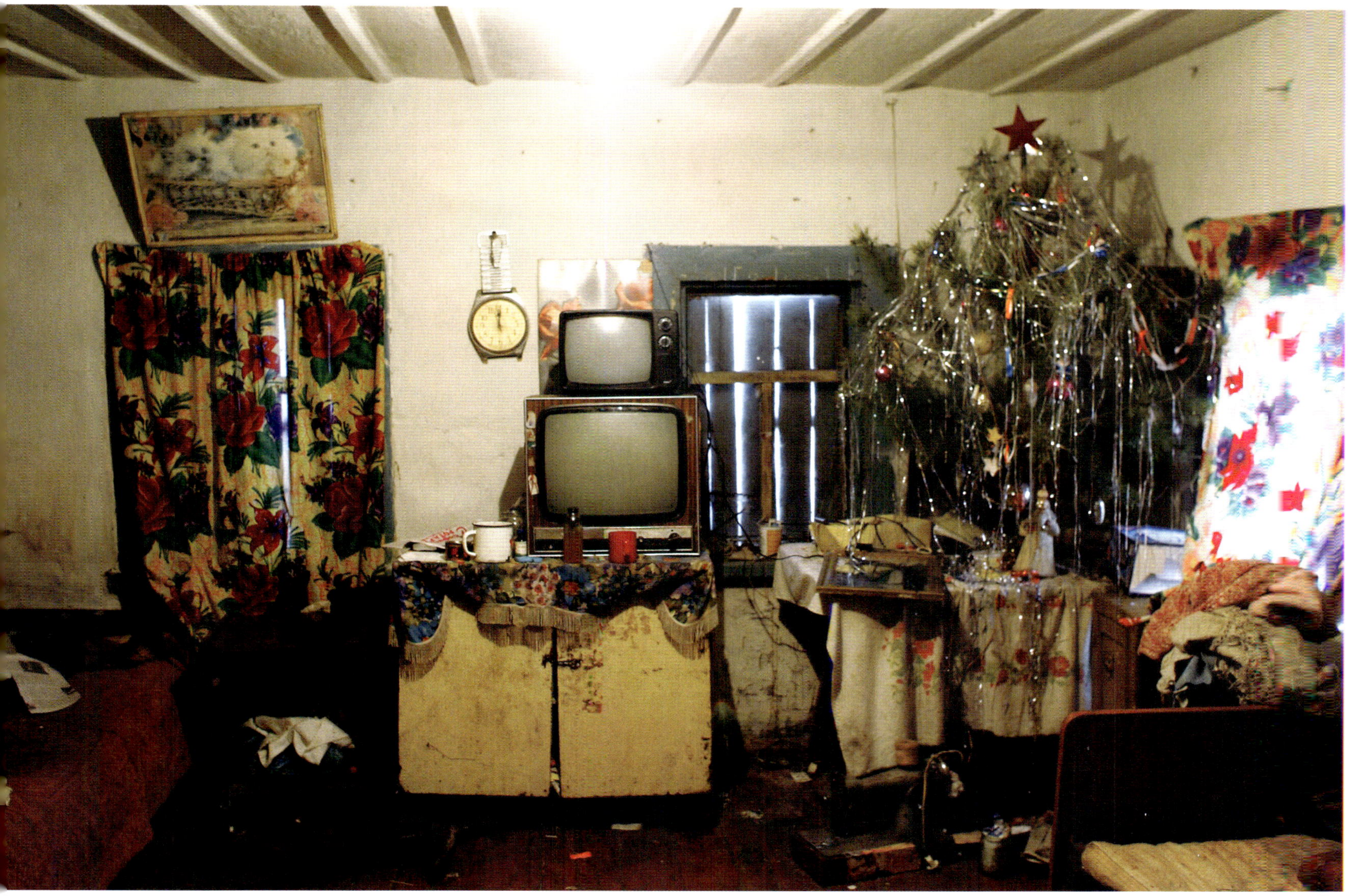

Village House, Chernobyl

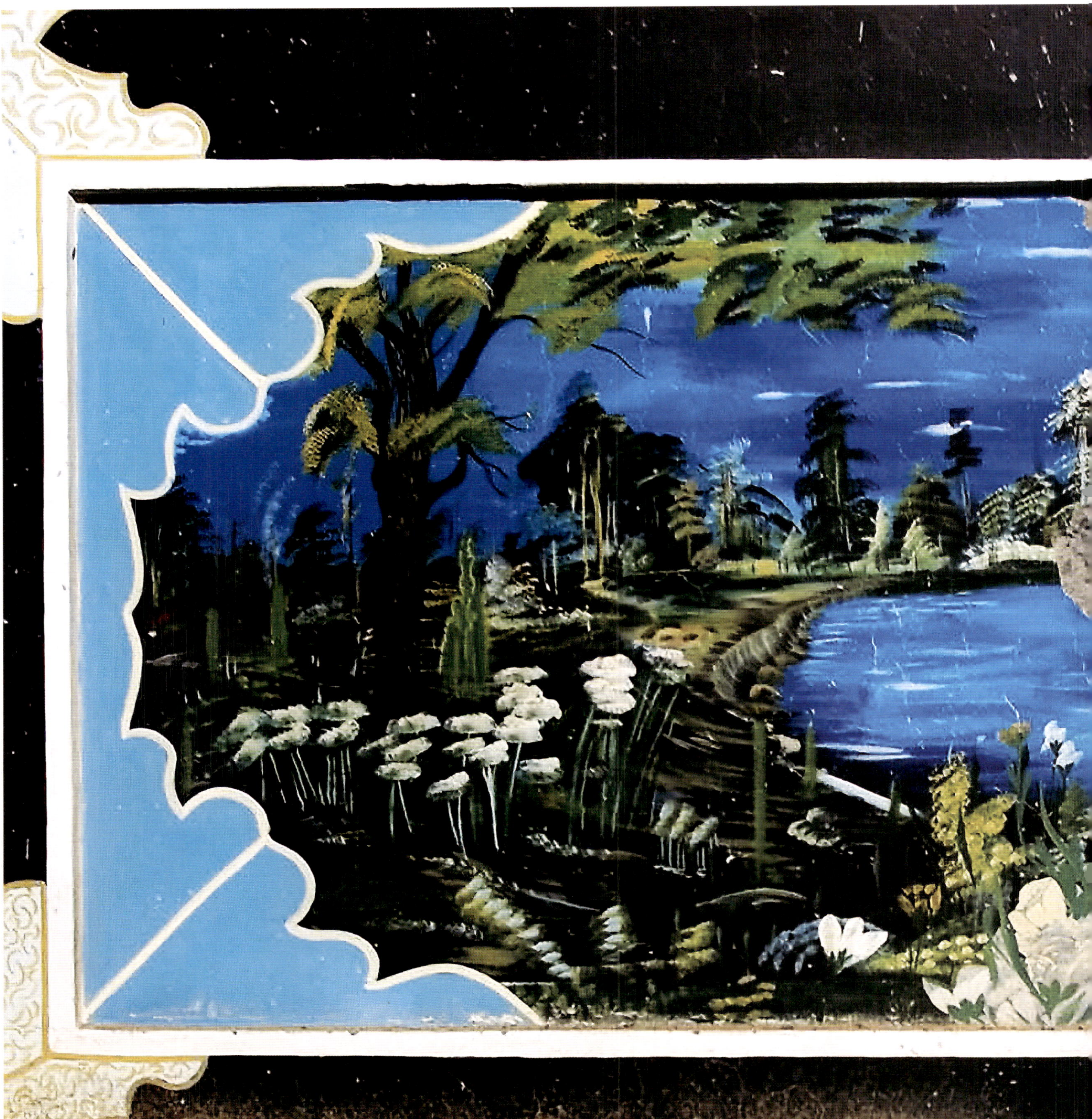

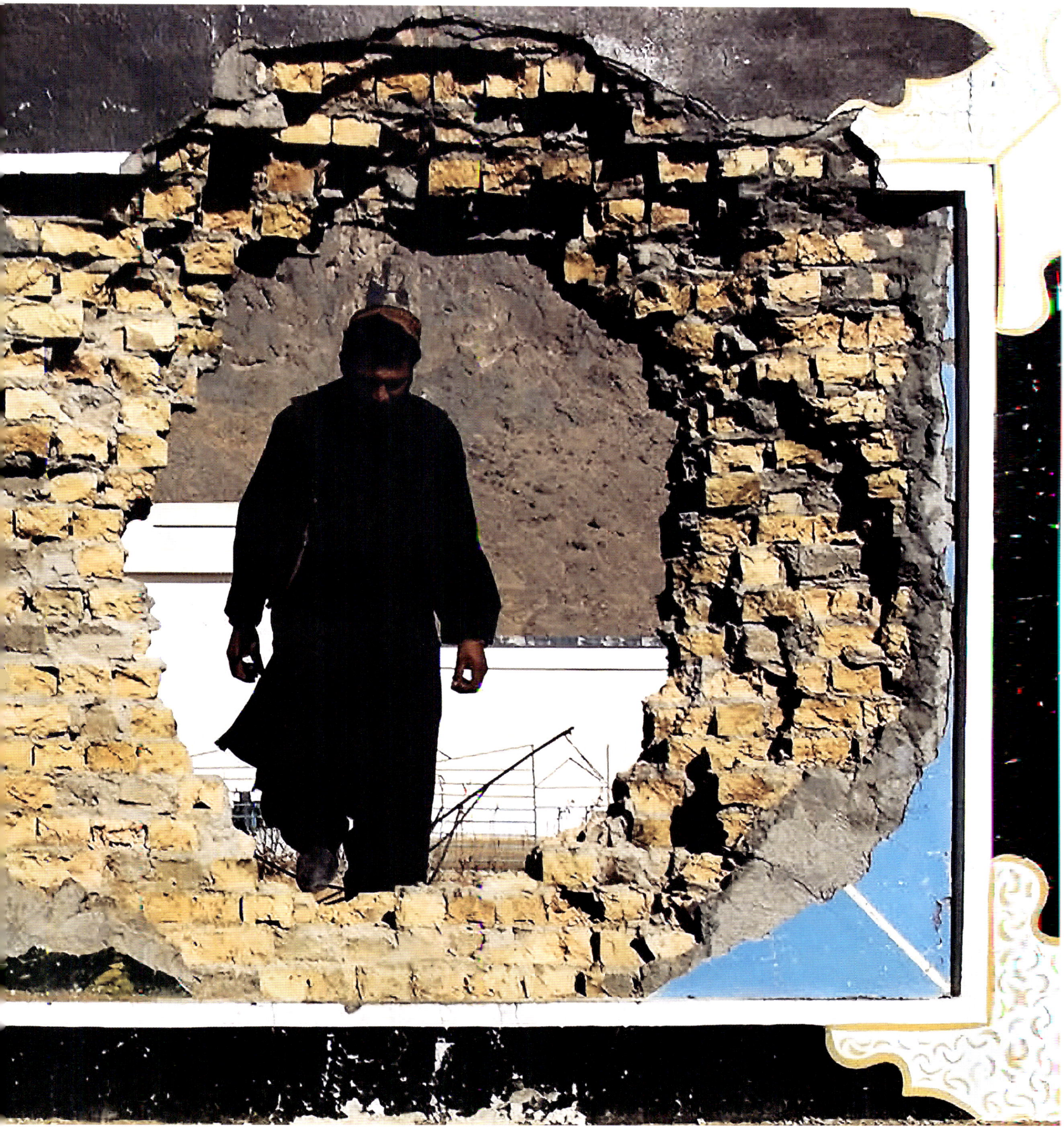

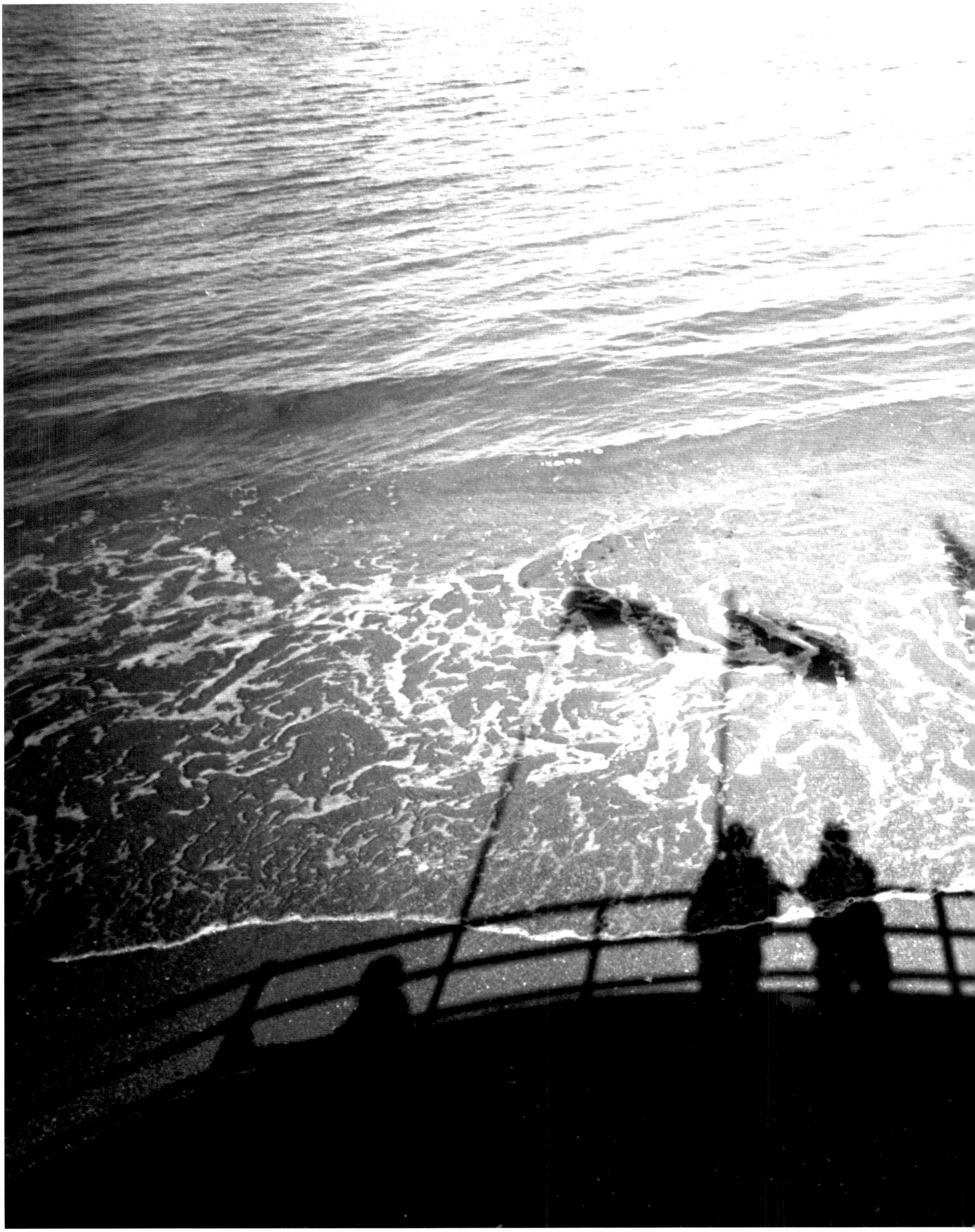

George S. Zimbel

Boardwalk at Chipiona, Spain, 2002

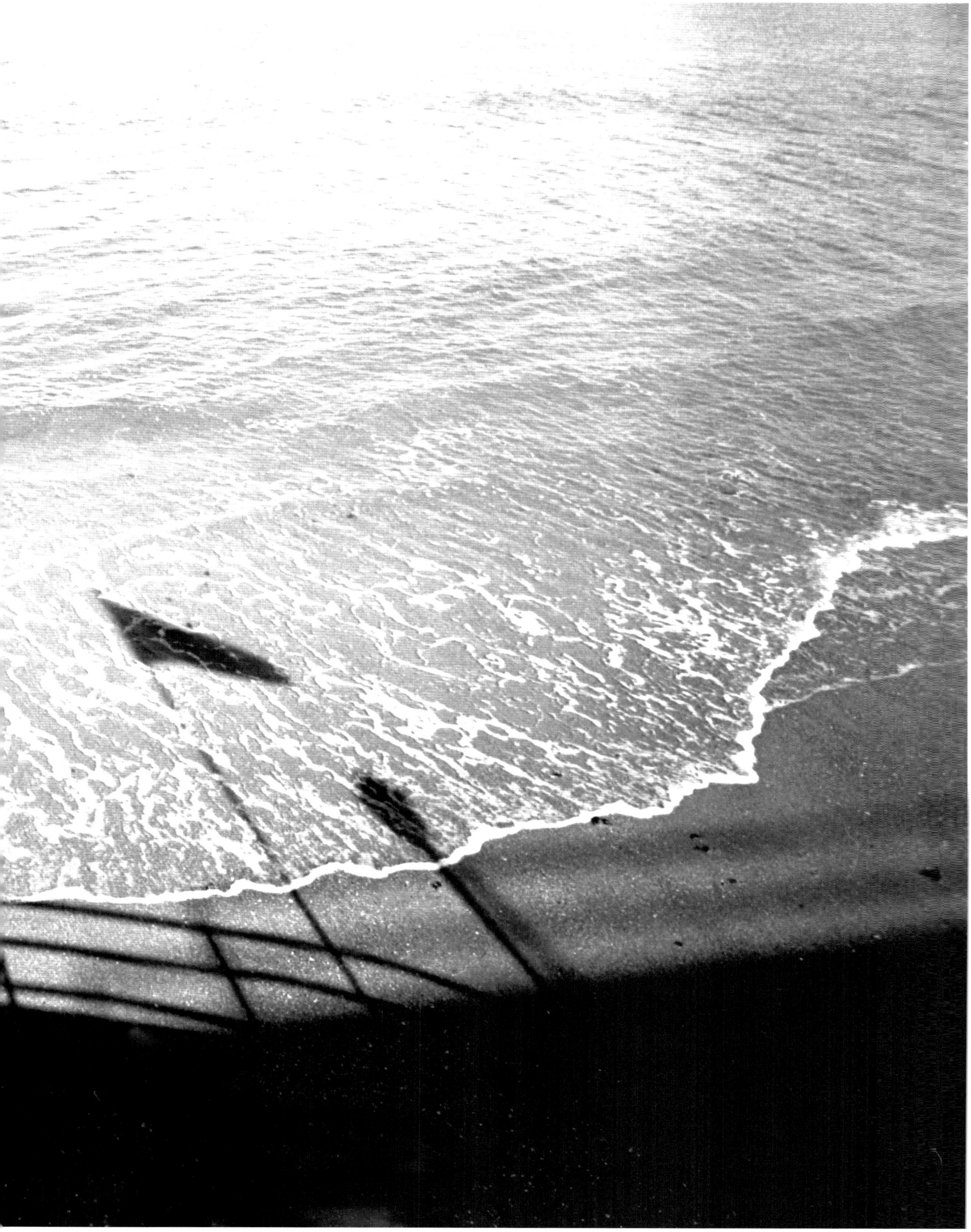

George S Zimbel

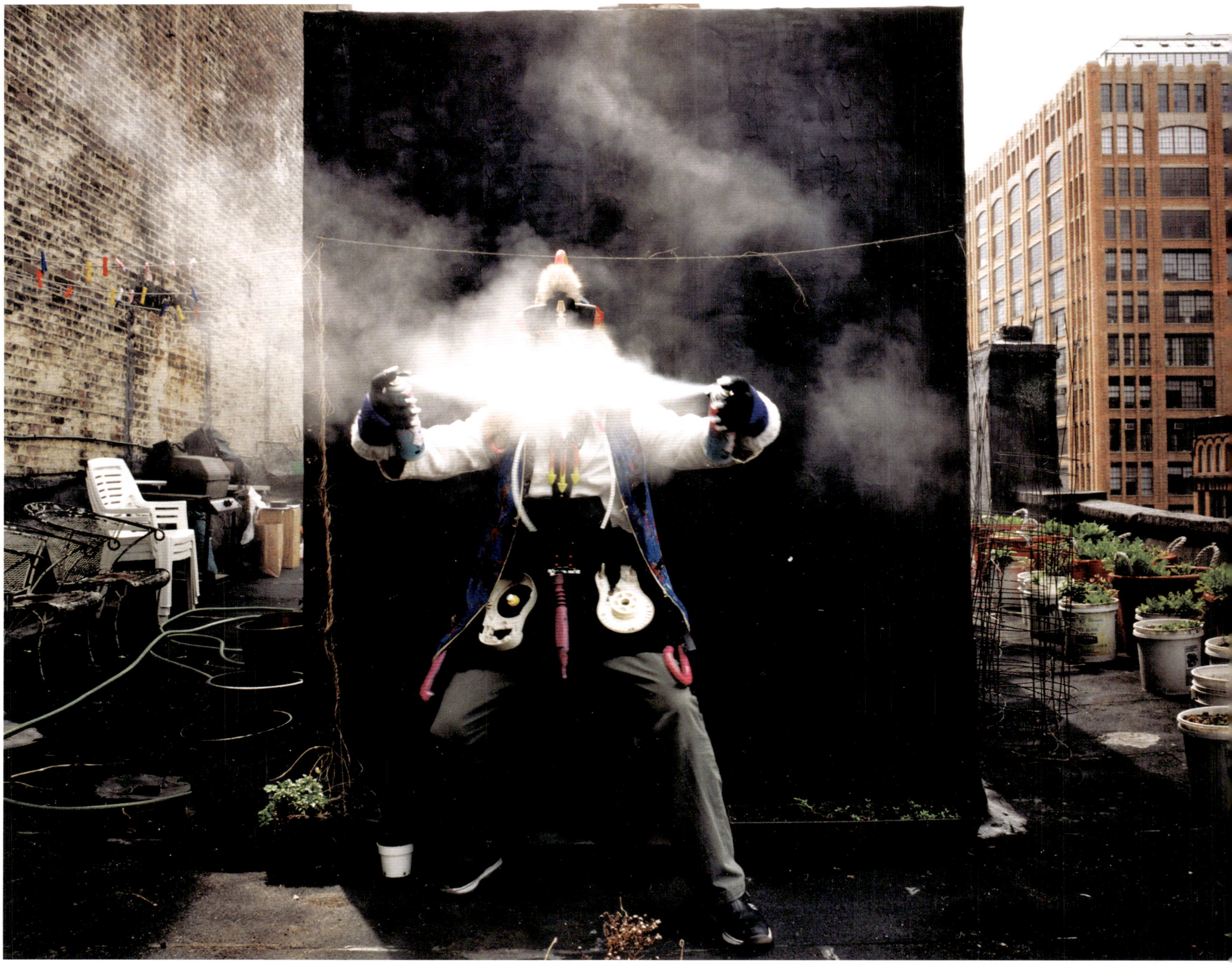

Rammallzee

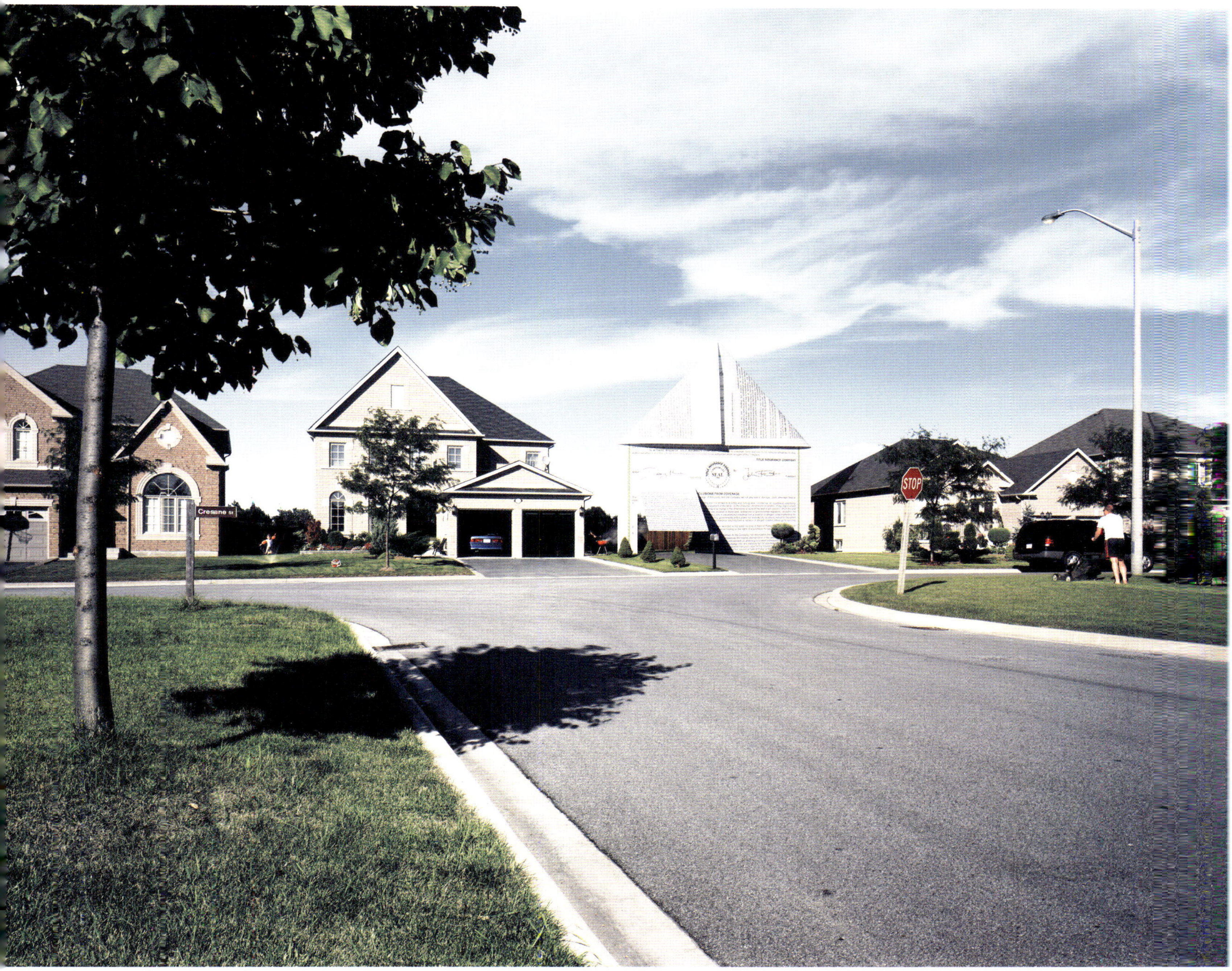

Land America Suburb Paper House

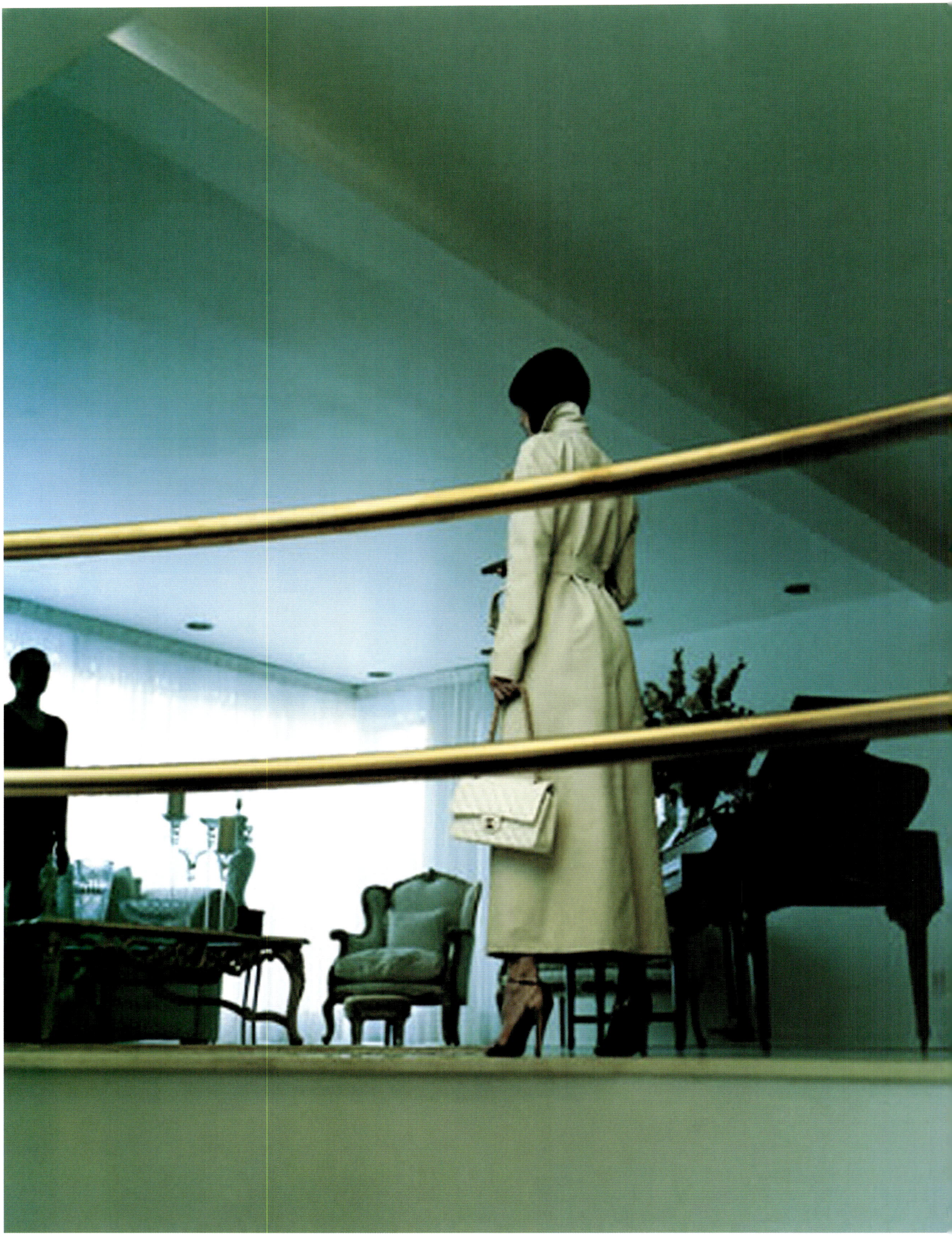

Agent Provocateur

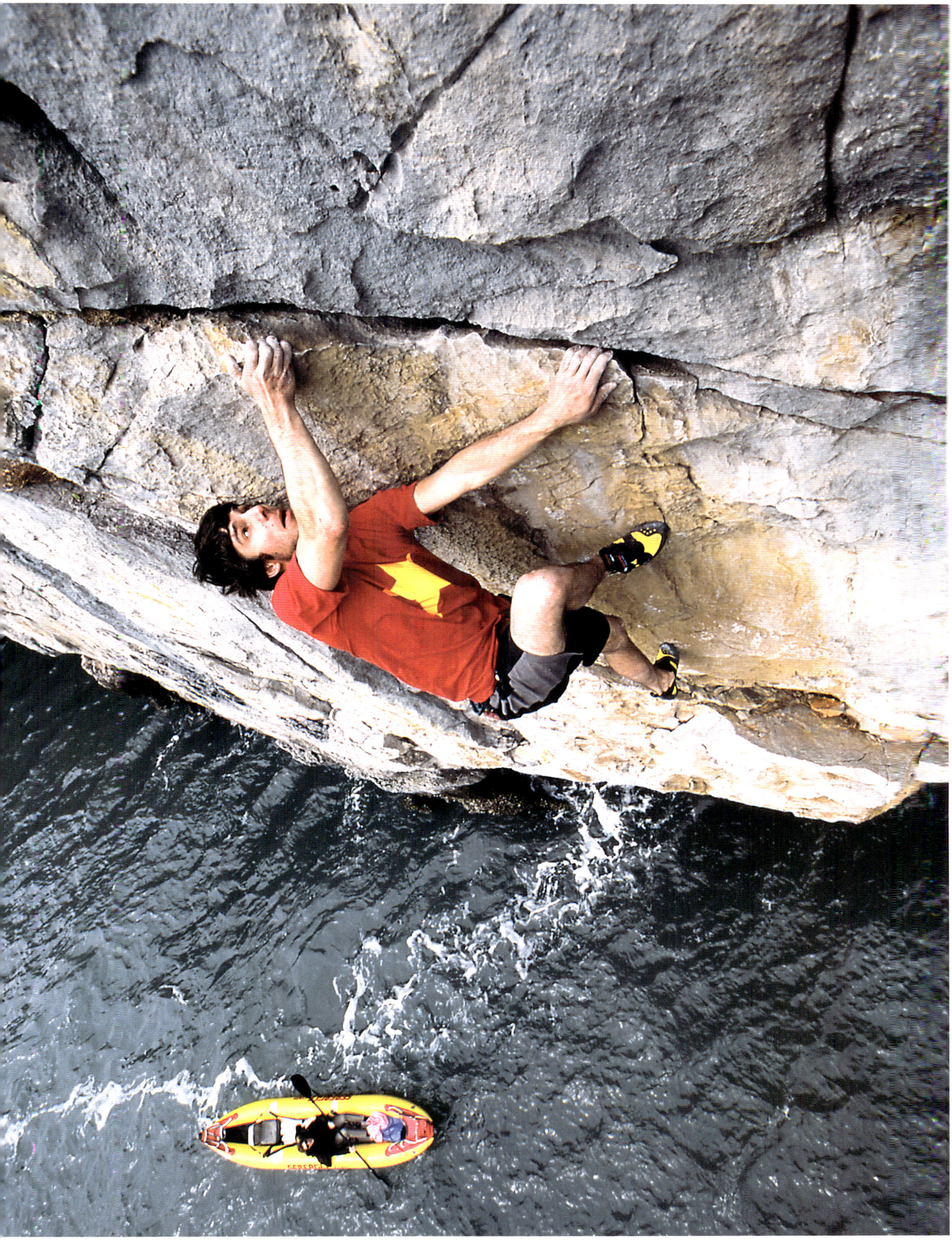

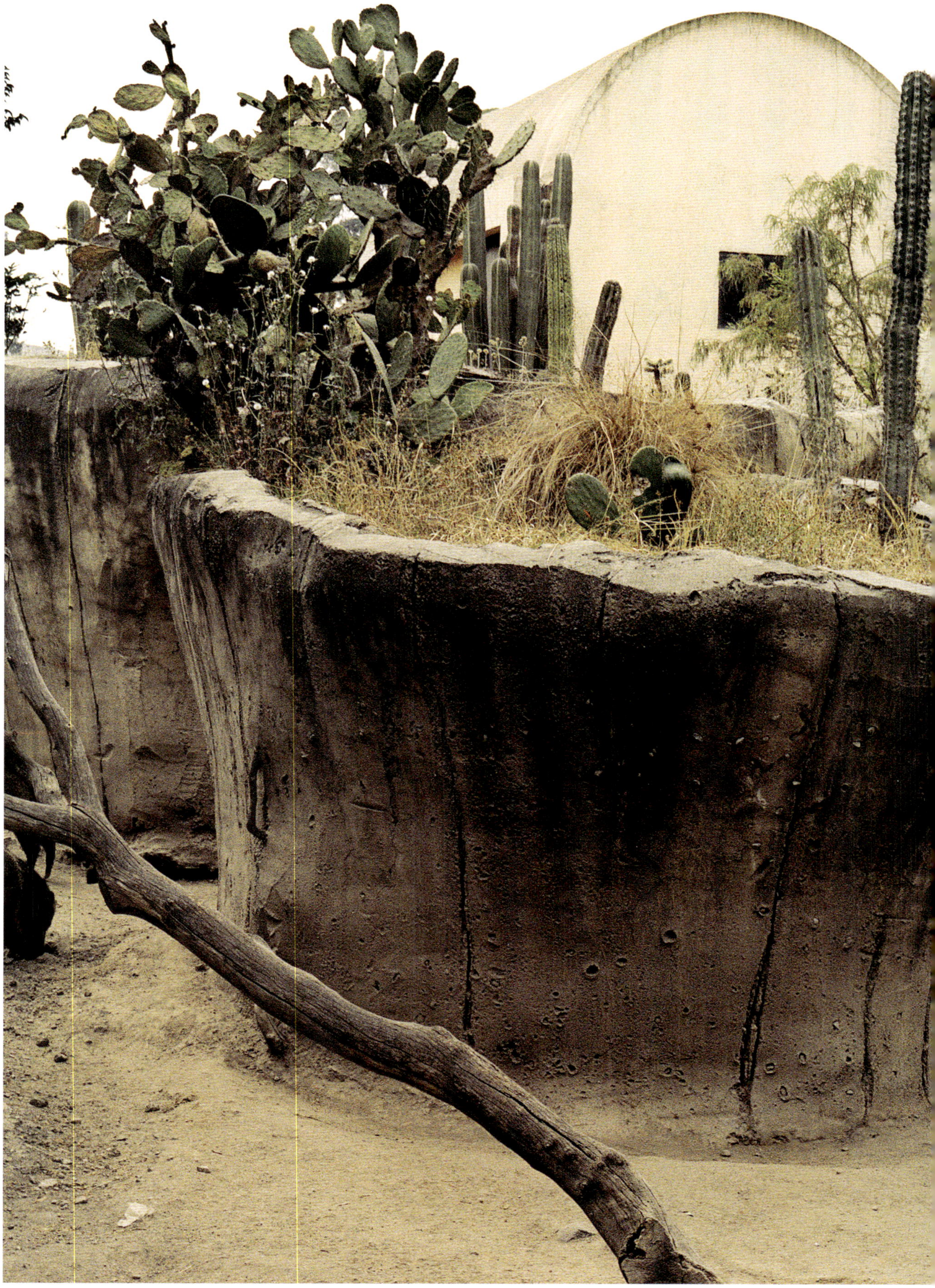

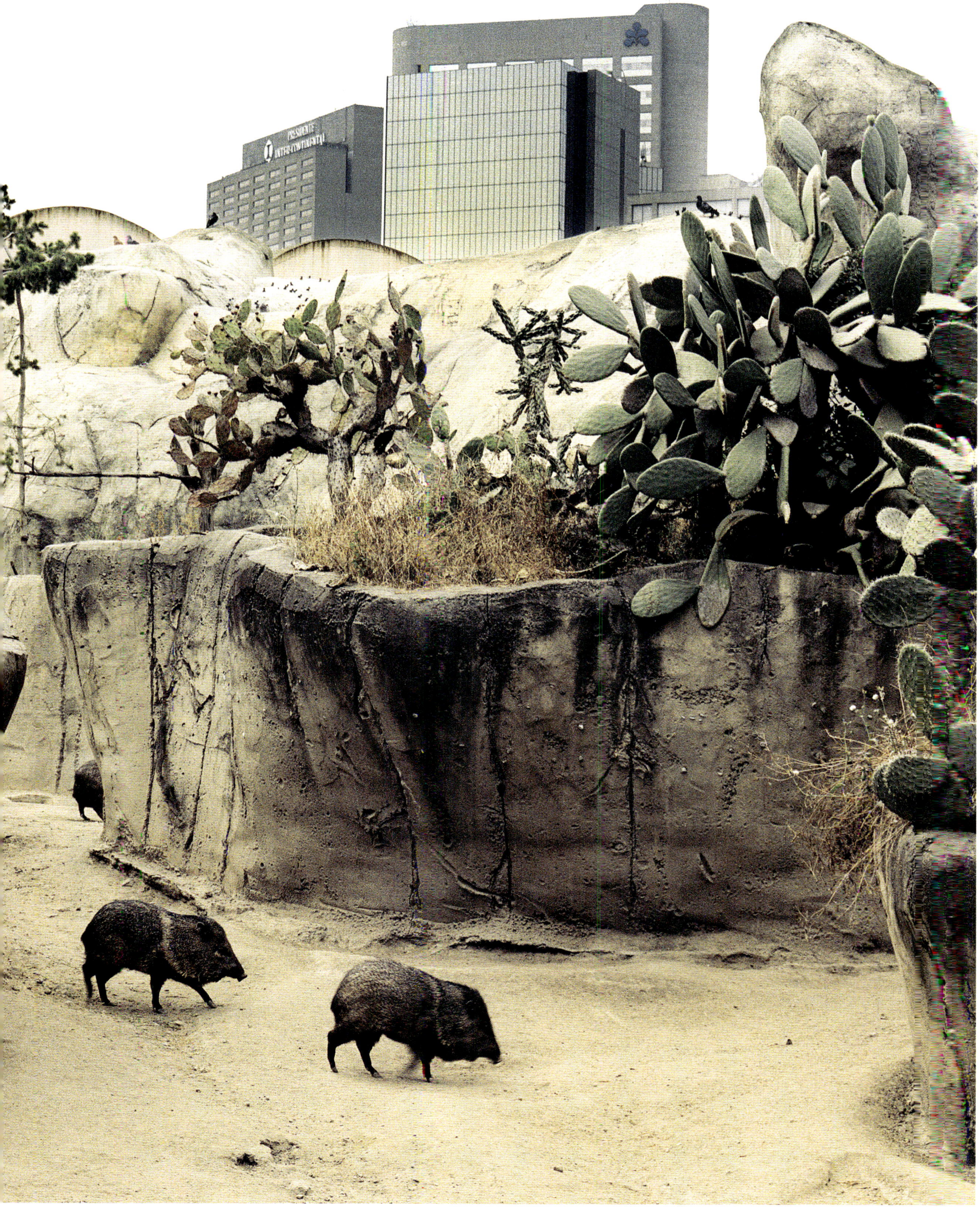

Zoo, Mexico City

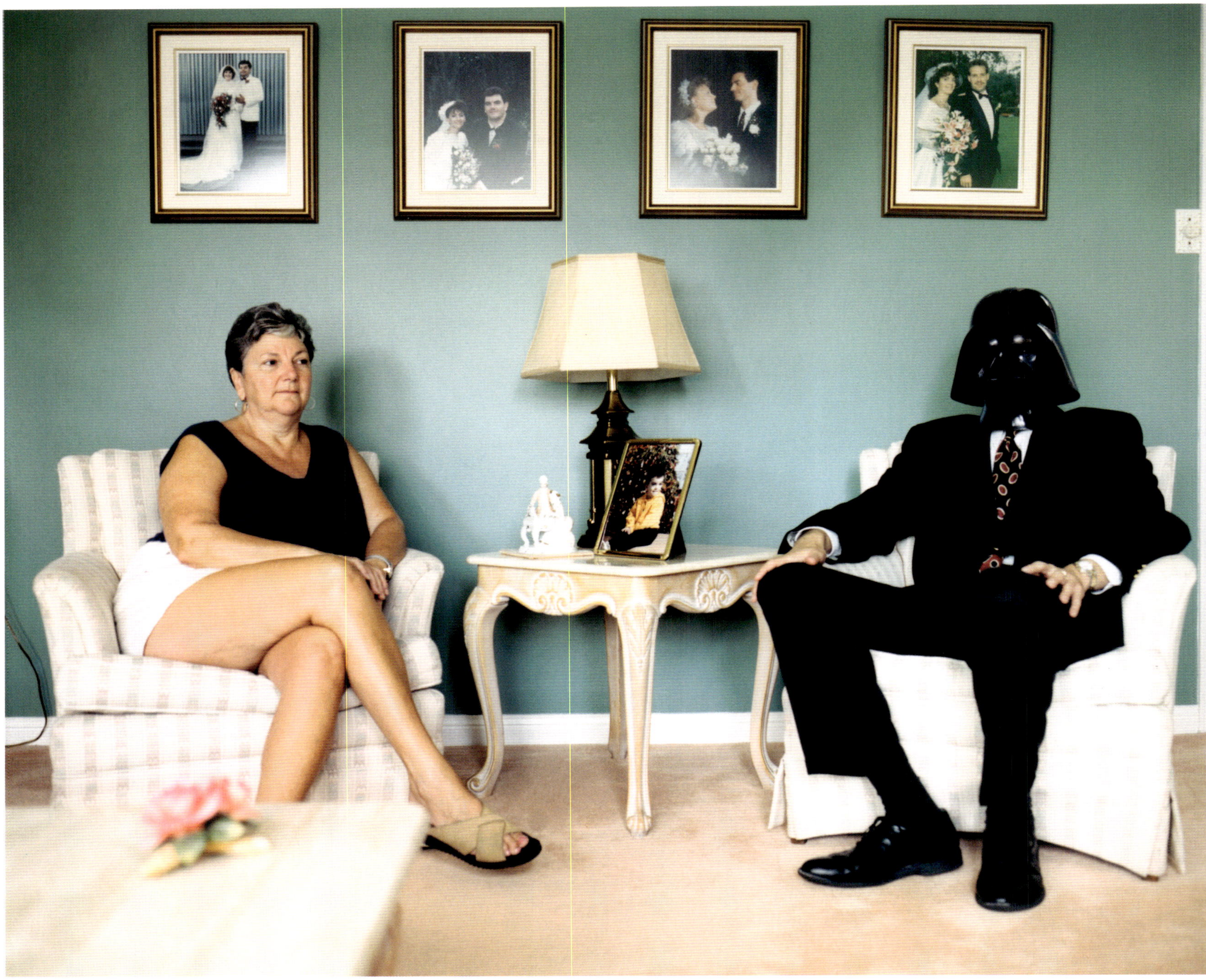

Mrs. Angelloti and Son

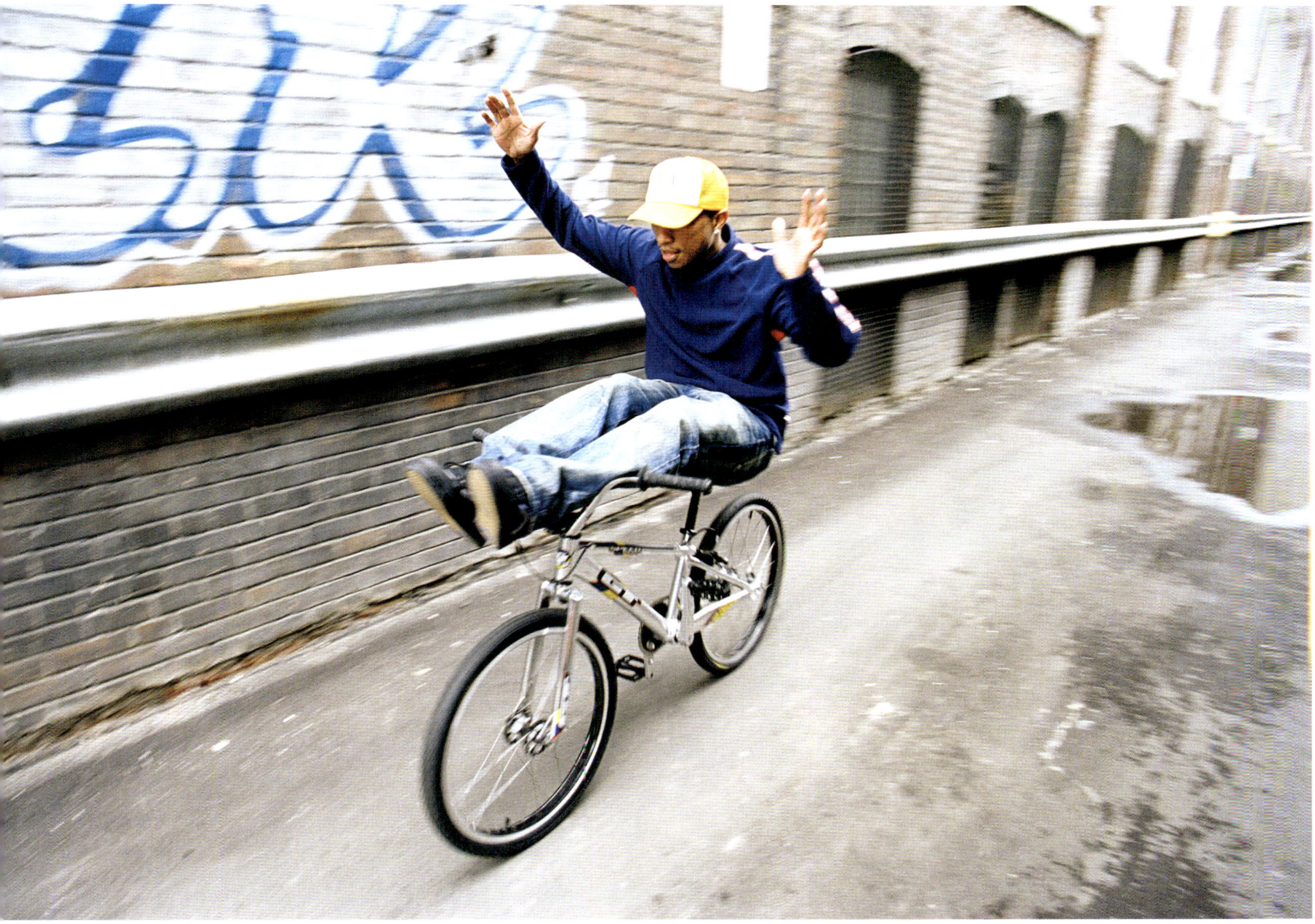

Pharrel Williams—No Hands, No Feet

Steve Carty

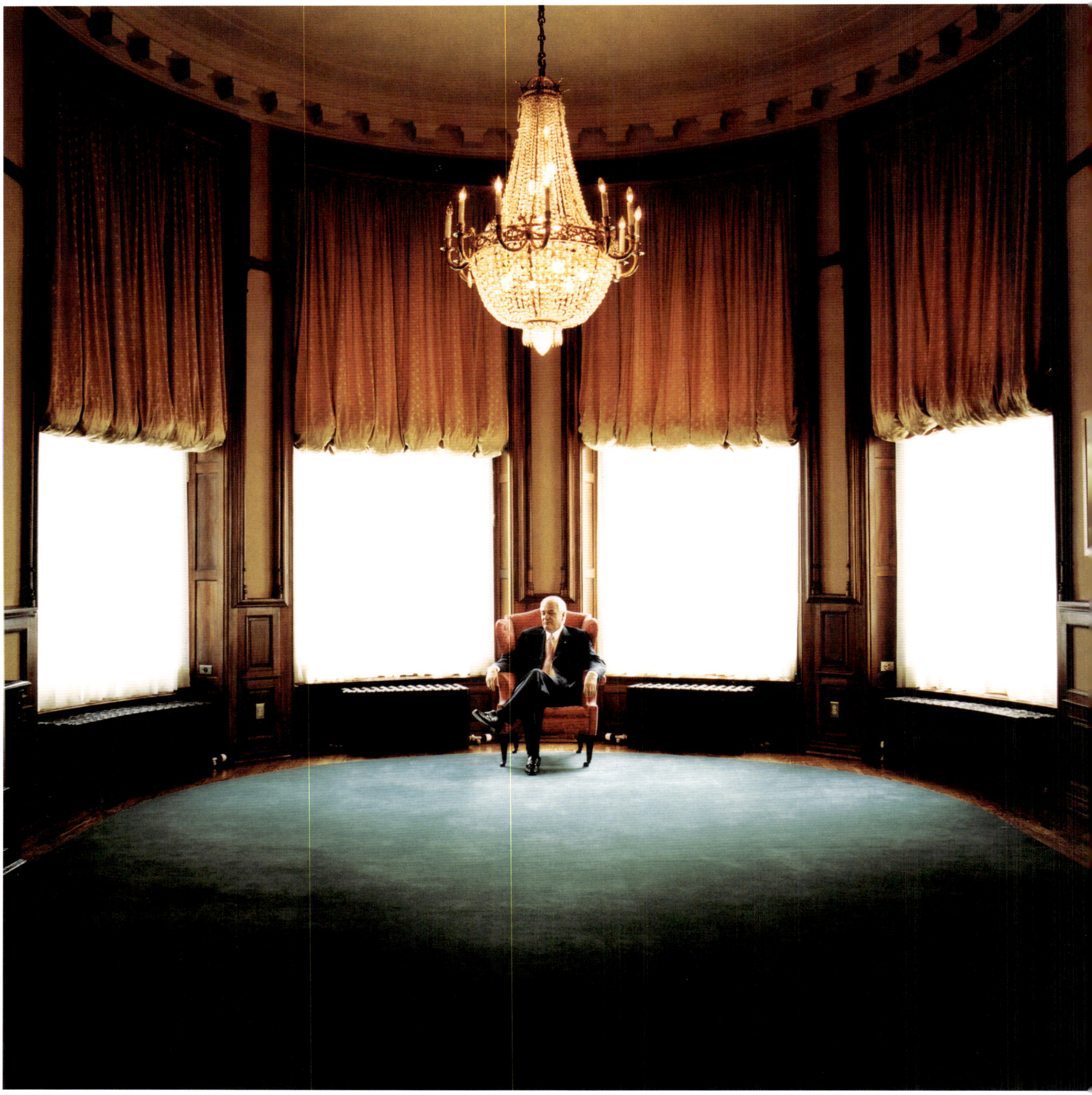

Lieutenant-Governor Bartleman

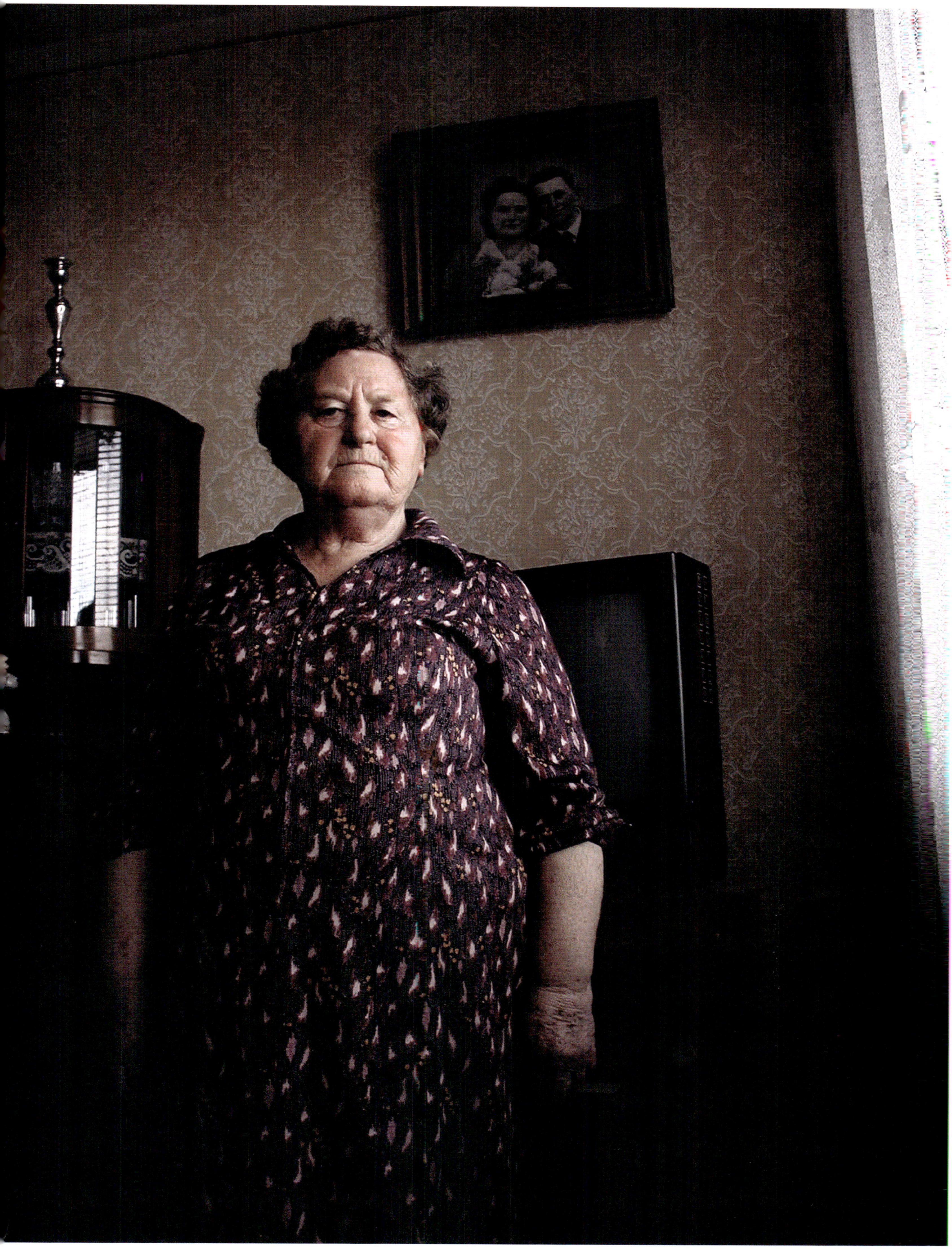

Old World from the series "We Endured")

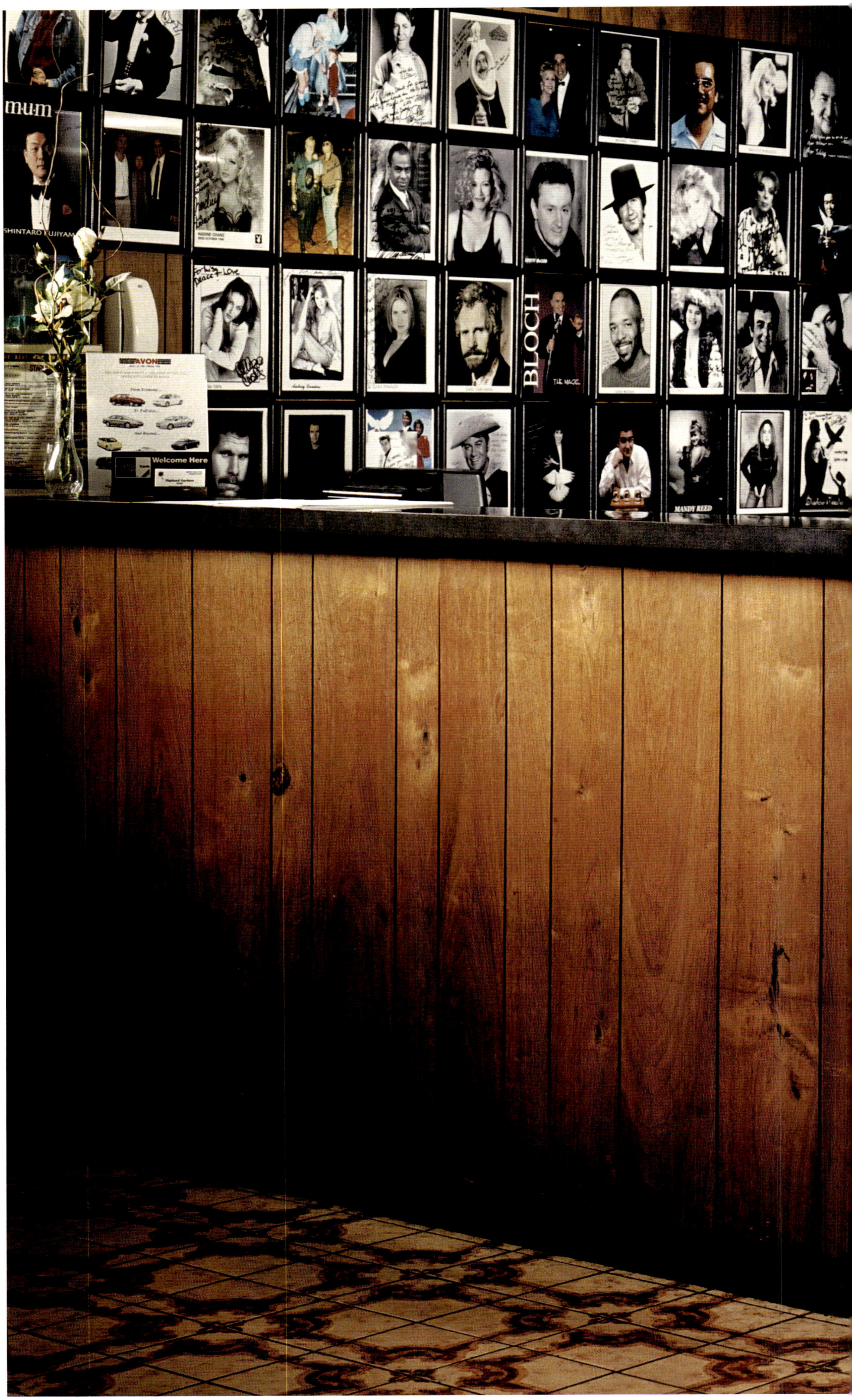

David Drebin

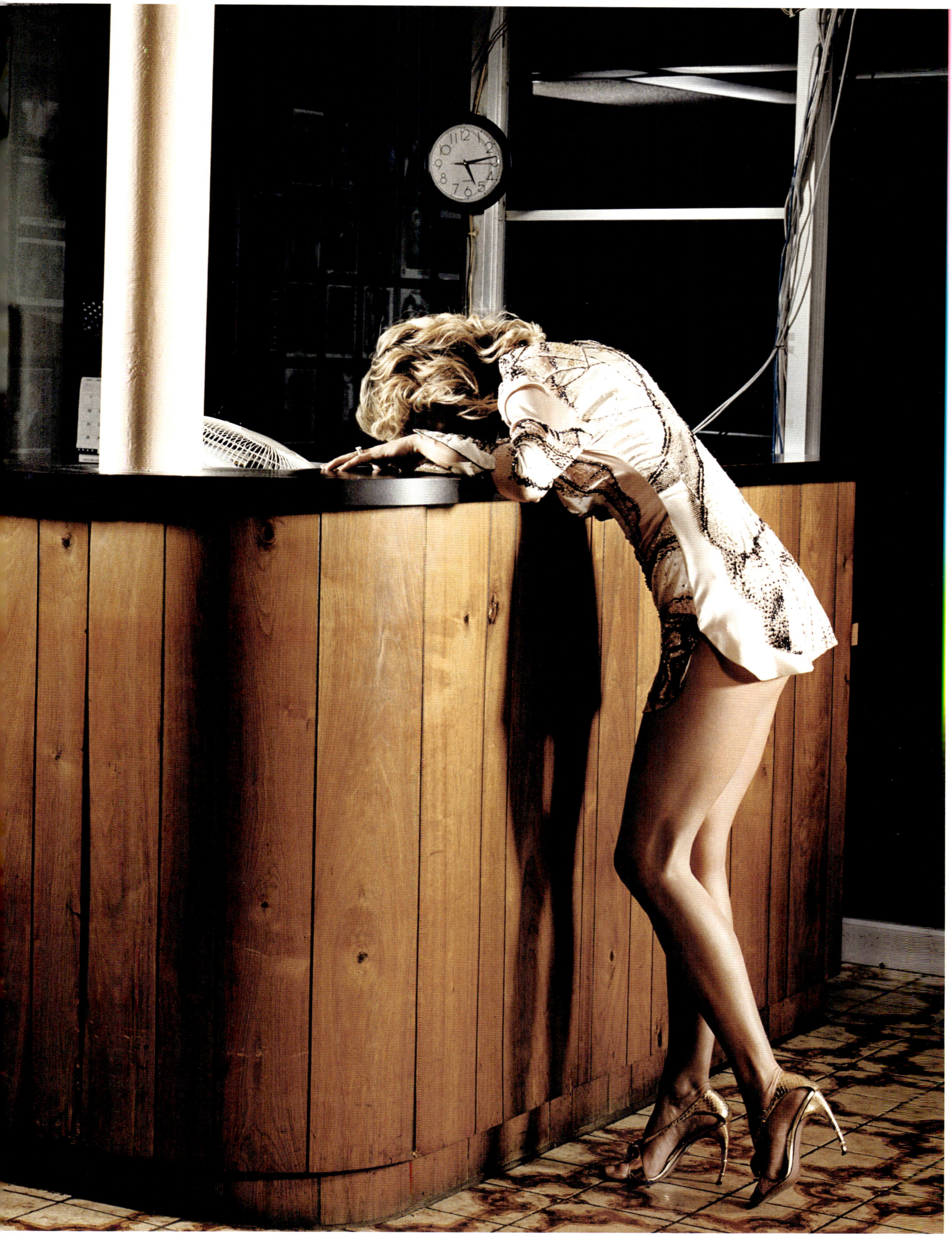

Girl on Bar

Davi[illegible]bin

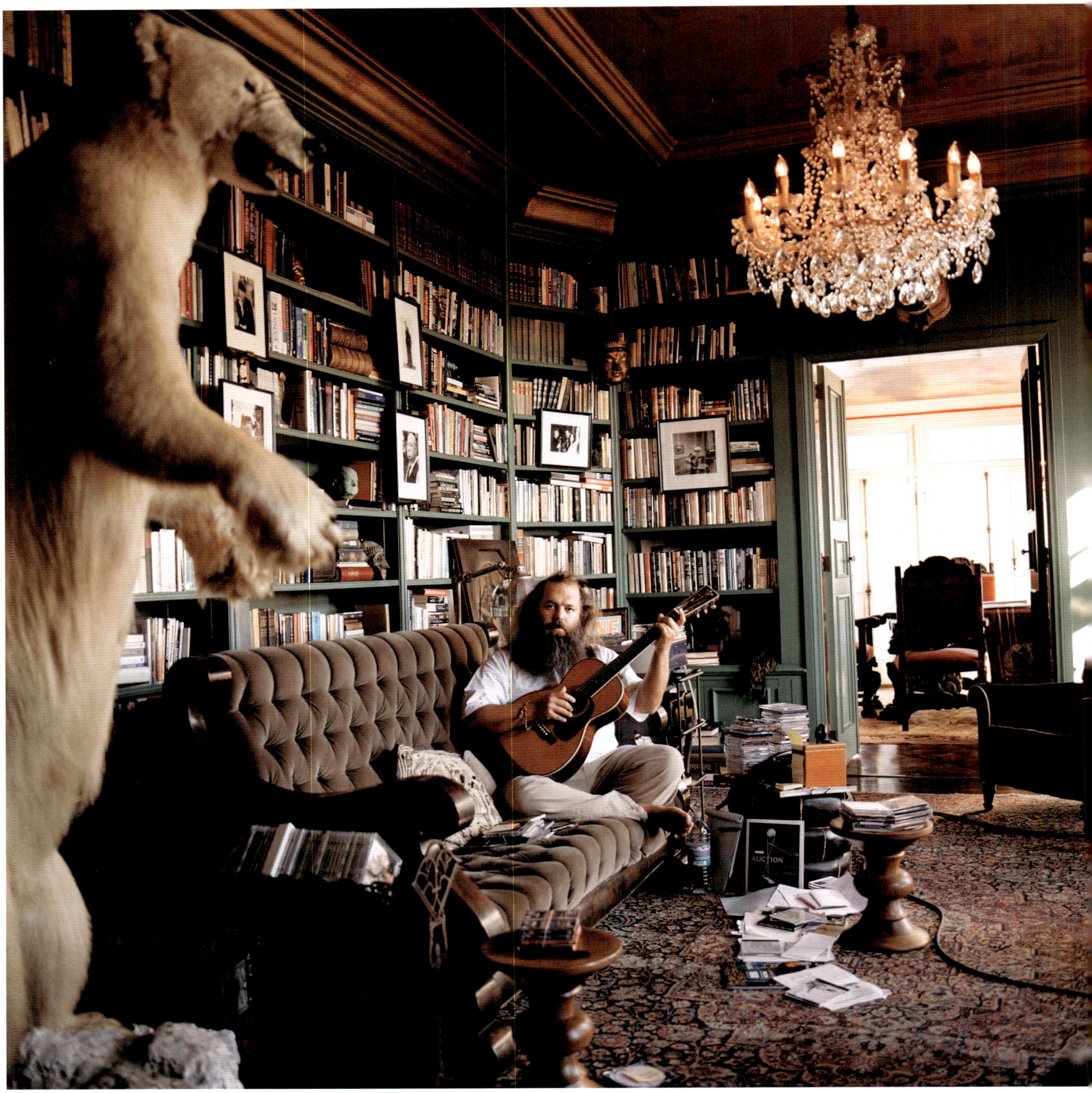

Rick Rubin

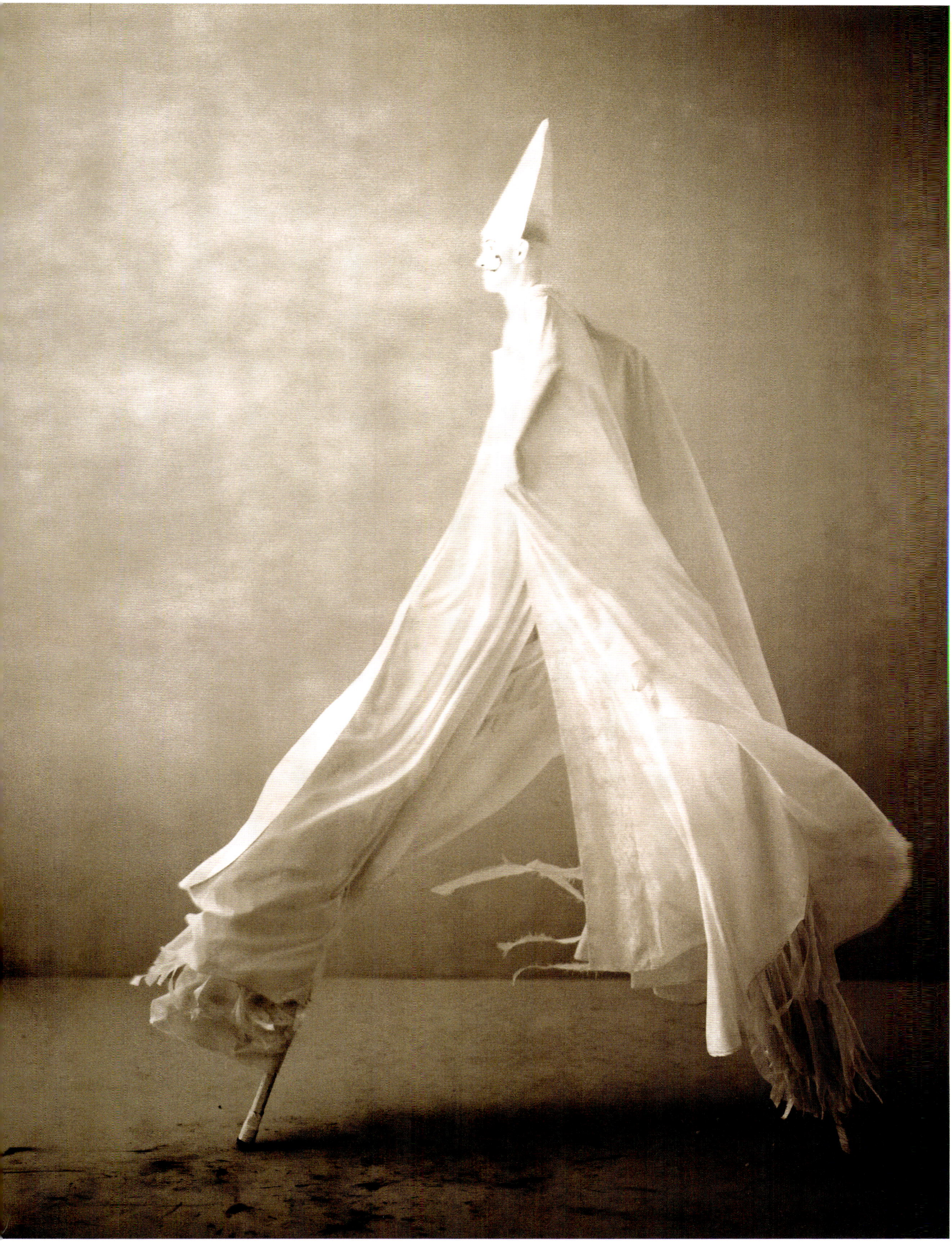

Stilts 2

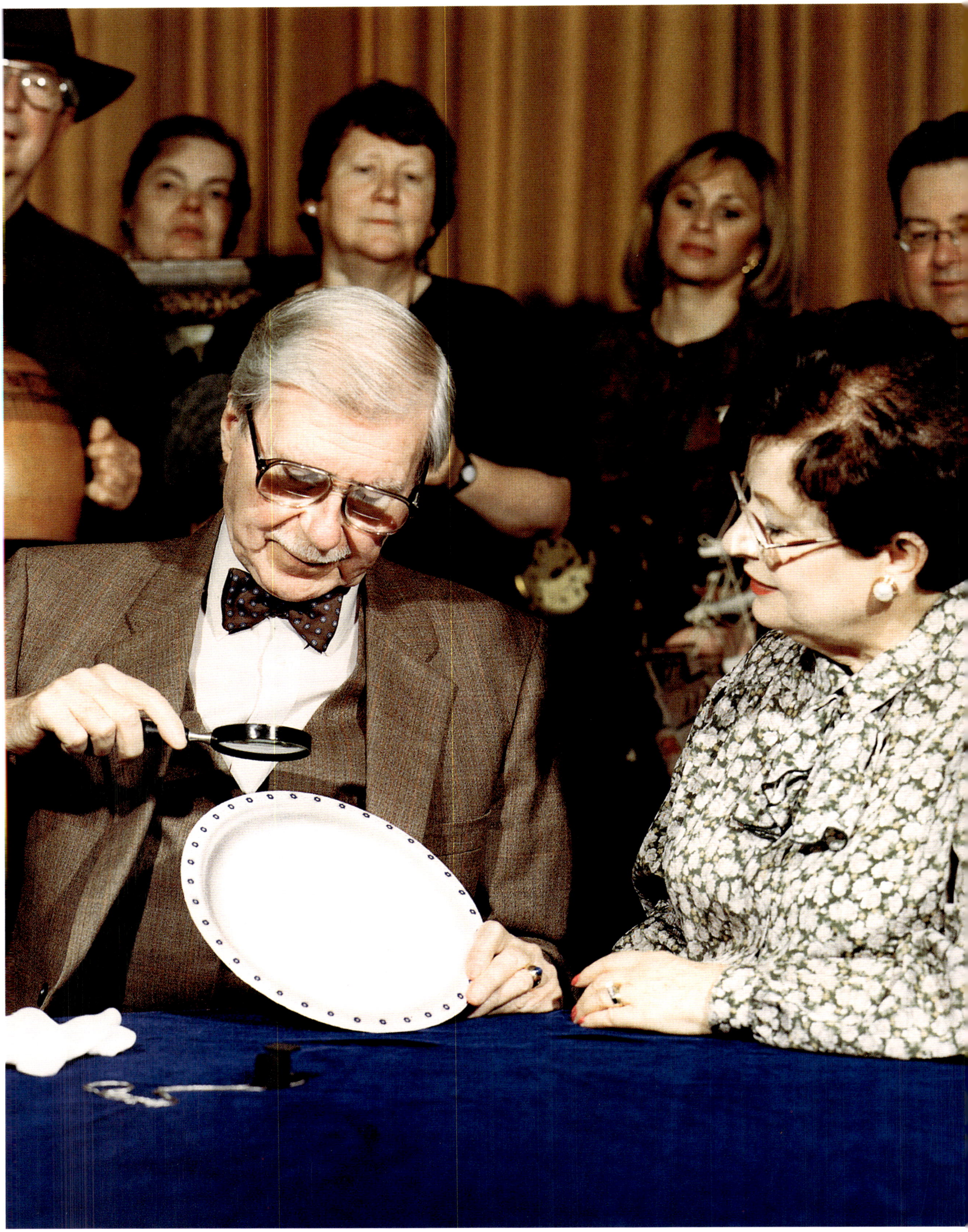

Chinet Road Show

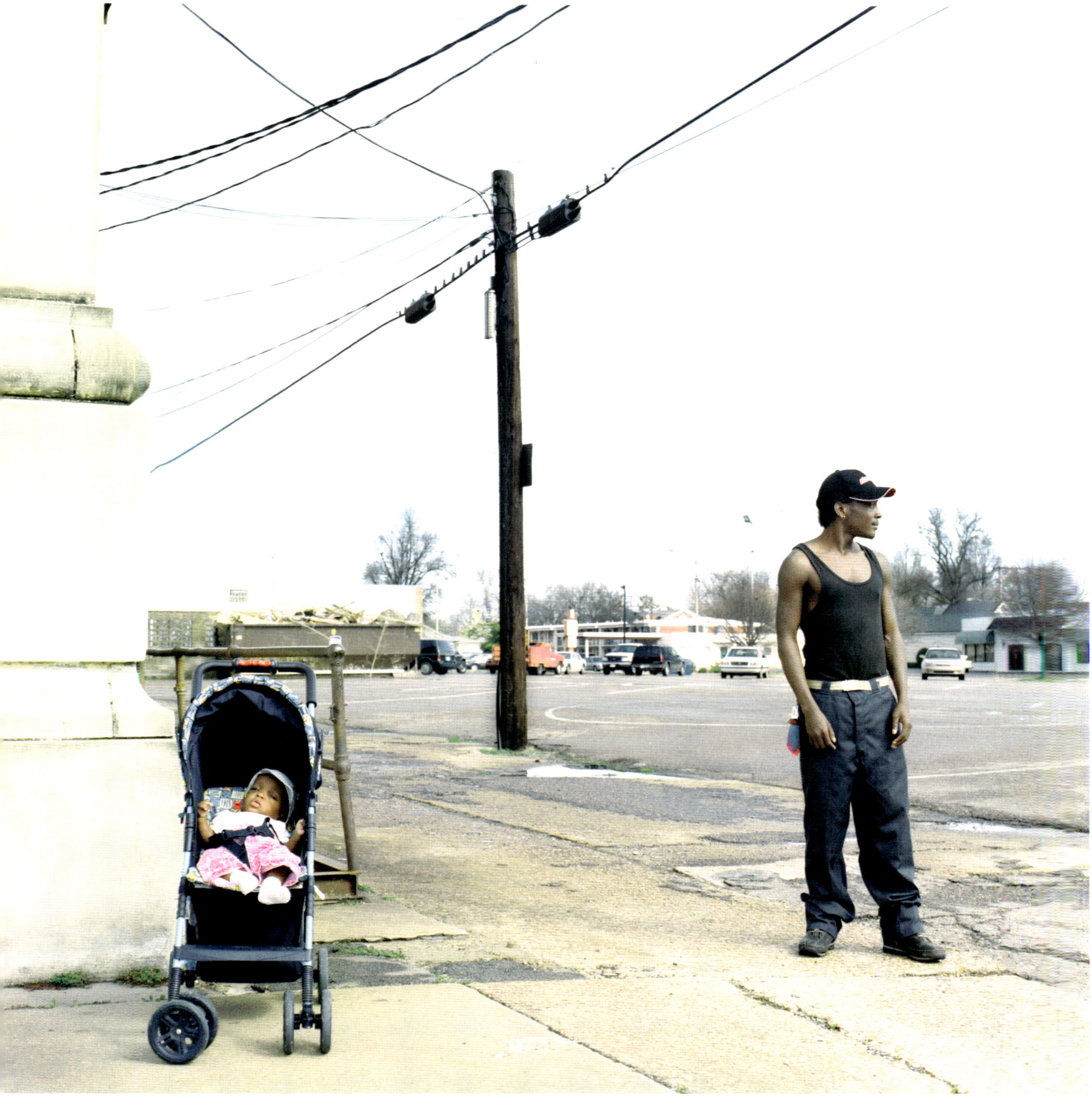

Kalvin Goodman & Daughter, Clarksdale, Mississippi

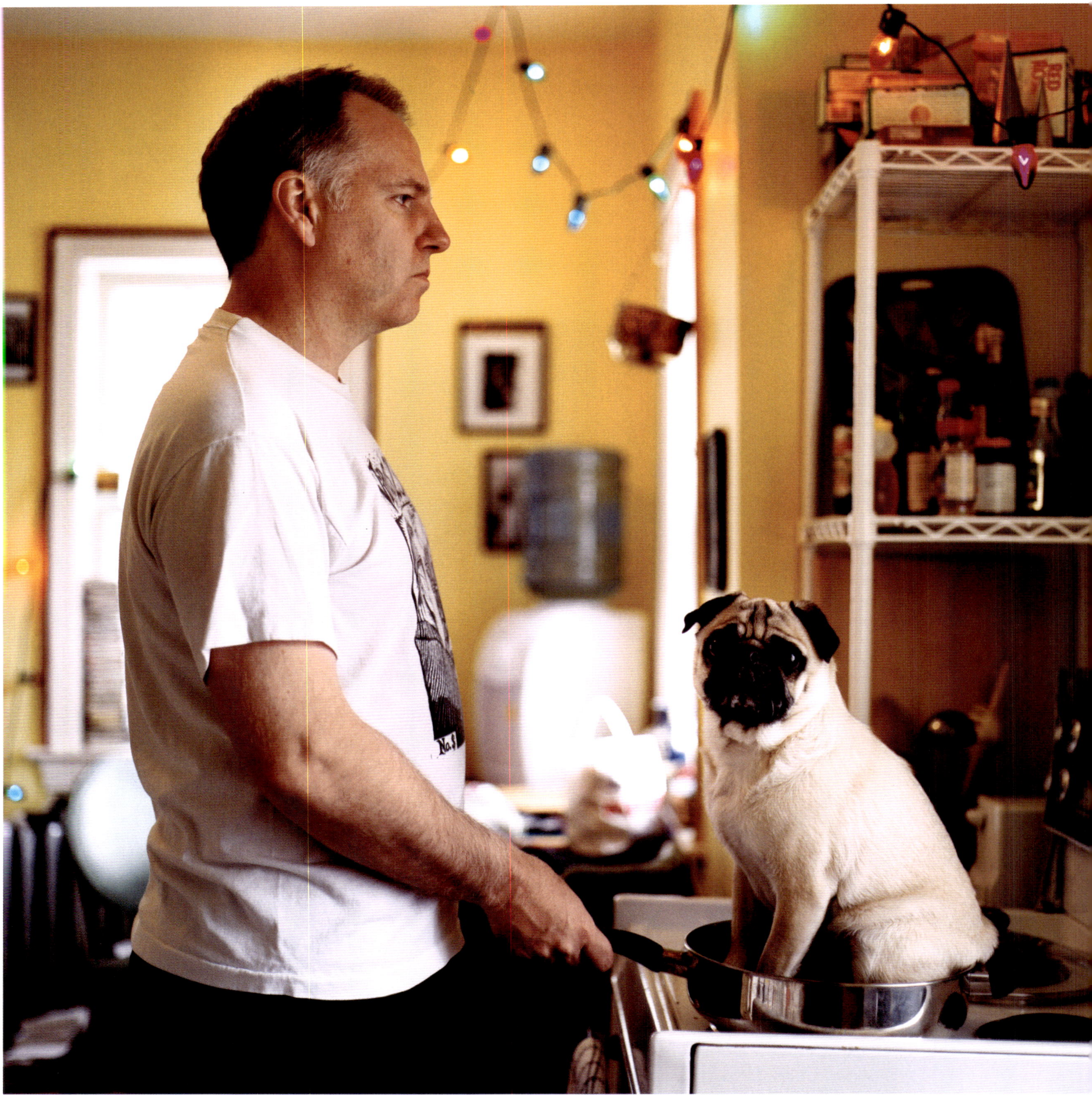

Guy Maddin

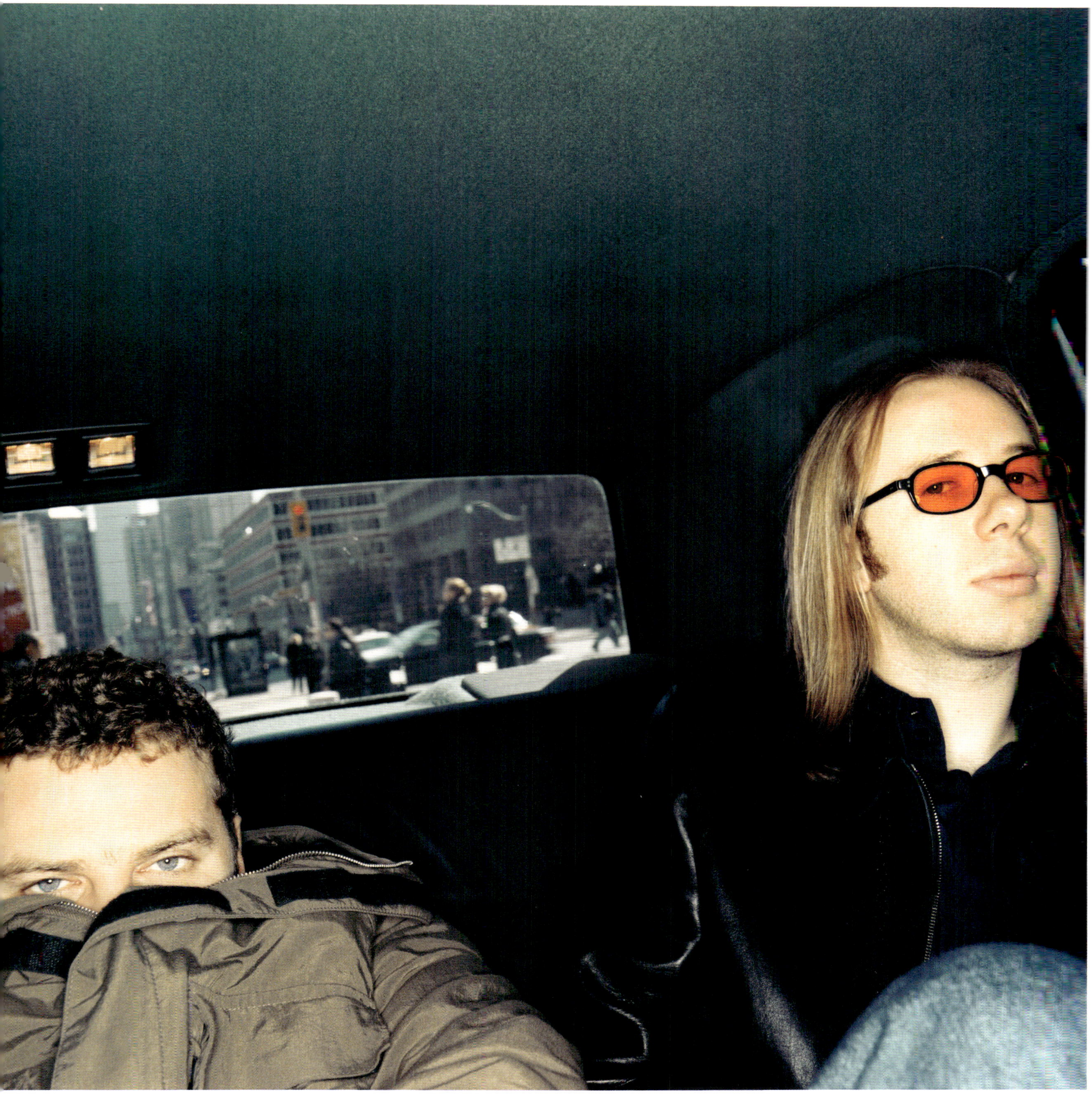

Chemical Brothers

Kathryn Caiters

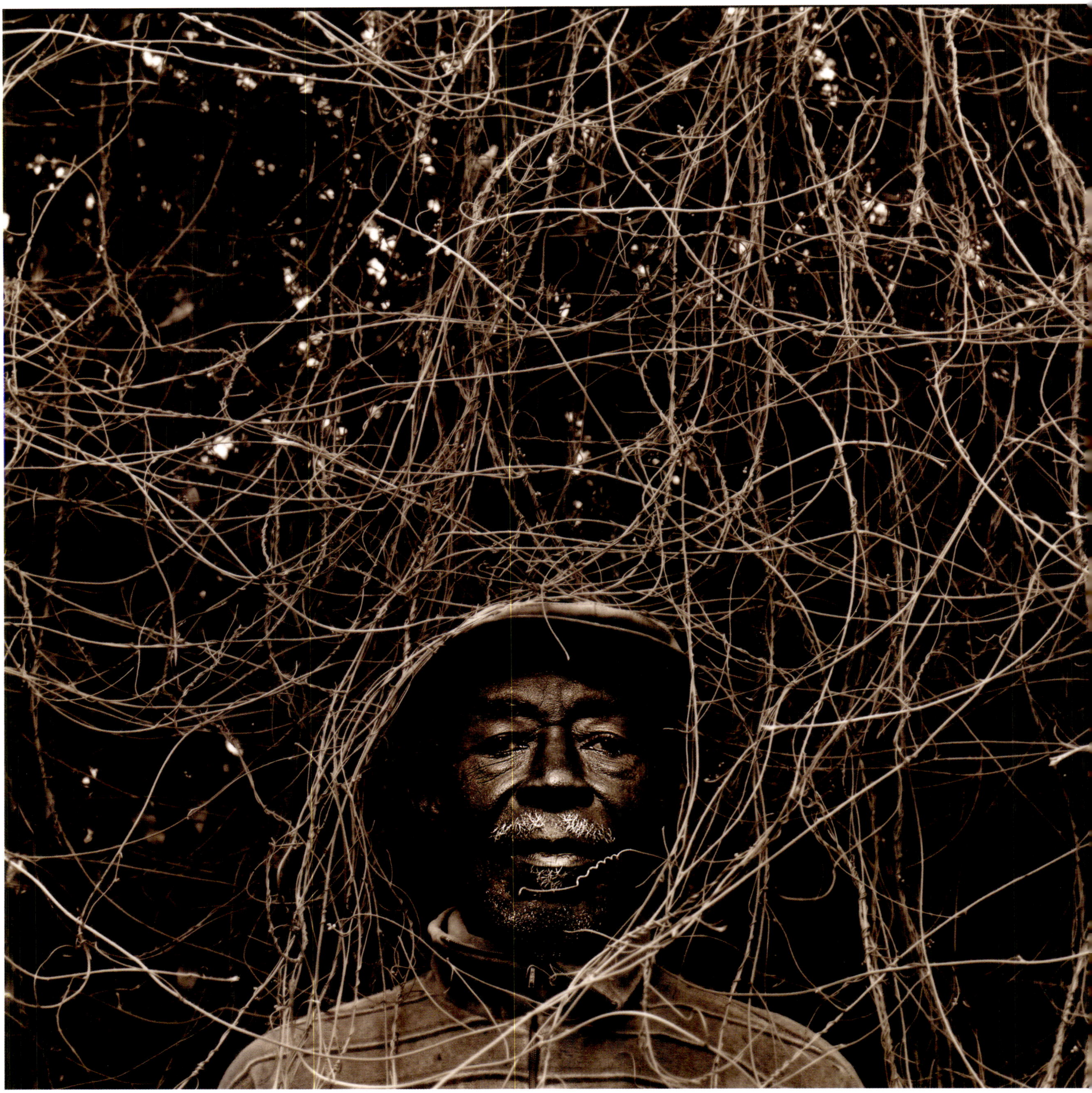

Edward Gajdel

Dr. Bob

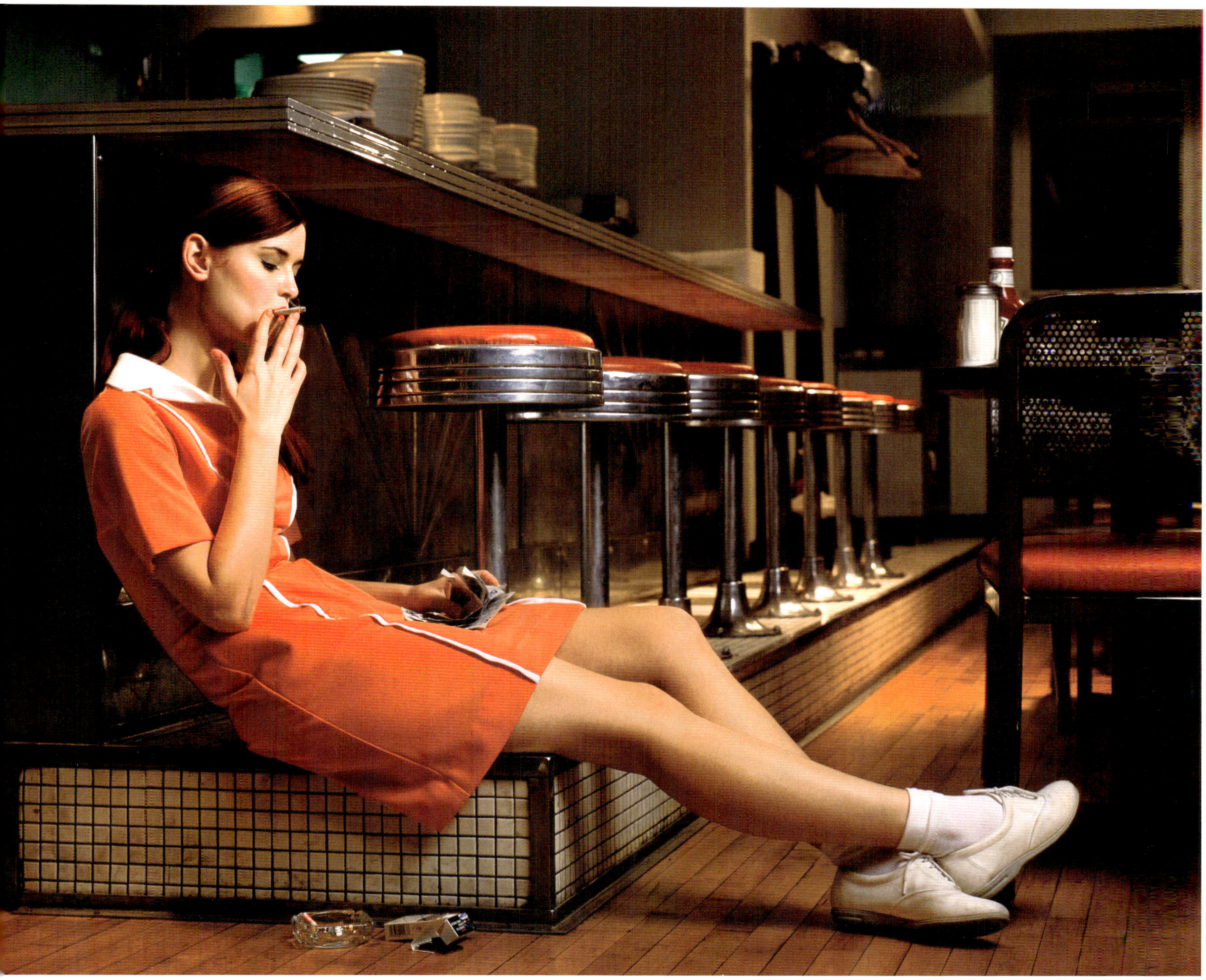

Waitress in Diner

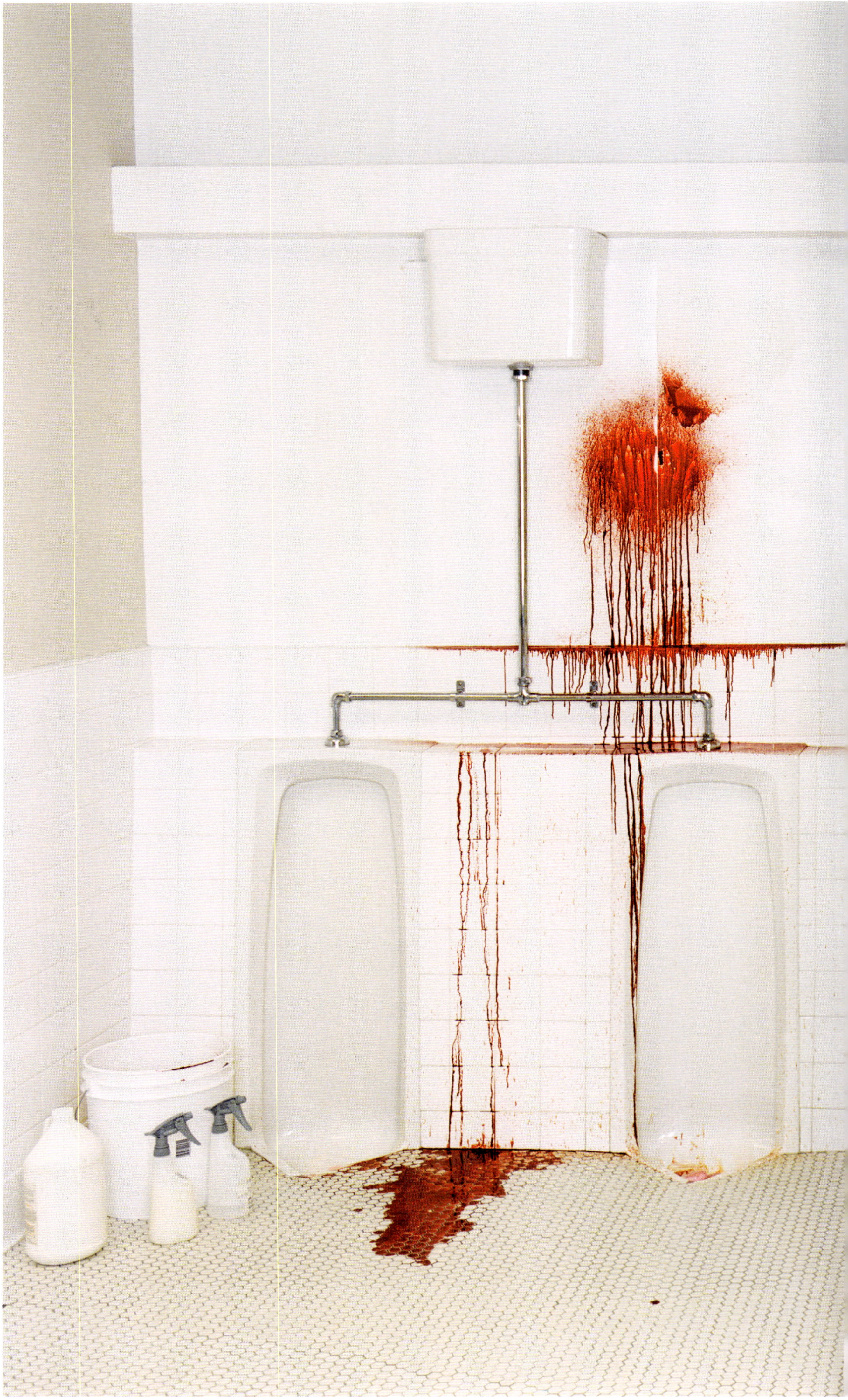

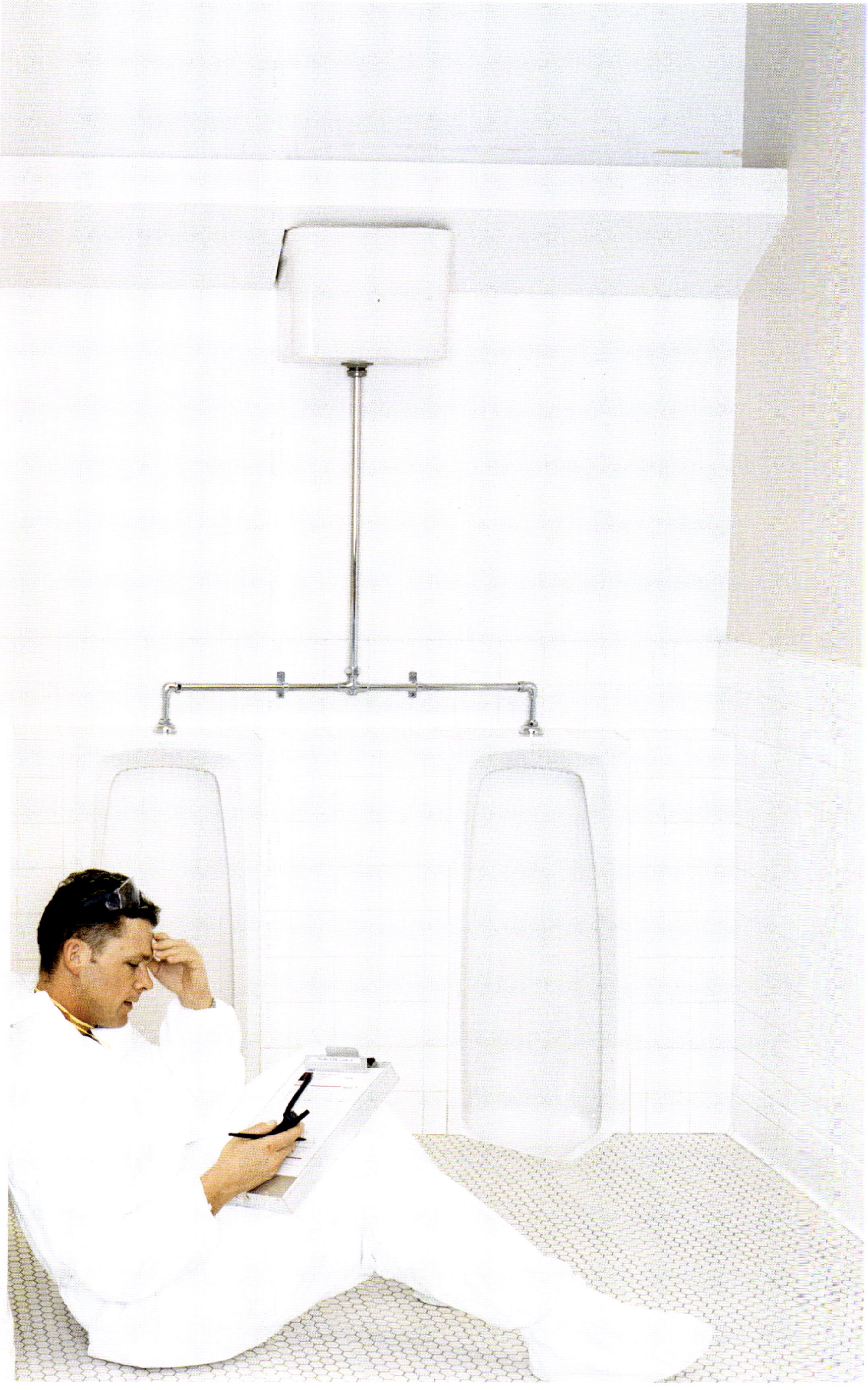

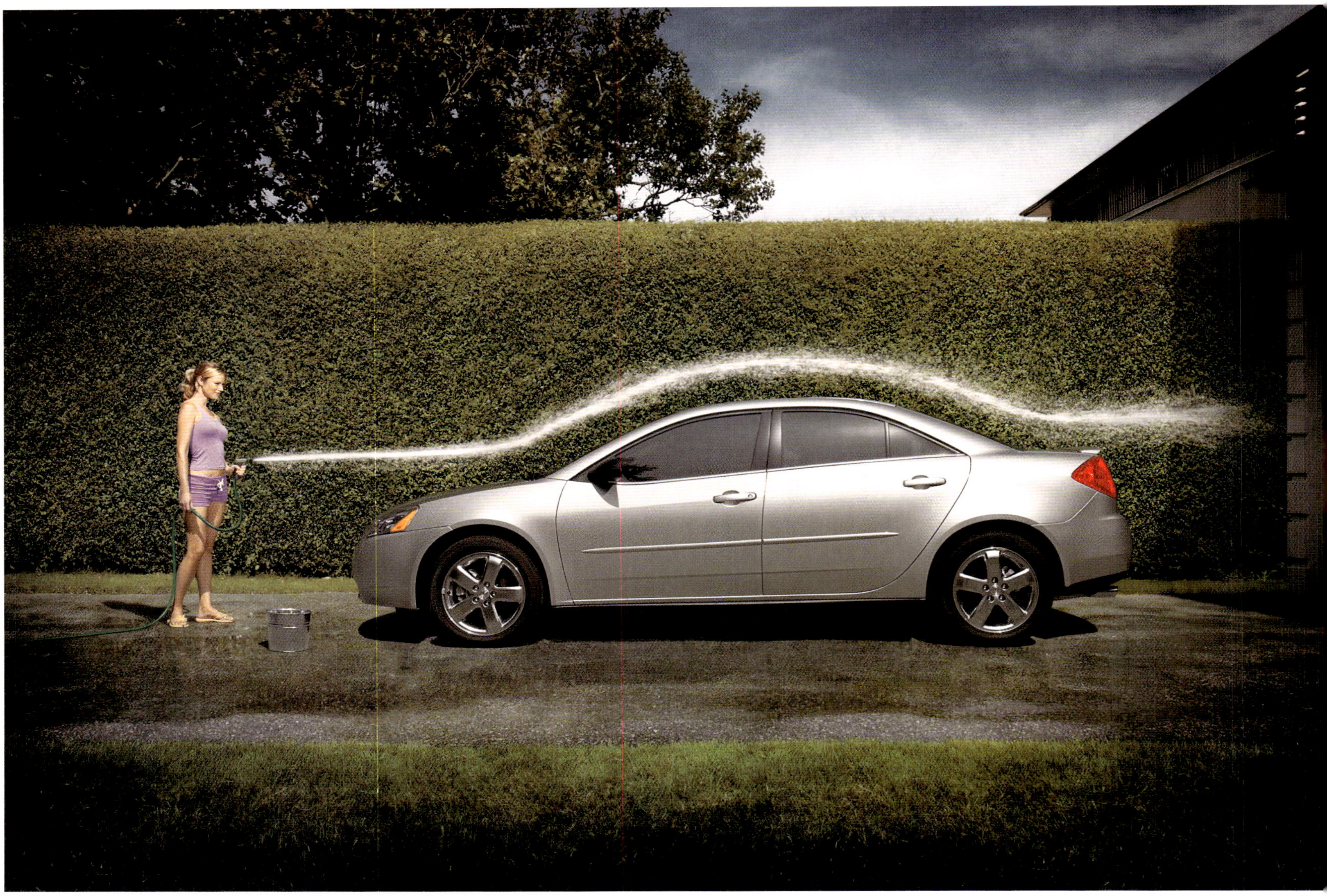

GMC Car Wash

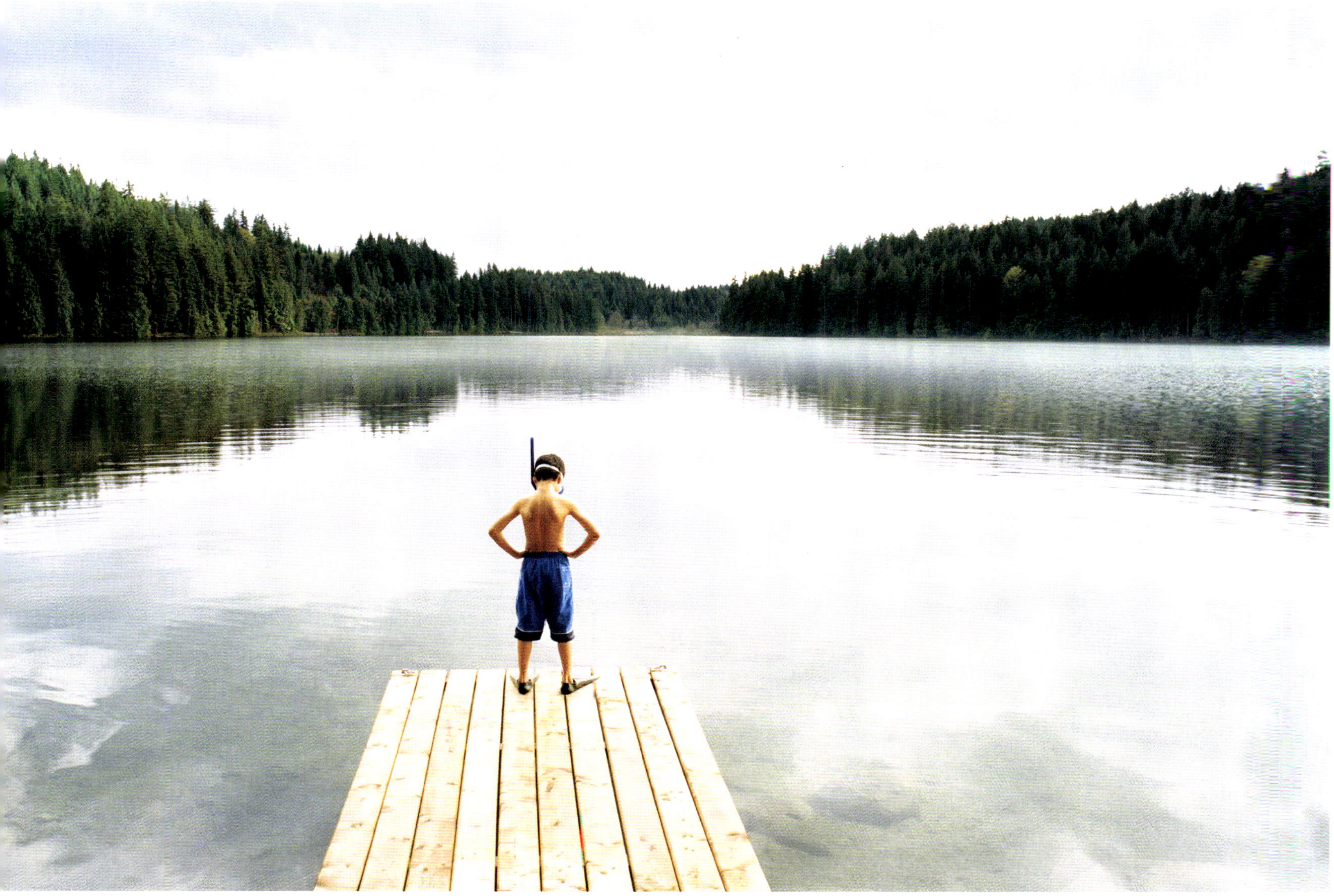

Sunrype Dock

Frank Boedl

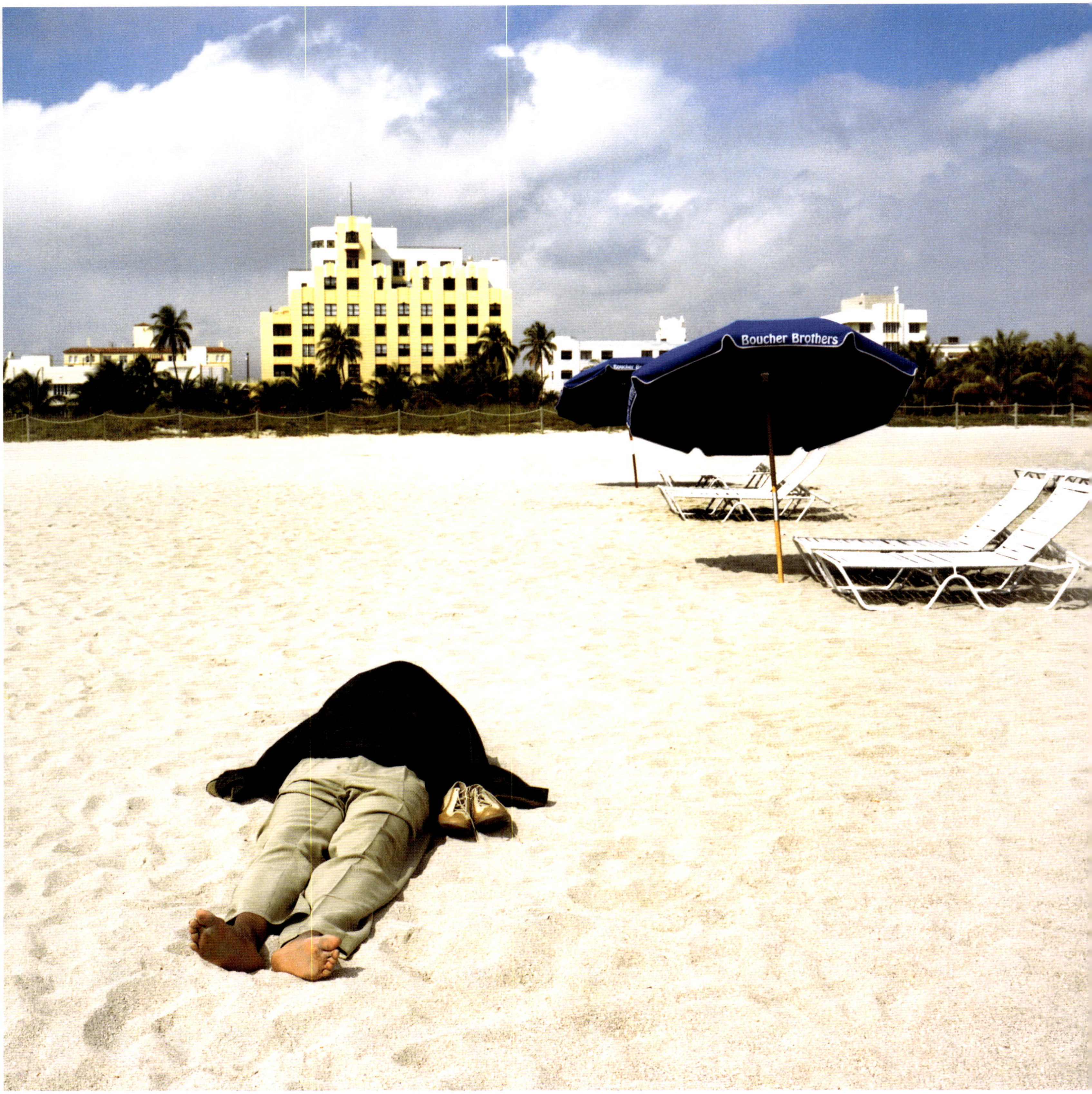
Boucher Brothers

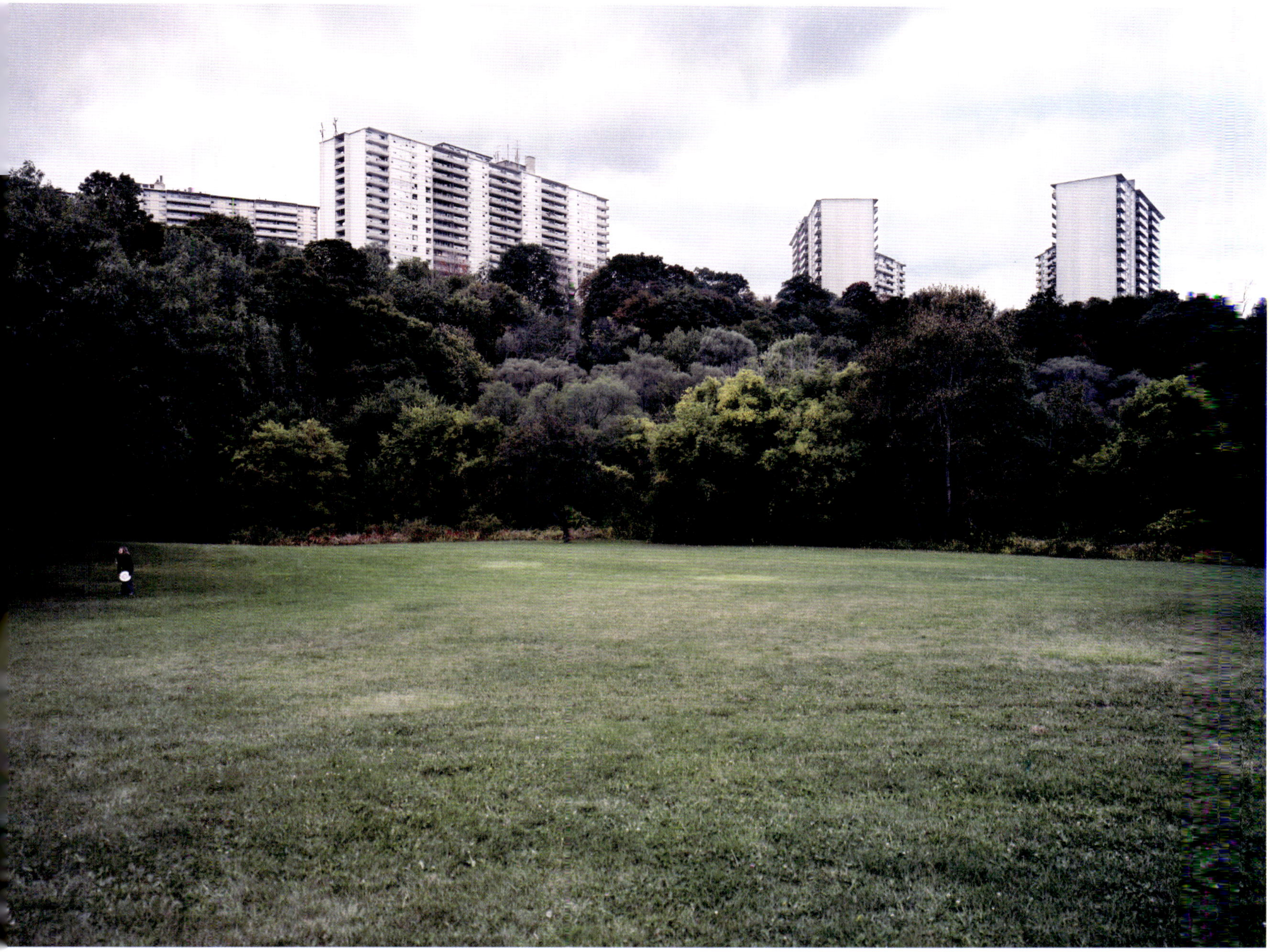

Leaside

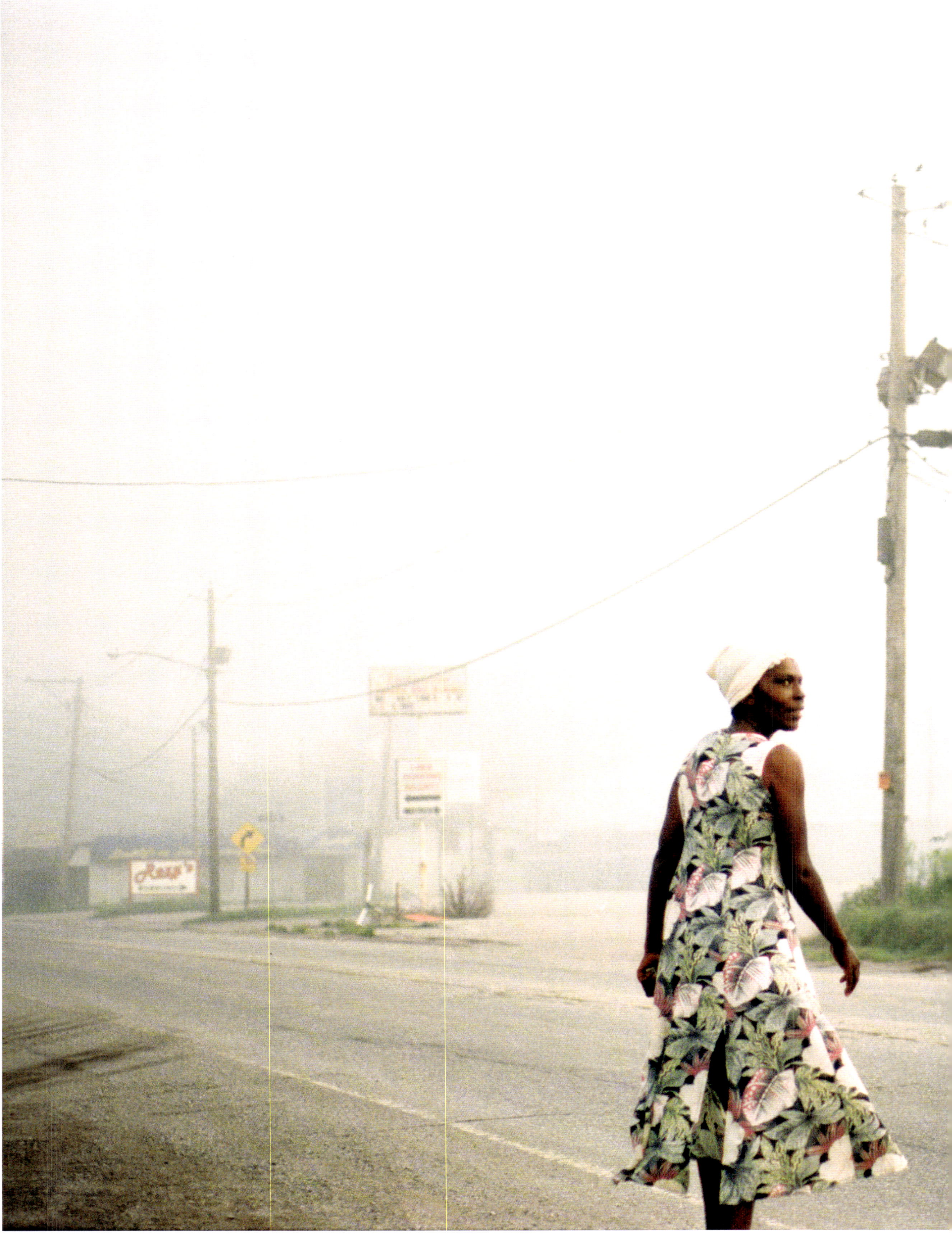

Woman in St. Louis

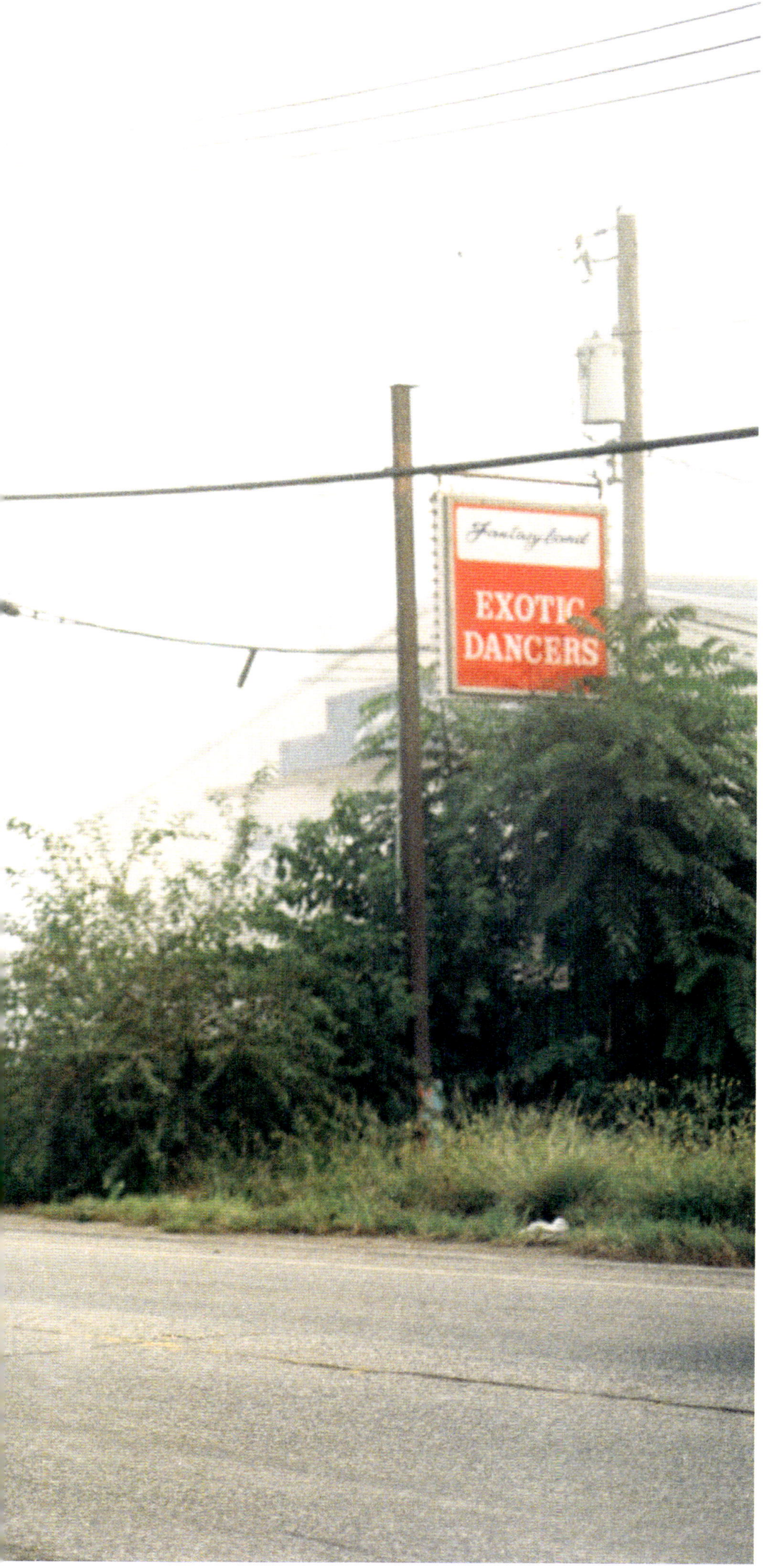
Fantasyland
EXOTIC
DANCERS

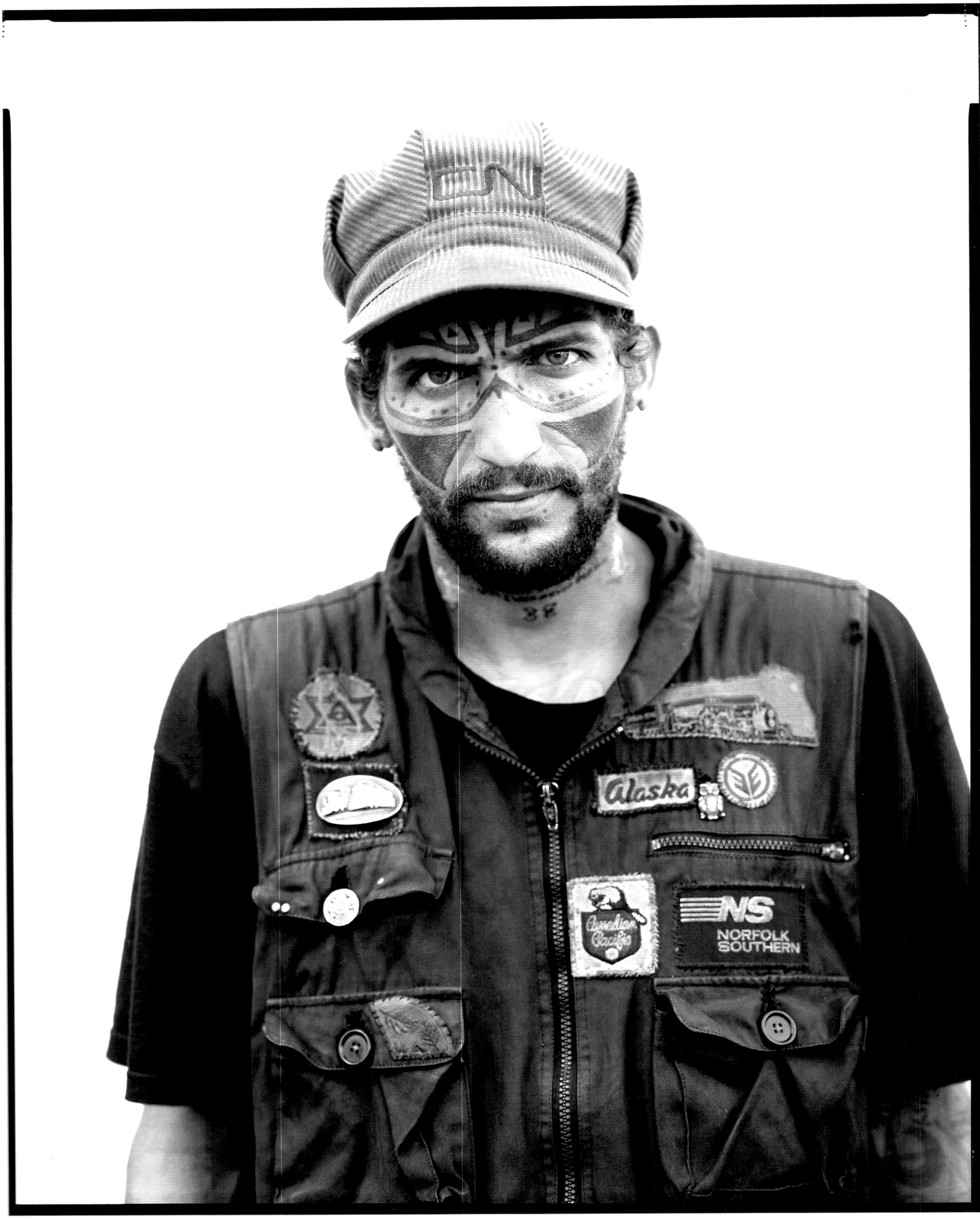

Eddie Railroader

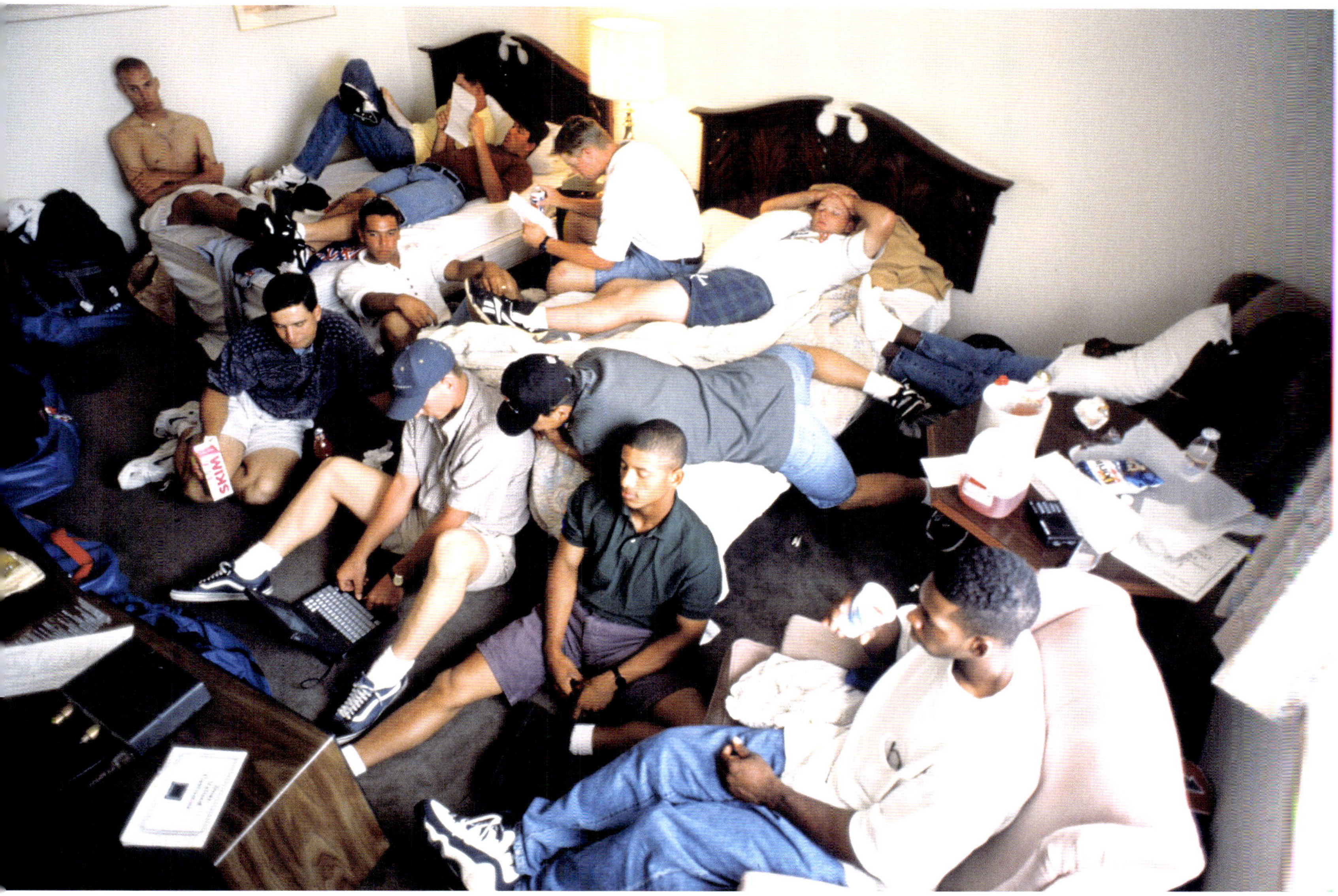
SKIM

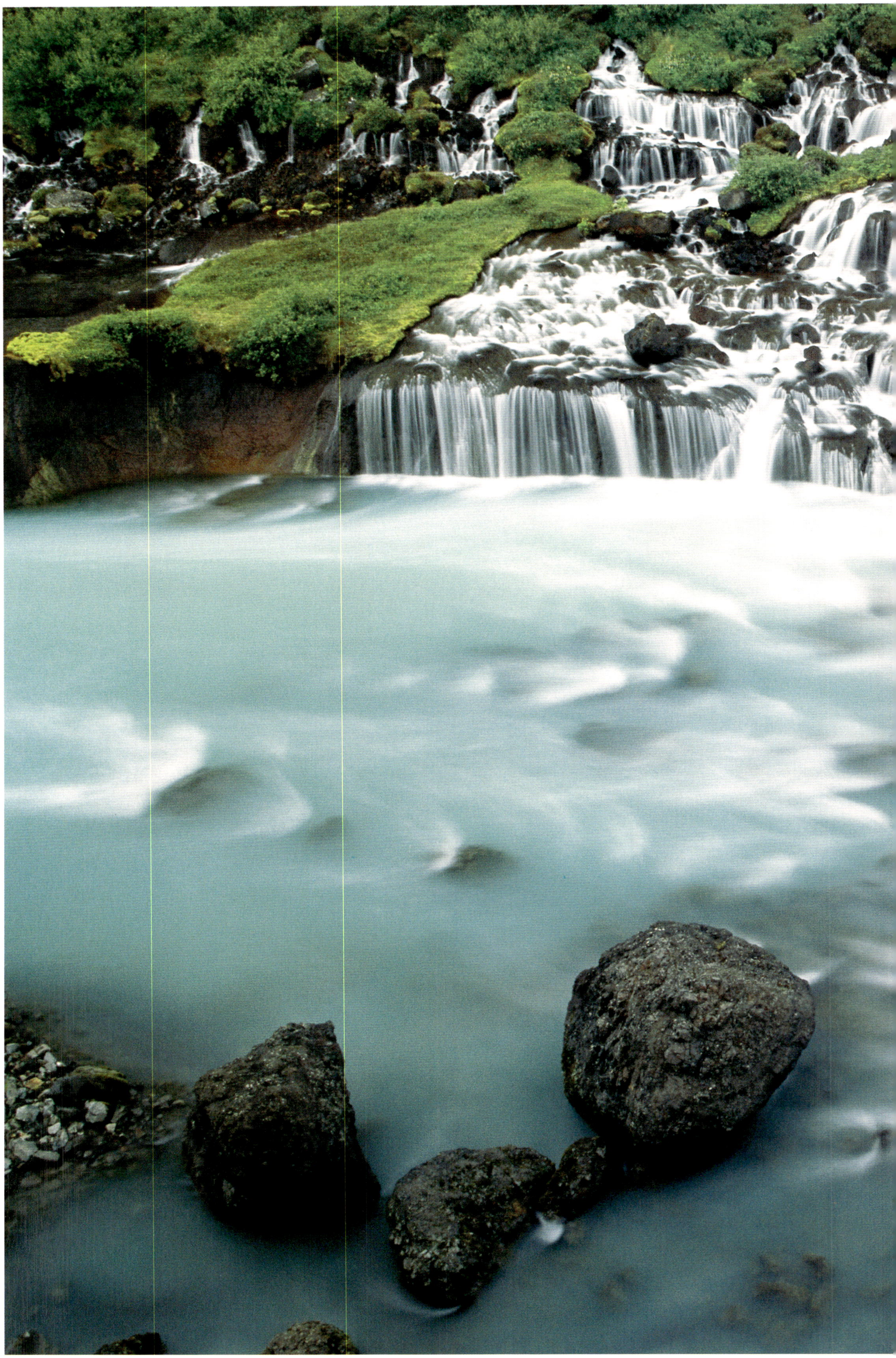

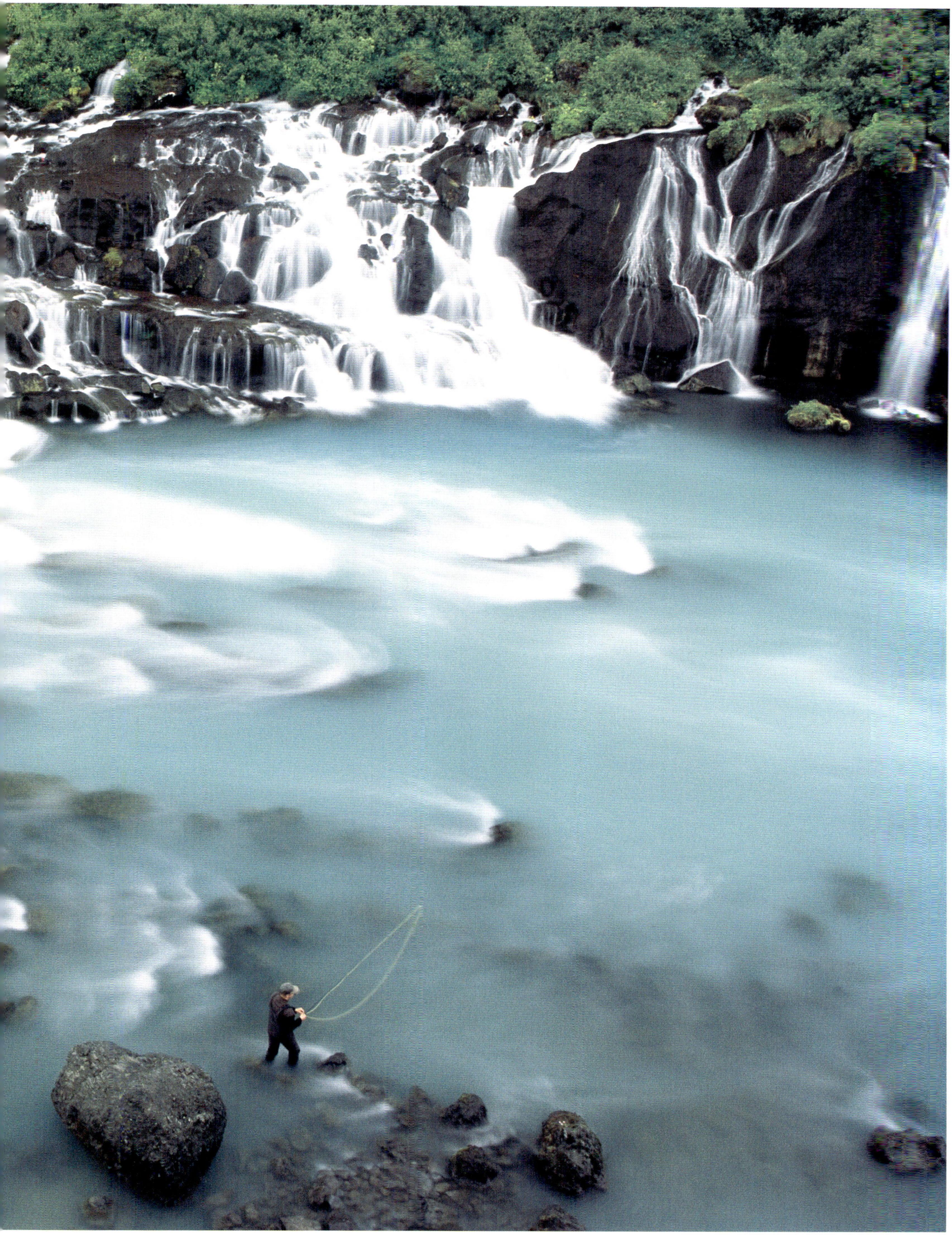

Icelandic Fishing

Paul Nicklen

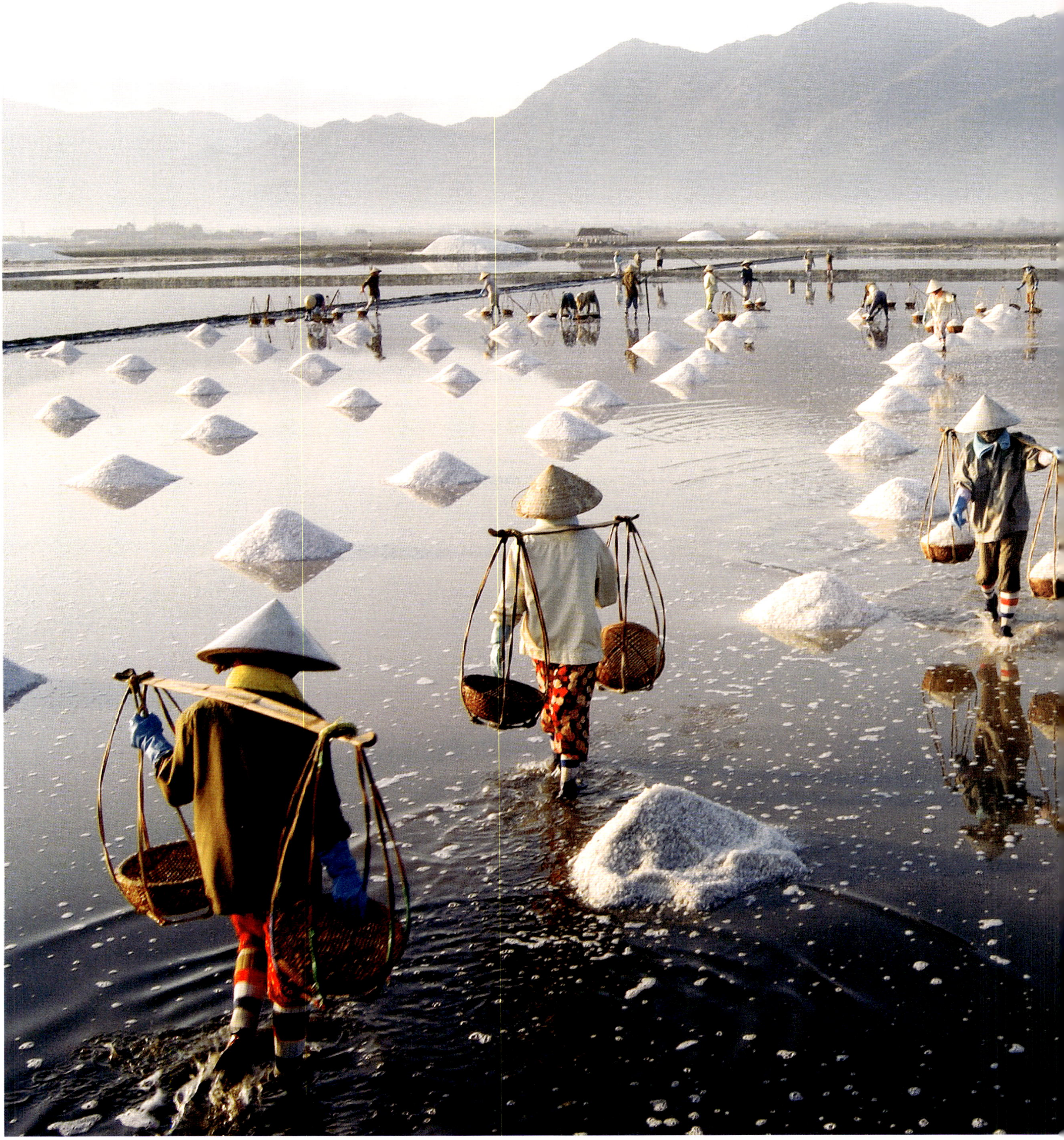

Salt Ponds #4

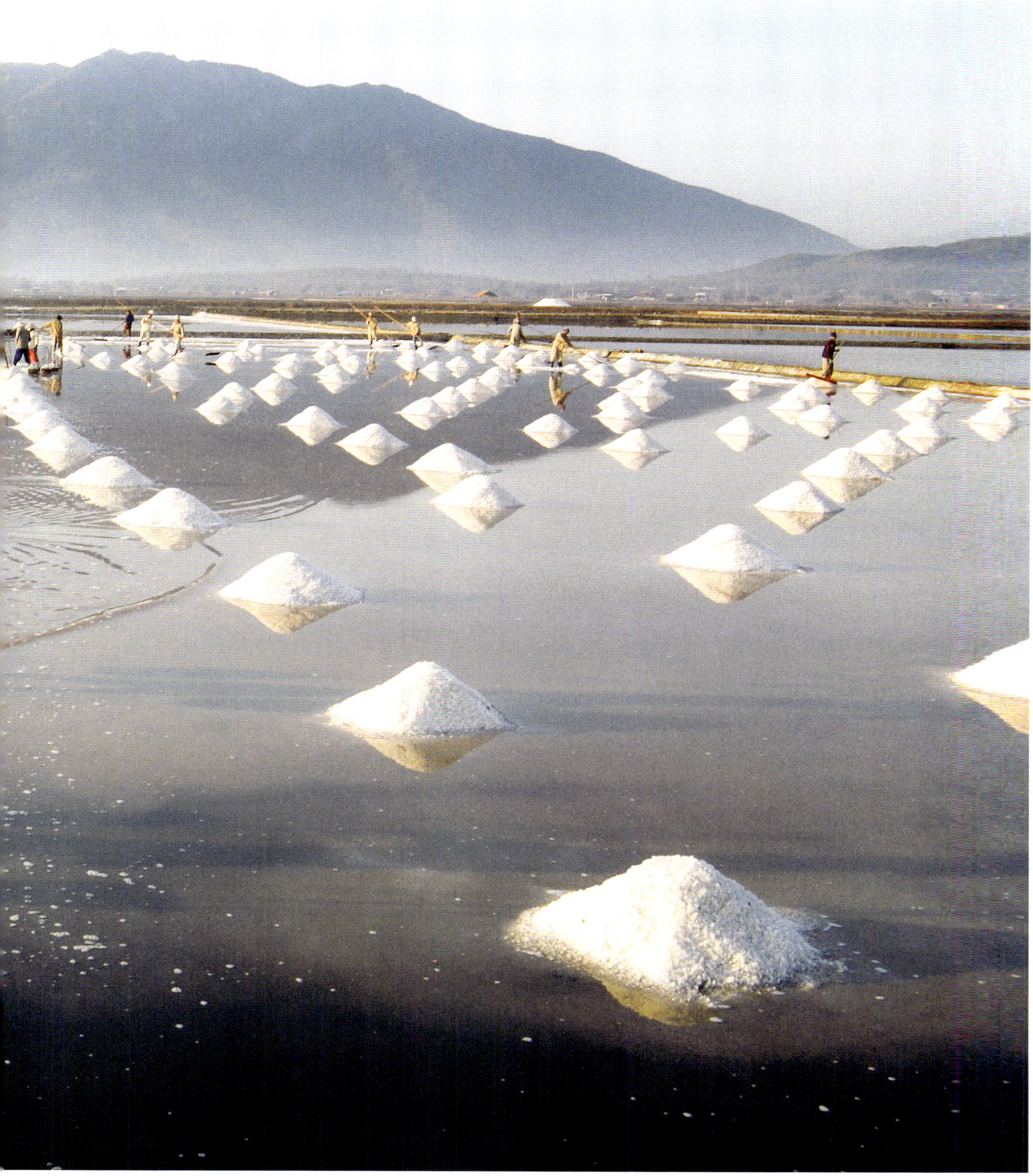

Jin Pan[illegible]u

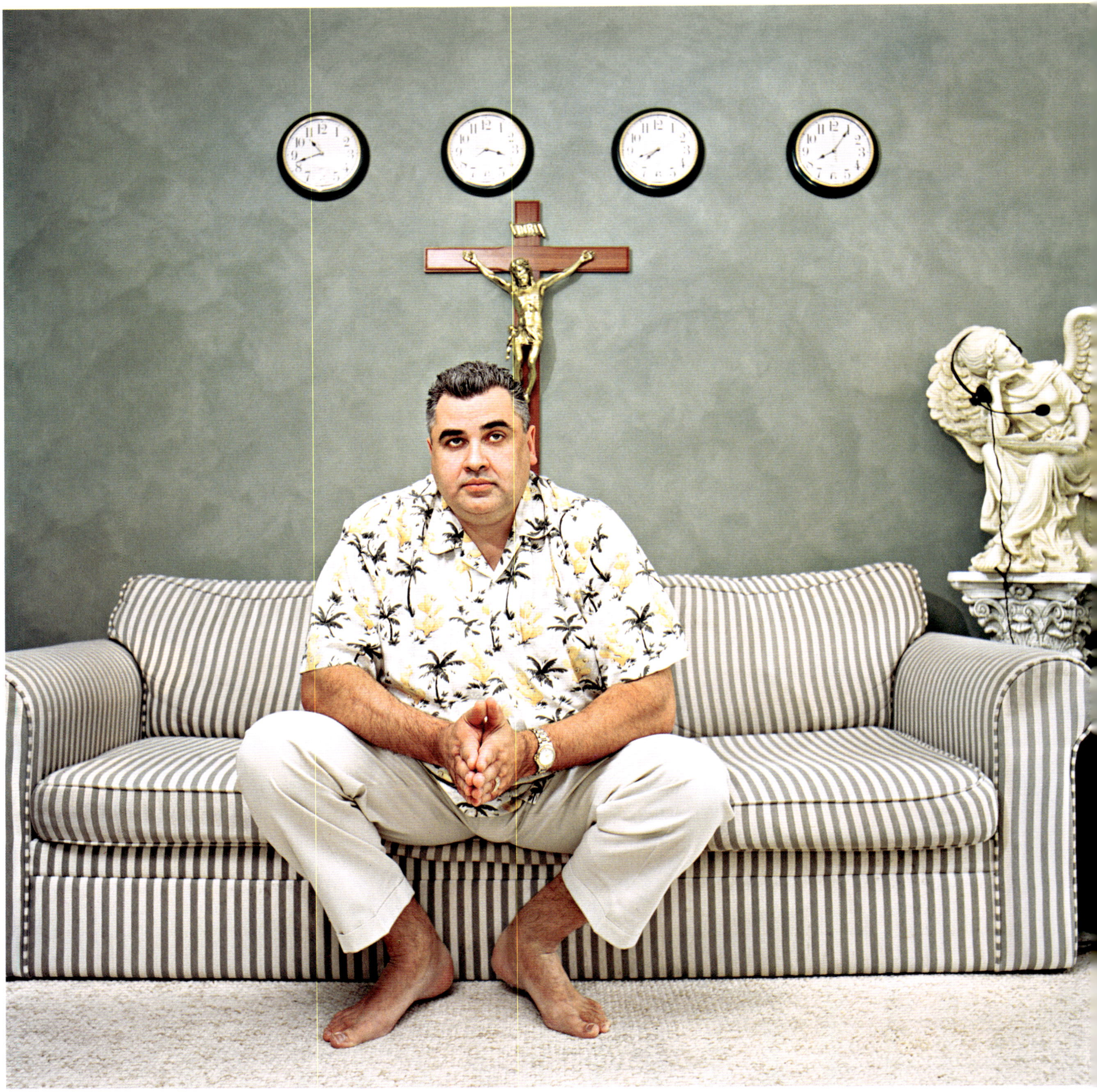

Brian Farnum

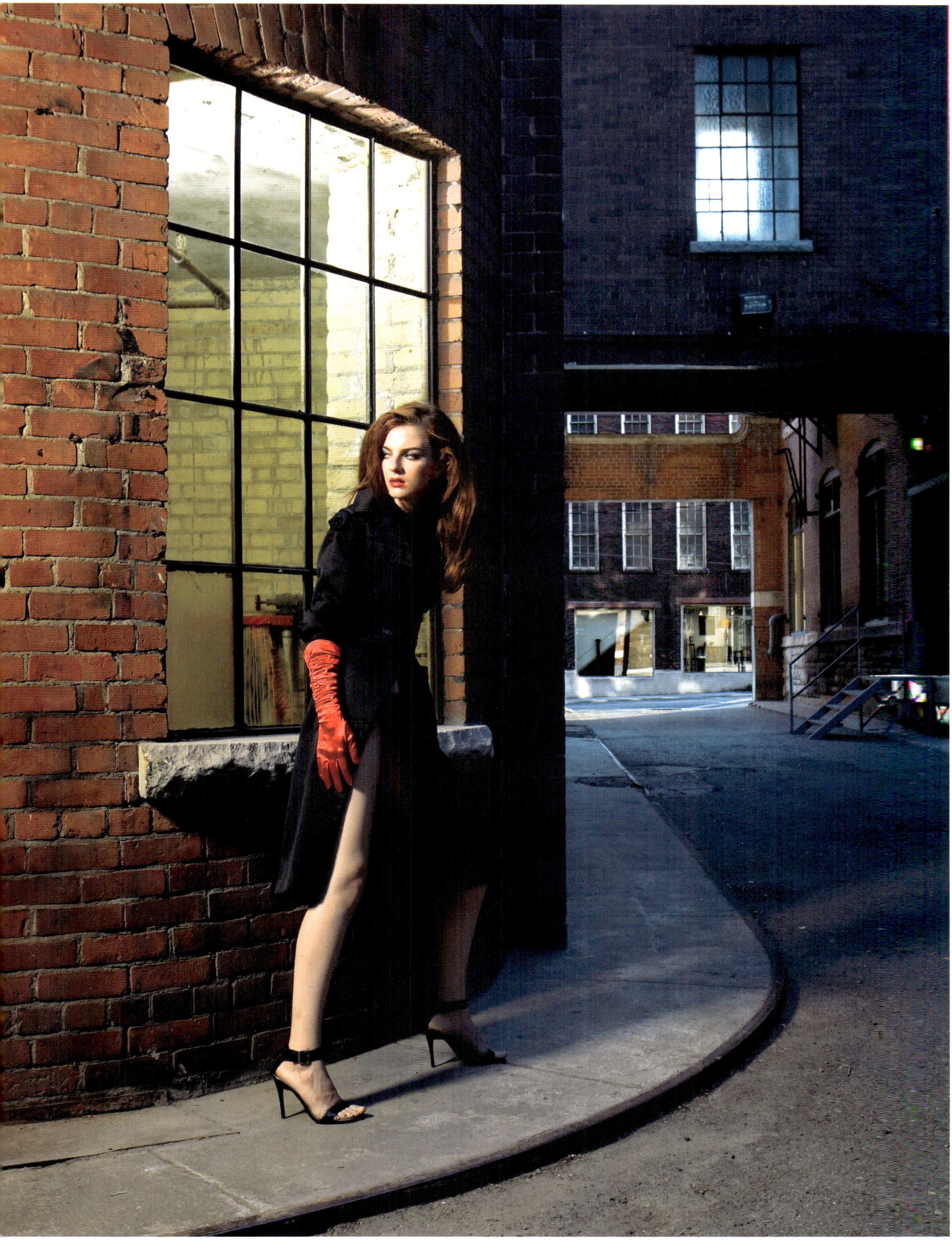

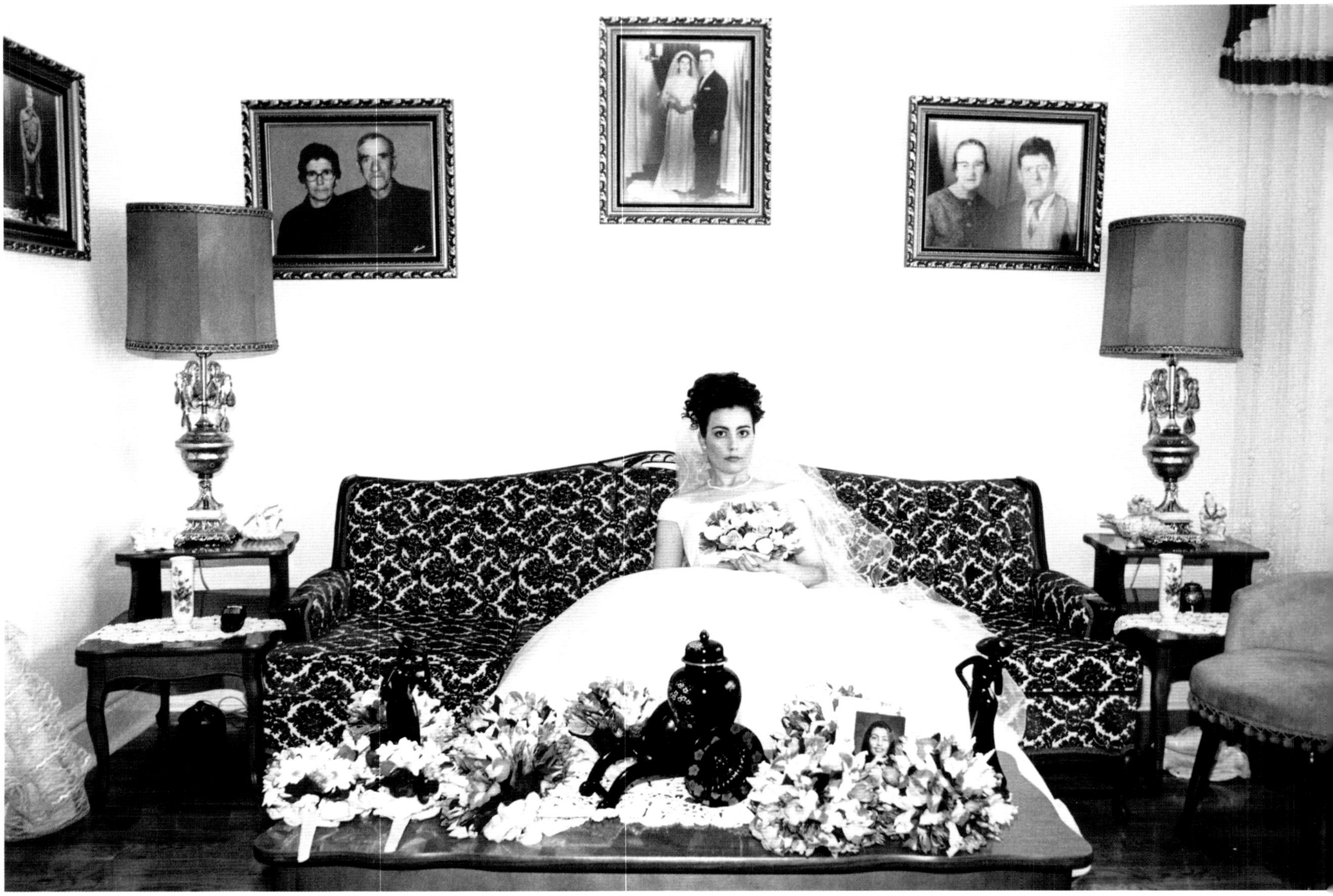

George Pimentel

Bride Sitting on Her Couch

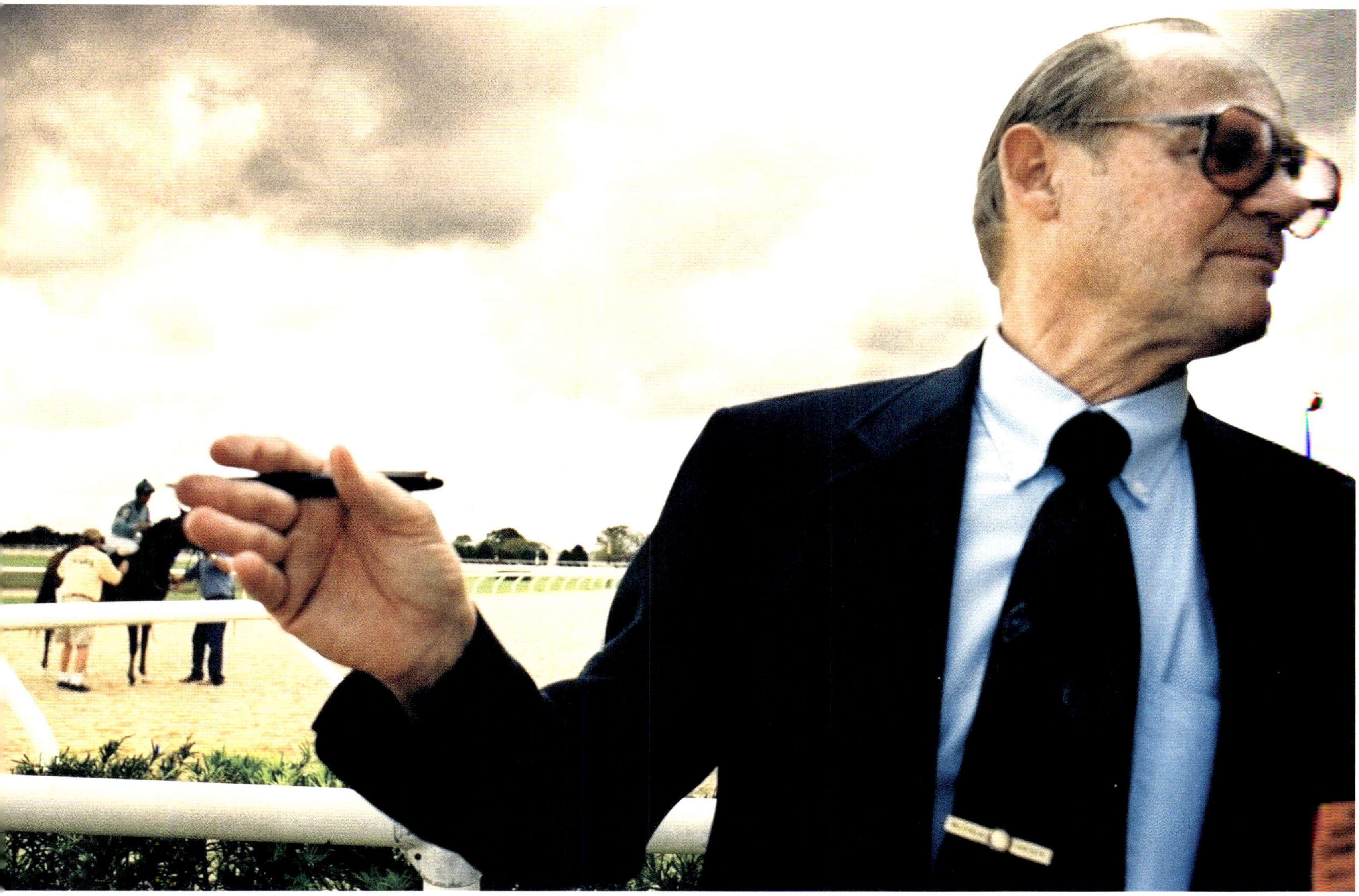

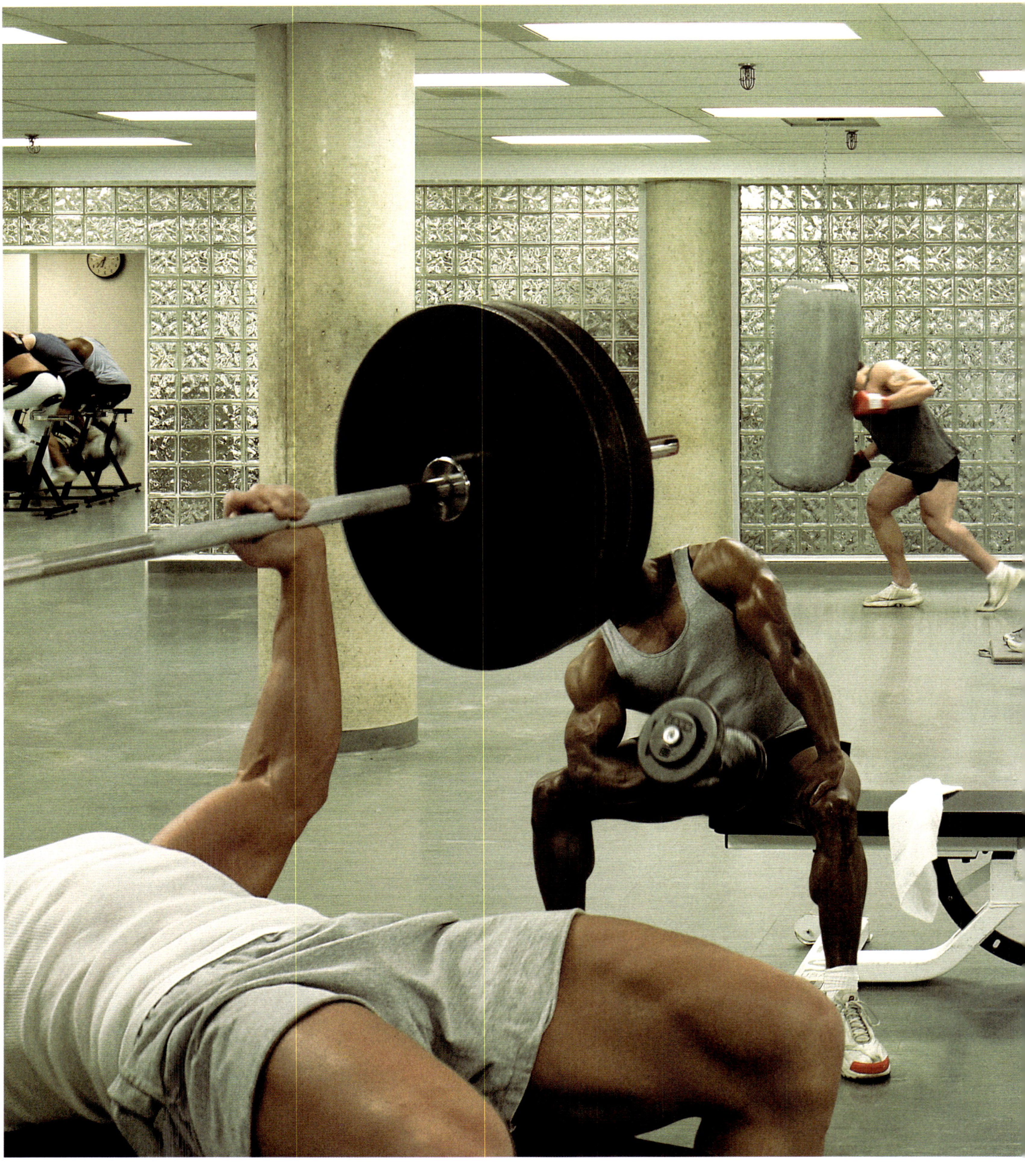

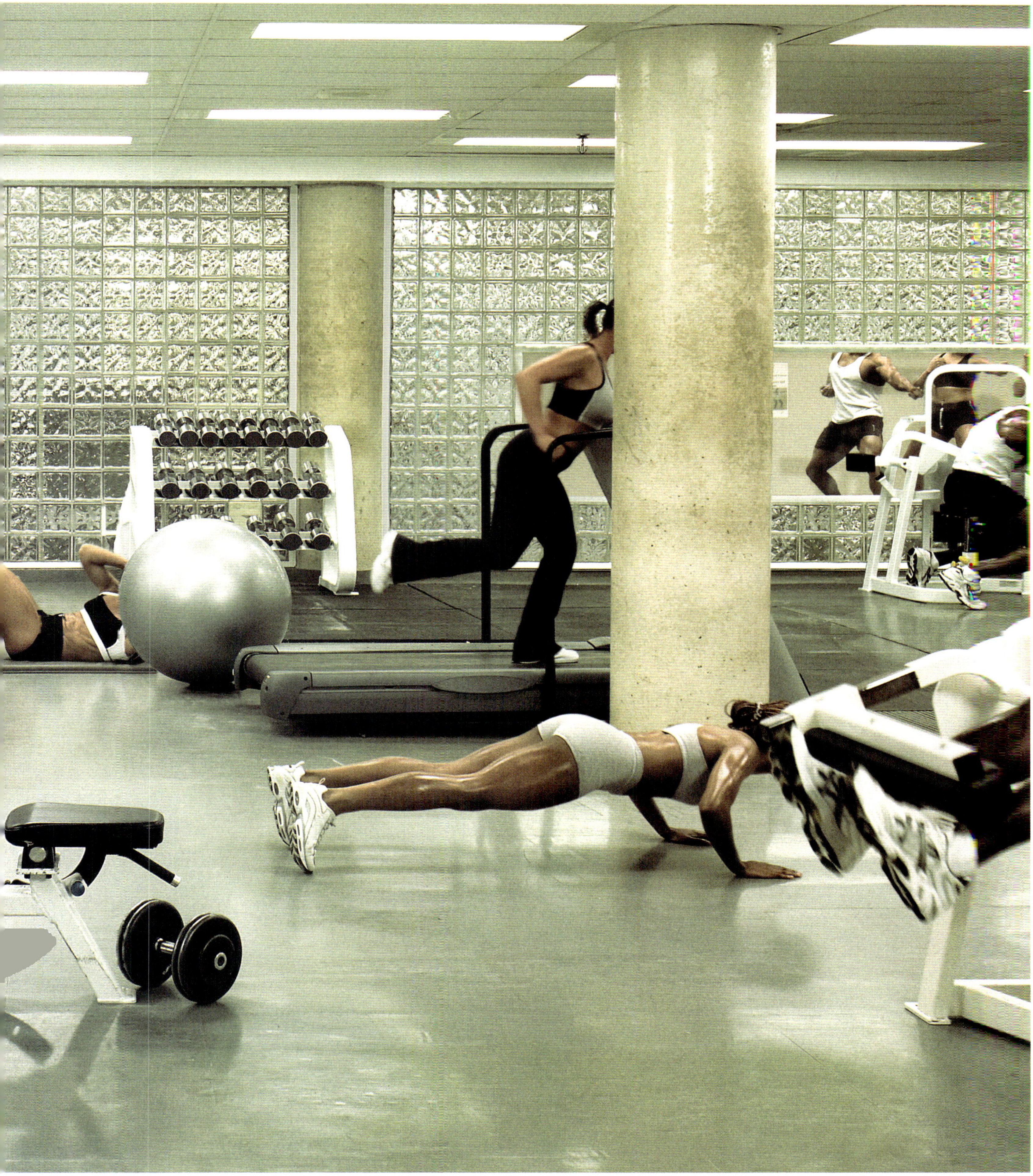

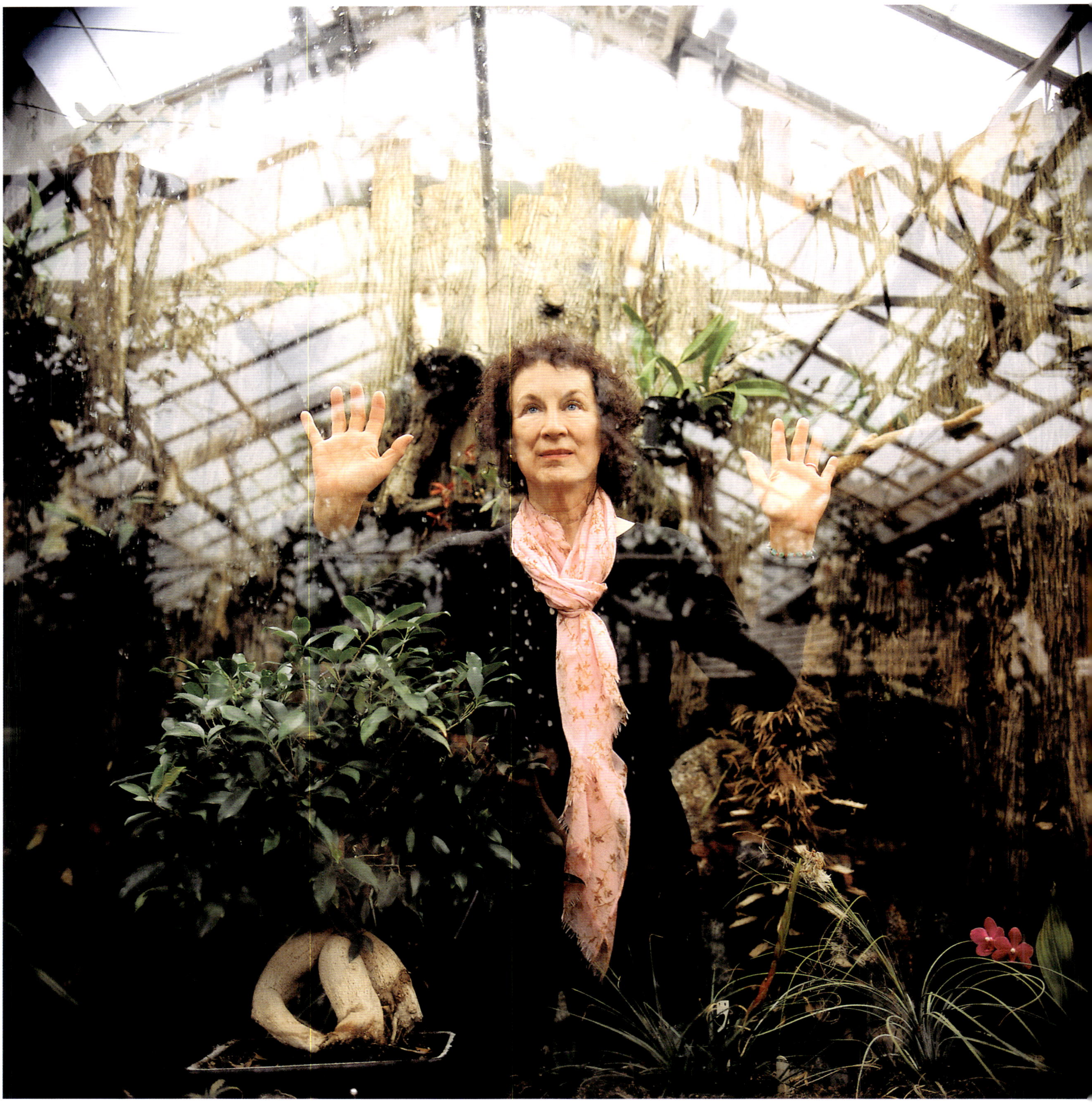

Margaret Atwood

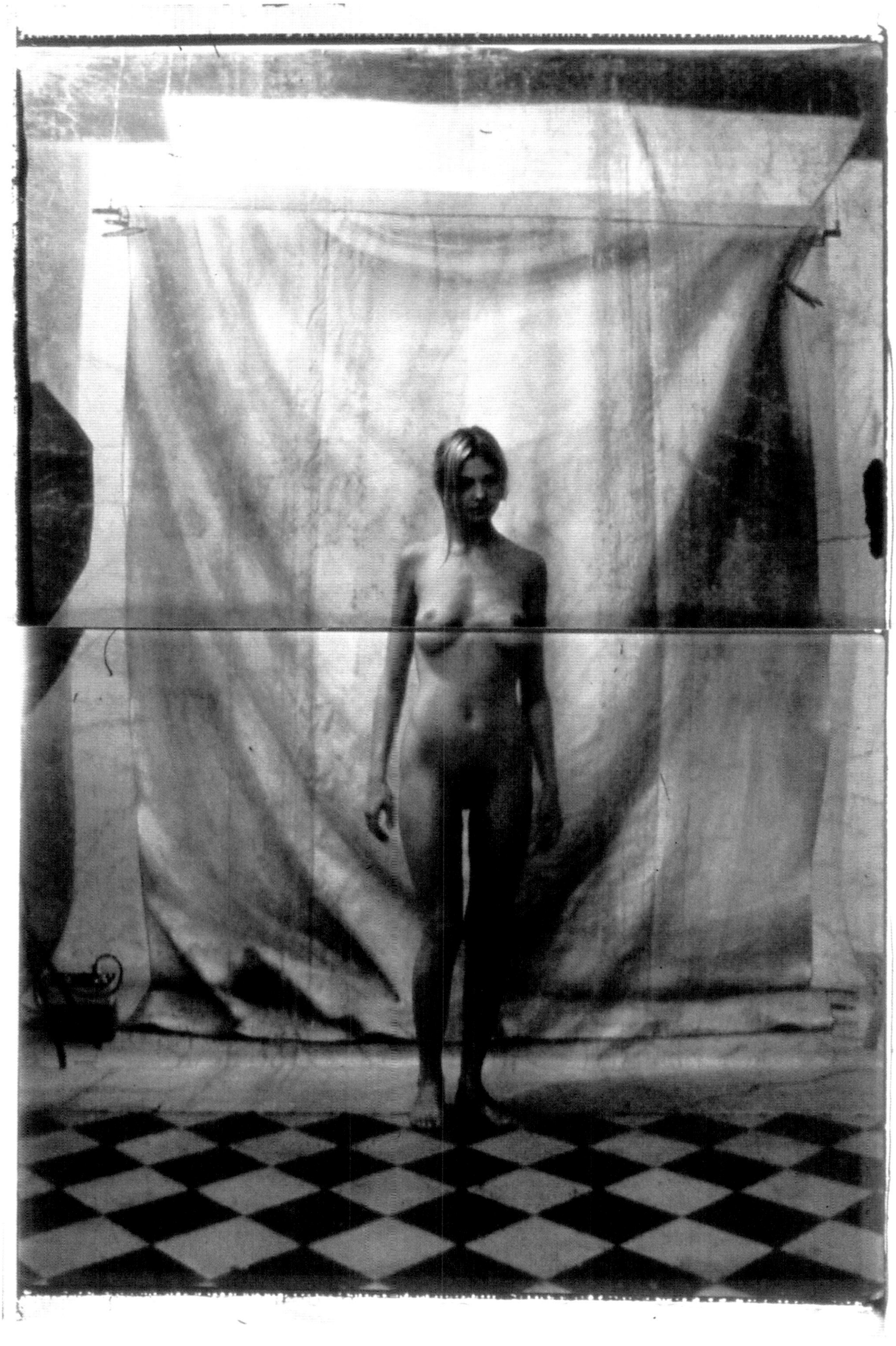

Dasha, Studio 307, 1999

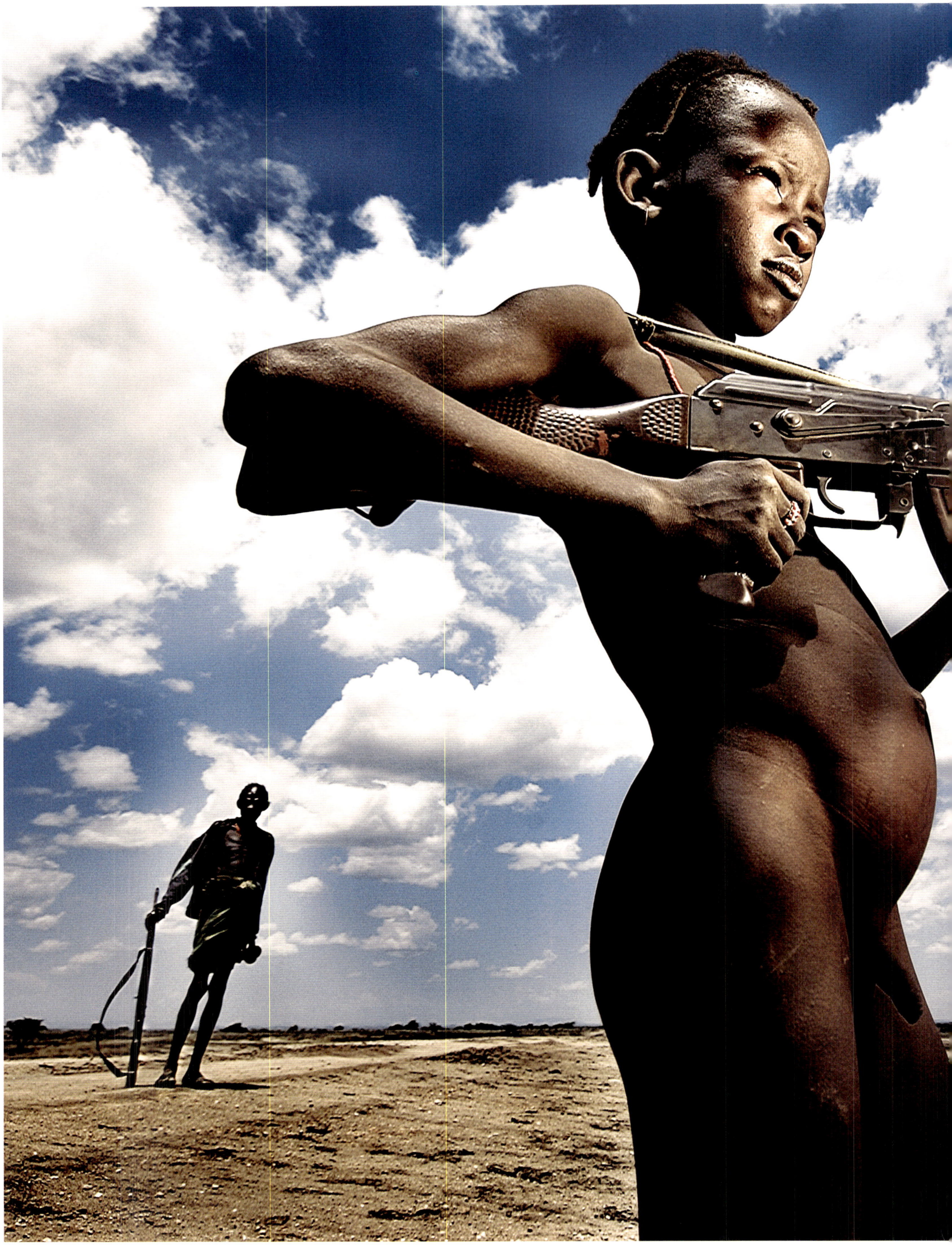

Liam Sharp

Boy With Gun

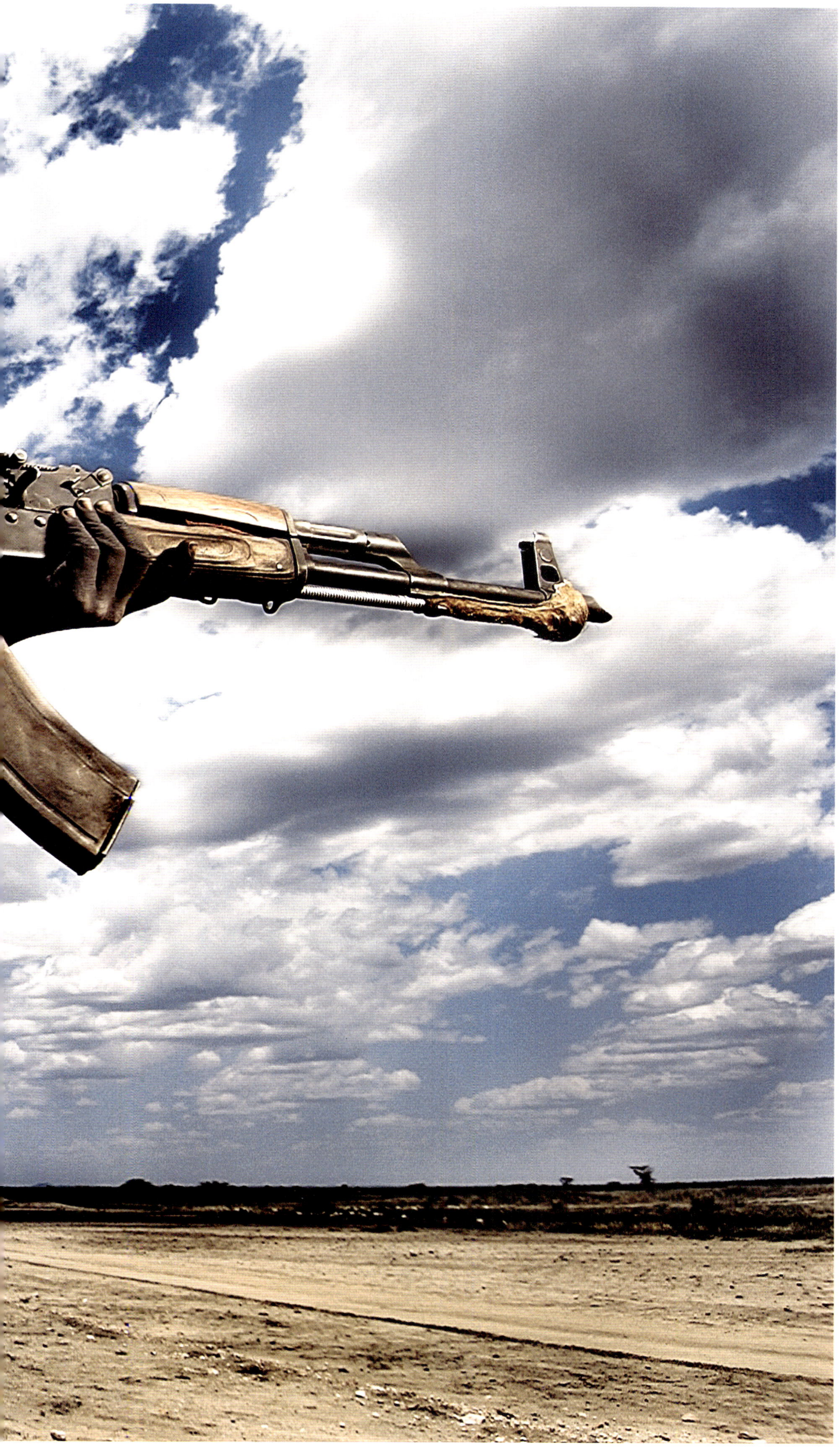

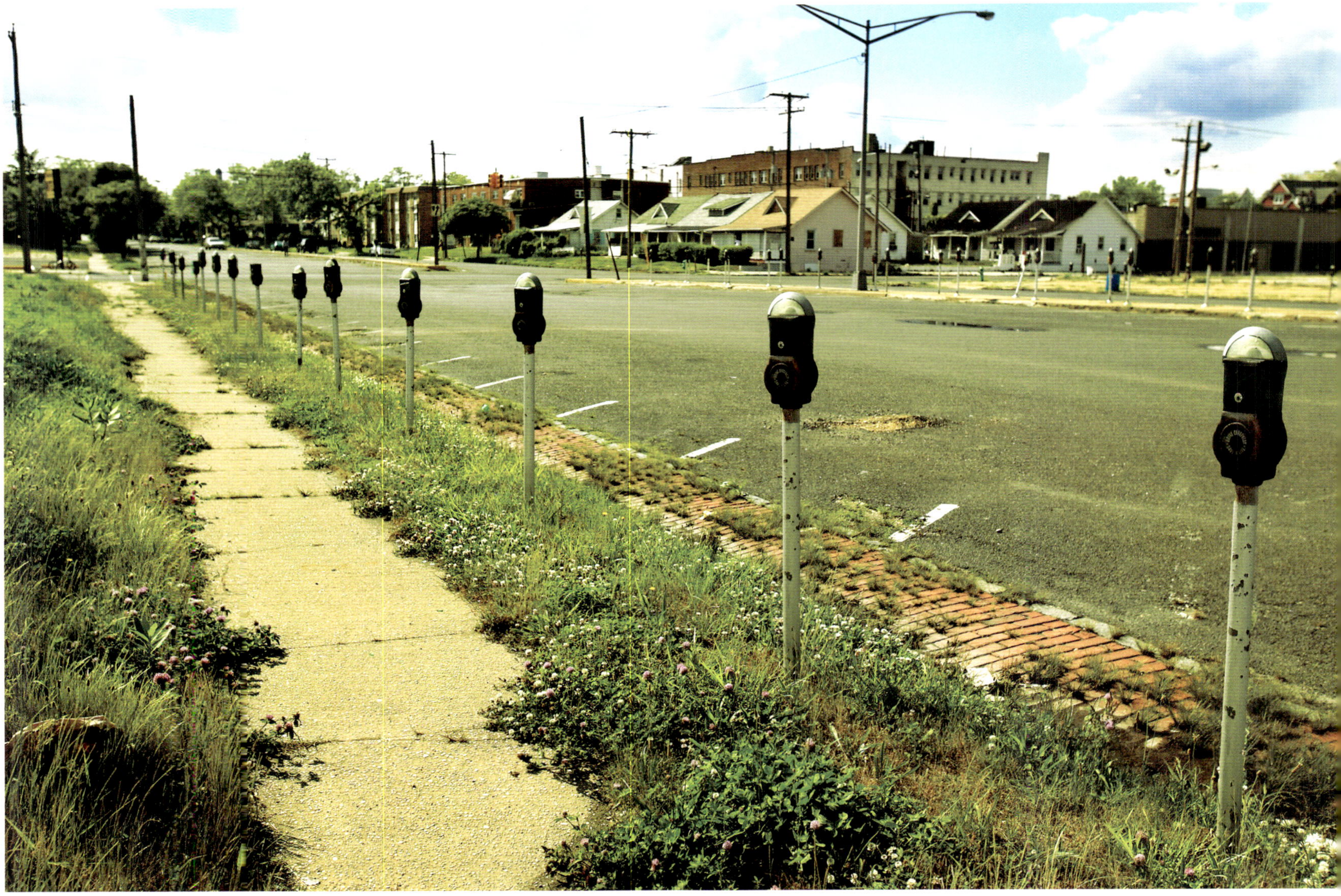

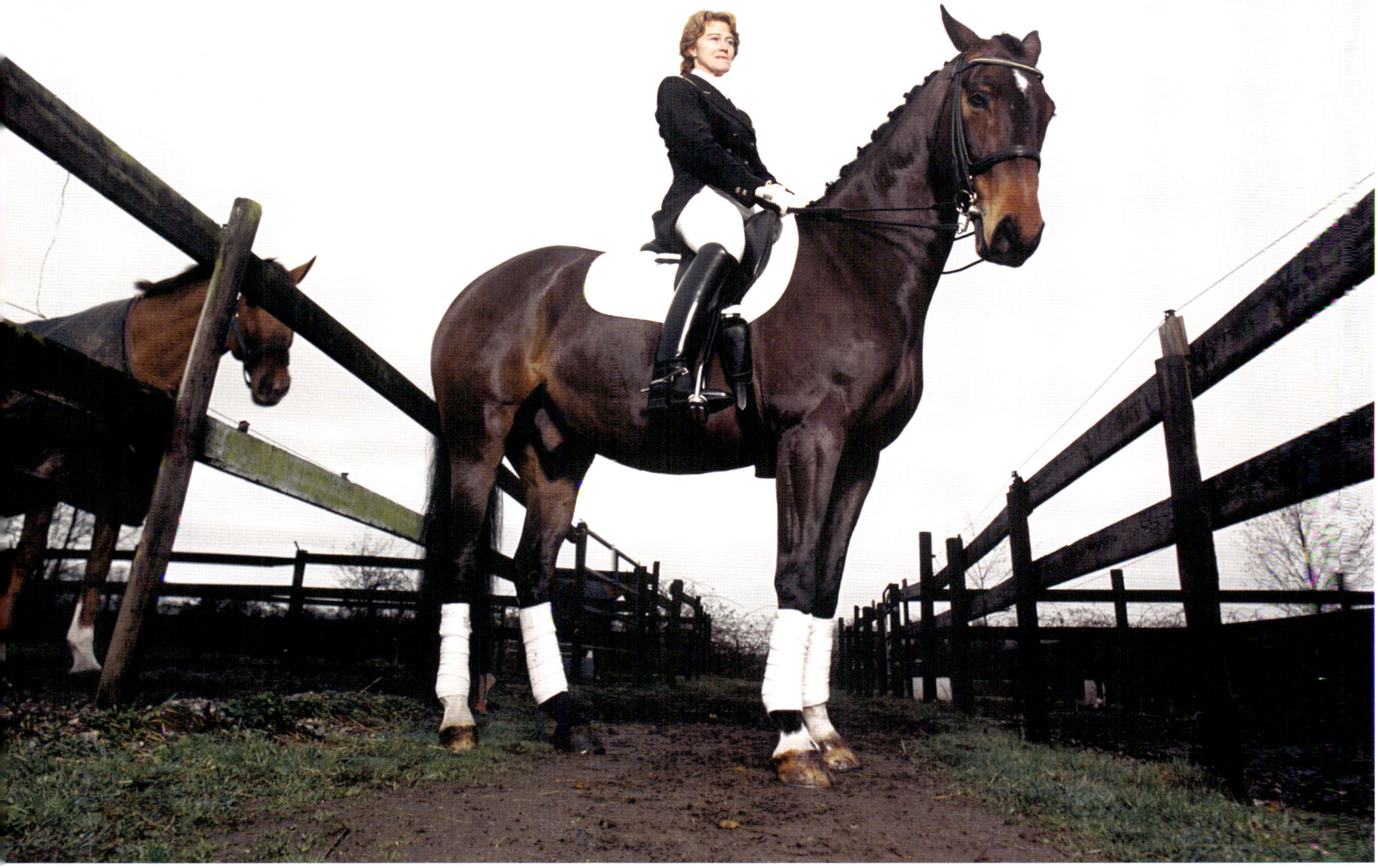

Champion

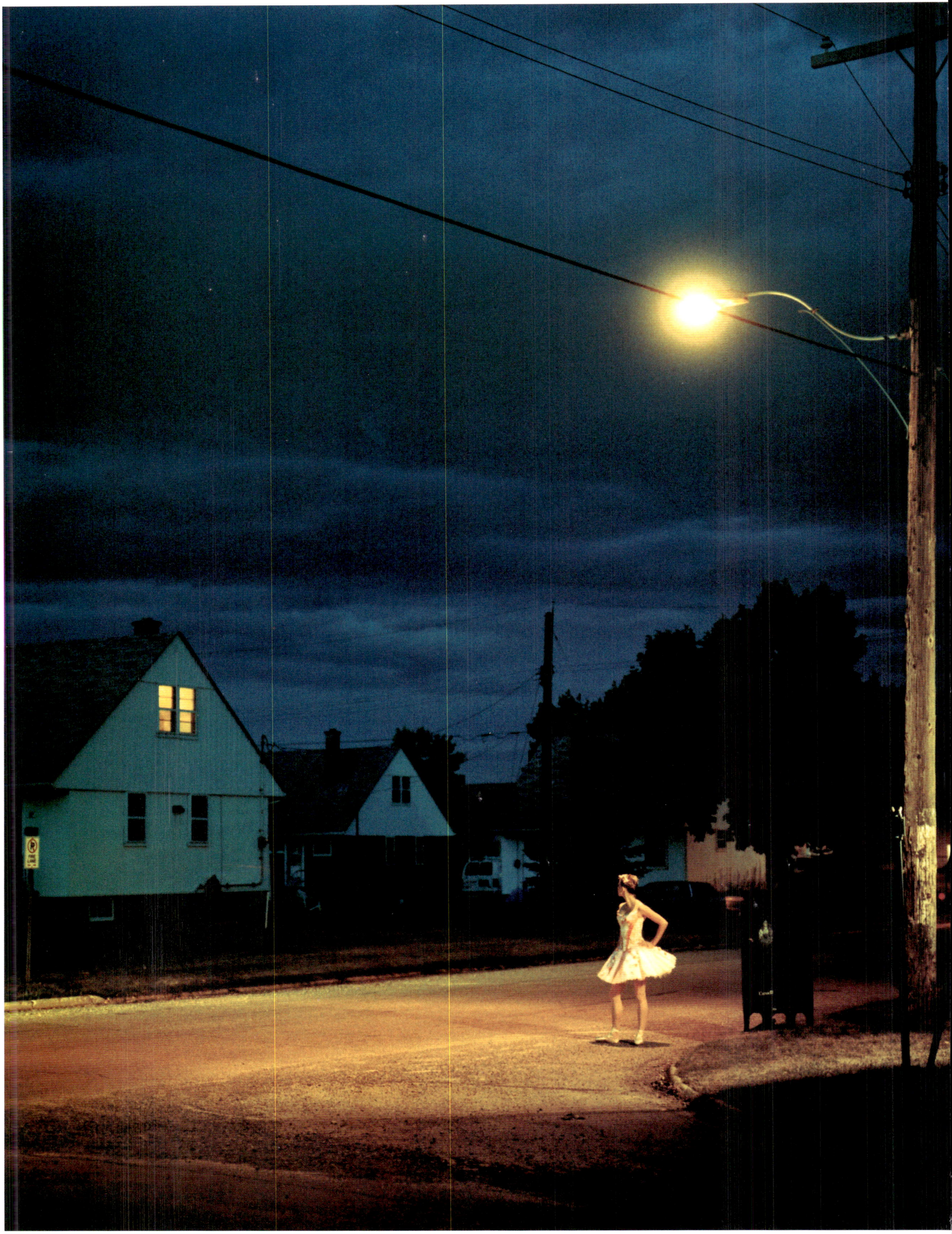

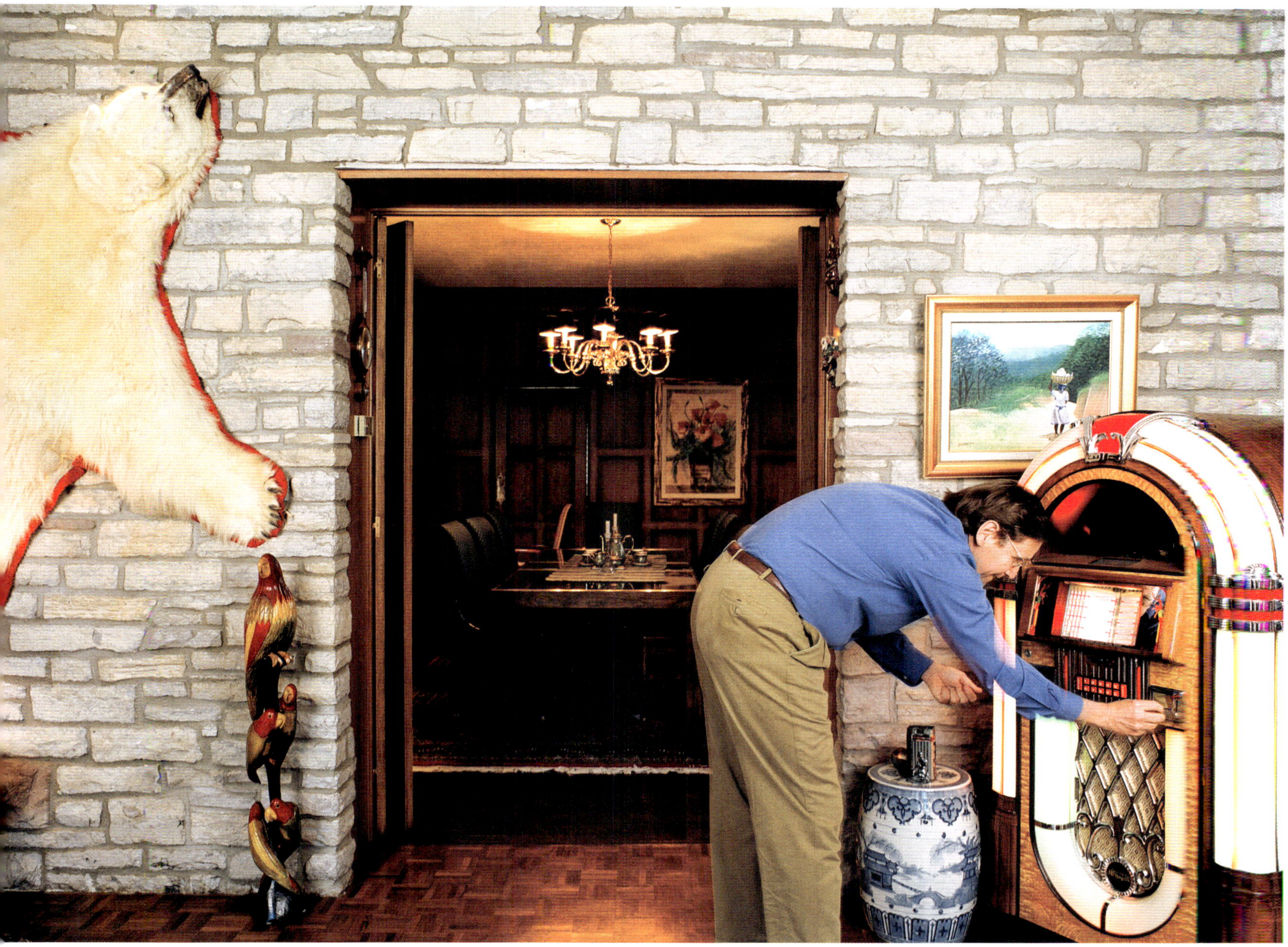

Rick Waugh

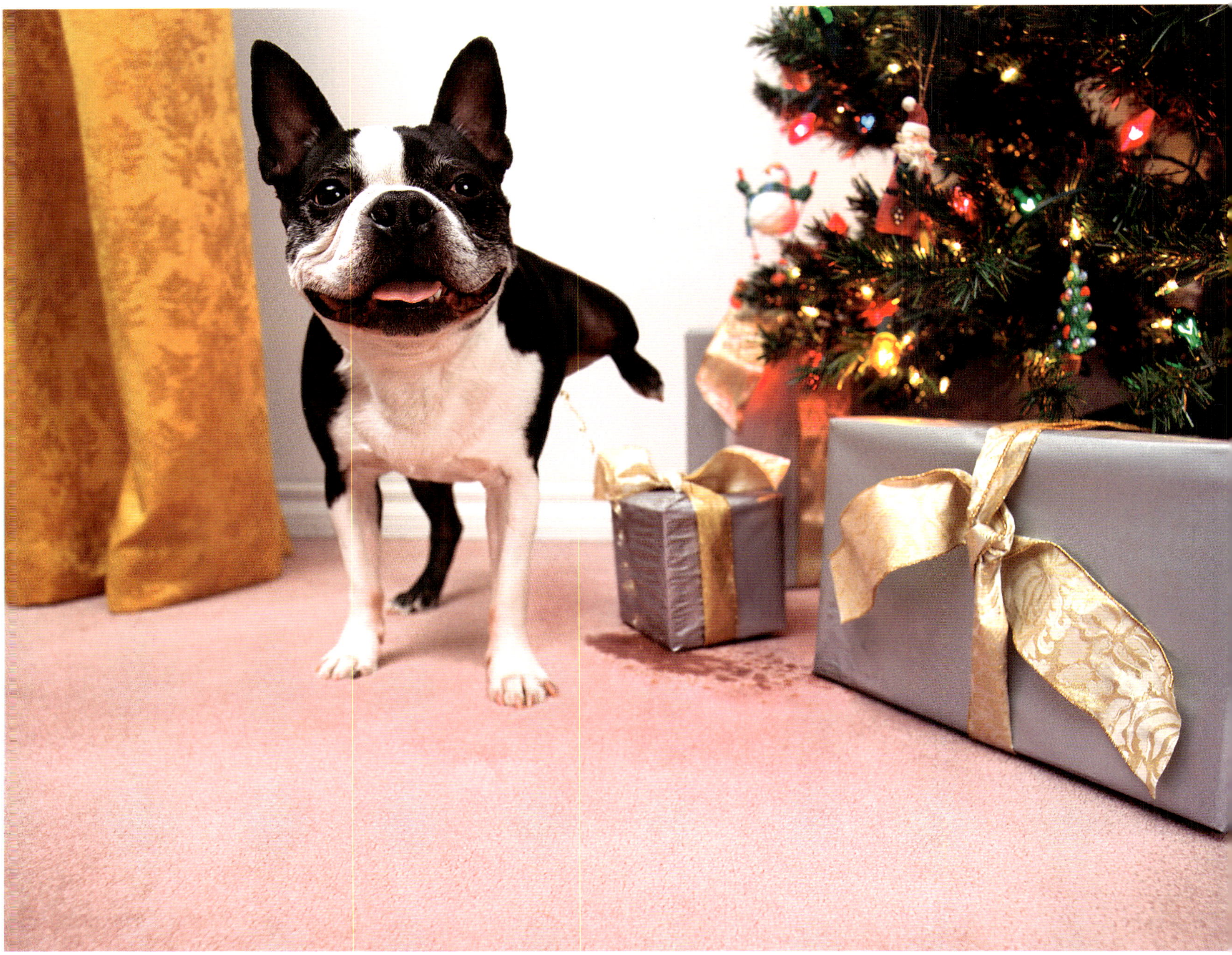

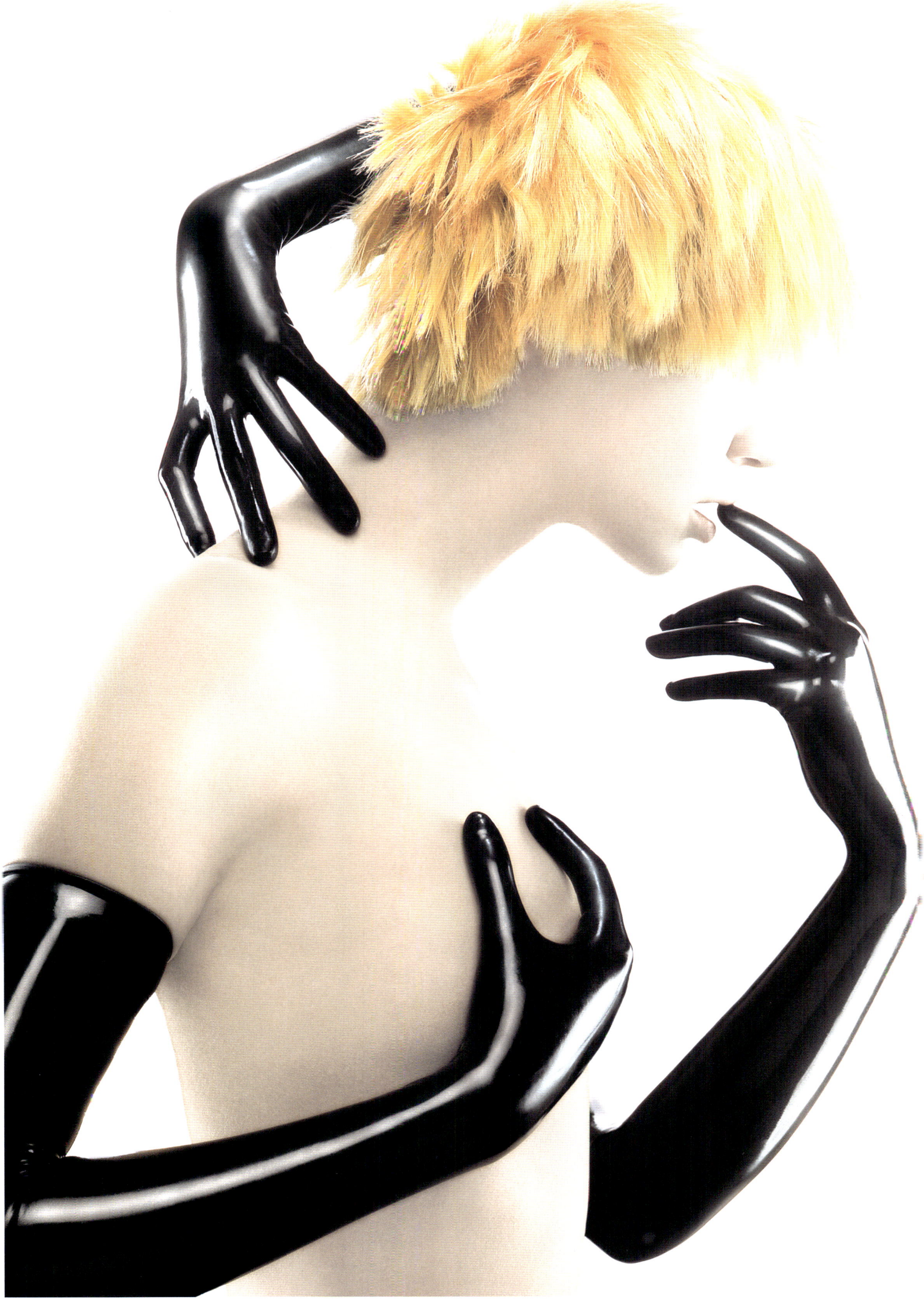

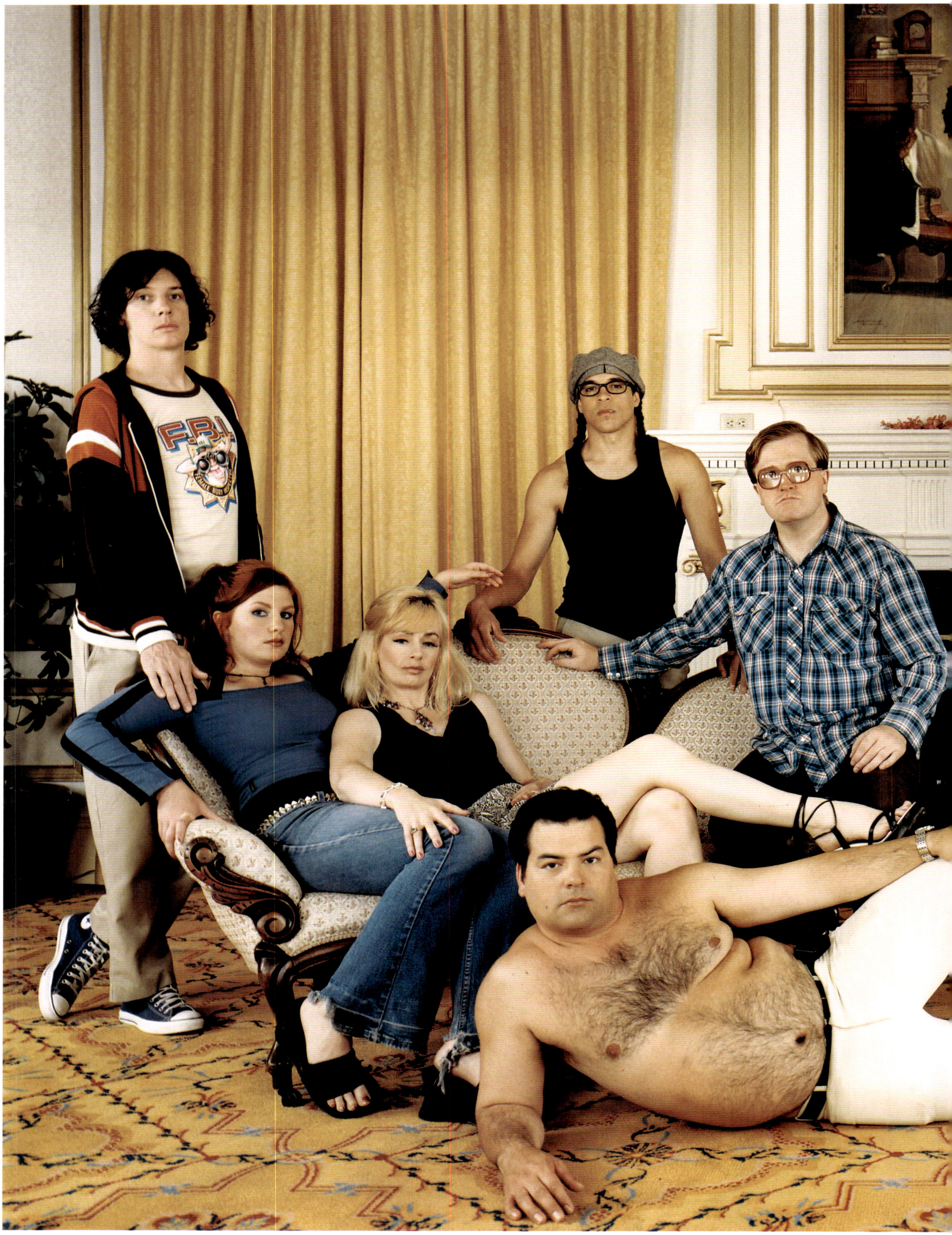

Trailer Park Boys

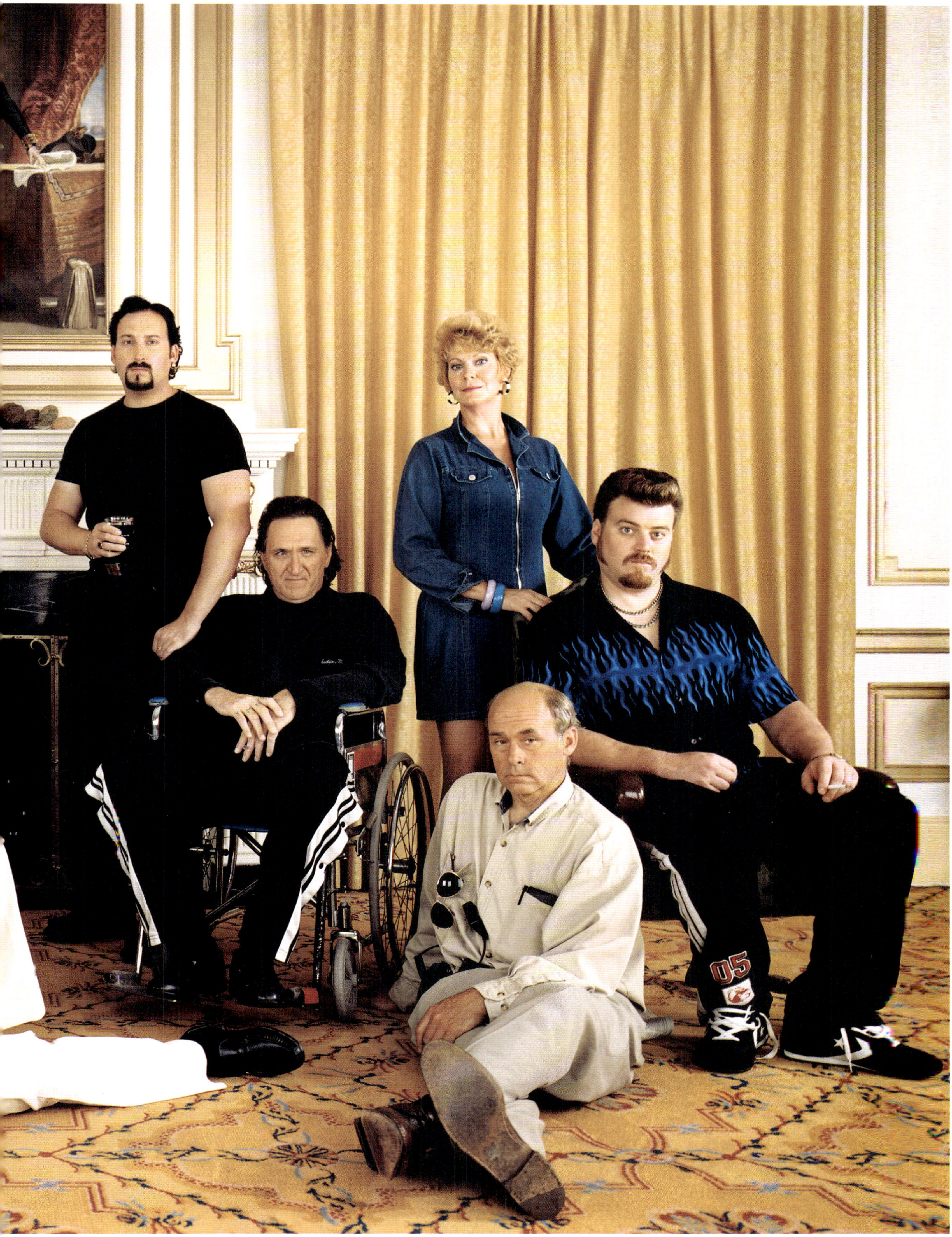

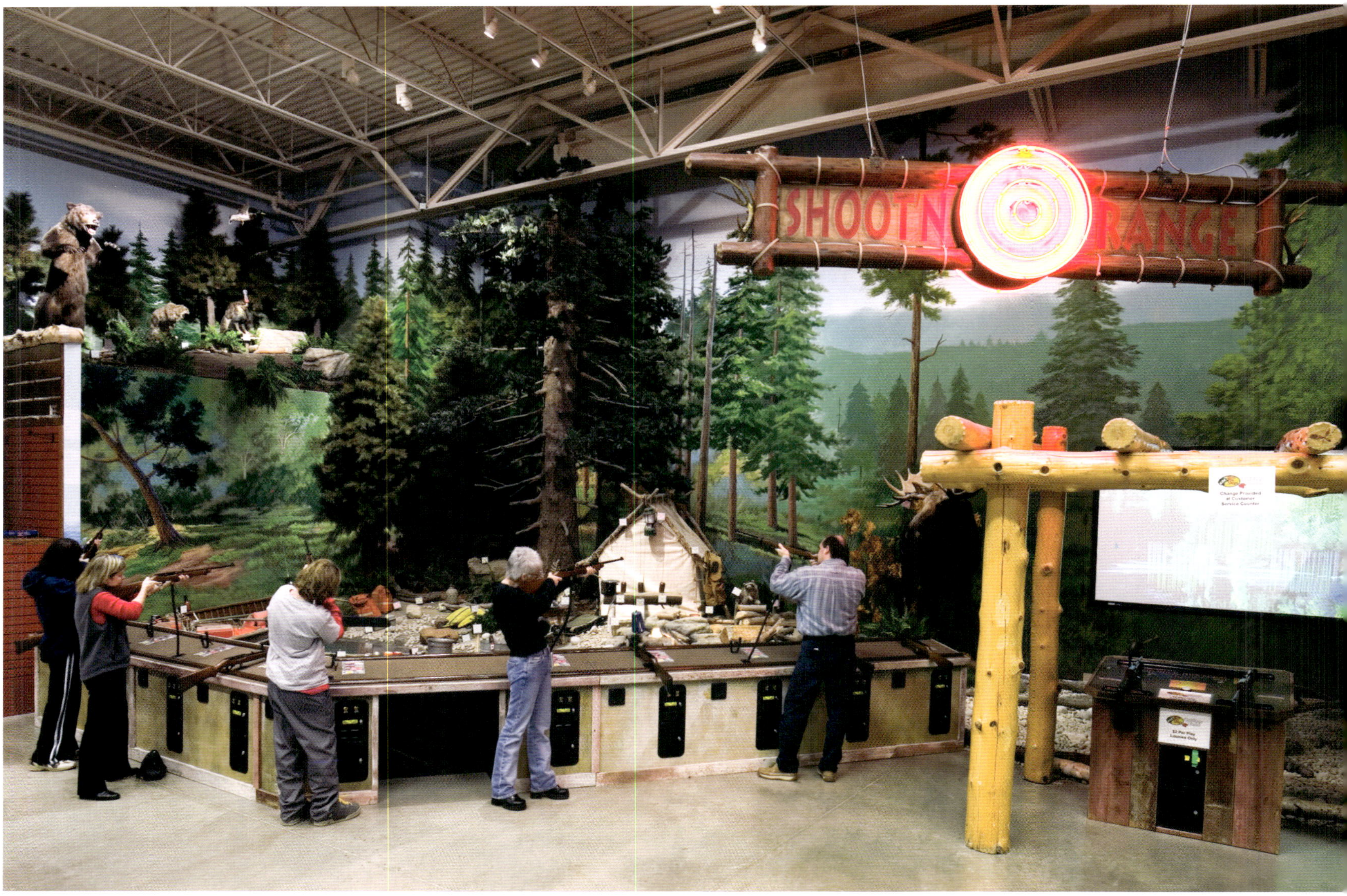
SHOOT'N
RANGE

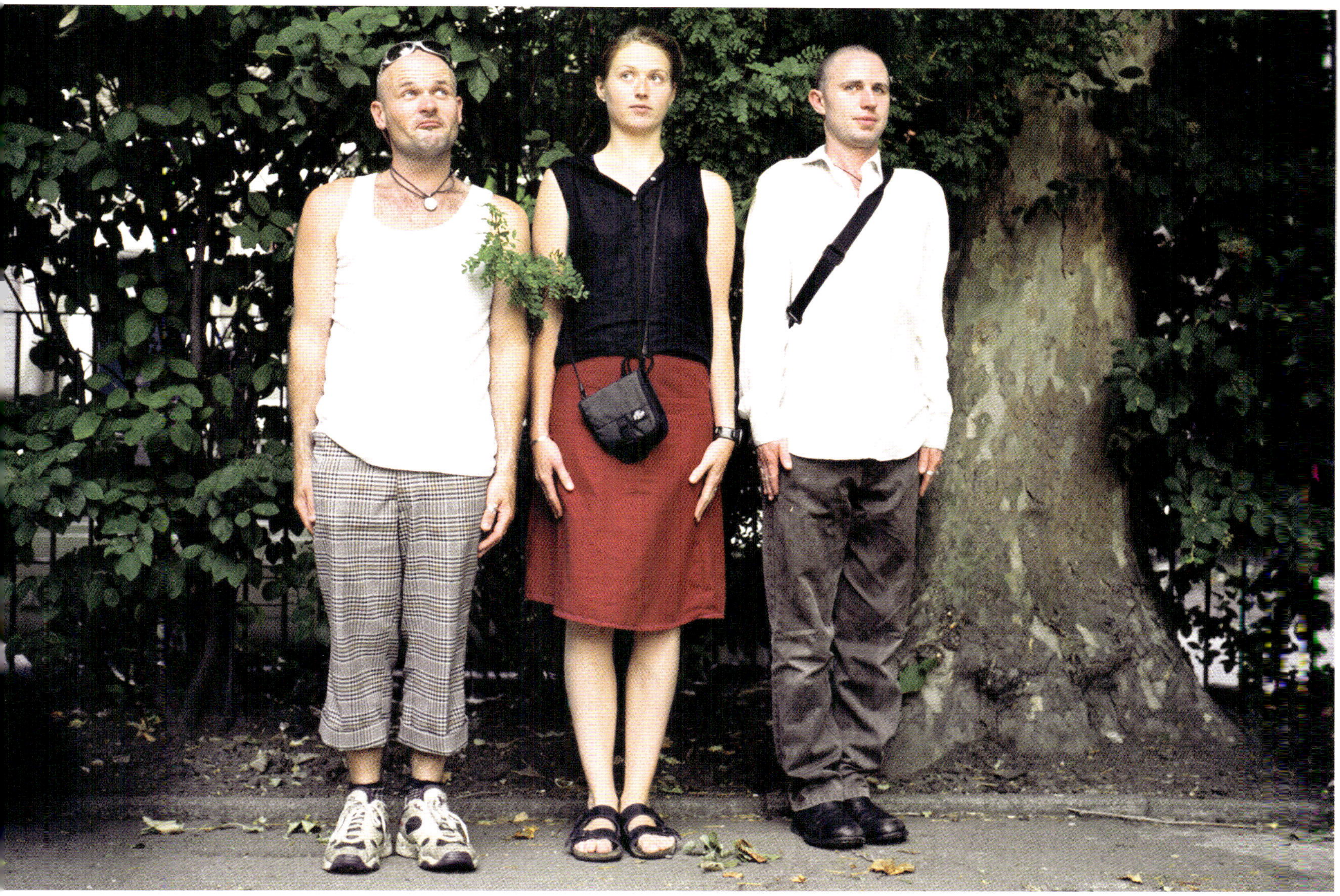

Three in Hoxton

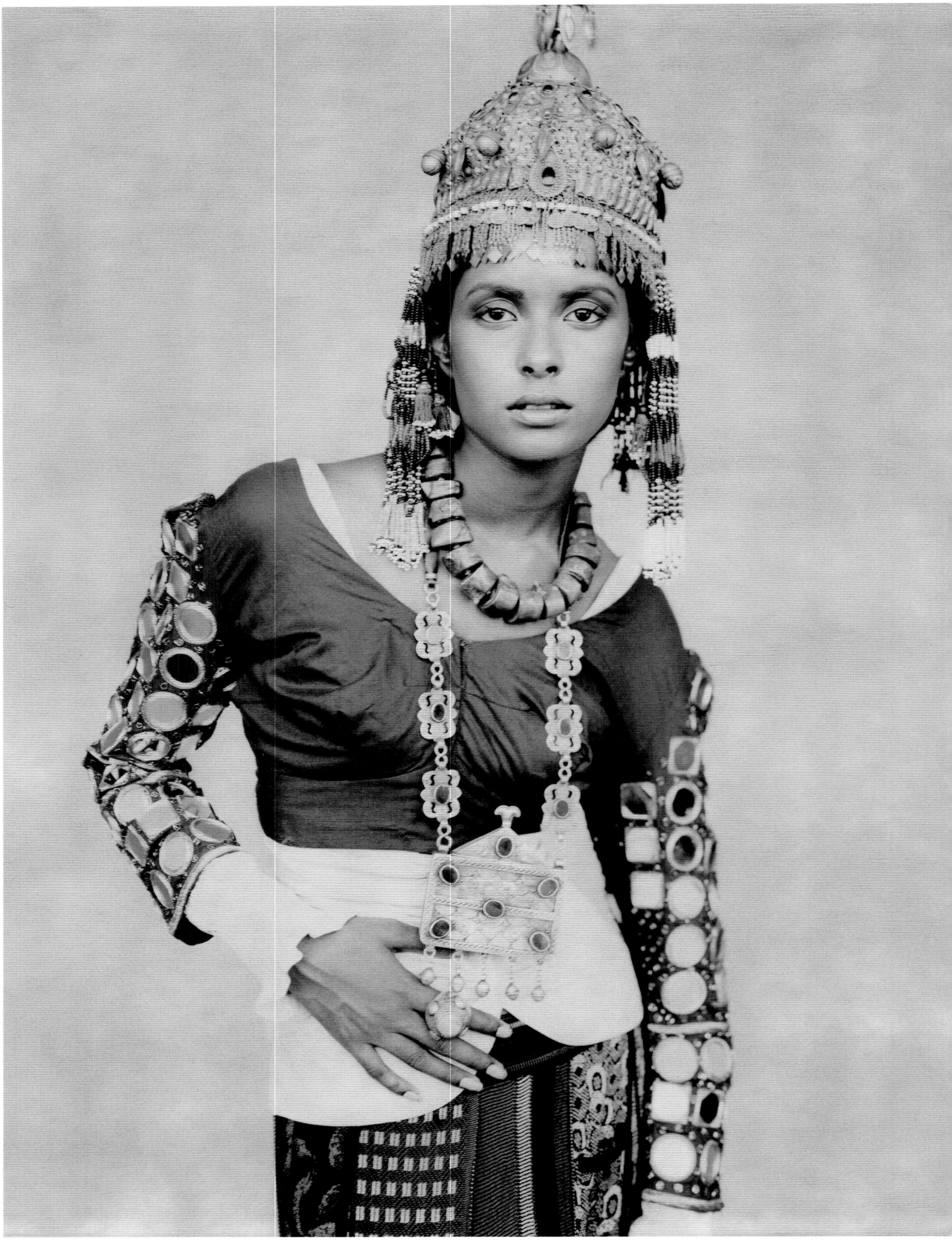

The Princess Regal

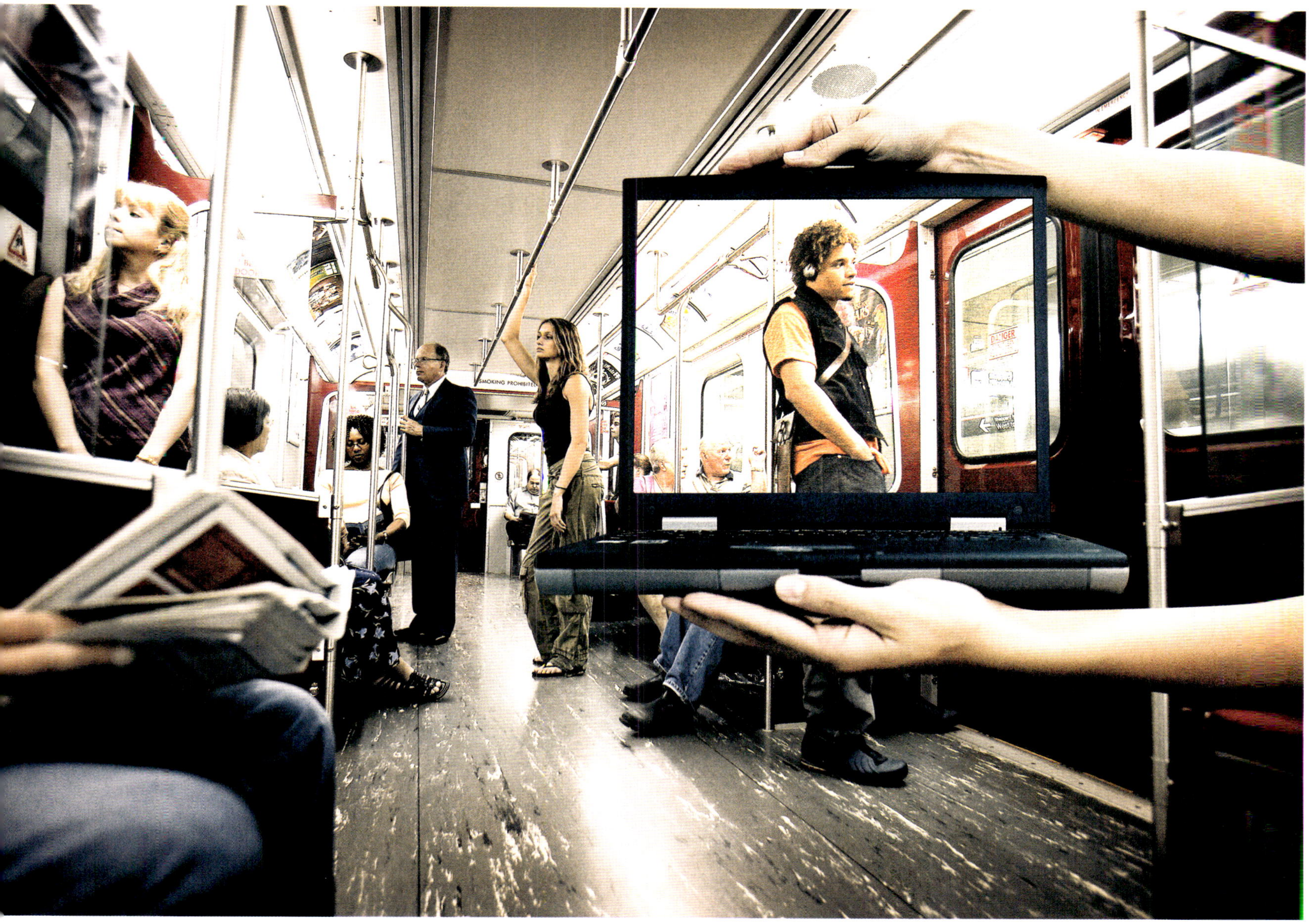

Untitled

Chris Woods

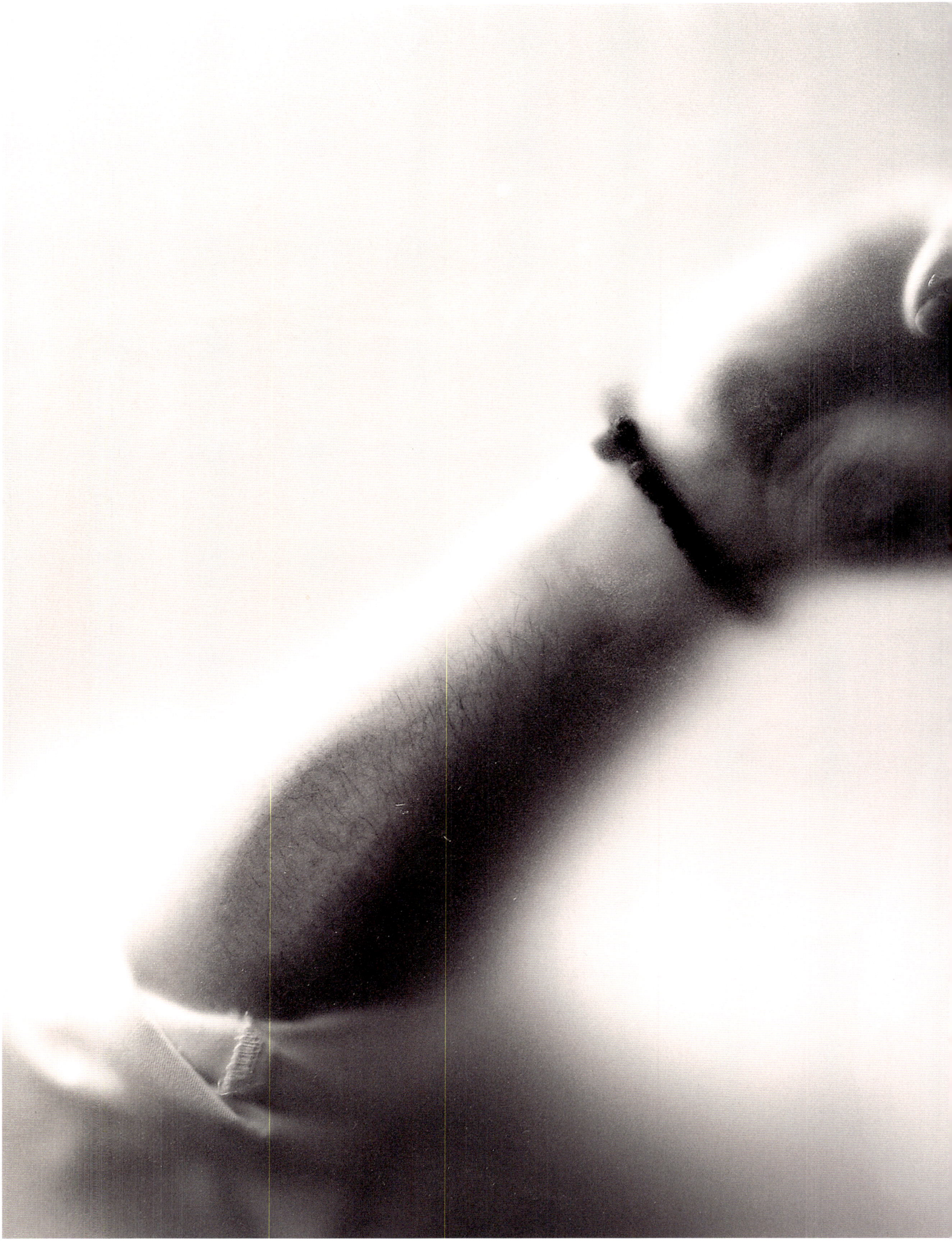

Mark Zibert

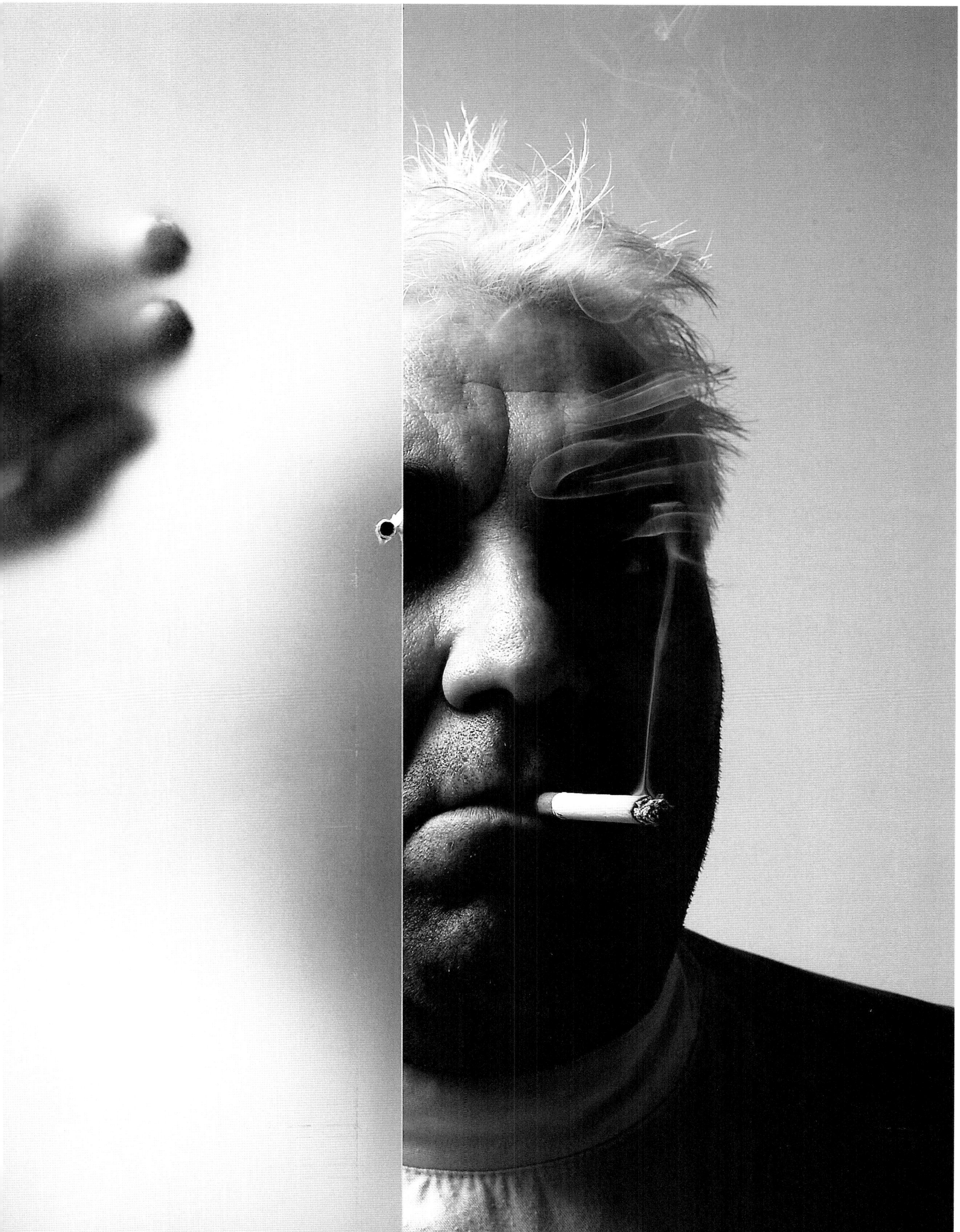

EMER

Alyssa Andrews, Jaret Belliveau, Patrick Blaeser, Kotama Bouabane, Lila Bujold, Miriam Cabell, Jamie Campbell, Ryan Carter, Becky Comber, Robyn Cumming, Danny Custodio, Kadija De Paula, Alice Dixon, Veronique Ducharme-Frappier, Carrie Duplessis, Adam Harrison, Vanessa Heins, Maayan Kasimov, Sasha Krieger, Sarah Mangialardo, Davida Nemeroff, Louis Perreault, Kerry Shaw, Graydon Sheppard, Joanna Simpson, Natalie Sorenson, Sarah Thorpe, Martin Verreault, Johanna Warwick, Elena Willis

GING

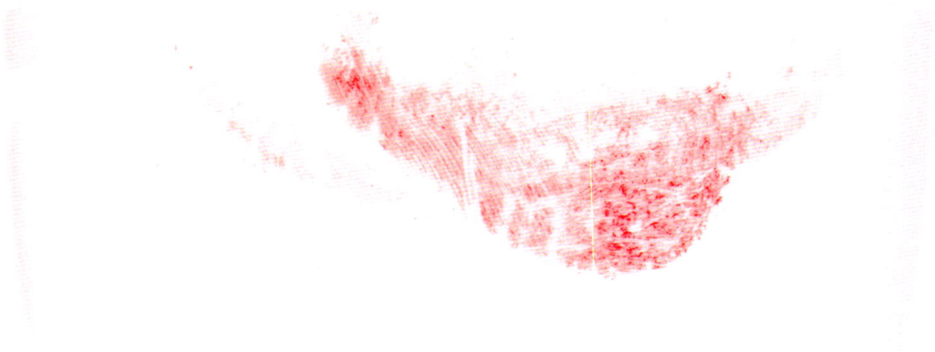

Alyssa Andrews

Carrie

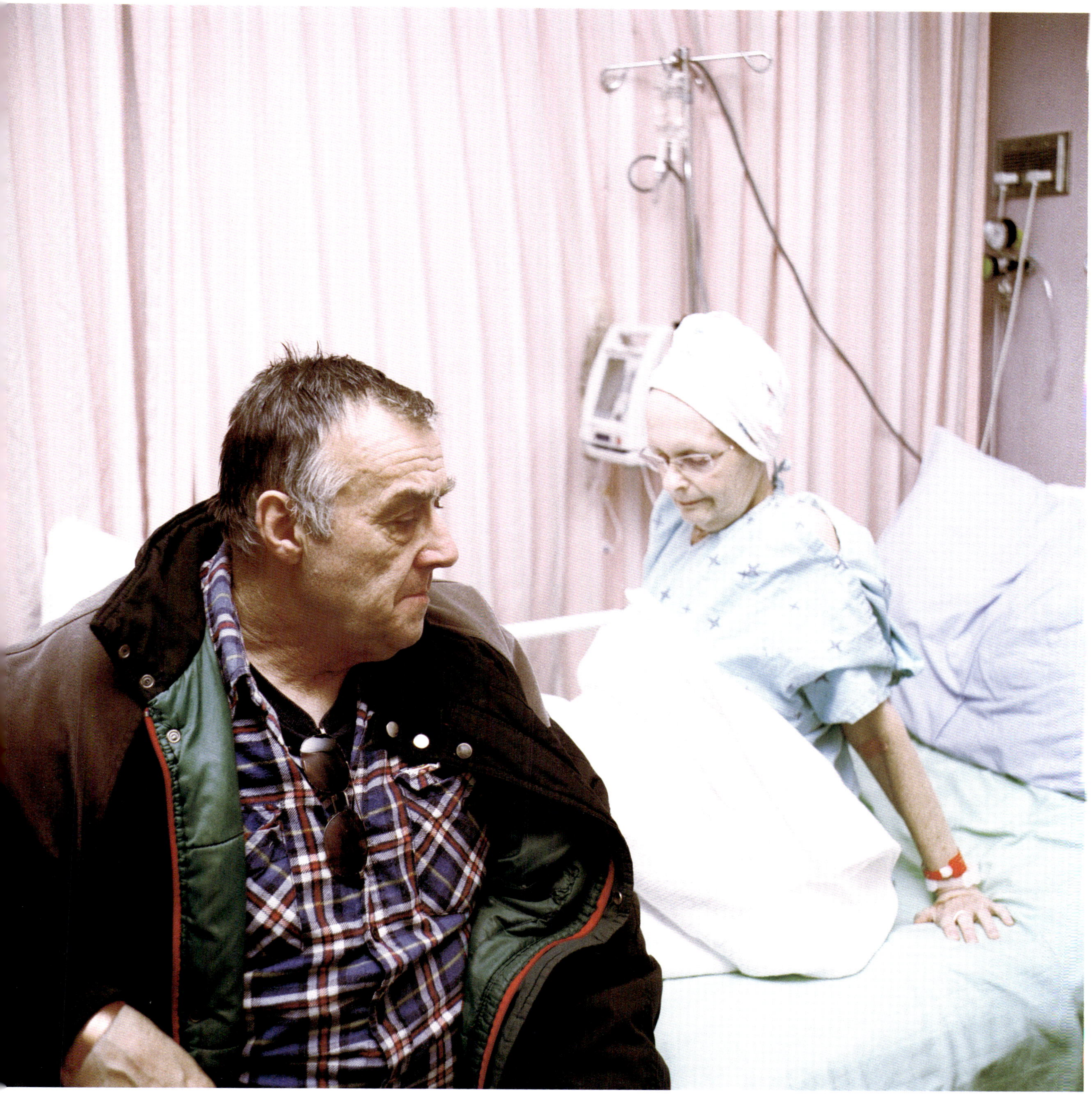

Re-admitted (attempting to increase nutrient levels)

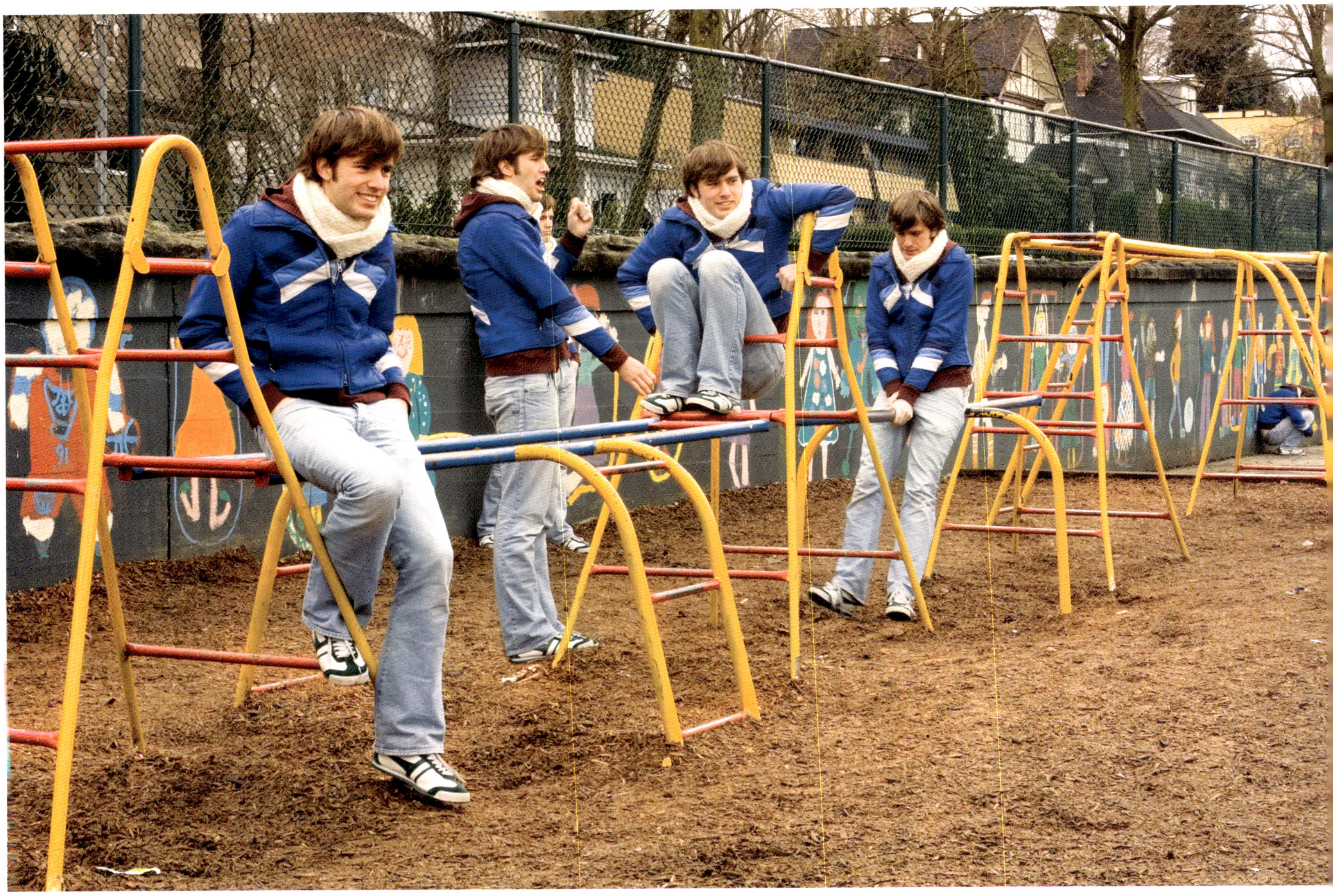

Monkey Bar Multiple 2

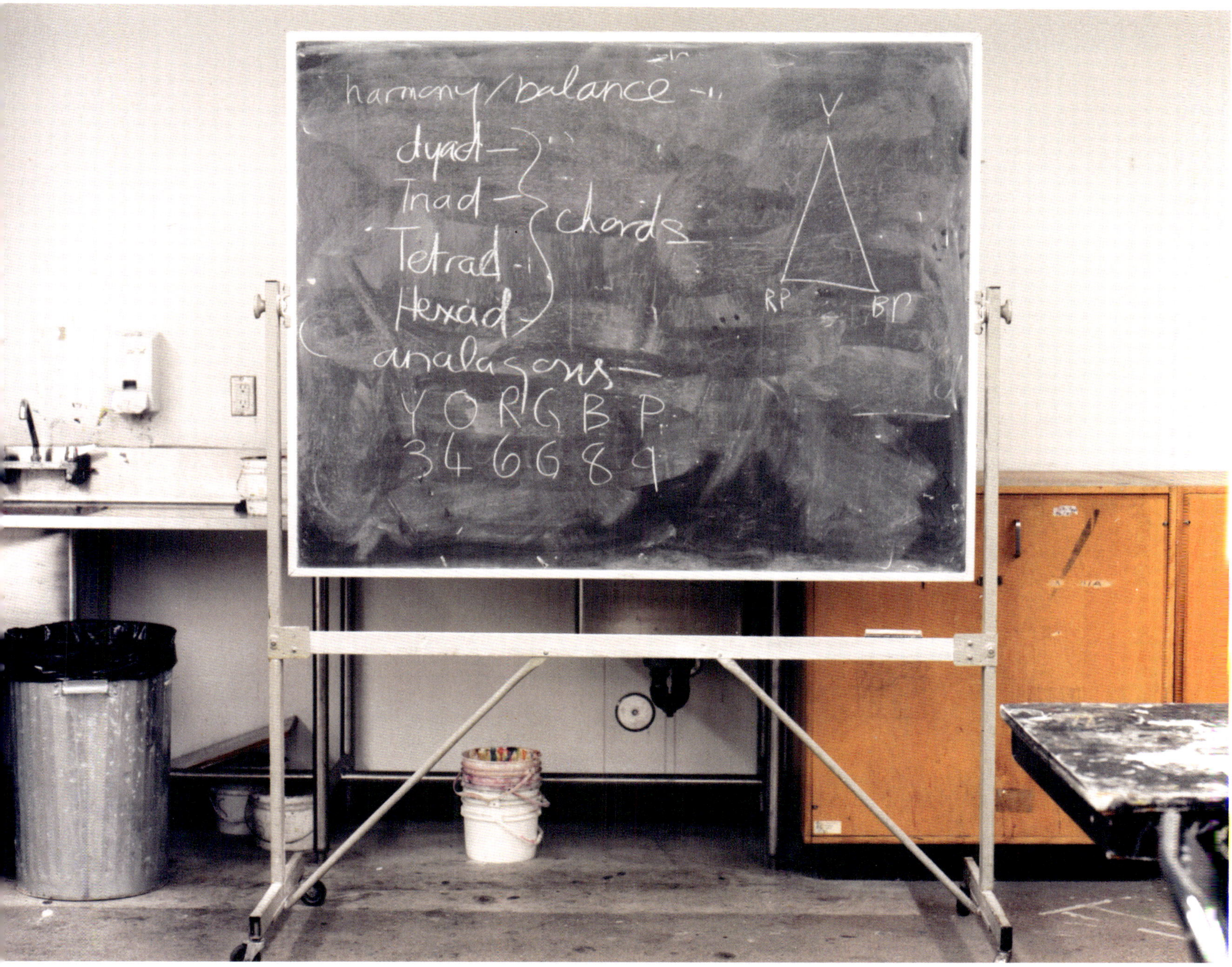

November 27-02, Rm. 1525

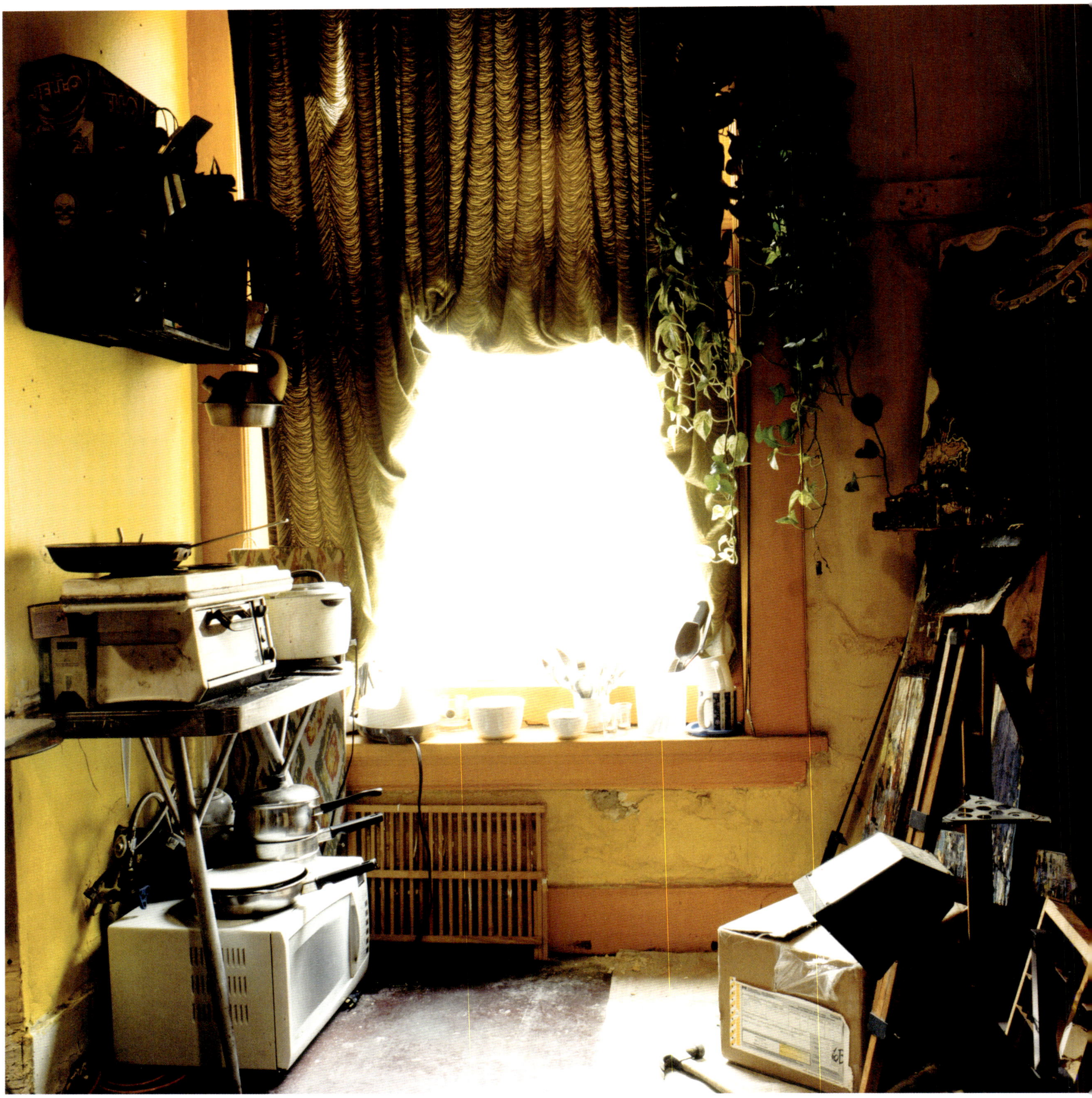

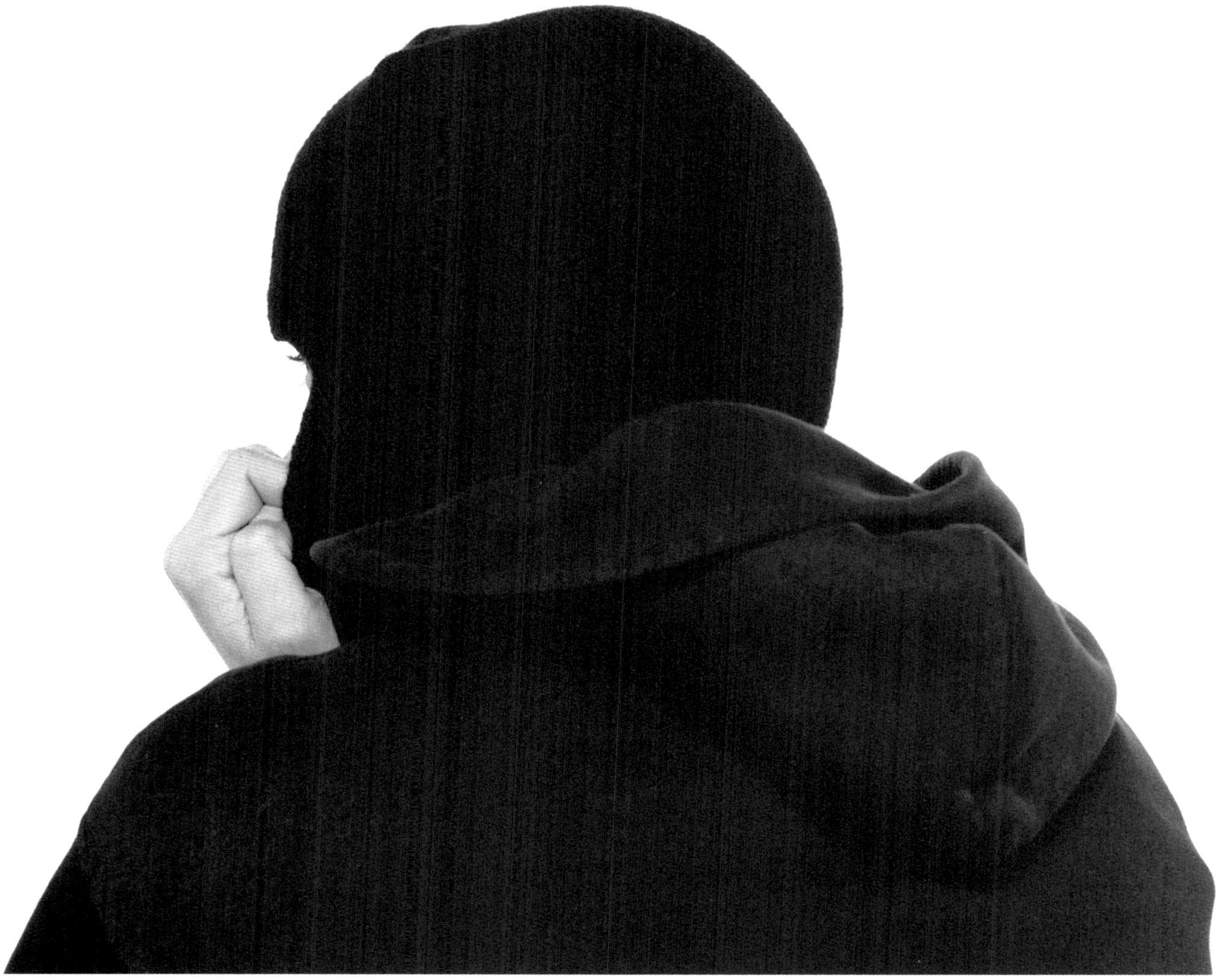

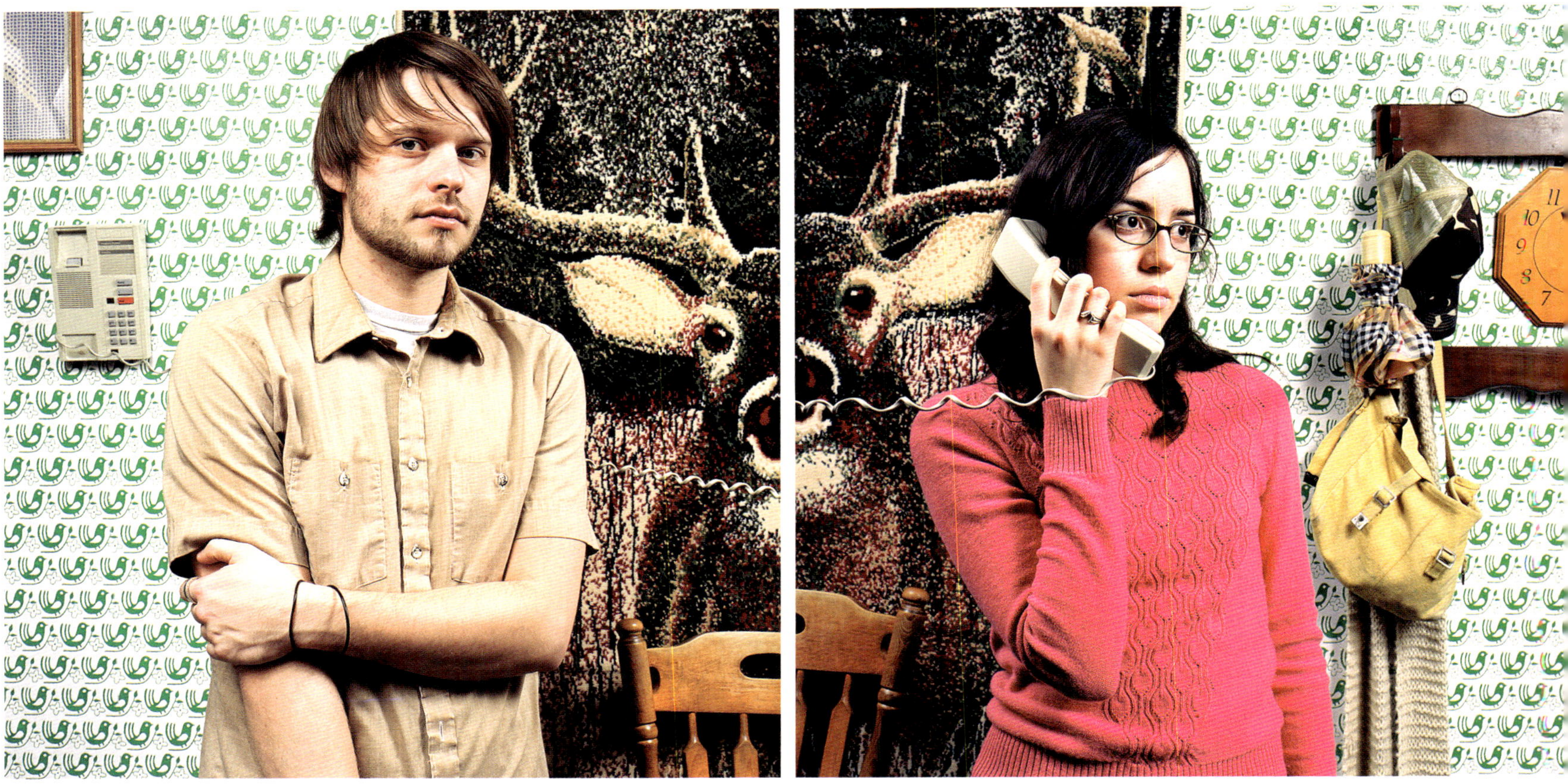

Jamie Campbell

Untitled

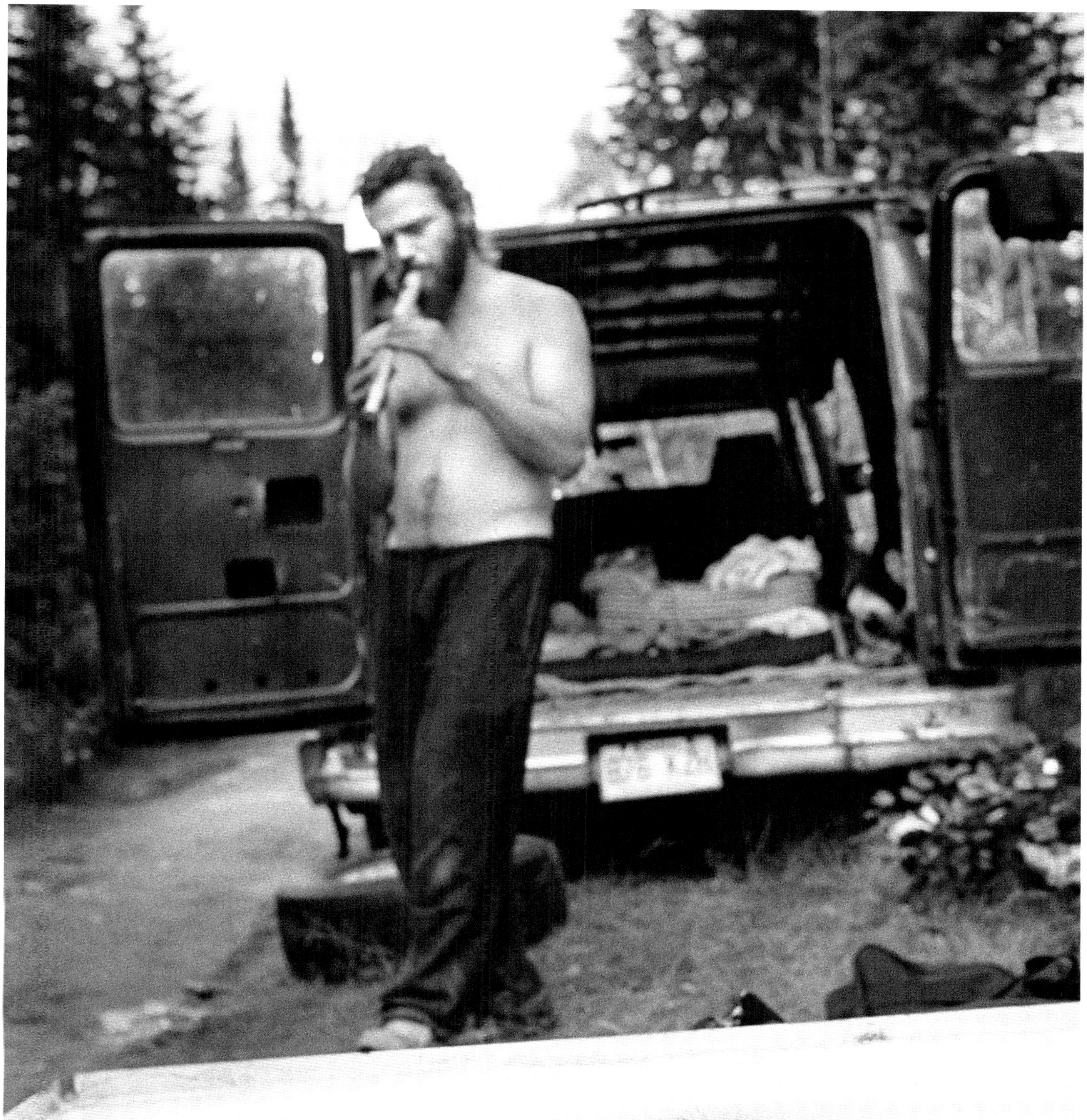

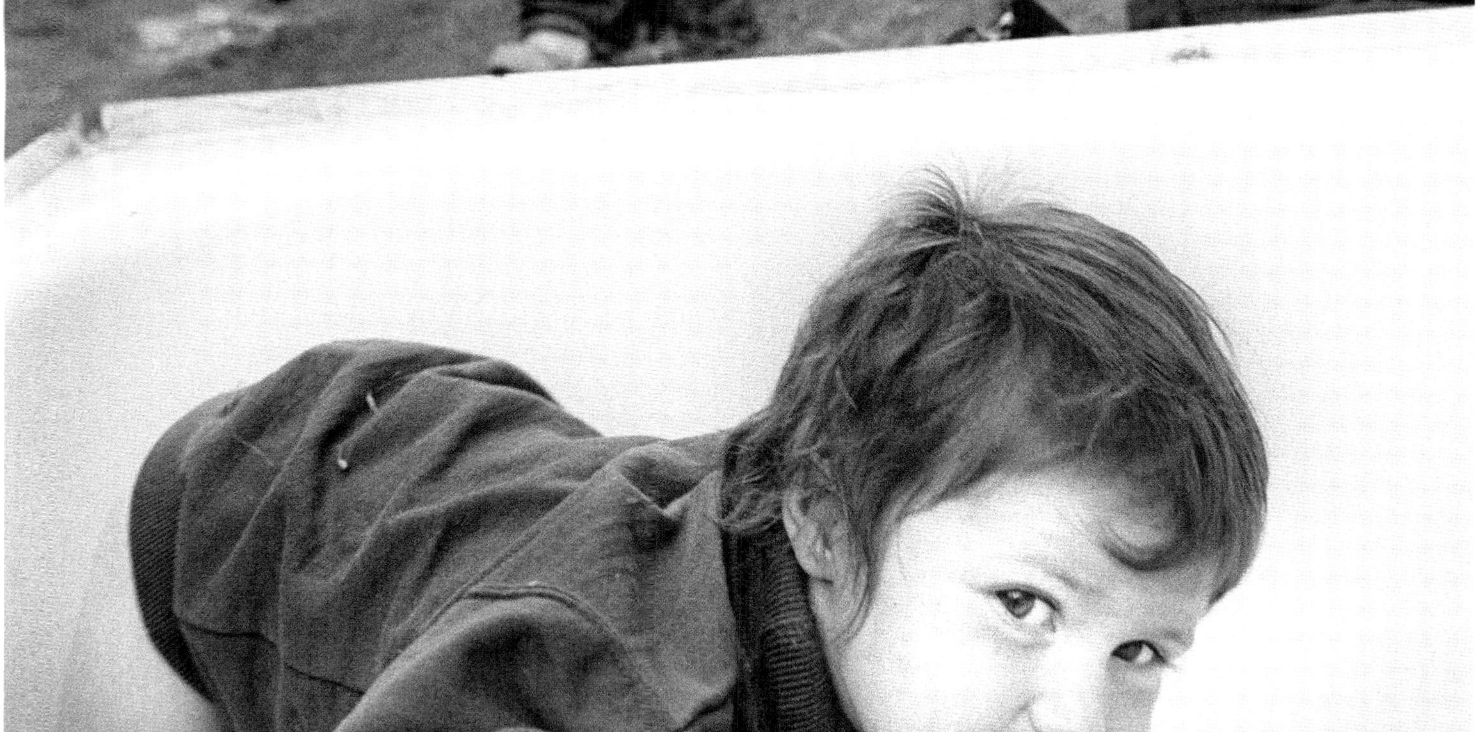

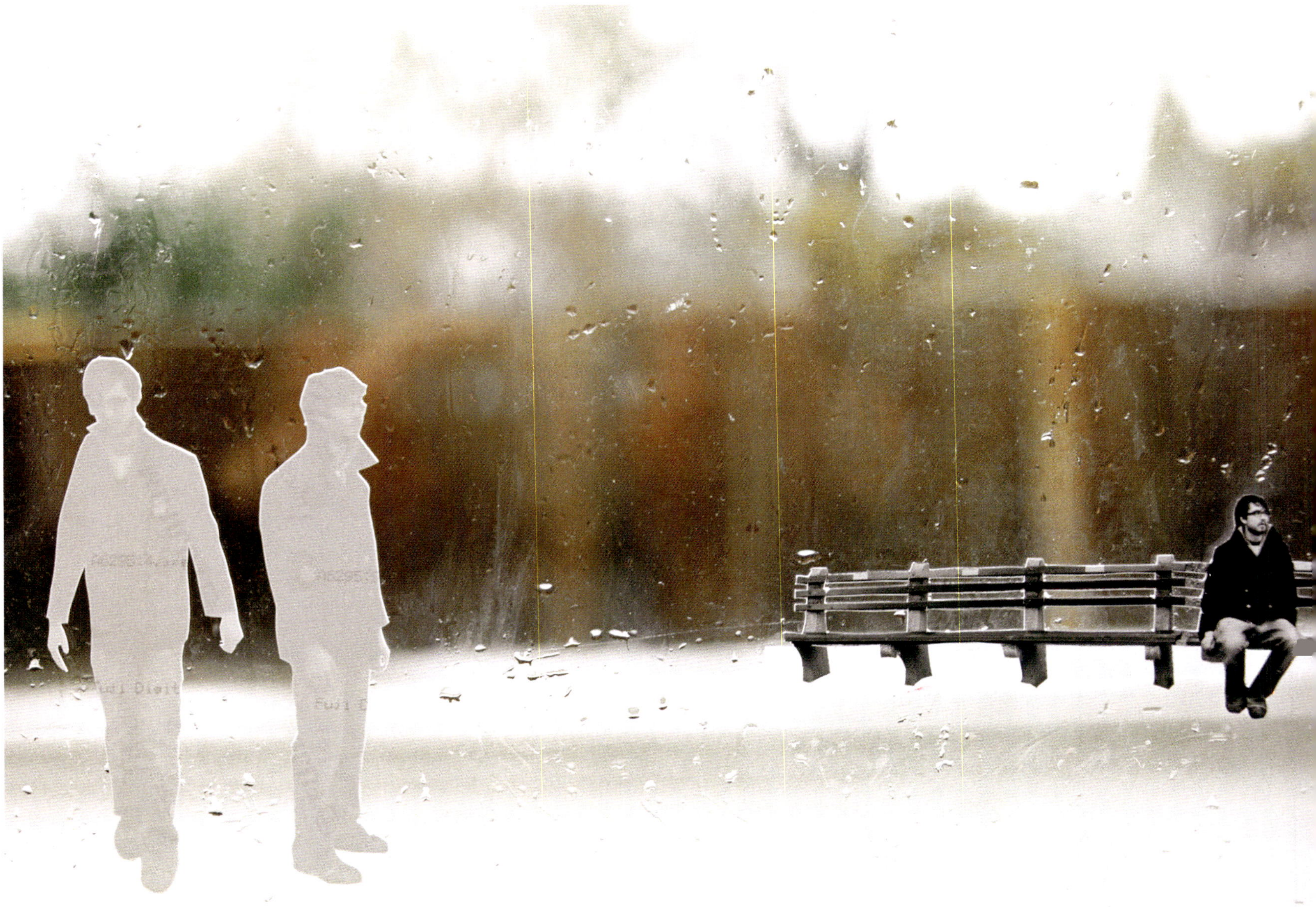

Becky Comber

Untitled

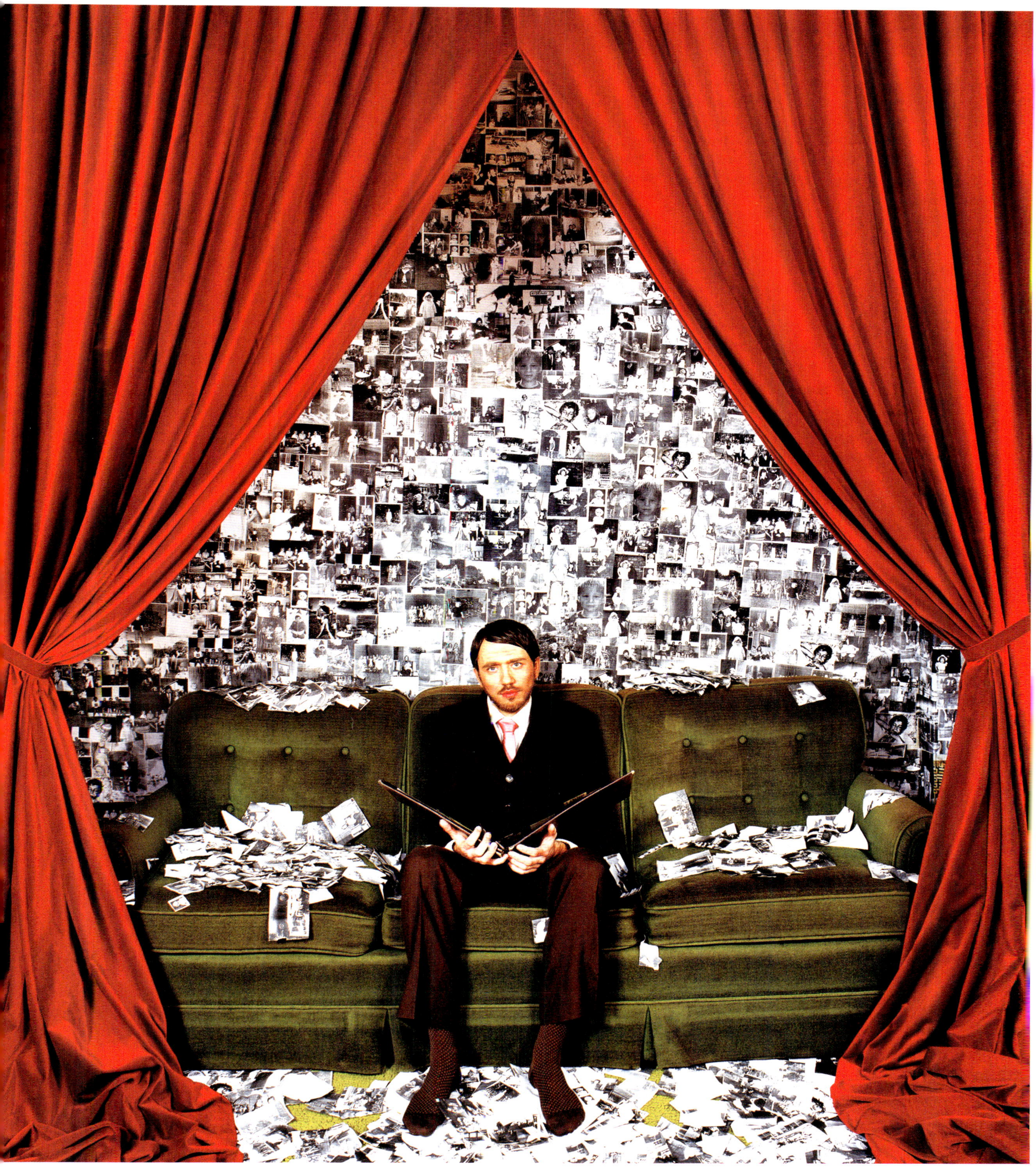

Untitled (from the series "In Place")

Robyn Cumming

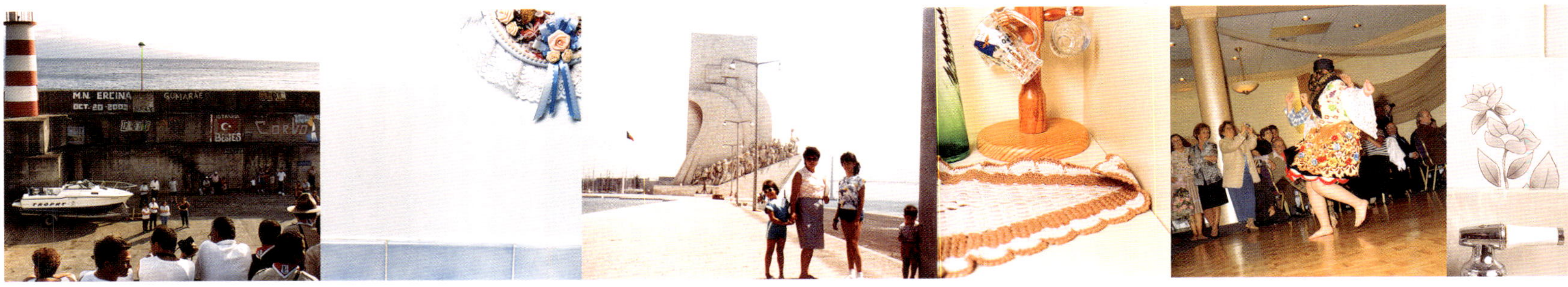

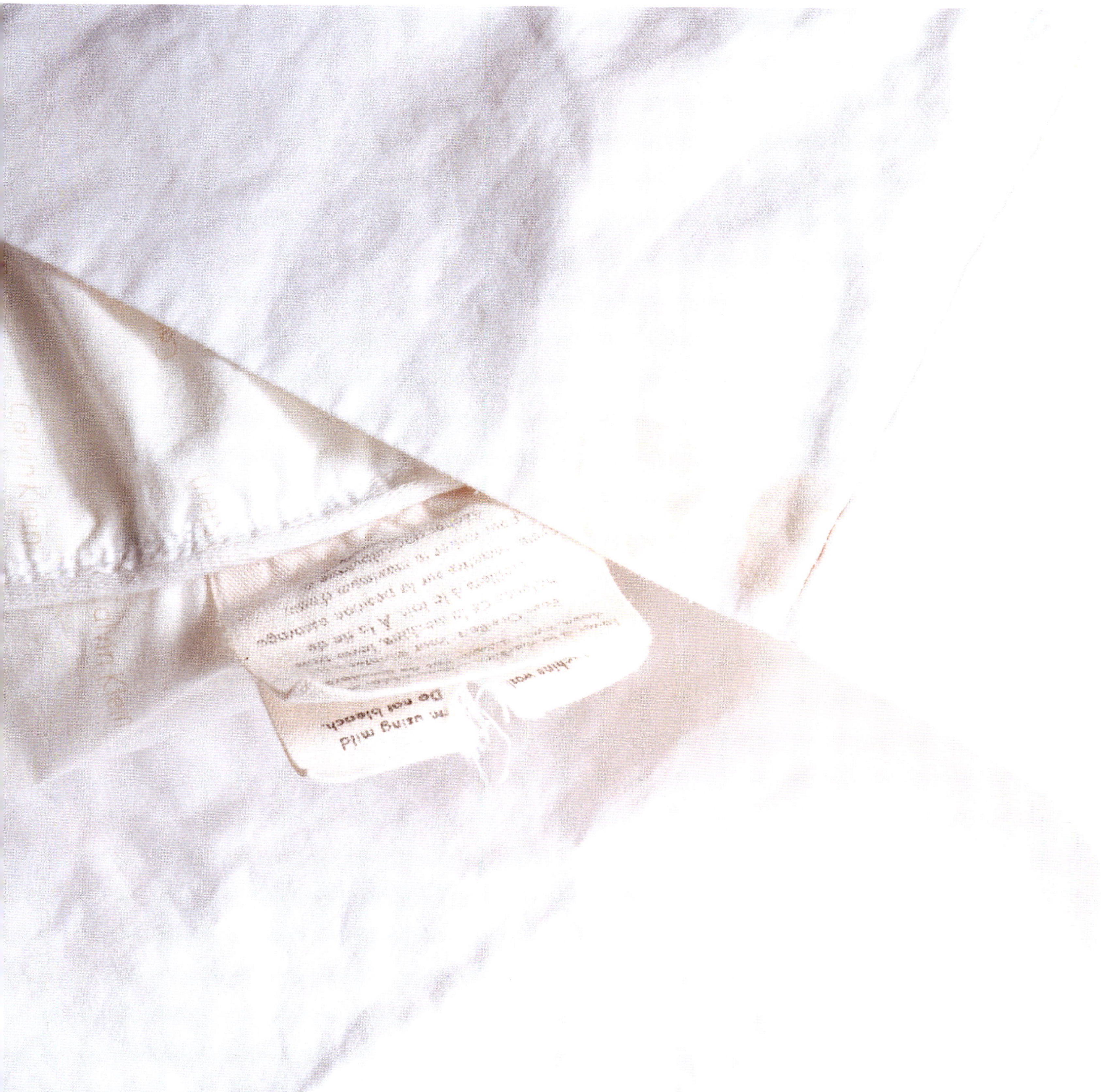

Pillow (from the series "White")

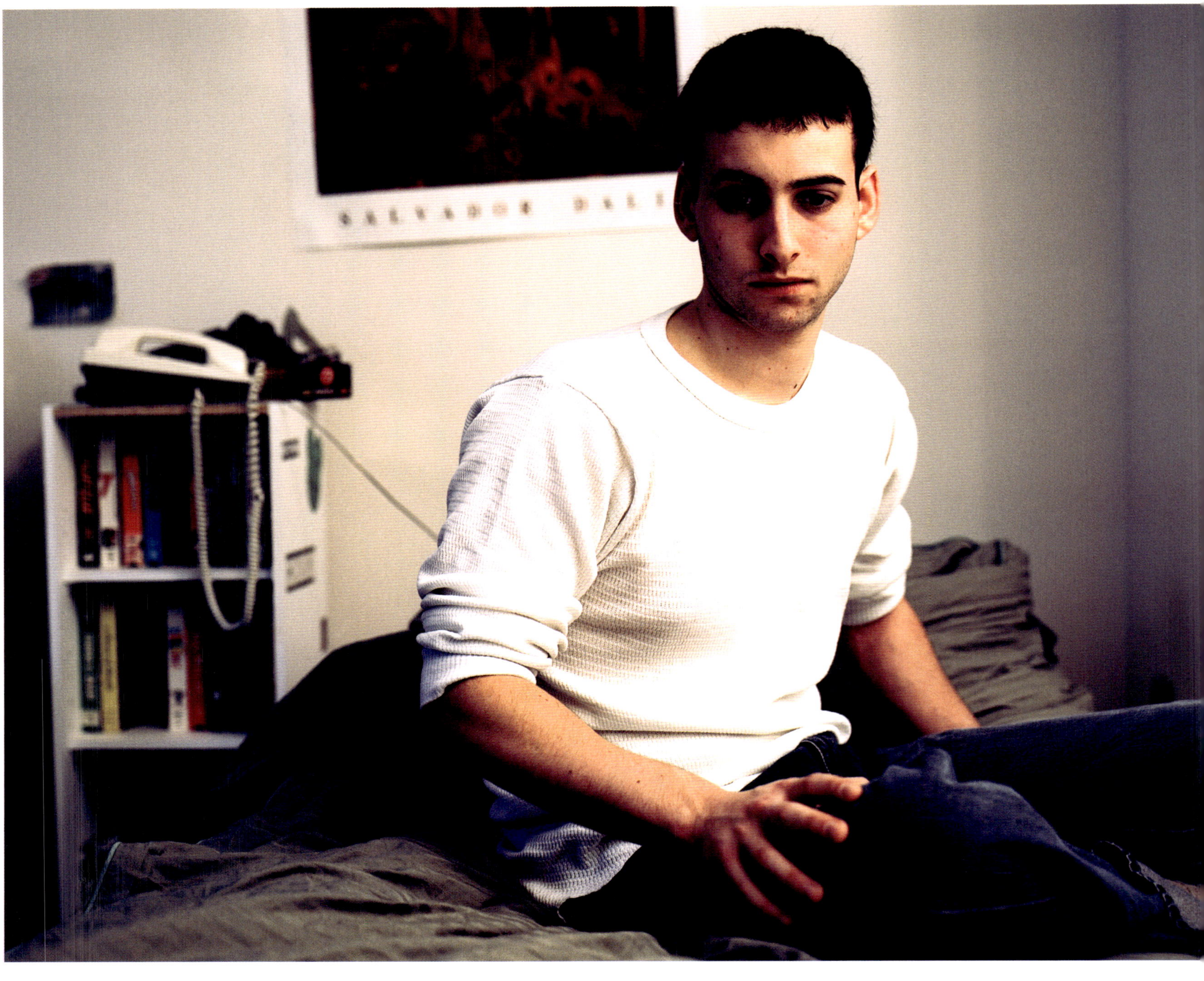
SALVADOR DALI

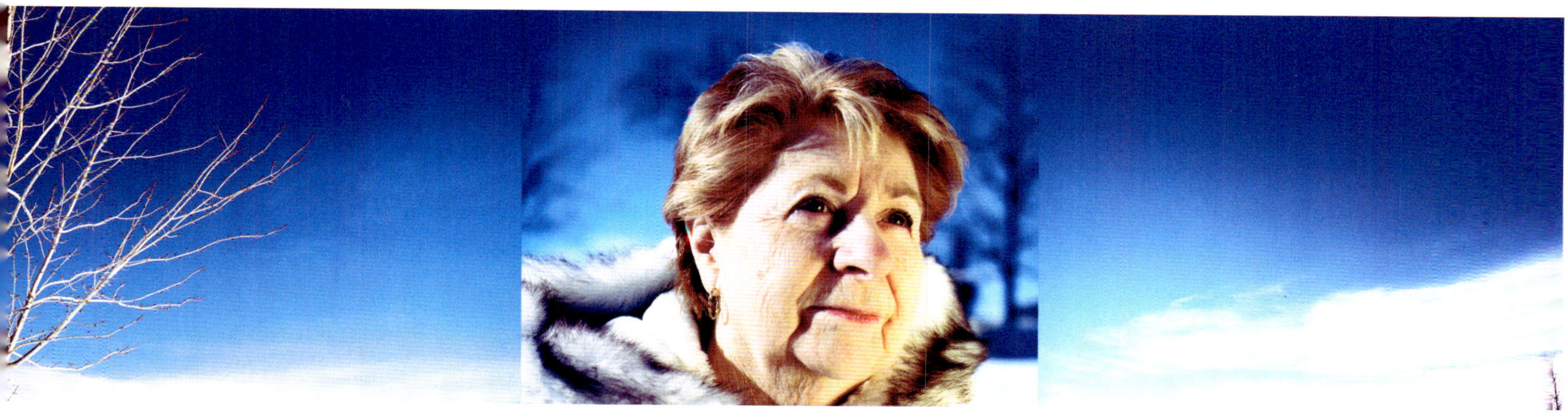

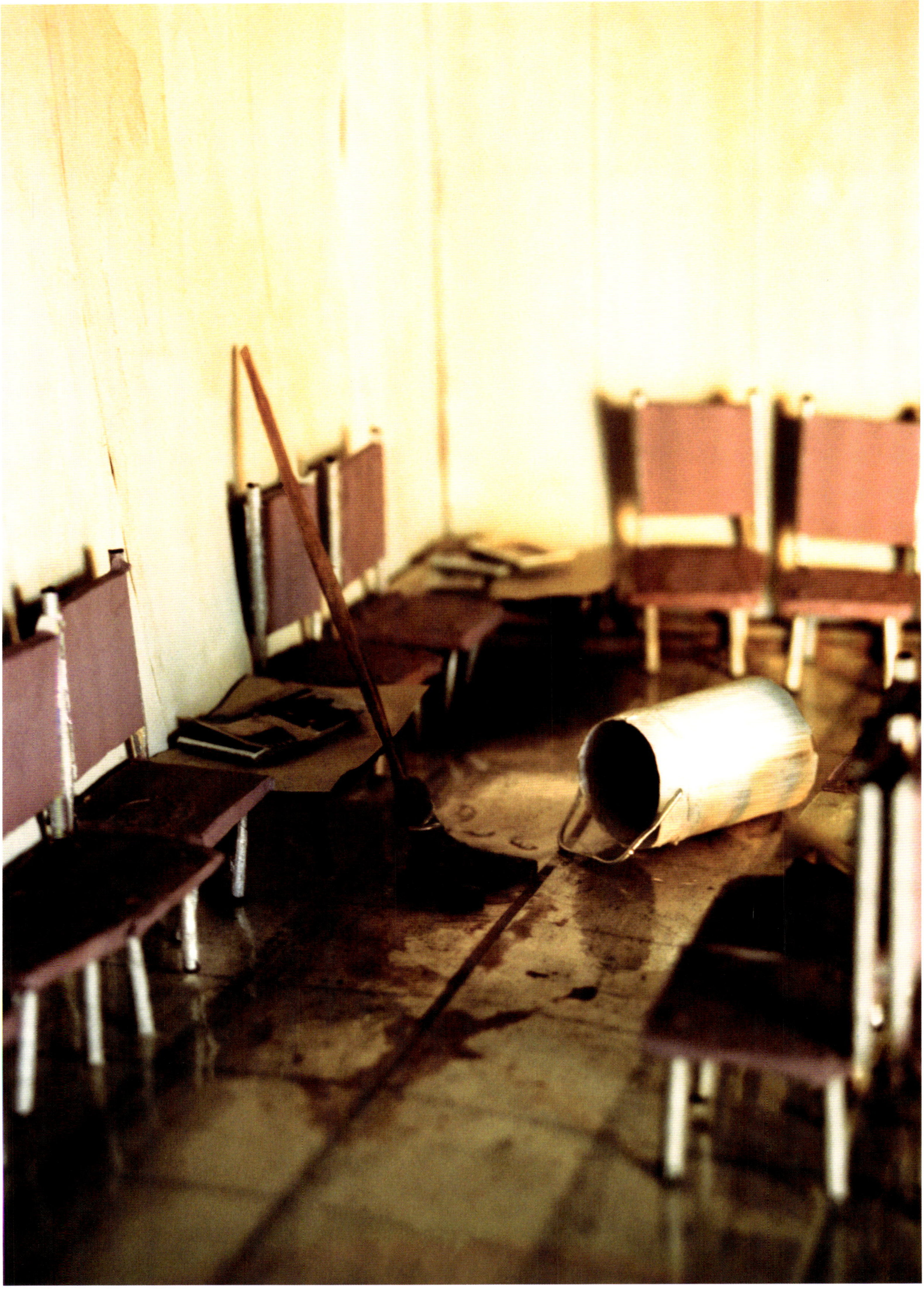

Carrie Duplessis

Waiting Room

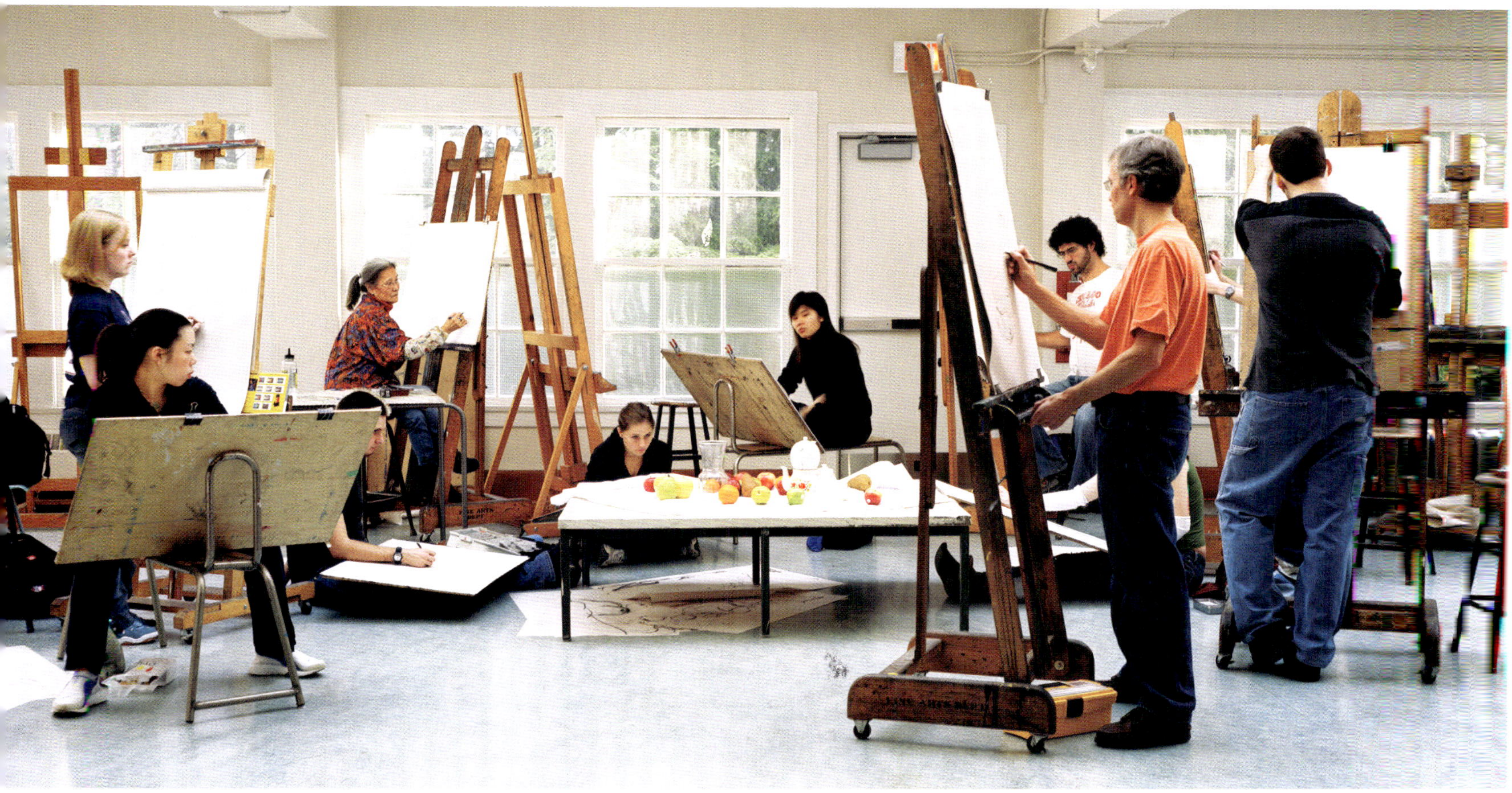

Drawing Class

Adam Harrison

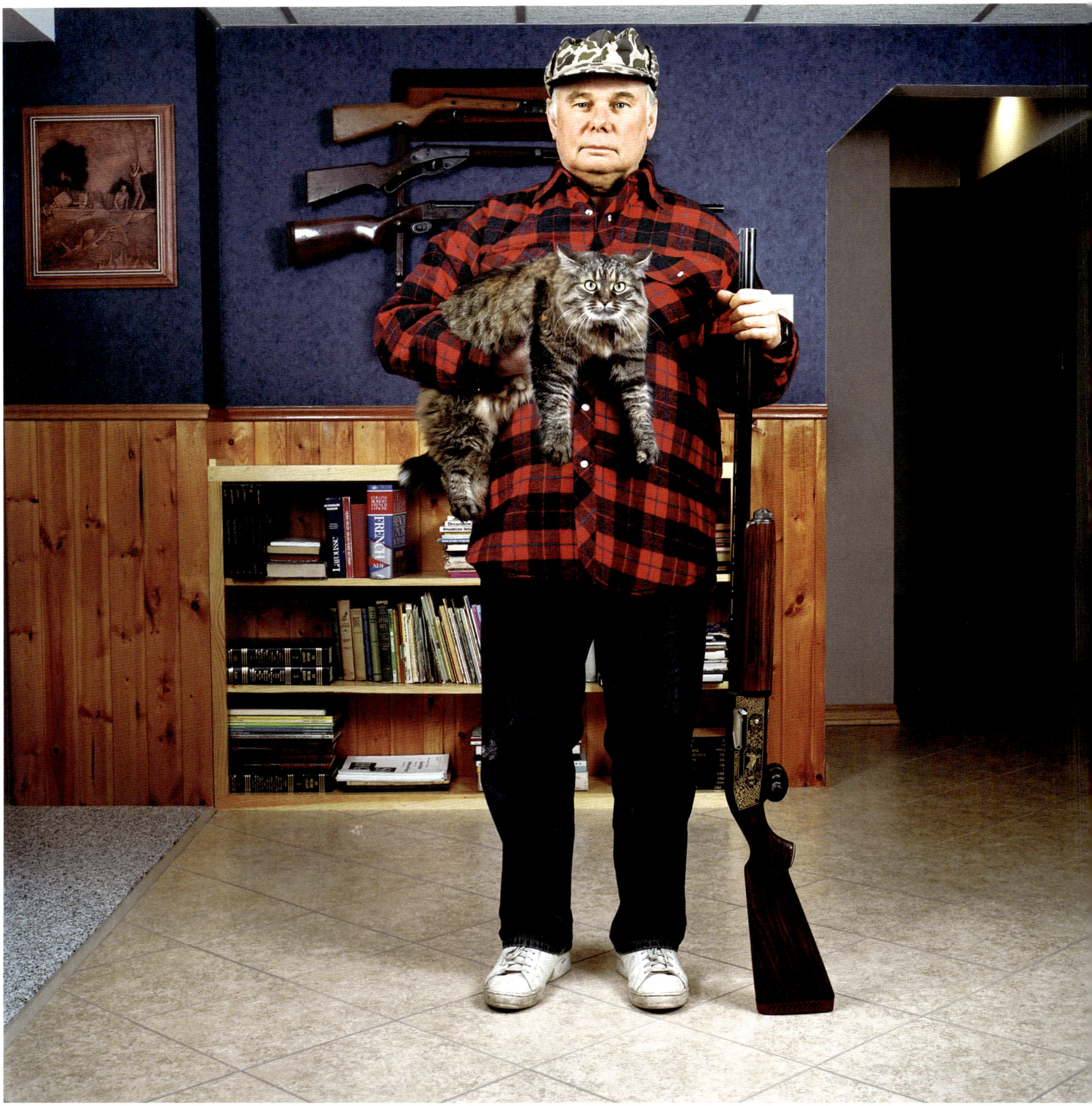

Ian and Ceader

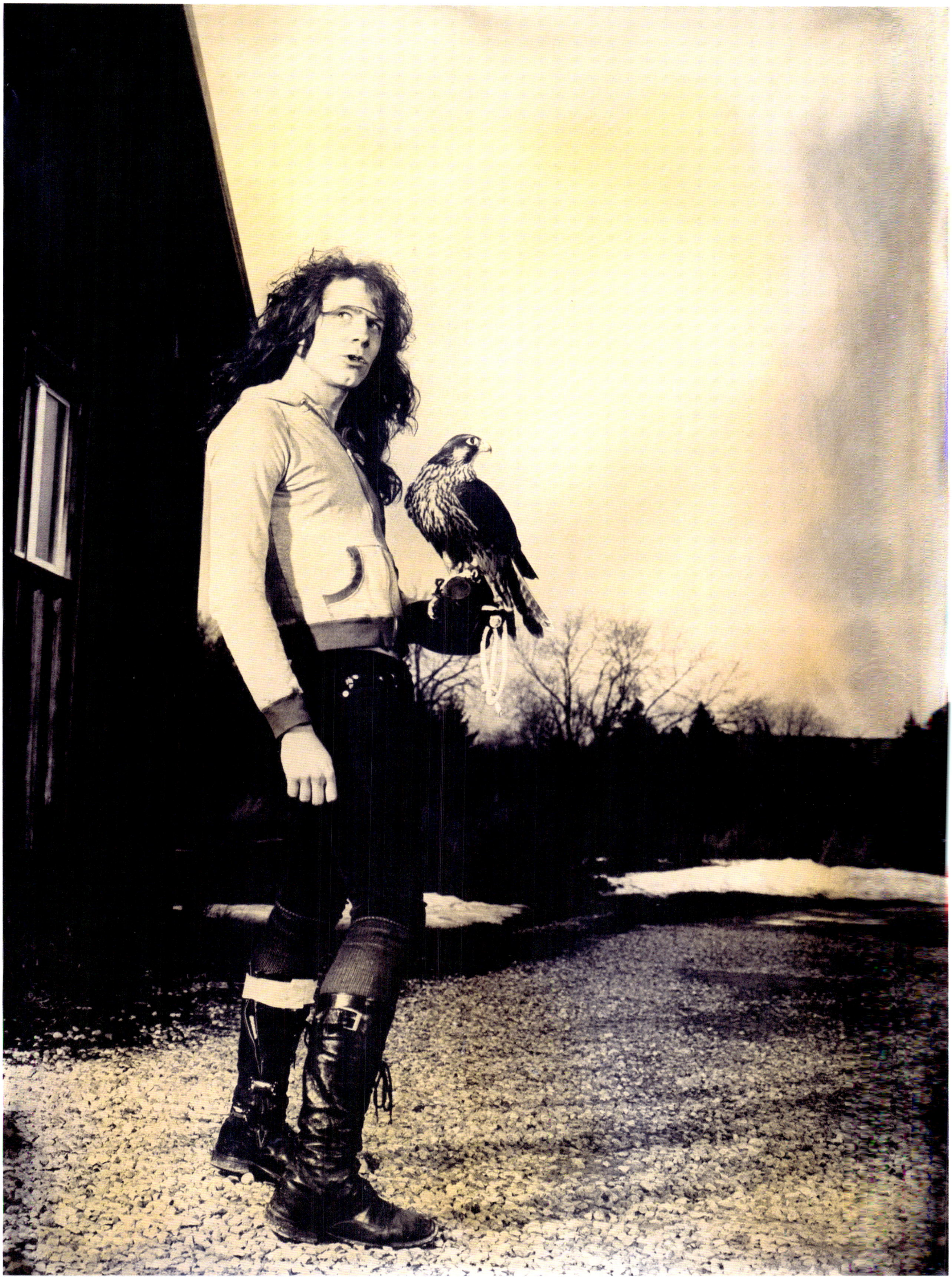

Untitled (from the series "Companions")

Maayan Kasimov

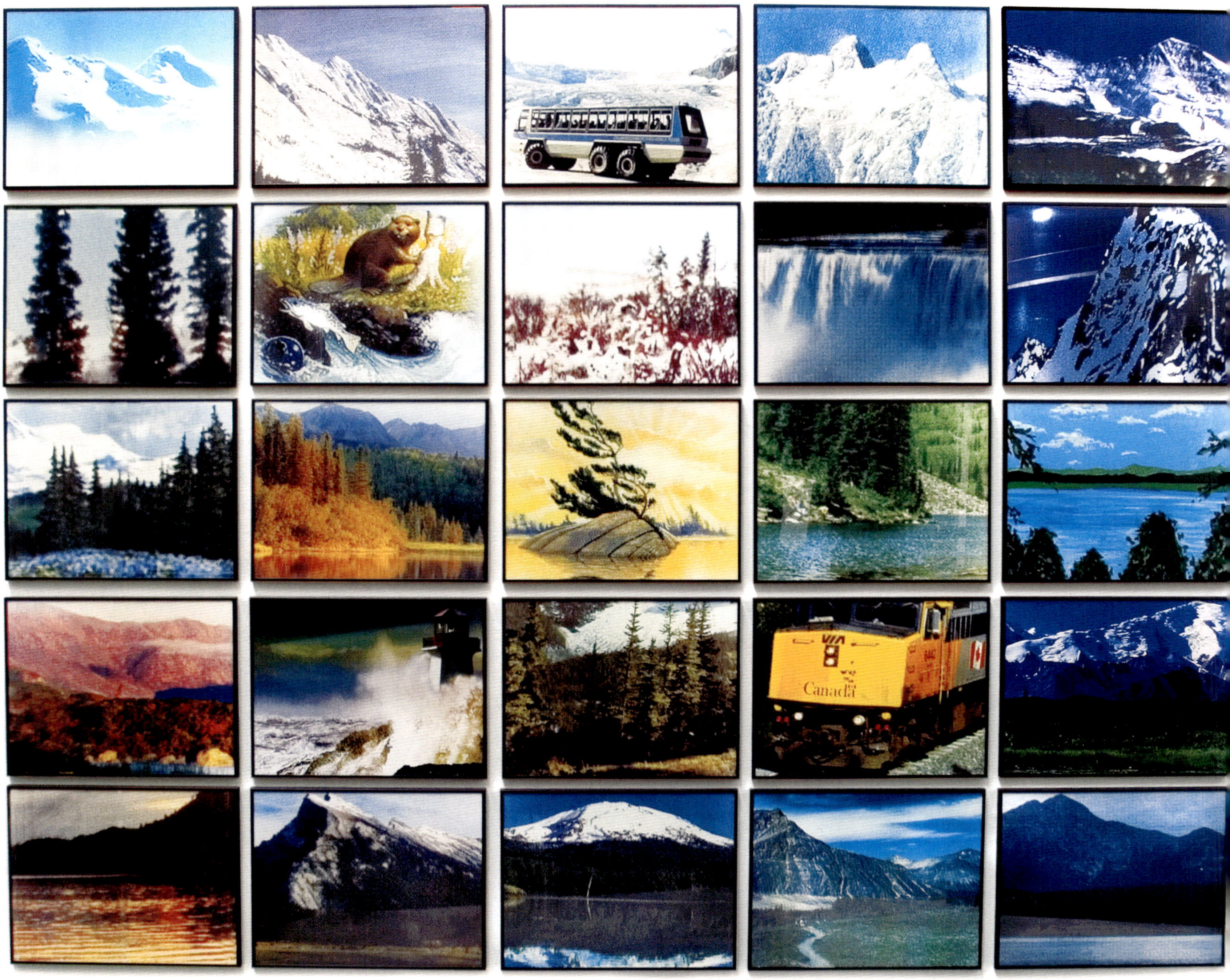
Canada

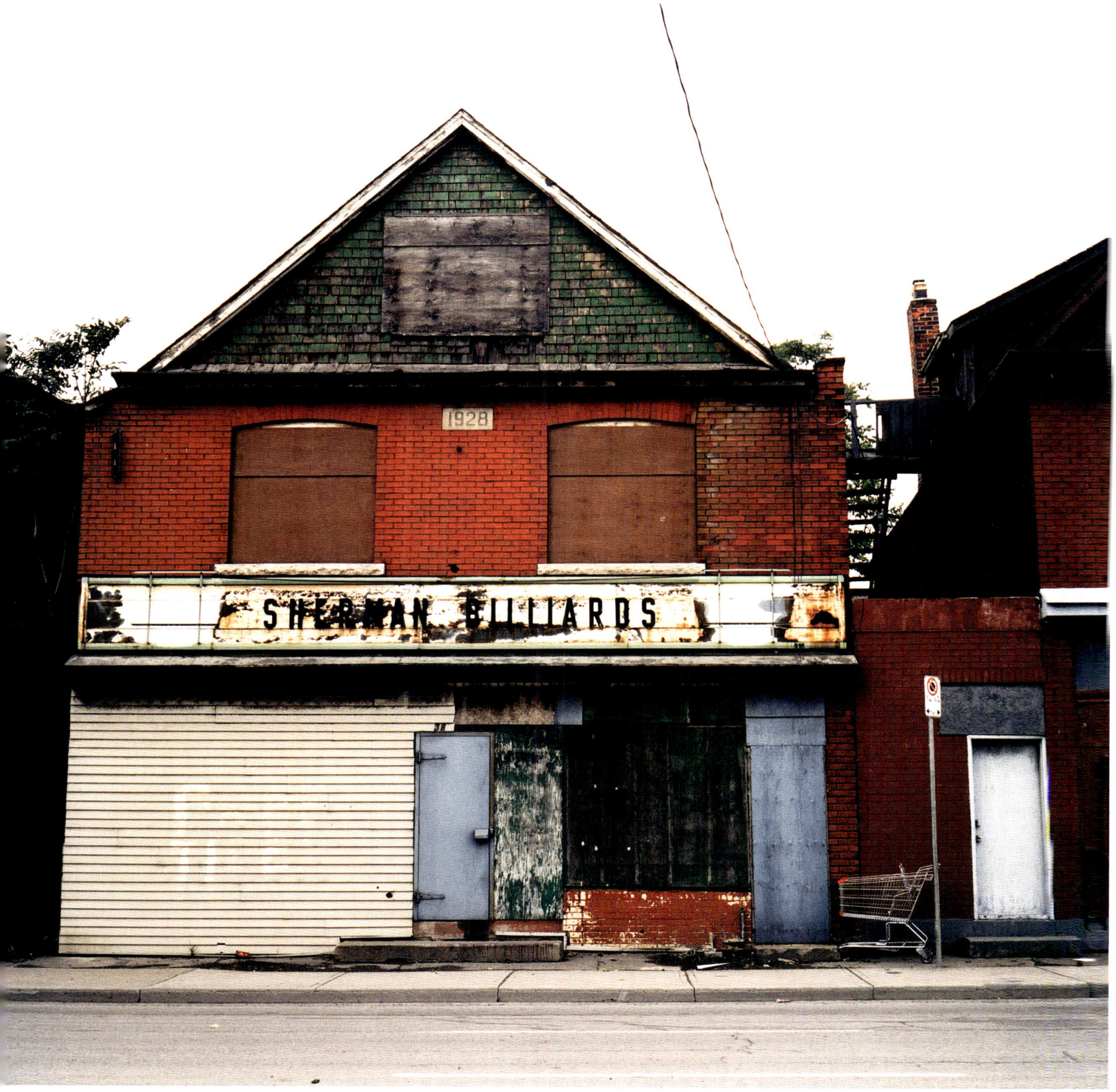

Sherman Billiards

Sarah Mangialardo

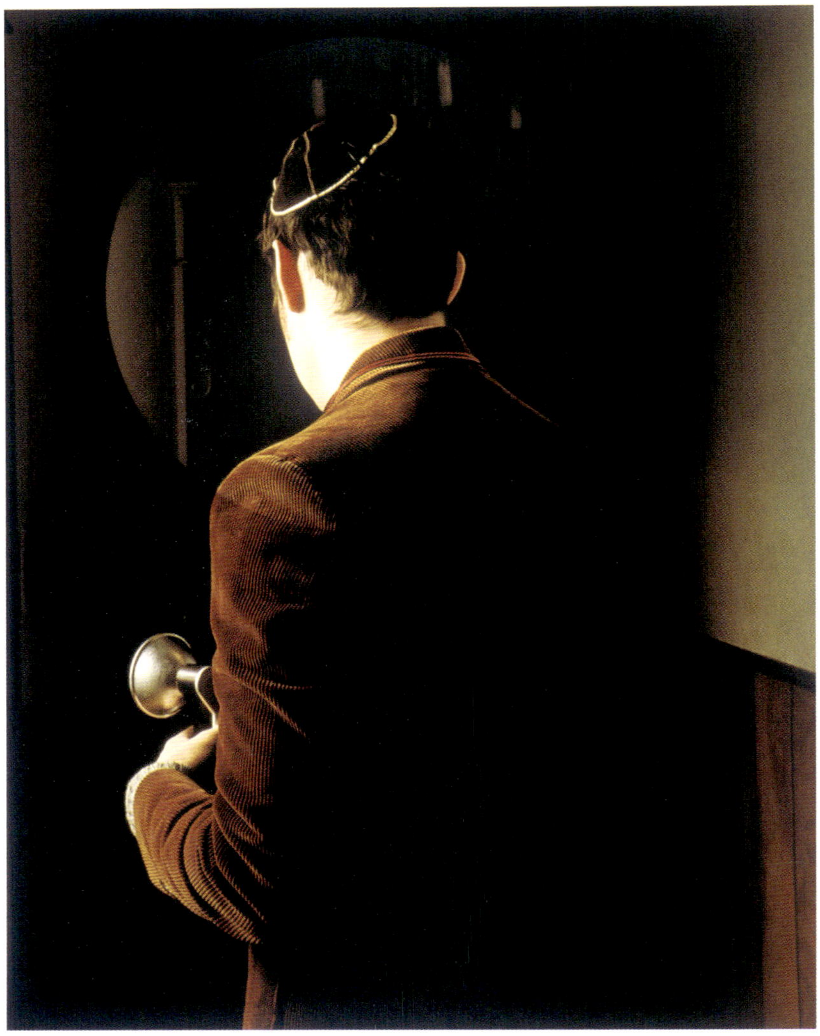

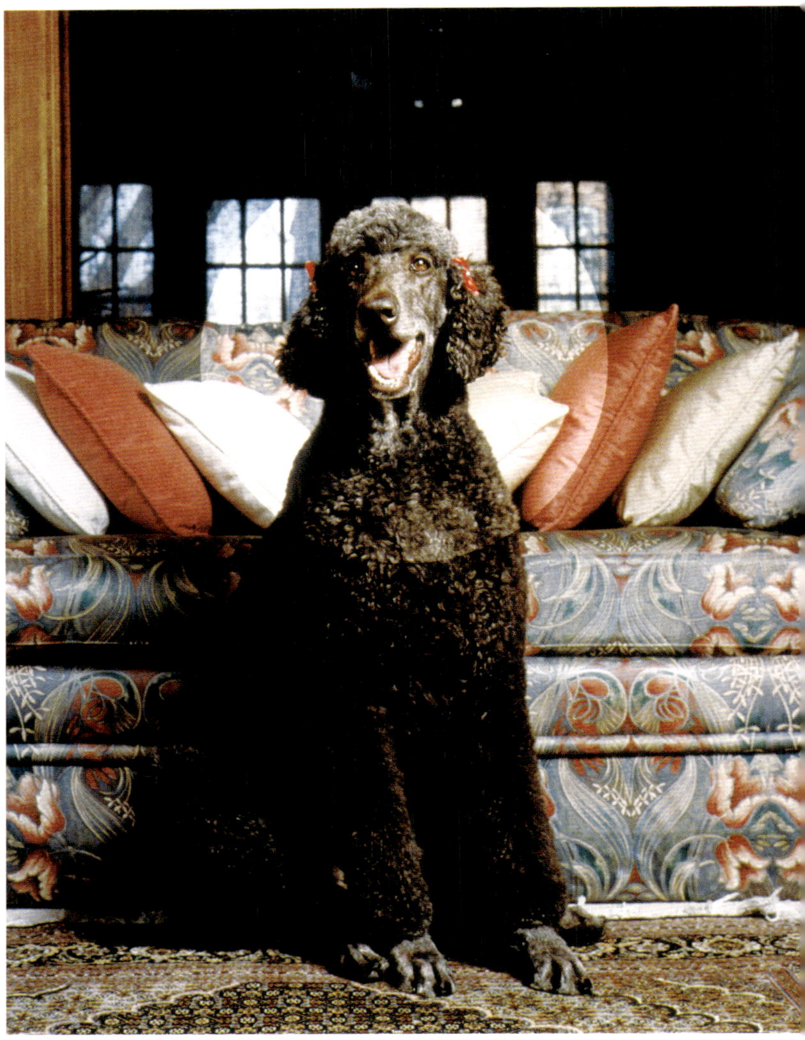

Sans titre (from the series "L'effacement")

Louis Perreault

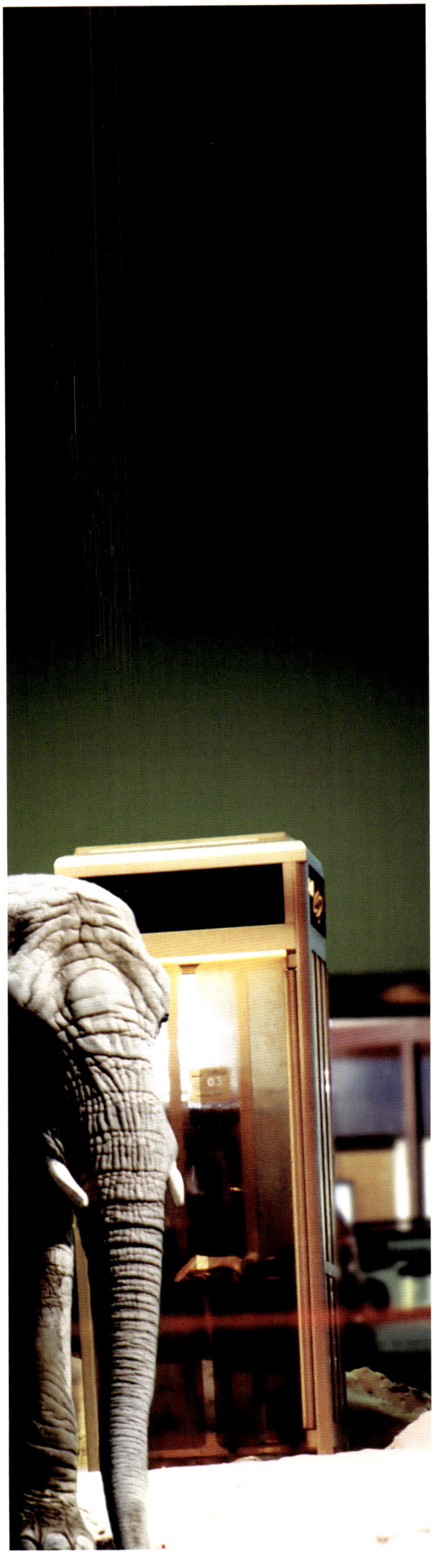

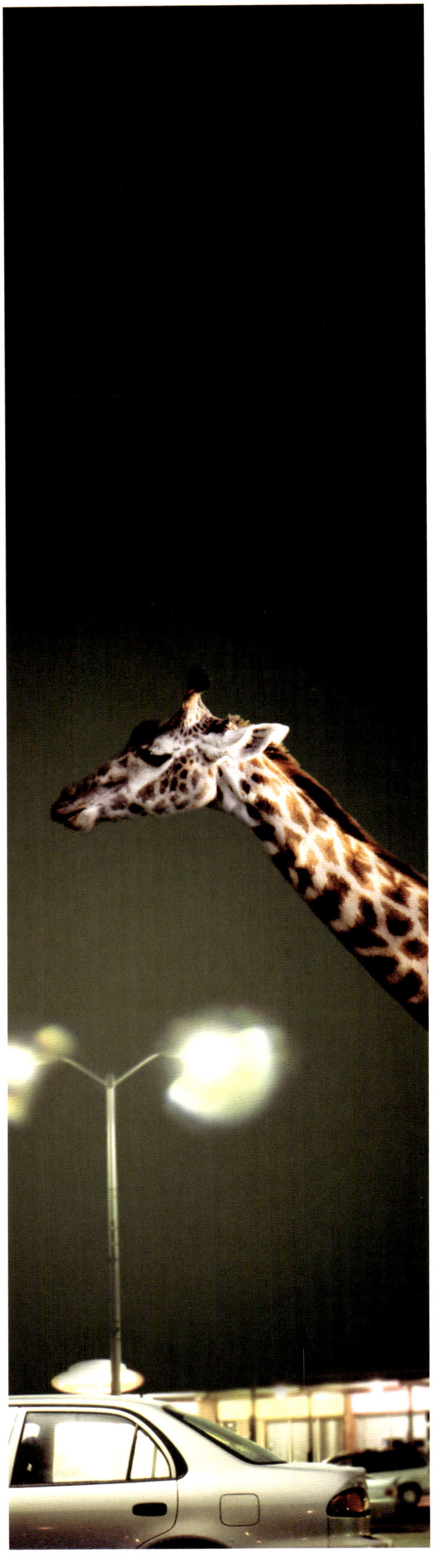

Elephant Booth / Giraffe

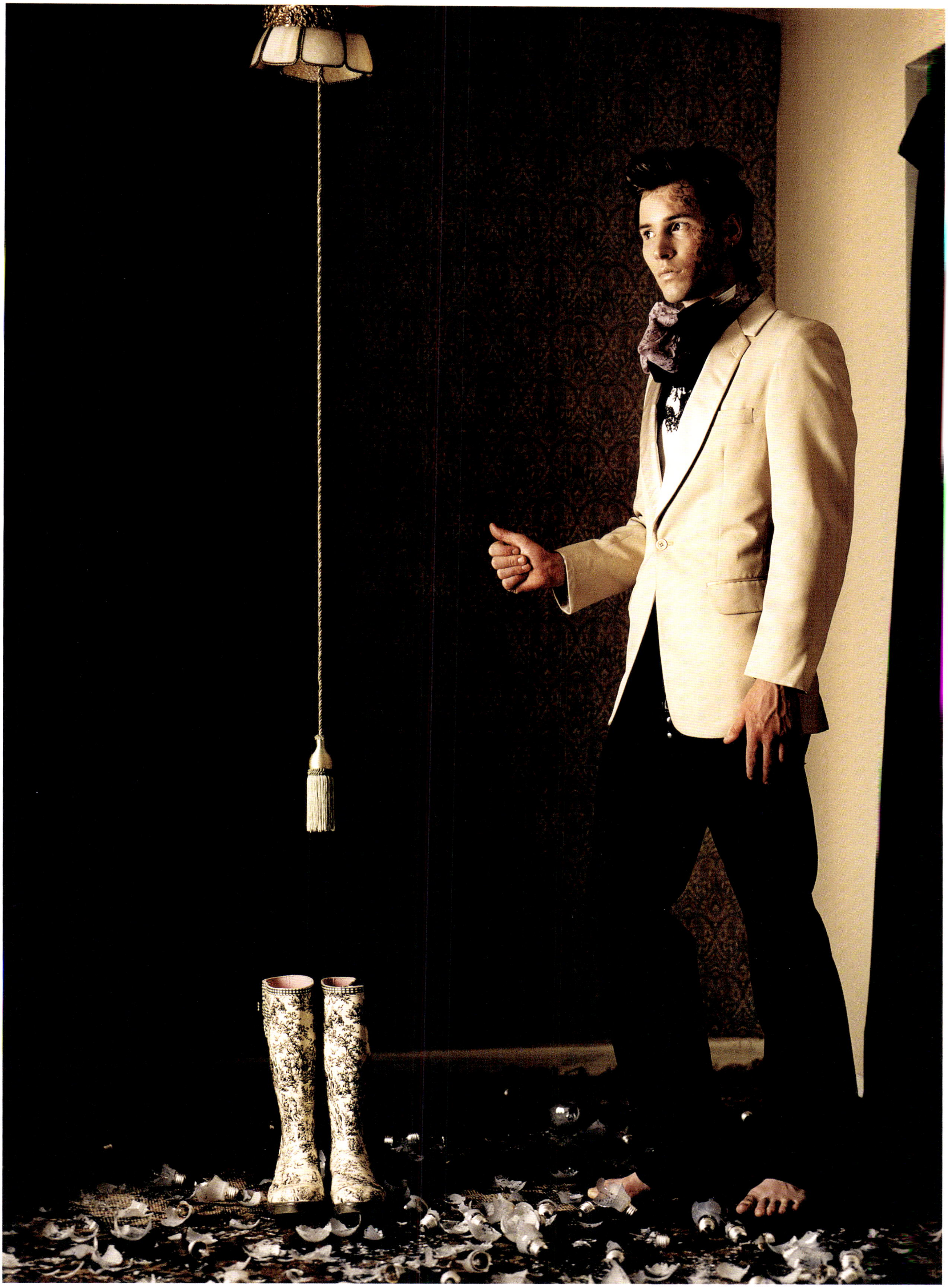

Knowledge (from the series "The Elusive")

Graydon Sheppard

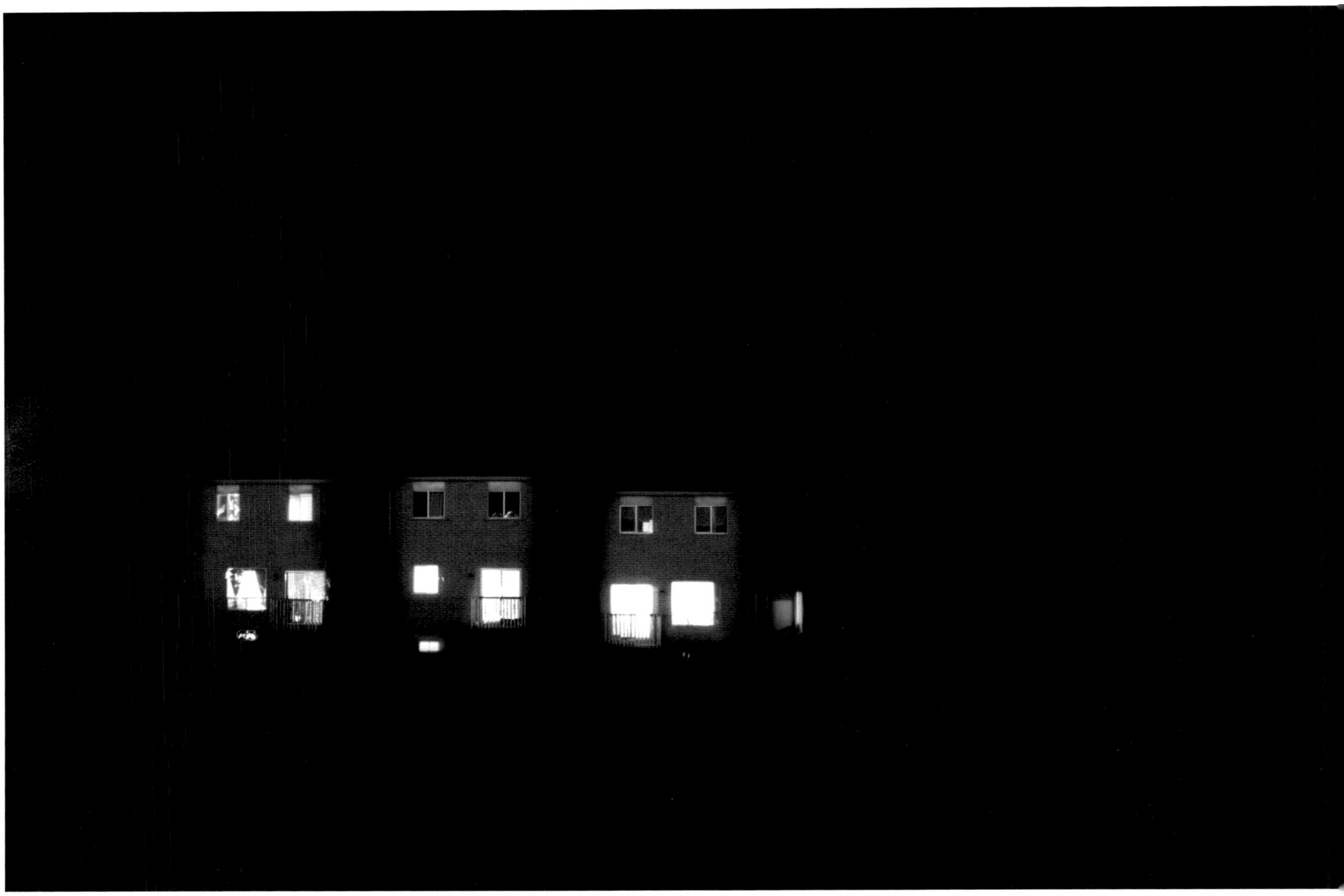

Joanna Simpson

Suburban Landscape # 3

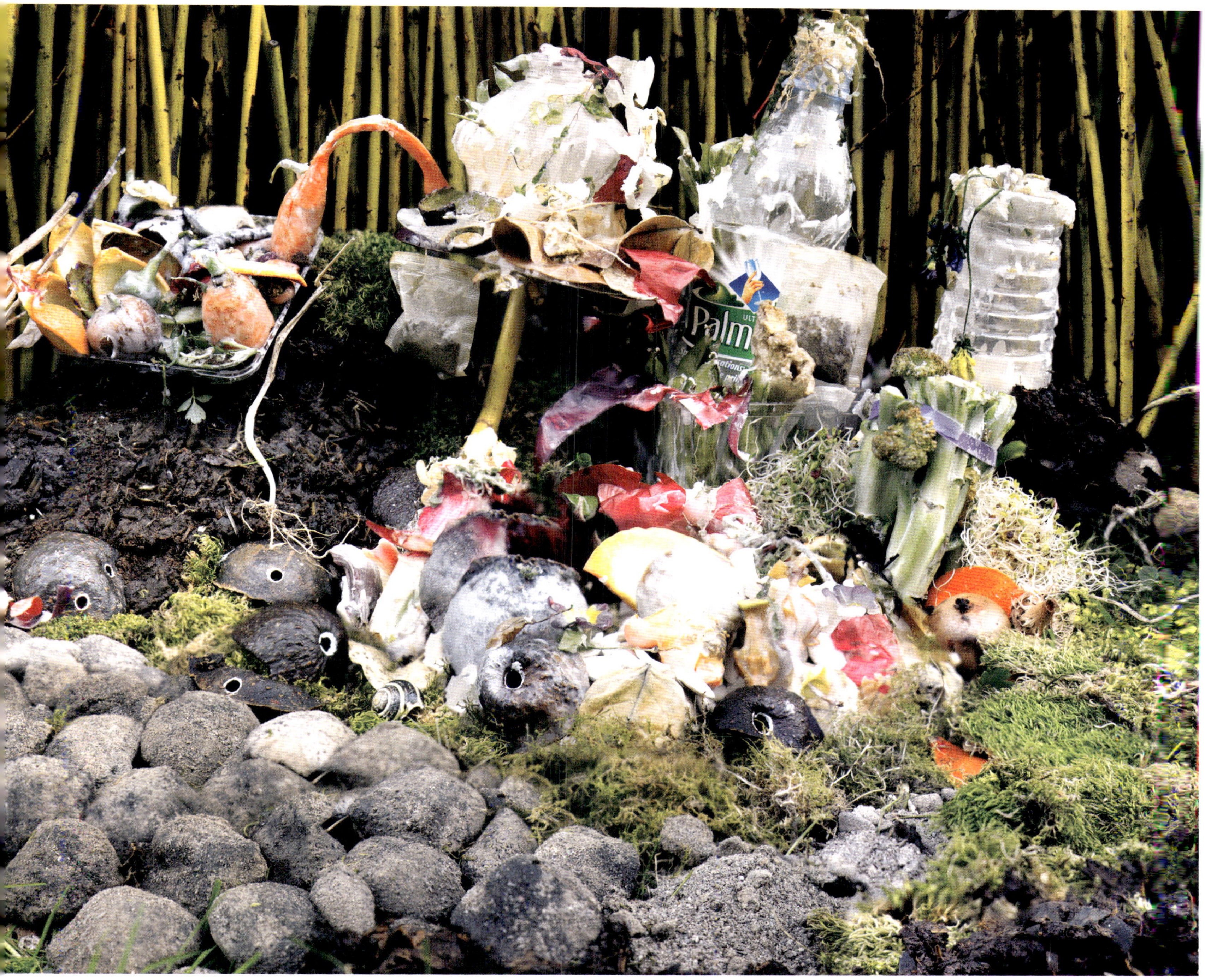
Palm

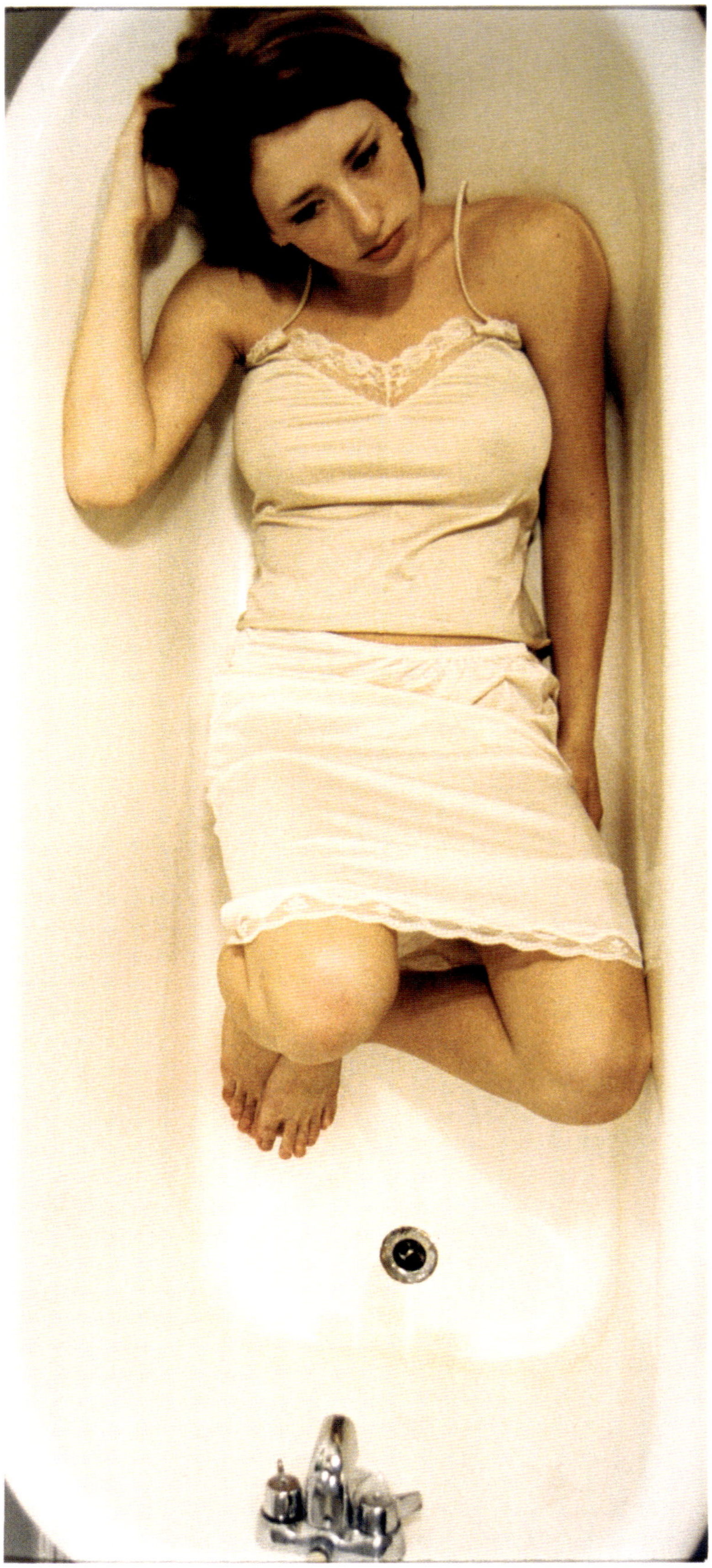

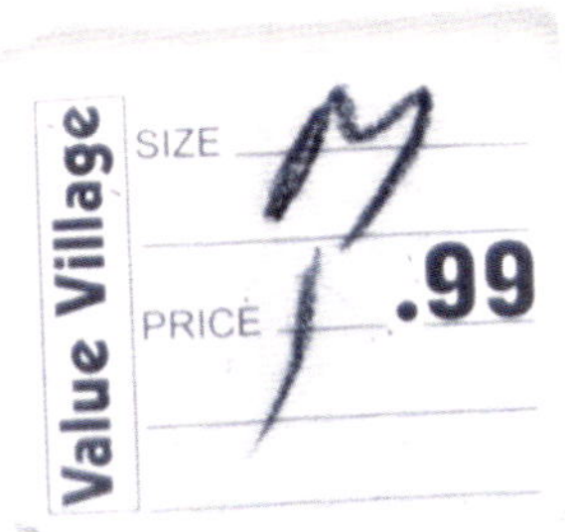

Sarah Thorpe

Untitled

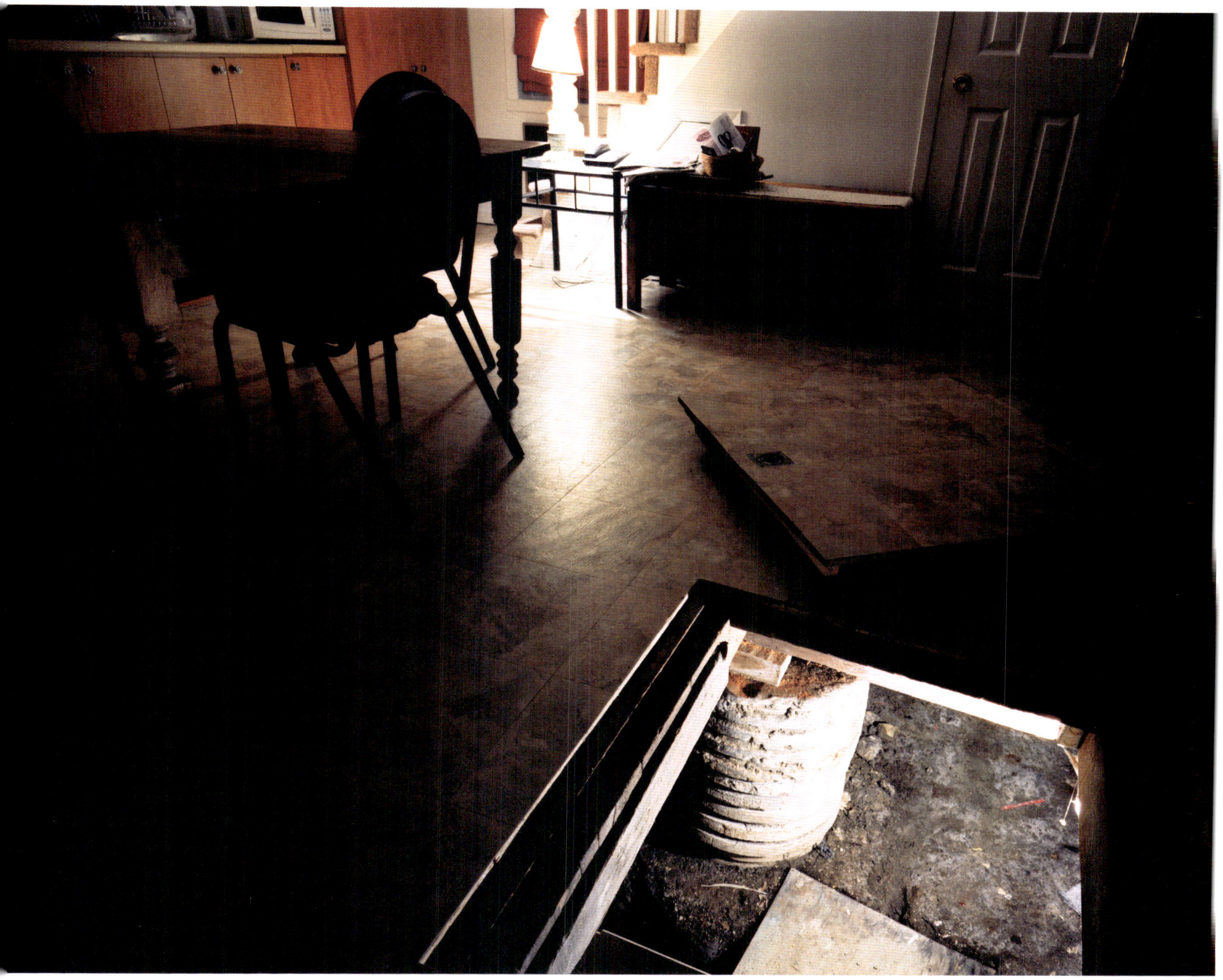

Untitled #4 (from the series "Like Home")

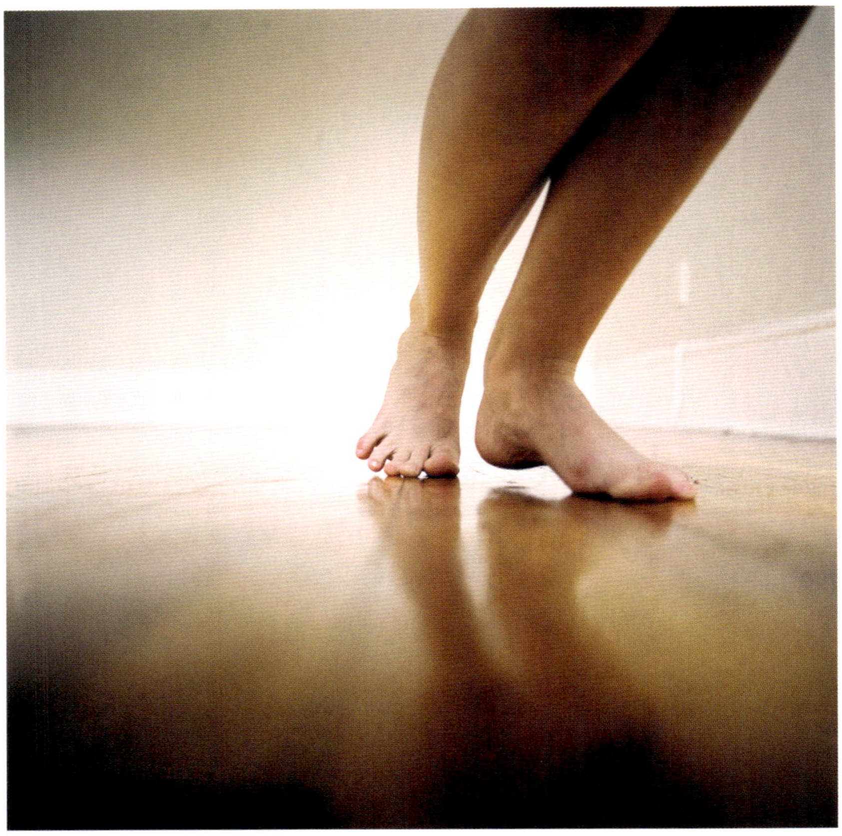

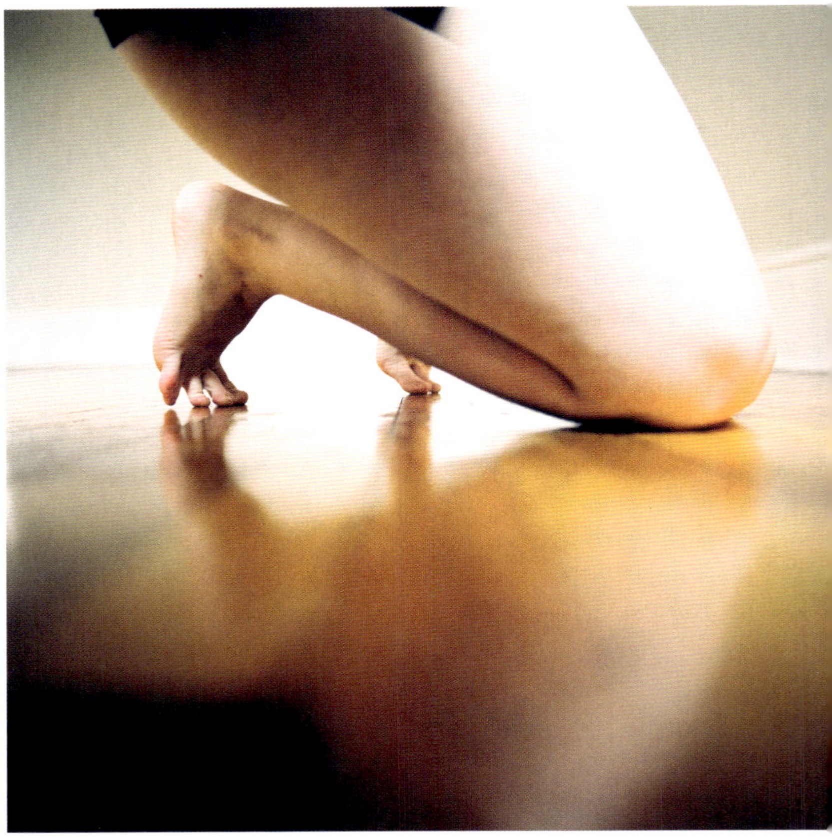

Feet and Knees

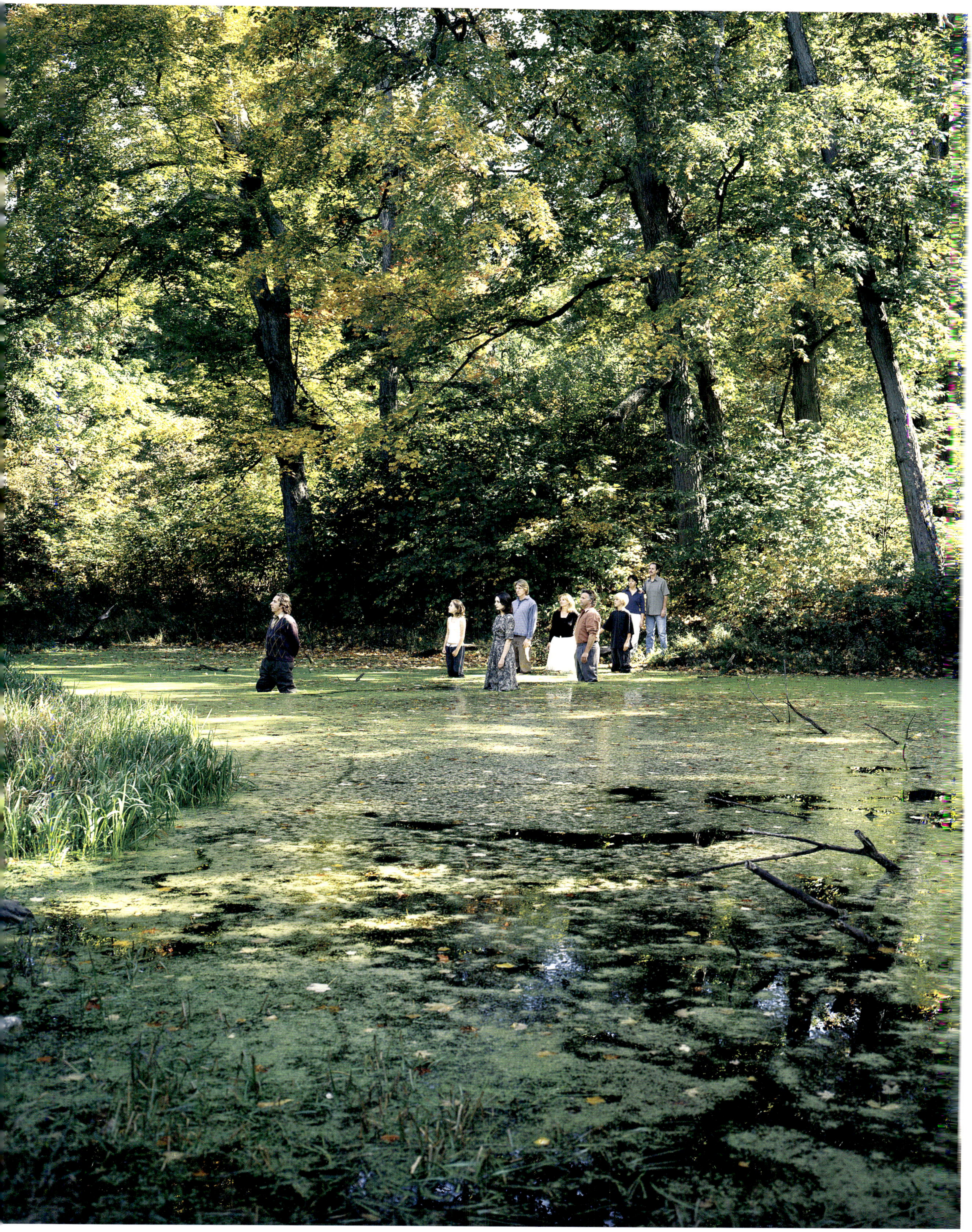

CONTRIBUTORS

Please visit the accompanying websites for complete contributor biographies.

FINE ART

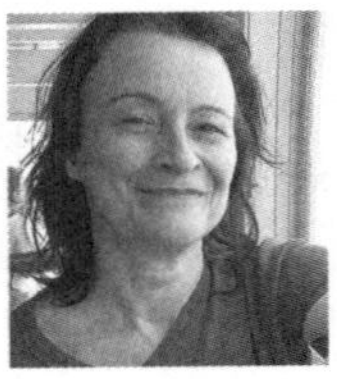

RAYMONDE APRIL

BORN Moncton, 1953 **RESIDES** Montreal **EDUCATION** Université Laval, Bacc. Arts Visuels (Arts Plastiques), Quebec City, 1975 **SELECTED SOLO EXHIBITIONS** *Raymonde April: bifurcations*, Centre culturel Yvonne L. Bombardier, Valcourt, Quebec, 2004; Manifestation internationale d'art de Quebec, 2005; *Tout embrasser*, Galerie d'art Leonard et Bina Ellen, Université Concordia, Montreal, 2001; *Les Fleuves Invisibles*, Musée d'art de Joliette, Joliette, Quebec, 1997–2001; *Raymonde April*, Galerie Rochefort, Montreal, 1993; *Raymonde April: Voyage dans le monde des choses*, Musée d'art contemporain de Montreal, Montreal, 1986 **BOOKS/PUBLICATIONS** *Raymonde April et Michèle Waquant: Aires de migrations/Migrations arecs*, Quimper, France: Le Quartier, centre d'art contemporain; *Montreal: Vox*, 2005; *Raymonde April: Soleils couchants*, Quebec, Editions J'ai VU, 2005; *L'eau renversée*, Editions Dazibao, Montreal, 2002; *Réservoirs Soupirs: photographies 1986–1992*, VU, Quebec, 1993 **WEBSITE** www.raymondeapril.com

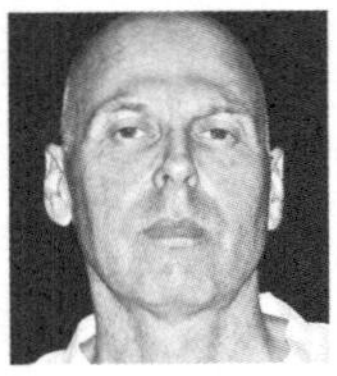

MICHEL ARCHAMBAULT

BORN Richelieu, Quebec, 1953 **RESIDES** Hemmingford, Quebec **EDUCATION** Studies in Visual Arts at Concordia University, Montreal, 1981–1984 **SELECTED SOLO EXHIBITIONS** *LandMark*, Artist in Residence at USINE C, A Multidisciplinary Centre, Montreal, 2005–2006; *Light of India*, Photography, Gallery Thérèse Dion Art Contemporain, Montreal, March 2005; *Oasis*, Photography, Video & Installation, Centre Expression, Quebec, October 1997; *Sculpture et autres inventions*, Photography & Sculptures, Musée national des beaux-arts du Quebec, October 1996 **SELECTED GROUP EXHIBITIONS** *Le Cheveu 12 Stories*, Photography, Gallery Espace, Montreal, September 2003; La Collection permanente, Musée national des beaux-arts du Quebec, 2002 **AWARDS** International Grant, The Gottlieb Foundation for 20 years of Sculptural Work; Grant A, Creative Grant from the Conseil des arts et des lettres du Quebec, 2001 **WEBSITE** www.theresedion.com

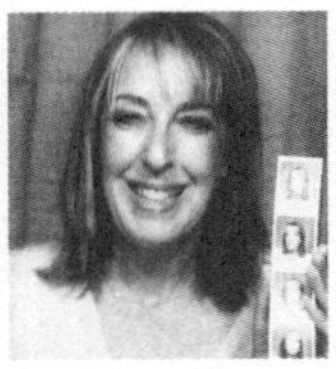

BARBARA ASTMAN

BORN Rochester, New York, 1950 **RESIDES** Toronto **EDUCATION** Ontario College of Art and Design, AOCA, Toronto, 1973; Rochester Institute of Technology, School for American Craftsman, Associates Degree, Rochester, New York, 1970 **SELECTED SOLO EXHIBITIONS** *The Clementine Suite*, The Koffler Gallery, Toronto, 2006; *Revisiting Red* and *The Clementine Suite*, Corkin Shopland Gallery, Toronto, 2005; *Barbara Astman: Clementine Part I*, The Art Gallery of Windsor, Windsor, Ontario, 2004 **SELECTED GROUP EXHIBITIONS** *Les Revenants*, Le Mois de la Photo, Montreal Arts Interculturels, Montreal, 2005; *Identities: Canadian Portraits*, McMichael Gallery, Kleinburg, Ontario, 2004; *Absolute Shape: Celebrating 50 Years of Collecting*, Mackenzie Art Gallery, Regina, 2003 **BOOKS/PUBLICATIONS** *Image & Imagination: Le Mois de La Photo a Montreal*, by Martha Lonford, McGill-Queens University Press, Montreal, 2005; *Barbara Astman: Personal/Persona, A 20-Year Survey Exhibition*, Art Gallery of Hamilton, Hamilton, Ontario, 1995; *Canadian Art in the Twentieth Century*, by Joan Murray, Dundurn Press, 1999; *By a Lady: Celebrating Three Centuries of Art by Canadian Women*, by Maria Tippet, Penguin Books Canada, 1992 **REPRESENTATION** Corkin Shopland Gallery (Toronto) **WEBSITES** www.barbaraastman.com, www.corkinshopland.com

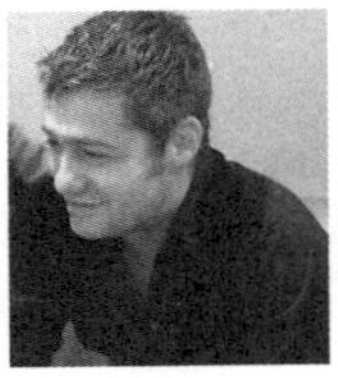

NICOLAS BAIER

BORN Montreal, 1967 **RESIDES** Montreal **EDUCATION** Concordia University, Undergrad in Fine Arts, Montreal, 1993 **SELECTED SOLO EXHIBITIONS** *Tableaux de chasse*, Musée des beaux-arts de Montreal, 2006; *Scènes de genre, canadian tour*, Montreal, Saskatoon, Halifax, 2003–2006; *Recent Works*, Galerie TPW, Toronto, 2001; *Travaux récents*, Galerie René Blouin, Montreal, 2001 **SELECTED GROUP EXHIBITIONS** *The space of making*, Neuer Berliner Kunstverein, Berlin, Germany, 2005; *Repères: art canadien contemporain, dix ans d'acquisition*, Musée des beaux-arts de Montreal, 2004 **BOOKS/PUBLICATIONS** *Nicolas Baier*, co-published by Musée d'art contemporain de Montreal and Musée des beaux-arts de Montreal, 2006; *Zeitgenossische Fotokunst Aus Kanada*, NBK, Berlin, Germany, 2005; *Scènes de genre*, solo exhibition catalogue, Musée d'art contemporain de Montreal, 2003 **WEBSITE** www.nicolasbaier.com

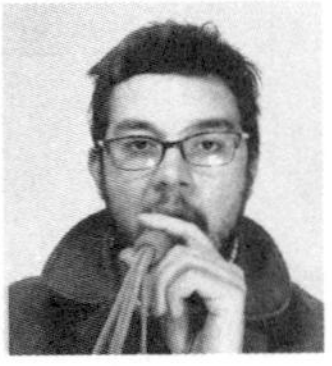

DEAN BALDWIN

BORN Orangeville, Ontario, 1973 **RESIDES** Toronto **EDUCATION** Concordia University, M.F.A., Montreal, 2003; York University, B.F.A. (Honours), Toronto, 1997 **SELECTED SOLO EXHIBITIONS** *House Hold*, Gallery 44, Toronto, 2004; *Facemaker*, Katharine Mulherin Contemporary Art Projects, Toronto, 2003 **SELECTED GROUP EXHIBITIONS** *Off Grid*, The Ottawa Art Gallery, Ottawa, 2005; *Wallpaper*, The Gladstone Hotel, Toronto, 2005 **WEBSITE** cbcradio3.com/issues/2004_04_30/

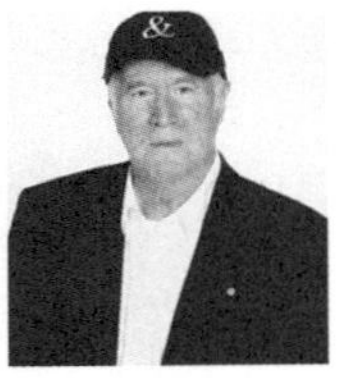

IAIN BAXTER

BORN Middlesborough, England, 1936 **RESIDES** Windsor, Ontario **EDUCATION** Washington State University, Painting, 1964, Master of Fine Arts; University of Idaho, Education, 1962, Master of Education; University of Idaho, Zoology, 1959, Bachelor of Science **SELECTED EXHIBITIONS** *Iain Baxter, Landscape Works*, Walter Phillips Gallery, Banff, Alberta, 1999; *Baxter—Any Choice Works*, 1965–1970, Art Gallery of Ontario, Toronto, 1982; *N.E. Thing Co. Ltd.*, National Gallery of Canada, Ottawa, 1969; *Global Village*, Montreal Museum of Fine Art, Montreal, 2003; *Light Boxes and Vacuum Forms*, Corkin Shopland Gallery, Toronto, 2005 **BOOKS/PUBLICATIONS** Boettiger, Suzaan, *Earthworks—Art and the Landscape of the 60s*, 2003; *Thirteen Essays on Photography*, Canadian Museum of Contemporary Photography, Ottawa, 1991; Fleming, Marie L., *Baxter—Any Choice Works*, Art Gallery of Ontario, Toronto, 1982; *Pluralities/1980/Pluralites*, National Gallery of Canada, Ottawa, 1980; Lippard, Lucy R., *Six Years: The Dematerialization of the Art Object from 1966 to 1972*, Praeger Publishers, Inc., New York, 1973; McShine, Kynaston, *Information*, Museum of Modern Art, New York, 1970; *N.E. Thing Co. Ltd.*, X Biennial Sao Paulo, National Gallery of Canada, Ottawa, 1969 **AWARDS** Royal Canadian Academy, 1973; Officer of the Order of Canada, 2002; Governor General's Award in Visual and Media Arts 2004; Honorary Doctorate, University of British Columbia, 2004; Order of Ontario Molson Prize, 2005 **REPRESENTATION** Corkin Shopland Gallery (Toronto) **WEBSITE** www.corkinshopland.com

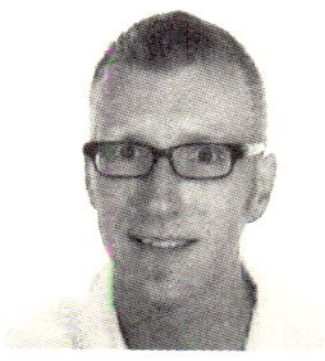

MARCO BOHR

BORN Wiesbaden, Germany, 1978 **RESIDES** Toronto **EDUCATION** Royal College of Art, M.A., London, England, 2005–Present; Nihon University, Pg Cert, Tokyo, 2004; Ryerson University, B.F.A. (Honours), Toronto, 2003; Napier University, exchange winter semester, Edinburgh, Scotland, 2002 **SELECTED SOLO EXHIBITIONS** *Uniforms*, Days Photo Gallery, Tokyo, 2004; *No Ball Games*, Ryerson Gallery, Toronto, 2003 **SELECTED GROUP EXHIBITIONS** *reGeneration: 50 Photographers of Tomorrow*, Musee de l'Elysee, Lausanne, Switzerland, 2005; *Connect the Dots*, Multi-media Group Show travelling across Canada, 2004 **BOOKS/PUBLICATIONS** *reGeneration: 50 Photographers of Tomorrow*, Thames & Hudson, 2005 **WEBSITE** www.macobo.com

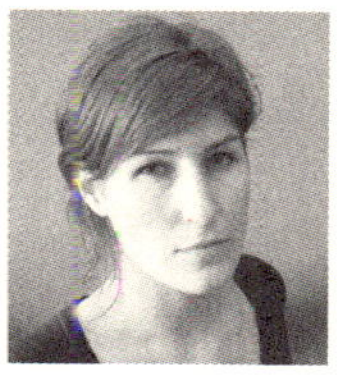

DIANE BORSATO

BORN Toronto, 1973 **RESIDES** Toronto **EDUCATION** York University, B.F.A., Toronto, 1997; Concordia University, M.F.A., Montreal, 2001; New York University, M.A. in Performance Studies, New York, 2003 **SELECTED SOLO EXHIBITIONS** *Moving the Weeds Around*, eyelevel gallery, Halifax, 2005; *How to Eat Light*, Mois de la Photo, Montreal, 2005; *How a Dead Hare Explains Pictures*, Museum of Contemporary Canadian Art, Toronto, 2004; *Worm Things to Chew for the Dead*, Contact Photography Festival, Gallery TPW, Toronto, 2004 **SELECTED GROUP EXHIBITIONS** *Sleeping With Cake*, Truck Contemporary Art, Calgary, 2005; *The Twitching Project*, National Museum of Fine Arts, Quebec, 2003; *The Flower Immersion Project*, La Torre de Los Vientos, Mexico City, 2002

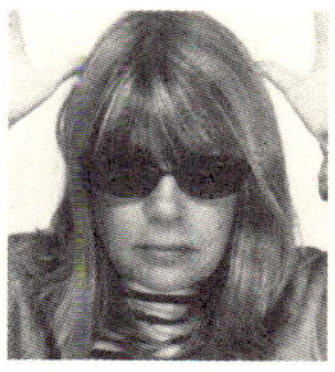

DIANNE BOS

BORN Hamilton, Ontario, 1956 **RESIDES** Calgary **EDUCATION** Mount Allison University, B.F.A., Sackville, New Brunswick, 1978 **SELECTED SOLO EXHIBITIONS** *Sound and Light*, Whyte Museum of the Canadian Rockies, Banff, Alberta, 2005; *Camere Illuminati*, University of Waterloo Art Gallery, Waterloo, Ontario, 2002 **SELECTED GROUP EXHIBITIONS** *Alberta Biennial of Contemporary Art*, Walter Phillips Gallery, Banff and Edmonton Art Gallery, 2005; *International Pinhole Exhibition*, Festival Visionaria, Sienna, Italy, 2002 **AWARDS** National Magazine Award, Gold, 2005; Alberta Foundation for the Arts Grant, 2002 and 2003 **WEBSITE** www.diannebos.com

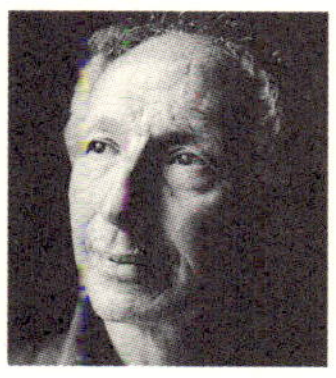

ROBERT BOURDEAU

BORN Kingston, Ontario, 1931 **RESIDES** Ottawa **EDUCATION** Queen's University, Kingston, Ontario, Bachelor of Art History; University of Toronto, Bachelor of Architecture **SELECTED SOLO EXHIBITIONS** *The Sixties: Photography In Question*, Canadian Museum of Contemporary Photography, 2006; *Le Grand Palais and The Distillery District*, Corkin Shopland Gallery, Toronto, 2005; *New to View: Recent Acquisitions in Photography*, The Art Institute of Chicago, 2003 **BOOKS/PUBLICATIONS** *Up and Down*, Vereins-und Westbank Collection, Hamburg, Germany, 2000; *Robert Bourdeau: Industrial Sites*, published by Jane Corkin Gallery, Toronto, 1998; *Children in Photography*, by Jane Corkin and Gary Michael Dault, Firefly Books, 1990; *Photographs: 150 Years*, edited by Jane Corkin, published by Jane Corkin Gallery, 1989; *The Photograph as Object 1843–1969: Photographs From the Collection of the National Gallery of Canada*, National Gallery of Canada, 1969 **AWARDS** Royal Canadian Academy of Arts, 1983 **REPRESENTATION** Corkin Shopland Gallery (Toronto) **WEBSITE** www.corkinshopland.com

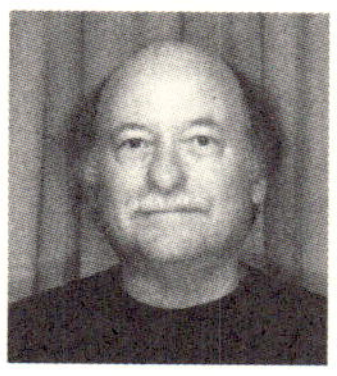

JIM BREUKELMAN

BORN Pointe-à-Pierre, Trinidad, 1941 **RESIDES** Vancouver **EDUCATION** Rhode Island School of Design, B.F.A. in Photography, Providence, Rhode Island, 1966 **SELECTED SOLO EXHIBITIONS** *Mesocosm*, State Gallery, Vancouver, 2005; *After Life*, State Gallery, Vancouver, 2003; *Hot Properties*, The Dunlop Art Gallery, Regina, 1988 **SELECTED GROUP EXHIBITIONS** *Real Pictures: Photographs From the Collection of Claudia Beck and Andrew Gruft*, Vancouver Art Gallery, Vancouver, 2005; *Image & Light/History & Influence*, Charles Scott Gallery, Vancouver, 2000; *Pacific Northwest Photography Now*, Whatcom Museum of History & Art, Bellingham, Washington, 2003 **REPRESENTATION** State Gallery, Vancouver

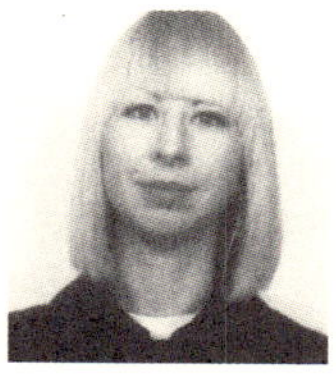

KARIN BUBAS

BORN Vancouver, 1976 **RESIDES** Vancouver **EDUCATION** Emily Carr Institute of Art & Design, Photography Program, Vancouver, 1988 **SELECTED SOLO EXHIBITIONS** *Ivy House*, Monte Clark Gallery, Toronto, 2004, and Vancouver, 2003 **SELECTED GROUP EXHIBITIONS** *Real Pictures: Photographs From The Collection of Claudia Beck and Andrew Gruft*, Vancouver Art Gallery, 2005; *About Time*, Canadian Embassy, Washington D.C., 2005 **AWARDS** Vancouver Arts Award, 2005; Canada Council C Grant, 2004; B.C. Cultural Grant, 2003 **REPRESENTATION** Monte Clark Gallery (Vancouver, Toronto) **WEBSITES** www.karinbubas.ca, www.monteclarkgallery.com

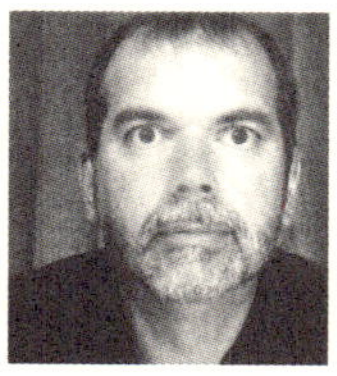

ROBERT BURLEY

BORN Picton, Ontario, 1957 **RESIDES** Toronto **EDUCATION** School of the Art Institute of Chicago, M.F.A. in Photography, Chicago, 1986; Ryerson University, B.A.A. in Media Studies, Toronto, 1980 **SELECTED SOLO EXHIBITIONS** *Great Lakes*, Stephen Bulger Gallery, Toronto, 2006; *Instruments of Faith*, Eric Arthur Gallery, Toronto, 2005; *Engineering the Picturesque*, The Canadian Museum of Contemporary Photography, Ottawa, 2001 **SELECTED GROUP EXHIBITIONS** *Sense of the City*, Canadian Centre for Architecture, Montreal, 2005; *New Toronto City Hall & Nathan Phillips Square*, Ballenford Books, Toronto, 2003; *The Urban Character*, Triennale of Milan, Milan, Italy, 2003 **BOOKS/PUBLICATIONS** *Viewing Olmsted: Photographs by Robert Burley, Lee Friedlander and Geoffrey James*, Canadian Centre for Architecture, Montreal, 1996; *Airfield: Airport on the Prairie*, The Chicago Historical Society, Chicago, 1988; *Seeing People—Seeing Places: Contemporary Photography from Ontario*, Visual Arts Ontario, Toronto, 1984 **AWARDS** Ryerson University, SRC Creative Grant, 2003; Ontario Arts Council, Mid-Career Grant, 2003 **REPRESENTATION** Stephen Bulger Gallery (Toronto) **WEBSITES** www.ccca.ca, www.bulgergallery.com

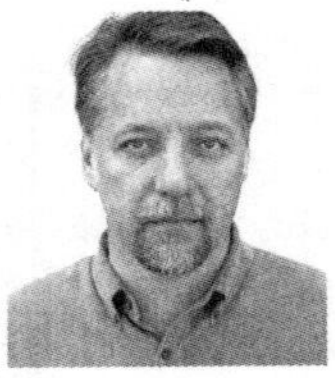

EDWARD BURTYNSKY

BORN St. Catharines, Ontario, 1955 **RESIDES** Toronto **EDUCATION** Ryerson Polytechnical University, B.A. in Photographic Arts, Toronto, 1982; Niagara College, Diploma in Graphic Arts, Welland, Ontario, 1976 **SELECTED SOLO EXHIBITIONS** *Manufactured Landscapes*, Art Gallery of Ontario, Toronto, 2004; *Manufactured Landscapes*, Musée d'art contemporain de Montreal, Montreal, 2004; *Asian Quarries*, Nicholas Metivier Gallery, Toronto, 2004; *Landmarks*, Oakville Galleries, Centennial Square, Oakville, Ontario, 2003 **BOOKS/PUBLICATIONS** *Burtynsky—China*, Steidl, 2005; *Manufactured Landscapes* by Lori Pauli, 2004 **AWARDS** TED Prize, 2004; The Rencontres d'Arles Outreach Award, 2004 **REPRESENTATION** Nicholas Metivier Gallery (Toronto) **WEBSITES** www.edwardburtynsky.com, www.metiviergallery.com

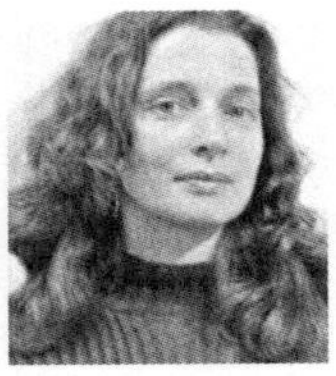

OLGA CHAGAOUTDINOVA

BORN Khabarovsk, Russia, 1968 **RESIDES** Montreal **EDUCATION** Concordia University, M.F.A. in Photography, Montreal, 2005-Present; Emily Carr Institute of Art and Design, B.F.A. in Photography, Vancouver, 2005; Republican Institute for Humanities, Graduate Study, Specialty Historical Culturology, St. Petersburg, Russia, 1998; Far East Pedagogical Institute, B.A. in Russian Language and World Literature, Khabarovsk, Russia, 1993 **SELECTED GROUP EXHIBITIONS** *Picture This*, Emily Carr Institute of Art and Design, Vancouver, 2005; *Fantasy Show*, Concourse Gallery, Vancouver, 2004; *Leaving Lotus Land*, Concourse Gallery, Vancouver, 2003

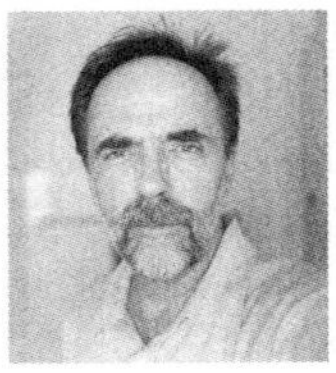

SERGE CLÉMENT

BORN Valleyfield, Quebec, 1950 **RESIDES** Montreal **EDUCATION** Cégep du Vieux Montreal, 1970 **SELECTED SOLO EXHIBITIONS** *Au Passage Patience*, Corkin Shopland Gallery, Toronto, 2003; *Vertige-Vestige* (travelling exhibition), Centro de Fotografia, Salamanca, Spain, Urania Gallery, Barcelona, Spain, Centre Photographique d'Île de France, Pontault-Combault, France, Encontros da Imagem, Braga, Portugal, 1998-1999; *Cité Fragile*, Mois de la Photo, Canadian Cultural Centre, Paris, 1994; *Photographie au présent*, Bibliothèque nationale de France, Paris, 1997; *Carnets de Voyage*, Canadian Museum of Contemporary Photography, Ottawa, 1994 **SELECTED BOOKS/PUBLICATIONS** *Sutures*, Les 400 coups, Montreal, 2003; *Fragrant Light*, preface by Gordon Baldwin, Curator, J. Paul Getty Museum, California, Les 400 coups, Montreal, 2000; *Vertige-Vestige*, Les 400 coups, Montreal, 1998; *Halloween 1995*, Les 400 coups, Montreal, 1997; *Six Photographes Contemporains*, Canada 8e Encontros da Imagem, Braga, Portugal, 1994; *Une Tradition Documentaire? Quelle Tradition? Quel Documentaire?* Serge Alaire, Mois de la Photo à Montreal, Maison de la Culture Notre-Dame-de-Grâce, Montreal, 1993; *La Collection: tableau inaugural*, 1992; *Cité Fragile*, photographs by Serge Clément, text by Francois Jalbert, Vox Populi, Montreal, 1992 **REPRESENTATION** Corkin Shopland Gallery (Toronto) **WEBSITE** www.corkinshopland.com

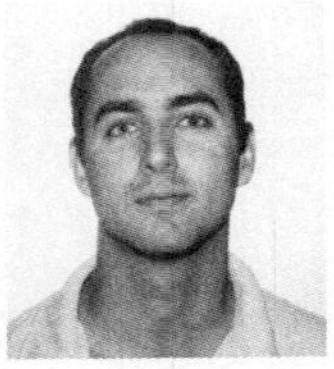

SCOTT CONARROE

BORN Edmonton, 1974 **RESIDES** London, Ontario **EDUCATION** Nova Scotia College of Art and Design, M.F.A., Halifax, 2005; Emily Carr Institute of Art and Design, B.F.A., Vancouver, 2001 **SELECTED SOLO EXHIBITIONS** *Harbour*, Mt. St. Vincent University Art Gallery, Halifax, 2005; *Average Pictures*, Anna Leonowens Gallery, Halifax, 2005, and Photo Passage, Toronto, 2005; *Bridgeworks*, State Gallery, Vancouver, 2002 **SELECTED GROUP EXHIBITIONS** *Exhibit A*, St. Mary's University Art Gallery, Halifax, 2004, Sir Wilfred Grenfell University Gallery, Cornerbrook, 2005, and Prefix Institute, Toronto, 2005; *Stay Warm*, Atelier Frankfurt, Frankfurt, Germany, 2005; *Juventus*, Ukrainian Institute of Modern Art, Chicago, 2004 **AWARDS** Galen Kuellmer Young Artist Fellowship, 2005; B.C. Arts Council Scholarship, 1997, 2004; Koerner Foundation Award, 2003 **WEBSITE** www.oneeggisenough.com

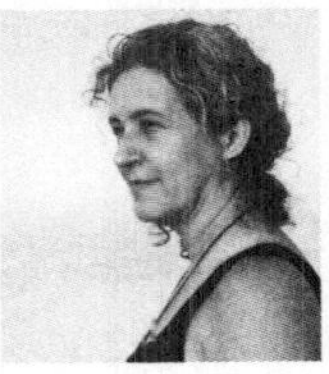

SUSAN COOLEN

BORN Halifax, 1955 **RESIDES** Montreal **EDUCATION** Columbia College Chicago, M.F.A. in Photography, Chicago, 2002; Concordia University, B.F.A. in Photography, Montreal, 1995; Nova Scotia College of Art and Design, Bachelor of Design in Communication Design, Halifax, 1977 **SELECTED GROUP EXHIBITIONS** *Beyond Science*, Fundación Metrònom, Barcelona, Spain, 2004–2005; *Peace of Mind*, Cafka '04, Kitchener, Ontario, 2004; *In the Light of: Six Contemporary Artists Explore the Work of William Henry Fox Talbot*, Kitchener-Waterloo Art Gallery, Kitchener, Ontario, 2003; *Sphere*, Presentation House Gallery, Vancouver, 2003 **BOOKS/PUBLICATIONS** *Terre océáne*, Dazibao Publications, Montreal, 2003; *Mementos*, Columbia College, Chicago, 2005 **WEBSITE** www.susancoolen.com

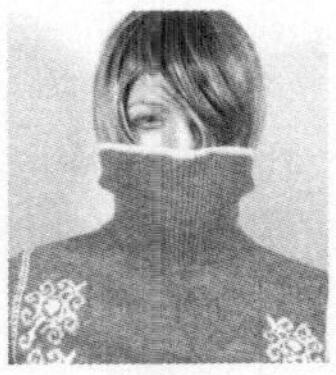

STEPHANIE CORMIER

BORN Montreal, 1970 **RESIDES** Toronto **EDUCATION** Ontario College of Art and Design, B.F.A., Toronto, 2005–Present **SELECTED EXHIBITIONS** *Nova Young Art Fair*, Ashley Gallery, Pittsburgh, 2006; *Projekt 30*, projekt30.com, 2005; *Propagandista*, Toronto Free Gallery, Toronto, 2004; *Electric Eye*, Sis Boom Bah, Toronto, 2004 **WEBSITE** www.stephaniecormier.com

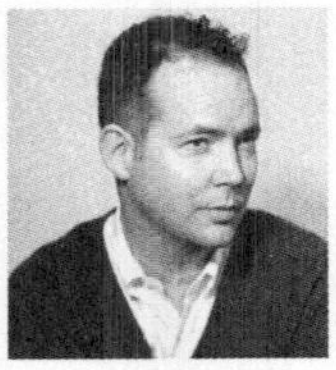

DOUGLAS COUPLAND

BORN Baden-Sollingen, Germany, 1961 **RESIDES** Vancouver **EDUCATION** Emily Carr Institute of Art and Design, Diploma in Sculpture, Vancouver, 1984 **SELECTED EXHIBITIONS** *I Like the Future and the Future Likes Me* and *Retranslation*, The Monte Clark Gallery, Toronto, 2005; *Super City*, The Canadian Institute for Architecture, Montreal, 2005, and Canada House, London, England, 2004 **REPRESENTATION** Monte Clark Gallery (Vancouver, Toronto) **WEBSITES** www.coupland.com, www.monteclarkgallery.com

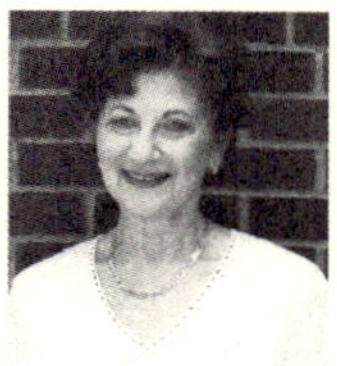

JACKIE CYTRYNBAUM

BORN Montreal, 1939 **RESIDES** Montreal **EDUCATION** Concordia University, B.A., Montreal, 1982 **SELECTED SOLO EXHIBITIONS** *Music in the Metro*, Photomedia Center, Erie, Pennsylvania, 2005 **SELECTED GROUP EXHIBITIONS** Florence International Biennale of Contemporary Art, Florence, Italy, 2003; *The Romantic Eye*, Montreal Museum of Fine Art, Montreal, 2003; *Moving*, Drabinsky Gallery, Toronto, 2002 **BOOKS/PUBLICATIONS** *After Mother Goose*, self-published, 1999; *Bequia*, self-published, 1992 **AWARDS** Florence International Biennale of Contemporary Art, Photography, 2003 **WEBSITE** www.jackiecytrynbaum.com

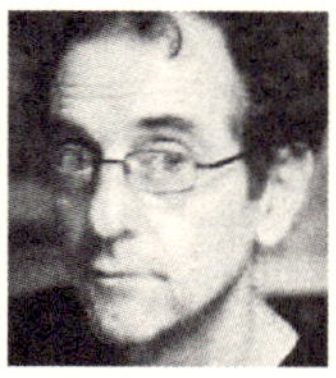

ANDREW DANSON DANUSHEVSKY

BORN Bournemouth, England, 1945 **RESIDES** Halifax **EDUCATION** University of Guelph, Recreation, Guelph, Ontario, 1967 **SELECTED SOLO EXHIBITIONS** Danielson Gallery, Toronto, 2000; Fotogalerie Friedrichschain, Berlin, 1999 **SELECTED GROUP EXHIBITIONS** *Toronto Portraits*, Martin-Gropius-Bau, Berlin, 2004; *Newfoundland Portraits*, National Gallery of Guyana, Guyana, 2003; Canadian High Commission, Port of Spain, Trinidad & Tobago, 2003; Biblioteca Luis Angel Arango, Bogotá, Colombia, 2003 **BOOKS/PUBLICATIONS** *Unofficial Portraits*, Doubleday Canada, 1987; *Face-Kao*, Hpf Press, 1996 **AWARDS** Department of Foreign Affairs (via KWAG) Broken Ground Exhibition, Berlin and Prague 2004; Canada Council Outreach Grant, 2002 **WEBSITES** www.nervebyte.com, www.danushevsky.com

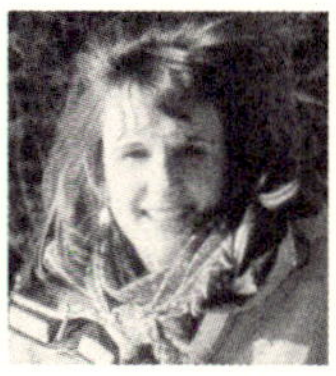

SUSAN DOBSON

BORN Moncton, 1965 **RESIDES** Guelph, Ontario **EDUCATION** University of Guelph, M.F.A., Guelph, Ontario, 1997; Ryerson Polytechnical Institute, B.A.A., Toronto, 1988 **SELECTED SOLO EXHIBITIONS** *Open House*, Fotoseptiembre, Centro Nacional de las Artes, Mexico City, 2005; *Open House*, Blue Sky Gallery, Portland, Oregon, 2005; *Open House*, Art Gallery of Calgary, 2004–2005 **SELECTED GROUP EXHIBITIONS** KWAG Biennial, Kitchener-Waterloo Art Gallery, Kitchener, Ontario, 2005; *Transitive: Toronto Artists in St. Petersburg*, Kabat Wrobel Gallery, Toronto, 2005 **AWARDS** Canada Council for the Arts, Creation/Production Grant, 1999, 2001, 2003; Ontario Arts Council, Grant for Individual Visual Artists, 1998, 1999, 2000, 2001, 2003; Gold National Magazine Award, 2001 **REPRESENTATION** Tatar Gallery (Toronto) **WEBSITES** www.susandobson.com, www.tatargallery.com

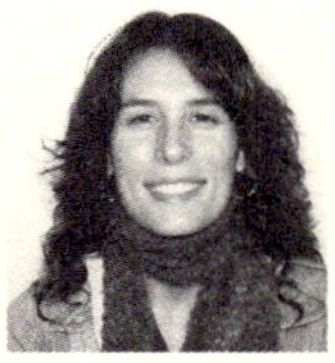

KATYUSKA DOLEATTO

BORN Turin, Italy, 1971 **RESIDES** Toronto **EDUCATION** Ryerson University, B.F.A in Photography, Toronto, 2004 **SELECTED GROUP EXHIBITIONS** *Illuminations*, Prime Gallery, Toronto, 2005; *Portfolio*, Ryerson Gallery, Toronto, 2003-2004; Hollinger Collins, Montreal, 2004; *Imago Recenseo*, Sis Boom Bah, Toronto, 2004; *The Toronto Outdoor Art Exhibition*, Nathan Phillips Square, Toronto, 2003-2004; *Pho-To Show*, Praxis Gallery, Toronto, 2004 **AWARDS** Imperial Tobacco Canada Arts Grant, 2004; Maximum Exposure Excellence in the Arts Award, 2004; Oakville Gallery Award, 2003; The School of Image Arts Bursary, Ryerson University, 2003; The 4th Annual International Polaroid Contest, 2003; The Steichenlab Award for Best Overall Colour Photography, 2002 **WEBSITE** www.hollingercollins.com

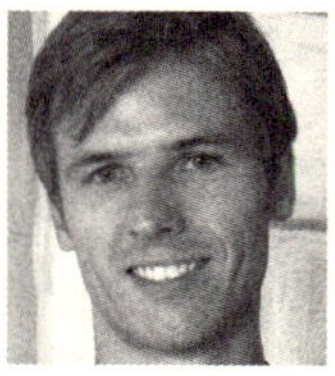

JAKUB DOLEJŠ

BORN Prague, Czech Republic, 1975 **RESIDES** Toronto **EDUCATION** Academy of Art, Architecture and Design, M.F.A., Prague, Czech Republic, 1998 **SELECTED EXHIBITIONS** *Little Histories of Modern Art*, Mois de la Photo, Montreal, 2005; *Perception*, Skew Gallery, Calgary, 2005; *AutumnFall*, Angell Gallery, Toronto, 2004; *East International*, Norwich Gallery, Norwich, U.K., 2004 **AWARDS** Canada Arts Council, 2005 and 2003; Ontario Arts Council, 2004; Toronto Arts Council, 2003 **REPRESENTATION** Angell Gallery (Toronto) **WEBSITE** www.jakubdolejs.com, www.angellgallery.com

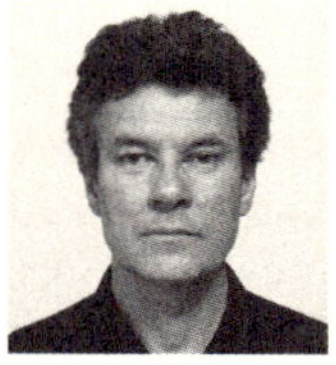

DAVID DONALD

BORN Toronto, 1955 **RESIDES** Toronto **EDUCATION** Queen's University, B.F.A., Kingston, Ontario, 1981; Queen's University, B. Ed., Kingston, Ontario, 1983; Ontario College of Art and Design, Toronto, 1989-1993 **SELECTION SOLO EXHIBITIONS** *Camera Obscura*, Members' Gallery, Gallery 44, Toronto, 2004; *Historia Naturalis*, The Photo Passage, Harbourfront, Toronto, 2004 **SELECTED GROUP EXHIBITIONS** *Dislocation Relaunch Exhibition*, Volkswagen Fotogalerie, Hong Kong; LEE Ka-sing Gallery, Toronto, 2004; *Details*, Gallery 1313, Contact Photography Festival, Toronto, 2003 **BOOKS/PUBLICATIONS** *Historia Naturalis: Photographs by David Donald*, EN Press, Toronto, 2004 **AWARDS** Ontario Arts Council Exhibition Grant, 2004; Diana Myers Award for Bookmaking, Ontario College of Art and Design, Toronto, 1992 **WEBSITE** www.daviddonald.ca

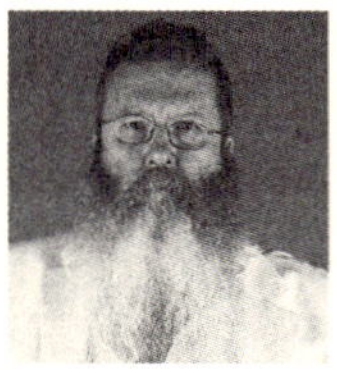

EVERGON

BORN Niagara Falls, Ontario, 1946 **RESIDES** Montreal **EDUCATION** Rochester Institute of Technology, M.F.A., Rochester, New York, 1974; Mount Allison University, B.F.A., Sackville, New Brunswick, 1970 **SELECTED SOLO EXHIBITIONS** *Cynicisme*, Galerie VU, Quebec City, 2005; *Evergon*, Edward Day Gallery, Toronto, 2004 **SELECTED GROUP EXHIBITIONS** *Unstilled Lives: Destiny Deacon*, Leonard & Bina Ellen Gallery, Montreal, 2005; *Le Corps Gay* Travelling Tour, University of Toronto, 2004 **BOOKS/PUBLICATIONS** *Porcelaine, Carte grise a Evergon*, Dazibao, Montreal, 2003; *Evergon 1987–1997*, The National Museum of Photography, Film and Television, Bradford, England, 1997; *Loitering With Intent*, Australian Centre for Photography, Sydney, 1999; *Ramboys: A Bookless Novel and Other Fiction*, The Ottawa Art Gallery, Ottawa, 1995; *Evergon 1971–1987*, Canadian Museum of Contemporary Photography, Ottawa, 1988

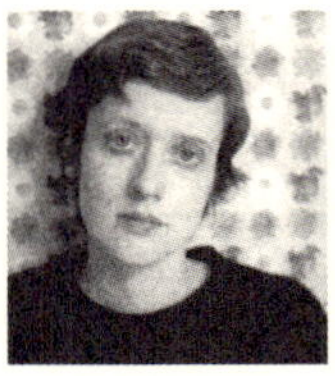

JANIETA EYRE

BORN London, England, 1966 **RESIDES** Toronto **EDUCATION** University of Toronto, B.A. in Philosophy, Toronto, 1988 **SELECTED SOLO EXHIBITIONS** Salamanca Ciudad de Cultura, Spain, 2006; *Staging*, Contemporary Art Museum, St. Louis, Missouri, 2002; National Gallery of Iceland, Reykjavik, 1999 **SELECTED GROUP EXHIBITIONS** Art Gallery of Ontario, Toronto, 2004; *The Amazing and the Immutable*, Florida Contemporary Art Museum, Tampa, Florida, 2004 **WEBSITE** www.janietaeyre.com

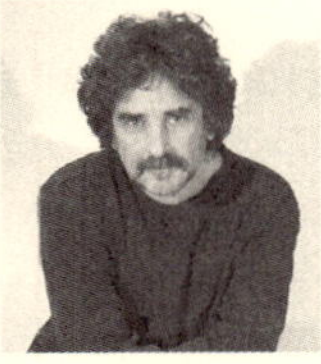

MICHAEL FLOMEN

BORN Montreal, 1952 **RESIDES** Montreal **EDUCATION** Self-taught **SELECTED SOLO EXHIBITIONS** *Teeming*, Ricco/Maresca Gallery, New York, 2005; *Trout Will Rise for Some Hats*, Sterling College, Craftsbury, Vermont, 2003 **SELECTED GROUP EXHIBITIONS** *Oil and Water*, Mois de la photo, Montreal, 2005; *What's New*, Diana Lowenstein Fine Arts, Miami, 2005 **WEBSITE** www. hastedhunt.com

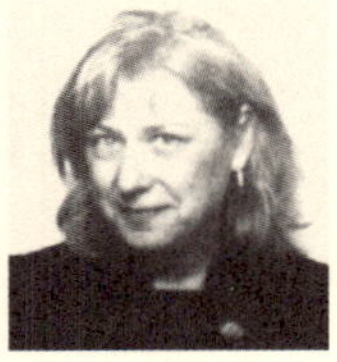

DEBRA FRIEDMAN

BORN Toronto, 1955 **RESIDES** Toronto **EDUCATION** School of the Art Institute of Chicago, M.F.A., Chicago, 1985 **SELECTED EXHIBITIONS** *The Very Image: Case Studies*, York Quay, Toronto, 2001; *House/Home*, Photo Passage, Toronto, 1999; Pikto Gallery, Toronto, 2003 **BOOKS/PUBLICATIONS** *Picture This*, KidsCan Press, 2003 **AWARDS** Polaroid Corporation Award, 1993; Ontario Arts Council, Project Cost, 2005 **WEBSITE** www.debrafriedman.com

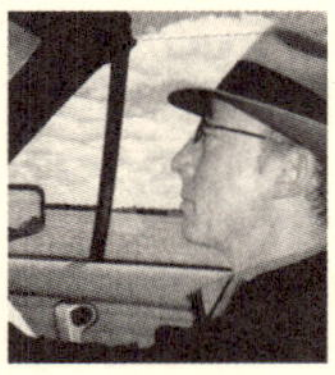

ELDON GARNET

BORN Toronto, 1946 **RESIDES** Toronto **EDUCATION** York University, M.A., Toronto, 1973; University of Toronto, B.A., Toronto, 1969 **SELECTED SOLO EXHIBITIONS** *Eldon Garnet*, Amsterdams Centrum voor Fotografie, Amsterdam, 2002; *The Fallen Body*, Saidye Bronfman Centre, Montreal, 2000; Canadian Museum of Contemporary Photography, Ottawa, 1998 **SELECTED GROUP EXHIBITIONS** *Hitchcock and Art*, Centre Georges Pompidou, Paris 2001; Montreal Museum of Fine Arts, Montreal, 2000; *Happy End*, Kunsthalle Dusseldorf, Dusseldorf, Germany, 1996 **BOOKS/PUBLICATIONS** *Impulse Archaeology*, University of Toronto Press, 2005; *The Melodious Child/Dust*, Museum of Contemporary Canadian Art, Christopher Cutts Gallery, Toronto, 2002; *Eldon Garnet*, Amsterdams Centrum voor Fotografie, CD catalogue, Amsterdam, 2002; *The Fallen Body*, Canadian Museum of Contemporary Photography, Ottawa, 1998; *Reading Brooke Shields: The Garden of Failure*, Semiotext[e], New York, 1995; *The Narrative Body*, Autonomedia, New York, 1992; *Today Tonight Tomorrow*, Impulse Society for Cultural Productions, Toronto, 1989; *I Shot Mussolini*, Impulse Editions/Summerhill Press, Toronto, 1987 **WEBSITE** www.eldongarnet.com

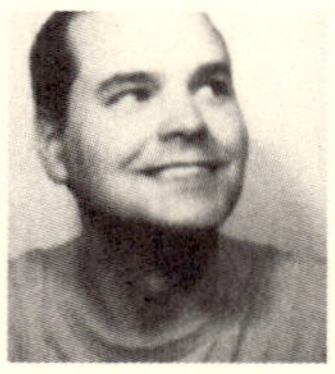

CHAD GERTH

BORN Southbridge, Massachusetts, 1975 **RESIDES** Chicago, Illinois **EDUCATION** The School of the Art Institute of Chicago, M.F.A. in Studio Arts, focusing on Photography, Chicago, 2003; Ryerson University, B.F.A. in Still Photography, Toronto, 1999 **SELECTED GROUP EXHIBITIONS** *Things Fall From the Sky*, Evanston Art Center, Evanston, Illinois; California Museum of Photography, Riverside, California, 2005; *Wallpaper*, Gladstone Hotel, Toronto, 2005; *Protégé Honours Exhibition*, The Design Exchange, Toronto, 2003; *Lighten Up*, Gallery 312, Chicago, 2003 **AWARDS** Community Arts Assistance Program Grant, Chicago, 2004; Protégé Honours Award, Arts Toronto, 2003 **REPRESENTATION** Corkin Shopland Gallery (Toronto) **WEBSITES** www.chadgerth.com, www.corkinshopland.com

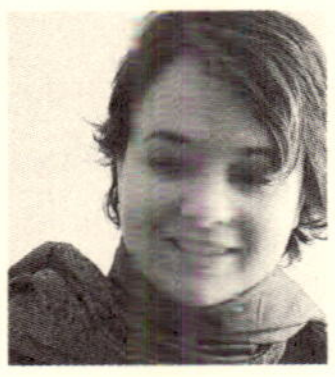

BARBARA GILBERT

BORN Quebec City, 1970 **RESIDES** Toronto **EDUCATION** Concordia University, M.F.A., Montreal, 2000; Concordia University, B.F.A., Montreal, 1994 **SELECTED SOLO EXHIBITIONS** *Parlours*, Red Head Gallery, Toronto, 2002; *Come On Up to the House*, Red Head Gallery, Toronto, 2002; *Ever After*, Bourget Gallery, Montreal, 2000; *Discomfort*, Bourget Gallery, Montreal, 1999 **AWARDS** Canada Council for the Arts, Grants to Professional Artists, 2002; Toronto Arts Council, Visual Artists Level 1, 2002

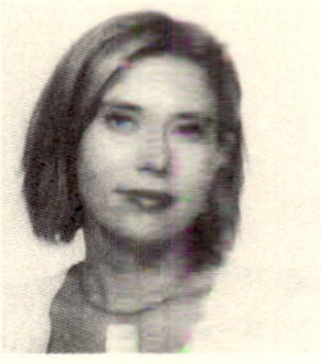

RITA GODLEVSKIS

BORN Calgary, 1978 **RESIDES** Toronto and Melbourne, Australia **EDUCATION** R.M.I.T., Masters in Creative Media, Melbourne Australia, 2005; Ryerson University, Bachelor of Arts, Toronto, 2000 **SELECTED SOLO EXHIBITIONS** P.I.T. Space Gallery, Melbourne **SELECTED GROUP EXHIBITIONS** R.M.I.T. Barker-Rance Contemporary Art, Prize Exhibition, Melbourne, 2005; *The Life of Water*, The Photosensitive Photographers Group touring Canada, 2005; *ACP Project Wall*, Australian Centre for Photography, Sydney, 2004; *Body of Water*, Contact Festival, Luft Gallery, Toronto, 2002; *Divide and Conquer*, Contact Festival, Prisma Gallery, Toronto, 2000 **WEBSITE** www.ritagodlevskis.com

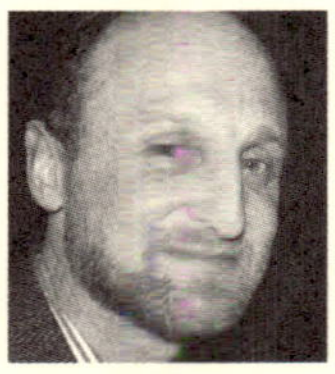

RAFAEL GOLDCHAIN

BORN Santiago, Chile, 1953 **RESIDES** Toronto **EDUCATION** York University, M.F.A., Toronto, 2000; Ryerson Polytechnical Institute, B.A.A., Toronto, 1980 **SELECTED SOLO EXHIBITIONS** *Familial Ground*, Rosella Junck Gallery, Berlin, Germany, 2005; *Familial Ground*, Rosella Junck Gallery, Venice, Italy, 2005; *Familial Ground*, MacIntosh Gallery, University of Western Ontario, London, Ontario, 2005 **SELECTED GROUP EXHIBITIONS** Mois de la photo a Montreal, Saidye Bronfman Centre, Lianne and Dany Taran Gallery, Montreal, 2005; *Broken Ground*, Galerie Vaclav Spaly, Prague, Czech Republic, 2004 **BOOKS/PUBLICATIONS** *About Face*, Thames and Hudson, Museé de L'Eliseé, Lausanne, 2006; *Canadian Art in the 20th Century*, Dundurn, 1999; *Nostalgia for an Unknown Land*, Lumiere Press, Toronto, 1989 (monograph) **WEBSITE** www.zonezero.com /exposiciones/fotografos/goldchain/index.html

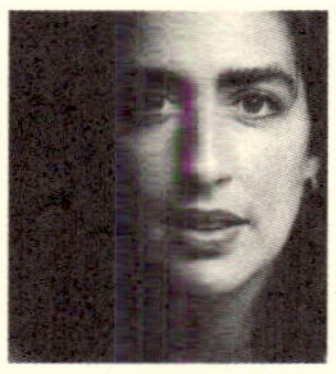

NATHALIE GOSSELIN

BORN Ithaca, New York, 1969 **RESIDES** Montreal **EDUCATION** M.F.A. in Photography, University of Saskatchewan, Saskatoon, 2002; B.F.A. Major in Photography, Concordia University, Montreal, 1996; B.A.Sc. in Classical Studies, Major in Archaeology, Queen's University, Kingston, Ontario, 1992 **SELECTED SOLO EXHIBITIONS** *Bodies of Light*, Espace trois, Montreal, 2005; *Simulacra*, Snelgrove Gallery, Saskatoon, 2002 **SELECTED GROUP EXHIBITIONS** *Tout Près/So Close*, Trafic, Abitibi-Téminscamingue, Quebec, 2005 **MEMBERSHIP** Atelier Fovea, a Montreal-based photographers' collective, Montreal, since 2004 **AWARDS** Graduate Scholarship, University of Saskatchewan, Saskatoon, 2000–2002; Quebec Arts Council, Production Grant, Montreal, 1999

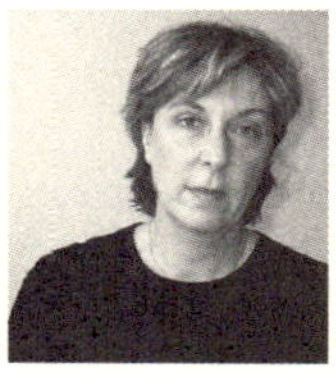

ANGELA GRAUERHOLZ

BORN Hamburg, Germany, 1952 **RESIDES** Montreal **EDUCATION** Kunstschule Alsterdamm, Diploma in Graphic Design, Hamburg, 1974; University of Hamburg, Bac in Literature, Hamburg, 1974; Concordia University, Masters in Photography, Montreal, 1982 **SELECTED SOLO EXHIBITIONS** *Reading Room for the Working Artist*, Olga Korper Gallery, Toronto, 2004; *Sententia I-VXII* and *Schriftbilder*, The Power Plant, Toronto, 1999; *Sententia I-VXII*, Albright-Knox Art Gallery, Buffalo, New York, 1999; *Angela Grauerholz: Photographies*, Musée d'art contemporain de Montreal, 1995 **SELECTED GROUP EXHIBITIONS** Sydney Biennial, 1990; Documenta IX, 1992; Carnegie International, 1995 **BOOKS/PUBLICATIONS** *Angela Grauerholz/Aporia*, Oakville Galleries, Oakville, Ontario, 1995; *Angela Grauerholz—Texte zum Werk*, Eckhard Schneider ed., Hannover Kunstverein, Hanover, Germany, 1995; *Angela Grauerholz photographies*, Paulette Gagnon, Musée d'art contemporain de Montreal, 1995; *Angela Grauerholz Photographien*, Friedrich Meschede, Chantal Pontbriand, Westfälischer Kunstverein, Münster, Germany, 1991 **REPRESENTATION** Olga Korper Gallery (Toronto) **WEBSITE** www.olgakorpergallery.com

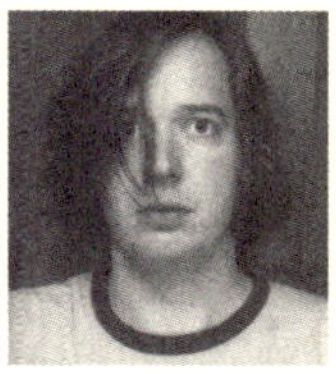

COLWYN GRIFFITH

BORN Ottawa, 1971 **RESIDES** New York **EDUCATION** Dawson College Institute of Photography, Montreal, 1994-1996; Carleton University, B.A. in Film Studies, Ottawa, 1994 **SELECTED SOLO EXHIBITIONS** *Eye Candy 3*, Carleton University, Ottawa, 2003-2004 **SELECTED GROUP EXHIBITIONS** *Image & Imagination*, Le Mois de la Photo, Montreal, 2005; *Hot Mush & Cold North*, Ottawa Art Gallery, Ottawa, 2005; *Proof 10*, Gallery 44, Toronto, 2003; *Show 2000*, Canadian Embassy of Japan, Tokyo, 2000 **BOOKS/PUBLICATIONS** *Souvenir of Canada 2*, Douglas & McIntyre, 2004; *Image and Imagination*, McGill-Queen's University Press, 2005 **AWARDS** Canada Council for the Arts, Mid Career Grant, 2005; Canada Council for the Arts, Emerging Grants, 2003 and 2000 **WEBSITE** www.colwyngriffith.com

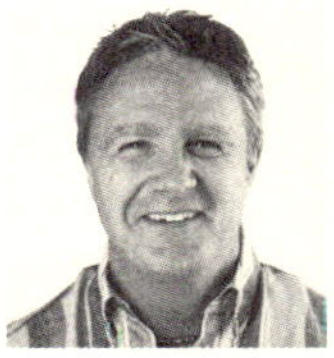

FRANK GRISDALE

BORN Edmonton, 1954 **RESIDES** Edmonton **EDUCATION** University of Alberta, B.A., Edmonton, 1978 **SELECTED SOLO EXHIBITIONS** *Waiting for the Light*, The Photography Room, Grand Rapids, Michigan, 2003, Yukon Arts Centre, Whitehorse, 2003, and Royal Museum of Alberta, Edmonton, 2002; *Mountain Photographs*, Jasper Park Lodge Gallery, Jasper, Alberta, 2002 **WEBSITE** www.FrankGrisdale.com

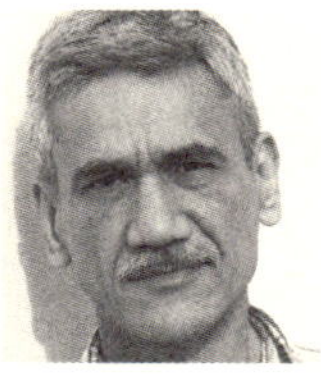

SUNIL GUPTA

BORN New Delhi, India, 1953 **RESIDES** London, England and New Delhi, India **EDUCATION** M.A. in Photography, Royal College of Art, London, England, 1983; Diploma in Photography, West Surrey College of Art & Design, Farnham, England, 1981; Lisette Model & Philippe Halsman (photography), The New School, New York, 1978; B.Comm., Concordia University, Montreal, 1977 **SELECTED SOLO EXHIBITIONS** *Sunil Gupta*, Museum of Contemporary Photography, UC Riverside, California, 2005; *Sunil Gupta*, Canadian Museum of Contemporary Photography, Ottawa, 2005; *Pictures From Here*, Visual Arts Gallery, Habitat Centre, New Delhi, India, 2004; *Homelands*, Stephen Bulger Gallery, Toronto, 2004 **SELECTED GROUP EXHIBITIONS** *Faces in the Crowd*, Whitechapel Art Gallery, London, England, 2004-2005 **BOOKS/PUBLICATIONS** *Pictures From Here*, Autograph/Chris Boot, London, 2003 **AWARDS** India Habitat Centre Awards for Excellence 2004, Best Photography Show, *Pictures From Here*, Visual Arts Gallery, 2004; Artist in Residence, Light Work, Syracuse, New York, 2003; AHRB Fellowship in Creative & Performing Arts, University of Southampton, England, 2000-2003 **REPRESENTATION** Stephen Bulger Gallery (Toronto) **WEBSITE** www.sunilgupta.net, www.bulgergallery.com

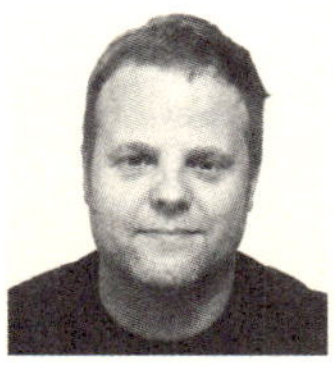

TONI HAFKENSCHEID

BORN Rotterdam, The Netherlands, 1959 **RESIDES** Toronto **EDUCATION** Gerrit Rietveld Academy, Photography, Amsterdam, The Netherlands, 1989 **SELECTED SOLO EXHIBITIONS** [illegible], Marcia Wood Gallery, Atlanta, Georgia, 2005, Aron Packer Gallery, Chicago, 2005, and Robert Birch Gallery Contact Festival, Toronto, 2004 **SELECTED GROUP EXHIBITIONS** *Neverlands*, Maison de la culture Frontenac, Montreal, 2005; *Part/Object*, University of St. Francis, Chicago, 2005 **AWARDS** Toronto Arts Council Grant, 2004; Ontario Arts Council Grant, 2003; Netherlands Arts Council Project Grant, 2002 **WEBSITE** www.thphotos.com

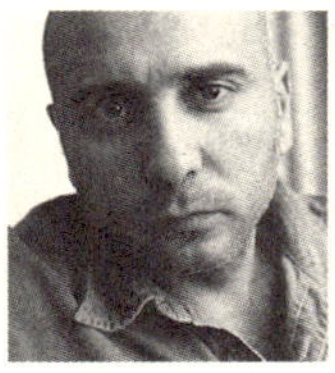

RAWI HAGE

BORN Beirut, Lebanon, 1964 **RESIDES** Montreal **EDUCATION** Concordia University, B.F.A. Major in Photography, Montreal, 1998 **SELECTED SOLO EXHIBITIONS** *Nazar*, 11th Noorderlicht Photofestival, Fries Museum, Leeuwarden, The Netherlands, 2004; *Artistes Against the Occupation*, Chikyu-Do gallery, Tokyo, 2004; *Artistes contre l'occupation*, Montreal [illegible] interculturelle, Montreal, 2003; *In Solidarity*, The Khyber Centre for the Arts, Halifax, 2003 **AWARDS** The Canada Council for the Arts, Visual Arts-Travel Grant, Japan, 2004; Conseil des arts et des lettres du Quebec, Visual Arts-Travel Grant, Carthagena, Colombia, 2000-2001

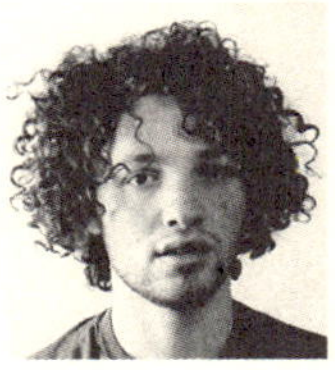

ADAD HANNAH

BORN New York, 1971 **RESIDES** Montreal **EDUCATION** Concordia University, M.F.A., Montreal, 2004; Emily Carr Institute of Art and Design, B.F.A., Vancouver, 1998; Emily Carr College of Art and Design, Fine Arts Diploma, 1994 **SELECTED SOLO EXHIBITIONS** *Cuba Still (Remake)*, Gallery B-312, Montreal, 2005 **SELECTED GROUP EXHIBITIONS** *Room 112*, WRO 05 11th International Media Arts Biennial, Poland, 2005; *Museum Stills*, G39, Cardiff, Wales, 2005; *Museum Stills*, Viper Basel, Basel, Switzerland, 2004; *Stills*, Loop 04, International Video Art Fair, Barcelona, Spain, 2004 **AWARDS** Images Festival Installation/New Media Award, Toronto, 2004; Bogdanka Poznanovic Award for Best Installation or New Media Work, 5th Videomedeja International Video Festival, Novi Sad, Serbia and Montenegro, 2004 **WEBSITE** www.adadhannah.com

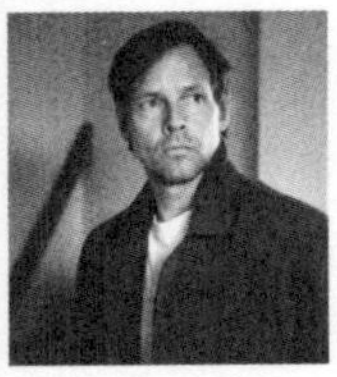

ARNI HARALDSSON

BORN Reykjavik, Iceland, 1958 **RESIDES** Vancouver **EDUCATION** University of British Columbia, M.F.A., Vancouver, 1990; Emily Carr College of Art & Design, Diploma In Interdisciplinary Studies, Vancouver, 1983 **SELECTED SOLO EXHIBITIONS** *Up & Down: Downtown Eastside Architecture*, Artspeak, Vancouver, 2003; *La Tourette*, Galerie Le Bleu du Ciel, Lyon, France, 2002 **SELECTED GROUP EXHIBITIONS** *Real Pictures: Photographs From the Collection of Claudia Beck and Andrew Gruft*, Vancouver Art Gallery, 2005; *Future Cities*, Art Gallery of Hamilton, Hamilton, Ontario, 2004 **BOOKS/PUBLICATIONS** *Up & Down: Downtown Eastside Architecture*, Artspeak, Vancouver, 2003; *La Tourette*, Editions Su-cure Sale, Lyon, France, 2002; *Firminy*, Contemporary Art Gallery, Vancouver, 2001 **AWARDS** Canada Council Creation/Production Grant, 2004; Canada Council Travel Grant, 2002; Conseil des arts et des lettres du Quebec, Research & Creation Grant, 2000

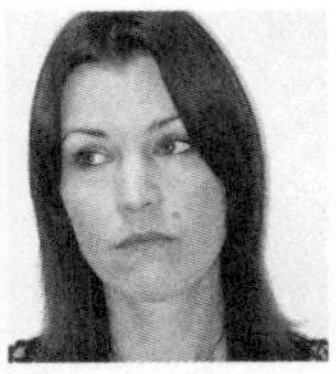

ISABELLE HAYEUR

BORN Montreal, 1969 **RESIDES** Montreal **EDUCATION** Université du Quebec à Montreal, M.F.A., Montreal, 2002; Université du Quebec à Montreal, B.F.A., Montreal, 1996 **SELECTED SOLO EXHIBITIONS** *America y america: conversaciones polares*, Galeria Arte X Arte (Fundacion Luz y Alonzo Castillo), Buenos Aires, Argentina, 2005; *Verge*, Agnes Etherington Art Centre, Kingston, Ontario, and Prefix ICA, Toronto, 2005; *Destinations*, Massachusetts Museum of Contemporary Art, North Adams, Massachusetts, 2004–2005 **SELECTED GROUP EXHIBITIONS** *Territoires urbains*, Musée d'art contemporain de Montreal, 2005–2006 **BOOKS/PUBLICATIONS** *Territoires urbains*, Musée d'art contemporain de Montreal, 2005; *Destinations*, Centre de recherche urbaine de Montreal, 2004 **AWARDS** OFQJ-Champ Libre Prize, 2004; The Contact Prize for Emerging Photography Artist, 2001 **WEBSITE** www.isabelle-hayeur.com

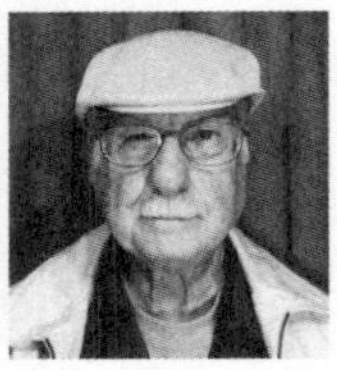

DAVE HEATH

BORN Philadelphia, Pennsylvania, 1931 **RESIDES** Toronto **SELECTED SOLO EXHIBITIONS** *Dave Heath*, Hereford Photography Festival, Hereford, England, 2002; *Dave Heath*, Howard Greenberg Gallery, New York, 2001; *Dave Heath: 1940s to 1960s*, Stephen Bulger Gallery, Toronto, 2000 **SELECTED GROUP EXHIBITIONS** *Wonderland*, Noorderlicht, The Netherlands, 1999 **BOOKS/PUBLICATIONS** *Dave Heath's Art Show*, Anonymous Press, 2005; *Korec*, Lumiere Press, 2004; *A Dialogue With Solitude*, Community Press, 1965, Lumiere Press, 2000; *Extempore*, Lumiere Press, 1988 **REPRESENTATION** Stephen Bulger Gallery (Toronto) **WEBSITES** www.photographerinterviews.ifihadahifi.com, www.bulgergallery.com

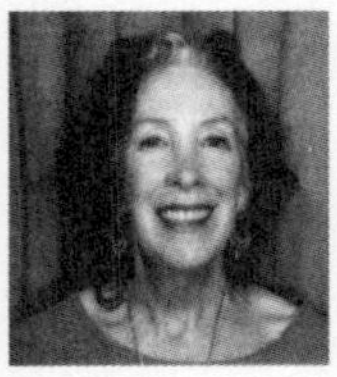

MARTHA HENRICKSON

BORN U.S.A., 1942 **RESIDES** Toronto **EDUCATION** Brooklyn Museum Art School, 1960; Arts Student League, 1965 **SELECTED SOLO EXHIBITIONS** *View From a Train*, Jane Corkin Gallery, Toronto, 2000 **BOOKS/PUBLICATIONS** *Awakenings*, by Thomas and Martha Henrickson, Arterial Books, Toronto, 1977; *The Organic Zucchini*, by Thomas and Martha Henrickson, Arterial Books, Toronto, 1977 **AWARDS** Ontario Arts Council, 1988, 1985 and 1984; Canada Council, 1987 **REPRESENTATION** Corkin Shopland Gallery (Toronto) **WEBSITE** www.corkinshopland.com

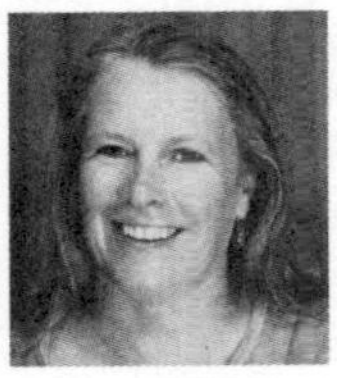

APRIL HICKOX

BORN Toronto, 1955 **RESIDES** Toronto **EDUCATION** Ontario College of Art and Design, AOCA, Graduate Studies Program, Photography and Printmaking, Toronto, 1977 **SELECTED SOLO EXHIBITIONS** *April Hickox: Point Pelee*, Billboard, Exhibition and DVD, Art Gallery of Windsor, Windsor, Ontario, 2003; *Landscape and Memory*, Leo Kamen Gallery, Toronto, 2003; *Porcelain, Crystal, Glass*, Leo Kamen Gallery, Toronto, 2002; *Glance*, Leo Kamen Gallery, Toronto, 2001 **SELECTED GROUP EXHIBITIONS** *Evoking Place*, Robert McLaughlin Gallery, Oshawa, Ontario, 2003; *Reality of the Fantasy: Truth and the Photographic Image*, curated by Shirley Madill, Art Gallery of Hamilton, Hamilton, Ontario, 2002; *Evoking Place*, McMaster Museum of Art, Hamilton, Ontario, 2002; *Evoking Place*, Canadian Museum of Contemporary Photography, Ottawa, 2001; *Photography Narrative*, Art Gallery of Ontario, Toronto 2001; *The Very Image*, Harbourfront Centre, Toronto, 2002; *Our Voices*, The Ryerson Gallery, Toronto, 2000; *Landscape Photography*, Tom Thomson Memorial Gallery, Owen Sound, Ontario, 2000 **BOOKS/PUBLICATIONS** *When the Mind Hears*, Vu centre d'animation et de diffusion de la photographie, Quebec, 1995 **AWARDS** Ontario Arts Council Senior Artist Grant, 2004; Canada Council B Grant, 2001 and 1998 **WEBSITE** www.aprilhickox.com

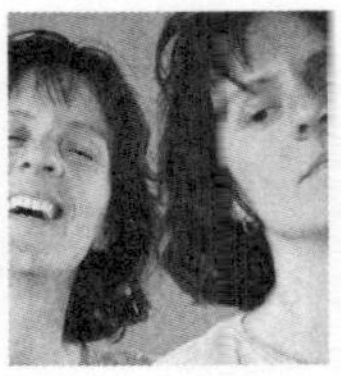

BETTINA HOFFMANN

BORN Berlin, Germany, 1964 **RESIDES** Montreal **EDUCATION** Hochschule der Künste, M.F.A., Berlin, Germany, 1992; California Institute of the Arts, Los Angeles, 1990 **SELECTED SOLO EXHIBITIONS** *La Ronde*, Galerie Michael Cosar, Düsseldorf, Germany, 2005; *Loop*, Video Art Fair, Gallery Michael Cosar, Barcelona, Spain, 2004; *Spoilsport/Trouble-fête*, Liane and Danny Taran Gallery, Saidye Bronfman Centre, Montreal, 2004; *The Social Reason*, Gallery TPW, Toronto, 2003 **SELECTED GROUP EXHIBITIONS** *Document*, Kunsthalle Dominikanerkirche, Osnabrück, Germany, 2005; *Sans souci*, Gallery B-312, Montreal, 2004 **BOOKS/PUBLICATIONS** *Feintes, doutes & fictions: réflexions sur la photographie et les nouvelles technologies*, Éditions J'ai VU, 2005; *Autoportraits dans la photographie canadienne contemporaine*, Éditions J'ai VU, 2004; *Spoilsport/Trouble-fête*, Liane and Danny Taran Gallery, Montreal, Saidye Bronfman Centre for the Arts, Montreal 2004; *Ich bin ich weil mein kleiner Hund mich kennt*, Copyright, Berlin, 2002; *Fotografie an der Schwelle zum neuen Jahrtausend*, Staatliche Galerie Moritzburg Halle, 2000 **AWARDS** Canada Arts Council Grant, 2005; Special Award (Video La ronde), VAD Festival Internacional de Vídeo i Arts Digitals, Girona, Spain, 2004; Conseil des arts et des lettres du Quebec Grant, 2003 **WEBSITE** www.bettinahoffmann.net

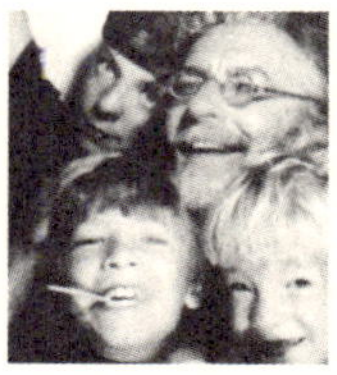

THADDEUS HOLOWNIA

BORN Bury Saint Edmunds, England, 1949 **RESIDES** Moncton **EDUCATION** B.A., Communications and Fine Arts, University of Windsor, 1972; Professor and Head of the Faculty of Fine Arts, Mount Allison University, 1977 **SELECTED SOLO EXHIBITIONS** *The Newfoundland Project*, Art Gallery of Newfoundland and Labrador, 2006; *Walden Pond Revisited*, Corkin Shopland Gallery, Toronto, 2004-2005; *Extended Vision*, Centro de la Imagen, Mexico City; Tom Thomson Gallery, Owen Sound, Ontario; McMichael Canadian Art Collection, Kleinberg, Ontario; Beaverbrook Art Gallery, Fredericton; St. Mary's University Art Gallery, Halifax; Owens Art Gallery, Mount Allison University, Sackville, N.B.; Art Gallery of South Western Manitoba, Brandon, Manitoba; Canadian Museum of Contemporary Photography, Ottawa, 1998-2002; *Drawing With Light*, Calgary Science Centre; Art Gallery of Nova Scotia, Halifax; The Canadian Museum of Contemporary Photography, Ottawa, 2000-2001 **BOOKS/PUBLICATIONS** *Dykelands*, with poems by Douglas Lochhead, McGill-Queen's University Press, Montreal, 1989; *Anatomy of a Pipeline*, text by Robert Enright, Owens Art Gallery, Sackville, N.B., 2003; *Extended Vision: The Photography of Thaddeus Holownia 1975-1997*, Canadian Museum of Contemporary Photography, Ottawa, 1998; *Beau*, Canadian Museum of Contemporary Photography, Ottawa, 1992; *Eight Landscape Photographers*, McMichael Gallery, Kleinburg, Ontario, 1991; *Headlighting*, text by Penny Cousineau, Mount St. Vincent University Art Gallery, Halifax, 1991; *Walden Pond Revisited*, Corkin Shopland Gallery, Toronto, 2004 **REPRESENTATION** Corkin Shopland Gallery (Toronto) **WEBSITE** www.corkinshopland.com

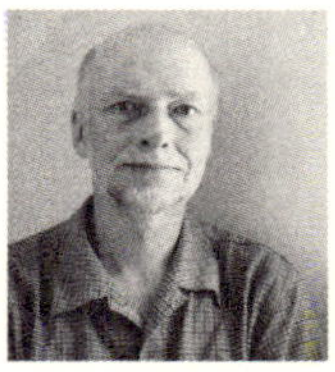

VID INGELEVICS

BORN Toronto, 1952 **RESIDES** Toronto **EDUCATION** M.F.A. Programme, York University, Toronto, 2005-Present **SELECTED SOLO EXHIBITIONS** Stephen Bulger Gallery, Toronto, 2006; Public art installation, Museum Subway Station, Contact Photography Festival, Toronto, 2004; Stephen Bulger Gallery, Toronto, 2001; Koffler Gallery, Toronto, 2000 **SELECTED GROUP EXHIBITIONS** *The Space of Making*, Neuer Berliner Kunstverein, Berlin, 2005; *Mémoire morte, mémoire vive*, Dazibao, Montreal, 2002; *Substitute City*, Power Plant, Toronto, 2001; *Photography and Engagement*, Foto Biënnale Rotterdam, Nederlands Foto Instituut, Rotterdam, The Netherlands, 2000 **REPRESENTATION** Stephen Bulger Gallery (Toronto) **WEBSITES** www.web.net/artinfact, www.bulgergallery.com

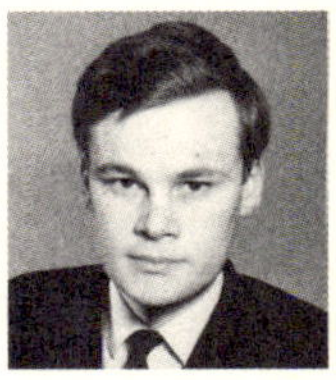

GEOFFREY JAMES

BORN St. Asaph, Wales, 1942 **RESIDES** Toronto **EDUCATION** Self-taught **SELECTED SOLO EXHIBITIONS** *Forgotten Zones*, Americas Society, New York, 2004; *Past, Present, Future*, University Art Centre, University of Toronto, 2003 **SELECTED GROUP EXHIBITIONS** *Deceits and Fantasies*, *Contemporary Photography and the Garden*, American Federation of Art (travelling to various U.S. museums), New York, 2004; *Future Cities*, Art Gallery of Hamilton, Hamilton, Ontario, 2004 **BOOKS/PUBLICATIONS** *Past, Present, Future*, University Art Centre, Toronto, 2003; *Place*, Douglas & McIntyre, Vancouver, 2001; *Paris*, Collection de L'Esplanade, Paris, 2001 **AWARDS** The Gershon Iskowitz Prize, 2002; The Roloff Beny Prize, 2002 **REPRESENTATION** Nicholas Metivier Gallery (Toronto) **WEBSITE** www.metiviergallery.com

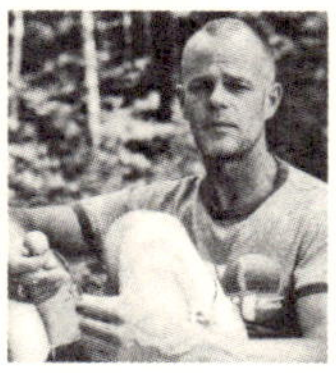

LOUIS JONCAS

BORN Winnipeg, 1959 **RESIDES** Montreal **EDUCATION** University of Ottawa, B.F.A., 1994; Concordia University, M.F.A., Montreal, 2004 **SELECTED SOLO EXHIBITIONS** *Naturels*, Pierre-Francois Ouellette Art Contemporain, Montreal, 2004 **SELECTED GROUP EXHIBITIONS** *La Manif d'art 3*, La Biennial de Quebec, Montreal, 2005; *Dead Nature*, The Ottawa Art Gallery, Ottawa, 2005; *Nature Rearranged*, organized by the National Gallery of Canada, Mackenzie Art Gallery, Regina; Beaverbrook Museum, Fredericton; Joliette Museum of Art, Joliette, Quebec, 1999-2000 *Rituals and Transformations*, National Gallery of Canada Ottawa, 1995 **WEBSITE** www.pfoac.com

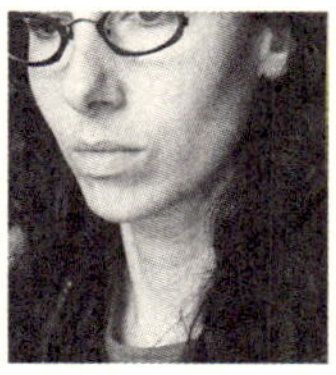

LISA KLAPSTOCK

BORN Kamloops, B.C., 1968 **RESIDES** Toronto **EDUCATION** Self-taught in photography; Simon Fraser University, B.A. in Communications, Vancouver, 1994 **SELECTED EXHIBITIONS** *Threshold*, I Space, Chicago, 2006; *liminal*, Kamloops Art Gallery, Kamloops, B.C., 2006; *Threshold*, Musée de la Photographie, Charleroi, Belgium, 2005; *liminal*, Southern Alberta Art Gallery, Lethbridge, Alberta, 2004; *Threshold*, VU Centre de Diffusion et de Production de la Photographie, Quebec, 2004; *Living Room*, Odense Photo Triennial Denmark, 2003 **BOOKS/PUBLICATIONS** *Lisa Klapstock: liminal* by Alison Nordstrom and Scott McLeod, co-published by Southern Alberta Art Gallery, Kamloops Art Gallery, and Tom Thomson Memorial Art Gallery, 2006 **WEBSITE** www.lisaklapstock.com

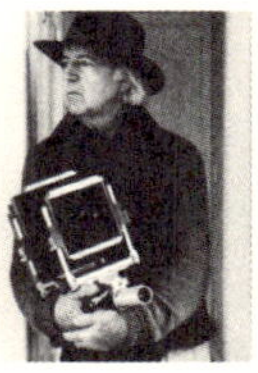

ERIC KLEMM

BORN Wadern, Germany, 1939 **RESIDES** Salt Spring Island, B.C. **EDUCATION** Art School Trier, Germany, 1956-19[illegible] **RECENT EXHIBITIONS** *Photo Synthesis*, Art Spring Gallery, Salt Spring Island, B.C., 2005; *Metamorphosis*, [illegible] Wagner Contemporary, Toronto, 2005, and Gallery Jones, Vancouver, 2005; *Artists for Tsunami Victims*, Salt Spring Island, B.C., 2005 **WEBSITE** www.ericklemm.com

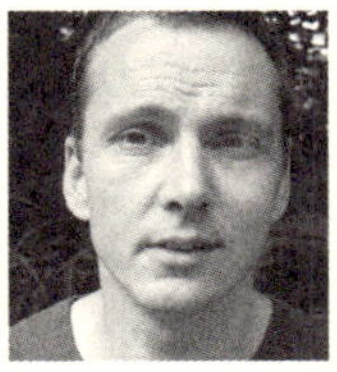

THOMAS KNEUBÜHLER

BORN Solothurn, Switzerland, 1963 **RESIDES** Montreal **EDUCATION** Concordia University, M.F.A., Montreal, 2003 **SELECTED SOLO EXHIBITIONS** *Plattform*, VU Centre de Diffusion et de Production de la Photographie, Quebec City, 2005; *Skol*, Centre des Arts Actuel, Montreal, 2004 **SELECTED GROUP EXHIBITIONS** *VIA Conception*, Friederichsbau, Biel, Germany, 2004; *Lieux anthropiques*, Casa Vallarta, Guadalajara, Mexico, 2003 **AWARDS** Conseil des arts et des lettres du Quebec, Bourse de Création, 2005; Canada Council for the Arts, Production Grant, 2004 **WEBSITE** www.voxphoto.com

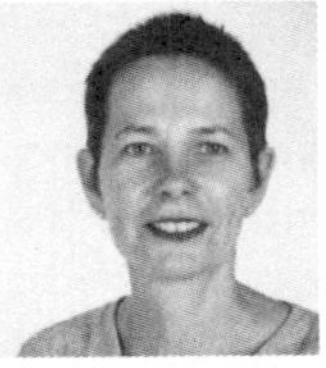

KATHERINE KNIGHT

BORN Ottawa, 1955 **RESIDES** Toronto **EDUCATION** University of Victoria, M.F.A., 1984; Nova Scotia College of Art and Design, B.F.A., Halifax, 1980 **SELECTED SOLO EXHIBITIONS** *Buoy*, L'Été photographique de Lectoure, Lectoure, France, 2005; *Wind and Water*, Ottawa Art Gallery, 2004; *Aerostat*, Michel Gibson Gallery, London, Ontario, 2001; *I became unconscious*, Museum London, London, Ontario, 2001 **AWARDS** Duke and Duchess of York Prize, 2000 **WEBSITE** www.kmknight.com

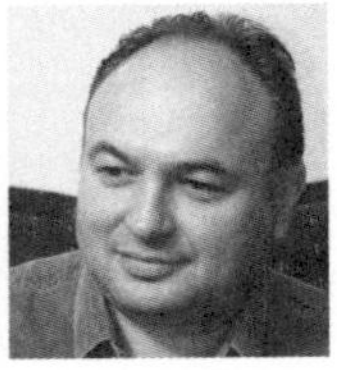

VICTOR KORCHENKO

BORN Krasnodar, Russia, 1961 **RESIDES** Oakville, Ontario **EDUCATION** Self-taught **SELECTED SOLO EXHIBITION** *Forest*, Yakut Gallery, Moscow, 1993 **SELECTED GROUP EXHIBITION** *Found on Volga*, Rutgers University, New Jersey, 1992 **WEBSITE** www.korchenko.com

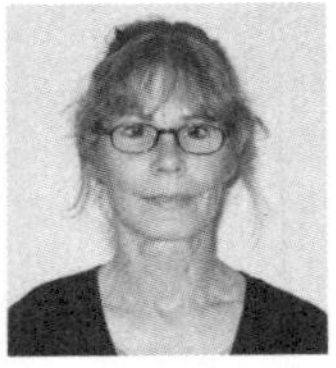

SUZY LAKE

BORN Detroit, Michigan, 1947 **RESIDES** Toronto **EDUCATION** Concordia University, M.F.A., Montreal, 1980 **SELECTED SOLO EXHIBITIONS** *L'Été photographique de Lectoure*, Centre de Photographie, Lectoure, France, 2005; *Suzy Lake 1973–2005*, Hallwalls Gallery, Buffalo, New York, 2005; *Whatcha Really Really Want...*, Paul Petro Contemporary Art, Toronto, 2004; *Attitudes et Comportements*, Musee Regionale du Rimouski, Rimouski, Quebec, 2002 **SELECTED GROUP EXHIBITIONS** *WHACK! The Feminist Revolution 1965–1980*, Los Angeles Museum of Contemporary Art, 2006; *Lecture Notes*, Mount Saint Vincent University Gallery, Halifax, 2004; *Identities: Canadian Portraits*, McMichael Canadian Art Collection, Kleinburg, Ontario, 2004; *Point and Shoot*, Dazibao Gallery, Montreal, 2004 **BOOKS/PUBLICATIONS** *Faking Death: Canadian Art Photography Since 1955* by Penny Cousineau-Levine, McGill-Queen's University Press, 2003; *Canadian Art in the Twentieth Century*, by Joan Murray, Dundurn Press, Toronto, 1999; *Journal of Canadian Studies*, Refiguring Wilderness, Vol. 33, No. 2, Authority is an Attribute...Revisited, 1999 **AWARDS** Canada Council Experienced Artist Grant, 2005; Canada Council Travel Grant, 2005; Foreign Affairs Exhibition Grant, 2005; Canada Council Experienced Artist Grant, 2003; Chalmers Development Award, Ontario Arts Council, 2002; Ontario Arts Council Exhibition Assistance Grant, 2002

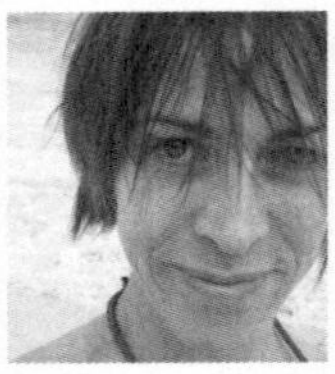

LAURA LETINSKY

BORN Winnipeg, 1962 **RESIDES** Chicago, Illinois **EDUCATION** Yale University, M.F.A., New Haven, Connecticut, 1991; University of Manitoba, B.F.A., Winnipeg, 1986 **SELECTED SOLO EXHIBITIONS** *Now, Again*, Galerie Kusseneers, Antwerp, Belgium, 2005; *Hardly More Than Ever*, Edwynn Houk Gallery, New York, and Stephen Bulger Gallery, Toronto, 2004; *Laura Letinsky*, Bank Art, Los Angeles, 2004 **SELECTED GROUP EXHIBITIONS** *Truth Matters: The Meaning of Objects*, Houston Center of Photography, Houston, Texas, 2004; *Locating Intimacy: The Space Between*, SF Camerawork, San Francisco, 2000 **BOOKS/PUBLICATIONS** *Now, Again*, Galerie Kusseneers, 2005; *Hardly More Than Ever*, The Renaissance Society, 2004; *Eating Architecture*, Ed. Jamie Horwitz and Paulette Singley, MIT Press, Massachusetts, 2004; *Blink*, Phaidon Press, 2002; *Venus Inferred*, University of Chicago Press, 2000 **AWARDS** Richard Driehaus Foundation Award, 2003; John Simon Guggenheim Fellowship, 2002; Anonymous Was a Woman Award, 2001 **REPRESENTATION** Stephen Bulger Gallery (Toronto) **WEBSITES** www.edwynnhoukgallery.com, www.bulgergallery.com

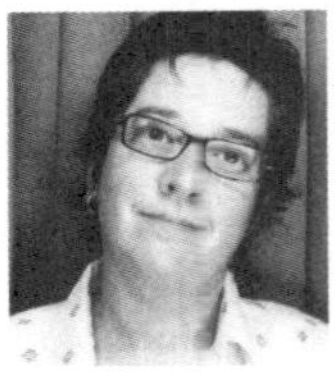

NINA LEVITT

BORN Toronto, 1955 **RESIDES** Toronto **EDUCATION** University of Illinois, M.F.A., Chicago, 1997 **SELECTED SOLO EXHIBITIONS** *Little Breeze*, Doris McCarthy Gallery, University of Toronto, 2004; *Little Breeze*, Oboro, Montreal, 2004 **SELECTED GROUP EXHIBITIONS** *The Uncanny: Experiments in Cyborg Culture*, Mendel Art Gallery, Saskatoon, 2003; *The Found & the Familiar: Snapshots in Contemporary Canadian Art*, Confederation Art Centre, Charlottetown, 2003 **BOOKS/PUBLICATIONS** *Gravity + Duet: Video Installations*, Toronto Photographers Workshop, 1999 **WEBSITES** www.ninalevitt.com, www.oboro.tv, www.ccca.ca

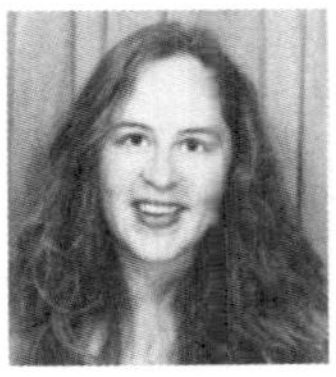

JENNIFER LONG

BORN Comox, B.C., 1974 **RESIDES** Toronto **EDUCATION** Ryerson University, B.A.A. in Photography, Toronto, 1998 **SELECTED SOLO EXHIBITIONS** *A Selection of Doubts*, Galerie Poller, Frankfurt am Main, Germany, 2005; *Shifting*, Luft Gallery, Toronto, 2004; *bedded*, ODD Gallery, Dawson City, Yukon, 2003 **SELECTED GROUP EXHIBITIONS** *extreme*, Station Gallery, Mousonturm, Frankfurt, Germany, 2004; *Body of Water*, Luft Gallery, Toronto, 2002; *Punch*, LEE Ka-sing Gallery, Toronto, 2001 **AWARDS** Emerging Artist Project Grant, Ontario Arts Council, 2004; Emerging Artist Project Grant, Canada Council for the Arts, 2003 **WEBSITE** www.jenniferlong.ca

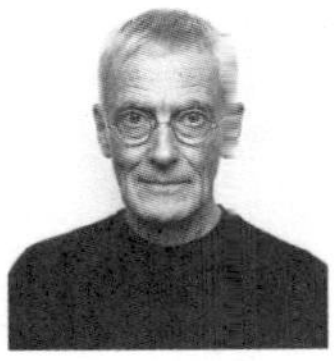

ARNAUD MAGGS

BORN Montreal, 1926 **RESIDES** Toronto **SELECTED SOLO EXHIBITIONS** *Werner's Nomenclature of Colours*, Susan Hobbs Gallery, Toronto, 2005; *Joseph Beuys, 100 Profile Views*, Art Gallery of Hamilton, Hamilton, Ontario, 2005; *Christo*, Art Gallery of Ontario, Toronto, 2005; *Dusseldorf Photographs*, Goethe Institute, Toronto, 2004; *Orford String Quartet*, Agnes Etherington Art Centre, Kingston, Ontario, 2004; Susan Hobbs Gallery, Toronto, 2003 and 2001; *Arnaud Maggs: Notes Capitales*, Canadian Cultural Centre, Paris, France, 2000 **SELECTED GROUP EXHIBITIONS** *Facing History*, Wharf Centre d'art contemporain de Basse-normandie, Hérouville Saint-Clair, France, 2005; *Making Faces: The Death of the Portrait*, Hayward Gallery, London, England, 2004; *Facing History*, Canadian Cultural Centre, Paris, France, 2004; *Identities: Canadian Portraits*, McMichael Canadian Art Collection, Kleinburg, Ontario, 2004; *Je t'envisage*, Musée de l'Elysée, Lausanne, Switzerland, 2004; *The Bigger Picture: Portraits From Ottawa*, The Ottawa Art Gallery, 2003; *Facing History*, Presentation House, Vancouver, 2001; *2000 and Counting, Part II*, National Gallery of Canada, Ottawa, 2001; *Memory: Transcribing Loss*, Art Gallery of Victoria, 2001; *The Bigger Picture: Contemporary Photography Reconsidered*, Art Gallery of Ontario, Toronto, 2001; Susan Hobbs Gallery, Toronto, 2001; *Mémoire et archive*, Musée d'art contemporain, Montreal, 2000; *Logo City*, Blackwood Gallery, Mississauga, Ontario, 2000 **BOOKS/PUBLICATIONS** *Arnaud Maggs: Notes Capitales*, Catherine Bedard and Russell Keziere, Canadian Cultural Centre, Paris, 2000; *Facing History: Portraits From Vancouver*, Vancouver: Presentation House Gallery/Arsenal Pulp Press, 2002; *Facing History: Portraits From Vancouver*, Canadian Cultural Centre, Paris, 2004; *The Bigger Picture: Portraits From Ottawa*, Ottawa Art Gallery, 2004; *Logo City*, Barbara Fischer, Blackwood Gallery, Toronto, 2000 **AWARDS** Lynch-Staunton Award, The Canada Council, 1984; Gershon Iskowitz Prize, 1991; Toronto Arts Award (Visual Arts), 1992 **REPRESENTATION** Susan Hobbs Gallery (Toronto) **COLLECTION** The Robert McLaughlin Gallery (Oshawa) **WEBSITE** www.susanhobbs.com

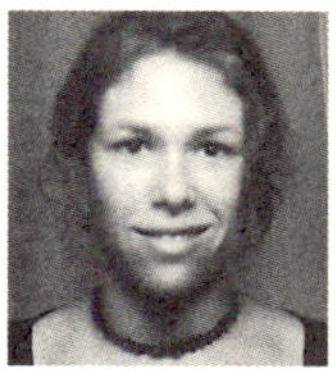

AMANDA MARCHAND

BORN Montreal, 1968 **RESIDES** New York and Montreal **EDUCATION** San Francisco Art Institute, M.F.A. in Photography, San Francisco, 2001; Queen's University, B.A. in Literature, Kingston, Ontario, 1990 **SELECTED SOLO EXHIBITIONS** *The Density of Air*, Bolinas Art Gallery, Bolinas, California, 2005; *415/514*, San Francisco City Hall, San Francisco, 2004; Traywick Gallery, Berkeley, California, 2003 **SELECTED GROUP EXHIBITIONS** *New Faces in Contemporary Art*, Gallery 44, Kansas City, Missouri, 2004 **AWARDS** Grant recipient, Conseil des arts et des lettres du Quebec, 2005; MacDowell Colony fellow and grant recipient, New Hampshire, Massachusetts, 2004; Headlands Center for the Arts, Residency/M.F.A. Studio Award, Marin, California, 2001-2003; Merit Scholarship, San Francisco Art Institute, 1999-2001 **WEBSITE** www.traywick.com/gallery/marchand

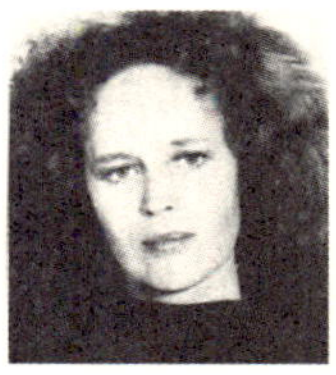

CAROL MARINO

BORN U.S.A., 1943 **RESIDES** Algonquin Park **EDUCATION** University of Pittsburgh, Creative Writing, B.A., 1964 **SELECTED SOLO EXHIBITIONS** *Nonfoundland*, Corkin Shopland Gallery, Toronto, 2006; *New Work*, Jane Corkin Gallery, Toronto, 2001; *From the Collection: Flowerpieces*, Canadian Museum of Contemporary Photography, 2000; *Flora Photographica: The Flower in Photography From 1835 to the Present* (travelling exhibition), Curator: William Ewing, 1992-1994; Musée des beaux-art, Montreal; Vancouver Art Gallery **BOOKS/PUBLICATIONS** *Life Forces, Photographs by Carol Marino*, Edited by Michael Bell, 1987; *The Female Eye*, The National Film Board, Ottawa, 1975; *12 Canadians, Contemporary Canadian Photography*, edited by Jane Corkin, 1980 **REPRESENTATION** Corkin Shopland Gallery (Toronto) **WEBSITE** www.corkinshopland.com

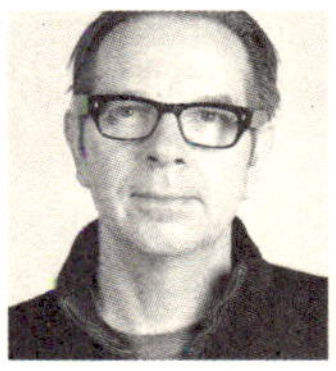

JOHN MASSEY

BORN Toronto, 1950 **RESIDES** Toronto **EDUCATION** Ontario College of Art, Experimental Arts, Toronto, 1974 **SELECTED SOLO EXHIBITIONS** *This Land*, Canadian Cultural Centre, Paris, 2005; *This Land*, The Spoke Club, Toronto, 2005; *As the Hammer Strikes*, Contemporary Art Gallery, Vancouver, 2005; *Phantoms of the Modern*, Bailey Fine Art, Toronto, 2004; *The House That Jack Built* (retrospective), Canadian Museum of Contemporary Photography, Ottawa, 2004; Galerie de l'UQAM, Montreal, 2005 **SELECTED GROUP EXHIBITIONS** *This Much is Certain*, Royal College of Art, London, England, 2004; *The Possibility of the Impossible*, Frankfurter Kunstverein, Frankfurt, Germany, 2003 **BOOKS/PUBLICATIONS** *Phantoms of the Modern*, Bailey Fine Art, Toronto, 2005; *The House That Jack Built*, Canadian Museum of Contemporary Photography, Ottawa, 2004; *Once Upon a Time*, Olga Korper Gallery, Toronto, 2000

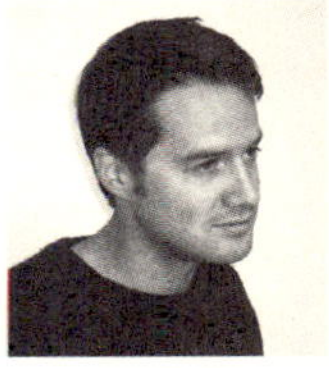

SCOTT MCFARLAND

BORN Hamilton, Ontario, 1975 **RESIDES** Vancouver **EDUCATION** University of British Columbia, B.F.A., Vancouver, 1997 **SELECTED SOLO EXHIBITIONS** *Another Photography*, Regan Projects, Los Angeles, 2005; *Gardens*, Monte Clark Gallery, Vancouver/Toronto, 2004 **SELECTED GROUP EXHIBITIONS** *Faking Death*, Jack Shainman Gallery, New York, 2006; *Clickdoubleclick*, Haus der Kunst, Munich, Germany, 2006 **BOOKS/PUBLICATIONS** *Coastal Cabin*, Contemporary Art Gallery, Vancouver, 2003; *Zeitgenossische Fotokunst Aus Kanada*, NBK, Berlin, Germany, 2005 **REPRESENTATION** Monte Clark Gallery (Vancouver, Toronto) **WEBSITE** www.monteclarkgallery.com

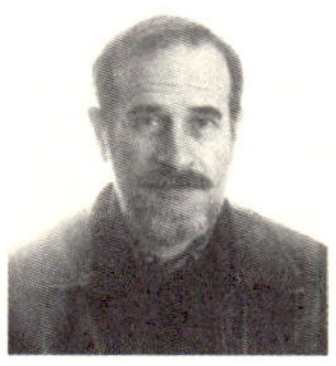

DAVID MILLER

BORN Montreal, 1949 **RESIDES** Montreal **EDUCATION** Self-taught **SELECTED SOLO EXHIBITIONS** *Arizona Landscapes*, Eleanor London Library, Montreal, 2004 **SELECTED GROUP EXHIBITIONS** *Obsolescence*, Centre de la Culture Marie-Uguay, Montreal, 2005; *The 60s—Montreal Thinks Big*, Canadian Centre for Architecture, Montreal, 2004; *Bringing to Order: Form and Expression*, CMCP, Ottawa, 2002 **BOOKS/PUBLICATIONS** *The 60s—Montreal Thinks Big*, Canadian Centre for Architecture, Montreal, 2004; *Regards sur un paysage industriel: le canal de Lachine*, Centre Canadien d'Architecture, Montreal, 1992; *An Industrial Landscape Observed: The Lachine Canal*, Canadian Centre for Architecture, Montreal, 1992; *L'or et la pierre: Un régard critique sur l'architecture des banques*, Centre Canadien d'Architecture, Montreal, 1991 **WEBSITE** www.voxphoto.com

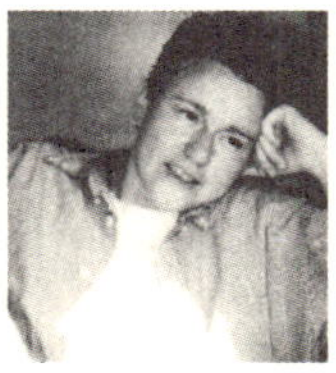

LORI NEWDICK

BORN Canada, 1968 **RESIDES** Toronto **EDUCATION** University of Guelph, M.F.A. Photography, 1999-2001; Ontario College of Art & Design, Toronto, Photography (Honours) 1996-1999; University of Toronto, Philosophy and English Literature, 1988-1991 **SELECTED SOLO EXHIBITIONS** *Lucky*, Corkin Shopland Gallery, Toronto, 2005; *Lure*, Kamloops Art Gallery, Kamloops, B.C., 2003; *Felonious*, Macdonald Stewart Art Centre Gallery, Guelph, Ontario, 2001; *Faculty Show*, University of Western Ontario, London, Ontario, 2002; *Future/Perfect*, Center for Photography at Woodstock, Woodstock, New York, 2000 **BOOKS/PUBLICATIONS** *Glimpse*, Lori Newdick, Gallery TPW, Toronto, 2002; *Felonious: Lori Newdick*, Macdonald Stewart Art Centre Gallery, Guelph, Ontario, 2001; *Desire*, Bedlam, OCAD Press, Toronto, 19[illegible]; *Women & Desire*, Bedlam, OCAD Press, Toronto, 19[illegible]; *Erotica*, Bedlam, OCAD Press, Toronto, 1997; *Representations Suites*, Flux, Laser Reproductions, Toronto, 19[illegible] **AWARDS** Canadian Federation of University Women Graduate Scholarship, 2000; Ontario Graduate Scholarship, 2000; University of Guelph Board of Graduate Studies Scholarship, 2000; Graduate Studio Scholarship, Professional Art Dealers Association of Canada, 2000; University of Guelph Graduate Entrance Fellowship, 1999; University of Guelph Board of Graduate Studies Research Scholarship, 19[illegible]; University of Guelph Delpha Award, 1999; University of Guelph Board of Graduate Studies Scholarship, 19[illegible]; OCAD Medal of Excellence in Photography, 1999; OCAD Student Union Scholarship for Excellence, 1999; Agfa Canada Photography Scholarship, 1999; Eugene A. Pogetta Excellence in Photography Scholarship, 19[illegible]; Dorothy Hoover Research Scholarship Honourable Mention, 1999; Polaroid Canada Photography Scholarship, 19[illegible]; Nora E. Vaughan Excellence in Photography Scholarship, 1998 **REPRESENTATION** Corkin Shopland Gallery (Toronto) **WEBSITE** www.corkinshopland.com

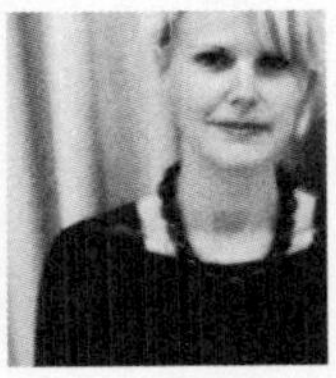

LINDSAY PAGE

BORN Toronto, 1974 **RESIDES** Chicago **EDUCATION** School of the Art Institute of Chicago, M.F.A., Chicago, 2004-Present; Ryerson University, B.F.A., Toronto, 2003 **SELECTED GROUP EXHIBITIONS** *Disappearing Acts*, Gallery TPW, Toronto, 2003; *Punch*, LEE Ka-sing Gallery, Toronto, 2004; *Collections*, Photo Passage, Toronto, 2003; *Bindings*, Luft Gallery, Toronto, 2004 **WEBSITE** www.lindsaypage.com

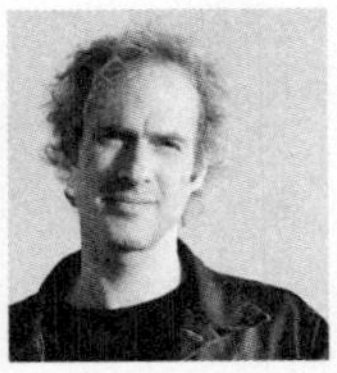

ALAIN PAIEMENT

BORN Montreal, 1960 **RESIDES** Montreal **EDUCATION** Université du Quebec a Montreal, M.F.A. in Visual Arts, 1987; Université du Quebec a Montreal, B.F.A. in Visual Arts, 1983 **SELECTED SOLO EXHIBITIONS** *Interior Views*, Leo Kamen Gallery, Toronto, 2004; *Le monde en chantier*, Musée national des beaux-arts du Quebec, Quebec, 2004; *Surfacing*, Tinglado 2, Tarragona, Spain, 2004; *Living Chaos*, Presentation House, Vancouver, 2004 **SELECTED GROUP EXHIBITIONS** *Faking Death*, Jack Shainman Gallery, New York, 2006; *The Space of Making*, Neuer Berliner Kunstverein, Berlin, 2005; *Espaces Vitaux/Extravagances*, Aeroport Trudeau, Dorval, Montreal, 2004-2005; *La vie, c'est la vie : plaisir, passions, émotions*, La Biennial de Montreal, 2002 **AWARDS** Gold Medal, Homes & Gardens, National Magazine Awards, 2004; Prix Grafika, Montreal (Museum Exhibition Design) 2003; Prix Louis Comtois, Montreal, 2002 **WEBSITE** www.alainpaiement.com

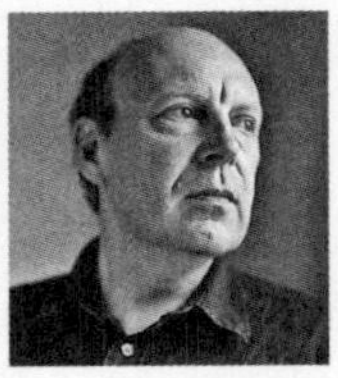

STEVE PAYNE

BORN Harbour Grace, Newfoundland, 1953 **RESIDES** Toronto **EDUCATION** Memorial University of Newfoundland, General Arts, St. John's, Newfoundland, 1974; Ryerson Polytechnical Institute, Photographic Arts, Toronto, 1977 **SELECTED SOLO EXHIBITIONS** *Motel*, Prefix Institute of Contemporary Art, Toronto, 2003; *House Music*, Robert Birch Gallery, Toronto, 2002; *Seas of Leaving*, The Photo Passage, Toronto, 2001; *Motel*, Robert Birch Gallery, Toronto, 1996 **AWARDS** Ontario Arts Council Grants: 2001, 1996, 1994 **WEBSITE** www.stevepaynephoto.com

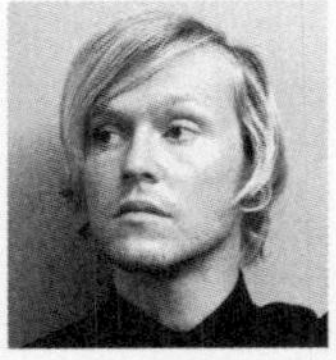

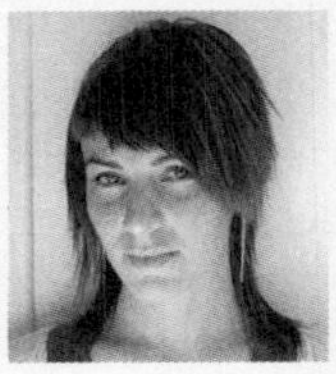

NICHOLAS & SHEILA PYE

BORN Nicholas—Torquay, England, 1976; Sheila—Hamilton, Ontario, 1978 **RESIDE** Toronto **EDUCATION** Nicholas—Ontario College of Art and Design, Undergraduate Degree in Photography, Toronto; Concordia University, M.F.A. in Cinema Production, Montreal; Sheila—Ontario College of Art and Design, Undergraduate Degree in Integrated Media, Toronto; Concordia University, M.F.A. in Cinema Production, Montreal; The Canadian Film Centre, Director's Lab Program **SELECTED EXHIBITIONS** European Media Arts Festival, Osnabruck, Germany, 2005; Sixtyseven Gallery, New York, 2005; *Almost Young*, Angell Gallery, Toronto, 2005; *Rencontres internationals, Paris/Berlin*, Paris, 2005; 404 Arte Contemporanea, Naples, Italy, 2006 **AWARDS** De Seve Graduate Award, 2005; European Media Arts Festival, Best of Selection, for *The Paper Wall*, 2005; Canadian Film Centre's Worldwide Short Film Festival, Best Experimental Film, 2004; Ontario-Quebec Exchange Fellowship, Full Graduate School Scholarship, 2004 and 2003; Mel Hoppenheim School of Cinema Cinematic Excellence Award, 2004; Toronto Outdoor Art Exhibition, Best in Show Photography, 2002; Photography Faculty Award, OCAD, 2002; Photography Students Choice Award, OCAD, 2001; George A. Reid Award, OCAD, 2000 **WEBSITE** www.nickandsheila.com

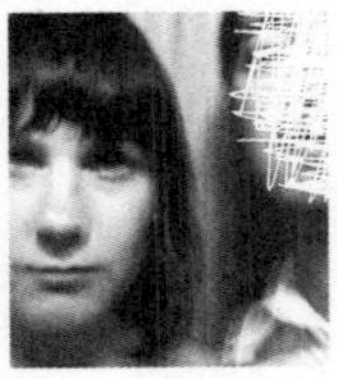

ELISE RASMUSSEN

BORN Edmonton, 1977 **RESIDES** Chicago **EDUCATION** School of the Art Institute of Chicago, M.F.A., Chicago, 2005-Present; Ryerson University, B.F.A. in Photography (Honours), Toronto, 2004 **SELECTED SOLO EXHIBITIONS** *Green Eyes*, Dyan Marie Art Projects, Toronto, 2005; *Proof 12*, Gallery 44, Toronto, 2005; *10 Days in July*, Gallery TPW, Toronto, 2005; *The Night Series*, The Ryerson Gallery, Toronto, 2005 **AWARDS** School of the Art Institute of Chicago, Merit Scholarship, 2005; Tobacco Canada's Art Council Grant, 2004 **WEBSITE** www.eliserasmussen.com

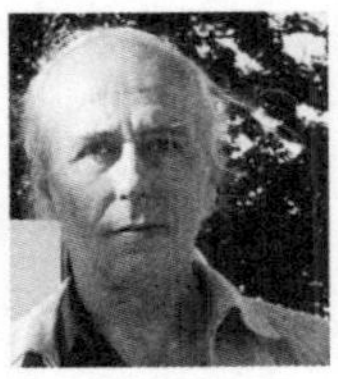

MARK RUWEDEL

BORN Bethlehem, Pennsylvania, 1954 **RESIDES** Vancouver and Long Beach, California **EDUCATION** Concordia University, M.F.A., Montreal, 1983; Kutztown State College, B.F.A., Kutztown, Pennsylvania, 1978 **SELECTED SOLO EXHIBITIONS** *Westward*, Stephen Bulger Gallery, Toronto, 2005; *Selections From the Ice Age Project*, Gallery Luisotti, Santa Monica, California, 2003; *Written on the Land*, Presentation House Gallery, North Vancouver, 2002 (touring through 2006) **SELECTED GROUP EXHIBITIONS** *Lewis and Clark Territory*, Tacoma Art Museum, Tacoma, Washington, 2004; *Temporal Surfaces*, Vancouver Art Gallery, 2003 **BOOKS/PUBLICATIONS** *Mark Ruwedel: Written on the Land*, Presentation House Gallery, North Vancouver, 2002; *The Italian Navigator*, Art 45, Stephen Bulger and Francoise Paviot, Montreal, 2001; *The Hanford Stretch*, self-published, Montreal, 1993 **AWARDS** Canada Council A Grant, 2001 and 1999 **REPRESENTATION** Stephen Bulger Gallery (Toronto) **WEBSITE** www.bulgergallery.com

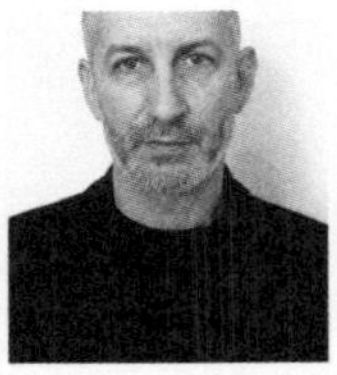

CHUCK SAMUELS

BORN Montreal, 1956 **RESIDES** Montreal **EDUCATION** Concordia University, M.F.A., Montreal, 1987 **SELECTED SOLO EXHIBITIONS** *InSiteOut*, Galerie Dazibao, Montreal, 2003; *Moving Images*, Music Gallery, Toronto, 1999 **SELECTED GROUP EXHIBITIONS** *Translating Grace*, Rosedale United Church, Toronto, 2005; *Les 20 ans du CIAC*, La Biennial de Montreal, Montreal, 2004; *essence/image*, University of Waterloo Art Gallery, Waterloo, Ontario, 2003 **BOOKS/PUBLICATIONS** *Weston & the Post-Modernists*, Alison Nordström, Image, the Magazine of George Eastman House, Vol. 43, No. 1, 2005; *Faking Death: Canadian Art Photography and the Canadian Imagination*, Penny Cousineau-Levine, McGill-Queen's University Press, Montreal, 2003; *Before the Camera—An Essay on the Works of Chuck Samuels*, Nina Levitt, Vol. 3, 2001 **AWARDS** Canada Council, Travel Grant, 2002; Conseil des arts et des lettres du Quebec, Research & Creation Grant, 2000 **WEBSITES** www.ccca.ca, www.voxphoto.com/fondsdocumentaire.html

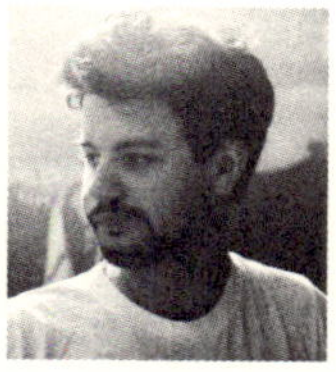
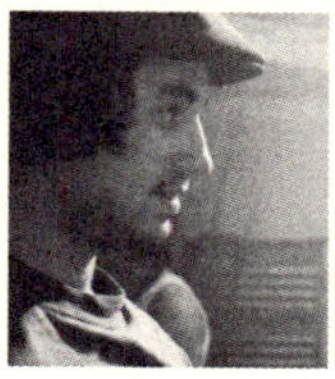

CARLOS & JASON SANCHEZ

BORN Carlos—Montreal, 1976; Jason—Montreal, 1981 **RESIDE** Montreal **EDUCATION** Carlos—Concordia University, B.F.A. Major in Photography, Montreal, 2001; Jason—Concordia University, Interdisciplinary Studies, Montreal, 2000 **SELECTED SOLO EXHIBITION** Torch Gallery, Amsterdam, The Netherlands, 2005 **SELECTED GROUP EXHIBITIONS** *Re-presenting Representation VII*, Arnot Art Museum, New York, 2005; *The Space of Making*, Neuer Berliner Kuntsverein, Berlin, Germany, 2005; *Oracle of Truth*, Aeroplastics Contemporary, Brussels, Belgium, 2005 **BOOKS/PUBLICATIONS** *Disruptions: Subversion and Provocation in the Art of Carlos and Jason Sanchez*, Christopher Cutts Gallery, 2005 **AWARDS** Type B Grant, Conseil des arts et des lettres du Quebec, 2005; Travel Grant, Canada Council for the Arts, 2004 **WEBSITE** www.carlosandjasonsanchez.com

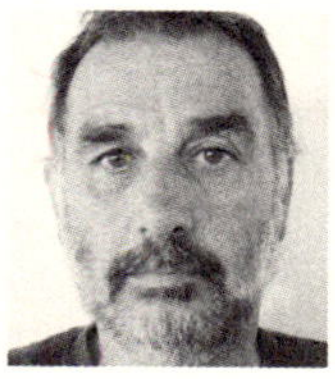

MICHAEL SCHREIER

BORN Vienna, Austria, 1949 **RESIDES** Ottawa **EDUCATION** Diploma in Photographic Arts, Ryerson Polytechnical Institute, Toronto, 1971; M.F.A., Concordia University, Montreal, 1975 **SELECTED SOLO EXHIBITIONS** *Time Line/In Two Parts, Tears for an Empty Desert, Portraits in Silence*, Peak Gallery, Toronto, 2004 **SELECTED GROUP EXHIBITIONS** *Theatre of the Moment*, Carleton University Gallery, Ottawa, 2003 **SELECTED REPRESENTATION** National Gallery of Canada; Canadian Museum of Contemporary Photography; Visual Studies Workshop, Rochester, New York; *Light Work*, University of Syracuse, New York

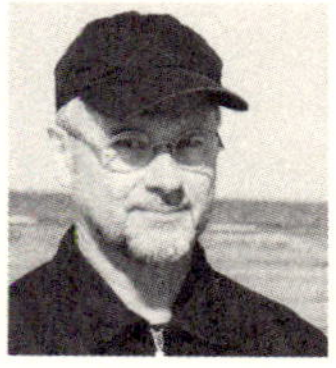

VOLKER SEDING

BORN Berlin, 1943 **RESIDES** Toronto **EDUCATION** Hannover School of Art, Germany, Apprenticeship with Master Photographer Klaus Berger, 1962-1965 **SELECTED SOLO EXHIBITIONS** *Façades*, Joseph Bellows Gallery, La Jolla, California, and Stephen Bulger Gallery, Toronto, 2004; *Façades*, Ariel Meyerowitz Gallery, New York, 2003; *Still Lifes*, Photo Eye Gallery, Santa Fe, New Mexico, 2000 **SELECTED GROUP EXHIBITIONS** *Faces, Places, Traces: New Acquisitions to the Photographs Collection*, National Gallery of Canada, Ottawa, 2004 **AWARDS** The Ontario Arts Council, Senior Arts Grant, 1999; The Canada Council A Grant, 1997; The Canada Council B Grant, 1994; The Toronto Arts Council, 1992 **REPRESENTATION** Stephen Bulger Gallery (Toronto) **WEBSITE** www.bulgergallery.com

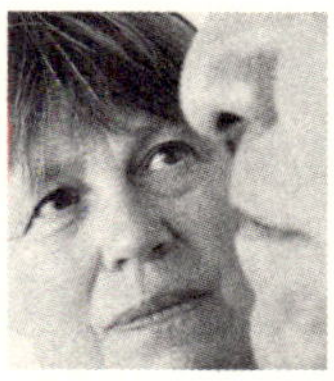

SANDRA SEMCHUK

BORN Meadow Lake, Saskatchewan, 1948 **RESIDES** Vancouver and Cochin, Saskatchewan **EDUCATION** University of New Mexico, M.A., Albuquerque, New Mexico, 1983; University of Saskatchewan, B.F.A., Saskatoon, 1970 **SELECTED EXHIBITIONS** *Poundmakers Garden* (collaborations with James Nicholas), Godfrey Dean Art Gallery, Yorkton, Saskatchewan, 2005; *Enemy Aliens* (collaborations with James Nicholas and Zeelia), Harbourfront Centre Gallery, Toronto, 2005; *how far back is home*, Canadian Museum of Contemporary Photography, Ottawa, 1995 (travelled nationally and internationally until 1998) **BOOKS/PUBLICATIONS** *Marking Time*, Dan Ring, Mendel Art Gallery, Saskatoon, 2005; *Autoportraits dans la photographie canadienne*, Andre Gilbert, J'ai VU, Quebec, 2004; *Facing History, Portraits From Vancouver*, Karen Love, Canadian Cultural Centre, Paris, 2002; *Faking Death, Canadian Art Photography and the Canadian Imagination*, Penny Cousineau Levine, McGill-Queen's University Press, Montreal, 2003 **AWARDS** Canada Council A Grant, 1993 **WEBSITES** art-history.concordia.ca/eea/artists/semchuk.html, www.eciad.ca/~ssemchuk

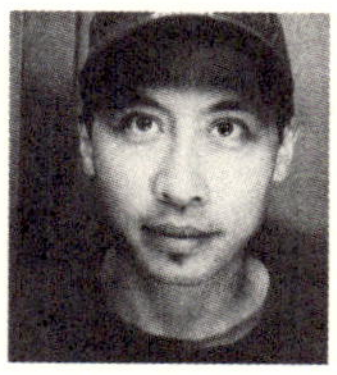

DEREK SHAPTON

BORN Toronto, 1971 **RESIDES** Toronto **EDUCATION** Self-taught **SELECTED GROUP EXHIBITIONS** *Wide Open*, Eckenr[illegible] Gallery, Vail, Colorado, 2002-2003; *Sense of Space* Noorderlicht Photofestival Main Exhibition, Groningen The Netherlands, 2001; *Decked: an exhibition of skate culture*, Art Gallery of Ontario, Toronto, 2000; *Drive By Shooting*, Sis Boom Bah Gallery, Toronto, 2000 **PUBLICATIONS** *Sense of Space*, Exhibition Catalogue, 2001; **AWARDS** National Magazine Award for Portraiture, 2002; National Magazine Award for Photojournalism, 1999 **WEBSITE** www.derekshapton.com

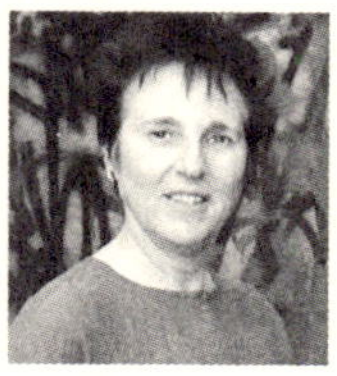

CHERYL SOURKES

BORN Montreal, 1945 **RESIDES** Toronto **EDUCATION** McGill University, B.Sc., 1966 **SELECTED SOLO EXHIBITIONS** *Cam Work*, Southern Alberta Art Gallery, Lethbridge, Alberta, 2006, Tom Thomson Memorial Art Gallery, Owen Sound, Ontario, 2006; *Public Camera*, Peak Gallery, Toronto, 2005; *Cam Cities*, Museum of London, London, Ontario, [illegible] **SELECTED GROUP EXHIBITIONS** *NXT. Message*, Koffler Gallery Toronto, 2005; *Transitive*, Kabat Wrobel Gallery, Toronto 2005; *Bossy Bitches: Sweet Shit*, Lennox Contemporary Toronto, 2005; *Corabbleation*, Surface Gallery, Nottingham England, 2004 **BOOKS/PUBLICATIONS** *Public Camera*, Stuart Reid, Cheryl Simon, Southern Alberta Art Gallery & Tom Thomson Memorial Art Gallery, 2006; *Suspect*, edited by John Knechtel, MIT Press and Alphabet City Media, [illegible] *Image and Inscription: An Anthology of Contemporary Canadian Photography*, edited by Robert Bean, YYZ Press, 2005 **AWARDS** Ontario Arts Council Exhibition Grant, 2004; Toronto Arts Council A Grant, 2003 **WEBSITE** www.cherylsourkes.com

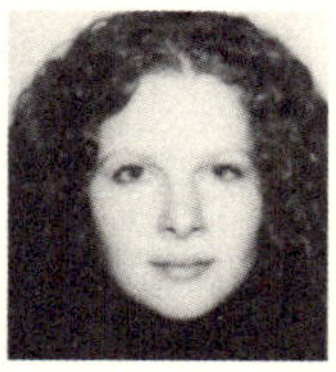

LISA STINNER

BORN Toronto, 1977 **RESIDES** Winnipeg **EDUCATION** The School of the Art Institute of Chicago, M.F.A. in Photography Chicago, 2003; University of Manitoba, B.F.A. (Honours) Winnipeg, 2001 **SELECTED SOLO EXHIBITION** Platform Ga[illegible] Centre for the Photographic and Digital Arts, Winnipeg, 2006 **SELECTED GROUP EXHIBITIONS** *Projekt30*, www.projekt30.com, New York, 2005; *Here and Back*, James Baird Gallery, St. John's, 2004; *Gilded Lily*, 1R Gallery, Chicago, 2004 **AWARDS** Lila Acheson Wallace Foundation, Reader's Digest Scholarship, 2003; Manitoba Arts Council, Visual Arts B Grant, 2003; The Art Institute of Chicago, Trustee Scholarship, 2001-2003 **WEBSITE** www.lisastinner.com

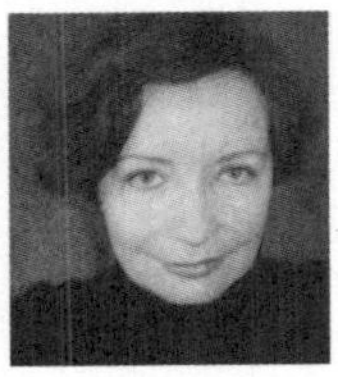

F. LESLIE THOMPSON

BORN Regina, 1952 **RESIDES** Toronto **EDUCATION** University of Illinois, M.F.A. in Art and Design, Urbana-Champaign, Illinois, 1978; Ivey School of Business, University of Western Ontario, M.B.A., London, Ontario, 1980; York University, B.A. in Visual Arts (Honours), Toronto, 1975 **SELECTED SOLO EXHIBITIONS** *Erase Me*, Southern Alberta Art Gallery, Lethbridge, Alberta, 2005; *Death Without Bodies*, *Chthonic Light*, Justina M. Barnicke Gallery, University of Toronto, 1997, 2002; *Chthonic Light*, Acadia University Art Gallery, Wolfville, N.S., 2000 **SELECTED GROUP EXHIBITION** *Persistent Documents*, Canadian Embassy Gallery, Tokyo, 2000 **BOOKS/PUBLICATIONS** *Erase Me*, monograph, Seraphim Editions, 2004; *Chthonic Light*, monograph, Treetop Press, Toronto, 1997; *Le mois de la photo Montreal*, catalogue, Vox populi, *Persistent Documents*, 1995; *Deux Ex Machina*, Galerie101 Gallery, Ottawa, 1994; *Women's Photography Daybook*, 1992, 1993, 1995, Second Story Press; *Exposure*, catalogue, Art Gallery of Ontario, Toronto, 1975 **AWARDS** Canada Council, 1993, 1995, 1997; Ontario Arts Council, 1975, 1976, 1978, 1993, 1994, 1996, 1997, 2003, 2004; Banff Centre for the Arts, 1990, 1991, 1999, 2001, 2002, 2003, 2004; Ontario Ministry of Culture, Recreation and Tourism, 1993; City of Glasgow, Scotland, 1993 **WEBSITE** www.f.lesliethompson.com

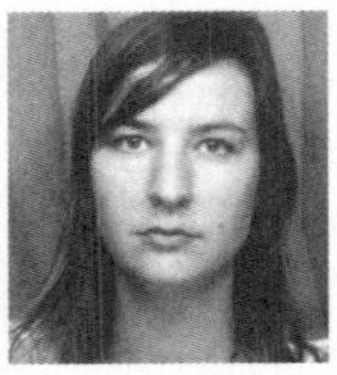

EVE K. TREMBLAY

BORN Val-David, Quebec, 1972 **RESIDES** Montreal **EDUCATION** Concordia University, B.F.A. Major in Photography, Montreal, 2000 **SELECTED SOLO EXHIBITIONS** *Tales Without Grounds*, BUIA Gallery, New York, 2006; *Mimi et Jeanne*, VU, Quebec, 2006; *Transitional Area*, White Space, Zürich, 2005; *Honeymoons* (in association with Michel de Broin), Gallery 44, Toronto, 2003; Pierre-François Ouellette, Montreal, 2004; Fototeca de Cuba, Havana, 2005; *À la recherche des placebos*, Circa, Montreal, 2002; *Les dédales d'Ariane*, L'Oeil de Poisson, Quebec, 2001; *L'Éducation sentimentale*, Occurrence, Montreal, 2000 **SELECTED GROUP EXHIBITIONS** *Canada Dreaming*, curator Justin Hoffman, Kunstverein Wolfsburg, Germany, 2005; *Faking Death*, curator Penny Cousineau-Levine, Jack Shainman, New York, 2006; *Salut les filles*, curator Loren Lerner, McCord Museum, Montreal, 2005; *L'Écho des Limbes*, curator Nathalie de Blois, Leonard Elen Bina Gallery, Montreal, 2005 **AWARDS** Canada Council Grant, 2003; Quebec Art Council, 2003, 2004, 2005 **ARTIST RESIDENCIES** Iaab, Christoph Merian Stiftung, Basel, Switzerland, 2003; ceaac, Strasbourg, France, 2005 **PUBLICATIONS** *CV photo*, *Ciel Variable*, *Spirale*, *EtC*, *Parachute*, *Esse*, *Border Crossing*, *Canadien Art*, *Mix Magazine* **WEBSITE** www.evektremblay.com

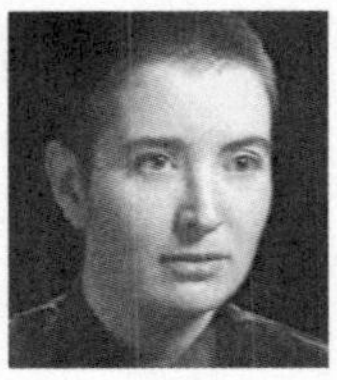

TOBARON WAXMAN

BORN Toronto, 1970 **RESIDES** New York **EDUCATION** School of the Art Institute of Chicago, M.F.A. in Performance, Chicago, 2002 **SELECTED EXHIBITIONS** *block of ice + 1/60* (performance installation), Paved Art New Media, Saskatoon, 2006; *portraits of severin* (photo), Toronto Alternative Art Fair International, 2005; *untitled diptych* (photo/collaboration), Prüss & Ochs Gallery, Asian Fine Arts Berlin, 2003 **AWARDS** Franklin Furnace Performance Art Award, 2004; Canada Council for the Arts Creation Grant, 2003, 2005; Technology Award for Students With Disabilities, Ontario Ministry of Education and Training, 1998 **WEBSITE** www.artic.edu/~twaxma

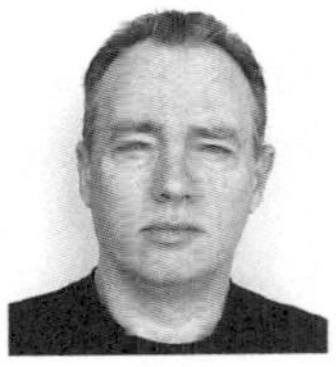

CARL ZIMMERMAN

BORN Hamilton, Ontario, 1951 **RESIDES** Marble Mountain, N.S. **EDUCATION** Self-taught **SELECTED SOLO EXHIBITIONS** *Unbuilt: Visionary Building in Colonial P.E.I.*, Confederation Centre Art Gallery, Charlottetown, 2005; *Untitled: Recent Work by Carl Zimmerman*, Owens Art Gallery, Mount Allison University, Sackville, N.B., 2000; *Lost Hamilton Landmarks*, Art Gallery of Hamilton, Hamilton, Ontario, and St. Mary's University Art Gallery, Halifax, 1997–1998 **SELECTED GROUP EXHIBITIONS** *The Unblinking Eye*, Irish Museum of Modern Art, Dublin, 2002–2003; *Westward Ho, a Guided Tour*, HX: Halifax Exhibition of International Contemporary Art, Halifax, 2000 **AWARDS** Canada Council B Grant, 2004; Canada Council B Grant, 2003; Irish Museum of Modern Art Residency 2001; Pollack/Krasner Foundation Grant, 2000 **BOOKS/PUBLICATIONS** *The Irish Museum of Modern Art, The Collection*, Irish Museum of Modern Art, Dublin, 2005; *Gravity and Grace, Selected Writings on Contemporary Canadian Art*, Gil McElroy, Gaspereau Press, 2001; *Lost Hamilton Landmarks*, Carl Zimmerman, Robin Metcalfe, St. Mary's University Art Gallery, Halifax, 1997 **REPRESENTATION** Stephen Bulger Gallery (Toronto) **WEBSITE** www.bulgergallery.com

DOCUMENTARY + PHOTOJOURNALISM

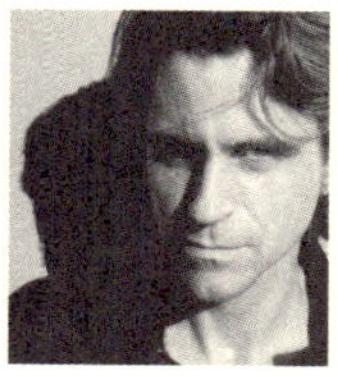

PATRICK ALLEYN

BORN Montreal, 1967 **RESIDES** Montreal **EDUCATION** Université du Quebec à Montreal, Communication Studies, 1986-1991 **SELECTED GROUP EXHIBITIONS** *Ordre public/ désordre mondial*, Le Mois de la photo à Montreal (Montreal international photographic biennial), 2003; *Le Centre-Sud, des gens et des maisons*, l'Écomusée du fier monde, 1999 **CLIENTS** *Recto Verso*, *Journal Alternatives*, *Reflet de Société*

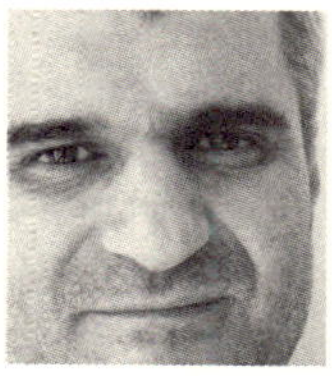

BENOIT AQUIN

BORN Montreal, 1963 **RESIDES** Montreal **EDUCATION** New England School of Photography, Boston, 1985-1988 **SELECTED SOLO EXHIBITIONS** *La Pêche*, Mission photographique de Gaspésie à L'Espace F de Matane, Montreal, 1998; *Haïti Chérie*, Galerie Occurrence, Montreal, 1997 **SELECTED GROUP EXHIBITIONS** *Ordre Public/ Désordre Mondial*, Biennale de photographie de Montreal, 2003; *Quartier Centre-Sud*, Écomusée du fier monde, Montreal, 1999 **CLIENTS** *La Presse*, CBC, *Maclean's*, *Canadian Geographic* **WEBSITE** www.benoitaquin.com

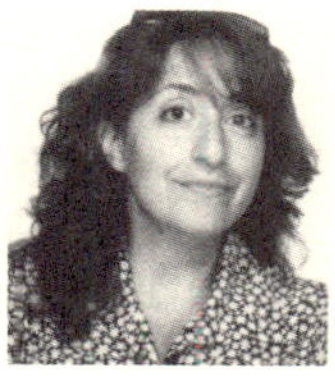

TOBI ASMOUCHA

BORN Vancouver, 1968 **RESIDES** Toronto **EDUCATION** Ryerson University, B.A.A. in Still Photography, Toronto, 1992 **SELECTED SOLO EXHIBITIONS** *Road Signs*, Balzac's Café, Contact Photography Festival, Toronto, 2005; *Toronto's Little Kabul*, Levity Café, Contact Photography Festival, Toronto, 2003 **SELECTED GROUP EXHIBITIONS** *Life of Water*, Allen Lambert Galleria, Toronto, 2005; *Toronto School of Art Faculty Retrospective*, The Spoke Club, Toronto, 2004; *Destination Toronto*, Allen Lambert Galleria, Toronto, 2004 **AWARDS** Gold National Magazine Award, "Arrivals," *Toronto Life*, 2003; National Magazine Award Honourable Mention, "Little Kabul," *Toronto Life*, 2002 **CLIENTS** *Canadian Geographic*, *Toronto Life*, *National Post Business*, *Golf Canada*, *Canadian Aviator*, *ON Nature* **WEBSITE** www.tobiphoto.com

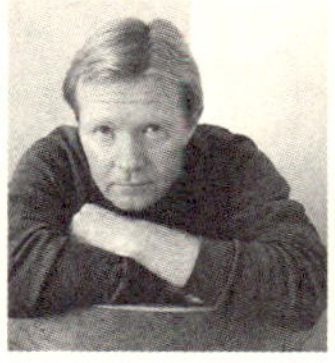

BRIAN ATKINSON

BORN Winnipeg, 1961 **RESIDES** Fredericton, N.B. **EDUCATION** B.A. in Sociology, Lethbridge, Alberta, 1982 **SELECTED SOLO EXHIBITIONS** *Connection at St. Croix*, Gallery Connection, Fredericton & Sunbury Shores, 2004; *Sustaining the Gaze: When Images Tremble*, University of New Brunswick, 2003; *Into the Fire: Guatemala's Mayans Return*, Saint John Museum, 1999 **BOOKS** *Fredericton*, Nimbus Books, 2002; *Fantastic New Brunswick*, Nimbus Books 2003; *Sustaining the Gaze: When Images Tremble*, Broken Jaw Press, 2004 **CLIENTS** *Canadian Geographic*, *Equinox*, CARE International, New Brunswick Tourism and Parks, Doctors Without Borders, *The Globe and Mail*, *Ottawa Citizen* **WEBSITE** www.brianatkinson.ca

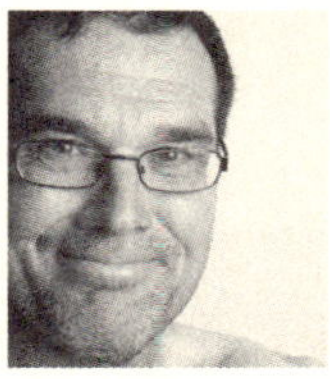

DAVID BARBOUR

BORN Winnipeg, 1952 **RESIDES** Ottawa **EDUCATION** University of Regina, B.A. in Geography, 1973; The Banff School of Fine Arts, Photography Program, 1976 **SELECTED SOLO EXHIBIT** *Havana*, Ottawa School of Art, 2003 **SELECTED GROUP EXHIBITS** *The Bigger Picture, Portraits From Ottawa*, Ottawa Art Gallery, 2004; *Havana*, Carleton University Art Gallery, Ottawa, 1999 **AWARDS** Mid-Career Canada Council Grant, 2000 **WEBSITE** www.davidbarbour.com

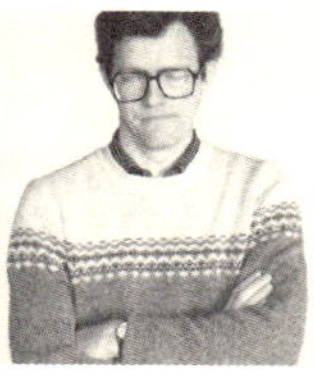

PHIL BERGERSON

BORN Toronto, 1947 **RESIDES** Toronto **EDUCATION** York University, B.F.A. in Painting and Printmaking, Toronto, 19[illegible]; Ryerson Polytechnical Institute, Diploma in Photographic Arts, Toronto, 1970 **SELECTED SOLO EXHIBITIONS** *Shards of America*, Canadian Museum of Contemporary Photography, Ottawa, 2004, and Stephen Bulger Gallery, Toronto, 20[illegible]; *Messages From New York*, MacLaren Art Centre, Barrie, Ontario, 2002; *Shards of Civilization*, Nickle Arts Museum, Calgary, 2001 **BOOKS/PUBLICATIONS** *Shards of America*, New York, 2004 **AWARDS** Ryerson Research Grants, 2[illegible] and 2002; Ontario Arts Council Exhibitions Grant, 2[illegible] **REPRESENTATION** Stephen Bulger Gallery (Toronto) **WEBSITES** www.philbergerson.com, www.bulgergallery.com

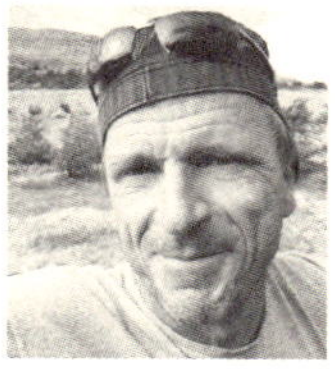

NORMAND BLOUIN

BORN Montreal, 1955 **RESIDES** Montreal **EDUCATION** Self-taught **SELECTED SOLO EXHIBITIONS** *Haiti Chérie*, Musée National de Port-Au-Prince, Haiti, 2002; *War and Peace*, Galerie TM, Montreal, 2001 **SELECTED GROUP EXHIBITIONS** *Life of Water*, Allen Lambert Galleria, Toronto, 2005 **CLIENTS** *The Montreal Gazette*, *La Presse*, *Le Journal de Montreal*, *L'Express*, *Le Monde* **WEBSITES** www.agencestockphoto.com, www.portfolios.com/normandblouin

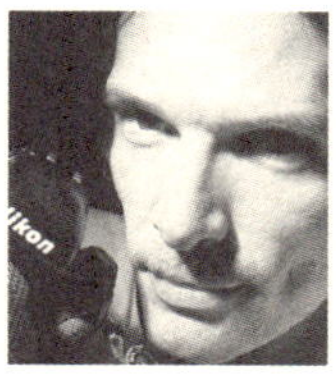

OLIVIER BOËLS

BORN France, 1968 **RESIDES** Brazil **EDUCATION** Self-taught **SELECTED SOLO EXHIBITIONS** *Os Povos da Chapada*, B[illegible] do Artesão, São Jorge, Goiás, Brazil, 2005; *Sangue [illegible] de Coragem: A contemporaneidade Kalungas*, Conjunto Cultural da Caixa, Brasília D.F, Brazil, 2004; *C[illegible] Sagradas: imagens de transcendência*, Centro Cultural de Caixa, São Paulo, Salvador, 2003; French Embassy in Brasília, Brazil, 2004; *Holy Ashes/Cendres Sacrées*, Alliance Française, Toronto, 2001 **SELECTED GROUP EXHIBITIONS** *A Volta ao Mundo em 80 Fotos (Around the World in 80 Pictures)*, Outdoor Exhibition, Avenidas das Nações Unidas, São Paulo, Brazil, 2005 **CLIENTS** *Caminhos da Terra*, *Marie Claire* Brazil, *Jornal de Brasília*, *Caros Amigos*, *Fome Zero*, Ministry of Social Development **AWARDS** World Press Photo, Category: Nature and Environment, 200[illegible]; Premio Pierre Verger, Category: Ensaio fotografico, 200[illegible]; 1er Premio Foto Arte, Category: Political and Social, 2004 **WEBSITES** www.avoltaaomundoem80fotos.com.br, www.contrast-photo.com, www.etnofoco.com

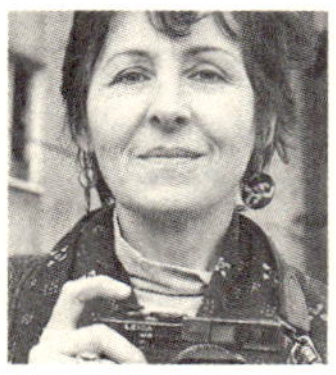

ELAINE BRIÈRE

BORN Nanaimo, B.C., 1946 **RESIDES** Vancouver **EDUCATION** University of British Columbia, 1968 **SELECTED SOLO EXHIBITIONS** Mayor's Conference on Poverty, Roundhouse, Vancouver, 2004; *Ground Zero: The WTO*, Tacoma History Museum, Massachusetts, 2001 **SELECTED GROUP EXHIBITIONS** *Documents & Dreams*, BFly Atelier Gallery, Vancouver, 2003; *Portrait V2K*, Vancouver Museum, Vancouver, 2000 **WEBSITE** www.elainebriere.ca

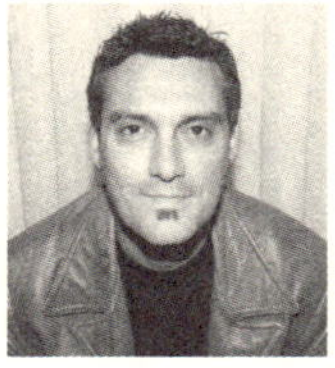

ADRIAN BROWN

BORN Shoreham-by-Sea, England, 1963 **RESIDES** London, England, and Vancouver **EDUCATION** Self-taught **CLIENTS** Sipa Press, Bloomberg News Hong Kong, Bloomberg News London, Canadian Press, *Toronto Star*, *Vancouver Sun*, *The Globe and Mail*, *Saturday Night*, *Cnewsworld Magazine*, *Zi Magazine* **WEBSITE** www.photo28.com

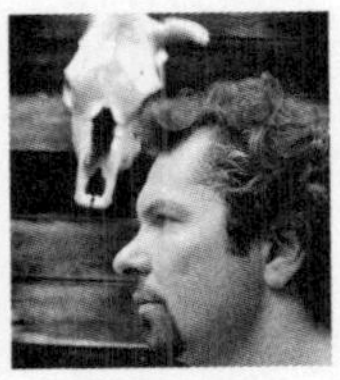

DAVID CAMPION

BORN Huddersfield, U.K., 1965 **RESIDES** Deroche, B.C. **SELECTED SOLO EXHIBITIONS** *Where Fire Speaks*, Geist Gallery, Contact Photography Festival, Toronto, 2003; *Arboretum*, XENO Gallery, Vancouver, 2002 **SELECTED GROUP EXHIBITIONS** *Real Pictures*, Vancouver Art Gallery, Vancouver, 2005; *Documents & Dreams*, Bfly Atelier Gallery, Vancouver, 2003; *Exile*, Artropolis Show, Vancouver, 2003; *Best of Vancouver*, New West Gallery, Vancouver, 1999; *Repercussions*, Helen Pitt Gallery, Vancouver, 1999 **BOOKS/PUBLICATIONS** *Where Fire Speaks*, Arsenal Pulp Press, 2002; *The Company of Others*, Arsenal Pulp Press, 2005 **AWARDS** Hubert Evans Prize, Best Non-fiction Book, B.C. Book Awards, 2003; Gold Medal, Photo Essay Category, Western Magazine Awards, 2002 **CLIENTS** *Geist Magazine*, *Adbusters*, *Canadian Geographic*, *The Boston Globe*, *Reader's Digest*, *Maclean's*, *The Globe and Mail* **WEBSITE** www.feetontheground.ca

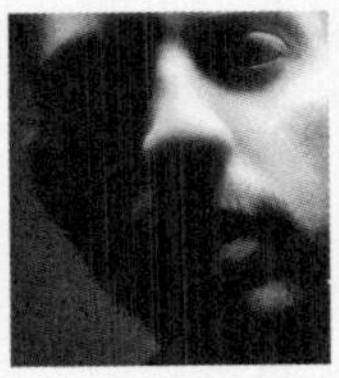

WILLIAM CICCOCIOPPO

BORN Toronto, 1969 **RESIDES** Toronto **EDUCATION** University of Victoria, Bachelor of Arts in Cultural Anthropology, 1993 **AWARDS** *Applied Arts* Photography & Illustration Annual, 2004; National Magazine Awards, Silver in Best Portrait, 2003; *Applied Arts* Photography & Illustration Annual, 2002; *Applied Arts* Photography & Illustration Contest, 2001 **CLIENTS** *Canadian Business*, *Canadian Geographic*, *The Globe and Mail*, *Maclean's*, *Money Sense*, *National Post Business Magazine*, *Nuvo*, *Report on Business*, *Saturday Night*, *Time Out New York*, *Toronto Life* **WEBSITE** www.cyclopsimages.com

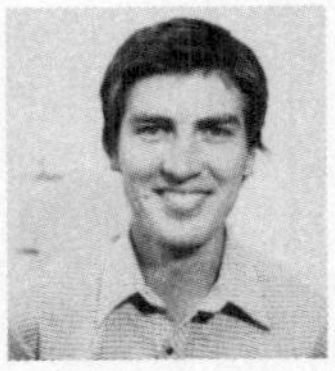

JOHN CULLEN

BORN Burlington, Ontario, 1976 **RESIDES** Toronto **EDUCATION** Dalhousie University, B.A. in English, Halifax, 1994–1998; Brooks Institute of Photography, Santa Barbara, California, 2000 **CLIENTS** *Canadian Geographic*, *Report on Business*, *The Globe and Mail*, Redwood Custom Communications, Butterfield & Robinson **WEBSITE** www.johncullenphotographer.com

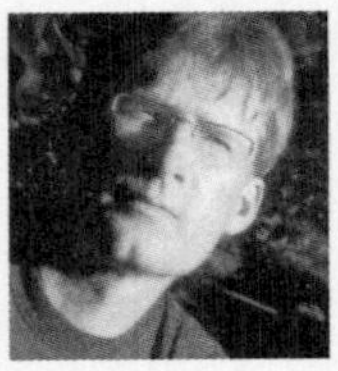

WILLIAM DEKAY

BORN London, Ontario, 1962 **RESIDES** Weldon, Saskatchewan **EDUCATION** Ryerson University, Bachelor of Applied Arts in Photography, Toronto, 1985; Staff Internship at National Geographic Society, Washington, D.C., 1986 **AWARDS** Pulitzer Prize Finalist for *Detroit Free Press* Staff Entries, 1990, 1991; Shortlisted for Roloff Beny Photography Book Award, *Down Home, A Journey Into Rural Canada*, 1999; Gold National Magazine Award, Photojournalism, 1999 **WEBSITE** www.williamdekay.com

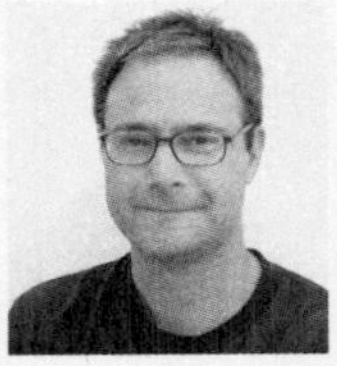

J. KEVIN DUNN

BORN Calgary, 1966 **RESIDES** Penticton, B.C. **EDUCATION** Alberta College of Art, Major in Photographic Arts, 1986–1989; Photojournalism Internship, *The Calgary Herald*, 1986–1989; University of Calgary, M.F.A., 1985–1986 **SELECTED SOLO EXHIBITIONS** *Of Smoke, Sweat & Honey—The Bee Project*, The Kelowna Art Gallery, Kelowna, B.C., 2004; *Railway*, The University of Toronto, 2004; *Valley 2000: A Photographic Record of Life in the Okanagan*, The Kelowna Art Gallery, Kelowna, B.C., 2000; *Along the Way—My Life as a Dog*, The Nanaimo Art Gallery, Nanaimo, B.C., 2000 **AWARDS** The B.C. Arts Council Grant, 2004; Canada Council for the Arts Grant, 2000 **WEBSITE** www.jkevindunn.com

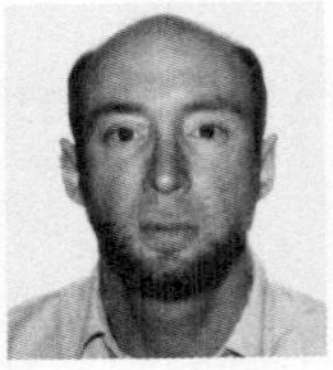

ETHAN EISENBERG

BORN Toronto, 1963 **RESIDES** Toronto **EDUCATION** Concordia University, M.F.A. in Photography, Montreal, 1993; University of Toronto, B.A. in Philosophy, Toronto, 1986 **SELECTED SOLO EXHIBITIONS** *Holyland, Photographs From the Time of the Peace Process*, 1994–1997 Photo Passage, Harbourfront, Toronto, 1998; *Christian Tourism in Jerusalem*, Alliance Francaise, Toronto, 2003; *Holyland*, Justina Barnicke Gallery, Toronto, 2003; *Holyland*, Maison de la Culture Rosemont, Montreal, 1997 **AWARDS** Canada Council B Grant, 2000 and 2004; Ontario Arts Council Project Grant, 1995, 1999 and 2004 **CLIENTS** *CV Photo*, *The Globe and Mail*, *Maclean's*, *U.S. News and World Report* **WEBSITES** www.jerusalemphoto.com, www.musarium.com

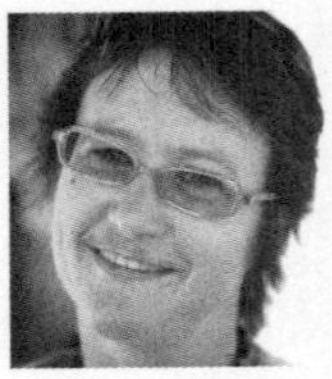

PAMELA GAWN

BORN Wellington, New Zealand, 1960 **RESIDES** Toronto **EDUCATION** Ryerson University, B.A.A. Media Studies, Toronto, 1985; Sheridan College, Advanced Television and Film Program, Oakville, Ontario, 2003 **SELECTED SOLO EXHIBITIONS** *Lost and Found at the Gladstone Hotel*, The Gladstone Hotel Atrium, Toronto, 2004; *Reflecting Irony*, Rustic Cosmo, Contact Photography Festival, Toronto, 2001 **SELECTED GROUP EXHIBITIONS** *The Collective Metropolis*, The Creit Building, Toronto, 2005; *Global Imagining*, Tokyo Metropolitan Museum of Modern Art, UNESCO, 1987; *Unparalleled Views*, Sparkes Gallery, Toronto, 1986; *Narratives*, The Women's Cultural Building, Toronto, 1985; *Sojourn*, Gallery 76, Toronto, 1984 **CLIENTS** The National Film Board, Toronto International Film Festival, Cinema Canada, Canadian Union of Public Employees, YWCA Toronto **WEBSITE** www.pamelagawn.com

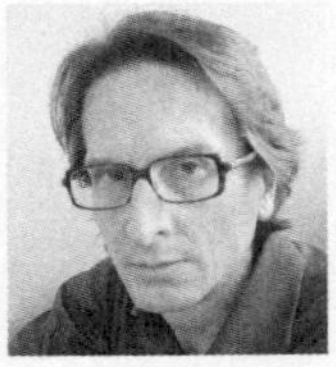

GREG GIRARD

BORN Vancouver, 1955 **RESIDES** Shanghai **EDUCATION** Self-taught **SELECTED SOLO EXHIBITION** *Phantom Shanghai*, Monte Clark Gallery, Toronto, 2005 **SELECTED GROUP EXHIBITIONS** *Hong Kong–Shanghai*, Lille 2004 European Cultural Capital, Lille, France, 2004; *Kowloon Walled City*, Columbia University Graduate School of Architecture Gallery, New York, 2003; *Cities of the 21st Century*, Bauhaus, Dessau, Germany, 2000 **BOOKS/PUBLICATIONS** *City of Darkness: Life in Kowloon Walled City*, Watermark Publications, 1993, 1999, 2000 and 2002 **CLIENTS** *Time*, *Newsweek*, *Fortune* **REPRESENTATION** Monte Clark Gallery (Vancouver, Toronto) **WEBSITES** www.greggirard.com, www.monteclarkgallery.com

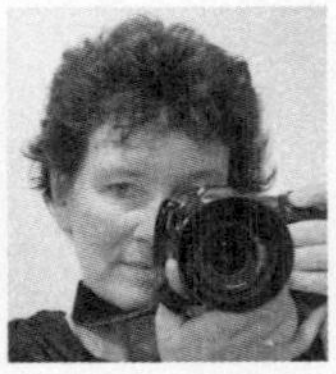

PATTI GOWER

BORN Calgary, 1960 **RESIDES** Toronto **EDUCATION** Waterloo University, B.Sc. Kinesiology, Waterloo, Ontario, 1984; Loyalist College, Diploma in Photojournalism, Belleville, Ontario, 1989 **SELECTED GROUP EXHIBITIONS** *Protecting Peace*, BloWup Gallery, Montreal, 2004; *Documents and Dreams*, Narrative 360 Exhibition, Vancouver, 2003; Toronto Contact Photo Festival, 2002, 2003 and 2005 **AWARDS** Atkinson Fellowship on Social Policy, 2001–2002; National Newspaper Award for Feature Photography, 1994 **WEBSITE** www.pattigower.com

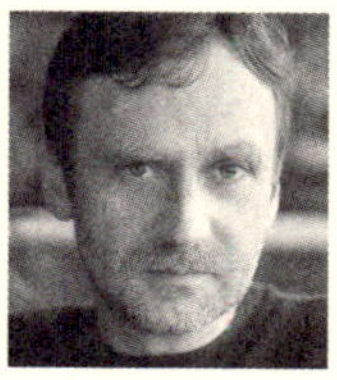

CHRISTOPHER GRABOWSKI

BORN Warsaw, Poland, 1954 **RESIDES** Vancouver **EDUCATION** Master Photographer Diploma, UPAP, Warsaw, 1986 **SELECTED SOLO EXHIBITIONS** *Kites, Guns and Dreams*, Vancouver, Montreal, Toronto and Halifax, 2004–2005; *The Gift*, Gallery WM, Amsterdam, The Netherlands, 2000 **AWARDS** Western Magazine Awards, 2004; Michener-Deacon Fellowship, 1999; Advertising and Design Club of Canada, 1996 **CLIENTS** *The Globe and Mail*, *The Washington Post*, *Financial Times*, *El Mundo*, *Utne Reader*, *Neue Zurcher Zeitung*, *Maclean's*, *Ottawa Citizen*, *Geist* **WEBSITE** www.mediumlight.com

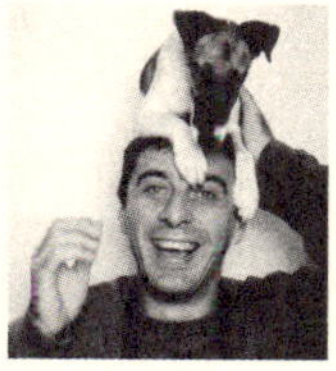

PATRICE HALLEY

BORN Paris, 1962 **RESIDES** Wycliffe, B.C. **EDUCATION** Ecole de la Chambre de commerce de Paris, Diploma in Commercial and Advertising Photography, Paris, 1980 **SELECTED SOLO EXHIBITIONS** *Far North*, BloWup Photo Gallery, Montreal, 2003; *Twenty Years of Assignments*, Centre 64 in Kimberley and The Key City Theatre in Cranbrook, B.C., 2003; *Le Nord Canadien*, Musée Pablo Picasso, Antibes, France, 1992 **BOOKS/PUBLICATIONS** *Canada's Last Wild Horses*, Editions de l'Homme, Quebec, 2006; *Far North*, Editions de l'Homme, Quebec, 2003; *Sentinels of the St. Lawrence*, Editions de l'Homme, Quebec, 2002; *Arctic Borealis Adventures*, Editions Barthelemy, France, 1991 **AWARDS** Northern-Light Awards, 2004, 2001, 2000, 1999 and 1998; Lowell Thomas Award, 1998; Canadian National Magazine Award, 1996 **CLIENTS** *Animan*, *Actualité*, *British Columbia Magazine*, *Canadian Geographic*, *Figaro*, *National Geographic*, *Paris Match*, *Photo Life*, *Time*, Aeroplan, Applied Communications, Arctic Adventures, Canadian Tourism Commission, Cie générales des eaux (France), Communications Daz, Cossette, Delta Hotels, Laval University, Louis XIV (France), Marketel, Precision Drilling, Result Communications, Ski Rossignol, Telebec, Tourisme Quebec, Tourism Ontario North, Travel Alberta, TWA **WEBSITE** www.patricehalley.com

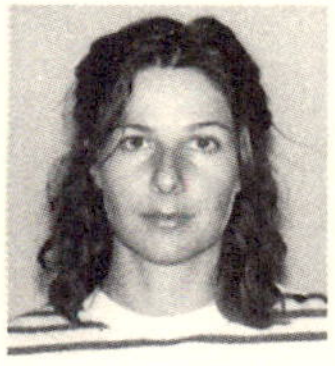

NAOMI HARRIS

BORN Toronto, 1973 **RESIDES** New York **EDUCATION** York University, Undergraduate School (Printmaking and Photography), Toronto, 1997; International Centre of Photography, Photojournalism and Documentary Photography, New York, 1998 **SELECTED SOLO EXHIBITIONS** *White Picket Fences, Swinging in Suburbia*, Fotofestiwal, Lodz, Poland, 2005; *American Swinger*, Jack the Pelican Presents, Brooklyn, New York, 2004; *Haddon Hall Hotel*, Pikto Gallery, Contact Photography Festival, Toronto, 2004 **SELECTED GROUP EXHIBITIONS** Schweppes Photographic Portrait Prize 2005, National Portrait Gallery, London, U.K., 2005; World Press Photo—Joop Swart Masterclass 'Pride' Foam, Fotografiemusem Amsterdam, The Netherlands, 2004; *Encontros da Imagem*, Sixteenth Annual Photo Festival Braga, Portugal, 2002 **AWARDS** Represented Canada at the World Press Joop Swart Masterclass in Amsterdam, 2004; Gold National Magazine Award, Photojournalism, 2003; 30 Emerging Photographers to Watch as selected by *Photo District News*, U.S.A., 2002; International Prize for Young Photojournalism from Agfa and Das Bildforum, Germany, 2001; Finalist for the Eugene Smith Award, U.S.A., 2001 **CLIENTS** *The New York Times Magazine*, *New York Magazine*, *Mother Jones*, *Newsweek*, *ESPN the Magazine*, *The London Sunday Times Magazine* **WEBSITE** www.naomiharris.com

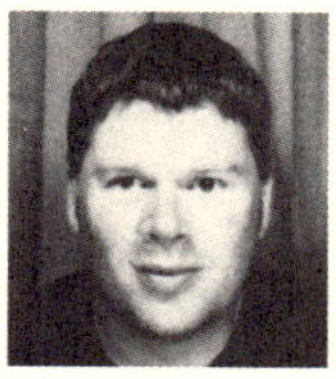

BRIAN HOWELL

BORN Vancouver, 1966 **RESIDES** Vancouver **EDUCATION** Ryerson University, B.A.A. in Still Photography, Toronto, 1994 **SELECTED SOLO EXHIBITIONS** *One Ring Circus*, Gas Gallery, Contact Photography Festival, Toronto, 2004 *Jean Buchan's Bansi*, Pimentel Gallery, Contact Photography Festival, Toronto, 2002 **SELECTED GROUP EXHIBITIONS** *Documents & Dreams*, View Point Gallery, Halifax, 2004 *Documents & Dreams*, BFly Atelier Gallery, Vancouver 2003 **BOOKS/PUBLICATIONS** *One Ring Circus*, Arsenal Pulp Press, 2002 **CLIENTS** *Geist*, *Saturday Night*, *Maclean's*, *Toronto Report on Business*, *The Globe and Mail*, *National Post* **WEBSITE** www.brianhowellphotography.com

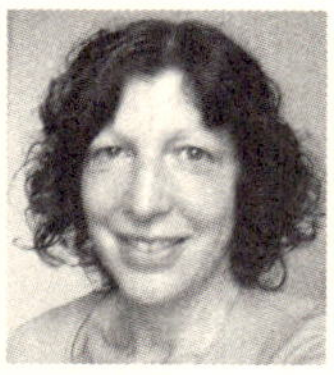

RUTH KAPLAN

BORN Montreal, 1955 **RESIDES** Toronto **EDUCATION** Ryerson University, B.A.A. in Photography, Toronto, 1981; Concordia University, Major in Photography and Painting, Montreal, 1977 **SELECTED SOLO EXHIBITIONS** *Bathers*, Quai de la Batterie, Arras, France, 2004; *Bathers*, Stephen Bulger Gallery, Toronto, 2003; *Bathers*, CMCP, Ottawa, 2001 **SELECTED GROUP EXHIBITIONS** *Toronto Grid Project*, York Quay Gallery, Toronto, 2003; *Whereabouts*, York Quay Gallery, Toronto, 2002; *Toronto 5*, Havana, Cuba, 2001 **AWARDS** Ontario Arts Council Exhibition Assistance Grant, 2003; Canada Council B Grant, 2001 **REPRESENTATION** Stephen Bulger Gallery (Toronto) **WEBSITES** www.ruthkaplan.com www.bulgergallery.com

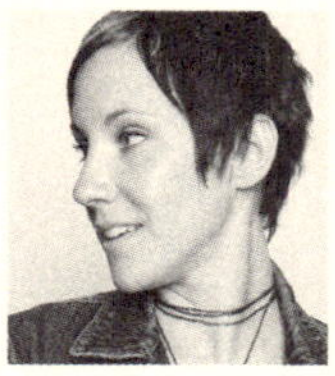

RAINA KIRN

BORN Toronto, 1977 **RESIDES** Toronto **EDUCATION** Dawson College, Commercial Photography Program, Montreal, 1998–2001 **SELECTED GROUP EXHIBITIONS** *First Truth*, Contact Photography Festival, Toronto, 2005; *Tsunami Relief*, Propeller Gallery, Toronto, 2005; *Provoke*, The Drake Hotel, Toronto, 2004; *Photographic Works*, Coop Gallery, Toronto, 2003; *Moving Pictures*, Bfly Atelier Gallery, Vancouver, 2003 **WEBSITE** www.rwphotographic.com

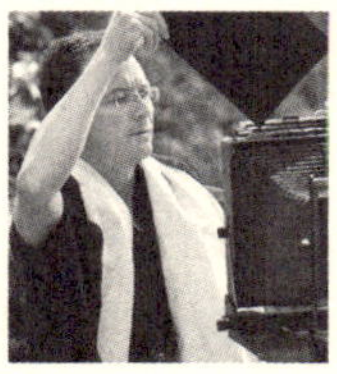

TODD KOROL

BORN Gilbert Plains, Manitoba, 1965 **RESIDES** Calgary **EDUCATION** Self-taught **SELECTED SOLO EXHIBITIONS** *Black & White*, Webster Gallery, Calgary, 1999; *Wanderings*, Black & White Gallery, Calgary, 1997; *Street Roaming*, Black & White Gallery, Calgary, 1996; *Sports*, Earl's Gallery, Saskatoon, 1991 **SELECTED GROUP EXHIBITIONS** *Alberta Landscapes*, Image 54 Gallery, Calgary, 2005; Artist group show, Image 54 Gallery, Calgary, 2005; *Artwalk*, Image 54 Gallery, Calgary, 2004; *Montana 24/7*, Dana Gallery, Missoula, Montana, 2004; *For the Love of the Children*, Crossroads Gallery, Calgary, 2003 **BOOKS/PUBLICATIONS** *Montana 24/7*, DK Publishing, 2004; *America 24/7*, DK Publishing, 2003; *Canada, Coast to Coast*, Reader's Digest, 1998; *A Day in the Life of the NHL*, HarperCollins, 1996; *Back Roads and Getaway Places*, Reader's Digest, 1994; *Harvest*, Fifth House, 1992 **AWARDS** Western Canadian News Photographers Association; Canadian Community Newspaper Association; National Press Photographers Association **CLIENTS** *Sports Illustrated*, *Maclean's*, *Canadian Geographic*, *Reader's Digest*, *Time*, *National Geographic*, *Paris Match*, Nexen, Stony Plain Records, *National Post Business Magazine*, *The Globe and Mail* **WEBSITE** www.toddkorol.com

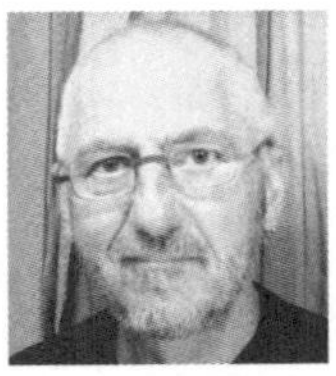

WOLF KUTNAHORSKY
BORN Germany, 1951 **RESIDES** Toronto **EDUCATION** Ryerson University, B.A. in Photography, Toronto, 1977 **MAIN STORIES** Documentaries on Third World issues; Aboriginal life in Australia; Nuclear industry in Romania and Canada **CLIENTS** *Time*, Scholastic Canada, *Canadian Geographic*, *Report on Business*, *Cottage Life*, United Church of Canada **WEBSITE** www.wolfphotos.ca

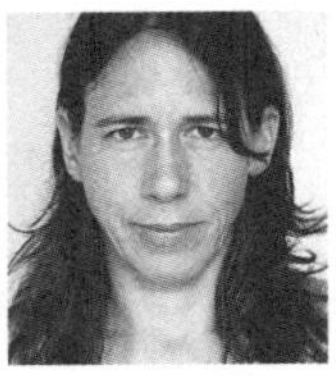

RITA LEISTNER
BORN Toronto, 1964 **RESIDES** Toronto **EDUCATION** The International Centre of Photography, Diploma in General Studies in Photography, New York, 2000; University of Toronto, M.A. in Comparative Literature, Toronto, 1990 **SELECTED SOLO EXHIBITIONS** *Portrait of Lamiya Aidan Kahumayes*, faceLIFT Series, Kitchener-Waterloo Art Gallery, Kitchener-Waterloo, Ontario, July, 2005; *Crazy Horse (American Cavalry in Iraq)*, Steve Wiley Gallery, Savannah, Georgia, 2004; *Photographs of Cambodia*, Foreign Correspondents' Club, Cambodia, 1999 **SELECTED GROUP EXHIBITIONS** *American Women Wrestlers*, Perpignan, France, and Contact Photography Festival, Toronto, 2003 **BOOKS/PUBLICATIONS** *Unembedded: Four Independent Photojournalists on the War in Iraq*, Chelsea Green, 2005; *Suspect*, MIT Press and Alphabet City Media, 2005 **MAIN STORIES** Portrait stories include American Women Wrestlers; A U.S. Cavalry Troop in Iraq; The gravediggers of Najaf during the August 2004 siege; The women patients of Baghdad's al Rashad Psychiatric Hospital; Cambodian-American ex-cons deported to Cambodia **CLIENTS** *Time*, *Newsweek*, *Rolling Stone*, *Colors*, *The Walrus*, *Maclean's* **WEBSITES** www.ritaleistner.com, www.reduxpictures.com

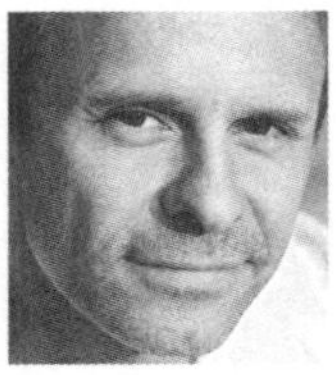

ROGER LEMOYNE
BORN Montreal, 1958 **RESIDES** Montreal **EDUCATION** Concordia University, B.A. in Cinema Production, Montreal, 1979 **SELECTED SOLO EXHIBITIONS** *24 Photos From Afghanistan, Iraq and Kosovo*, Maison de la Culture, Mont-Royal, Montreal, 2003; *Visa Pour l'Image*, slideshow Les Enfants et la Guerre, Perpignan, France, 2001 **SELECTED GROUP EXHIBITIONS** *Kites, Guns and Dreams* (travelling exhibitions), Vancouver, Montreal, Toronto, 2004–2005; *Imagenes Havana*, Centro Desarrollo de las Artes Visuales, Havana, Cuba, 2003 **BOOKS/PUBLICATIONS** *Details Obscurs*, les 400 Coups, 2005 **MAIN STORIES** Coverage of conflicts in Eastern Congo; Coverage of Kosovo, Middle East crisis **AWARDS** The Alexia Foundation Professional Grant, 2004; Pictures of the Year International, 3rd Place Magazine Photographer of the Year, 2004; World Press Photo, 2nd Place, People in the News, 1999 **CLIENTS** *Life*, *Saturday Night*, *Time*, *Maclean's*, UNICEF, CIDA, Redux Pictures **WEBSITE** www.rogerlemonye.com

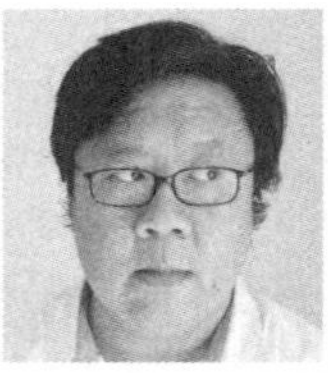

FRED LUM
BORN Toronto, 1962 **RESIDES** Toronto **EDUCATION** Ryerson Polytechnical Institute, First Year Photographic Arts, 1980 **MAIN STORIES** "Behind Closed Doors: The Struggle Over Homecare"; "Canada's Apartheid: Are Aboriginal People Second-class Citizens?"; "China Rising" **AWARDS** Placed in NPPA, ECNPA Contests and CP Picture of the Month; Society of Newspaper Design Award of Excellence for Photojournalism, 2002 **WEBSITE** www.theglobeandmail.com

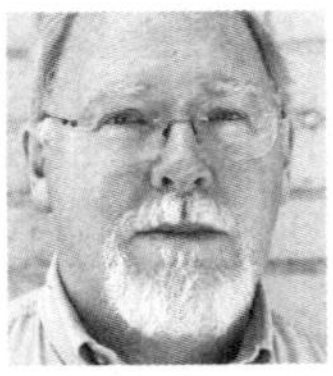

IAN MACEACHERN
BORN Glace Bay, N.S., 1942 **RESIDES** London, Ontario **EDUCATION** Self-taught **SELECTED SOLO EXHIBITIONS** *Ian MacEachern Photographs*, Stephen Bulger Gallery, Toronto, 2004; *Photographs of Saint John, 1963–1973*, Handworks Gallery, Saint John, 2002–2004 **SELECTED GROUP EXHIBITIONS** *Summer Review*, Stephen Bulger Gallery, Toronto, 2004; *Queen Street*, Stephen Bulger Gallery, Toronto, 2003 **BOOKS/PUBLICATIONS** *Velvet Underground in Hamilton*, Barry Lord, artscanada, 1967; *Ian MacEachern's Photographs of Saint John*, artscanada, 1967; *Grass Roots Art in Canada*, artscanada, 1969; *Us Too, A Photographic Essay by Ian MacEachern*, Diane P. Rogers and Robert J. Clark, Inside World Politics, Macmillan of Canada, 1969; *The People in Ian MacEachern's Pictures*, Barry Lord, artscanada, 1970 **AWARDS** Toronto Art Directors Club Award, 1975; Canada Council Visual Arts Grant, 1971 **CLIENTS** artscanada, *Canadian Magazine*, *Chatelaine*, *The Imperial Oil Review*, *London Magazine*, *Maclean's*, *Ontario Living*, *Quest*, *Saturday Night*, *Shell News*, *The Star Weekly Magazine*, *Site Sound*, *Time* **REPRESENTATION** Stephen Bulger Gallery (Toronto) **WEBSITES** www.ianmaceachern.com, www.bulgergallery.com

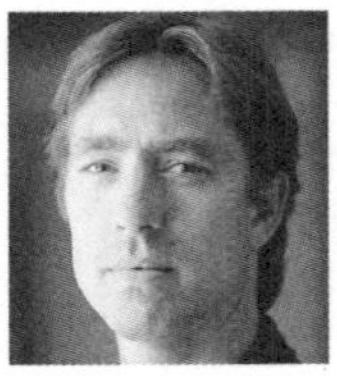

BRYAN MCBURNEY
BORN Halifax, 1967 **RESIDES** Toronto **EDUCATION** Ryerson University, B.A. in Visual Arts, Toronto, 1996; Bezalel Academy of Art and Design, Jerusalem, Israel, 1994–1995 **SELECTED GROUP EXHIBITIONS** *Panorama*, Spin Gallery, Toronto, 2004; *Gallery and Invited Artists Exhibition*, Spin Gallery, Toronto, 2004; *Shock and Awe*, Spin Gallery, Toronto, 2004 **MAJOR STORIES** Iran Generation of Change; Israel/Palestine Conflict; The Intifada; King Hussein Funeral; Kosovar Refugees; Iranian Elections; Lebanon Transition **CLIENTS** *Newsweek*, *L'Express*, *Focus Magazine*, *The Guardian/Observer*, *The Washington Post*, *The Boston Globe*, *Die Zeit* **WEBSITE** www.bryanmcburney.com

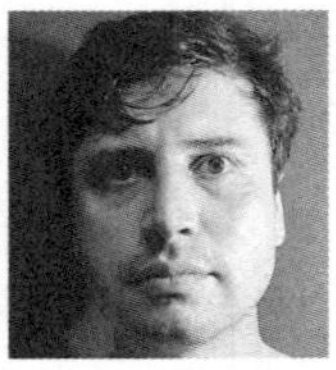

FERNANDO MORALES
BORN Santiago, Chile, 1972 **RESIDES** Toronto **EDUCATION** Institute of Superior Studies in Communications ALPES, B.A. in Photojournalism, Santiago, Chile, 1993 **SELECTED SOLO EXHIBITION** *In the Barrio*, Queen East Studio-Gallery, Toronto, 2005 **SELECTED GROUP EXHIBITIONS** *Salvador Allende Arts for Peace*, De Leon White Gallery, Toronto, 2004; Art Amici Gallery, Austin, Texas, 2003; Paper & Ink Gallery, Austin, Texas, 2003 **AWARDS** ECNPA Picture Story of the Year, Third Place, 2004; Best Agence France Presse Photo, 2001; NBC's Editor's Choice, 2001 **CLIENTS** *The Globe and Mail* **WEBSITES** www.moralesimages.com, www.queeneastgallery.com

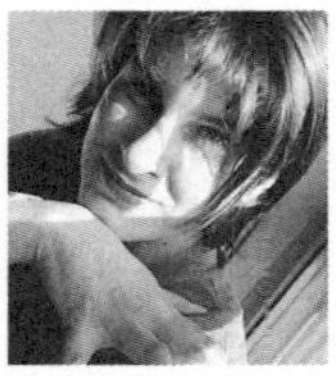

CHRISTINNE MUSCHI
BORN Hamilton, Ontario, 1965 **RESIDES** Montreal **EDUCATION** Ryerson University, Bachelor in Applied Arts (Honours), Toronto, 1998 **SELECTED GROUP EXHIBITIONS** *Life of Water*, PhotoSensitive, Allen Lambert Galleria, BCE Place, Toronto, 2005; *I Read Montreal*, Joe Lis Montreal, McGill College, Montreal, 2005; *Protecting Peace*, BloWup Gallery, Montreal, 2004; *Power of Reflection*, Saidye Bronfman Centre, Montreal, 2001 **MAIN STORIES** Trucking Little America; Katherine 90; Oxfam aid in Africa; Grey Cup; Fina World Aquatics; Federal Election; Queen's Royal Visit **CLIENTS** Reuters, *The Globe and Mail*, *National Post*, *Maclean's*, *Toronto Star*, *The New York Times*

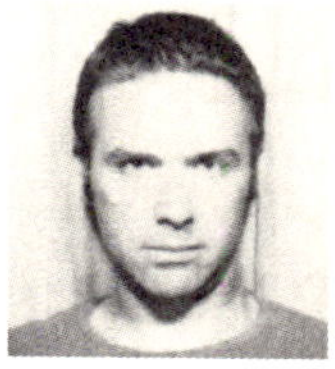

SANDY NICHOLSON

BORN Sydney, Australia, 1973 **RESIDES** Toronto **EDUCATION** Royal Melbourne Institute of Technology, B.A. in Photography, Melbourne, Australia, 1995 **SELECTED SOLO EXHIBITIONS** *Suburban Fetish*, Tatar Alexander Gallery, Toronto, 2001; *Lifts*, Tatar Alexander Gallery, Toronto, 2003 **SELECTED GROUP EXHIBITIONS** *Suburban Fetish*, World Press Photo Exhibitions, 2004; *Lifts*, Canberra Contemporary Art Space, Canberra, Australia, 2002; *Pools as Part of Moral Hallucinations*, Museum of Contemporary Art, Sydney, Australia, 2000 **MAIN STORIES** "Toronto, A Great Place to Die," *Toronto Life*, 2005; "Masons," *Toro*, 2005; "Bruce Mau," *The New Yorker*, 2005; "Margaret Atwood," *Financial Times Magazine*, 2004 **CLIENTS** Nike, Hutchison Global Communications, Bank of Montreal, Dove, GlaxoSmithKline, *Financial Times Magazine*, *Wired*, *Saturday Night*, *Rolling Stone*, *AdBusters*, *Communication Arts*, *American Photography* **REPRESENTATION** Tatar Gallery (Toronto) **WEBSITES** www.sandynicholson.com, www.tatargallery.com

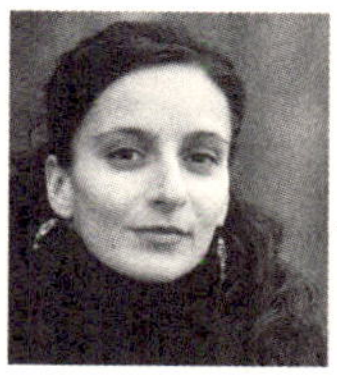

FARAH NOSH

BORN Edmonton, 1974 **RESIDES** Vancouver and New York **EDUCATION** Western Academy of Photography, Diploma in Photojournalism, 2002; University of British Columbia, B.A., Major Geography, Minor Religious Studies, 1998 **MAIN STORIES** Iraq coverage, 2002–2005; Project to document the Haida nation's struggle to keep the endangered Haida language alive **CLIENTS** *Toronto Star*, *The Globe and Mail*, *The New York Times*, *Time*, *National Geographic Traveller*, *Life* **WEBSITE** www.farahnosh.com

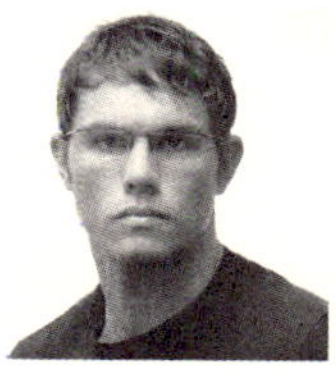

LUCAS OLENIUK

BORN Saskatoon, 1978 **RESIDES** Toronto **EDUCATION** University of Saskatchewan, B.A. (Honours) in English, Saskatoon, 2000 **MAIN STORIES** The Native struggle in Western Canada; Hurricanes Ivan and Katrina **AWARDS** National Newspaper Award, 2004 **CLIENTS** *Toronto Star*

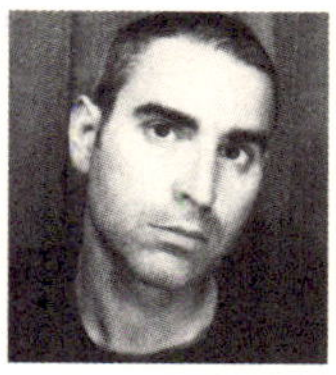

LOUIE PALU

BORN Toronto, 1968 **RESIDES** Toronto **EDUCATION** Ontario College of Art and Design, Diploma in Communication and Design, Toronto, 1991 **SELECTED GROUP EXHIBITIONS** Ping Yao International Photography Festival, Ping Yao, China 2005; Visa Pour L'Image, Perpignan, France, 2004 and 2005; Internationale Fototage, Mannheim/Ludwigshafen, Germany, 2005; George Eastman House, Rochester, New York, 2005 **AWARDS** Society of Newspaper Design Silver Medal, 2005 **WEBSITE** www.louiepalu.com

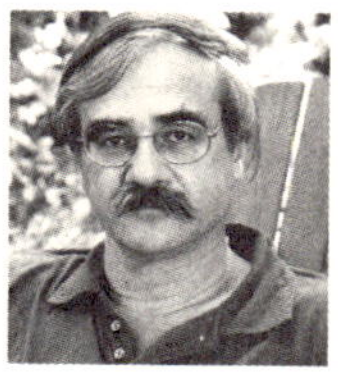

VINCENZO PIETROPAOLO

BORN Maierato, Italy, 1951 **RESIDES** Toronto **EDUCATION** Self-taught **SELECTED SOLO EXHIBITIONS** *Essential Workers: Mexican Farm Workers in Canada*, Art Gallery of Windsor, Windsor, Ontario, 2004; *Vincenzo Pietropaolo, A 30-Year Retrospective*, Stephen Bulger Gallery, Toronto, 200[illegible]; *Growing Cultures*, Royal Ontario Museum, Toronto. 200[illegible]; *Harvest Pilgrims*, El Atrio, Embassy of Canada, Mexico, later travelling through the Caribbean, the United States, and Canada, 1996–2001 **BOOK/PUBLICATIONS** *Not Paved With Gold*, Between the Lines Press, Toronto, 2006; *Making Home in Havana*, Text: Cecelia Lawless, Rutgers University Press, New York, 2002; *Canadians at Work*, Canadian Auto Workers Union, 2000; *Canadiens au travail*, Canadian Auto Workers Union, 2000; *Kensington*, Text: Jean Cochrane, Boston Mills Press, Erin, Ontario, 20[illegible] *Celebration of Resistance*, Between the Lines Press Toronto, 1999; *Toronto, A Colour Guide*, Formac Publishing Co. (four editions), Halifax, 1997–2003 **CLIENTS** City of Toronto, City Home Corporation, Heritage Toronto, Toronto Community Foundation, CN Tower/La Tour CN, HOK Canada, Canadian Auto Workers, Canadian Union of Public Employees, National Labour College (Washington), National Film Board of Canada, College of Nurses of Ontario, Urban Strategies, Inc., Ministry of Citizenship, Ontario, St. Stephen's Community House **REPRESENTATION** Stephen Bulger Gallery (Toronto) **WEBSITE** www.bulgergallery.com

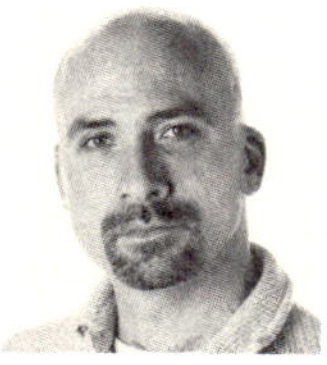

PETER POWER

BORN Labrador City, Newfoundland, 1965 **RESIDES** Hamilton, Ontario **EDUCATION** Loyalist College, Diploma in Photojournalism, Belleville, Ontario, 1999 **MAIN STORIES** Toronto's mentally ill; Terminally ill cancer patients; Tent City residents; 18-month documentation of young men undergoing facial reconstruction; Three Olympic Games Zapatista uprising, Mexico, 1994 **AWARDS** National Newspaper Awards, 1996 and 2002; Governor General's Michener Award for Public Service Journalism, 1998 National Press Photographer's Association, Region Two, Photographer of the Year, 1994, 2001, 2002; Eastern Canadian Newspaper Association, Photographer of the Year, 1994 **WEBSITE** www.peterpower.ca

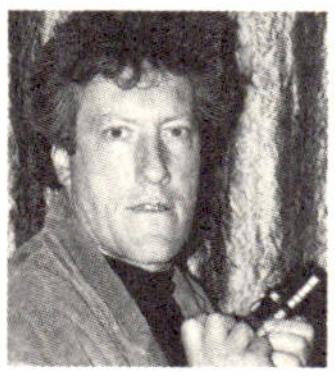

DUANE PRENTICE

BORN Montreal, 1960 **RESIDES** Victoria **EDUCATION** L.B. Pearson College, Metchosin, B.C., 1977–1979, International Baccalaureate; University of Victoria, B.Sc., 1984–1987; Missouri School of Journalism Short Course 1998; Bruce Barnbaum Workshop, 1993 **SELECTED SOLO EXHIBITION** *In the Crucible*, InterUrban Gallery, Vancouver, 2004 **SELECTED GROUP EXHIBITIONS** *Labyrinthes '05*, On Canvas Gallery, Victoria, 2005; *AngKor Series and Transformations*, Vancouver Art Crawl, Vancouver, 2003; *Crucible*, Iraqi Photographic Society International Press, Baghdad, Iraq, 2002; *M.I.L.K. (Moments of Intimacy, Laughter and Kinship)*, Science Museum, London, England, 2001 **MAIN STORIES** *In the Crucible*, a five-year project documenting the lives of 30 people and families living in the Downtown Eastside of Vancouver; Sudan: Médecins Sans Frontières **AWARDS** *Applied Arts Magazine*, Photojournalism, 2004; *Applied Arts Magazine*, Nature and Environment, 2004; NPPA Honourable Mention, Feature Story, 2001 **WEBSITE** www.nomadicvisions.com

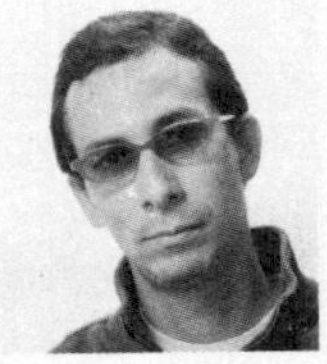

PEDRO RUIZ

BORN Caracas, Vénézuéla, 1970 **RESIDES** Montreal **EDUCATION** l'Université Centrale du Vénézuéla, B.A. in Communications, Caracas, Vénézuéla, 2002 **SELECTED GROUP EXHIBITIONS** Semaine culturelle vénézuélienne à la maison de la culture Frontenac, 2005; Mega exposición Arte Venezolano del Siglo XX, Galería de Arte Nacional, Vénézuéla, 2005; Festival Víctor Jara, Montreal, 2004; Mega exposición Arte Venezolano del Siglo XX, Museo de Arte de Maracay, Vénézuéla, 2004; L'Expo 2000 Hannover, l'Allemagne, 2000 **BOOKS/PUBLICATIONS** Co-auteur du livre *Oficio de familia*: la photographie journalistique vénézuélienne dans le XXième siècle, Accent Éditorial, 2004 **MAIN STORIES** "Le Farc: Camper et aimer et survivre," San Vicente del Caguan, Colombie; "L'incertitude, toujours au coin de l'œil," Barrios de Caracas, Vénézuéla; "Jusqu'à ce que le corps supporte," L'hôpital Pérez de de Leon, le Périphérique de Coche et le Périphérique de Catia, Vénézuéla; "11 avril, 2002 coup d'État," Caracas, Vénézuéla; "Dans le plafond de la forêt," Amazonas, Darién, Bresil, Panama, Vénézuéla; "Or à contra-jour," Fleuve Caroni, Vénézuéla; "Metiers de famille," Edoviña, Vénézuéla; "Cuando la carne no es de vaca," Caura, Vénézuéla; "Lumières d'eau apprivoisée," Lac Titicaca, Pérou **WEBSITE** www.pedroruiz.com

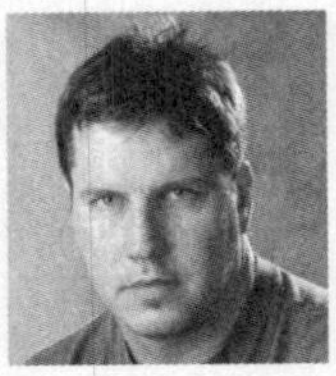

STEVE RUSSELL

BORN Sudbury, Ontario, 1967 **RESIDES** Toronto **EDUCATION** Loyalist College, Diploma in Photojournalism, Belleville, Ontario, 1995 **SELECTED GROUP EXHIBITIONS** *Photosensitive's Destination*, BCE Place, Toronto, 2003; *Photosensitive's Water*, BCE Place, Toronto 2005 **MAIN STORIES** Swissair crash; The turning of the millennium in Tonga; 2000 Sydney Summer Olympics; Elections in Zimbabwe **AWARDS** Eastern Canadian New Photographer Association, Photographer of the Year, 1999, 2002 and 2003; Eastern Canadian New Photographer Association, Picture of the Year, 2003; Society for News Design Awards of Excellence, 1999, 2002, 2003 and 2004

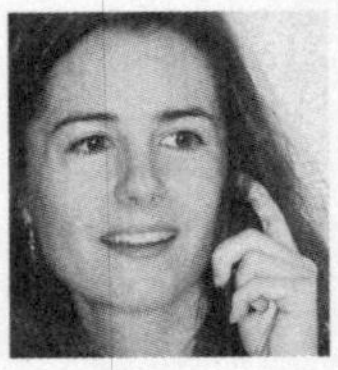

ANDREA RYDER

BORN Toronto, 1965 **RESIDES** New York **EDUCATION** New York University (in association with the International Centre for Photography), M.A. in Studio Art, 2003; Concordia University, B.F.A., a double minor in Photography and Print Media, Montreal, 1996-1999; Trent University, B.A. in Cultural Studies and French, Peterborough, Ontario, 1989 **SELECTED SOLO EXHIBITIONS** *The Hebrew Pentecostals*, The Interfaith Center of New York, 2004; *Entourage*, The International Center for Photography, 2003; *Old Cars in Ontario* and *The Worker Series*, Festival Iberoamericano, Holguin, Cuba, 1999 **SELECTED GROUP EXHIBITIONS** *NYU's Master's Thesis Show*, 80 Washington Square Gallery, New York, 2003; *A Commons Show*, New York University, New York, 2003; *Reciprocity Failure*, Open City, Montreal, 1999 **WEBSITE** www.andrearyder.com

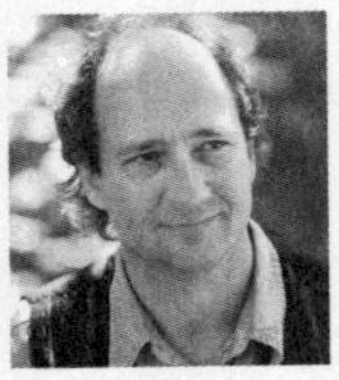

ROBERT SEMENIUK

BORN Big Valley, Alberta, 1949 **RESIDES** Bowen Island, B.C. **EDUCATION** University of Alberta, Edmonton, B.A., 1971; York University, Toronto, Master of Environmental Studies **SELECTED SOLO EXHIBITIONS** *War Affected Children*, Retrospective, Canadian War Museum, Ottawa, 2002-2003; *Landmines*, Arts Centre, Maputo, Mozambique, 2000; *Landmines*, Okanagan Art Gallery, Penticton, B.C., 1999; *Landmines*, Canadian Museum of Contemporary Photography, 1997 **BOOKS/PUBLICATIONS** *Among the Inuit*, Raincoast, 2006 **WEBSITE** www.robertsemeniuk.com

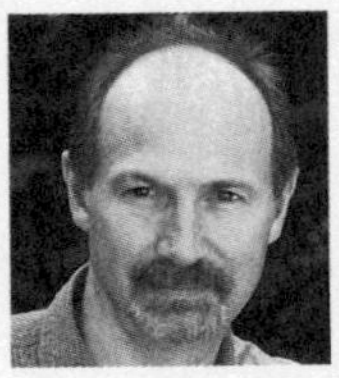

PETER SIBBALD

BORN York County, Ontario, 1957 **RESIDES** Georgina, Ontario **EDUCATION** Queen's University, B.A. in Sociology, Kingston, Ontario, 1980; Queen's University, B.Ed (Intermediate-Senior Math/Science plus ESL), Kingston, Ontario, 1983 **SELECTED SOLO EXHIBITIONS** Quebec Summit of the Americas 2001; The Photo Passage at Harbourfront Centre, Toronto, 2002; *Home Front*, Jet Fuel, Contact Photography Festival, Toronto, 1998 **SELECTED GROUP EXHIBITIONS** *Oka, été 1990/Oka, Summer 1990*, Red Deer and District Museum and Archives, Red Deer, Alberta, 2002; *Oka, Summer 1990*, The Little Gallery, Prince Albert, Saskatchewan, 2001 **MAIN STORIES** The Innu, The Oka Crisis and the Relationship Between the First Peoples and Non-Natives in Canada; Home Front and The Making of a Family; Sprawl 905—Changing Land Use in Southern Ontario **AWARDS** Canada Council Project Assistance to Visual Arts, Craft and Architecture recipient, The May 17 Photo Collective, 2002; Alexia Foundation for World Peace, Special Recognition, 2001 **CLIENTS** *Business Week*, *Canadian Geographic*, *Forbes*, *Maclean's*, *Time* **WEBSITE** www.petersibbald.com

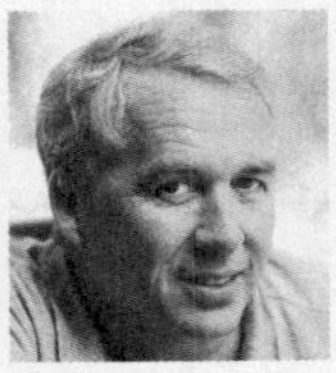

DAVID LEONARD SIDAWAY

BORN London, Ontario, 1955 **RESIDES** Montreal **SELECTED GROUP EXHIBITIONS** *I Read Montreal/Joe Lis Montreal*, McGill College, Montreal, 2005; The Life of Water, Allen Lambert Galleria, BCE Place, Toronto, 2005 **MAIN STORIES** Ice Storm; Stanley Cup; Grey Cup; Royal Tours of Queen Elizabeth and the Queen Mother to Quebec; Famine of Ethiopia **CLIENTS** *The Montreal Gazette*, United Press Canada, Reuters, *The Globe and Mail*

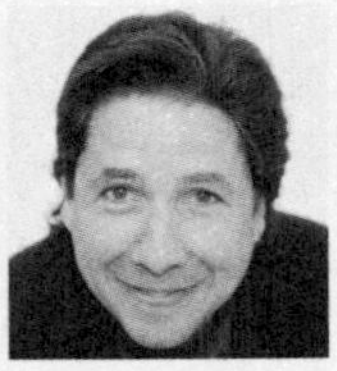

STEVE SIMON

BORN Montreal, 1960 **RESIDES** New York **EDUCATION** Concordia University, B.A., Communications/Journalism, Minor in Fine Art, 1985; Dawson College, Diploma of Collegial Studies in Professional Photography, Montreal, 1997 **SELECTED SOLO EXHIBITIONS** *Contemporary American Photography*, Seventh Internationale Fototage, Mannheim/Ludwigshafen, Manneheim, Germany, 2005; *American Photographs*, Escuela Argentina De Fotografia, Buenos-Aires, Argentina, 2004; *Empty Sky*, Realtime Gallery, Toronto, 2004; *Allegiance*, The Half King, New York, 2002 **BOOKS/PUBLICATIONS** *The Republicans*, Charta Art Books, Milan, 2006; *Empty Sky—The Pilgrimage to Ground Zero*, Les Editions International, Montreal, 2002 **AWARDS** The Global Health Council Photography Award, 2004; Art Directors Club of New York Award of Merit, 2003; Alfred Eiesenstaedt Award for Magazine Photography, 2000; National Press Photographers Association Picture of the Year, 1999; Canadian News Photographer of the Year, sponsored by The Canadian Press, 1993 **WEBSITE** www.stevesimonphoto.com

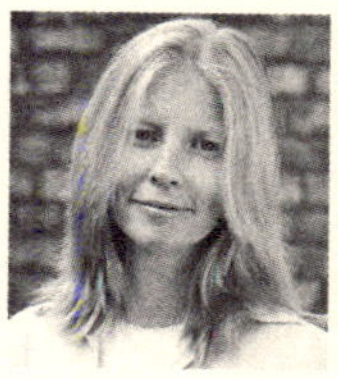

LANA SLEZIC

BORN Toronto, 1973 **RESIDES** Kabul, Afghanistan **EDUCATION** University of Western Ontario, London, Ontario, Honours B.A. in Kinesiology, 1997; Loyalist College, Photojournalism Degree, 1999 **SELECTED SOLO EXHIBITIONS** *Afghan Women*, Sponza Palace Gallery, Dubrovnik, Croatia, 2005; *Never Conquered*, BloWup Gallery, Montreal, 2005 **SELECTED GROUP EXHIBITIONS** *Kites, Guns and Dreams*, Photo Passage Gallery, Harbourfront, Toronto, 2005 **MAIN STORIES** Book project on Afghan women; A project on Dubrovnik, Croatia **CLIENTS** *Time*, *Paris Match*, *The New York Times*, *The London Times*, *British Vogue*, *Marie Claire*, *The Sunday Times Magazine*, *The Sunday Telegraph*, *The Guardian*, *The Sunday Herald*, *The Observer*, *Institutional Investor Magazine*, *The Australian*, *The Independent*, *The Globe and Mail*, *Canadian Geographic*, *Maclean's*, *The Daily Telegraph*, Getty Images, Panos Pictures, Global Aware, UNICEF, Catholic Relief Services **WEBSITE** www.lanaslezic.com

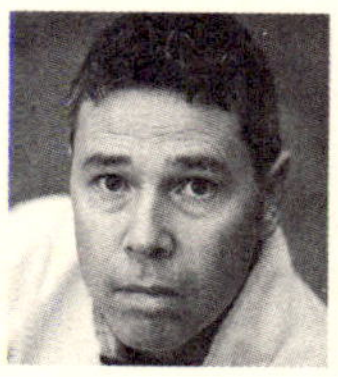

LYLE STAFFORD

BORN Vanguard, Saskatchewan, 1959 **RESIDES** Vancouver **EDUCATION** Self-taught **BOOKS/PUBLICATIONS** *2/15, The Day the World Said No to War*, AK Press/Hello NYC, 2003 **MAIN STORIES** Ugandan child soldiers, 2002; Elizabeth II royal tour, 2002; Pickton Farm murders, 2002; Kenyan AIDS researchers, 2002; Philippines elections, 1998 **CLIENTS** *The Globe and Mail*, Reuters, *National Post*, *Toronto Star*, *Wish* magazine **WEBSITE** www.lylestafford.com

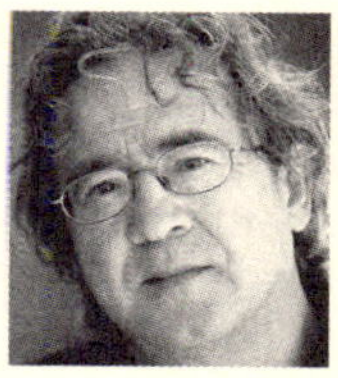

ANDREW STAWICKI

BORN Poland, 1948 **RESIDES** Mississauga, Ontario **EDUCATION** College of Photography, Poland, 1969 **SELECTED SOLO EXHIBITIONS** *A People Apart*, Wellington-Cooke Gallery, Toronto, 1995; *Fashions From Paris, Milan and New York*, Queen's Quay Terminal Gallery, Toronto, 1992 **SELECTED GROUP EXHIBITIONS** *PhotoSensitive: Life of Water*, Allen Lambert Galleria, BCE Place, Toronto, 2005; *Destination Toronto*, Allen Lambert Galleria, BCE Place, Toronto, 2004; *HIV Positive—AIDS Through a New Lens*, First Canadian Place Gallery, Toronto, 2002; *Child Poverty—A National Disgrace*, First Canadian Place Gallery, Toronto, 2001; *Braille = Equality*, Parliament Hill, Ottawa, 2000; *Gdansk, Celebrating 100 Years*, PEKAO Gallery, Toronto, 1997; *Them = Us*, Royal Ontario Museum, Toronto, 1997; *A Hand of Hope*, Queen's Quay Terminal Gallery, Toronto, 1995; *Precious Time*, The Hospital for Sick Children, Toronto, 1994; *It's in Their Eyes*, Toronto City Hall, Toronto, 1992 **BOOKS/PUBLICATIONS** *Life of Water, PhotoSensitive*, PhotoSensitive, 2005; *Photosensitive, 10-Years Work*, PhotoSensitive, 1999; *Precious Time, The Hospital for Sick Children*, PhotoSensitive, 1990; *A People Apart*, Somerville House, 1995 **AWARDS** Society of Newspaper Design Awards, Gold Medal, 1998; CAPIC Award, Gold Medal, 1991 and 1992; National Newspaper Award, Features Category Winner, 1993 and 2000 **WEBSITE** www.photosensitive.com

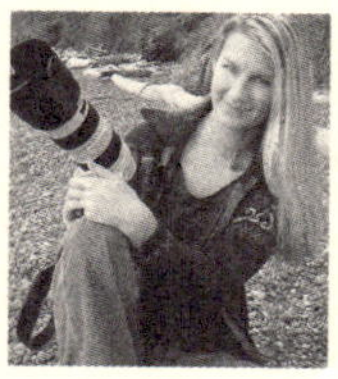

DEDDEDA STEMLER

BORN Esterhazy, Saskatchewan, 1975 **RESIDES** Victoria **EDUCATION** Western Academy of Photography, Diploma in Photojournalism and Journalism, Victoria, 2000-2001; University of Calgary, B.A. Sociology, Calgary, 1993-199[illegible] **SELECTED GROUP EXHIBITIONS** *Tsunami: Aftermath in Phuket*, National Geographic IMAX Theatre and Royal B.C. Museum, Victoria, 2005; *Tsunami: Aftermath in Phuket*, Mayfair Shopping Centre, Victoria, 2005; *Black and White Photography*, On Canvas Art Gallery, Victoria, 2005 and 2003; *Fine Art Photography*, Sooke Fine Arts Show, Sooke, B.C., 2003; Professional Photographers Association of British Columbia Salon, Vancouver, 2001 **AWARDS** Western Canadian News Photographer Association, 2005, 200[illegible] and 2003; *Photo Life* magazine, 2002; Professional Photographers Association of British Columbia, 20[illegible] **WEBSITE** www.deddeda.com

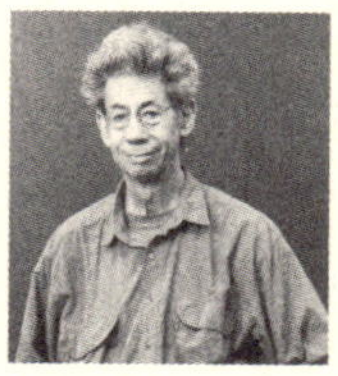

GABOR SZILASI

BORN Budapest, Hungary, 1928 **RESIDES** Montreal **EDUCATION** Self-taught **SELECTED SOLO EXHIBITIONS** *Gabor Szilasi: Photographies, 1954-1996*, Musée des beaux-arts de Montreal and Stephen Bulger Gallery, Toronto, 1997; *Gabor Szilasi-Szilasi Gábor*, Hungarian House of Photography, Budapest, 2003; *Noir et blanc sur les Impatients*, Centre Les Impatients, Montreal, 200[illegible] **SELECTED GROUP EXHIBITIONS** *Exchanging Views: Quebec 1939-1970*, Canadian Museum of Contemporary Photography, 1999; *Vertiges: duos photographiques*, Bordeaux, France, 2002 **BOOKS/PUBLICATIONS** *Gabor Szilasi: Photographies, 1954-1996*, McGill-Queens University Press, Montreal-Kingston, 1997; *I AM (Photographer Gabor Szilasi's Journey Into a World Seldom Visited)*, Editions Les Impatients, Montreal, 20[illegible] **REPRESENTATION** Stephen Bulger Gallery (Toronto) **WEBSITES** www.voxphoto.com, www.bulgergallery.com

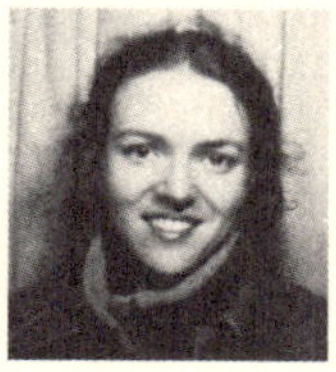

AMANDA TETRAULT

BORN Montreal, 1977 **RESIDES** Montreal **EDUCATION** Dawson College, Diploma of Collegial Studies in Professional Photography, Montreal, 1997 **SELECTED SOLO EXHIBITIONS** *Phil and Me*, Trolley Gallery, and ZooArtFair, London, England, 2004 **SELECTED GROUP EXHIBITIONS** *Impressions of Moscow*, Bobards, Montreal, 1998 **BOOKS/PUBLICATIONS** *Phil and Me*, Trolley Books, 2004 **AWARDS** Conseils des arts et des lettres du Quebec Artists Grant, 2005; Visual Arts Fellow, Fine Arts Work Centre, Massachusetts, 20[illegible]; *Phil and Me* shortlisted for the John Kobal Photography Book Award, 2005; Canada Council of the Arts Emerging Artist Grant, 2001 **CLIENTS** *The Observer*, *Saturday Night*, *The Globe and Mail*, *The Montreal Gazette*, *Photo Event* **WEBSITE** www.amandatetrault.com

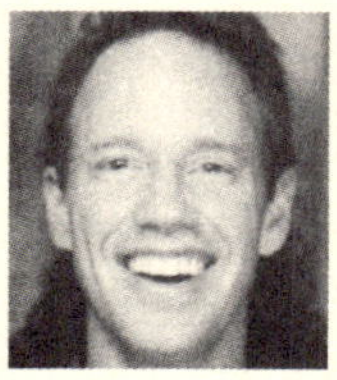

DAVID TRATTLES

BORN Ottawa, 1970 **RESIDES** Ottawa & Toronto **EDUCATION** Self-taught **SELECTED SOLO EXHIBITION** Yukon Art Centre, Novara di Sicilia, Sebnitz Germany, 2005 **SELECTED GROUP EXHIBITIONS** *Legacy*, CBC, Contact Festival, touring Canadian cities, 2005; *Project Malta*, touring U.S., Australia, 2004-Present; *Citylights*, Krakow, Poland, 2005; *Canadiana*, touring Venezuela, Guyana, Panama, 2004; *Dreamworks*, Vancouver, Halifax, 2004 **BOOKS/PUBLICATIONS** *Project Malta*, Progress Press, 2005 **AWARDS** National Magazine Award Nomination, 1996 and 2002; Kodak North American Print Competition, First Prize, 1998 **CLIENTS** CIDA, *Canadian Geographic*, *The Globe and Mail*, *Maclean's* **WEBSITES** www.davidtrattles.com, www.photomediterraneo.com

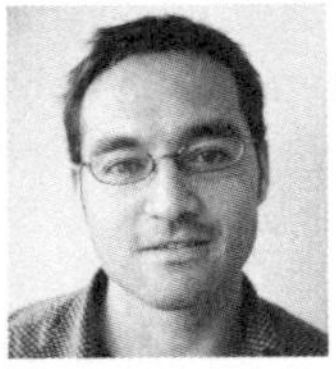

KEVIN VAN PAASSEN

BORN Calgary, 1971 **RESIDES** Toronto **EDUCATION** Southern Alberta Institute of Technology, Diploma in Journalism Arts, Calgary, 1996 **MAIN STORIES** Anniversary of 9/11 terrorist attacks; Regent Park housing project **CLIENTS** *The New York Times*, *USA Today*, *The Globe and Mail*

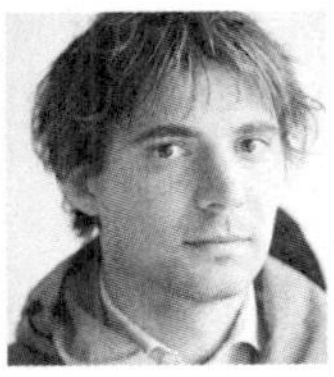

CHRISTOPHER WAHL

BORN Toronto, 1972 **RESIDES** Toronto **EDUCATION** Self-taught **CLIENTS** Federal Express, The Dow Jones, Nike, Etrade, IBM, The Rolling Stones **WEBSITE** www.christopherwahl.com

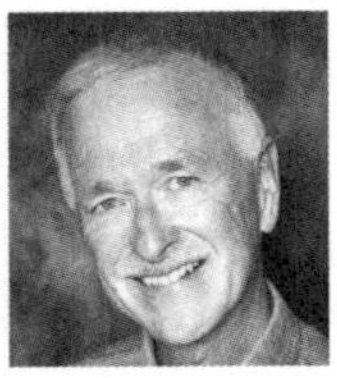

GEORGE WEBBER

BORN Drumheller, Alberta, 1952 **RESIDES** Calgary **EDUCATION** The University of Alberta, Bachelor of Arts in Political Science, Edmonton, 1973; Carleton University, Bachelor of Journalism (Honours), Ottawa, 1974 **SELECTED SOLO EXHIBITIONS** *A World Within*, Photospace, Calgary, 2005; *Portraits and Landscapes: Photographs by George Webber*, Travelling exhibition, 2003–2004; *The Blood Reserve*, Eleanor London Public Library, Montreal, 2003; *Startling Ordinary*, Art Gallery of Hamilton, Hamilton, Ontario, 2002; *Requiem*, Folio Gallery, Calgary, 1995 **BOOKS/PUBLICATIONS** *People of the Blood*, Fifth House, 2006; *A World Within: An Intimate Portrait of the Little Bow Hutterite Colony*, Fifth House, 2005; *Footprints on the Land: Tracing the Path of the Athabasca Chipewyan First Nation*, Athabasca Chipewyan First Nation 2003; *Requiem: The Vanishing Face of the Canadian Prairie, Folio Gallery, 1995;* Hospital: A Portrait of the Calgary General, The Calgary General Hospital, 1982 **AWARDS** National Magazine Awards, Silver Award, 2002; Elected to Royal Canadian Academy of Arts, 1999; Ford of Canada Photographic Grand Prix, 1992 **CLIENTS** *Canadian Geographic*, *Doubletake*, *Geist*, *Saturday Night*, *Photolife*, *Leica Fotographie*, *Lenswork Quarterly*, *Hasselblad Forum*, *CV Photo*, *Legacy* **WEBSITE** www.ccca.ca (search for George Webber)

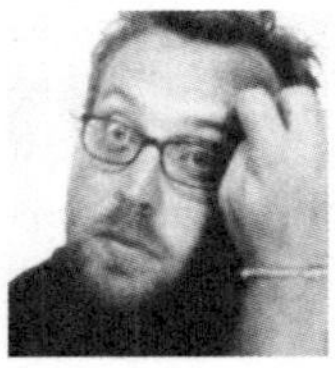

DONALD WEBER

BORN Toronto, 1973 **RESIDES** Toronto **EDUCATION** Ontario College of Art and Design, Honours Diploma in Environmental Design, Toronto, 1996; Loyalist College, Honours Diploma in Photojournalism, Belleville, Ontario, 2001 **SELECTED GROUP EXHIBITIONS** *Drinking in Chernobyl*, Fuel Gallery, Mississauga, Ontario, 2005; *Life of Water*, Allen Lambert Galleria, BCE Place, Toronto, 2005; *The Hidden Sitter*, Gladstone Gallery, Toronto, 2005; *Welcome to My Country*, 3 Storey Gallery, Toronto, 2004; *Stoking the Star Making Machinery*, Horseshoe Tavern, Toronto, 2004; *Barnstorm XVI*, The Bath House, New York, 2003 **MAIN STORIES** Criminal underclass of the ex-Soviet cities; Kurdistan, Middle East **AWARDS** World Press Photo Masterclass Nominee, 2006; Society of Newspaper Design Gold Medal of Excellence for Photography, 2005; ECNPA Pictures of the Year, 2004; Society of Newspaper Design Award of Excellence for Special Coverage, 2004 **CLIENTS** Getty Images, *The Globe and Mail*, *The Guardian*, *The Independent*, *La Presse*, *Le Monde*, *The London Times*, *The Los Angeles Times*, *Maclean's*, *National Post*, *The New York Times*, *Newsweek*, *Rolling Stone*, *Time*, *Outpost Magazine* **WEBSITE** www.donaldweber.com

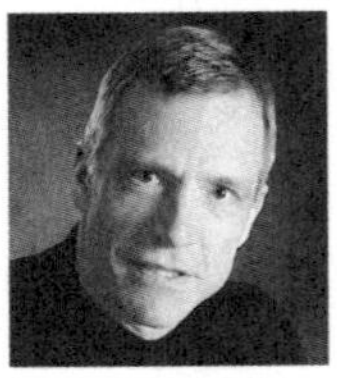

BERNARD WEIL

BORN Toronto, 1958 **RESIDES** Toronto **EDUCATION** Sheridan College, Diploma in Applied Photography, Oakville, Ontario, 1979 **SELECTED SOLO EXHIBITIONS** *Visa pour l'Image*, International Festival of Photojournalism, Perpignan, France, 2004 **MAIN STORIES** Hurricanes Katrina and Rita; Olympics in Atlanta and Sydney; War in Afghanistan; New York World Trade Centre attack; Los Angeles and Quebec City riots; Peru cholera epidemic; Fashion collections in Milan, London, Paris and New York

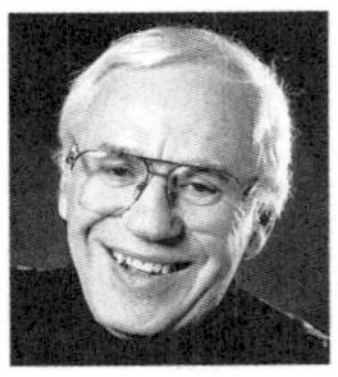

GEORGE S. ZIMBEL

BORN Woburn, Massachusetts, 1929 **RESIDES** Montreal **EDUCATION** The Photo League, 1949; Columbia College, New York, B.A., 1947–1951; Alexy Brodovitch Workshop, New School, New York, 1951 **SELECTED SOLO EXHIBITIONS** *George S. Zimbel: Documentary Photographer, Works 1947–2004*; Canadian Embassy Prince Takamado Gallery, Tokyo, 2005; *Before, During & After: The Photographs of George S. Zimbel*, Confederation Centre Art Gallery and Museum, Charlottetown, 2004; *A Survey From Five Decades of Photographs*, Stephen Bulger Gallery, Toronto, 2002; *New York 1947–2000*, Columbia University, 2001; *Documents*, John Cleary Gallery, Houston, 2000; *Retrospective*, IVAM, Valencia, Spain, 2000; *Still Movies*, Brock University, 1997 **SELECTED GROUP EXHIBITIONS** *I Wanna Be Loved by You: Photographs of Marilyn Monroe From the Leon and Michaela Constantiner Collection*, Brooklyn Museum, Brooklyn, New York, 2005; *Bright Lights Big City*, Winston Wachter Fine Art, Seattle, 1999; *Photographs*, Swan Galleries Auction, New York, 1999; *Exchanging Views: Quebec, 1939–1970*, Canadian Museum of Contemporary Photography, Ottawa, 1999; *Gallery Artists Exhibition*, Shapiro's Gallery, San Francisco, 1999; *The Sixties*, Bonni Benrubi Gallery, New York, 1999; *New Acquisitions*, Museum of Fine Arts, Houston, 1996; *American Politicians: Photographs From 1843–1993*, Museum of Modern Art, New York, 1994 **AWARDS** Roloff Beny Book Awards, 2002; CAPIC Lifetime Achievement Award, 2001; Life Member of American Society of Media Photographers, 1994 **BOOKS/PUBLICATIONS** *George S. Zimbel* (Monograph), Institute Valencia D'art Modern, Valencia, Spain, 2000; *American Politicians*, Musuem of Modern Art, New York, 1994; *McGill, A Celebration*, McGill-Queen's University Press, 1991; *Children in Photography, 150 Years*, Firefly, 1990; *Schoolhouse*, Walter McQuade, 1961; *Child Psychology*, Arthur Jersild M.D., Prentice Hall, 1960 **REPRESENTATION** Stephen Bulger Gallery (Toronto) **WEBSITE** www.bulgergallery.com

EDITORIAL + COMMERCIAL

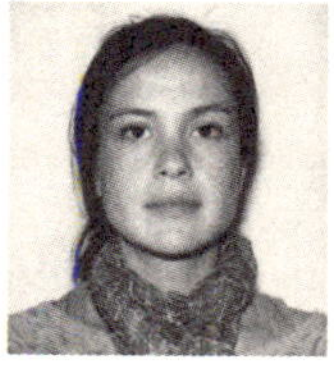

KEETJA ALLARD

BORN Toronto, 1969 **RESIDES** New York **EDUCATION** Self-taught **CLIENTS** U.S.A.—*Domino, Cosmo Girl, Nylon, Soma*; Japan—*Esquire, Relax, Paper Sky, Invitation, Composite, Buzz, Rock'n On*; Europe—*British Vogue, Beaux Art, Sleek, Allegra, Maxi, Der Telegraph, NME*; Australia—*Poly Oxygen, Vive* **WEBSITE** www.keetjaallard.com

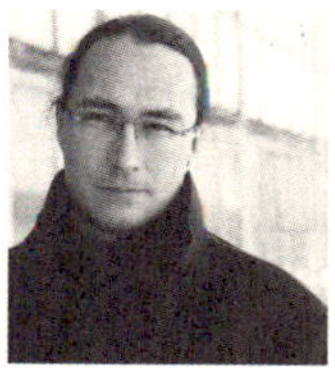

LJUBODRAG ANDRIC

BORN Belgrade, Yugoslavia, 1965 **RESIDES** Toronto **EDUCATION** University of Belgrade, Yugoslavia, English Literature, 1989 **CLIENTS** Audi, Volvo, Nokia, Bank of Montreal, Honda, Nissan Infinity, IBM, AMTRAK, Corona, Unisys, Renault, Solvay, VW, P&G, Unilever, Disney **AWARDS** *Communication Arts*, ADC NY, ADC Italy, *Archive*, *Applied Arts*, ADCC 2003–2005 **WEBSITE** www.andric.biz

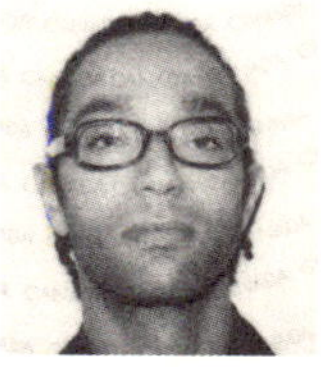

RICHARD BERNARDIN

BORN Chicago, 1972 **RESIDES** Montreal **EDUCATION** Self-taught **SOLO EXHIBITION** *Edification Corporelle*, Gallery TM, Montreal, 2001 **SELECTED GROUP EXHIBITIONS** International Fashion Photography Festival—*Masterminds of Mode*, Kobe Fashion Museum, Kobe (Japan), 2000–2001; *Rouge—Sang neuf à découvrir*, Galerie SAS, Montreal, 2001; *La Mode Nu*, Gallery 23, Prague, Czech Republic, 2000; *Fashion Photography 2000*, ZAO Gallery, New York, 2000 **BOOKS** *BEKA*, R14, Montreal, 2006; *Sensation*, Steidl, Göttingen (Germany), 2003; *Masterminds of Mode*, H20 Company Ltd., Tokyo, 2000; *Naked Eye*, Rice Publications, Montreal, 1999 **MAIN STORIES** "Dawn Till Dusk," *FQ Magazine*, September 2005; "Enigma," *Lush Magazine*, May 2005; "Play Ball," *Elle* Canada, May 2005 **CLIENTS** Le Bon Marché, La Caisse de Depot et de Placement, Bombardier Aeronautique, BBDO/Nolin, L'Order des Chiropracticien du Quebec, Diesel Marketing **WEBSITE** www.richardbernardin.com

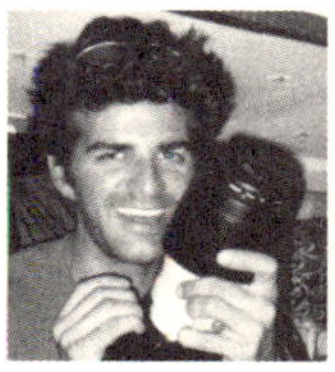

PAUL BRIDE

BORN Toronto, 1970 **RESIDES** Squamish, B.C. **EDUCATION** Self-taught; Algonquin College, Diploma in Social Science, Ottawa, 1995 **SELECTED EXHIBITIONS** *Southern Exposure*, Gallery 888, Toronto, 2001; *Rich Reflections*, Spin Gallery, Toronto, 2002 **CLIENTS** Patagonia, Arc'teryx, Cascade Designs, FiveTen, Bluewater, Julbo, Sea Eagle, *Alpinist, Rock & Ice, Climbing, Gripped, Pacific Yachting*, Beautiful British Columbia, *Canoe & Kayak* **WEBSITE** www.paulbride.com

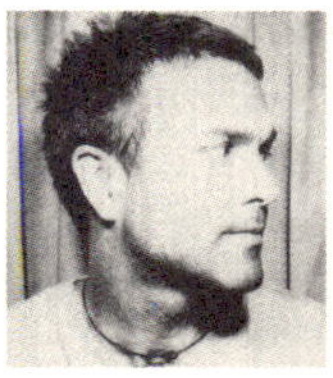

LORNE BRIDGMAN

BORN Toronto, 1963 **RESIDES** Toronto **EDUCATION** Emily Carr Institute of Art and Design, B.A. in Photography, Vancouver, 1994 **MAIN STORIES** "Cowards or Heroes?" *Glasgow Herald Sunday Magazine*; "Terminal City," *Toronto Life*; "Lost!" *Outpost* **CLIENTS** Michelin, Bell, I-Star, Avaya, Rogers, RBC, Scotiabank, Roy Thomson Hall, Purolator, Maritime Life, Instinet, Canada Post, Toronto Stock Exchange, Air Canada, ESPN, Alternative Fick, Labatt **WEBSITE** www.lornebridgman.com

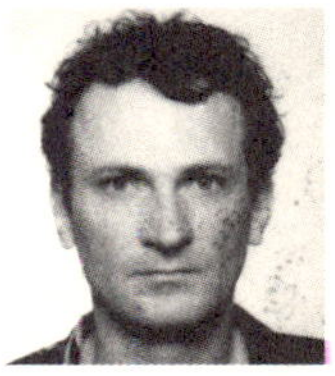

CHRIS BUCK

BORN Toronto, 1964 **RESIDES** New York **EDUCATION** Ryerson Polytechnical Institute, B.A. in Photography, Toronto, 1987 **SELECTED EXHIBITIONS** *The Sound of Music*, Other Music Record Store, New York, 2002; *FanClub*, Saba Gallery, New York, 1998 **AWARDS** Photo annuals for *Communication Arts, American Photography, Photo District News* **CLIENTS** Microsoft, *Moviefone*, Citibank, *Esquire, Premiere, Blender, Toro, Saturday Night, The New York Times Magazine* **WEBSITE** www.chrisbuck.com

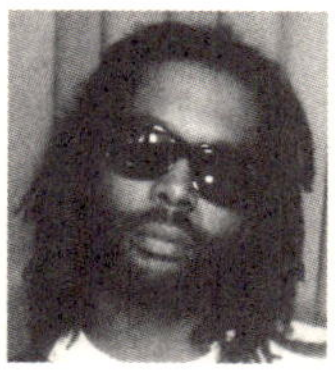

STEVE CARTY

BORN Toronto, 1970 **RESIDES** Toronto **EDUCATION** Self-taught **SELECTED EXHIBITIONS** *Hip Hop Immortals*, Galerie Patricia Dorfmann, Paris, 2004; *Hip Hop Immortals*, Das Moskau, Berlin, 2004; *Naked in the House*, IT Nightclub, Toronto, 2000 **BOOKS** *Hip Hop Immortals Remix Edition*, Sock Bandit Productions, New York, 2003; *Foto Pozytyw #11*, Nov. 2003 **CLIENTS** CBC, *American Photo, Jane, InTouch Weekly, Girlfriend* (U.S. & New Zealand), *Flare, Maclean's, Fashion18, Saturday Night, Maxim, Cosmo Girl U.K., TChad, Pound, Foto Pozytyw, National Post, Toro*, Smirnoff, Adidas, Reebok, MCA Records, Virgin Records, Lounge Clothing, Limb Apparel **WEBSITE** www.stevecarty.com

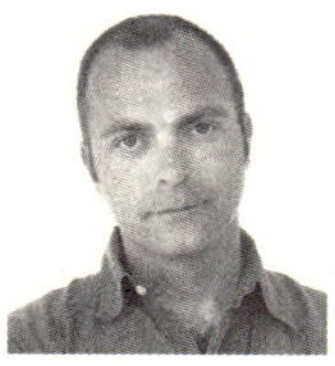

DAN CREMIN

BORN Hampstead, England, 1968 **RESIDES** Toronto **EDUCATION** Self-taught **MAIN STORIES** "Native Son," *Esquire*, 2001; "The Player," 2003, "The Electric Horseman," 2004, "Adventures in Diplomacy," 2004, all *Toronto Life*; "Starting From [Ground] Zero," *Azure*, 2003 **CLIENTS** *Canadian Business, National Post Business, Esquire, EnRoute*, Chapters/Indigo, Teranet, *Bizarre* **WEBSITE** www.dancremin.com

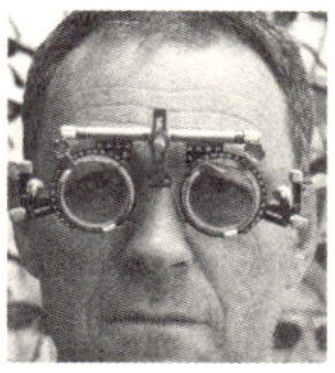

YURI DOJC

BORN Czechoslovakia, 1946 **RESIDES** Toronto **EDUCATION** Ryerson, Photo Arts Diploma, 1973 **SELECTED EXHIBITIONS** *We Endured*, Slovak Embassy, Washington D.C., 2001; *We Endured*, Pittsburgh, 2002; *Amorous Nature*, Tecumsa Gallery, Toronto, 2003 **BOOKS/PUBLICATIONS** *Marble Women*, Firefly Books, 1993; *American Dreams*, Limelight Media, 1993; *Eros e Fotografia—Yuri Dojc*, Gruppo Editoriale L'Espresso, 2003; *Nudi*, Federico Motta Editore, 2004 **MAJOR STORIES** "We Endured," "Amorous Nature," "Toronto City of Nations," "Portraits of Bravery" **AWARDS** Three Gold awards at PDN, Three Gold awards from Capic, Applied Arts Awards, CA Awards **CLIENTS** Magazines and ad agencies around the world **WEBSITE** www.yuridojc.com

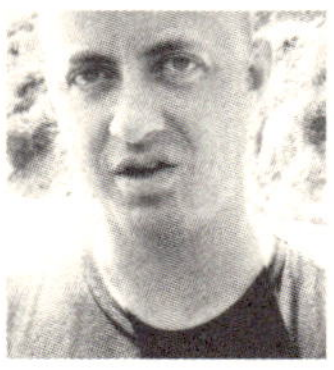

DAVID DREBIN

BORN Toronto, 1970 **RESIDES** New York **EDUCATION** Parsons School of Design, B.F.A., New York, 1996 **SELECTED SOLO EXHIBITIONS** *David Drebin*, Camerawork, Berlin, 2005; *Unbounded Youth*, Fahey Klein Gallery, Los Angeles, 2005; *David Drebin*, Gallery One, Toronto, 2004; *Love You Too*, Gallery One, Toronto, 2002 **CLIENTS** *Rolling Stone, Vanity Fair, The New York Times Magazine, Le Monde, The London Sunday Times*, British *Marie Claire, Elle* **WEBSITE** www.daviddrebin.com

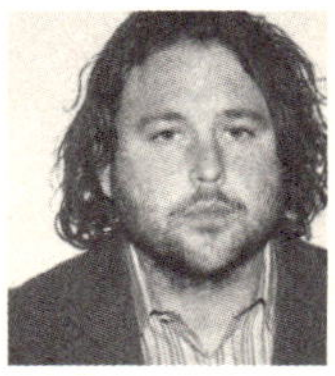

BRYCE DUFFY

BORN Prince George, B.C. **RESIDES** Los Angeles and Silverton, B.C. **EDUCATION** Ryerson University, Photography & Film, 1991–1993 **SELECTED GROUP EXHIBITIONS** *Surf Style*, 111 Minna Gallery, San Francisco, 2003 **BOOKS/PUBLICATIONS** *Blue Earth, Pictureality*, 2001 **CLIENTS** *Rolling Stone, Premiere, Entertainment Weekly*, Microsoft, Nike, IBM **WEBSITE** www.bryceduffy.com

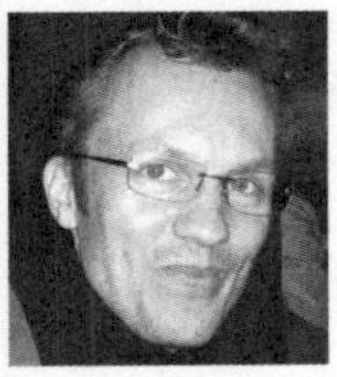

COLIN FAULKNER

BORN Halifax, 1963 **RESIDES** Toronto **EDUCATION** Fanshawe College, Diploma in Photography, 1987 **CLIENTS** Holt Renfrew, LCBO, Keilhauer, *Wish*, *Cargo*, *Outside*, *Texas Monthly* **WEBSITE** www.faulknerphoto.com

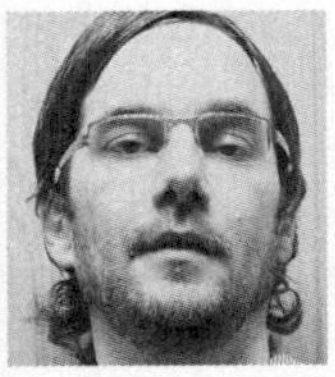

TOM FEILER

BORN Welland, Ontario, 1963 **RESIDES** Toronto **EDUCATION** Ryerson Polytechnical Institute, Photography, Toronto, 1986 **SELECTED SOLO EXHIBITIONS** *Old Nice Snap*, Elevator Gallery, Toronto, 2000 **CLIENTS** Sony, Microsoft, Bell, HP, Home Depot, *Saturday Night* **WEBSITES** www.tomfeiler.com, www.westsidestudio.com, www.radkefilms.com

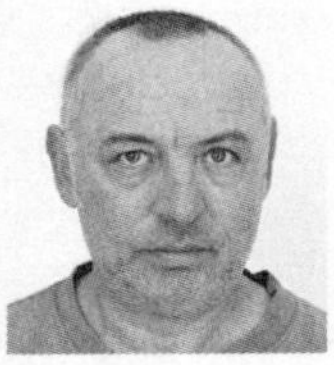

TONY FOUHSE

BORN Ottawa, 1954 **RESIDES** Ottawa **EDUCATION** Algonquin College, Photography, Ottawa, 1975; Visual Studies Workshop, Rochester, N.Y., 1982 **SELECTED GROUP EXHIBITIONS** Angel City Gallery, Los Angeles, 2004; SAW Gallery, Ottawa, 2004; Galerie Bouchon, Paris, 2004; Upcoming: Gallery La Petite Mort, Ottawa, 2006 **MAIN STORIES** "Nothing Out of the Ordinary," *Report on Business* **AWARDS** National Magazine Award, 2004; Advertising and Design Association, 2004 **CLIENTS** *Report on Business*, *Maclean's*, *CA Magazine*, *Canadian Business*, *Reader's Digest*, *Ottawa Magazine*, Canada Post, AT&T, PeopleSoft, CBC **WEBSITE** www.tonyfoto.com

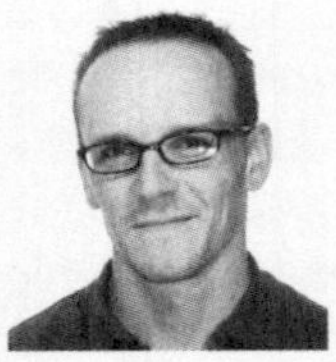

THOMAS FRICKE

BORN Hamilton, Ontario, 1969 **RESIDES** Winnipeg **EDUCATION** University of Toronto, B.A., Philosophy major, Political Science minor, Toronto, 1992; Ryerson University, First Year Photographic studies, French River, P.E.I., summer 1991 **SELECTED GROUP EXHIBITIONS** Outworks Art Gallery, Winnipeg, 2005 **AWARDS** National Magazine Award, 2003 **CLIENTS** *The New York Times*, *Saturday Night*, *Canadian Geographic* **WEBSITE** www.fricke.ca

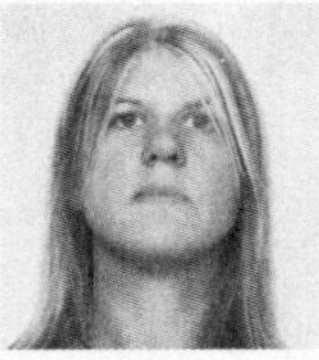

KATHRYN GAITENS

BORN Vancouver, 1966 **RESIDES** Toronto **EDUCATION** Ryerson University, B.F.A. in Photography, Toronto, 1992 **SELECTED GROUP EXHIBITIONS** *Life of Water*, Photosensitive, BCE Place, Toronto, 2005; *Close*, Now Lounge, Contact Photography Festival, Toronto, 2002; *Eight Ball*, Silent Auction, Canfar, Toronto, 2000 **CLIENTS** *Time Canada*, *Maclean's*, *People*, German *Men's Health*, *Stern Magazine*, *Air and Space*, *Now Magazine* **WEBSITE** www.gaitensphotography.com

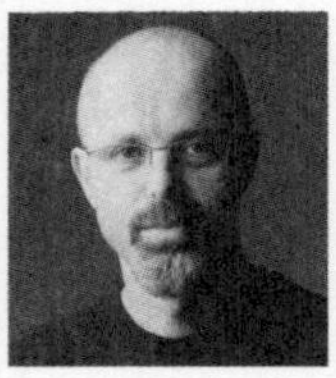

EDWARD GAJDEL

BORN Sokolka, Poland, 1958 **RESIDES** Toronto **EDUCATION** University of Calgary, Art History, 1978; Northern Alberta Institute of Technology, Edmonton, 1980 **SELECTED GROUP EXHIBITIONS** Edward Day Gallery, Toronto, 2003; Alternative Pik, New York, 2002; The Art Gallery of Ontario, Toronto, 2001; Saba Gallery, New York, 1996 **MAIN STORIES** Photojournalistic Exposés on Fox Hunting; NAFTA (travelled with Mexican Presidents); Plum Island (U.S. Disease Control Centre) **CLIENTS** *Time*, Price Waterhouse Coopers, Coca-Cola, *GQ*, *Rolling Stone*, *InStyle*, *Esquire*, ESPN **AWARDS** *Communication Arts*, World Press Organization, *American Photography Annual*, Advertising and Design Club of Canada **WEBSITE** www.edwardgajdel.com

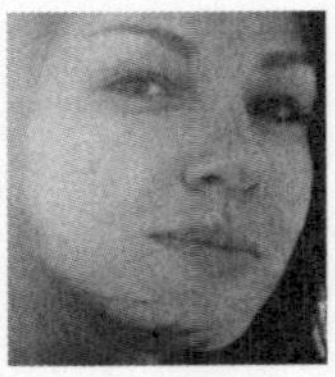

REGINA GARCIA

BORN Mexico, 1974 **RESIDES** Toronto **EDUCATION** Alberta College of Art and Design, Photography, Calgary, 1993–1997 **CLIENTS** Universal Music, Ford, Alliance Atlantis, *Toronto Life*, *Report on Business*, *Maclean's*, *Azure* **WEBSITE** www.reginagarcia.com

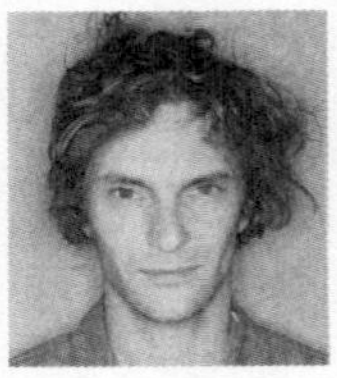

MARK GILBERT

BORN Nottingham, England, 1969 **RESIDES** Vancouver **EDUCATION** University of Western Ontario, Liberal Arts Degree, London, Ontario, 1992 **CLIENTS** Mercedes, Honda, Toshiba, Visa, AT&T, *Elle*, *GQ*, *Toro*, *Dutch* **WEBSITE** www.markgilbert.com

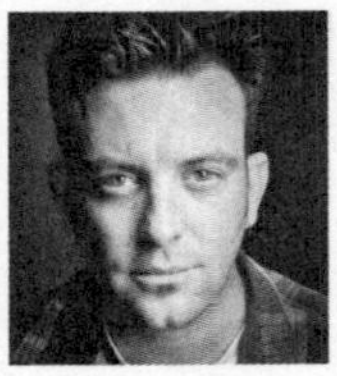

CHRIS GORDANEER

BORN Mississauga, Ontario, 1969 **RESIDES** Toronto **EDUCATION** Self-taught; Sheridan College, Photography, Oakville, Ont., 1989–1991 **SELECTED SOLO EXHIBITIONS** *Cuba*, Elevator Gallery, Toronto, 2001 **SELECTED GROUP EXHIBITIONS** Westside Studio, Contact Photography Festival, Toronto, 2000 and 2003 **AWARDS** *Communication Arts* Photo Annual, 1996–2006; ADCC, 1996–2006; Graphis Photo, 1998–2006; Gold Lions, Cannes, 1999 **CLIENTS** Nike, Bell, Chivis Regal, Coca-Cola, GMC, Honda, Dodge, Ford, Acura, Harry Rosen **WEBSITE** www.chrisgordaneer.com

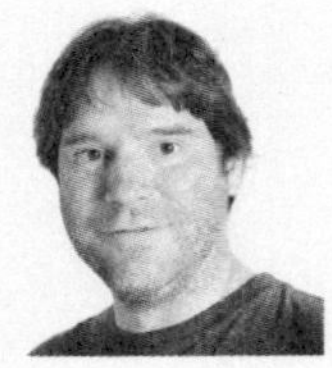

FRANK HOEDL

BORN Yellowknife, 1966 **RESIDES** Toronto **EDUCATION** Diploma in Applied Photography, Sheridan College, Oakville, Ont., 1987 **CLIENTS** United Way, Covenant House, BMW, Toyota, Mercedes, Lexus, Nissan, Honda, Infiniti, Unilever, Sportchek, Sunrype, Bud Light, Shoppers Drug Mart, Newfoundland & Labrador Tourism, Rogers, Bell, Purina, Sprite, Smirnoff **AWARDS** Gold & Silver Pencils, 2004; Gold, Silver, Merit, Marketing Awards 2003 and 2004; Best of Show, Extra Awards, 2005; Cannes Silver Lion, 2002; New York Festivals, 2002; D&AD, 2003 **WEBSITES** www.frankhoedl.com, www.westsidestudio.com

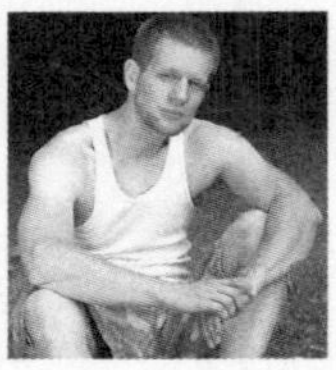

JOHN HRYNIUK

BORN London, England, 1969 **RESIDES** Toronto **EDUCATION** Self-taught **SELECTED GROUP EXHIBITIONS** *Naked in the House*, Gallery Bibianne, Toronto, 2004; *Exposure*, Hereford Photography Festival, U.K., 2003; Berlin Photography Festival, Martin-Gropius-Bau, 2002 **BOOKS/PUBLICATIONS** *Our Beautiful Children*, HarperCollins, New York, 2002; *Friendship: A Celebration of Humanity*, HarperCollins, New York, 2001 **CLIENTS** *Rolling Stone*, *The New York Times Magazine*, *The London Sunday Times*, *The Advocate*, *Report on Business* **WEBSITE** www.inthedarkroom.com

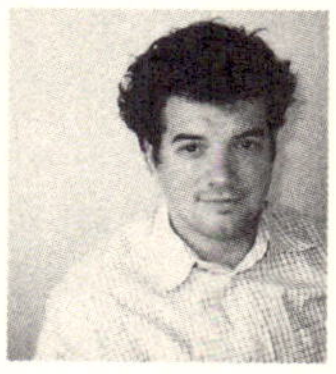

ANDREJ KOPAC

BORN Victoria, 1968 **RESIDES** Toronto **EDUCATION** Concordia University, M.A., Montreal, 1998; University of Victoria, B.A., Victoria, 1992 **MAIN STORIES** *Report on Business*—"Hydro Privatization," 2002, "Divorce," 2004, "Stinson Real Estate Developer," 2005; *Saturday Night*—"Karim Rashid Home," 2002; *Canadian House & Home*—"50s Revival," 2002, "Finkleman Home," 2004, "Melody Barn" 2005; *Azure Magazine*—"Concrete Renovation," 2001, "Totum Gym," 2003, "Drake Hotel," 2004; *Wish Magazine*—"Condo Loft Story," 2004, "Wychwood Home," 2004 **CLIENTS** Allard Johnson, *Azure*, *Canadian Business*, *Canadian House & Home*, Canadian Tire, Concrete Design Communications, *EnRoute Magazine*, *Frame Magazine*, GM Canada, Grey Worldwide, Holt Renfrew, HOOPP, L.A. Ads, Leapfrog Design Communications, Leo Burnett, Lever, M2 Design NYC, Marshall Fenn Communications, McLaren McCaan, Novartis, Ogilvy & Mather NYC, Ove Design, *President's Choice Magazine*, Q30 Design, Karim Rashid, *Report on Business Magazine*, Rogers Publications, *Saturday Night Magazine*, *Style at Home Magazine*, TD Bank, 3rd Uncle Design, Up Country Canada, Wescast Industries, *Wish Magazine*, The Wolf Group, Young & Rubicam NYC **WEBSITE** www.andrejkopac.com

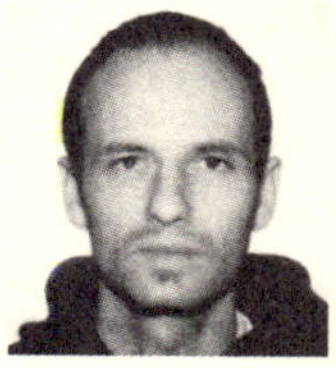

EAMON MACMAHON

BORN Toronto, 1976 **RESIDES** Toronto **EDUCATION** Applied Photography, Sheridan College, 1998 **SELECTED SOLO EXHIBITIONS** *Window Seat*, The Embassy, Toronto, 2005; *Hidden Door*, Pikto Gallery, Toronto, 2005; *Sleepwalking*, The Drake Hotel, Toronto, 2004; *Sleepwalking*, The Photo Passage, Harbourfront Centre, Toronto, 2004 **SELECTED GROUP EXHIBITIONS** *Tree Box*, The Drake Hotel, Toronto, 2005; *Wegway Magazine* Juried Photography Show, Steamwhistle Roundhouse Gallery, Contact Photography Festival, Toronto, 2004 **MAIN STORIES** "Afterglow," *The Walrus*; "Fantasies Made Fresh," *Maisonneuve Magazine*; "The Silence Issue," *Coupe Magazine*; "The Other Muskoka," *Toronto Life* **CLIENTS** *The Walrus*, *Maisonneuve Magazine*, *Coupe Magazine*, *Toronto Life*, World Wildlife Fund, Random House, Intrawest **WEBSITE** www.eamonmacmahon.com

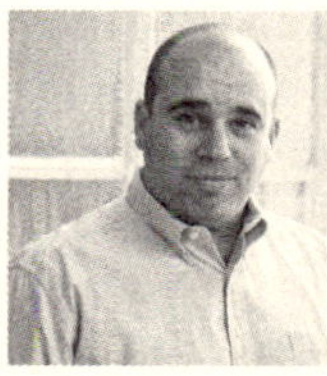

BRUCE MACNEIL

BORN Sydney, N.S., 1965 **RESIDES** Toronto **EDUCATION** University of Victoria, 1999; University of Cape Breton, N.S., 1983-1985 and 1993-1994; St. John's College, Annapolis, Maryland, 1989 **SELECTED SOLO EXHIBITIONS** *Home and Away*, Fred Gallery, Halifax, 2005; *A Couple in a Room*, Helsinki Gallery, Toronto, 2005; *Women*, Tricera Gallery, Toronto, 2004; *Men*, Pikto Gallery, Toronto, 2004 **MAIN STORIES** "Destinations and Departures," a presentation of the diverse family life on Toronto's Jameson Avenue; "Down on the Downtown East Side" **CLIENTS** *Report on Business*, *Toronto Life* **WEBSITE** www.brucemacneil.com

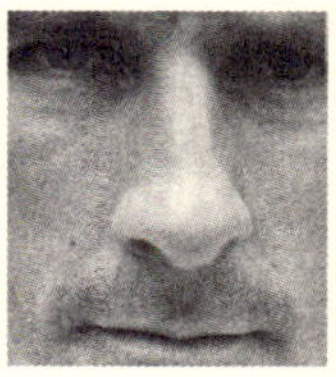

CHRISTOPHER MORRIS

BORN Ottawa, 1965 **RESIDES** Vancouver **EDUCATION** Carleton University, 1985 **CLIENTS** *Maclean's*, *Time*, *Newsweek*, *Forbes*, *Stern*, *People*, *The New York Times*, *Der Spiegel* **WEBSITE** www.christophermorris.com

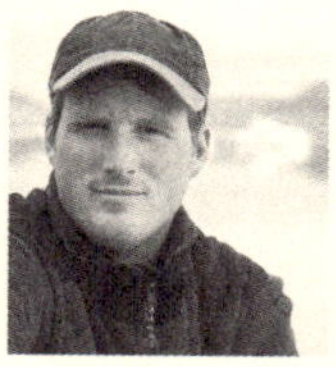

PAUL NICKLEN

BORN Tidsdale, Saskatchewan, 1968 **RESIDES** Whitehorse **EDUCATION** University of Victoria, 1990 **BOOKS** *Seasons of the Arctic*, Douglas and McIntyre, 2000 **MAIN STORIES** "Where Have All The Salmon Gone?" *National Geographic*, July 2003; "Northern Exposure," *National Geographic*, January 2004; "A Coral Reef Wilderness Revisited," *National Geographic*, February 2004 **AWARDS** World Press Awards, 2004, Atlantic Salmon, Science and Nature; POYi, 2004, Atlantic Salmon; POYi, 2005, Arctic Science; BBC Wildlife Photographer of the Year, 2000 and 2001; Nature's Best 2002 **CLIENTS** *National Geographic*, *Patagonia*, *GEO BBC Wildlife*, *Canadian Geographic*, *Natural History International Wildlife* **WEBSITE** www.paulnicklen.com

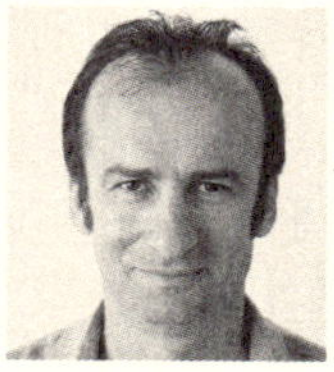

JIM PANOU

BORN Greece, 1959 **RESIDES** Toronto **EDUCATION** Ryerson University, B.A.A. in Photographic Studies, Toronto, 1983 **SELECTED GROUP EXHIBITIONS** *Salt Harvest*, Drabinsky Gallery, Toronto, 2003; *Masala! Mhendi! Masti!*, York Quay Gallery Number II, Harbourfront Centre, Toronto, 2002; *After the Mela and Other Observations of India*, Drabinsky Gallery, Toronto, 2002; Toronto International Art Fair, Drabinsky Gallery, Toronto, 2001 **AWARDS** The Canadian Council for the Advancement of Education, Gold Medal, 2000 **CLIENTS** *Saturday Night*, *Report on Business Magazine*, *Canadian Art*, *National Post*, *The Washington Post*, *The Los Angeles Times*, Sony, HSBC, BMO, Nike, Ikea, University of Toronto, Chrysler, General Motors **WEBSITE** www.jimpanou.com

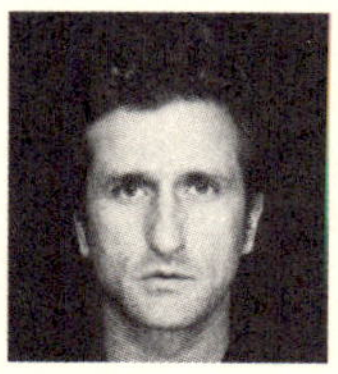

JAMES PATTYN

BORN Tillsonburg, Ontario, 1970 **RESIDES** Toronto **EDUCATION** Sheridan College, Applied Photography Program, Oakville, Ontario, 1993 **SELECTED GROUP EXHIBITIONS** *Peace of Mine*, Elevator Gallery, Toronto, 1999; *A Journey in Progress*, Jet Fuel, Toronto, 1996 **MAIN STORIES** "The First-Timer" and "In Praise of Plonk," *Saturday Night* **CLIENTS** *Toronto Life*, *Report on Business*, Universal Music, *2 for Life* **WEBSITE** www.jamespattyn.com

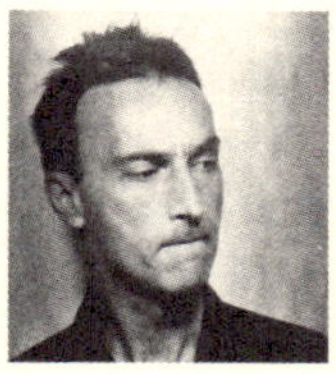

HILL PEPPARD

BORN New Westminster, B.C., 1955 **RESIDES** Toronto **EDUCATION** Self-taught **AWARDS** KRW Award, Gold, 2001; Advertising & Design Club of Canada, 1994 and 1995 **CLIENTS** Warner Music Canada, Sprint Canada, Sony, Flecken 5th Avenue NYC, Nettwerk Productions, Oracle Publishing, Olympia & York, Paula Lishman International, Prentice Hall, EMI Music Canada, du Maurier Arts, CanWest, Butterfield & Robinson, Bank of Montreal, *EnRoute*, *Saturday Night*, *Report on Business*, *Chatelaine*, *Canadian Business*, *Flare*, *Profit*, *Canadian Living* **WEBSITE** www.hillpeppard.com

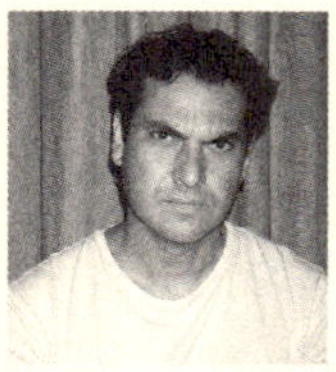

GEORGE PIMENTEL

BORN Toronto, 1967 **RESIDES** Toronto **EDUCATION** Ryerson University, B.A.A. in Photographic Arts, Toronto, 1992 **SELECTED GROUP EXHIBITIONS** *Retrospective of Celebrity Culture*, Roots Store, 2003; *5 Seconds With a Movie Star*, Pimentel Gallery, 2003; *Documents and Dreams*, Canadian Documentary Group Exhibition, 2003 **CLIENTS** *People*, *US Weekly*, *Rolling Stone*, *New York Post*, *Entertainment Weekly*, *Hollywood Reporter*, *Flare*, *Maclean's* **WEBSITE** www.wireimage.com

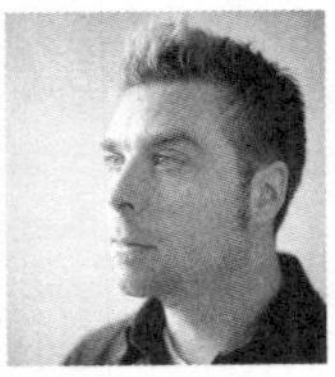

SHANNON ROSS

BORN Toronto, 1972 **RESIDES** Toronto **EDUCATION** McGill University, B.A. in English Literature, 1996 **CLIENTS** *Toronto Life*, *Toro*, *Maclean's*, Redwood Custom Communications, Ogilvy & Mather **WEBSITE** www.shannonross.com

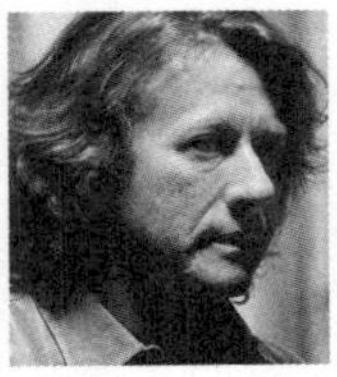

PHILIP ROSTRON

BORN England, 1955 **RESIDES** Toronto **EDUCATION** Salisbury College of Art, England, 1975 **CLIENTS** Alpo, Aveeno, Babybel, Baby Dove, Bell Canada, City of Toronto, Coca-Cola Canada, Dairy Board of Ontario, Energizer, FedEx, Fuji, GayLea, General Motors, Glad, HomeSense, Johnson & Johnson, Laughing Cow, MADD, McCains, Michelin, Molson Breweries, National Bank of Canada, Proctor & Gamble, Reitmans, RBC Visa, Rogers, Ryerson, Salvation Army, Scottie's, Sleeman Breweries, Tim Hortons, Timex, Toshiba, World Wildlife Fund, Wrigley's **AWARDS** Clio Award—2005, 2001, 2000, 1998, 1995, 1990, 1986, 1985; *Communication Arts*—2005, 2004, 2000, 1999, 1998, 1997, 1995, 1994, 1992, 1991; *Archive* (200 Best Ad Photographers Worldwide)—2004/2005; D and AD; New York Art Directors; London International; Mobius Award; *Applied Arts*, 2005; Cannes, 1996; Advertising and Design Club of Canada—2004, 2003, 2001, 2000, 1997, 1996, 1995, 1993, 1992, 1988, 1986, 1985, 1984; Canadian Association of Photographers & Illustrators in Communications (CAPIC)—1999, 1998, 1996, 1995, 1994, 1993, 1992, 1991 **WEBSITE** www.instilproductions.com

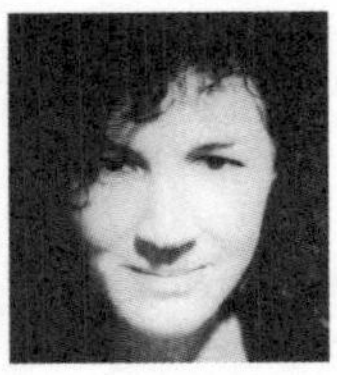

DEBORAH SAMUEL

BORN Vancouver, 1956 **RESIDES** Santa Fe, New Mexico **EDUCATION** Limerick College of Art & Design, Art Fundamentals, Limerick, Ireland, 1974; Sheridan College, Applied Photography, Oakville, Ontario, 1977 **SELECTED SOLO EXHIBITIONS** *Dog*, Drabinsky Gallery, Toronto, 2004; *Dog + Pup*, Special Photographers Gallery, London, England, 2002 **SELECTED GROUP EXHIBITIONS** *The Dog Show*, Conduit Gallery, Dallas, Texas, 2003; *A Thousand Hounds*, UBS Paine Webber, New York, 2002 **BOOKS / PUBLICATIONS** *Dog*, Chronicle Books, 2001; *Pup*, Chronicle Books, 2002 **CLIENTS** *Maclean's*, *GQ*, *Rolling Stone*, *Musician*, *The Los Angeles Times Magazine* **WEBSITE** www.deborahsamuel.com

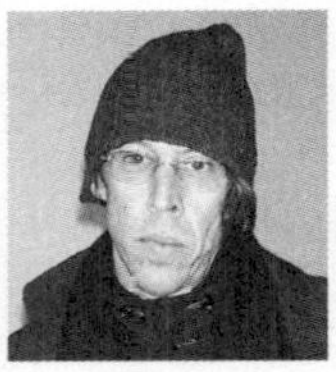

NIGEL SCOTT

BORN Jamaica, 1955 **RESIDES** New York **EDUCATION** Ontario College Of Art, Photography Program, Toronto, 1975 **SELECTED EXHIBITIONS** *Polarity*, Jane Corkin Gallery, 2004; *Nigel Scott*, Gallery T.Y.K-TWO, Tokyo, 2000; Festival de la Photo de la Mode, Biarritz, France, official selection, 1996 **BOOKS** *Sakura Girl*, Satoshi Yagioka, Kamishoba Co., Japan, 2003; *Nigel Scott*, Homareya, Nomura Yoshio, Japan, 2002; *Venus: Masterpieces of Erotic Art*, Michelle Olley (ed.), Thunder's Mouth Press, 2000 **CLIENTS** *Vogue* France, *De Peche Mode*, *Elle* France, *Harper's Bazaar*, *Glamour* France, *City and Country Home*, *Max* France, *Marie Claire Bis*, *Cosmopolitan* France, *Jardin des Mode*, *Life* **REPRESENTATION** Corkin Shopland Gallery (Toronto) **WEBSITE** www.corkinshopland.com

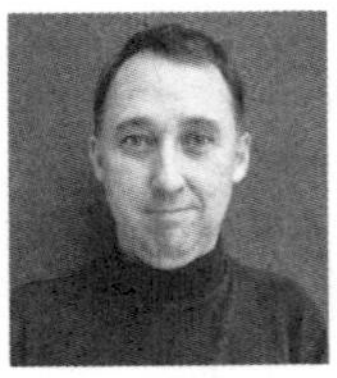

LIAM SHARP

BORN London, England, 1958 **RESIDES** London, England, and Toronto **EDUCATION** Professor, George Brown College, Toronto, 1991-1997; Professor, Humber College, Toronto, 1997-1998 **SELECTED SOLO EXHIBITIONS** *Thank You India*, Contact 2000, Gallery Out, Toronto; *First Contact*, Elevator Gallery Toronto, 2000; *Clash*, Alliance de Francais, Toronto, 2003 **SELECTED GROUP EXHIBITIONS** *Red Havana Reflections of the Past*, Club Lucky Gallery, Contact 2002; *Photorama*, Gallery TPW, Toronto, 2000; *Open City*, 2001 **BOOKS/ PUBLICATIONS** *Photo Graphis*, 2005; *Graphis Profile*, 2005 **AWARDS** KRW Awards Best Cover Photography Silver, 2003; *Applied Arts*, Magazine Award, 2004; PDN Photography Annual, 2004 **CLIENTS** Royal Bank, St. Michael's Hospital, Toronto Hospital for Sick Children, West Park Hospital, St. John's Hospital, Mount Sinai Hospital, Dove Soap U.K., Coram U.K., Graff Diamonds U.K., University of Toronto, IESO Ontario, Ontario Investment Service, Fields Institute,. Rogers, Enwave, Blumont Capital, Teknion, Ontario Energy Board, Manulife, Fortis, LCBO, *Fader Magazine*, *Report on Business Magazine*, *Profit*, *Today's Parent*, *Canadian Lawyer Magazine*, *CIO Magazine* **WEBSITE** www.liamsharp.com

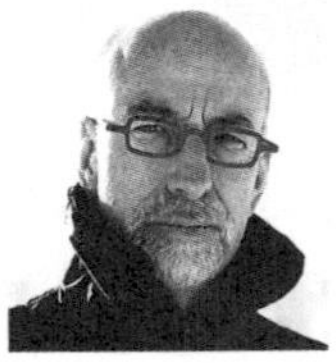

GEORGE SIMHONI

BORN Israel, 1951 **RESIDES** Toronto **EDUCATION** Sheridan College, Diploma in Applied Photography, Oakville, Ontario, 1975 **SELECTED EXHIBITIONS** Westside, Contact Photography Festival **CLIENTS** Chase Bank, Chrysler, Coca-Cola, Ford Motor Company, General Motors, Honda, Mackenzie Financial, MasterCard, Rogers, Visa, Walt Disney **WEBSITE** www.georgesimhoni.com

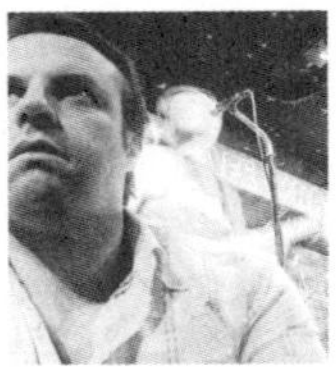

PETE SOOS

BORN Vancouver, 1966 **RESIDES** Vancouver and Toronto **EDUCATION** One-year program at a photography school in Victoria, 1997 **SELECTED GROUP EXHIBITIONS** *25X1*, Lumen Gallery, Vancouver, 2005 **CLIENTS** *Toro*, *Saturday Night*, *Surface*, *Maclean's*, *Report on Business Magazine*, *Profit*, *National Post Business*, Bell, Sunoco, Imperial Margarine, B.C. Hydro **WEBSITE** www.petesoos.com

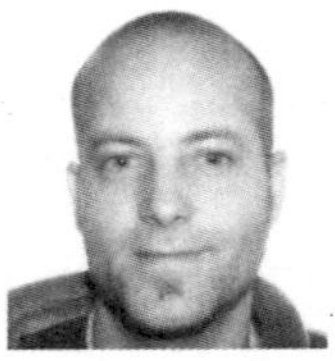

CLAY STANG

BORN Calgary, 1970 **RESIDES** Toronto **EDUCATION** Alberta College of Art and Design, B.F.A. in Photography, Calgary, 1998 **AWARDS** Advertising & Design Club of Canada; *Applied Arts*; AR100; *Communication Arts* Design Annual; *Communication Arts* Photography Annual; IPA Awards; PDN Photography Annual **CLIENTS** BMG, BOS, Coca-Cola, Cossette, Grip, Leo Burnette, Lowe Roche, MacLaren McCann, MTV, O&M, RCA Records, Rethink, Sony Music, TBS **WEBSITE** www.claystang.com

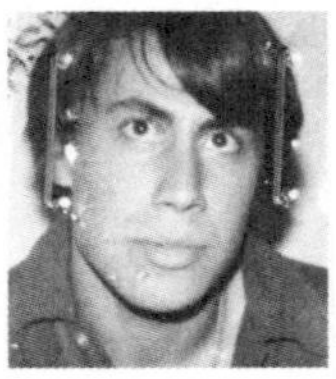

KRISTOFF STEINRUCK

BORN Vancouver, 1976 **RESIDES** Toronto **EDUCATION** University of British Columbia, B.A., English Literature and Fine Arts, 1999 **SELECTED GROUP EXHIBITIONS** *Third Rail*, Gladstone Hotel, Toronto, 2003; *Outtakes*, BCE Place, Toronto, 2003; *Swarm*, UBC Gallery, Vancouver, 1999 **MAIN STORIES** "The Selling of Place," "Invisible Geography," *EnRoute*, October 2005; "Scott Brison vs. Peter Mackay," *Saturday Night*, September 2004; "Things Fall Apart," *Slam*, New York, December 2002; "Religion and the Right," *Maclean's*, March 18, 2002 **CLIENTS** *Maclean's*, *Saturday Night*, *EnRoute*, *Report on Business*, *The Los Angeles Times*, *XXL* **WEBSITE** www.kristoffsteinruck.com

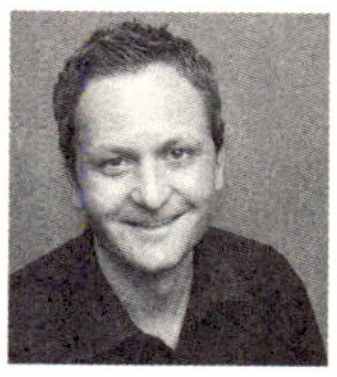

CHAL STILES

BORN Edmonton, 1970 **RESIDES** Calgary **EDUCATION** Alberta College of Art & Design, B.F.A. Major in Photography, Calgary, 1998 **AWARDS** ACAD Board of Governors Award, 1998 **CLIENTS** YWCA, Royal Bank, Westjet, Husky, Suncor, Western Canadian Lotto Corporation, Calgary Stampede, *Maclean's*, *Canadian Business Magazine*, *Report on Business Magazine*, *Toro*, *Profit* **WEBSITE** www.chalstiles.com

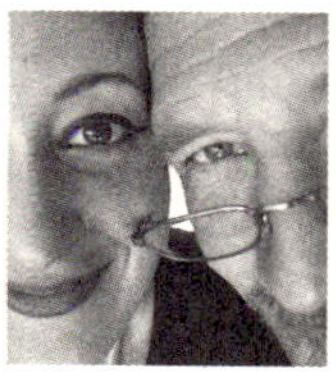

LEDA & ST. JACQUES

BORN Leda—Rome, Italy, 1971; St. Jacques—Hull, Quebec, 1953 **RESIDE** Montreal **EDUCATION** Leda—University of Ottawa, B.Sc. Fine Arts, 1998. St. Jacques—Algonquin College, Diploma in Photography, Ottawa, 1975 **SELECTED GROUP EXHIBITIONS** *Hommage à l'anonymat*, Domtar Building, Montreal, 2001 **AWARDS** Lux Contest, Grand Prize Fashion and Beauty Editorial, 2004; *Applied Arts*, Fashion and Beauty I, II & III, 2004 **CLIENTS** Buffalo, *Elle Canada*, *Elle Quebec*, Harry Rosen, RW & CO, Cossette Communication, Diesel **WEBSITE** www.productionsleloi.com

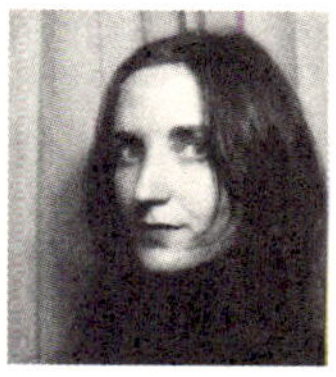

MACKENZIE STROH

BORN Prince George, B.C., 1971 **RESIDES** New York **EDUCATION** M.F.A., Studio Arts/Photography, Concordia University, Montreal, 2003; B.F.A., Intermedia, Emily Carr Institute of Art and Design, Vancouver, 1998 **SELECTED SOLO EXHIBITIONS** *Girls, Girls, Girls*, Galerie La Centrale, Montreal, 2003; *The Body in Question, A Portrait of the Medical Industry*, Vancouver Community Arts Council, Vancouver, 1998 **SELECTED GROUP EXHIBITIONS** *Faking Death*, Jack Shainman Gallery, New York, 2006; *Portraits*, National Arts Club, New York, 2005; *Expressions*, Centre d'exposition de Saint-Hyacinthe, Saint-Hyacinthe, Quebec, 2005; *Sous L'Oeil de la Photographe, Portraits de Femmes 1898–2003*, Le Centre d'Exposition de Val D'or, Val d'Or, Quebec, 2004; *Porcelaine*, Dazibao, Montreal, 2003 **CLIENTS** *Details*, *The New York Times Magazine*, *New York Magazine*, *Toro*, *Paper*, *The Sunday Telegraph Magazine* (London), *The Guardian Weekend Magazine* (London), *Jane*, *Nylon*, *Maclean's*, *The Look*, *Toronto Life*, *34 Magazine*, *Time Out New York*, *Report on Business Magazine* **WEBSITE** www.mackenziestroh.com

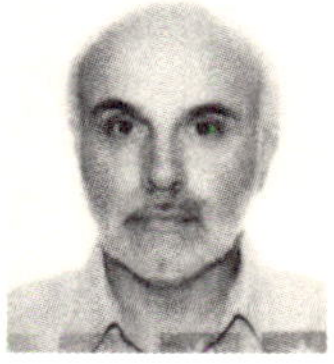

CHRIS THOMAIDIS

BORN Dernovany, Greece, 1953 **RESIDES** Toronto **EDUCATION** Self-taught **CLIENTS** Abbott Pharmaceuticals, Concord, Adex, Ernst & Young, Expedia, H.J. Heinz, Hewlett-Packard, Impressum, Ontario Hydro, *Report on Business*, *Saturday Night*, *Tapestry*, *New Opera* **WEBSITE** www.thomaidis.com

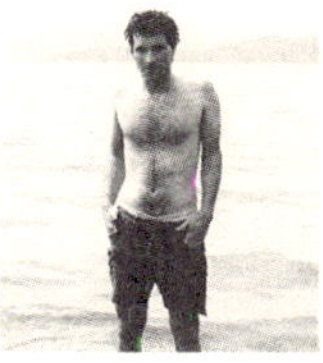

JOHANN WALL

BORN Vancouver Island, 1972 **RESIDES** Vancouver **EDUCATION** University of Victoria, Department of Writing Program, 1991–1993; Western Academy of Photography, Program, Victoria, 1998 **SELECTED SOLO EXHIBITIONS** *Baiser*, Xeno Gallery, Vancouver, 2004 **SELECTED GROUP EXHIBITIONS** *Artroplis*, CBC Building, Vancouver, 2004; *Provoke*, Alibi, Vancouver, 2004; *25X1*, Lumen Gallery, Vancouver, 2005 **CLIENTS** *Nylon*, *Fader*, *Fashion*, *Fashion18*, *Butter*, *The Guardian Weekend Magazine*, *Spin*, CBC **WEBSITE** www.johannwall.com

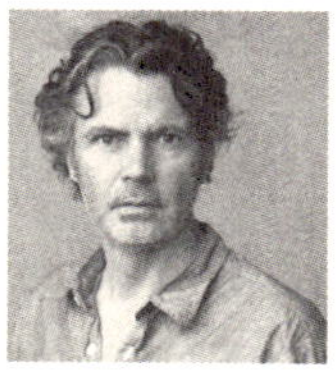

GEORGE WHITESIDE

BORN Hamilton, Ontario, 1956 **RESIDES** Toronto **EDUCATION** Ontario College of Art and Design, Photo Electric Arts, Toronto, 1979 **SELECTED SOLO EXHIBITIONS** *Photographs*, Spin Gallery, Toronto, 2004 **SELECTED GROUP EXHIBITIONS** *Translations*, Fluid, Toronto, 2003; *Core*, John Carter, Toronto, 2001; *Exxposed*, Circa, Toronto, 2001 **AWARDS** Art Directors' Club, Gold, 2003; National Magazine Awards, Gold, 2002 **CLIENTS** Marlowe, Holt Renfrew, The Bay, Hyperion Books, *Fashion*, *Gourmet* **WEBSITE** www.georgewhiteside.com

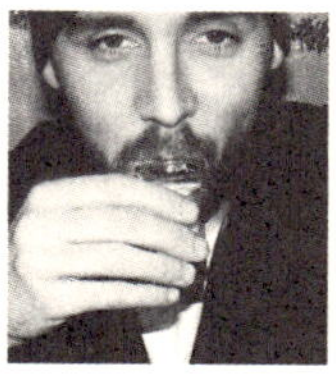

CHRIS WOODS

BORN Barrie, Ontario, 1974 **RESIDES** Toronto **EDUCATION** Self-taught **CLIENTS** Kia, Volvo, VW, Cadillac, Infiniti, Honda, Range Rover, Corvette, Yamaha, Shaw, Labatt, Molson, Astro, Powerbar, Sony, Harry Rosen, Pizza Hut, Rogers, CIBC, BMO, TD, Pepsi, Bell Canada, Microsoft MSN, Advil, Zellers, Absolut, Purolator, *Rolling Stone*, *Interview*, *Maclean's*, *Fashion*, *Fashion18*, *X-Ray*, *Zink*, *Harry Rosen*, *Gig*, *Time Out New York*, *Saturday Night*, *Canadian Business Magazine*, *InStyle*, *Vogue* France **WEBSITE** www.chriswoods.ca

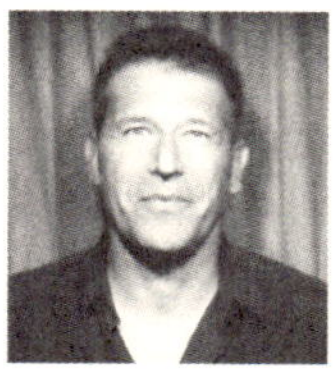

HARRY ZERNIKE

BORN Stamford, Connecticut, 1965 **RESIDES** New York **EDUCATION** International Centre of Photography, Certificate in Photojournalism and Documentary Photography, New York, 1999; Rhode Island School of Design, Bachelor of Architecture, Providence, Rhode Island, 1989; Rhode Island School of Design, Bachelor of Fine Arts, Providence, Rhode Island, 1988; Simon's Rock College, Associate in Arts, Great Barrington, Massachusetts, 1984 **SELECTED GROUP EXHIBITIONS** *Fellows*, ICP, New York, 2005; *Plan and Digression*, ICP, New York, 2003; *8½ x 11*, Jen Bekman Gallery, New York, 2003; *Made in New York*, Jen Bekman Gallery, New York, 2003 **BOOKS/PUBLICATIONS** *In Search of America*, Peter Jennings & Todd Brewster, Hyperion, 2002; *The Phaidon Atlas of Contemporary World Architecture*, Phaidon Press, 2004; *New New York: Architecture of a City*, Rizzoli, 2004 **CLIENTS** *The New York Times Magazine*, *Time*, *Mother Jones*, *Report on Business*, *Fast Company*, *Scientific American*, *National Geographic Adventure*, *American Way*, *Architectural Record*, *Interior Design*, *Organic Style*, *Dwell*, *Metropolis*, *Premiere* **WEBSITE** www.harryzernike.com

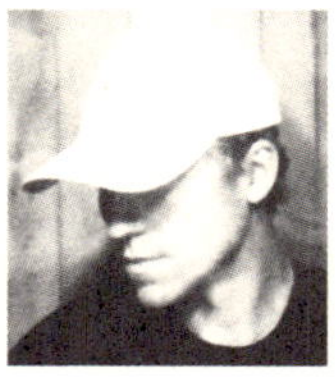

MARK ZIBERT

BORN Toronto, 1977 **RESIDES** Toronto **EDUCATION** Sheridan College, Applied Photography, 1998 **CLIENTS** Nike, Timberland, Adidas, Arrow, Toyota, Ford, Hyundai, Mercedes Benz, Toronto International Film Festival, Sims Snowboards, Nokia, *Life*, ESPN, *Toro*, *Toronto Life*, *The Look*, *Maclean's*, *Report on Business* **WEBSITE** www.markzibert.com

EMERGING

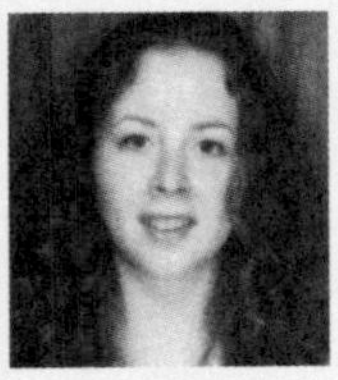

ALYSSA ANDREWS
BORN 1982 **RESIDES** Montreal **EDUCATION** Sir Wilfred Grenfell College, Memorial University of Newfoundland, B.F.A. (Visual Arts), Corner Brook, Newfoundland, 2004

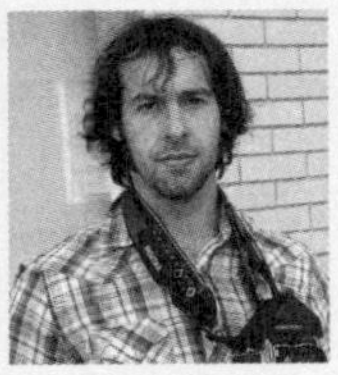

JARET BELLIVEAU
BORN 1981 **RESIDES** Moncton, N.B. **EDUCATION** Nova Scotia College of Art and Design, B.A. in Photography, Halifax, 2001–Present

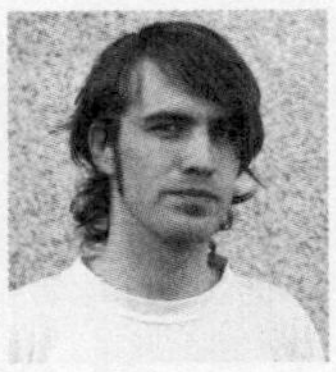

PATRICK BLAESER
BORN 1981 **RESIDES** Vancouver **EDUCATION** Emily Carr Institute of Art & Design, B.F.A. in Photography pending, 2005; University of British Columbia, First year of B.A., 2000–2001

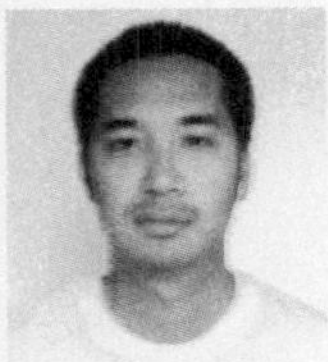

KOTAMA BOUABANE
BORN 1980 **RESIDES** Toronto **EDUCATION** Ontario College of Art & Design, Undergraduate studies completed, Toronto, 2003

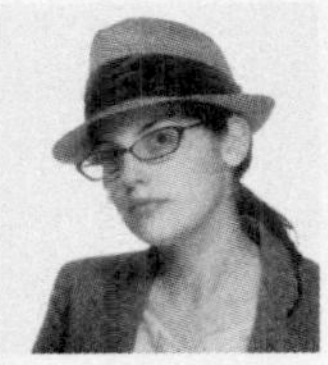

LILA BUJOLD
BORN 1983 **RESIDES** Richmond, B.C. **EDUCATION** Emily Carr Institute of Art & Design, Third year of B.F.A., Major in Photography, 2002–Present

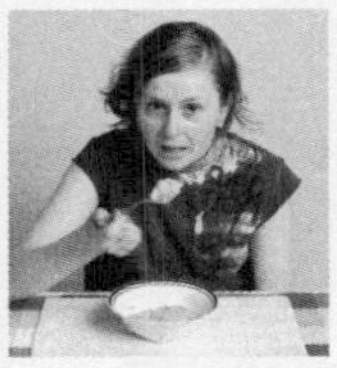

MIRIAM CABELL
BORN 1981 **RESIDES** Toronto **EDUCATION** Ryerson University, Photography, Toronto, 2002–Present **WEBSITE** www.mimicabell.com

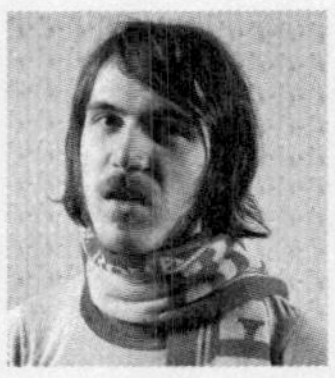

JAMIE CAMPBELL
BORN 1983 **RESIDES** Toronto **EDUCATION** Ryerson University, Photography, Toronto, 2002–Present **WEBSITE** www.jamiecampbell.suddencalm.net

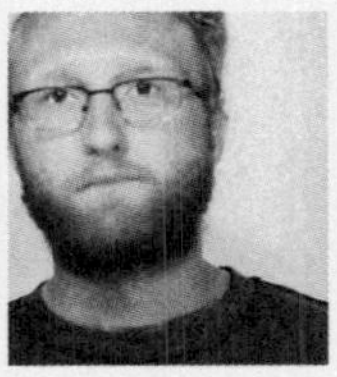

RYAN CARTER
BORN 1981 **RESIDES** Toronto **EDUCATION** Humber College, Diploma in Creative Photography (Honours), Toronto, 2003 **WEBSITE** www.ryan-carter.com

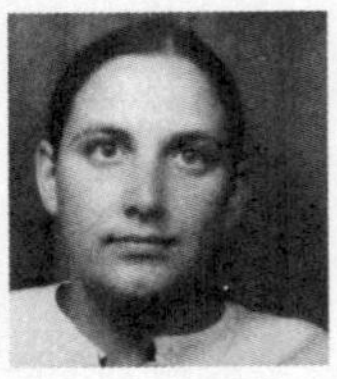

BECKY COMBER
BORN 1982 **RESIDES** Toronto **EDUCATION** Ryerson University, B.A. in Photography, Toronto, 2005

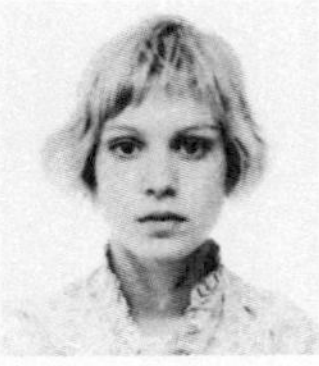

ROBYN CUMMING
BORN 1981 **RESIDES** Toronto **EDUCATION** Ryerson University, B.F.A. in Photography, Toronto, 2004 **WEBSITE** www.robyncumming.com

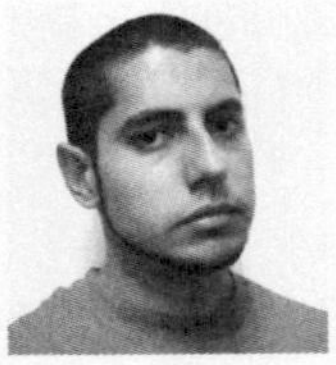

DANNY CUSTODIO
BORN 1982 **RESIDES** Toronto **EDUCATION** Ontario College of Art & Design, B.A. in Photography, Toronto, 2005

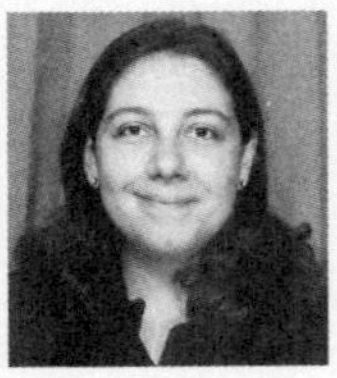

KADIJA DE PAULA
BORN 1980 **RESIDES** Toronto **EDUCATION** Ontario College of Art & Design, B.F.A. in Photography, Toronto, 2005 **WEBSITE** www.kadijadepaula.com

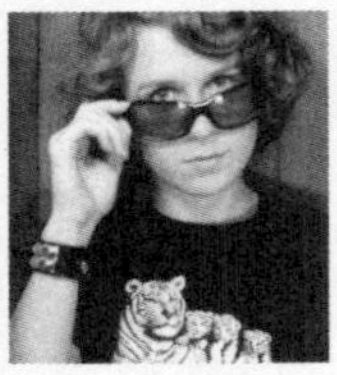

ALICE DIXON
BORN 1980 **RESIDES** Toronto **EDUCATION** Ryerson University, B.F.A. in Photography, Toronto, 2003 **WEBSITE** www.portfolios.com/alicedixon

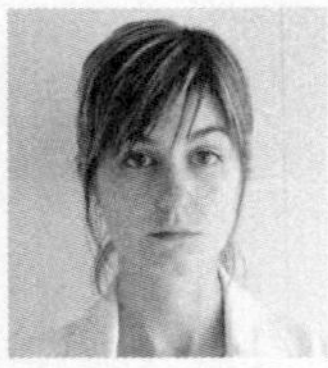

VERONIQUE DUCHARME-FRAPPIER
BORN 1983 **RESIDES** Montreal **EDUCATION** Concordia University, B.F.A. in Photography, Montreal, 2004–2005; Emily Carr Institute of Art and Design, B.F.A. in Photography, Vancouver, 2003–2004

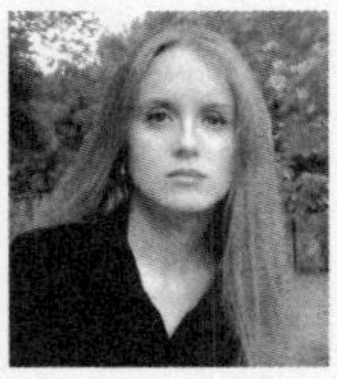

CARRIE DUPLESSIS
BORN 1981 **RESIDES** Ajax, Ontario **EDUCATION** Ontario College of Art and Design, B.F.A. in Photography, Toronto, 2005

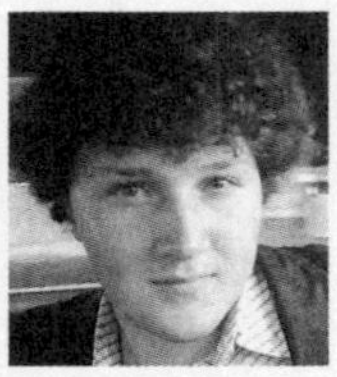

ADAM HARRISON
BORN 1983 **RESIDES** Vancouver **EDUCATION** Self-taught **WEBSITE** www.aharrison.com

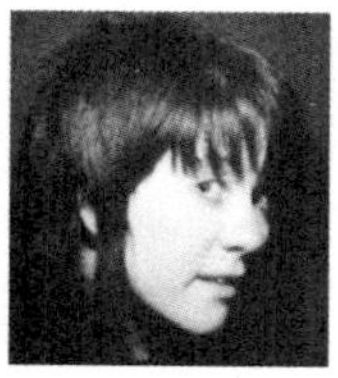

VANESSA HEINS
BORN 1984 **RESIDES** Toronto **EDUCATION** Ryerson University, B.F.A. in Photography, Toronto, 2005

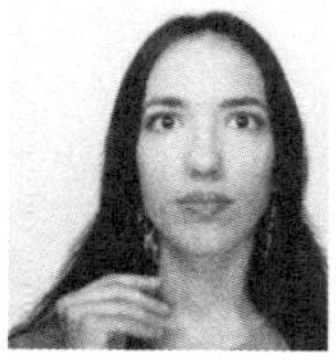

MAAYAN KASIMOV
BORN 1981 **RESIDES** Toronto **EDUCATION** Ryerson University, B.F.A. in Photography, Toronto, 2004 **WEBSITE** www.ambrotos.ca

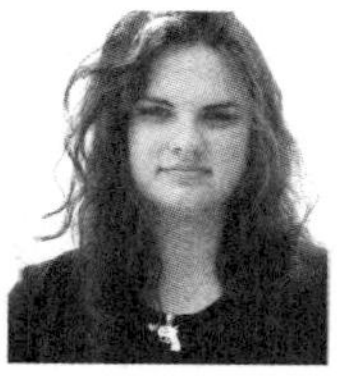

SASHA KRIEGER
BORN 1983 **RESIDES** Vancouver **EDUCATION** Emily Carr Institute of Art & Design, B.F.A. in Photography, Vancouver, 2005

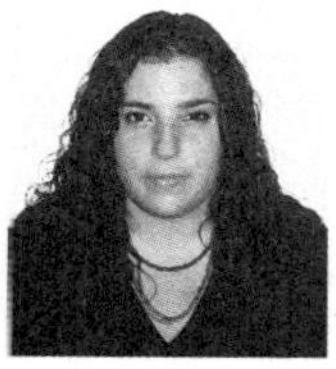

SARAH MANGIALARDO
BORN 1981 **RESIDES** Toronto **EDUCATION** Ryerson University, B.F.A. in Photography (Honours), Toronto, 2005

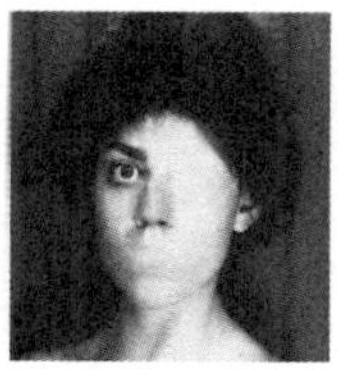

DAVIDA NEMEROFF
BORN 1981 **RESIDES** Toronto **EDUCATION** Ryerson University, B.F.A. in Photography (Honours), Toronto, 2004 **WEBSITE** www.afikomen.ca

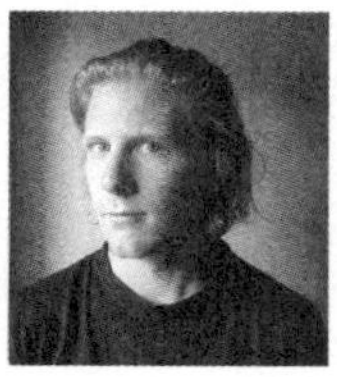

LOUIS PERREAULT
BORN 1979 **RESIDES** Sherbrooke, Quebec **EDUCATION** Concordia University, B.F.A. in Photography, Montreal, 2003-Present; Dawson College, D.E.C. Professional Photography, Montreal, 2005; Cégep de Sherbrooke, D.E.C. Social Sciences, Montreal, 1998 **WEBSITE** www.louisperreault.com

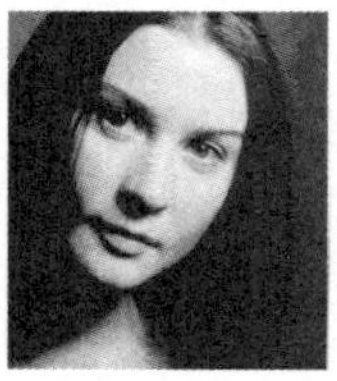

KERRY SHAW
BORN 1980 **RESIDES** Toronto **EDUCATION** York University, B.F.A. in Visual Arts (Honours), Toronto, 2004 **WEBSITE** www.kerryshaw.com

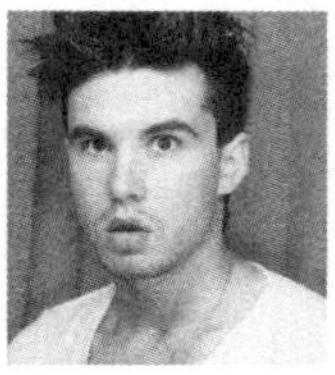

GRAYDON SHEPPARD
BORN 1982 **RESIDES** Toronto **EDUCATION** Ryerson University, B.F.A. in Photography (Honours), Toronto, 2005 **WEBSITE** www.graydonsheppard.com

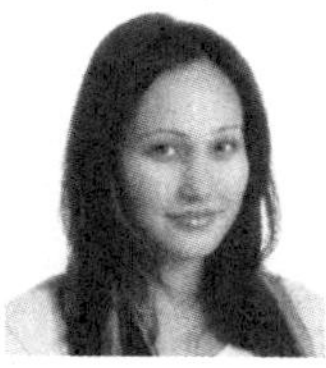

JOANNA SIMPSON
BORN 1981 **RESIDES** Toronto **EDUCATION** Ontario College of Art & Design, B.F.A. in Photography, Toronto, 2005

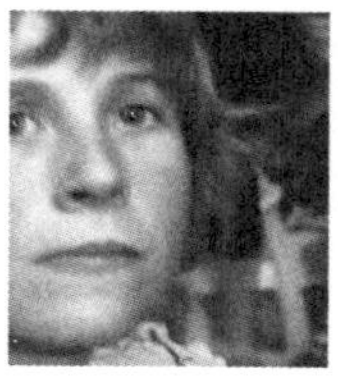

NATALIE SORENSON
BORN 1979 **RESIDES** Vancouver **EDUCATION** Emily Carr Institute of Art & Design, B.F.A. in Photography, Vancouver, 2005; Memphis College of Art, Photography Major, Memphis, Tennessee, 2001 **WEBSITE** www.nataliesorenson.com

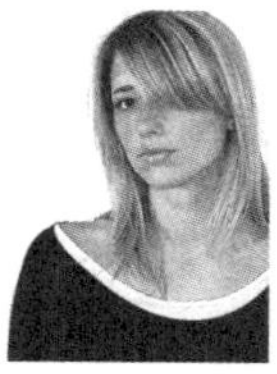

SARAH THORPE
BORN 1979 **RESIDES** Windsor, Ontario **EDUCATION** University of Windsor, B.F.A., 2004-Present; Ontario College of Art & Design, Diploma in Photography & Printmaking, 1998-2002

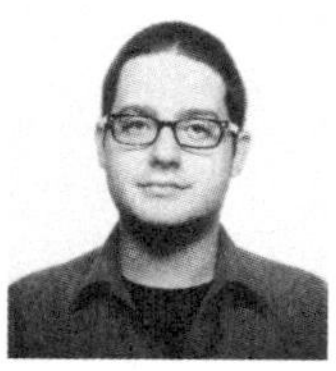

MARTIN VERREAULT
BORN 1980 **RESIDES** Montreal **EDUCATION** Concordia University, B.F.A. in Photography, Montreal, 2002

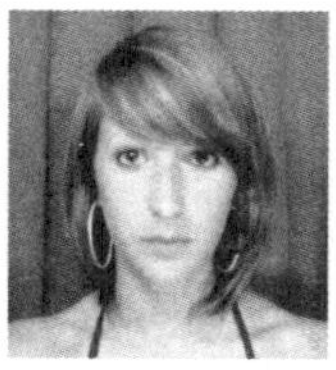

JOHANNA WARWICK
BORN 1983 **RESIDES** Toronto **EDUCATION** Ryerson University, B.F.A. in Photography, Toronto, 2002-Present **WEBSITE** www.johannawarwick.com

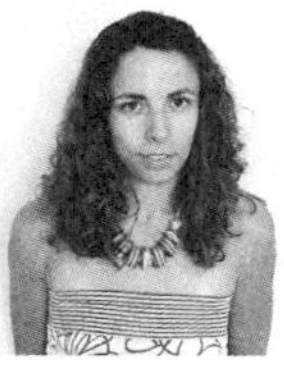

ELENA WILLIS
BORN 1979 **RESIDES** Montreal **EDUCATION** Concordia University, B.F.A. in Photography, Montreal, 2001-2004 **WEBSITE** www.elenawillis.com

JURORS

FINE ART

Maia Sutnik	Photographic Curator, Art Gallery of Ontario
Ann Thomas	Curator of Photography, National Gallery

DOCUMENTARY

Stephen Bulger	Director, Stephen Bulger Gallery
Catherine Dean	Photo Editor, *Toronto Life*
Margaret Williamson	Photo Director, *Canadian GEO Magazine*

PHOTOJOURNALISM

Erin Elder	Photo Director, *The Globe and Mail*
Timothy Neesam	Producer, CBC Radio 3
Lesley Sparks	Photo Project Director

EDITORIAL

Donna Braggins	Art Director, *Maclean's*
Carmen Dunjko	Designer / Editor
Clare Vander Meersch	Photo Editor, *Report on Business Magazine*

COMMERCIAL

Felicia Cohen	Photography Director, Masterfile Stock Agency
Myles McCutchin	Photo Editor, *Toro Magazine*
Judith Tatar	Director, Tatar Gallery

EMERGING

Adrienne Lai	Emily Carr College of Art and Design
Jennifer Long	Director, Gallery 44
Gaetane Verna	Art Gallery of Bishop's University

ACKNOWLEDGEMENTS

We would like to thank the following people for championing Magenta:
Charlie Coffey
Alan Convery
Scott Mullin

A big thank you to the people who helped build and create this publishing house:
Barbara Gilbert
Sophie Hackett
Lynna Landstreet
Gilbert Li

Special thanks to the following photographers who generously donated a print to our endowment fund:
Karin Bubas
Greg Girard
Rafael Goldchain
Colwyn Griffith
Toni Hafkenscheid
Vid Ingelevics
Ruth Kaplan
Eric Klemm
Thomas Kneubühler
Katherine Knight
Andrej Kopac
Roger Lemoyne
Jennifer Long
Davida Nemeroff
Sandy Nicholson
Lindsay Page
Louie Palu
Carlos & Jason Sanchez
Derek Shapton
Lana Slezic
Mackenzie Stroh

And everyone else:
Stephanie Allen (and her Mom)
Ruth Alves
Sara Angel
Monica Appugliesi
Grant Arnold
Bruce Bailey
Tony Barone
Hannah Baysden
Réjean Beaudin
Kaye Beeston
Jet Belgraver
Pauline Bohnec
Chris Boot
Bruce Borysiuk
Chris Bucci
Sarmite D. Bulte
Manny & Louise Camilleri
Frank Cassellis
Clarity
Kristin Cochrane
Jane Corkin
Douglas Coupland
Geordie Daglish
Geoffrey Dawe
Connie Deckert
Jill Delaney
Alice Dixon
Robert Enright
Jane Francisco
Stephen Franklin
Lynn Fraser
Jane Friedman
Nelson French
Dean Gabourie
Patrick Gagnon
Vicki Goldberg
Margot Gordon
Sam Grosso
Dolores Gubasta
Michael Hall
Pam Hamilton
Maurice Henri
Bill Huffman
Victoria Jackman
Andrea Janus
Bill Jeffries
Paul Jerinkitsch
Gerry Jordan
Stanley Katz
Jennifer Kean
Robert Kearns
David Kent
Darcy Kileen
Sandy Kim
Lisa Klimek
John Knechtel
Karen Machtinger
Maisonneuve Magazine
Helen Malkin
Belinda Martin
Sanaz Mazinani
Reford McDougal
Emily McInnes
Scott McIntyre
Leah McLaren
Scott McLeod
Peggy Miller
Marie Moliner
Liz Mullen
Michael Naccarato
Manny Neubacher
Aimee Nishitoba
Gregory Nixon
Angela Novosel
Michael O'Byrne
David Oiye
Alexandra Oliver
Stephen Osborne
Doug Pepper
John Petcoff
Alysha Rajkumar
Bonnie Rubenstein
Nanette Sanson
Julie Schaper
Michael Schellenberg
Marcus Schubert
Shirley Ann Spiteri
Douglas Steiner
Robin Steinfeld
Sharon Switzer
Margaret Thomas
Cuong Tran
Laas Turnbull
Rodney Vander Meersch
Derek Webster
Chris Whitern
Rhonda Wilson
Marsha Winn
Jake Wozniak
Vanessa Wyse
Gillian Yates

CONCEPT
MaryAnn Camilleri

DESIGN
The Office of Gilbert Li

PHOTO EDITORS
MaryAnn Camilleri
Catherine Dean
Erin Elder
Sophie Hackett
Clare Vander Meersch

EDITOR
Doug Wallace

COPY EDITOR
Michaela Cornell

FRENCH TRANSLATION
Chantal Morris

LOGO
Astrolab Design / Rob Mattan

PREPRESS
Clarity

© 2006 The Magenta Foundation

The Magenta Foundation
151 Winchester Street
Toronto, Ontario, Canada M4X 1B5
www.magentafoundation.org

All rights reserved. No part of this publication may be reproduced, stored in a retrieval system or transmitted in any form or by any means, electronic, mechanical, photocopying, record or otherwise, without the prior permission of the publisher.

Library and Archives Canada Cataloguing in Publication

Camilleri, MaryAnn, 1966-
Carte blanche : photography, 1 / MaryAnn Camilleri.

Includes bibliographical references and index.
Introduction in English and French.
ISBN 0-9739739-0-0

1. Photography—Canada. 2. Photography, Artistic. 3. Photographers—Canada. 4. Photographers—Canada—Biography. I. Magenta Foundation II. Title.

TR26.C34 2006 779'.0971 C2006-900014-X

Printed and bound in China by
C & C Offset Printing Co., Ltd.

Distributed in Canada by
Douglas & McIntyre Ltd.
2323 Quebec Street, Suite 201
Vancouver, British Columbia, Canada V5T 4S7
www.douglas-mcintyre.com

Distributed in the United States by
Consortium Book Sales & Distribution
1045 Westgate Drive
St. Paul, Minnesota, U.S.A. 55114-1065
www.cbsd.com

10 09 08 07 06 1 2 3 4 5